Film Making in 1930s Britain

BY THE SAME AUTHOR

The History of the British Film 1929–1939

Film Making in 1930s Britain

RACHAEL LOW

London
GEORGE ALLEN & UNWIN
Boston   Sydney
Published in association with the
British Film Institute

© George Allen & Unwin (Publishers) Ltd 1985
This book is copyright under the Berne Convention. No reproduction
without permission. All rights reserved.

George Allen & Unwin (Publishers) Ltd,
40 Museum Street, London WC1A 1LU, UK

George Allen & Unwin (Publishers) Ltd,
Park Lane, Hemel Hempstead, Herts HP2 4TE, UK

Allen & Unwin Inc.,
Fifty Cross Street, Winchester, Mass 01890, USA

George Allen & Unwin Australia Pty Ltd,
8 Napier Street, North Sydney, NSW 2060, Australia

First published in 1985

Published in association with the British Film Institute

British Library Cataloguing in Publication Data

Low, Rachel
    Film Making in 1930s Britain.
    1. Moving-pictures—Great Britain—History
and criticism
    I. Title
    791.43'0941   PN1993.5.G7
    ISBN 0-04-791042-9

Set in 10½ on 11½ point Baskerville by Grove Graphics, Tring
and printed in Great Britain by Anchor Brendon, Tiptree, Essex

Contents

Illustrations

The most striking stills from the most important films have been reproduced many times. Rather than repeat them I have tried to convey some general impression of the British film industry as a whole, with the various companies, some of the film makers and stars, the comics, the work of the art directors, the unexpected realism of many of the films and the way the overall look of the films changed between the beginning of the period and the end.

I am in debt to the Stills Department of the British Film Institute for making most of the illustrations available. For the shot of Gracie Fields in *Sally in Our Alley* I am indebted to John East.

Foreword

by Sir Richard Attenborough

The British film industry has been through many cycles and phases since the first commercial screening of a moving picture almost ninety years ago.

It may well prove that the 1980s, with the benefit of hindsight, will be as major a turning point in our history as the decade Rachael Low chronicles so thoroughly and with such perception in this book.

The pre-war period is fascinating and instructive for all manner of reasons – not least because the characters, many of them giants of the cinema, who spring so vibrantly from these pages are, in the main, no longer here to tell their own story. By fleshing out these pioneers during their most active and creative years and depicting them against the social, economic and technological conditions of an epoch of fundamental change, Miss Low gives an overview that is tremendously helpful in understanding what is happening today.

The long term effect of talkies and, to a lesser extent, colour – introduced in the thirties – was just as radical and far-reaching as recent innovations such as video, cable and satellite communication will prove to be in the 1980s and beyond.

This book, for me, is particularly illuminating for two reasons. From a purely personal point of view, it charts the decade immediately preceding my own first encounter with feature film making as a young, nervous and inexperienced actor in 1942.

More importantly, however, by describing the pitfalls of hasty and ill-conceived legislation that resulted in the infamous quota quickies of the pre-war years, Miss Low illustrates vividly the potential for good or ill that government may exert over our industry, whilst failing to place feature films correctly in context with other performing arts.

For example, only two years after the implementation of the second Quota Act in 1938 which, while it cured one set of problems created a whole series of others, the Council for the Encouragement of Music and the Arts – later the Arts Council – was formed. Whilst recognising the phenomenal ascendancy of British music, live theatre and ballet at the beginning of the forties, only in the mid-sixties did it acknowledge film, by initiating an allocation for documentaries on the work of painters.

It is true that the ultimately somewhat anachronistic Eady Fund did prove, over a long period, to be of considerable value to the indigenous film industry. But now that the Fund has been abolished, one of its principal beneficiaries, the National Film Finance Corporation, is to be re-constituted on a basis that is, to say the least, somewhat questionable. This, coupled with the policy of treating feature films as though they were indivisible from any other manufacturing industry – with the minor exception of NFFC grants emanating from the Exchequer which, over the years, have been little more than derisory, highlights the imperative need for a long term solution.

It is greatly to be hoped, in the light of today's resurgence of the British feature film both at home and as an export, that present and future administrations have learned the folly of improvised stop-gap measures and will finally grant our industry the status and sustained support it has been so cruelly denied since its inception in 1896.

What emerges with great clarity from Miss Low's book is that those pioneers who cared desperately about quality productions had to struggle against tremendous odds. That so many did fight, did care and won through to lay the foundations of an indigenous industry of which we can be truly proud, should be a continuing source of inspiration to us all

9 October 1984

Introduction
and Acknowledgements

Many years ago, when I began a series of books on the development of the British film industry, of which this is the seventh, the history of the film was not taken seriously as an academic subject. It was a question of starting from scratch, interviewing veterans of all branches of the industry from the beginning of the commercial showing of films in this country in 1896, and looking for documentary evidence concerning the whole field of production, distribution and exhibition, film technique, official and unofficial regulation and organisation.

Gradually more and more information became available and, of course, the later the period being studied the more activity there was to study. Some years ago, with the help of a research fellowship at Lucy Cavendish College, Cambridge, awarded by the Calouste Gulbenkian Foundation, I began research into the British film industry in the 1930s. Work on this has continued with the generous support of the British Film Institute. Two books based on this research appeared in 1979, *Documentary and Educational Films of the 1930s* and *Films of Comment and Persuasion of the 1930s*. In the intervening years a number of other writers have brought out useful studies of particular aspects of the subject or of individual film makers. But until now there has been no full account of the decade to put the cinema and its problems into a historical perspective and trace the power struggles within the developing industry.

This book gives an overall picture of the feature industry between the coming of the talkie in 1929 and the outbreak of the Second World War in 1939. In doing so, incidentally, it clarifies the nature and causes of the speculative boom in production and the subsequent crisis in the mid-thirties. Without a historical perspective these have been much misunderstood and, surprisingly, the part played by the Aldgate Trustees has been neglected. An idea has gained acceptance that Korda's success with *The Private Life of Henry VIII* in 1933 was responsible for a boom in investment and that his extravagance at Denham subsequently caused financial interests in the City of London to lose confidence in production as a field for investment. Certainly Korda was extravagant and certainly his chief backer, the Prudential Assurance Company, took fright during 1937. But it was the unfortunate results of the Aldgate operation which alerted them and others, and caused something like a panic in the City. It was the Aldgate producers, not Korda, who were at the centre of the scandal and it was their activities that gave rise to the legal action which followed.

Financial considerations are fundamental to the story. Despite a persistent drain to Hollywood there has never been a shortage of film-making talent in Britain. It is production finance that has been hard to find. The economic facts of life enabled American producers to make so much profit in their own home market that they could afford the best of everything, whereas their British counterparts, with a much smaller public near at hand, had to watch costs. Cost and quality are not synonymous, of course, and everyone can point to good low-budget films. But shoestring masterpieces are rare, and because British pictures had to be relatively cheap they suffered in comparison with their American rivals. A share of the American market, which would have made more lavish production economically viable, was denied to them. For, although isolated British films enjoyed occasional successes in America, regular nation-wide circuit distribution at a fair rental was in the hands of the big Hollywood companies, who naturally saw little reason to assist their competitors. By the late twenties the American advantage had been reinforced by exploitation methods which even had the British market so tied up that British producers had difficulty in finding playing dates for their films in their own country.

The 1927 quota legislation intended to solve all the industry's problems was a failure. Film production doubled during the thirties, but the increase consisted almost entirely of cheap and inferior films, the famous quota quickies and others not much better, which took advantage of the protected market and went far to ruin the reputation of British production as a whole. Much time was spent during the mid-thirties trying to devise a better system, and the second Quota Act, which was passed in 1938, did succeed in killing the quota quickies. It is interesting that despite their economic handicaps the serious producers made pictures throughout the decade which were popular with British audiences. They presented a varied and interesting body of film which was quite separate from the quota output, as examination of both forms of production will show. The story of these quality producers, of the quota merchants, and of the American importers who made, sponsored or acquired British film footage for their legally required quota, reminds us again and again that the problems of the British film industry stemmed from the disparity in size of the British and American markets. All the big British producers tried to break into the American market during the thirties in order to counter the Americans' overwhelming competitive advantage, and by 1939 both Korda and Wilcox seemed on the verge of success.

As for the films themselves, since this is the study of an industry rather than a critical assessment a detailed critical analysis would be out of place. All the same, an account of any branch of show business must try to convey some idea of what it was all about. A broad survey of the films and those who made them, an extensive study rather than an intensive one, is needed to establish a frame of reference so that individual contributions can be seen in context. This was the age of stars like Jessie Matthews, Merle Oberon, Anna Neagle, Leslie Howard, Michael Redgrave and Jack Buchanan; of comics like Gracie Fields, George Formby, Will Hay and Jack Hulbert. Michael Balcon, Korda, Hitchcock, Wilcox and Victor Saville were leading film makers and the young Carol Reed, David Lean and Michael Powell were showing new talent. There was also a westward drift as British actors and technicians were drawn away to Hollywood, and eminent refugee film makers arrived in Britain from Nazi Europe. Films by these and many others, good and bad, are discussed against the economic background of production. The film index at the end of the book is included in order to make the material upon which this survey is based available to others, and makes no claim to be comprehensive, although I believe it to be reasonably accurate.

Between the conversion to talkies and the outbreak of war both the studios and the cinemas were transformed, most of the changes taking place in a few short, confusing and anxious years. The talkie revolutionised film making, causing dramatic changes in the continuity structure, and even to the physical appearance, of the films. Stories told in pictures, with a few inset titles which could easily be translated, had been acceptable in any country. But stories depending heavily on the spoken word brought new problems. Many producers strove to retain the international currency of the cinema by production of the so-called 'multilingual' films, but by 1939 the ordinary British filmgoer knew only the English-speaking stars of British and American pictures. The ease with which they had previously accepted stories and personalities from many European countries was a thing of the past. At the same time well educated people, who had previously looked down on the cinema, increasingly went to film societies and small specialised or repertory cinemas showing the best films from all over the world. The thirties were the age of the super-cinema, with the 'atmospherics', the Odeons, and lavishly decorated picture palaces of every description, and showmen had a monolithic philosophy, hoping to draw more and more people into the same cinemas to see the same films. In fact, fragmentation of the audience had already begun with the advent of a more selective public.

I would like to express my gratitude for the help and encouragement I received down the years from the late Sir Michael Balcon, Thorold Dickinson, Baynham Honri and Paul Rotha. My thanks are also due to Brenda Davies, formerly Information Officer of the British Film Institute, and to Jeremy Boulton, formerly of the National Film Archive, as well as to the Calouste Gulbenkian Foundation and the Governors of the British Film Institute.

RACHAEL LOW

Chapter 1

Exploitation

The cinema, like spectator sports and tourism, is one of the great recreation industries of the twentieth century. By the time the talkies arrived in Britain in 1929 many millions of people throughout the world went to the pictures regularly. It was estimated in the mid-thirties that an average of 18½ million cinema tickets were sold in Britain every week.

The estimate, in an industry notoriously short of statistical information, was made by Simon Rowson. Rowson, who had started his career many years before as a statistician, had entered films in his thirties as a renter and, greatly admired in the trade for his academic attainments, for many years tried single-handed to pin down the elusive statistics of an industry not keen on disclosing its business to others. Some of his value judgements have to be treated with reserve, for as a statistician he was concerned with quantity rather than quality. For example, he considered the quota legislation of 1927 a success because it led to an enormous increase in British film production, ignoring the appalling quality of most of that increase.[1] Nevertheless his work is a mine of information, carefully gathered and meticulously defined. By now the cinema was widely accepted as a respectable part of society and Rowson was to address several august bodies on the subject during the thirties. He read papers at a Royal Empire Society dinner, to the British Kinematograph Society, the British Association, the Royal Statistical Society and the Royal Institute of International Affairs. By far the most comprehensive and important paper was that read to the Royal Statistical Society on 17 December 1935, describing the film exhibition business as it was in the year 1934.

To get a detailed picture of cinema admissions he based his calculations on two sets of figures, the yield of entertainment duty, which included tax from legitimate theatres and other forms of amusement as well as cinemas, and the number of admission tickets of various prices sold for use in a number of certified halls, that is to say cinemas licensed under the 1909 fire precautions legislation. In the paper he referred to the study as covering a large proportion of the cinemas in the United Kingdom, and the figure was said elsewhere to be 2,000, which turned out to be approximately 43 per cent of the total. The figures were obtained from the Excise Department, which issued adhesive labels to be used with tickets, and from legally authorised ticket printers. His main conclusions about admissions were that they numbered 963 million in 1934, or an average of 18½ million a week; that a total of £41,120,000 was taken at the box office, of which about £6,800,000 went on entertainment duty; and that the vast majority of the tickets sold were for the cheaper seats. Nearly 80 per cent of them cost 1/- or less, including entertainment duty, and 43 per cent as little as 6d or less. What he could not tell from the figures was the frequency of people's visits or the actual size of the cinema-going public. It was clear that many people paid a weekly visit to the pictures and indeed that many went more often than that. An indication of this was contained in the results of a questionnaire filled in by 124,837 of the people visiting Sidney Bernstein's Granada cinemas in 1933–4, which suggested that 37.4 per cent of them went once a week but that 57.7 per cent went even more often.

Rowson's figures were the first authoritative statistical survey of the number, size and distribution of the cinemas in Britain and their takings. From time to time different bodies quoted conflicting figures of the number of cinemas. The Cinematograph Exhibitors' Association used a low figure, claiming that its membership included virtually all regular six- or seven-day cinemas, but it seems from Rowson's investigation that it actually included only 85 per cent. Western Electric, concerned with the installation of sound reproduction equipment for the talkies, used a much higher figure; as they were looking for custom it may well be that their figure was high because it included halls and legitimate theatres used only for occasional shows and cinemas which were temporarily closed. In the House of Commons Leslie Hore-Belisha, for the Board of Trade, said in reply to a parliamentary question that on 30 April 1933 there were 4,331 cinemas operating in Great Britain, but as this probably referred to licences issued a true picture would have to take account of cinemas closing and changing hands. It is necessary to remember that the number of cinemas in the country was fluctuating all the time. After the introduction of the talkie in 1929 many less prosperous cinemas were unable to make the transition and were closed down, most of the others were closed temporarily for alteration and a growing number of new ones were opened. Rowson took the two trade directories, *Kine Year Book* and *Cinema Buyers' Guide*, both of which claimed to have a complete list, giving the sound system used in each cinema and the number of seats in many of them. By combining the lists and checking up on discrepancies he formed a more accurate and complete list and was able to fill in the missing information about seats by applying to the sound equipment companies, who had made their own records of seating capacity when they conducted their acoustic surveys. In this way Rowson was able to give a definitive account of regular six- or seven-day cinemas at the date of collection by the two directories. He found that there were 4,305 such cinemas, with 3,872,000 seats. Most of the cinemas, or 70 per cent, with just over half the seats, were small and had only 1,000 seats or less. In the

London County Council area this was not so marked, 55 per cent of the cinemas with only 31 per cent of the seats falling into this category.

The acoustic requirements of the talkies were not met by many of the early auditoriums and the cost of adaptation and equipment hit many small exhibitors very hard. Times were bad anyway in 1929 and the early thirties. There was mass unemployment, the dole was cut in October 1931 and there were widespread wage·cuts. The Chancellor of the Exchequer, Philip Snowdon, who had cut the rate of entertainment duty in 1924, now put it up again and at the same time both the rate and the spread of income tax were increased. As a result people had less to spend on going to the pictures and, despite the early attraction of the talkies, rentals and service charges for equipment were too much for many small showmen.

To make matters worse the big renters handling the desirable new sound films were able to insist on sharing terms, or percentage rentals, often at very high levels and often with guaranteed minimum payments. If the film did not come up to expectations at the box office the exhibitor lost, but if it did unexpectedly well there was no windfall to compare with the old days of flat rates and the exhibitor, compelled to disclose his takings, had to pay up.

The secrecy of the box office had always been jealously guarded, and there was great resentment of the new system. To prevent 'ticket irregularities', by which they meant fraudulent returns, the two big trade organisations formed a joint investigation committee, with inspectors to police the system. The Kinematograph Renters' Society, dominated by the American majors, was a small, united and aggressive body with a couple of dozen members, who held all the cards and kept the exhibitors in line with very real threats of boycott. The Cinematograph Exhibitors' Association, with from three to four thousand members, was an ineffective body which tried to represent at the same time the interests of the many small independent showmen and of the big circuits. The latter were themselves associated with renting companies and their interests were totally different to those of the small showmen. The CEA's disunity and lack of support for joint action was as marked as the unity of purpose and effectiveness of the KRS. The sole concession made by the joint investigating committee was to offer a flat rate instead of a percentage to cinemas with weekly takings of £125 or less. It is revealing that even as late as 1935 the CEA estimated that 1,250 cinemas or nearly 30 per cent of Rowson's total took less than £50.

The big circuits did not need the protection of the CEA, for their bargaining power was so great that they were able to get bookings paying only 20 or 25 per cent of their takings to the renters, but the small men had to pay up to 40 or 50 per cent for their super films, or 33⅓ per cent for an ordinary feature without any supporting programme. Charges for discs, during the early years when some companies still did sound-on-disc, were an additional burden. In the middle of 1930 the CEA tried to rally its members to refuse to pay, in order to get guaranteed minimum payments and disc charges abolished. J. C. Graham of Paramount, the American President of the KRS, refused to countenance joint talks between the two bodies, saying that such talks would be useless as the KRS did not tell its members how to conduct their business. The CEA accordingly tackled the renters individually. Some were agreeable but some insisted that guarantees were essential 'in exceptional cases', by which they meant when they suspected exhibitors of lying about their returns. Several wished to retain disc charges. As for J. C. Graham, he simply said that he would run his business as he saw fit.[2] The CEA tried to persuade its members to continue their resistance and later claimed that this had been partially successful, and in March 1931 W. R. Fuller of the CEA asserted that charges had been reduced from between 50 and 60 per cent to between 38 and 45 per cent. But a boycott was not a weapon the CEA was ever able to use effectively and in reality there was little the independent cinemas could do if they wanted a film. Charlie Chaplin's *City Lights* in 1931 caused much bitterness. Neighbouring showmen were angry when the Dominion Theatre, not yet converted into a cinema, booked it for twenty weeks at 60 per cent to United Artists with a guarantee of £40,000, creaming off much of the business it would do in the London area.[3] United Artists wanted 50 per cent from other exhibitors and the Gaumont-British circuit refused to pay, trying to get it for 40 per cent. The CEA advised its members to stand out for 33⅓ per cent in the case of large halls and 25 per cent for the smaller ones. But John Maxwell of the large ABC circuit booked it at 50 per cent, saying that it was his duty to the public, and Oscar Deutsch expressly dissociated himself from an attempt by the Midlands branch of the CEA to boycott the film. With a box-office winner like *City Lights* no unity could be expected from exhibitors. But even in the case of less outstanding films they had to take the renters' terms or go without, and those who could paid up.

In early 1933 the CEA, lowering its sights a little, was trying to establish a ratio of 40 to 60 per cent in the exhibitor's favour. At a conference in Birmingham a resolution not to book at a higher rate was adopted by the members. But once again it was proved that the CEA was too big and heterogeneous a body for united action, and towards the end of 1935 it was admitted that the Birmingham resolution had been a failure.

Meanwhile many exhibitors blamed their financial difficulties not so much on the high cost of programmes as on competition from new cinemas. As early as August 1931 some exhibitors in Manchester sought to persuade the magistrates not to issue any new licences on the grounds of 'saturation'. This word, like 'overseating' and 'redundancy', was to become familiar during the next five years. Elaborate calculations based on the number of seats and performances a week and the head of population sought to establish a ratio beyond which no new licences would be issued in an area. What no one mentioned was that every time a new modern cinema opened it was because the old ones had not kept up with the times, and that if new cinemas were not allowed it would be the public who lost. New openings increased as the decade went on. At the same time the CEA claimed that 420 cinemas closed in the years 1932, 1933 and 1934. The authorities' initial response to pleas about overseating was to point out that licensing under the 1909 Act was for safety, not for the protection of vested interests.* Late in 1933 the Liverpool JPs did turn down two applications although the reason given was that of site difficulties, not redundancy. Councils were, however, entitled to refuse applications without stating their grounds for doing so, and in August 1934 at last Wells, and later a number of other towns, gave in to pleas of redundancy. Two years later it was openly admitted that an application from Union Cinemas at Darlington had been turned down because there were six other cinemas within 300 yards of the site. But as it was to be a modern cinema with 2,000 seats and Union thought well enough of its prospects to make the investment, it must be assumed that the refusal was protecting inferior cinemas. As a rule, however, the authorities were unsympathetic to such requests. Towards the end of 1936 one exhibitor tried to arouse interest in getting government intervention, but nothing was done and the complaints gradually died away.

Two methods by which independent exhibitors repeatedly tried to defend themselves against high rentals were co-operative booking and co-operative production.

Thomas Ormiston's attempt in 1927 to give the independents something approaching the bargaining power of the big circuits by forming a co-operative booking agency had been effectively stopped by the flat refusal of KRS members to supply films to any exhibitor joining such a group. Unlike the CEA, the KRS was well able to operate a boycott and made it very plain that they would do so, yet there were many similar attempts by exhibitors during the thirties. Every now and then a plan would be announced, followed shortly afterwards by a repetition of the KRS position. One of the more important was the Film Industries Co-operative Society, which was proposed in July 1931. The structure planned was typical, with member cinemas contributing the capital and receiving interest, doing all their booking through it at a 1 per cent booking fee; one of the directors was to handle booking, which it was hoped would be at a 25 per cent rental, and assurances were given that all business would be kept private and confidential. The scheme was to go into operation when membership had reached 200. But even if enough independents had overcome their extreme reluctance to disclose their finances the scheme had no chance, for the KRS simply made their usual pronouncement in December 1931 and that was that. Then, when a certain Mr Urquhart was appointed to book for a firm

* The Cinematograph Act of 1909 explained that the licensing authorities were 'The Council of the County or County Borough, but as a rule these powers are, in the first instance at least, exercised by a committee . . . The County or County Borough Council may delegate these powers to the local justice'.

in Scotland, the KRS made it known early the following year that they were not prepared to deal with a booking agent without a substantial financial interest in the firm in question. Before long another leading exhibitor, C. P. Metcalfe, suggested that the CEA itself might either be turned into a limited liability company or form a subsidiary and operate a booking scheme. This proposal, however, threatened to split the CEA in two, as the big circuits were unlikely to welcome the creation of what would amount to a new large circuit and rob them of the competitive advantage for which they had been formed. Discussions led nowhere.

In the mid-thirties the Gaumont-British circuit had acquired a financial interest in H & G Cinemas, owned by Major Gale and Sid and Philip Hyams. Early in 1935 the KRS, which J. C. Graham had so pointedly said did not tell its members how to conduct their business, instructed them not to book to H & G through Gaumont-British until that firm had explained itself to the KRS. H & G had no option but to call off the booking arrangement, which they did in April, upon which the KRS gave its members permission to resume booking. Some months later Gaumont-British, in what was described as a £700,000 deal, acquired three H & G supers in London – the Troxy at Stepney, the Troc-ette in Tower Bridge Road and the Trocadero at Elephant and Castle. The properties were held by Gaumont Super Cinemas, which was registered as a private £400,000 company in August 1935 with Gale and the Hyams, and Mark and Maurice Ostrer and A. W. Jarrett of Gaumont, on the board. Booking was to be conducted by Major Gale. Next month the KRS took a full-page advertisement in the trade press, stating that renters would only book to agents owning a majority control of the share capital of a company, and that they were investigating 'scores of cases'. Later it specifically instructed its members not to book to the three supers. Gaumont Supers sought an injunction to prevent them from enforcing the ban and there was talk of it being a conspiracy in restraint of trade. Gaumont, of course, had its own renting business, which was a member of the KRS, and it was persuaded to drop the action early the following year, but the issue of legality which had been raised demanded further examination. Early in 1938 the question of exhibitors' combines and KRS boycotts was raised in Parliament, and later the Cinematograph Films Council created under the new quota legislation in 1938 took the matter up. Talks were held with the KRS but it surprised no one that agreement had not been reached by the time that war broke out in September 1939.

An alternative to co-operative booking as a way of reducing rentals was co-operative production backed by the exhibitors themselves, and various schemes for this were proposed during the thirties. Like booking combines, all proved unsuccessful. An abortive scheme in 1933 called the Empire Co-operative Friendly Society was typical. It was intended to produce twelve films a year at the old Whitehall studio at Elstree, costing from £10,000 to £20,000 each. Member exhibitors would choose from a list of possible

PLUNDER

Farce from the Aldwych Theatre, filmed by Tom Walls in 1930 for B & D, with little alteration. Ralph Lynn and Tom Walls in centre stage, Mary Brough seated, with Robertson Hare.

PLUNDER

Ralph Lynn and Tom Walls in their usual roles as 'young men-about-town'.

JOURNEY'S END
David Manners, Billy Bevan and Colin Clive in the successful film of a hit play: theatrical drama of life in the trenches.
Directed in Hollywood by James Whale for Gainsborough-Welsh Pearson in 1930.

SUSPENSE
A less successful film, but a more adult and realistic treatment of the same subject, directed by Walter Summers
in 1930 at Elstree.

WHY SAILORS LEAVE HOME
Leslie Fuller, a British music hall comic with large heavy face and a lugubious style. With Eve Gray. The film was directed by fellow comic Monty Banks at Elstree in 1930.

THE LYONS MAIL
The actor manager Sir John Martin-Harvey appeared for Julius Hagen in a mini-spectacular film of his favourite stage part, made at the tiny Twickenham studio in 1930.

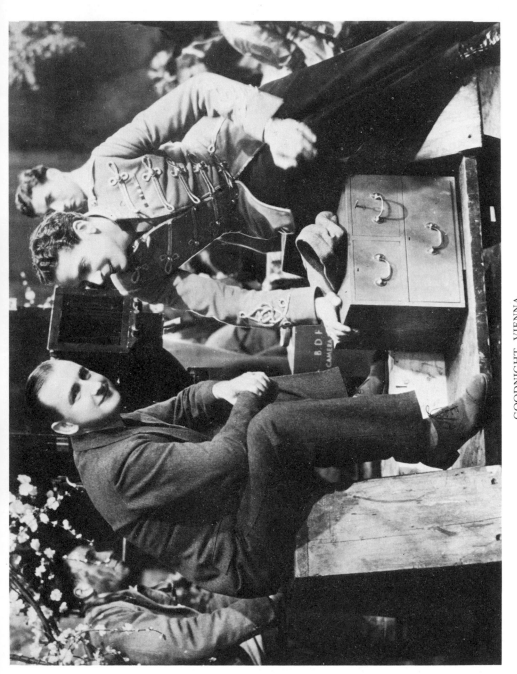

GOODNIGHT, VIENNA

Herbert Wilcox and Jack Buchanan on the set late in 1931.

films which should be made. They would contribute to the cost of each film, and be entitled to book it before other exhibitors at a rental of 33⅓ per cent.

The scheme fell through. Like later schemes, it had two fundamental weaknesses. The exhibitors' problem was not an absence of cheap, mediocre films, which this kind of operation was likely to produce, for the market was already overstocked with these owing to quota production. What they really wanted was to be able to book high-quality features at lower rentals than those currently charged, and the scheme did nothing to make this possible. Secondly, the idea that if exhibitors selected which films were to be made from a list then these would be more likely to do well at the box office, a belief which has recurred many times down the years, was very unrealistic.

In the late summer of 1936 the solicitor and Conservative MP A. C. N. Dixey circularised exhibitors about a plan essentially the same as the earlier one and based on the same misconceptions; 350 member cinemas were estimated to be the minimum needed to start the operation, and fifteen films a year were planned. This time it was claimed, moreover, that a number of films which were already made or in production would be available to launch the scheme. An agreement was made in April 1937 for studio space and services at the small Rock studio at Elstree, and five of the six films eventually put out as British Independent Exhibitors Distribution films were, in fact, simply Joe Rock productions. The standard of production was very poor and only Michael Powell's fine independent production *The Edge of the World*, for which Rock had fortuitously provided backing and which seemed oddly out of place in such company, had any merit. Despite much big talk, BIED never got more than 300 members and was dogged by trouble. Dixey resigned at the end of the year and the company was taken over by another low-grade producer, Norman Loudon of Sound City, but was in the hands of the receivers by October 1938.

The production of top-quality films which could then be hired at reasonable rentals by independents would have cost far more than the small exhibitors who needed them could afford, but the idea of exhibitor-financed production continued to have an appeal and even John Maxwell of British International Pictures suggested something along similar lines in the summer of 1939. As a postscript, after the war had started a group of producers and exhibitors, including Michael Balcon and Sidney Bernstein, got up a scheme largely through the initiative of Richard Norton whereby guaranteed bookings would enable producers to raise production finance. Bernstein wrote a pamphlet published privately which outlined an exhibitor-financed system very like the Dixey scheme, producing twelve pictures a year, with 400 member cinemas in an exhibitors' co-operative having CEA representation.[4]

It was not only the cost of film hire which worried small showmen. The cost of both producing and showing sound films was far higher than that of silent films and a rise in the price of admission would have been justified, but the industry continued to think of the cinema as entertainment for the masses at rock-bottom prices. Technical standards, and standards of comfort and elegance, improved greatly. The thirties were the heyday of the super cinema, and competition was fierce. Many cinemas were big, but on the whole the trend towards the really enormous halls seen at the end of the silent film era – such as the Davis Theatre at Croydon, opened in December 1928 and with 3,900 seats one of the biggest in Europe – was halted by the acoustic demands of the talkie. From 1,500 to 2,500 seats was said to be a more suitable size. Some, however, still aimed to astonish the public with their size and opulence, like the Trocadero at Elephant and Castle, which was so big that at its opening one foggy day in December 1930 the fog was said to be almost as thick inside as it was outside.

Much trouble was taken to make the new or converted picture palaces the last word in luxury and magnificence, and there were a number of architects and interior designers who specialised in them.* Some care was given to their facades although not to their lumpish sides and backs, which, with their bleak windowless walls and ugly roofs, did little for the environment. It was inside that imagination ran riot. Intricate coffering of walls and ceilings, decorative grills, illuminated panels and alcoves and luxurious seating, carpets and drapes were common. Many cinemas were built with stages, for variety shows were sometimes included with the films, although this, like the double feature, led to extremely long performances of three or even four hours and was the subject of much criticism from renters. Underlying the magnificence of these palatial buildings was the idea that the film, the occasion for the outing, was only part of the total experience and that a touch of grandeur was part of the fantasy for a largely underprivileged public. There were three main types of decorative flights of fancy. Traditional theatres in adaptations of classical and baroque styles were common, less so the modern theatres influenced by the more riotous aspects of art deco. But it was the atmospheric cinemas that caught the imagination. In these, the interior gave an illusion of a palace, garden or some other exotic setting with the appropriate domes, minarets, balconies or vistas; the proscenium arch, the exits, galleries and lighting effects were incorporated into some fantastic scene from Spain, Italy or the Middle East, the reality of which the audience, who in the thirties got no further than the British seaside for their holidays, would never see. Some were mainly *trompe-l'œil* murals or bas-reliefs but the more spectacular included solid architectural detail.

Atmospherics had been popular in America for some years before they reached Britain in 1929. Not everyone liked them. In January 1930, the same month that the new Tivoli opened at Portsmouth disguised as a Spanish courtyard, *Kine Weekly* expressed some disapproval of atmospherics as

* The architecture and design of British cinemas have been admirably described in great detail by David Atwell in *Cathedrals of the Movies*.

obtrusive, expensive and, a strangely practical note, dust traps. By contrast '*l'art moderne*' seemed preferable for it was uncluttered, cheaper and, presumably, dust-free. By 1933 a more modern and understated style influenced by cubism and cool art deco was making a growing impact. It was not yet associated with Oscar Deutsch's Odeon circuit, which was still very small. In fact in that year the 700-seat Odeon at Lancing opened with an auditorium designed, by Mrs Lily Deutsch, as an old-world garden, the dado a stone wall with flowers and trees painted above it, and the ceiling as the sky. Before long, however, the Odeons adopted a quintessential thirties look, streamlined and plain, the apotheosis of the antiseptic style for which *Kine Weekly* seemed to hanker. A rapidly growing circuit of medium-sized halls, Odeon created a house style aimed at comfort rather than luxury, and good taste rather than magnificence. With exteriors in either brick or the well-known cream faience tiles, with slim vertical towers or fins and characteristic lettering, there was an overall similarity also in the simple interiors with their pastel art deco detail.

To digress, the rise of the Odeon circuit, which finally rivalled ABC and Gaumont-British, with Deutsch's highly original approach to exhibition was one of the success stories of the thirties. The son of an immigrant from Hungary who set up a prosperous family scrap-metal business in Birmingham, he had entered the film business in the twenties in association with two other members of the large Jewish community in the Midlands, his former school friends Michael Balcon and Victor Saville. Whilst these two moved over to production, Deutsch acquired two Coventry cinemas in 1925 and before long was a prominent provincial exhibitor. He founded Cinema Service to run his expanding circuit and provide centralised services for his cinemas, and at the Birmingham suburb of Perry Bar he first used the name 'Odeon' for one of his cinemas in 1930. Each new cinema was a separate company, the bulk of the money for the site being raised by the sale of preference shares to local business interests likely to benefit from the existence of a cinema in the community. A small number of ordinary shares would be held by Deutsch and his associates W. G. Elcock and F. S. Bates. A rent charge on the site and later a mortgage on the building, raised chiefly from insurance and finance companies, would pay for the building itself, but the policy of local involvement was deliberate and every effort was made to establish the cinema as a focus for the neighbourhood, with ceremonial openings attended by local dignitaries. Deutsch sited his cinemas in new suburbs and dormitory towns previously without them. These were being spread across the country by ribbon builders in the twenties and thirties and the sites, which were relatively inexpensive, avoided competition with established circuits. When the conversion to talkies occurred Deutsch's technical expert, Sidney Swingler, conducted research at the laboratories of British Thomson-Houston, as a result of which in 1931 Deutsch founded Sound Equipment to market the successful BT-H system of sound reproduction, which he installed in his own cinemas.

By 1933 the circuit, with 26 cinemas, was the eighth biggest in Britain, and in October Odeon Theatres was registered as a private £100 company to replace Cinema Service. A London office was opened in November. Still based in Birmingham, the circuit also included a number of cinemas in the south-east and a number that, having been acquired rather than built, had names other than Odeon. Newly built ones, however, were all called Odeon and from now on evolved the characteristic contemporary architecture and decorative style which created a brand image for the company similar to that of the chain stores then extending across the country. Early in 1935 the capital was put up to £200,000, almost all the ordinary shares owned by Deutsch himself. The two other directors remained, but the operation was very much Deutsch's personal business and according to the articles of association he was to be the permanent managing director, with a perpetual casting vote. An attractive figure in the development of cinema exhibition, with an individual and intelligent approach, despite bad health he made the local Odeon a comfortable feature of suburban life, providing value for money rather than spectacular showmanship.*

The Odeon style was more in touch with contemporary life than the atmospherics. At the time many regarded the latter with amused tolerance as vulgar displays for common people. The more sophisticated cinemas in the West End of London did not go further than the semi-atmospheric. Theodore Komisarjevsky, a highbrow and aristocratic stage producer-designer who designed a number of bizarre settings for Bernstein's Granada circuit, had little opinion of the public for whom he created them. His oft-quoted remark 'The commercial cinema not only caters for imbeciles; it breeds them'[5] suggests that the bad taste of his conceptions was an expression of condescension to the audience. Deutsch, with his emphasis not on fantastic surroundings but on reasonable standards of comfort and ambience in which to concentrate on the film, showed greater respect both for the films and for the people.

The great palaces, the comfortable modest halls and the struggling flea-pits were full for comparatively few of their weekly performances, of course. Deutsch and Rowson were two who were concerned to push up weekly admissions by persuading more of the population to go to the cinema. Estimating that some 5 million out of a population of 40 million went to the cinema once a week or more, Deutsch considered another £300,000 could easily be taken at the box office by attracting new customers. Rowson said in his Royal Statistical Society paper that cinemas were only a third full on average. In 1936 he calculated that 3,800,000 seats and 19,500,000 admissions gave a rate of 5·1 full houses a week, whereas the comparable figure for the United States was over 7 full houses. Like Deutsch he considered that an increase of 1 per cent or £370,000 was feasible and suggested publicity like the 'Eat More Fruit' campaign of the time. Both

* For later development of the company see under United Artists.

accepted without question, as did the entire industry, that progress lay in getting more and more people in to the same cinemas to see the same films.

This monolithic philosophy, however, with its limiting effect on film content, was already out of date. As cinemagoing spread upwards in society different tastes emerged, and specialised cinemas and film societies began to cater for them. There were several attempts to pinpoint the preferences of regular cinemagoers. Both *Film Weekly* and *Picturegoer*, the latter the biggest of the fan papers with a circulation of 100,000, held annual ballots amongst their readers. Bernstein conducted several rather more elaborate polls in an effort to draw systematic conclusions about his patrons' opinions, as distinct from his box-office results. But the problem with the monolithic cinema, with everyone seeing all the films, was that by its very nature it had to please the least discriminating. A writer in *Kine Weekly* complained that 'the cheapest and most obvious gags are the ones that get the laughs: the sloppier the sentimentality the more certain the tears'.[6] Cyril Ray talked of 'a semi-educated public . . . the film of today presents, with supreme technical efficiency, a theme of unparalleled triviality'.[7] Under the circumstances, as Charles Tennyson, the poet's grandson, remarked in the discussion following Rowson's address to the Royal Statistical Society, it was surprising how good a lot of the films were. But there were still many amongst the better educated sections of society who would have agreed with Liberal MP Isaac Foot and many Wesleyan Methodists in their frequent condemnation of the cinema, or the poet John Drinkwater when he asserted that 'Nothing has done so much to vulgarise the taste of the world as the cinema'.[8] On the other hand there were also plenty of signs of society's growing acceptance of the cinema. Big premières were attended by diplomats, politicians and aristocrats as well as by intellectuals. The Federation of British Industries put on a gala film show for delegates to the Imperial Conference in 1930. A big dinner to launch a new version of *Phantom of the Opera* was attended by many famous members of the establishment. When Douglas Fairbanks and Mary Pickford visited Britain in 1929 it was with Lady Mountbatten that they stayed, and when Chaplin came in 1931 he gave a party at which he entertained such celebrities as Lord and Lady Astor, Lady Oxford and Winston Churchill.

If such straws in the wind showed that many educated people were now prepared to take films seriously, it did not necessarily mean that they would join the regular fans who went to the pictures whatever was on. The founding of film societies enabled them to select their films, and by 1938 it was estimated[9] that there were over a hundred of them. More important was the appearance of specialised repertory cinemas showing revivals of good films. The Shaftesbury Avenue Pavilion in London had been run by Stuart Davis as an art house showing repertory and unusual films in the late twenties. When his lease ran out in 1929 Paul Rotha and others obtained his mailing list and secured support from his regular patrons for a film group, founded in October 1930, to hire another hall and run it as a rep cinema.

They were unsuccessful, but the idea was taken up by the exhibitor Eric Hakim, whose Academy Cinema in Oxford Street opened early in 1931, under the management of Elsie Cohen, with a six-week season of French films. Later a season of unusual films there included *Earth*, early work by Chaplin and *The Cabinet of Dr Caligari*. There were other rep cinemas in London, but the Academy was outstanding in finding worthwhile films from all over the world. Foreign films, widely shown in silent days with translated titles, had disappeared from the ordinary cinema since the advent of the talkie except in the unsatisfactory form of multilinguals (q.v.). The best of them now began to reappear in these specialised cinemas, and the well educated tended to prefer them to run-of-the-mill American or British films. Similar cinemas gradually appeared in other large towns. In 1933 the little Everyman Theatre in Hampstead was converted to a rep cinema of 285 seats by J. S. Fairfax-Jones, who had earlier founded the Southampton film society, and proved very successful in this rather special residential area of London, which was a centre of *avant-garde* artistic activity. The Curzon Cinema, opened in early 1934 near Park Lane by the Marquis of Casa Maury, set new standards of comfort and elegance, with a purist approach to the film which disdained distractions like interval music or supporting programmes. In 1936 Studios One and Two opened very near the Academy in Oxford Street with two small cinemas in one building, the second with only 300 seats.

The days of the monlithic system were numbered. Its fragmentation was delayed by the coming of war in 1939 and the mass audience, presented with a mass product, actually increased enormously during the next few years, admissions soaring in a way that neither Deutsch nor Rowson would have dared to hope for. Yet the process had already begun. Rep cinemas, film societies, television (not yet in the home to any great extent but already greatly feared by the exhibitors) small, intimate plural cinemas – in fact all the means except video and cable television by which people would be able to exercise a more personal choice of film in future – were already threatening the cinema as it then was.

Chapter 2

The Organisation of Labour

With some four thousand cinemas in the country, staffed by cleaners, ushers, projectionists, box-office staff, electricians and managers, a large number of people were earning their living in the cinemas by 1929. Long hours, low pay and little or no provision for such things as overtime, paid holidays or conciliation machinery made it a depressing industry in which to work.

Two large trade unions, both affiliated to the TUC, competed for members throughout the thirties. The National Association of Theatrical Employees, which also included workers in legitimate theatres and music halls, aimed at industry-wide representation of all cinema workers and was prepared to let members retain their craft union cards as long as they were represented in their dealings with the film industry employers by the NATE.[1] The Electrical Trades Union wished to recruit electricians and projectionists only, and had an early studio agreement with BIP for those working at Elstree and Welwyn. Both unions wanted to include workers in the studios as well as those in the cinemas.

The coming of the talkie focused attention on the projectionists, who now required greater skill and deserved better pay. An organisation for projectionists was already in being. When talkies came in and the big sound companies were talking toughly about boycotting cinemas with poor sound performance the Guild of British Projectionists and Technicians was organised in May 1929 to set up inspection and training schemes. Its stated aims were 'to uphold the status of Projectionists through efficiency and good service'.[2] It sought recognition from the Cinematograph Exhibitors' Association as the voice of the projectionists, but as a craft organisation rather than as a trade union. In May 1931 it was registered as a limited company, which meant that it was legally unable to negotiate as a union.

NATE did little in 1930 apart from concluding its first studio agreement at Elstree over carpenters' rates of pay.[3] The ETU, on the other hand, was very active on behalf of projectionists. In the early summer of 1930 a new branch in Manchester, claiming that projectionists there had to work between 60 and 75 hours a week for between 24/- and £2, threatened to strike unless the CEA granted them a 48-hour week. The CEA was unwilling to recognise any union at all, asking instead that cases of exploitation should be referred to it individually. In the autumn ETU operators in Liverpool held a lightning strike, but the North-West CEA still refused to recognise the union. Despite official CEA policy, though, the Manchester branches of the ETU and CEA nearly reached an agreement. This was for a 48-hour week, agreed overtime, one week's holiday for every six months and a minimum pay of £4 in grade-A cinemas and less for B and C halls, as well as some provision for conciliation. The CEA headquarters, however, censured the branch for this and it withdrew. The ETU then considered calling out 150 operators and 100 electricians, claiming that this was 95 per cent of the Manchester operatives.* Next the Liverpool ETU members came out. As so often happens, both sides claimed success. The Secretary of the Birmingham branch of the union claimed that conditions were bad there also, with chief operators getting only £2 5s 0d, but again the CEA refused to discuss the matter. Later in the year, however, agreement was reached in Liverpool and conflict seems to have died away for a while.

From now on, although the ETU continued to press for a 48-hour week and was less willing to compromise than NATE, leadership in the struggle passed to the latter. Next year the Labour Minister of Labour, Margaret Bondfield, promised to look into the wages and working conditions of cinema employees, but nothing was done. At the TUC Conference Hugh Roberts, the General Secretary of NATE, moved a resolution which was adopted, urging the government to institute an inquiry into pay and conditions. He called exhibitors 'the most relentless and unscrupulous individuals the world has ever seen'. The attempt to involve the government in regulation of the industry continued to be part of NATE policy but was resisted by successive governments. Roberts was replaced as Secretary of NATE in 1932 by Tom O'Brien, a former stage electrician and a union official who had belonged to NATE since 1919, and who was to lead it vigorously and successfully for many years.

In November 1931 a joint conciliation board was formed by the London and Home Counties Branch of the CEA and the London Trades Council, which included the ETU, NATE, the Musicians' Union and the Guild of Projectionists. This was to play an important part in laying the basis for later national negotiations. Preliminary proposals were announced in the spring of 1933. These included a 60-hour week for male uniformed staff, 54 for women, 55 for projectionists, time and a half for overtime work, not more than 5 hours to be worked on Sunday, double rates for Sunday work and a week's holiday a year. These mild proposals caused consternation at some branches of the CEA although many in the unions felt they did not go nearly far enough. After further discussion the final recommendations were published in April 1934. The classes of hall were defined, an AA hall being one with average weekly takings of £1,000 or more, and A hall takings

* This seems unlikely as *Kine Year Book* lists 119 cinemas in Manchester at the time.

of £500 to £1,000, a B hall £300 to £500 and a C hall under £300. Pay rates ranged from £5 5s 0d a week for a first projectionist in an AA hall down to £1 2s 6d for a third projectionist in a C hall, and from £5 for a stage manager in an AA hall to 15/- for a cleaner in a C hall. Hours were to be 60 a week for a man and 55 for a woman if not working on a Sunday, or 55 for a man and 50 for a woman if Sundays were being worked.

These proposals were an advance on the worst of existing conditions but many cinemas already had better terms and both unions rejected them. The ETU was strongly critical of the proposed hours. At a mass meeting called by both unions O'Brien of NATE called again for a national inquiry and legislation for a trades board, with wages and conditions backed by law, and urged more cinema workers to join the unions. According to him, 6,500 cinema workers then belonged to NATE out of a possible 20,000.[4] Cinema workers joining the ETU were very much fewer, and even in 1936 in its memorandum to the Moyne Committee it only claimed 1,000.

The Joint Conciliation Board's proposals were finally adopted by the CEA's London and Home Counties branch, NATE and the Musicians' Union for a twelve-month trial period beginning in September 1935, covering some 10,000 people. O'Brien was prepared to settle for what he could get, and considered the attitude of the ETU, which continued to demand a 48-hour week, as unrealistic. At the TUC Conference in September, this time at Margate, an ETU resolution condemned the agreement and demanded that the industry should be brought under the provisions of the Trade Boards Act as a sweated industry. The resolution, condemned by O'Brien, was shelved.

Meanwhile in February 1935 the General Council of the TUC had at last sent a deputation to the Home Secretary which included representatives of NATE, the ETU and the TUC, seeking an inquiry and legislation. The predictable reply was that wages were a matter for the unions and the employers to settle. It was added that if the Cinematograph Act of 1909 were to be revised at any time some regulation of working conditions might be included.

By 1935 the new Association of Cine-Technicians was starting to organise the studio technicians, and both the other unions turned their attention to manual workers in production. The NATE Annual Report of July 1935 spoke of an agreement with ABPC and of 'influence' rather than agreements with Gaumont-British, Stoll, Fox-British and London Film Productions, and asserted that the terms of many studios were already up to union rates of pay and conditions. In September it called for the reaffirmation of O'Brien's policy, which he claimed had pushed up wages in the studios by £100,000 in the last twelve months. In October an agreement already reached with Gaumont-British informally in June was made public. It covered plasterers, carpenters, electricians, props, painters, stage-hands and others over wages, overtime and other matters.[5] The 1936 report mentioned agreements also with London Films and British Lion. In his evidence to the Moyne Committee in 1936–7 O'Brien claimed the union had about 5,000 members in the studios, although out of a total membership of 8,421 in 1936[6] this seems surprisingly high. Meanwhile in August 1935 the ETU had brought about a strike of electricians at BIP. Work was brought to a standstill for four days, but the union decided to concentrate on building up branches for projectionists in the big cities in future and leave the studios to others.

NATE was growing much faster and now changed its name to the National Association of Theatrical and Kine Employees. At the Plymouth TUC Conference in 1936 an ETU resolution urging a 48-hour week yet again was amended to bring it into line with TUC policy in favour of a 40-hour week, so even here the ETU lost the initiative. In the south-east the arrangements recommended by the Joint Conciliation Board were working well, but many exhibitors and CEA branches still refused to recognise either union and one unionist attacked them for using 'the language of slave-owners of 150 years ago'.[7] Again it was discussed whether the government should be asked to schedule exhibition as a sweated industry.

1937 was a year of great progress for NATKE. Agreement was reached with the AC-T defining their respective spheres in the studios and providing for mutual support and joint action. Leaving the higher technicians to the AC-T, it had wage agreements for other workers with all the main studios and with the Gaumont-British, ABC, Odeon and County circuits, as well as a number of CEA branches. In 1937 the TUC Conference was held at Norwich, and NATKE pressed for official support of the film industry both on ideological grounds and as a source of employment, urging that regulation of hours and conditions should be included in the quota legislation then being discussed. In October 1937 the Film Industry Employees' Council was formed by all the unions, including one which represented artistes, to take part in the discussions leading to the Films Act.

NATKE continued to reach agreements with CEA branches in 1937 and early 1938. These agreements, of course, covered the projectionists, whom the ETU regarded as their concern. NATKE usually accepted weekly hours of up to 54, but at the same time talks were held with the London Joint Conciliation Board on the possibility of securing a 48-hour week and a 12½ per cent rise in pay. By early 1938 there were 95 NATKE branches, 70 of them for projectionists, and a membership of 16,000. The union was on the way to securing recognition as an industry-wide negotiating force. In February 1938 it succeeded in signing an agreement, with the Leicester CEA, which included a normal working week of 48 hours. Significantly, it also included a two-year probationary period for projectionists pending a national agreement, as a first step towards controlling entry into the industry.

In early 1938 the ETU found that NATKE talks with local CEAs had prejudiced their position, for several CEAs refused to negotiate with them whilst talks with the other union were going on. The first was Hull in

February 1938, and when the same thing happened next month in London the ETU threatened to strike. In reply O'Brien publicly complained that the ETU action was meant to sabotage his own talks on the 48-hour week for all workers. Over Easter ETU members in Hull, London and Manchester went on strike, and the Gaumont-British studios at Islington were briefly shut down when fifteen projectionists and electricians struck, but they were soon replaced by NATKE and Guild members. The AC-T was sympathetic to the strikes and left-wing sources claimed that large numbers were involved, but O'Brien, who belittled them and said that the strikers were damaging the unions' cause, put the figure at only 300. The strikes lasted some weeks in London and Manchester and longer in Hull, and in both Manchester and London the employers were finally prepared to consider a 48-hour week.

By that time, however, the NATKE negotiations in favour of it seemed to be nearing success. For, although the larger union continued to make agreements allowing longer hours, the Joint Conciliation Board at last agreed to consider its proposals for a 48-hour week and a 12½ per cent rise in pay in June 1938. A general national draft agreement was presented for discussion at the next NATKE annual conference in July, covering the hours, conditions and pay of all cinema workers. For the first time a 48-hour week with no exceptions, and 45 for women, was claimed. An important clause, leading to a closed shop, was also introduced:

> It also provides that in case of any vacancy arising, the manager shall ask for a list of the unemployed members of the National Association of Theatrical and Kine Employees from the local secretary, and, if practicable, fill the vacancies from the said list, the management having the right to select or reject if unsuitable.
>
> In the event of a non-member of the N.A.T.K.E. being engaged, such employee shall be required to apply for membership of the Association at the end of the first week of employment.[8]

O'Brien called the draft agreement a national charter for the cinema worker and hoped that it would eventually be adopted by the CEA. But this did not happen, and its existence gave the government an excuse, if it needed one, for taking no action. Its half-promise of February 1935 to look into pay and conditions had led to nothing until, after much prompting, an official questionnaire was sent to 4,800 cinemas in October 1937. Two years later persistent questioning in Parliament by a Labour MP, Harry Day,* elicited the reply from Ernest Brown, the Minister of Labour, that inquiries were complete, but he insisted that matters were best left to the negotiations between joint bodies representing employers and employees which he heard were in progress. In exasperation Day demanded: 'How can that apply to cases where the people concerned do not belong to any

---

* Harry Day, a loyal and vociferous parliamentary watchdog for the film industry, died several months later in September 1939, aged 59.

association?' There was no reply.'⁹ Later in the month Brown repeated, 'We are anxious to promote harmonious discussions between the two sides of industry', at which Day asked if he was aware that some smaller cinemas would not let their employees join a union. Again, 'There was no answer'.¹⁰ A similar exchange took place the next month also.

The union had made remarkable progress under O'Brien's leadership. By the summer before the war it had 33 agreements covering 45,000 workers in 2,500 cinemas. There were also new hopes of continuing the organisation of studio workers, which had slowed down during the production slump, and of negotiating industry-wide agreements with the new employers' organisation. This was the Film Production Employers' Federation, which changed its name to British Film Producers' Association in 1939. The old Film Producers' Group of the British Federation of Industries had been prevented by its constitution from negotiating labour matters with the unions, and in any case by its very nature could not represent American production interests in Britain. The rise of the AC-T had made it essential that there should be a body that could negotiate on behalf of all producers and the new organisation was in being by early 1938. Later that year NATKE, ETU and the AC-T were considering the possibility of setting up an organisation to represent all workers in the production side of the industry, including higher, semi-skilled and unskilled workers. The first studio agreements reached by NATKE were with Nettlefold and Sound City early in 1939, covering skilled and artisan labour and including a 47-hour week.

Thus the unionisation of workers in the cinemas and of craft and manual workers in the studios made great progress during the thirties. The organisation of film technicians, however, was even more remarkable. By the early thirties there was already a small learned technical society. A branch of the American Society of Motion Picture Engineers, formed in London in 1928, broke away in January 1931 and established the British Kinematograph Society under the chairmanship of Simon Rowson. By the end of 1931 it had 188 members. Its aim was 'the dissemination of knowledge and the elucidation of technical problems within the Industry',¹¹ and it continued to flourish, although on a small scale, throughout the thirties and after. Like the Projectionists' Guild, it was concerned not with union matters but with status and excellence.

For the technicians were better educated and had careers rather than jobs, and although they worked long hours and were poorly paid in comparison with their Hollywood counterparts there is little sign in the early thirties that they shared the cinema workers' discontent. The nature of their work led to an absence of routine and a spirit of 'the show must go on', and excitement and ambition, especially among the youngers ones, kept them going when they were expected to work all night, to sleep at the studio if public transport had closed down, and to improvise endlessly to meet unexpected problems, especially on location. Printing and lab technicians

SALLY IN OUR ALLEY
Gracie Fields in her first film, which she was later to describe as a real story, not just one 'stitched around her'. With Florence Desmond. Produced by Basil Dean at Beaconsfield in 1931.

LOOKING ON THE BRIGHT SIDE
Archie Pitt persuaded Basil Dean to include this expensive set in Gracie Fields' third film. The two buildings moved unsteadily together across the Ealing stage until the lovers could embrace across the gap. Dean directed with Graham Cutts in 1932, and the art director was Clifford Pember.

A HONEYMOON ADVENTURE
More to Dean's liking were films shot on location. Benita Hume and Harold Huth are in the grounds of Dalcross
Castle, Inverness, in this 1931 film.

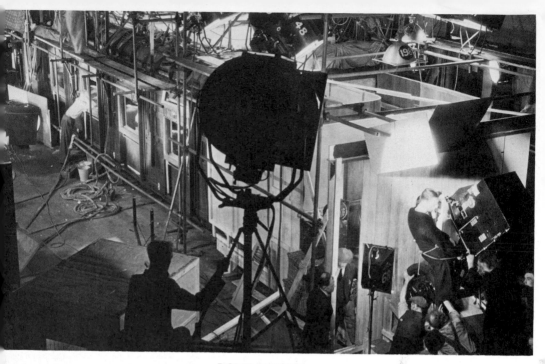

ROME EXPRESS

The railway carriage, wall and platform built at Shepherd's Bush in 1932 for a film whose action almost all took place on a train. Directed by Walter Forde, art director Andrew Mazzei.

JACK'S THE BOY

Jack Hulbert as a policeman on the lot at Welwyn in 1932. Director Walter Forde, art director Vetchinsky, cameraman Leslie Rowson; a Gainsborough film.

THE GOOD COMPANIONS

In a cosy English boarding house the touring concert artistes toast the troupe – Denis Hoey, Marjorie Binner John Gielgud, Percy Parsons, A. W. Baskcomb, Mary Glynne, Edmund Gwenn, Jessie Matthews, Viola Compto and Jack Hawkins. Victor Saville directed this important Gaumont-British film at Shepherd's Bush in 1932. A director Alfred Junge.

THE GOOD COMPANIONS

The concert party in action, in the film of J. B. Priestley's bestseller.

found life less rewarding, but later memoirs and recollections of those directly involved in production convey no sense of injustice but instead a perverse pride in how hard they had to work, and the flexibility with which they helped each other and met the demands of their jobs. Despite this, by the end of the decade they were almost entirely unionised. Being comparatively few in number they were easy to organise, and under the leadership of a keen left-wing group rapidly became an articulate and effective radical union. They were soon in a position to demand an elaborate scale of hours, pay and conditions, and manning levels and job demarcation which were later to prove costly to a British film industry always threatened with economic disaster. Two things boosted support for the new union: first the large number of refugee film makers from Nazi Europe working in British studios, and later the production slump of 1937–8.

In the early part of 1933 a group of Gaumont-British technicians, including the editor Sidney Cole, fell into the habit of meeting at a cafe in Shepherd's Bush to discuss film matters. According to R. J. Minney[12] it was at first simply a select band of top technicians without union aspirations. Adopting the name of the Association of Studio Workers, soon changed to the Association of Cine-Technicians, it turned into a more formal organisation, at first under the colourful and slightly disreputable Captain Cope, and then with help from Tom O'Brien became a fully-fledged trade union and met for the first time as such in February 1934.

At this meeting the employment of aliens in British studios was one of the chief topics, and it is ironic, if understandable, that throughout the thirties a constant refrain running through the deliberations of this very left-wing body was a desire to prevent European film makers, many of them refugees from Nazism, being freely employed in British studios. It was suggested that if the union had a register of members it would be less easy for employers to obtain a work permit for a foreigner by telling the Ministry of Labour that no British technician was available.[13] The exodus from Hitler's Europe from 1933 onwards included many well-known film makers and Michael Balcon and the Ostrers, among others, with their experience of Anglo-European co-production, were glad to take advantage of the presence of experienced directors, cameramen and designers. In 1933 and early 1934 there were between twenty and thirty working in British studios, most of them for Gaumont-Gainsborough, Korda and BIP. As many as ten were at Shepherd's Bush. The union's aims as published in *Kine Year Book* in 1934, while largely those of a craft guild concerned to safeguard standards and employment, included the phrase 'To check foreign employment if a Britisher is available capable of undertaking the work required by the Company'.

Starting with 98 members in 1933, the AC-T grew rapidly and numbered 605 by the end of 1935. Membership fluctuated, however, owing to the irregularity of employment in films. Not all technicians were on contract as some were employed on a picture-to-picture basis, a practice the union was not able to eradicate during the thirties. Membership included cameramen, editors, sound technicians, and members of the art and scenario departments and labs. A newsreel section was being formed in late 1935. George Elvin became General Secretary in January 1935, introduced by his brother Harold Elvin, a film enthusiast. George Elvin, son of the trade unionist and later President of the TUC. H. H. Elvin, had been Honorary Secretary of the British Workers' Sports Association and was a professional trade union organiser. Thorold Dickinson and Ivor Montagu became vice-presidents, and with backing from Labour Party supporters like Sidney Bernstein and the Ostrers the union was on its way. Its politics were further to the left than those of either the ETU or NATKE. Elvin himself was a Labour supporter but Sidney Cole and two of the most influential members, Ralph Bond and Ivor Montagu, were communists. Montagu, member of a wealthy and titled banking family, was a talented film maker who worked on Gaumont's *Wings Over Everest* in the summer of 1933 and soon became a key member of Balcon's production team. He and Bond, a documentary film maker, had together organised the import and distribution of the great Soviet silent films. Under a professional trade union organiser the union became more suave, changing its rather frank remark about foreigners' work permits to a discreet clause about 'Consultation with Authorities on employment of foreign technicians', and they succeeded in setting up an official employment bureau licenced annually by the LCC.

The resentment felt against aliens continued to be a unifying factor. In November 1935 the General Council issued a protest at the number of foreign technicians engaged in Britain and set up a committee to investigate it. The next spring a deputation, which included Elvin, Desmond Dickinson and Sidney Cole, complained to the Ministry of Labour that at any one time about a hundred foreign technicians exclusive of resident aliens were at work in Britain, standing in the way of promising British talent and causing unemployment. The following year it was claimed that 122 foreign technicians had applied for work permits in 1935 and all but 12 had been granted.

The figure of 110 permits must presumably refer to all forms of production, including, for example, short films and the colour advertising films of Dr Gaspar. As far as mainstream feature films made during the course of 1935 are concerned, examination of screen credits reveals that some 55 senior European film makers and 25 non-Europeans, mostly American, worked on them. Americans had always been employed in Britain, most of them not of top rank and not attracting any resentment from British film makers. It was the Ostrer policy of appointing Europeans to top jobs which had given the AC-T its rallying call, and this grew in strength as time went by and Korda's Hungarians and others, as well as Max Schach's less impressive but equally showy associates, seemed to dominate production. It became a bitter joke that to get a job in British films you only needed a foreign accent. Xenophobia was not the current sentiment in British left-wing circles, which were sympathetic to refugees from Nazism. But when the union complained, as it did in 1935, that not all foreign imports were able to pass their knowledge on to their British juniors because of language difficulties, and said in its 1939 report that 'refugees' blocked British promotion, it was clear that it was the Europeans, not the Americans, who were under attack.

The union continued to expand in 1936, taking part in the Moyne discussions, and had 1,200 members by the end of the year, claiming that this was almost 100 per cent of studio technicians. At the end of 1936 the union prepared a set of demands for selected studios which included a normal 48-hour week, overtime, two weeks paid holiday a year, sickness pay, 50 per cent of the money received by the studio for their services when hired to other studios and a £1 15s 0d minimum for juniors. At the end of December the first studio agreement was signed for a trial period of six months, predictably enough with Gaumont-British at Shepherd's Bush. This did not follow the terms of the standard demands but covered minimum rates for camera staff, sound editing, stills and continuity personnel and some of those in the sound department, and dealt with such matters as late work, location work, travelling expenses, termination of employment, holidays and sickness pay. The terms were in no way remarkable but it was a beginning, although in fact Shepherd's Bush closed down before the six months was up and was to remain shut for two and a half years.

At the same time AC-T turned its attention to the laboratory workers and in November 1936 asked the printing and lab companies for a meeting. The request was turned down. The next spring the union claimed that district meetings of lab members had promised support and the General Council now threatened action. Their demands included a 44-hour week spread over 5½ days, with overtime and night rates, limits on how many hours could be worked continuously, provision for travelling expenses when public transport was not running, and adequate wage fixing, with an average basic wage of £3 10s 0d. In May 1937 the AC-T met the employers' representatives under Neville Kearney's chairmanship and the proposals were circulated.

A month later, as we have seen, the AC-T signed an agreement with NATKE for mutual support and joint action. A joint consultative committee was formed as a result of which the Film Industry Employees' Council was set up in the autumn, with O'Brien as president and Elvin as secretary. It soon represented not only the AC-T and NATKE but also the ETU, the British Association of Film Directors, which was still in existence although not active, the Film Artistes' Association, representing mainly small-part players, and the newly formed Screenwriters' Association. Ivor Montagu was on the Council. Trade union forces had been strengthened in June by the appointment to the post of President of the AC-T of another member of an aristocratic family with many useful contacts, Anthony Asquith.

The FIEC claimed to represent 10,000 people engaged in film production, and it was felt that national collective bargaining was in sight. The official figure of those working in film production at the time was given in the Board of Trade Production Census late in 1938,[14] which put the number in the week ending 16 October 1937 at 9,529.* But 4,125 of these were artistes, who in fact were not yet very highly organised, and it was the other 5,404 who constituted the FIEC's real strength.

At the time there was considerable unemployment in the industry. The protracted discussions about the forthcoming quota legislation had led to great uncertainty and many companies were waiting to see what sort of production would be possible. At the same time a crisis of confidence among investors in the City contributed to the fall in production. In November 1937 Thorold Dickinson, with Anthony Asquith, Tom O'Brien and the cameraman Henry Harris representing labour and with Maurice Elvey representing the directors, formed an AC-T deputation to R. A. Butler, Parliamentary Secretary to the Ministry of Labour, to protest about the current unemployment in the film industry. Once more opposition to alien technicians played its part. Claiming that the number of unemployed members of the AC-T had risen from 40 to 200 in twelve months (which would have been 16 per cent of the membership of 1,200 previously mentioned), they sought a ruling that only one foreign technician might be employed on a film unless equivalent British technicians were also employed.

Nothing was done and unemployment continued to get worse, and early in 1938 the FIEC held a protest meeting at Gatti's restaurant in London which unanimously urged the government to amend the Films Bill in order to ensure production workers continuity of work and better pay and conditions. They referred to unemployment of 80 per cent among production workers, although it was not explained how this figure was reached. At the time many studios were closed, although this situation did not last. Shepherd's Bush remained closed, but most reopened after two or three months, when the new legislation came into being. However, production did not return to its former level, because changes in the quota laws had killed the quota quickie. The new system resulted in better, but fewer, films. But the labour unions were naturally more concerned with the volume of employment than with the quality of production.

The only response to Labour's request that regulation of conditions and pay be included in the Quota Act had been Section 34, which laid down that pay and conditions of employment in the film industry were not to be inferior to those in government employment. Shortly after it came into force this led to trouble. Because of the slump Pinebrook had been formed in January 1938 with plans for six £20,000 films to be made on a co-operative basis, with some of the participants working for low salaries and waiting

* In the Board of Trade evidence to the Moyne Committee it was stated that the only available evidence of the numbers actually engaged in production up to that time, 1936, was the 1931 Census of Population, which put the number at just over 6,000 excluding artistes and those out of work.

for a share of the returns. Probably the best known of these was *This Man is News*, made in the early summer of 1938 and said by Richard Norton of Pinebrook to have cost only £12,000.[15] The Labour MP Tom Williams promptly rose in the House to ask the President of the Board of Trade whether the company had complied with Clause 34, and mentioned the dissatisfaction of the union. Elvin issued a statement about 'a recent film' on which 70 hours a week had been worked with no overtime, with inadequate dinner money being paid after 8 p.m. and salaries which were from 17 to 35 per cent below the recognised rates. He mentioned one cameraman who received only 50 per cent of his salary and had to wait for the rest to come as a co-operative share of the distribution. Henry Harris, one of the deputation to R. A. Butler, was the film's lighting cameraman. As it happened, *This Man is News* was a box-office success and immensely profitable, grossing £58,000 according to Norton. But the union clearly had no sympathy with this form of production.

Later in the year it put forward a draft standard studio agreement for weekly paid staff, which after September 1938 was considered by a negotiating committee of the Studios Group of the BFPA. This laid down with great precision salaries, a working week of 47 hours with provisions for overtime, breaks, holidays, sickness pay, termination of service, payment for technicians lent to other studios, insurance, travelling and disputes procedures. The suggested pay rates are revealing for the light they throw on relative status in the studio. Directors and top technicians were on individual contracts, but the minimum weekly rates show the lighting cameraman as the aristocrat of the technicians with a minimum of £50 a week, the art director and grade-A editor coming far lower with £20 a week, grade-A sound recordist £16, camera operator and maintenance engineer £15, first assistant director £12 and stills cameraman £11. Other rates were as little as £2 or in one case £1 15s 0d. The draft also laid down who would get a screen credit and, significantly, minimum crews. This quietly introduced the basis for the manning levels of later years.[16]

With this draft agreement under consideration the new producers' organisation signed the first national collective agreement in February 1939, covering 14,000 lab workers in 14 labs. To last for two years, it was signed by two very upper-class negotiators, Asquith for the AC-T and the Hon. Captain Richard Norton for the employers. It established minimum wage rates from £1 a week for juvenile foyer girls to £7 10s 0d for optical printers and superintendents. The normal working week was to be 44 hours, or 47 in processing and newsreels, and not more than 16 hours were to be worked consecutively. Provision was made for overtime, night work, holidays with pay, sick leave and conciliation procedures.

With production somewhat restored after the new Quota Act, AC-T membership rose again to 1,389 in May 1938. But as the industry settled down in its new shape, with comparatively few films, the trend was reversed once more and the annual report in April 1939 recorded a fall to 1,212 and again made the claim that there was 80 per cent unemployment in production. Because of this, the report said, educational and training establishments had been approached to restrict entry. Restricted entry, the closed shop, demarcation and minimum crews were to be familiar characteristics of British film production after the war, and sprang directly from this struggle to cope with the unemployment caused by the production crisis and the new quota legislation.

The annual report published in April 1939 took a last swipe at the foreign technician. Scrutiny of the feature films in production between March 1938 and the month of publication of the report shows that the wave of refugees was virtually over. Most had already passed on to other countries, leaving about twenty in Britain, including, briefly, Erich Pommer, and a number of others who made Britain their home and continued to contribute to the film industry. American quota production in Britain now took the form of few, but important, pictures and the number of Americans working in Britain, also about twenty, included several senior producers and directors, each of them visiting the country for one production only.[17] As before, it was the European film makers who held key posts and attracted animosity and the report included the suggestion that 'whenever a technically good refugee enters the country . . . another not so good foreign technician, who is not a refugee, should at the first opportunity be refused permission for a further stay in this country'.

Chapter 3

The Quota

The 1927 quota legislation had a profound and damaging effect on the structure of the British film industry. Discussion of it continued throughout the early and middle 1930s in Parliament and in the trade, and when the Act expired in 1938 it was replaced by one with very different terms.

It was primarily intended to keep British production alive in the face of competition from American films. As the Board of Trade representative to the Moyne Committee said in 1936, 'The purpose of the 1927 Act was to build up a healthy film-making industry'. But the methods by which American films were exploited had caused difficulties for exhibitors, and in an effort to solve all the film industry's problems at once the legislators had lost sight of their primary aim. The renting subsidiaries of Hollywood producers had secured a grip on British screens during the twenties by insisting that a cinema owner who wanted to book one desirable picture must book a large block of other films, some unseen and some even unmade. By attempting to check advance and blind booking of this sort, and requiring renters and exhibitors to include a fixed percentage of British films in their programmes, it was intended to help both producers and exhibitors at the same time. But their interests were not indentical. The crucial importance of protecting British production was forgotten in the attempt to check booking abuses. This oversimplified approach was to have a disastrous effect on production as a whole whilst failing to stop block booking.

Under the 1927 Act, which was to run for ten years, renters were obliged to offer, and exhibitors to show, a proportion or quota of British film footage which rose by annual steps to 20 per cent in 1938. Block booking was not made illegal, but advance and blind booking, which were inseparable from it, were restricted. Seventy-five per cent of the salaries of those engaged in the production of any film was to go to British subjects, and the scenarist was to be British. Films made anywhere in the British Empire were eligible as quota. An Advisory Committee was appointed by the Board of Trade to assist it in the administration of the Act, but it was badly chosen and heavily weighted against the producers. The distinguished outsiders who represented the public interest were quite ineffective in comparison with the knowledgeable and hardbitten representatives of the renters; and, because of the large number of people employed in exhibition, the exhibitors were given twice as many representatives as the producers.

Importers of foreign films, and especially the London renting subsidiaries of the major Hollywood companies, now needed a large number of British films to balance their very big imports. Some announced grandiose plans for the production in Britain of films comparable in quality to their home product. To begin with a number of them acquired for distribution a handful of films from some of the best British producers. But there were far too few of them and in any case promoting the output of a rival, however small, was hardly good business. Before long they were making, sponsoring or acquiring an entirely new type of film made solely for quota, as cheaply and quickly as possible. Their aim was less to make a profit than to make as small a loss as possible. Before long these films came to be known contemptuously as quota quickies.

So British production expanded, but not in the way Parliament had intended. The films of reputable British producers continued to be distributed by their own renting subsidiaries or by renters with few or no imports, and were not affected by the quota system. But a large number of producers were soon in business solely to provide quota for importers. Some American firms supplied their own as economically as they could. Warner Brothers-First National with its studio at Teddington and Fox-British at Wembley ran their own mini-factories, while Paramount sponsored many units and individuals working in hired studios. There was also a very large number of small British units and partnerships which turned out film after film taken variously by all the big importers. In addition Australian, Canadian and extremely long Indian films, almost all of them silent, supplied the renters with footage which was not really expected to leave their shelves. For it was soon realised that although a renter was legally obliged to acquire British films 'for the purpose of renting', as the Act put it, he could not be penalised if no one actually booked them. In 1929, one importer, Film Booking Offices, chose the uninviting date of 27 December for the trade show of an 11,000-foot silent Indian film for which they had paid less than a shilling a foot. Another renter, Tiffany Productions, bought a silent comic item called *Auntie's Antics* which was registered as 1,092 feet but turned up as 5,114 for its Trade Show. Made for £114, it cost Tiffany £125. These were desperate cases. More common were short features of less than five reels, made in a couple of weeks and costing as little as 15/- a foot. Many films of just over 3,000 feet, the legal definition of a long film, were hastily concocted from music hall or other material by fringe producers. Every March renters still short of British footage as the quota year neared its end scrounged around for such stuff and there would be a rush of trade shows, sometimes as many as a dozen in a week, of films that no one seriously expected to be booked.

The result was that far more film was registered for renters' quota than the law required (see Appendix, Table 5). As importers fulfilled the whole of their legal obligation with specially made quota films, the quality British producers now had to compete not only with imported films but with low-cost quota as well. After a fall in production during one year owing to the difficulties of converting to sound, British output rose steadily from 130 features to 228 in ten years (see Appendix, Table 1).

According to John Maxwell in his evidence to the Moyne Committee in 1936, a well made British film needed at least 1,500 bookings to be a success. Rowson in his 1933 address to the Royal Empire Society said that a film must be seen by 7 or 8 million people before it was profitable. *Sunshine Susie*, for example, was seen by 10 million, *Rome Express* and *Jack's the Boy* by 11 or 12 million. It was paradoxical that, although more British films were being made than were legally required for renters' quota, there were frequent complaints from exhibitors that they were unable to get enough British films for their own quota. In fact what was in short supply was good-quality British production, but there were actually few defaulters and exhibitors' quota was exceeded to an even more marked extent than that of the renters (see Appendix, Table 6). In one year more than double the obligatory footage was screened.

Quota Year	Renters' British Quota		Exhibitors' British Quota	
	Statutory %	*Actual %*	*Statutory %*	*Actual %*
1931–2	12½	19·6	10	21·6
1932–3	15	20·3	12½	23·7
1933–4	17½	24·1	15½	26·1
1934–5	17½	23·8	20	27·4

There was much disagreement as to why this was so. It was said that some parts of the country had a greater partiality for British films than others. During the thirties the new style of modern, comfortable circuit cinema was driving many small, out-of-date halls out of business, and the low-cost quota pictures may have appealed to those in difficulty. Also, although there was no separate shorts quota, the many popular American shorts had to be registered as foreign footage and since most British shorts were not eligible for quota the imported shorts shown had to be balanced by British features. None of this seems to be an adequate explanation. Repeated denials by American renters that they compelled cinemas to take their quota pictures by block booking are hard to believe. It seems likely that cinemas showed American-owned quota films because they had to, and British quality films because they wanted to.

The lamentable reputation of quota films was soon recognised as damaging to the reputation of all British producers, and demands by MPs and others for official action began as early as November 1929. Sir Ernest Craig, Vice-President of the Kinematograph Renters' Society but also a producer, early suggested an alternative system. This had the support of many exhibitors and of Sir Philip Cunliffe-Lister, later Lord Swinton, who had been at the Board of Trade when the original Act was passed. Craig maintained that if films had to have a minimum production cost of £15,000, and if quota obligations applied only to renters, the latter would sponsor better films as the loss would be considerable if they were not booked.

For several years expressions of concern and various alternative proposals were met by official stonewalling and assurances that all was well. In Parliament, anxiety was expressed by MPs of all parties. The Conservative Cunliffe-Lister's proposal was supported by Liberal MP Geoffrey Mander, brother of the actor Miles Mander, who suggested a slightly lower minimum cost. It was backed also by Labour MP Harry Day, a professional showman himself and one of the few MPs of the time who did not have a public school and university background. Outside Westminster, the Film Producers' Group of the Federation of British Industries entered the fray with a memorandum to William Graham, President of the Board of Trade under the Labour government, suggesting a modest minimum cost of £150 per 100 feet, or about £10,000 for a normal feature film. The trade unions, also, were concerned to create a flourishing production industry in the interests of employment. An early proposal by the National Association of Theatrical Employees to increase the quota to 50 per cent was dropped in favour of the £10,000 minimum cost clause and other provisos as recommended in the TUC report of August 1931. Official replies showed an obtuseness which was quite astonishing. Early in 1930, W. R. Smith, Parliamentary Secretary to the Board of Trade, boldly claimed that the Act was fulfilling its purpose of increasing the production of films 'of high quality'. Graham, moreover, claimed that there was a better outlook for British talkies than ever before, as the world did not like the 'Yankee twang'. He consistently refused to do anything on the grounds that there was a lack of Parliamentary time 'for the remaining four years which they would be in office'.[1] In fact, both Graham and Smith lost their seats the following year in the election which threw the Labour government out. They were replaced by the Liberal Unionists Walter Runciman and Dr Leslie Burgin in the 1931 coalition under Ramsay MacDonald, but little had changed. Like his predecessor, Runciman refused demands for an inquiry into the working of the Act, and turned down a joint TUC and FBI delegation* which recommended the terms of the TUC report and the 'elimination of worthless films made especially in this country for Quota purposes'.

* The delegation included among others Sir Walter Citrine, general secretary of the TUC, the FBI chairman, Charles Tennyson, its secretary, Neville Kearney, and Michael Balcon and Simon Rowson.

But the Act was due to be renewed in the spring of 1938, and Runciman began to look into the situation in the summer of 1934. There was much controversy and discussion of alternative proposals during the next four years. The Cinematograph Exhibitors' Association, less concerned with the size of the quota than with the box-office pull of the films, proposed some sort of viewing panel and quality test rather than a minimum cost. Many small independent showmen seemed to have hoped rather wistfully that some unspecified quality test would guarantee box-office results. In discussions with the Board of Trade the CEA also came out in favour of Craig's renter-only quota.

On 23 March 1936 it was announced in the House of Commons that a departmental committee on cinematograph films was being set up by the Board of Trade under the chairmanship of Lord Moyne. Other members were the educationist A. C. Cameron, already involved in the establishment of the British Film Institute; the Hon. Eleanor Plumer, another BFI governor and the sister of a field-marshal; Dr J. J. Mallon; J. Stanley Holmes MP; and Lt-Colonel Sir Arnold Wilson. Mallon, Warden of Toynbee Hall and a well-known champion of the underdog, had very different views from those of Wilson who, with a background of army and overseas service, was a keen supporter of Fascism and Nazism. None of the large number of MPs who took a keen and knowledgeable interest in film matters was appointed to, or heard by, the committee and the only two members other than Wilson with any connection with films, the BFI governors, were more interested in their educational value than in the ramifications of the industry.

The committee took evidence from all sections of the industry during 1936. Film makers were represented by the FBI Film Producers' Group, a group of documentary film makers, and the labour unions. The FBI deputation consisted of Kearney, F. W. Baker of Butcher's Film Service, Alexander Korda, Norman Loudon of Sound City and Richard Norton of Pinewood. They were in favour of re-enacting the Act for another ten years but with higher quota figures, rising from 29 to 54 per cent for the renters and from 25 to 50 per cent for the exhibitors. Other recommendations were that films costing only 15/- a foot or less should not be eligible for quota, that a separate shorts quota should be introduced and that films from the Empire should be eligible for quota only under reciprocal arrangements. Maintaining that the insistence on a British scenarist was already a dead letter because of the ambiguity of the term, they, like others, felt that this proviso should be dropped. It was also recommended that renters should be prevented from 'pairing' cheap quota films with imported films, or in other words from block booking, although it was not suggested how this secret practice, denied by all, was to be stopped. It is noticeable that the two biggest producers in the country, ABPC and Gaumont-British, were vertical integrations with renting and exhibition interests, and although formally members of the FBI group they took little part in its deliberations and were more fittingly represented as this stage by the Kinematograph

Renters' Society delegation, on which Maxwell of ABPC was extremely active. He and Isidore Ostrer of Gaumont-British feared that a quota as high as that suggested by the FBI would cause the Americans to produce more in Britain and that the films would compete with the output of Elstree and the Gaumont studios. As an alternative, they suggested reciprocal deals whereby renters would be allowed to count any British films which they distributed abroad as quota footage.

The documentary film makers, Associated Realist Producers, with Paul Rotha as their spokesman, proposed a separate quota for short films and said that documentary films should be eligible for it. The Association of Cine-Technicians represented by George Elvin, like the producers, wanted to encourage a large volume of production, but favoured a lower quota than the FBI, with a renters' quota of 25 per cent and the exhibitors' quota half that, and a slightly higher minimum cost of £2 a foot, or £12,000. They also proposed a separate shorts quota, a proviso that all technicians should be British except the scenarist, and a plea for the employees to be represented on the Films Advisory Committee. The TUC submitted a memorandum which favoured the same large quota figures and lower minimum costs as the FBI. The Screenwriters' Association, which was represented by the Incorporated Society of Authors, Playwrights and Composers, was the only body wishing to retain the clause insisting on a British scenarist. In other words, all the recommendations were very predictable.

Amongst exhibitors, particularly the small independents whose views the CEA reflected, many would have liked the total abolition of the quota, and many more longed unrealistically for a guarantee of quality. For this to be secured by a minimum cost did not appeal to them, as they survived only by using low-cost films. The two big vertical combines ABPC and Gaumont-British, although they included the two biggest circuits, took no part in the CEA negotiations. Represented by W. R. Fuller and its President T. R. Fligelstone, the CEA proposed a viewing panel and quality test, reduction of exhibitors' quota, and a renters' quota so fixed that two films were available for every one required by exhibitors; the introduction of a shorts quota was opposed. Significantly, nothing was said about the restriction of block booking.

The case put by the KRS was crucial, and expressed with great vehemence by John Maxwell, a determined and angry fighter, and the managing directors of the London renting subsidiaries of three of the biggest Hollywood companies, Sam Eckman of M-G-M, J. C. Graham of Paramount and D. E. Griffiths of Warner Brothers-First National. This powerful trio of Americans handled many of the most popular films of the time. Claiming that the number of their imports demanded a combined quota of 51 films for that quota year, and that all the major American renters together needed 104, they asserted eloquently that production facilities and personnel in the United Kingdom were simply not sufficient to make so many good-quality films. With this unrealistically high quota, they claimed, they had no option but to make or acquire films as cheaply as possible. Maxwell, whose large output was not made for quota, admitted he was glad the quota films were so bad that they offered him no competition. But he supported the American view that if quota obligations were reduced to a reasonable figure of perhaps four or five films a year for each company it would be possible for them to make films of a quality comparable with their Hollywood product, costing from £30,000 to £50,000 each or approximately £7 a foot. With one voice the KRS deputation denied that quota films were forced on the exhibitors. Maxwell even backed the Americans in their claim that quota production was not actually intended for the market at all, but was regarded as an expenditure made simply to comply with the law. He told the committee that Graham estimated Paramount's loss on their quota films, each costing some £6,000, as £100,000 a year.[2] Simon Rowson estimated elsewhere that American renters as a group lost £500,000 a year on quota production. The films acquired by M-G-M were mostly so cheap that to regard them as a total loss would perhaps be reasonable. But it is hardly credible that Paramount, and presumably Warners and Fox-British, mounted their large production operations in Britain without intending to recoup anything on them. Allegations that the American renters linked high-mark American films with low-mark quota had rumbled on in the CEA from the beginning of the Act, and the FBI Producers' Group memorandum and evidence to the Moyne Committee stated unequivocally that renters did block-book their quota quickies. In an internal FBI memorandum of 27 May 1937 Kearney referred to 'the American renters registering and showing one super picture with ten programme pictures, and forcing the exhibitor to book the whole amount'.[3] A characteristically intemperate letter from Maxwell to Kearney refers to a remark that American companies distributed their quota films at a very low cost in order to undersell British pictures as 'rather a farcical statement'.[4] Block booking, pairing, and any other form of persuasion were virtuously and repeatedly denied by the KRS deputation. But even these protestations had a certain ambiguity. Maxwell said:

> I should think there are some advance understandings that are entered into, but not translated into contracts, verbal understandings, when, let us say, a renter has got a very good picture and the exhibitor wants it, and the renter says, 'I am having half a dozen others coming along. I expect you to take these if you take this one.' There may be a verbal arrangement of that kind, but British renters are as guilty of that as American, whenever they have a picture good enough to justify it.[5]

He added ingenuously that as such agreements were illegal exhibitors were free to break them. In reality, however, exhibitors had to do what renters told them to do, since the KRS was a small and united organisation which could easily cut off the supply of films to an exhibitor who stepped out of line. As we have seen, moreover, the very large use of British footage suggests that the films were indeed shown.

Whether or not the committee was convinced by these four powerful personalities, the Moyne Report, which was presented to Parliament on 23 November 1936, was to prove only the basis for further argument. Briefly, it recommended a quota for another ten years, to rise ultimately to 50 per cent by steps to be fixed each year by a very complex procedure. Despite the difficulty of devising an objective test of quality, the exhibitors' fear of a minimum cost was heeded and a quality test was boldly proposed. The ban on advance booking was removed; both block and blind booking were retained as offences, but for renters only, in the hope that exhibitors would identify those trying to impose them. Only a foolhardy exhibitor would do so. Great importance was attached to the creation of the powerful new Films Commission, appointed to supervise and if necessary to alter the terms of the Act, and to consider ways of raising production finance. Other changes were the introduction of a separate shorts quota and the dropping of the clause requiring the scenarist to be British.

Little of this plan survived in the legislation which eventually emerged some sixteen months later. Immediate reactions from various sections of the industry were again predictable, and largely irreconcilable. Early in 1937 Burgin urged producers, renters and exhibitors to sort out their differences so that legislation which would suit everyone could be framed. Once more the fact that their interests conflicted was ignored.

The CEA was pleased about the viewing panel but opposed the shorts quota and considered the eventual quota of 50 per cent too high. The FBI, pleased about the high quota and the inclusion of shorts, disapproved of the panel and continued to press for a minimum cost of £1 a foot; producers regretted that advance booking was not to be illegal and considered that the control of block booking would prove impracticable. The Association of Cine-Technicians, also in favour of a cost test rather than a quality test, felt it should be at the higher rate of £2 a foot. The KRS, also opposed to the viewing panel, sensibly pointed out that producers would be unwilling to spend money producing films which could be turned down later. They opposed a separate shorts quota and repeated their objection to a high quota on the grounds that a more realistic figure would enable them to undertake worthwhile production in Britain. They objected to the restrictions on blind booking and claimed that the penalty proposed, revocation of the licence, was too harsh. The measures to deal with block booking they simply dismissed as unworkable (while continuing to deny that it was practised). The only thing upon which all were agreed was dislike of the proposed films commission with its wide powers. In horror, *Kine Weekly* described the proposal as 'positively Socialist', and it immediately aroused opposition from both the CEA and the KRS. The AC-T was suspicious of power in the hands of people from outside the industry, and the FBI pleaded that representatives of the industry should be included. The Commission's powers of enforcement, which would have enabled it to tackle such matters as block booking and the KRS boycott of booking combines, were the crux of the matter. The eventual failure to establish such a commission was a victory for the KRS and the American firms which dominated it.

Big producers with divided loyalties like Maxwell and Ostrer, seeing a possible chance of overseas distribution for their films, continued to discuss the idea of reciprocal agreements, with renters released from quota obligations to the extent that they secured release abroad for British films. Rowson, also, began to push the reciprocity plan which he had proposed before. He now presented it to the FBI in the following terms:

> Exemption from quota obligation may be granted to the renter of any foreign films, in return for his substantial cash contribution to the production of any British picture, which will be distributed by an approved distributor in the country of origin of the imported pictures.[6]

The scheme was to apply to films made by companies under British control and costing £12,000 or more, to which a foreign company must have contributed at least £8,000. Such films were not to be eligible for the renter's quota in the United Kingdom as well as securing him exemption. Rowson believed that fewer but better films would be made under this scheme, which the FBI considered putting to the Board of Trade.

While discussions in Parliament continued, representatives of the exhibitors' and renters' organisations got together in an effort to resolve their differences, and in the spring of 1937 invited the FBI to join them. The Producers' Group met, including Mark Ostrer, Basil Dean, J. Arthur Rank, Alexander Korda, S. W. Smith of British Lion and Arthur Dent of ABPC, and appointed representatives to meet the others. But at the same time they privately decided to give general support to the Moyne proposals, although pressing for a cost clause of £2 a foot, reciprocity and even import restriction.[7]

Basil Dean, as chairman of the Producers' Group, was deeply engaged in the quota negotiations, working closely with Kearney and Norton, and was much harassed by Maxwell, forceful, touchy and long-winded and with a foot in both camps. It was at this point that the latter as well as several others with renting as well as producing interests, including C. M. Woolf, decided to throw in their lot with the Producers' Group and cease to take part in the negotiations as members of the KRS. Their presence in the Group, whose aims were not identical with theirs, greatly increased Dean's problems.

Unanimity was clearly impossible, and cracks began to appear even within the three main divisions of the industry. Many a small renter, importing the lesser American films, feared a cost test as much as the small exhibitor did. Paying £1,000 or so for an imported film, he might clear from £2,000 to £8,000 on it, but operating on such a level he would find it difficult to provide quota costing £10,000 or more. Argument also broke out in the FBI between what Maxwell called the 'quality producers' and British producers of quota quickies, who were threatened by measures like reciprocity which would reduce the volume of production. Kearney argued strongly that current output was far too large to be profitably absorbed by the market. He estimated in a memorandum dated 27 May 1937 that the 47 million people in the United Kingdom with 4,950 cinemas had been offered 745 English-language films in a year, whereas in America, with 137 million people and 18,000 cinemas, only 540 films had been on offer.[8] The figures require careful interpretation as an indication of how many booking slots would be available for each film, as there is no breakdown into first and second features or into cinemas changing their programmes weekly and those changing more frequently. But they do highlight the comparative profitability that was possible for American and British producers. Norman Loudon, however, being the owner of a hire studio which existed solely by virtue of quota production, promptly replied with statistics to prove that the large number of films on the British market were actually needed. Like much of the inflated British production sector he had no interest in the quality film with a chance of overseas distribution. The move for reciprocity as an alternative to the Moyne proposals grew, and on 2 June Dean, Woolf, Kearney and Maxwell put the plan to Burgin more or less as Rowson had outlined it, but applying it to films costing the lower figure of £10,000.

Uncertainty about the future of quota legislation, together with the crisis in production investment, led to a sharp fall in production in 1937. Official hopes that the various parts of the trade would reach agreement on a scheme of their own were in vain, and in June the next Secretary of the Board of Trade, the Conservative Oliver Stanley, announced an entirely new set of proposals. Much of the Moyne plan was abandoned, including the viewing panel, the powerful films commission and the flexible new way of fixing quota figures. A shorts quota was introduced but quota figures, 20 per cent rising to 30 per cent in ten years for renters and 15 per cent rising to 25 per cent for exhibitors, were lower. New proposals were made for a cost test of £2 10s 0d a foot with a minimum of £15,000, although provision was made to allow cheaper films if they had 'special exhibition value', and secondly some sort of reciprocity plan was envisaged.

Later in the summer a White Paper[9] based on the Stanley proposals introduced two entirely new ideas – labour costs and double quota. Quota figures were even lower, especially for exhibitors, rising from 15 to 30 per cent for renters and from 10 to 15 per cent for exhibitors. This figure, despite the current overfulfilment of quota by exhibitors, was in recognition that other clauses would in future lead to fewer films being made. Minimum costs, set at £1 a foot with a minimum of £7,500, were for the first time defined as labour costs, and estimated at half the total costs of a film. Thus the real minimum cost was £15,000. To encourage exports a film with labour

YES, MR. BROWN
Jack Buchanan with Margot
Grahame in an early musical
produced by Herbert Wilcox in
1932.

JOSSER IN THE ARMY
Like many music hall comics of
varying degrees of coarseness,
Ernie Lotinga transferred his
material to the screen in a series
of cheap comedies. This one was
made at Elstree in 1932.

TELL ENGLAND
In 1931 Anthony Asquith and Geoffrey Barkas finished their film of the Gallipoli campaign in the first world war. Made at Welwyn studios and on location at Malta, it included a magnificent battle sequence.

AUNT SALLY
Cicely Courtneidge with Sam Hardy in a Gainsborough film of 1933. Eager, sweet, a little coy, she seemed like a much-loved aunt to her many British fans.

TIMBUCTOO
Interesting shots of ritual dancing filmed by Walter Summers in 1933, inconguously sandwiched into a feeble B.I.P. comedy, aroused little interest and were even criticised as 'travel stuff'.

THE QUEEN'S AFFAIR
Anna Neagle and Fernand Graavey. Music, romance and glamour in an undeservedly forgotten light comedy directed by Herbert Wilcox in 1933. Sets by L. P. Williams and costumes by Doris Zinkeisen.

EVERGREEN
Jessie Matthews began a four year run of hit musicals with this film. Here she flits in her own inimitable manner around the pale, elegant apartment designed by Alfred Junge. Directed by Victor Saville in 1934.

EVERGREEN
Jessie Matthews and her co-star Barry Mackay on the set with her favourite director, Victor Saville.

costs of £3 a foot, or a film in the region of £45,000, was to count as double footage for quota purposes. Moreover, a renter acquiring such a film for export was to be excused from handling British quota film of equivalent length at home. Booking in advance of six months was still banned, and blind booking was to remain illegal but with stiffer penalties, and for renters only.

Many were disappointed by the new proposals. The labour unions on the whole had hoped for a strong commission with union representation, provision of production finance, a high quota and a large volume of production, and therefore jobs, none of which would ensue from this scheme. The AC-T in particular had hoped that a fair wages clause would be included, that 75 per cent of wages and salaries would be for British employees and that only one foreign technician would be allowed on a picture. The Film Industry Employees' Council of the AC-T and NATKE now sent a memo to the Board of Trade through Tom O'Brien and George Elvin, and held a mass protest meeting at the Victoria Palace in November 1937. Amendments to the Bill along those lines were moved in Parliament without success by three Labour Members, Tom Williams, Ellen Wilkinson and George Strauss, and by the Liberal Geoffrey Mander and the Conservative Kenneth Pickthorn. Sir Arnold Wilson also wanted a strong commission which would control a viewing panel and regularise censorship, and had also hoped that it would help to raise production finance, raise a levy to provide for training, possibly at university level, and perhaps also supervise hours and conditions of work. All these special interests were disappointed. At the same time minimum costs and the reduction in film supply resulting from the doubling and reciprocity clauses separated the big producers, renters and circuits, none of whom had anything to fear, from the small quota producers, the small importer-renters and the least successful independent showmen, all of whom depended on low-cost films. The notorious quickie producer George King left the FBI in a fury, protesting that films of his which cost only half the proposed minimum had no difficulty in securing from 1,000 to 1,300 bookings.

A dramatic change now took place. A bill dated 27 October following the terms of the White Paper was due to be presented to Parliament on 18 November, but at the last moment the Film Producers' Group of the FBI launched an entirely new scheme, over which argument raged whilst the Bill was taking its course through Parliament. Accepted by a committee of the group on 3 November and presented to a general meeting a couple of days later, it was unanimously approved, secured the agreement of the unions and was embodied in a memorandum to the Board of Trade, intended as the basis of an amendment, on 10 November. The news broke in the *Financial Times* on the 12 November, and *The Times* of 16 November carried an explanatory letter from Basil Dean headed 'An Eleventh Hour Proposal'.

Known as the Loudon scheme, although it was originally suggested by

J. B. Williams of the Screenwriters' Association, it was put forward by Norman Loudon to save the type of film made in his studios. Under it a film would be registered either for renters' quota or exhibitors' quota but not for both. As films registered by renters could not be used as exhibitors' quota they would be booked only on their merits and, as in the renters-only scheme of a few years before, the minimum cost would make it uneconomic to make films with no chance of being booked. As good quality films they could hope to be exported, and renters would be able to use the reciprocity clause to get part of their quota fulfilled by distributing the best British pictures abroad. Exhibitors' quota, on the other hand, would provide a 'sheltered market' for other British producers. The more expensive films, that is films with labour costs of £22,500 or more, could be used once as renters' quota and once as exhibitors' quota. The latter was to be 10 per cent in the first year and fixed thereafter in relation to the number registered the previous year.

The Loudon scheme, also known as 'separation of quotas', was superficially attractive and generally welcomed by the political left and the trade unions, as well as by film producers and technicians. But mention of a sheltered market was ominous, and opposition soon appeared. The exhibitor Sidney Bernstein, for example, maintained that it kept small producers and the owners of hire studios alive and, although this meant more jobs, the high-price films would be used for renters' quota and the exhibitors would be left with only inferior films for theirs. The Ostrers and Maxwell also believed this, although representatives of Gaumont-British and ABPC had been at the FBI meeting which had unanimously adopted the eleventh-hour proposal just twelve days before. After some acrimonious correspondence with Dean, Maxwell insisted on the group's meeting on 19 November, when he moved a resolution against the scheme. This was lost by fourteen to six and Maxwell, Maurice Ostrer, C. M. Woolf, John Corfield of British National and Bruce Woolfe left the meeting. Notwithstanding this the FBI afterwards issued a statement that the proposals had been affirmed by an 'overwhelming majority', opposed only by exhibitor-renters. Deputations and memoranda bounced back and forth.

In the House of Commons on 9 December Sir Adrian Baillie, a Conservative MP who was a director of British Technicolor, proposed an amendment introducing separation, which he called the 'split quota'. But Stanley, incidentally criticising Dean for his late change of attitude after supporting the Bill, presented the argument that under the new scheme renters would keep the best films and the exhibitors would find that in order to get their quota they would be forced to book inferior films. The amendment was defeated by 34 to 14 and no more was heard of the Loudon scheme. The very cheap films which had swollen British production, and with them many jobs, were doomed.

While this late battle was being fought another main issue, that of the films commission, was also being decided. Some MPs, including Tom

Williams and Geoffrey Mander, and also the FBI, continued to press for the strong commission of three to five people from outside the industry, with power to administer and suggest changes in the law, originally proposed by Moyne. Instead the government announced a film council of twenty-one people, which would report and advise the Board of Trade. The President of the latter claimed that this had the support of the whole trade except, significantly, the foreign renters. It was, in fact, more or less the Films Advisory Committee of the earlier legislation under a new name. There was widespread suspicion that the plan for a powerful commission had been dropped in response to American pressure. About the time of the Moyne Report there had indeed been rumours that the American State Department wanted quota concessions as part of a reciprocal trade treaty.[10] A year later an article in the magazine *This Week* claimed that pressure from Washington in connection with Anglo-American trade talks had induced the British government to abandon proposals which would have given the commission real power. Kearney wrote privately to Dean about this article: 'There is, I understand, a substantial basis of truth although the statement and deductions are wrong.'[11] Both Major Procter, the Conservative MP involved with the Schach companies, and Ellen Wilkinson questioned Stanley in the Commons as to whether there had been any official American pressure over the Bill, especially over the proposals for a commission and for split quotas, and whether it had been linked to discussions about an Anglo-American trade agreement. Stanley replied that American representations over films had indeed been received several times, but he denied the present implications. But Ellen Wilkinson later asserted that the 'representative of America's interest in this country' had boasted that American pressure had been applied to the government. Euan Wallace, moreover, replying in 1938 to a parliamentary question on behalf of the Board of Trade, admitted that the American government had made representations about certain provisions in the Quota Bill. A last attempt to secure a strong commission was made by Lord Strabolgi (previously Commander Kenworthy) in the Lords debate in March 1938. Clearly such a body would have been in a position to challenge the American renters who practised block booking and a boycott of booking combines, and it is easy to see why official American pressure should be enlisted against it. A proposal by the Liberal MP H. Graham White that finance for British production should be raised by a levy on imported films was also rejected because of American trade negotiations.

The current Act was due to be superseded by a new one on 1 April 1938, yet even at this late stage arguments and pamphlets continued. Late in February the President of the Board of Trade caused a sensation by announcing that the Bill would allow not only for doubling of quota registration but, in the case of even more expensive films, of trebling. As this would probably reduce production even further it was instantly attacked by both the CEA and the unions. There was an outburst of calculation.

The President of the CEA estimated that exhibitors would need 92 British films in the first year but that the doubling, trebling and foreign rights clauses might well mean that only 15 or 16 would be made.[12] The Americans, on the other hand, maintained that cost levels had been set too high and that few trebles would be made. Both Maxwell and the Americans, of course, had always maintained that Britain was not really capable of producing more than about 15 top-class pictures a year. In Maxwell's view there would be no shortage of film for the cinemas because a single top-class film would play for weeks, whereas quota films were minimally playable.

March 1938 saw the last annual rush to register the dregs of quota production, with ten British trade shows one week and twelve the next. The royal assent was given on 30 March, and the Cinematograph Films Act 1938 was in being.

Apart from the tripling clause it followed the terms of the White Paper closely. Two clauses affecting employment had been added in Parliament. Largely owing to the work of Tom Williams, it was laid down that the wages and conditions of employment of studio workers must not be inferior to those in government departments, and a clause introduced in the Lords required the Films Council to report on the possibilities of an apprenticeship scheme. Quota figures were similar to earlier ones, starting a little lower than they already were in view of current difficulties, the exhibitors' quota being reduced from 20 to 15 per cent. A shorts quota was introduced, and the quality and use of British shorts was to increase noticeably in the next few years. Renters' quota during the next ten years was to increase from 15 to 30 per cent for long films and from 15 to 25 per cent for shorts, and exhibitors' quota was to rise from 12½ to 25 per cent for long films and from 12 to 22½ per cent for shorts. Dominion films were no longer to be eligible for quota. The minimum labour costs of £7,500 followed the recommendation of the White Paper, and a measure of flexibility for quality was provided through the Films Council, which might advise the registration of a cheaper film if it was of special entertainment value, or disallow registration for renters' quota of a film passing the cost test but of insufficient entertainment value. The doubling and tripling clauses led to a registration system with four categories: films eligible for exhibitors's quota only; for renters' and exhibitors' quota; for exhibitors' quota and renters' double quota; and for exhibitors' quota and renters' triple quota.* Films with labour costs of £22,500 or more, that is £45,000 films, would count as double footage for renters' quota, and those with labour costs of £37,500, or £75,000 films, as triple footage; only 50 per cent of a renter's total footage might consist of such film. Under the reciprocity clause a renter acquiring the foreign rights of a £45,000 film for at least £20,000 could count its footage as quota even though it was already being used for quota in Britain, and if the rights were being acquired for £30,000 or more it could count as double quota; here again, only 50 per cent of a renter's footage could consist of such films.

* Respectively Br/E, Br/R, Br/DR and Br/TR.

Blind and advanced booking continued to be illegal, with stiffer penalties, including the revocation of licence, now applicable to renters only, but the small, strong film commission, which was to have been the chief weapon against block booking, had been dropped. The Cinematograph Films Council of twenty-one with advisory powers only perpetuated the earlier Films Advisory Committee with all its faults, including the overweighting of exhibitor representation.

Sir Frederick Whyte was chosen as its chairman. In his fifties and Director General of the English Speaking Union, he had been a Liberal MP in his twenties and since then had had a career in public service. Among the independent members were a sprinkling of MPs, none of them prominent in parliamentary debates about the film industry, Sir Walter Citrine of the TUC, the historian Philip Guedalla, the economist Professor Arnold Plant of the London School of Economics, Eleanor Plumer, and others. The renters were represented by the veteran F. W. Baker of Butcher's, reponsible for many feeble low-cost British films, and one of our American triumvirate during the earlier discussions, D. E. Griffiths of Warners. Against these two formidable professionals and the four leading exhibitors, film makers were somewhat surprisingly represented by John Grierson, who had played little part in the quota negotiations and who by May 1938 was already deeply involved in the planning of the National Film Board of Canada, where he was to move early in 1939 and live for some years, and by Captain the Hon. Richard Norton, who, stylish and socially gifted though he was, had earlier been responsible for many quota films. Labour was represented by A. M. Crickett of the Film Artistes' Association and G. H. Elvin of the AC-T.

There was a truce for a while but by the end of the year it was clear that all was not well. Production fell, as expected, from 225 new features registered in the previous quota year to 103 in the first year of the new Act. When this was raised in Parliament by Vice-Admiral Taylor, Oliver Stanley replied blandly that although the films were fewer in number they were of better quality. Certainly the quota quickie was dead. But of the sixty-two features registered from the 1 of April to the 30 of November 1938 only thirteen were at all memorable, while by the end of the first full quota year as many as twenty-five fell into the category eligible only for exhibitors' quota, including three from the firm owned by Council member F. W. Baker.

With the turn of the year the problems of the film industry were back in the limelight again. An article by the film critic Campbell Dixon in the *Daily Telegraph*[13] was headed 'Films Act Has Failed' and pointed out that everybody was prospering except the very film makers whom the Act had set out to help in the first place. Next morning the paper carried a bitter reply from Basil Dean saying 'I told you so'. Sadly Dean, who had worked so hard to get justice for the film makers, now retired from the industry altogether, writing to a colleague: 'For my part I am tired of knocking my head against a brick wall, and have given up all active work in films for the time being.'[14]

The possible failure of the Films Act was debated by the Lords in March 1939 when Lord Strabolgi suggested the setting up of a financial corporation to aid investment. The Films Council produced its first report at the end of the month but this was negative and unhelpful. Whilst noting empty studios and many unemployed, with production down in value from £5.7 million to £4.5 million, the Council decided against the increase in quota favoured by the unions and the new body which had superseded the Film Producers' Group, the British Film Producers' Association. It preferred to ascribe the drop in production to uncertainty preceding the Act and to the film investment scandal in the City, which had not yet come to court, than to the working of the Act.

But warnings that the Act would reduce film supply were certainly justified. Ten trebles and 21 doubles in the first year were the equivalent of 41 films unmade, and that on a total of only 103 films. However, although the number of films was only 48 per cent of the 1935–6 output, their footage was 63 per cent of it, since the typical quota quickie had been not only cheap but fairly short. The actual time British screens were occupied by British films was reduced very little, to 88 per cent of the 1935–6 figure (see Appendix, Tables 2 and 6). This was partly because there were many reissues, of course, but it was at least partly because, as Maxwell had predicted, big films had longer runs and more bookings. Anthony Asquith and George Elvin of the ACT, concerned as unionists with the volume of employment, claimed that the present situation would drive the best film makers out of the industry. But it can be argued that the cost clauses in the legislation drove out not the best but the worst, and that the artificial stimulus of the quota system had produced too many films. Unemployment was the price paid for killing the quota quickie.

More important, perhaps, was Asquith's warning that 78 of the 103 films were made by or to the order of Americans.[15] For one thing was clear: the power of the KRS and its dominating members, the American majors, was unshaken. Hollywood films would continue to be distributed in the United Kingdom by methods which included block booking and the boycott of booking combines. In its annual report the KRS said that finance would only be attracted to British production when films were made which were good and distinctively British and could make a profit at home. The last two words are significant. British producers still had no American market and, without this, their films would continue to be made on budgets which could not rival Hollywood production standards. In the Commons Stanley said in March 1939 that average labour costs in the first year of the Act had been £3 5s 0d. a foot, but it was commonly accepted that the American figure was £7. The outbreak of war transformed the situation, but had it not occurred what would the results of the new legislation have been? The American companies were now making good films in Britain instead of bad ones, but the fundamental economic problem for home producers, how to make films which would compare with those of Hollywood when they did not have a market of comparable size, was unsolved.

Chapter 4

The Censorship of Feature Films

The Home Office Model Rules of 1923 had recommended that local authorities should issue licences under the fire regulations of 1909 only to those cinemas which accepted the British Board of Film Censors classification of films. These were certified as U, or suitable for universal exhibition, or as A, suitable for exhibition to adults and to young people under sixteen only when accompanied by a parent or bona fide guardian. This system had been accepted by many local authorities by 1929. In December 1929 the Labour Home Secretary J. R. Clynes sent a circular letter to all licensing authorities urging even wider adoption of the rules and stronger enforcement. By early 1931, 65 per cent of the authorities had complied and, as this included most big towns, considerably more than 65 per cent of cinemas in the country were covered. Manchester, which refused to co-operate, held that if a film was fit to be seen at all it was fit for everybody, and had all films reclassified by its own watch committee; this gave U certificates to many films classed as A by the Board. All exhibition premises in Manchester, even those not normally requiring a fire licence, were brought under this control through the requirement of a fire-resisting enclosure. Manchester was alone in this, but there was plenty of local variation over individual films. Regional licensing authorities wishing to preserve some independence were not always repressive, and there were probably as many cases of films banned by the Board being allowed as there were of A films being banned. Greater tolerance was found especially in and around London, where the joint committee on censorship of the London County Council and Middlesex County Council was joined by the Surrey County Council in 1930 and Essex County Council and East Ham Borough Council in 1937. Film societies were for the most part subject to the same restrictions as the cinemas, in which, indeed, many of them met. Non-flammable substandard (less than 35mm wide) stock had been introduced in 1923, but as most films were at first only available on the highly inflammable 35mm nitrate base they continued to be subject to fire regulations.

Outward Bound, a serious American film showing life after death and thus breaking a cardinal rule of the Board, was naturally not given a certificate, but ninety authorities passed it for adult audiences. *Her Child*, originally called *Her Unborn Child* and described as an anti-birth-control film, was banned by the Board but the LCC, Middlesex and Surrey allowed it. It fared less well elsewhere: Dundee Town Council refused even to examine it and when two Dundee cinemas showed it they were closed down. Strong feelings were aroused by such matters and some were moved to hysterical incoherence by imaginary horrors, 'films of the most unutterable filth of terrible suggestions' (*sic*).[1] Debates during the thirties were on two issues: how the categories of certificate applied to young people, and the legal position of film societies. There was much misunderstanding about the certificates, many insisting that if U films were suitable for children then A films were by implication unsuitable, and it was illogical to let children see them if accompanied by a parent. By the end of the decade it had been established that an A certificate simply drew a parent's attention to the need for making an individual decision, and this system had been strengthened by introducing a new certificate for horror films which barred young people completely. In the case of film societies, as non-theatrical substandard shows increased in number the absence of a legal definition of "non-flam"* stock enabled a number of local authorities, backed by exhibitors fearful of competition and by various moral pressure groups, to try to control them by claiming that substandard film was, in fact, inflammable. In 1939 it was finally established that this was not so, and that substandard film shows were not subject to fire regulations or, consequently, to censorship.

The first battle was over film society freedom, and paradoxically took the form of a demand from the political left wing for the establishment of state censorship. First the Labour MP Harry Day asked the Home Secretary in the House of Commons in December 1929 if legislation could be introduced giving film societies the right to show films without certificates, in the same way that theatre clubs were free of the censorship of the Lord Chamberlain, and the Conservative MP G. S. Hall Caine asked the Home Secretary for legislation to provide a film censor responsible to Parliament. The Home Secretary invariably replied to such questions that censorship was a matter for the local licensing authorities and nothing to do with him.

Matters came to a head in 1930. The Film Society in London, select and expensive, was in a privileged position and able to show many imported films which had been passed by neither the Board nor by other licensing authorities. But when a left-wing working-class film society, the Masses

---

* At this time the film trade and licensing authorities used the term 'inflammable' in the sense given in the Oxford Dictionary, 'easily set on fire', to describe film stock which caught fire easily; 'non-flam' was used to describe film stock which was not easily set on fire. There was some disagreement as to whether the latter could be set on fire if the conditions were right, or not at all. This was settled by a definition set out by the British Standards Institution in 1939 as explained below. See page 66.

Stage and Film Guild, applied to the LCC for permission to show four films from Soviet Russia, the request was turned down. The films had already been allowed at the Film Society, but the Board of Censors maintained that they were liable to provoke a breach of the peace if shown publicly or, they added significantly, at a nominally private showing to which admission was so cheap that it was virtually open to all. All four films challenged the Board's taboos. *The Battleship Potemkin* and *Mother* both showed defiance of authority in a favourable light, *New Babylon* they considered brutal and indecent and *Storm over Asia*, a film about a puppet leader set up by the British interventionist army after the Revolution, touched upon such a delicate matter that it was not shown until at last, in 1935, the Middlesex County Council allowed it with a caption describing the military force as 'symbolical' rather than real.

The class and political bias of the refusal caused consternation. On the initiative of the Labour MP Fenner Brockway, a founder member of the Guild, the Parliamentary Film Committee was formed, which included two other Labour MPs, Ellen Wilkinson and George Strauss, and the Conservative W. E. D. Allen. This committee asked Clynes to consider setting up an official film censorship operating like the Lord Chamberlain's office. Ellen Wilkinson and the Labour MP J. F. Horrabin also questioned Clynes in the Commons but he replied as usual that the current position was satisfactory. Fenner Brockway, Horrabin, Harry Day and the Liberal Percy Harris continued to question him but he refused to be drawn. In April another Conservative, Sir Kingsley Wood, entered the fray from the other side, seeking more pressure on local authorities to ban films without certificates, but Clynes continued to disclaim responsibility.

The four films became a political *cause célèbre*. Next the Labour Council of West Ham, and later the watch committee in Leeds, passed *Mother* for exhibition in the ordinary cinemas. So did Rotherham Borough Council, the chairman adding, however, 'We, as a committee, were only surprised that anyone should be so foolish as to pay money to go and see it.'[2] But the LCC stuck to its guns and refused applications for *Mother* and *New Babylon*. Meanwhile Conservative MPs were dismayed that Soviet films should be available in Britain at all and harried the Home Secretary from the other side of the House, receiving the predictable answer that it was nothing to do with him. The Parliamentary Film Committee, and especially Ellen Wilkinson, became more and more convinced that a censor financed by the trade would always be reactionary and ban films from the Soviet Union, and that state censorship would be more equitable. In July 1930 they formed a deputation which included Fenner Brockway and Ellen Wilkinson, the Conservatives W. E. D. Allen and Lord Lymington, and the Liberals Sir Herbert Samuel and Geoffrey Mander, as well as Bruce Woolfe of British Instructional Films, Miss J. M. Harvey of the Film Society and Miss Hilda Browning of the Masses Stage and Film Guild. They pointed out to Clynes that conditions had changed since the start of the licensing and censorship system before the 1914 war, and suggested a select committee to consider revision. Clynes, with a truly remarkable talent for stalling, asked for a report on why the deputation wanted a select committee rather than a departmental one.

The fate of other early Soviet films was similar. They continued to be of interest to intellectuals and serious students of the cinema, partly because of the current hopes that the socialist experiment in Russia would prove politically liberating and, of more importance to film enthusiasts, because of the experiments and advances in film technique made in Russia. But not only were they in conflict with the Board's political assumptions, they also broke its rules, especially its support for established authority. Some well known films such as *Arsenal*, *Counter-Plan* and *Strike* were not even brought in to Britain, so obvious was it that they would be regarded as subversive. *Two Days*, a 1927 film in which a father and son take different attitudes to social progress, caused such an outcry when shown at a Merseyside hall that it was banned.[3] Among films refused certificates by the Board but shown at the Film Society was *Bed and Sofa*, shown in 1929 with cuts and later passed for the LCC area for adults only. About the position of women as affected by the housing shortage in Russia, it appeared to the Board as 'crude immorality'. *October*, described by Eisenstein as an ideological montage on events in St Petersburg in 1917 and of great interest for its experimental technique, was shown at the Film Society in 1934; banned by the Board for showing violence and brutality, it was passed for adults by the LCC. *The Ghost That Never Returns*, with its critical view of life in a South American prison, was of course banned by the Board as subversive but later passed by the LCC, Middlesex and Surrey. *The Blue Express*, shown at the Film Society in 1931, was sanctioned later for adults only by the LCC, but when a workers' film society in Manchester wanted to show it the watch committee turned it down. *Golden Mountains*, about a 1914 strike at Baku, stressed class solidarity and although shown at the Film Society in 1933 was not even submitted to the Board. *Alone*, shown at the Film Society in 1932, also received no certificate. Pudovkin's first sound film, *The Deserter*, was shown at the Film Society in November 1933. It included strikes and conflict with armed police and its theme, that a worker not taking part in the class struggle was a deserter, was unlikely to appeal to the Board. The LCC and Surrey, however, passed it for adults in 1935. Dovzhenko's beautiful film *Earth*, dramatising conflict with the kulaks and the establishment of collective farming, was shown at the Film Society in 1930 and a cut version was given a trade show in 1931 with an A certificate, but it seems that it was not much booked. According to C. A. Lejeune, by cutting shots of a woman in labour during the funeral procession the Board destroyed the message that new life replaces old. It was unthinkable to the elderly Board to show childbirth, however worthy the meaning.

MPs continued to press the Home Secretary for action from time to time and in March 1932 the Parliamentary Film Committee once more urged him to set up an inquiry. The Labour government had fallen and been succeeded by a coalition, and the new Home Secretary was none other than Sir Herbert Samuel, who had long been in favour of an official censor and was a member of the earlier deputation. But in office, advised by the permanent officials, he took the same view as his predecessor and told his former colleagues that there was no need for legislative change. It is possible, too, that with the change from a Labour government to a largely Conservative coalition, which was soon to be replaced by a traditional Conservative government, Ellen Wilkinson was no longer quite so sure that an official censor would be an improvement, and from now on the demand for one died away. However, she continued to suspect that the financial basis of the Board caused bias and even in 1938, when increasing fears of government interference were the subject at issue rather than complaints about the Board, she took the opportunity to raise the matter once more.

Meanwhile the merits of the system of two certificates, particularly in connection with young people, were under discussion. In his circular letter of December 1929 Clynes had asked for two new measures which would make it easier for people to see that young people under sixteen were allowed to see an A film only with a guardian. A notice board was to be displayed prominently outside the cinema indicating the category of each film being shown, and the censor's certificate for each film would be projected immediately before the film. It was already felt, however, that some exceptional films fitted neither category and in December 1929 Colonel Josiah Wedgwood, an Independent Labour member, suggested in Parliament that there should be a third category for films of scientific, educational and artistic value. Clynes replied, of course, that it was nothing to do with him. The LCC had already approached the Board itself about the possibility of a third certificate, C, for films especially suitable for children, but the President of the Board of Film Censors, Edward Shortt, had pointed out that this would make nonsense of the U certificate. People began to feel that the categories left something to be desired, especially in view of the ambiguous nature of the A certificate. Indeed, the Board's report for 1930 admitted in an unguarded moment: 'It cannot be denied that these films are unsuitable for children.'[4] The system was somewhat ineffective, anyway. Every cinema was familiar with the sight of young people waiting outside for someone willing to 'adopt' them temporarily. One Mrs Saviour obliged a Bristol cinema by escorting forty-five young people in to see the A film *Never the Twain Shall Meet*, for which transgression the cinema was fined £10.[5] But exhibitors stood to lose the custom of a large part of their working-class audience for A films if parents could not take their young children in with them. In the respectable name of parental responsibility the CEA opposed any attempt to ban under-sixteens from A films completely, but a movement to do so grew.

Especially keen on action were a number of women's organisations, including the National Federation of Women's Institutes. In May 1930 the National Council of Women, holding a conference on the cinema in Birmingham, passed a resolution calling on Clynes to appoint a court of inquiry to see how film censorship could be improved in the public interest. He refused on the usual grounds. The Birmingham conference accordingly formed their own Cinema Inquiry Committee consisting of doctors, JPs, ministers of religion, parents and teachers under the chairmanship of Sir Charles Grant Robertson, Principal and Vice-Chancellor of Birmingham University, a supporter of official censorship. Early in 1931 this committee asked the Birmingham Public Entertainments Committee to exclude under-sixteens totally from A films. The committee replied that it had no power to do so.

In Liverpool, however, a different view prevailed. In October 1930 the Liverpool JPs had resolved that in future under-sixteens could not see an A film even with their parents who, it was felt, were 'not always the best judges of what a child should see'.[6] Early in 1931 the Burlington Cinema was prosecuted for allowing some children to see *Red Pearls*. In defence the cinema claimed that the ban was unreasonable, but it lost the case and was fined. During 1931 and 1932 all appeals, formal and informal, failed to get the decision changed. Business suffered, and people who were able to visit cinemas in other towns did so. Both exhibitors and the public were angry. A deputation of exhibitors was seen by the Theatre and Public Entertainments Committee, which was not unsympathetic, and during this period many A certificates were reassessed as U at Liverpool.[7]

Other areas followed Liverpool's example briefly, among them Beckenham, Newcastle, Leicester, Sheffield, Hove and Bridgwater. The CEA, however, found that if it were carefully explained to each licensing authority in person that an A certificate did not indicate that a film had been declared unsuitable for young people, but was a way of drawing the parent's attention to the need to exercise his own judgement as to whether his child might see it, the authority would see the matter differently. All abandoned the total ban when the meaning of the certificate was explained to them in this way except Liverpool, which refused even to receive the CEA deputation, and Beckenham.

Beckenham was obdurate, and in January 1932 appointed its own panel of censors, which included representatives of all local organisations. Here again a lot of films were reassessed from A to U.[8] But the restrictions were sufficiently damaging to cause annoyance amongst exhibitors and the public and a petition was presented to the Home Secretary asking him to put pressure on the Council. In April Councillor Mr Evans decided to resign from both the Council and the Film Advisory Panel and fight an election on the issue. A successful protest meeting was organised by the CEA and the ratepayers, and a petition signed by 5,000 was presented to the Council. Mr Evans was returned unopposed, and requested the Council to drop the scheme. In July it was formally announced that the Home Office Model

Rules would be in force from the end of December 1932, and Mr Evans was the hero of the hour. The cinemas in Liverpool also continued to suffer in 1932. In October the magistrates' annual meeting decided by 40 votes to 30 to keep the ban in force. The North-West CEA in desperation wrote to explain the Board's system but the JPs did not bother to read the letter out at their meeting. The exhibitors finally wrote personally to each city councillor and at last the message got home. After two years of defiance the bench gave way and, like Beckenham, Liverpool dropped the ban at the end of 1932.

Meanwhile the Birmingham conference had continued trying with reports and deputations to do something about what they saw as the low moral standard of many films. The most they could get from Clynes was the establishment of a consultative committee of representatives of the local authorities, which was to keep in touch with the British Board of Film Censors, explaining their own position to it and learning in turn of the Board's objectives. It was after the election of 1931 that Clynes was replaced as Home Secretary by Herbert Samuel, and during the latter's tenure of office the consultative committee first met under the chairmanship of Sir Cecil Levita of the LCC. Its aim was a uniform system of censorship for the country as a whole and high standards of film in the interests of 'family entertainment'. Another conference of the Birmingham inquiry in February 1932 sent yet another deputation to the Home Secretary, but Samuel proved as good as the previous incumbent at sidestepping requests for action.

Individual films continued to encounter local differences. Somerset Maugham's *Rain* with Joan Crawford, *Are We Civilised?* and the Paul Muni film based on the life of Al Capone, *Scarface*, all heavily cut by the Board and issued as A films, encountered further difficulties in many areas. Gustav Ucicky's *Refugees*, about German refugees fleeing from the Russians, highly praised by Alistair Cooke,[9] was banned by the Board but allowed in one London cinema in 1934. The Sunday Entertainments Act of 1932, which permitted cinemas to open on Sundays 'subject to such conditions as the authority may think fit to impose', provided a wonderful opportunity for censorship which many authorities took. Croydon, under the initiative of its bishop, even set up its own censorship committee for the purpose and by October 1934 proudly claimed that in two years it had stopped 200 films from being shown.[10] The appearance of a new type of film, made to thrill the audience with fear, set the censors a fresh problem in which they saw the protection of the young as crucial. Bela Lugosi's *Dracula* in 1931, Boris Karloff's *Frankenstein* and the Frederic March *Dr Jekyll and Mr Hyde* in 1932 were given A certificates but caused public concern in many areas and were banned by a number of authorities. The Board took to describing such films as 'horrific' in its monthly lists, and by informal arrangement with the CEA a notice to this effect was displayed with the category boards in cinemas as a warning to parents.[11] The fashion continued, with such films as *The Mystery of the Wax Museum* and *King Kong* in 1933, *The Werewolf of London*

THE PRIVATE LIFE OF HENRY VIII

Alexander Korda's first spectacular success in Britain, made in 1933. The magnificent sets by Vincent Korda and costumes by John Armstrong created a sensation and started a fashion for costume films.

THE PRIVATE LIFE OF HENRY VIII

Charles Laughton looked like the Holbein portrait of Henry, but in this publicity shot four of his wives played by Wendy Barrie, Elsa Lanchester, Merle Oberon and Binnie Barnes, have a twentieth century air.

LORNA DOONE
Basil Dean filming on Exmoor in 1934.

CATHERINE THE GREAT
Douglas Fairbanks Jnr. and Flora Robson in Korda's production following *Henry VIII*, again designed by Vince
Korda and John Armstrong. Directed by Paul Czinner in 1934.

MAN OF ARAN
Michael Balcon waited patiently for Robert Flaherty to finish his beautiful but controversial documentary of the islanders' struggle to survive in Galway Bay. Made in 1934.

THE MAN WHO KNEW TOO MUCH

Reproducing Switzerland at Shepherd's Bush in 1934, director Alfred Hitchcock and art director Alfred Junge preferred the studio to location.

and *The Bride of Frankenstein* in 1935 and *Dracula's Daughter* and *Devil Doll* in 1936. By early 1937 it was said that eighteen films had been classed as horrific and *Kine Weekly* claimed that the vogue for making people's hair stand on end seemed to be over. This was premature, however, and in that year the Board instituted a special H certificate for films from which young people were to be banned entirely. Two other Hs were issued before the outbreak of war but neither was for a horror film. One was the Abel Gance anti-war film *I Accuse* and the other *On Borrowed Time*. This M-G-M film about an old man who tricked death showed the latter personified as the transparent 'Mr Brink', and it was considered not so much horrific as unsuitable for the young. By using the inappropriate H certificate for these two films the Board was trying to control the filmgoing of young people for other reasons, but no discussion of the basic principles of censorship could take place now until the war was over.*

However, this is to anticipate. Meanwhile freedom for the film societies was secured, not by appointing an official censor like the Lord Chamberlain as the Parliamentary Committee had hoped, but by freeing substandard film from the fire regulations. As the 1909 Act had not defined inflammable film, and as the acetate substandard film burnt slowly if actually held in a flame, it was possible to argue that shows using it did in fact need licences under the Act. Exhibitors, fearful of the competition offered by non-theatrical shows, urged local authorities to insist on this. The police in Manchester tried to prove that the 16 mm stock on which *The Road to Hell* was put out by the Socialist Film Council in 1933 would burn if left long enough in a hot fire, and that showing it would therefore require a licence.[12] The Model Rules of 1923 were shortly due for revision and the formation in 1934 of the American Legion of Decency, with its call for 'clean films', aroused new interest in censorship in Britain and encouraged those who wanted to extend it. In June 1934 both Surrey and Bristol tried to persuade the Home Office to include shows using substandard film in the scope of their licensing regulations.

During this year, however, an important court case vindicated the acetate film's right to freedom from control. *The Battleship Potemkin* and a film about the hunger marches in Britain were shown on substandard at the Miners' Hall at Bolden Colliery, near South Shields. The premises were unlicensed, but the police prosecuted the trustees on the grounds that the film stock was not really non-flammable and that a licence should therefore have been obtained. Many felt that the real motive of the prosecution was to discourage the showing of such films of left-wing origin to working-class audiences, and the defence was subsidised by the National Council for Civil Liberties and the British Institute of Adult Education. It was demonstrated that although the film smouldered it went out when the flame was removed,

---

* The first British H film, *The Dark Eyes of London* with Bela Lugosi, was trade shown in October 1939.

and the case was dismissed early in 1935. The Home Secretary announced in the Commons that he had no intention of applying the fire regulations to acetate film. But those who wished to tighten up censorship continued to be restive. The Birmingham Cinema Inquiry Committee had already sent yet another deputation, this time to the Prime Minister. Reckoning that 25 per cent of the films passed by the Board were unsatisfactory, and some even demoralising, they echoed Ellen Wilkinson's belief that the Board was not truly independent of the trade, and put in yet another plea for an official censor. The Prime Minister was sceptical, however. In the spring Surrey County Council approached the County Council's Association, and as a result the latter brought out a report in September recommending that representatives of the licensing authorities should be allowed to sit on the Board of Film Censors, and that non-flam film should be controlled 'in the interests of public safety and morality'.[13] Clearly the lesson of the Bolden Colliery case had not been learnt. In May the Archbishop of Canterbury led a deputation to the Prime Minister asking for an advisory committee to be set up, and in November Surrey finally issued regulations for the licensing of all film shows, whether on non-flam stock or not. Still insisting that the latter did burn, it challenged the 1909 Act by throwing the onus of proof that it did not on the applicant. Like the County Councils' Association it frankly bracketed safety with moral censorship, including in its regulations the demand that no film should be 'injurious to morality'. Birmingham followed Surrey's example.

There was active lobbying by the CEA for this to be extended to other towns, but nothing happened. Early in 1937 Harry Day, ever hopeful, asked the Home Secretary whether in view of the development of non-flammable stock since the 1909 Act he would appoint a departmental committee to draft new and clearer legislation. Instead, largely as a result of the Archbishop of Canterbury's intervention, an advisory committee of representatives of local government under the chairmanship of Lord Stonehaven was announced in July 1938 by the new Home Secretary, Sir Samuel Hoare. In June 1939 the British Standards Institution finally published a new standard, No. 850–1939, which for the first time defined safety film. This it did in terms of the maximum amount of nitrogen in the material, and by definition of the terms 'difficult to ignite' and 'slow burning'. A couple of months later, just before the outbreak of war, the Stonehaven Committee brought out a report which specifically established the right of film societies using substandard film to show films without censors' certificates. This was accepted by the Home Office, and although Surrey did not formally give up its regulations until the following year the fight was over.

So by the outbreak of war the uncertainty about the position of young people on the one hand and of substandard film societies on the other had been cleared up. The Board had refused to give certificates to some 140 films in the previous eleven years, 8 of them early Russian ones. Alterations had been demanded in several thousand. In addition, many scenarios and projects were discussed in advance of production, and altered or abandoned.*

Given that the Board's terms of reference were to see that films did not give offence, in order to save the film industry from trouble with licensing authorities, the attitudes and beliefs of the president, secretary and four examiners determined what was actually held to be offensive. J. Brooke Wilkinson, who was secretary from the Board's establishment before the 1914 war until his death in 1948, was in his sixties at this time and was considered a tough disciplinarian with considerable influence over the various presidents. The first, T. P. O'Connor, was a former journalist and MP, and died in office in November 1929. He had been appointed to the job when he was sixty-eight, and this turned out to be a precedent. His successor, Edward Shortt, a monocled barrister and MP and former Home Secretary, was the son of a clergyman, lived in Kensington and was sixty-eight when he was appointed. Lord Tyrrell of Avon, a former diplomat, was appointed in November 1935 at the age of sixty-nine and was to stay in the post until he died at eighty-one. All had been gentlemanly public servants unconnected with either popular entertainment or art, but mindful of the importance of public opinion and the stability of society. The identity of other members of the Board was kept secret at the time, although it was known that one vice-president was eighty-one when he died in 1930 'in harness'. And Shortt, speaking to the Women's Civic Club at Leeds, allowed his audience to know that the current examiners were two former army officers, a former politician and a 'woman with many years of social work on the LCC'. The public image was upper-class, responsible and conformist. The very nature of the job discouraged broadmindedness and experiment, and many of their decisions suggest naivety and excessive timidity, anticipating the protests of pressure groups to an exaggerated degree.

The early practice of publishing an annual list of reasons for which exception had been taken to films during the year, without mentioning the films by name, was given up in 1932. The report for that year commented a little stiffly: '. . . for some unaccountable reason, critics have seized upon isolated sentences in these exceptions, and, by taking them out of their context, have placed mischievous construction upon them.'[14] By the early thirties some of these reasons, given by people born in the 1860s or even earlier, may well have sounded somewhat ridiculous. Complaining of scenes introduced solely to impart a 'spicy flavour', the 1931 report had complained: 'There are certainly some Producers who delight to show the female form divine in a state of attractive undress . . .'. They continued to be guided by the rules established earlier.† There were a number of topics which were prohibited completely, but beyond that the members of the Board relied on their own judgement of

* For an interesting study of the examiners' objections to scenarios presented between November 1930 and December 1939, see Jeffrey Richards, 'The British Board of Film Censors and Content Control in the 1930s', in the *Historical Journal of Film, Radio and Television*, vol. 1, no. 2 (1981) and vol. 2, no. 1 (1983).

† See earlier volumes of *The History of the British Film*.

what was bad taste or likely to cause offence. Religion, sex, subversion and disrespect for authority greatly preoccupied these respectable elderly people.

One basic rule was that films must not offend people's religious beliefs or show the materialised form of Christ. The silent German film *Martin Luther* was banned in 1929 after the Board's request to cut scenes about indulgences, which it was thought might offend Roman Catholics, was refused. Later the film was trimmed by the renter and given an A certificate. Thomas Ince's 1916 *Civilization* in which Christ, reincarnated in the body of a soldier, crusades for peace in a warring world, had been allowed in Britain without a certificate by many local authorities, but when it was reissued as a sound film in 1931 even the LCC was unwilling to allow it unless the figure of Christ was cut, a manifest impossibility. Yet in 1936 Warner Brothers folksy modern dress bible story played by a negro cast, *The Green Pastures*, delayed for many months, was finally given a U certificate although the play itself had been banned by the Lord Chamberlain. An actor played 'de Lawd', a portrayal never otherwise countenanced by the Board. Passions were aroused all over the country both for and against it, many finding the naivety touching, others finding it cute, sentimental and patronising. Some felt that a U certificate was inappropriate because the film should not be regarded as ordinary entertainment, and the Christian Cinema Council maintained that children should not be allowed to see it. There was much talk about this pseudo-reverent film, yet in the same year Julien Duvivier's *Golgotha*, a serious film about the Passion and Crucifixion, went almost unnoticed. Passed only by Middlesex County Council, and then only for special showing, it aroused no interest in Britain.

Anything which threatened respect for established authority, whether social or political, was suspect. Films banned as subversive included von Sternberg's *An American Tragedy* and Pabst's *Die Dreigroschenoper*, both in 1931, and the Socialist Film Council's film *Blow, Bugles, Blow* in 1934. In 1937 two political films, *Millions of Us* and *I Would Today*, were turned down and Vigo's joyfully anarchic *Zéro de Conduite*, shown at the Film Society in November 1934, was allowed late in 1936 only by the LCC, Middlesex and Surrey. Aspersions must not even be cast on doctors, dentists, lawyers or officials, and Richard Massingham's funny short *Tell Me if it Hurts* was at first denied a certificate as 'offensive to the dental profession'. The social hierarchy must not be questioned. In 1934 B & D abandoned its film about Judge Jeffreys, *The Hanging Judge*, because it could not be made without showing British justice in an unfavourable light. The danger of white people, especially white women, appearing in a less than favourable light in films which might be 'seen by natives' was a constant worry to them. Even *Chelsea Life*, a 1933 film directed and written by the exemplary British father and daughter Sidney Morgan and Joan Wentworth Wood (previously the actress Joan Morgan), was given an A certificate because the heroine was shown 'in a state of inebriety'.[15] The censors were mindful of their international duty. Maurice Elvey gave up his planned *Relief of Lucknow* because the censor was 'advised by all authorities responsible for the Government of India' that it would stir up memories better forgotten, and in Parliament in December 1938 Sir Samuel Hoare said that the Secretary of State for India had 'advised the promoters not to proceed', a rare admission of official intervention. But national scruples were selective. In 1934 a British picture, *Forbidden Territory*, was based on a Dennis Wheatley thriller about the rescue of a young Englishman from prison in Siberia. Neil Maclean, a Labour MP, claimed in Parliament that it was anti-Russian and a deputation from the Friends of Soviet Russia asked that it should not be shown. Later the Maryport Communist Party in vain asked the exhibitors to withdraw it as a 'libel on the Soviet working man'. Russia was fair game, it seems. Yet two films were banned until after the outbreak of war for fear of offending Nazi Germany, considered a 'friendly nation' by the Board. *I Was a Captive of Nazi Germany* was based on a true account by an American woman journalist and, although shown in America and Canada in 1936, it was pronounced 'quite unsuitable for public exhibition in this country' by the Board as late as May 1939. A cut version was allowed by the LCC, Essex and East Ham just before the war but not passed by the Board until after war broke out. *Professor Mamlock*, a Russian film of 1938 about the persecution of a Jewish doctor in Nazi Germany, was shown in America and got a good press after being seen at the Film Society in London. It was described favourably by *Kine Weekly* in April 1939, but was refused a certificate on the grounds that it was 'not in the public interest'. On the eve of war a cut version was passed by the LCC, Essex and East Ham councils. Again, it was finally passed by the Board after war had broken out. It was later shown commercially with some success, although ironically by then Russia had signed a pact with Nazi Germany.

The Board preferred to err on the side of caution when it came to sex, and childbirth, birth control and prostitution were prohibited subjects. *Her Unborn Child* has already been mentioned. In 1933 a First National film starring Loretta Young called *Life Begins*, which was set in a maternity home, was banned by both the Board and the LCC; it was brought out again in 1935 under a new title, *Dawn of Life*, and was given an A certificate but was still banned by the LCC. In 1933 a Canadian drama on the theme of venereal disease, *Damaged Lives*, was also turned down. In 1934 the English-language version of the Czinner-Bergner film *Ariane* had yet another unacceptable theme, that of a girl loving an older man. And in the same year a Paramount film featuring Douglass Montgomery, *Eight Girls in a Boat*, gave offence by discussing the right of a single girl to have a baby, and was refused a certificate. It was later shown at a London cinema, to adults only, by permission of the LCC. Similarly *The Unborn*, an American film said by *Kine Weekly* to be about the 'sterilisation of the unfit',[16] was allowed only by the LCC, Middlesex and a few other authorities. The Czech film *Extase* was shown at the Film Society in 1933 but refused a certificate by the Board, for not only did it show a beautiful young wife desert an impotent husband but that wife, played by Hedy Lamarr, was briefly seen naked. Even in 1937 Middlesex County Council confirmed this ban on the grounds that sex was treated in a way that would offend public feeling, and Surrey was prepared to grant it an A certificate only if cut. It was finally allowed by the LCC in 1938, and in one cinema only. George Hoellering's celebrated and beautiful semi-documentary of the Hungarian plains, *Hortobagy*, was banned by the Board in 1936 although accepted with cuts by both Essex and the LCC. Graham Greene wrote that the 'leaping of the stallions, the foaling of the mares are shown with a frankness devoid of offence',[17] but the Board did not agree. Needless to say *The Birth of a Baby*, sponsored by the American Committee for National Welfare, was refused a certificate in 1939 as 'quite unsuitable for mixed audiences', although Middlesex and the LCC were prepared to consider applications for special shows at such places as maternity clinics. And in 1931 the English film *City of Shadows*, a pseudo-*exposé* of the lower depths in London, was at first refused a certificate because it touched on 'white slavery', but was later passed as an A film after a very public fuss created by George Bernard Shaw, who mischievously made it sound as if the Board were trying to keep the subject dark in case girls were discouraged from coming to London to find work as servants.[18]

The specifically sexual taboos were extended into a general squeamishness about all sorts of subjects felt obscurely to be nasty. The surrealist film of 1928 *La Coquille et le Clergyman*, shown with cuts at the Film Society in 1930, was refused a certificate on grounds which became a byword for naive prudery: 'So cryptic as to be almost meaningless. If there is a meaning it is doubtless objectionable.'[19] In 1931 the English version of Fritz Lang's *M*, with Peter Lorre as a compulsive child murderer, was given an A certificate only after many cuts, including the linchpin of the film, his final despairing speech in which he tries to explain how helpless he is to control his compulsion. Duvivier's 1931 *Poil de Carotte* was trade shown in 1933 but refused a certificate because it was about a child driven to suicide. The producers refused to cut it. When a Brighton exhibitor showed it and said in his defence that he catered for an intelligent audience and it had been recommended by the British Film Institute, he was fined £5. The same unacceptable idea of a child's despair was also present in *La Maternelle*, a film by Marie Epstein and Jean Benoit-Lévy about the attempted suicide of the unhappy child of a prostitute. Tod Browning's controversial *Freaks* of 1932 was banned, and the list of objections for that year in the Board's annual report mentions 'revolting monstrosities'. Paramount's 1932 version of the H. G. Wells novel *The Island of Dr. Moreau*, called *Island of Lost Souls* and disliked by Wells himself, was banned as sadistic. *Der Ammenkoenig*, shown in 1936, was acceptable only to the LCC and Middlesex.

Many censored films were ordinary commercial productions made by well-known companies with respected stars, and some were serious works of art, not intended to be what the Board called spicy. The spicy suggestiveness was more likely to be found in the performances of stars like Mae West and George Formby, who were careful to avoid forbidden subjects and were rewarded with U certificates. A book on censorship by Causton and Young published in 1930 complained of the Board, 'They shun the frank but permit the suggestive',[20] and in 1923 Dorothy Knowles wrote that while film societies were obliged to look to foreign films for serious, thoughtful cinema the Board was cheerfully passing many vulgar, silly and falsely sentimental films.[21] In his obituary of T. P. O'Connor, Brooke Wilkinson wrote that he had 'endeavoured to steer a middle course between prudery and licence',[22] and he later spoke of granting certificates only to films which would not give offence. The censors were always on the lookout for anything undesirable. But, as Shaw said in a broadcast, there is no such thing as an undesirable film, for one which was not desirable to a bishop might be so to someone else. He added that if there was to be an inquiry into film censorship 'people who consider sex sinful in itself must be excluded from it like other lunatics'.[23] Tastes may differ, but it was the tastes of the Board that set limits to what the whole of the British cinemagoing public might see. Its immense influence was negative, defining areas of reality which must not be admitted or discussed. Subjects people might disagree about, and which therefore might be assumed to be important to them, were banned. Causton and Young complained that 'in other words, the pace must be set by the half-witted'.[24] In 1936 the AC-T protested about remarks made by the President of the Board at a recent CEA conference. He had disapproved of films expressing political views, but the union pointed out that limiting film in this way prevented it from playing a useful part in the life of the nation. Impoverishment of intellectual content was the result of protecting the trade from harassment.

For the film industry's massive self-censorship did succeed in protecting it from the multiplicity of regional censorship requirements, and puritanical or reactionary pressure groups, fear of which had led it to set the Board up in the first place. There was some local variation, some instances of behind-the-scenes interference from central government, and individual renters, producers and exhibitors were inconvenienced by decisions of the Board. But on the whole the system worked in the industry's favour. As for the public, it seems to have been well enough pleased with the films it was getting. Cinema audiences grew and grew, and those who sought more thoughtful and challenging films in special cinemas and film societies remained a tiny minority.

Perhaps more harmful than prudishness and religious taboos were the politics of members of the Board and their diligence in detecting subversion. They never questioned the social and political assumptions of the extreme right wing, which apparently seemed to them to be normal, neutral, desirable and non-controversial. In this they certainly did not reflect public opinion for, although the Conservatives won the 1935 election, Labour had 8,325,491 votes to their 10,496,300, or nearly 45 per cent of their combined total, and there was in addition a strong Liberal Party. The prohibition of any serious treatment of social or political questions, the extraordinary lengths to which they would go to protect established authority of any sort not merely from attack but from disrespect, assumed that the status quo was perfect. Their attitudes to the Soviet films and the two anti-Nazi films are significant, with their acceptance that films from a socialist country were highly dangerous and that Nazi Germany was a friend of Britain. With an unofficial censorship so devoted to authority in all its forms there was little need for government participation, and throughout the decade Home Secretaries gave the same dusty answer to concerned MPs and pressure groups. Film censorship was not their business. But, deplorable as the negative and reactionary influence of the Board was, an official censor pursuing an active political policy might well have been worse.

Chapter 5
The Arrival of the Talkie

The silent film was completely superseded by the sound film in the early 1930s. To say that the film had never really been silent but had always had musical accompaniment is to miss the point of the transformation. Cinema music, even when cue sheets or special scores had been provided by the film makers, was not under their control and the film as they put it in the can carried only the image. It therefore had to tell its story by visual means. What producers now had was direct control of sound during the performance and, moreover, this sound included the human voice. The new films were not just sound films, they were talkies. Dialogue was to change the narrative structure of the film profoundly.

In the next ten years not only did continuity and the style of acting change a great deal, but the technical demands of sound cinematography affected the physical look of the film. Because the hiss of arc lights made a change to incandescent lighting necessary it was also necessary to change to panchromatic stock, which lost the deep focus of orthochromatic stock. Mechanical and optical research was intensified to meet new problems. Printing a sound-track down one edge of the films slightly reduced the width of the picture from a ratio of $1.33:1$ to $1.2:1$, with some loss of background, although, of course, the film now had a sound background which it had not had previously. Many found the nearly square picture displeasing, and Hollywood technicians in the Society of Motion Picture Engineers in 1932 reverted to the earlier shape by masking the top and bottom of the picture and using a new projection lens to enlarge the image on the screen. Sound also meant that cameras and projectors could no longer be turned by hand. Hand turning had previously allowed a good deal of flexibility, unacceptable now because pitch depended on speed. Film had to be projected at 24 frames a second to avoid the distortion of sound, and the speed was maintained by electrical means. One result was that earlier films made at speeds varying from 16 to 20 feet a second could not be run on modern projectors without appearing unnaturally fast and jerky. Cecil Hepworth and Sydney Wake of the Standard Kine Laboratories in 1931 devised a method of printing some frames twice, which appeared to slow down the movement,[1] although stretch printing, as it was called, was only a rough and ready method of correcting the varied speeds of the old films. So great were the changes in the film's appearance and structure that by the outbreak of war in 1939 even the best silent films looked antiquated and visual story-telling was a dead language. The films of the late thirties, on the other hand, would continue to be acceptable technically on their own terms for many years, and only their social attitudes and assumptions would date.

The change to sound was not unexpected. Experiments with both discs and sound-on-film had been going on for years. But it was Warner Brothers' use of Western Electric's Vitaphone system of wax discs for a musical accompaniment to *Don Juan* in 1926 that opened the door to commercial exploitation in America, and a multiplicity of reproduction systems rapidly appeared. Cinemas all over the United States were wired for sound. Next year the same company introduced a few words of dialogue into *The Jazz Singer*, and the rush to install sound became even greater. At the same time RCA demonstrated a sound-on-film system, Photophone, and Fox was exploiting another one known as Fox-Movietone. Two years later, in October 1929, there were between thirty and thirty-five talkies on offer in America and nearly 9,000 wired halls, and in Europe a big international combine had been formed by Tobis and Klangfilm to exploit the European market. There was no going back.

Britain read about the new wonders and listened to travellers' tales but was a couple of years behind America. Short sound-on-film revue items had been filmed for several years by British Phonofilms at the small Clapham studio using Lee De Forest's process, and these enjoyed a modest success at a couple of London cinemas. Gaumont-British had been developing their own sound-on-film process, British Acoustic. The American film *Seventh Heaven*, with music recorded on Movietone, was successfully shown at the New Gallery in London in 1927, although it was still beyond the reach of the ordinary cinema. Vitaphone was only demonstrated privately. The *Jazz Singer* had its British showing early in 1928, for release a year later, and a handful more talkies were shown in the course of the year. In the first eleven months of 1929, 215 of the 599 feature films offered had some sort of sound, and both RCA and Western Electric registered companies in Britain to market equipment. Interest was intense, but the widespread curiosity could not be satisfied until the right apparatus had been installed in the cinemas, and it was a time of great uncertainty and difficulty for the exhibitor. Would the sound film last, or prove a passing fad? If it lasted, would disc or sound-on-film prove more satisfactory, and which make? And how could showmen time the conversion of their cinemas in regard to the relative availability of silent and sound films? In the first eleven months of 1930 new silent films were in the minority for the first time. Only 193 were shown, and in 1931 this fell to 46. Before long only the occasional silent film was offered, usually from abroad, and in 1934 the censors noted that only two silent films had been submitted for censorship. The conversion of the cinemas proceeded alongside this disappearance of new silent films. In June 1929 only 400 British cinemas had been wired, including most of those in London's West End. By December a silent cinema was the exception in the London area although progress elsewhere was still slow apart from big cities like Birmingham, Leeds, Manchester and Aberdeen. According to the *Kine Year Book* annual directories, there were 685 cinemas in the United Kingdom which were wired for sound at the end of 1929, 2,523 a year later and 3,537 at the end of 1931.

By this time it was clear that sound-on-film was going to be more successful than disc. RCA had never used discs, while Western Electric, which ran both systems for a while, announced that they were giving up discs altogether in December 1931. From a producer's point of view disc recording, although at first it gave better results, was limiting as it made editing difficult and location filming inconvenient. But from the exhibitor's point of view discs were tempting. Many cinemas already had gramophone systems for accompaniments and interludes, and different systems of synchronisers and amplifiers proliferated for a few years. For the poorer showmen it seemed a cheap alternative. For a while, as producers went over to sound-on-film and a large number of cinemas found themselves left with disc systems, the gramophone companies found a source of profit in re-recording film tracks on to disc. There was a wide choice of reproduction system. Several local makes proved durable, such as Edibell and British Acoustic. British Thomson-Houston had 700 installations by 1932. British Talking Pictures, formed as a £500,000 company in August 1928 by the financier who had backed De Forest, I. W. Schlesinger, took over Phonofilms at Wembley early in 1929. Late in that year they combined with Klangfilm-Tobis, which had formed a British branch. Reproduction equipment was to be handled by BTP, but the company had a chequered career and in September 1938 it was taken over by British Acoustic, combining its 350 installations with British Acoustic's 650. There were many other less important ones.*
By October 1930 *Kine Weekly* claimed that its expert, R. H. Cricks, had analysed thirty systems, but few of them survived more than a year or two.

Not only did equipment firms fail but many small showmen failed with them. RCA and Western Electric were expensive, with their servicing and spares and leasing arrangements, and the less prosperous exhibitors turned to the other, 'interchangeable', systems, which were often inadequate, wrong for their particular halls, badly installed and often badly operated too.

---

* By late 1929 Butcher's Film Service had installed 115 Electro-cord systems. British Phototone had its AWH disc system with a synchronising apparatus for £100, which it was claimed would fit any other disc system; Filmophone were to sell about 100 machines in the next couple of years and Syntok Talking Films had yet another disc system, with parts which were said to be interchangeable.

Deploring what poor tone, lack of synchronisation and fading sound could do to the film, the American companies responsible for recording them took steps to improve sound reproduction. According to the Minister of Labour there were eighty-one American electrical engineers in Britain to install sound apparatus in the summer of 1929. Western Electric, after discussion with its American producer-licensees, declared that exhibitors with new and untried systems, often referred to as bootleggers, would not be allowed to rent sound films until these had been tested. The Cinematograph Exhibitors' Association pressed the authorities to declare this in restraint of trade, but a renters' sound inspection department was formed and operated for some months.

The whole business of exhibition was becoming much more complicated. The shape of the hall affected the acoustics, as did upholstery, recesses, pillars and panels, and the exclusion of outside noises brought problems of ventilation. The projectionist had more to think about with his monitor sheet, cue sheet, fader, tone control and a signalling device from the hall checking changes in volume due to changes in the number of people in the hall. He had to cope with low volume, ground noise, distortion or breaks in the film, and the overlap and fade-over of different projectors required rehearsal, to avoid changes in pitch at the switch-over due to a drop in the power supply. No wonder many exhibitors were reluctant to change, hoping it would all turn out to be a passing fancy. The showmen's leader, Gavazzi King, an old man now, maintained that sound was being foisted on an unwilling public by the big American bosses. One exhibitor spoke up at a CEA meeting. 'Ask yourself the question "How long will the British public put up with it?" I venture to say, "Not long!" ' he said.

By 1931 things were settling down. The novelty was wearing off, and the two big American sound companies brought down their prices. After several years of patent difficulties beween the Americans and Klangfilm-Tobis the situation was stabilised by an International Patents Conference in June 1930, and the Paris Agreement. The hiss or ground noise of early sound tracks was reduced by noiseless recording techniques made available by both Western Electric and RCA, and quickly adopted by British studios. The frequency range of recording was shortly to be extended by Western Electric's Wide Range, British Acoustic's Full Range, RCA's High Fidelity and British Thomson-Houston's new system. Great changes had taken place in a few short years.

Difficulties similar to those facing exhibitors faced producers also. Once they had seen a sound film most of them were keen to change over to sound production, but they had to decide what system to adopt, at what rate the market for silent films would decline and what to do with their recently completed silent films. Most of them synchronised some sort of sound-track, part or full talking or just music and sound effects, and issued both sound and silent versions of the latter. Between January and November of 1929 twenty-three of the 215 sound films trade shown were British, all of them shown in the second half of the year.*

George Pearson, unlike the other directors of his company, saw the importance of sound and did his best with *Auld Lang Syne*, featuring Sir Harry Lauder. Made as a silent film, it was extended by the inclusion of over 800 feet showing Lauder miming to existing records of his popular songs, recorded on sound-on-film by RCA with a new negative ingeniously cut and patched by Thorold Dickinson, Pearson's editor, to synchronise with the track. Both sound and silent versions, the latter lacking the song sequences, were registered in March 1929 and trade shown in April for release in December. However clever, this was neither a talkie nor a true sound film. The company unwisely continued to make silent pictures, and closed down shortly afterwards.

The first successful British talkie feature to be shown was made by Hitchcock, enough of whose *Blackmail*, trade shown in June 1929, was hastily re-shot in sound, using the music planned for the cinemas as accompaniment to the rest, for it to be put out as a full talking picture.† Just as *The Jazz Singer* was the effective turning point in America, *Blackmail*, which was a tremendous success both critically and at the box office, was regarded as a landmark in the history of the British film industry. Its imaginative use of sound has been described many times. After this, British International Pictures revamped its other silent films awaiting release, giving them sound-tracks of some sort, and turned over to serious sound production. By the end of 1930 it had eight sound stages, which used RCA and a system called Ambiphone, which was very like RCA but based on a patent belonging to BIP. They continued to use it throughout the thirties. The Gaumont-British system British Acoustic, which was also used throughout the decade, at first had the sound-track on a separate strip of film, but this was abandoned in December 1929. They were hard on the heels of BIP with Elvey's *High Treason*, shown in August. Herbert Wilcox's first sound production, *Black Waters*, actually shown before *Blackmail*, had been made in America by an American director and was not a British film. His new studio was for some years the only one in England to adopt Western Electric recording. Basil Dean's new studio at Ealing, the first in Europe to be designed from the start for sound, drew heavily on his American associates RKO for equipment, expertise and personnel, but did not open until late in 1931. Michael Balcon at Islington was caught with a large number of silent films which had to be revamped but Graham Cutts's silent film *The Return of the Rat*, trade shown in May and then, after the showing of *Blackmail* in June, remade in a much longer version with dialogue and sound effects, was highly praised. Sound production at Islington began late in 1929, on RCA. Unlike Gainsborough, both British Lion and British Instructional

---

* *Black Waters* and *Woman to Woman* were made in America and *The Crimson Circle* in Germany, and none of them were registered as British films.

† There was also a silent version.

Films were eager to begin sound production early, but neither was successful. The former eventually installed RCA after heavy losses on their stock of silent films. British Instructional had an early agreement with Klangfilm but their joint production with UFA, *A Throw of Dice*, made in India and shown in October 1929, had a sound-track on Breusing disc, and the sound section of Anthony Asquith's *A Cottage on Dartmoor* was also recorded in Berlin. Despite technical difficulties Klangfilm was finally installed at Welwyn, but delays and the cost of conversion were too much for the company and it was taken over by BIP, and Ambiphone was installed. The only other Klangfilm connection in Britain was at Wembley, where BTP had taken over the large international consortium, but it lasted only a few years and made few films. Julius Hagen installed RCA at Twickenham and was soon busy turning out French and English versions of his films.

Thus most British studios installed RCA. Western Electric, at first confined to Wilcox's studio at Elstree, was adopted by Worton Hall in 1934 and later by the important new studios at Denham and Pinewood.* The American systems charged producers high royalties of £100 a reel, reduced in 1936 to £60, but there were a number of other inexpensive British systems.† By far the most important was Visatone. This excellent sound-on-film system was developed by Captain Round out of Asdic submarine detection equipment used during the 1914 war. It was made for the Stoll company under licence from the Marconi Wireless Telegraph Company. Stoll's studio at Cricklewood was equipped with it and used for hire and the production of short films. Visatone was also used as a second string by a number of other studios.‡

Studios, equipment and methods of work changed dramatically. The noisy studios of the silent film days, with a number of units working side by side and the directors shouting their instructions as the cameras turned, had gone. Every stage had to be isolated from outside noises, and a number of companies constructed elaborate inner shells inside the walls of their former studios, although with experience it was later found possible to modify the heavy soundproofing of the earliest conversions.

Two contemporary descriptions, by John Scotland in 1930[2] and Bernard Brown[3] in 1931, give some idea of what went on in these studios. A red light outside the door warned people not to enter when shooting was in progress. All sounds were recorded at once in long continuous takes, so microphones were hung or hidden about the set according to the

---

* Smaller installations were at the British Movietone studio in Soho Square, British Paramount News at Acton and at Merton Park.

† Piezo Electric Sound was installed at the Marylebone studio and British Thomson-Houston established a re-recording studio in Wardour Street, called Studio Sound Service. The Edibell Sound Film Apparatus Company which Edison Bell tried to float failed, and was wound up early in 1931. Fidelytone was an inferior sound-on-film system which appeared in 1930 and was operated briefly at Worton Hall and Southall.

‡ Sound City, Rock studios, Twickenham, Wembley and small studios in Albany Street, Bushey, Hammersmith and Blackheath.

EVENSONG

Victor Saville directing Evelyn Laye in 1934, with Alfred Junge's recreation of Venice at Shepherd's Bush.

NELL GWYN

Anna Neagle, Cedric Hardwicke and Jeanne de Casalis in Wilcox's 1934 reply to Korda's historical spectacle. Art director L. P. Williams and costume designer Doris Zinkeisen, who both worked on many of his films.

AS YOU LIKE IT
Elizabeth Bergner with Sophie Stewart in a production designed by Lazare Meerson, with costumes by John Armstrong and Joe Strassner. Director by Paul Czinner in 1934.

THE SCARLET PIMPERNEL
Merle Oberon and Leslie Howard in a successful Korda production of 1934. Sets by Vincent Korda and costumes by John Armstrong, with Merle Oberon's costumes by Oliver Messel.

SING AS WE GO
Made by Basil Dean in 1934 at Ealing and on location at Blackpool, where the crowds were as fascinated by the film crew as they were by Gracie Fields. The film owed much to Thorold Dickinson, nominally its editor, and to the story by J. B. Priestley.

JEW SÜSS
Conrad Veidt in Balcon's lavish production in 1934 of the bestselling novel, with sets by Junge.

whereabouts of the actors, the elaborate sound effects machines previously used in big cinemas, and the orchestra if there was one. No longer could the director coax his players through their parts, so rehearsals were necessary, and total silence from the technicians during shooting. Because cameras made a noise when they were running, which was picked up by the microphones, they were at first enclosed with the camera operators in soundproofed padded booths or cabins. Both Scotland and Brown describe them, hot and stuffy, with the camera pointing through thick optically-worked glass. Sometimes on power-driven trolleys, sometimes on rails with a little movement forward and back, they had lost the free mobility of the silent film. Several of these unwieldy cameras, typically four, would take different angles on a set which could afterwards be edited to form a mute which was married to the continuously recorded sound-track. Needless to say it drastically reduced the elaborate cutting of the late silent film. Lighting was by incandescent light to avoid the hiss of the arc and Scotland wrote of huge incandescent globes giving out enormous heat, and frames of up to seventy smaller ones mounted on stands with compressed-air brakes. He described the power needed to feed them, the heat they generated in the studio and the equipment needed to cool and ventilate them. Incandescent light is 60 per cent red, and as the orthochromatic film stock was not equally sensitive to all colours and reproduced red as black it was necessary to change to panchromatic stock. Sound-track and mute were shot in synchronisation but printed separately, so some device was needed to restore synchronisation after printing. Already in October 1929 *Kine Weekly* noted: 'Some studios signalise the start of a sound shot by a man clapping two pieces of wood together in front of the camera and microphone.' Writing in *Close Up* in 1931, the film editor Dan Birt described three methods. Western Electric, he said, used a hole punched in the film in each camera gate, RCA two black-and-white boards hinged at one end, and Klangfilm a 'syrchronising mark at every foot. A neon lamp in each camera photographs footage numbers in morse on the edge of the film.'[4]

The sound engineer sat in the mixing or monitoring room watching the action through the window, usually high above the set but sometimes in a less satisfactory portable monitoring room down below. With headphones on, he sat in front of a mixing panel covered with switches, cutting and fading sound from the various microphones, adjusting the volume and passing it on to the sound recording machine or sound camera housed in another room. The sound engineer had many problems and great power. It was hard enough to achieve mere intelligibility. He demanded clear speech, nothing too high or low or too loud or soft, no jerky changes in tone or volume from mike to mike or from shot to shot, and music which was fairly constant in speed and pitch. Fading his mikes in and out to follow the action, he must achieve correct sound perspective, for it was soon discovered that an impression of distance could not be achieved simply by fading down the volume of close-up sound. The studio must be damped down to produce the reverberation time appropriate to the setting. This would be different, for example, in a well furnished room, an empty hall or the open air. Indeed, when outdoor scenes were shot in the studio the whole place must be damped, as sound does not reverberate outdoors. Different camera set ups on the same set presented different acoustic problems and required him to 'shift and shuffle his draperies', as Scotland put it, much as the lighting cameraman adjusts his lighting. Sound rehearsals were needed to check all this, and the demands of the conscientious sound man, struggling to achieve clarity, infuriated film makers used to freedom in their choice of set-up. Perfect clarity was not necessarily what the director wanted, and there are several examples of an indistinguishable buzz of background conversation in early sound films.

Sound on location presented special difficulties, with its extraneous noises, especially high wind noise, and mass of equipment. In 1931 Brown wrote that it was necessary to take several 'microphones, a recording amplifier, a film recorder, and camera equipment, a small developing kit, film magazines, a large amount of connecting cables and wire for telephones, and finally the power generators and the motors for driving cameras and recorders'.[5] All this might need two large trucks, or three if lamps and their generators were required for filming at night. Most sound production was carried on indoors, and as time went on the Schufftan and other special processes reinforced the tendency to stay in the studio. Early in 1932 *Kine Weekly* said that it had 'not been until fairly recently that recording out-of-doors has reached a really reliable standard of efficiency'. But outdoor production was possible from the beginning, and dialogue sequences were shot on Dartmoor and at Marble Arch for Basil Dean's *Escape* in 1930. Both Western Electric and RCA had light portable recording units by 1931.[6]

While techniques were still being mastered the results could sometimes be rather strange. At the dance in *The Flag Lieutenant*, the shuffle of foxtrotting feet on the deck seems louder than the music of the band. In *Rookery Nook* a door closes with a shattering metallic clang. In *The Flying Scotsman*, a silent film with a synchronised track, the angry voices of a café brawl are punctuated by silent punches. People turning away as they spoke always presented problems but when, in Hitchcock's *Juno and the Paycock*, characters talking with their backs to the audience remained fully audible, presumably because of a handy microphone, theatre critic James Agate complained that it was unnatural. Not all voices recorded equally well at this stage of technical development, and one of the actors in *White Cargo* is virtually unintelligible. Dupont's *Atlantic* made effective use of the sound of the sea, the melancholy hooting of the ship in distress, the noise of the alarm, running feet and the dance band, although sound perspective was not always convincing and cutting to the ballroom, with the dance band in full flood, produces the kind of shock that film makers rapidly learnt to avoid. Such imperfections were forgiven by the public in the new excitement of the talkies, and the cars, trains, birds, tramping feet, the sounds of battle and the screech of shells, planes, the rap at the door in *The W Plan* suggest the enthusiasm with which directors like Victor Saville grasped the new opportunities.

The stationary camera booth with mikes scattered about the set did not last long. Soon the camera was enclosed in a soundproof box called a blimp, leaving the controls outside the casing. On a silent trolley or dolly, it could be moved more easily; takes could be shorter and four cameras covering different angles were no longer necessary. At the same time a single mobile microphone became possible with the use of the boom. This was described slightly later:

> When recording talking sequences the microphone is usually suspended just over the heads of the actors on the end of a pole that looks like a gigantic fishing rod. The other end of the pole is mounted on a truck, so that it can easily be moved about, and means are provided for raising or lowering the microphone and swinging it in any direction.[7]

Both boom and blimp had, in fact, been in existence in America when sound production first began in Britain, and a book published in 1930 actually showed them in use in a Hollywood production of 1929.[8] *Kine Weekly* mentioned mobile cameras at Wembley in August 1929, claiming that they were specially quiet so that soundproofed cabins were not necessary. And when Basil Dean started production at Beaconsfield in 1930 he had an imported 'hooded camera' and travelling microphone. By 1933 the camera was moving about freely once more:

> Scenes in which the camera follows an actor about are done in various ways. The most usual is to mount the camera on a rubber-tyred trolley, which is pushed by hand. For elaborate travelling shots, and for outdoor scenes, a 'camera crane' is used. The crane is on wheels and is constructed so that the platform carrying the camera and operator can be moved up and down or sideways. In a recent British film the camera was outside a house and appeared to move up to a window and through the frame into a room. For this the whole window-frame was moveable, so that when the camera reached it the woodwork was caught up on the trolley and carried on into the room.*[9]

Later in the decade the sound engineer would sit at his monitoring desk mixing not several microphones, but a large number of different sound-tracks, to make the final sound-track of the film. Dubbing and post-synchronisation eventually came to mean recording new sound, whether sound effects or dialogue, while film which had already been shot was projected; re-recording came to mean making a new sound track by electrical means out of a number already made. But the terminology had not settled down in the early years and the words were used interchangeably. In fact

---

* Probably *Looking on the Bright Side*.

re-recording in the modern sense was not possible until introduced by American engineers in 1932. The term was used by Dan Birt in *Close Up* in September 1931 to describe post-synchronisation. The process was very familiar, as the way in which many silent films had been turned into rough-and-ready sound films. *Rich and Strange*, for example,. used foreign backgrounds with crowd voices and other sounds synchronised at Elstree. And Pitkin and Marston specifically mentioned the addition of fresh sound to film which already carried sound:

> This ·process of dubbing on orchestration or other sound effects, such as the shooting of guns, the squealing of pigs, the roaring of floods, etc.·, may be performed in the same way on a film which already carries both picture and dialogue records.[10]

By June 1932 *Kine Weekly* could assert that only studio dialogue was recorded with the picture, and that musical background and effects were made separately and added after editing. Much more elaborate effects could be achieved by dubbing. Birt, who worked on *Windjammer* and *Tell England*, both of which were shot silent on location and post-synchronised, wrote in 1931:

> Two tracks, taken separately, may be dissolved one into the other: fades may be made; sounds can be distorted by running them through the projector faster or slower than the speed at which they were taken. (This was how we obtained the background for the trench raid and the low-frequencies for the blowing up on 'Clara', in *Tell England*).[11]

He also said that *Tell England* had a track for the explosions made from a collection of suitable recordings plus 'background from another projector and voices from the floor'.

So long as directors had to record all sound when they filmed the action, cutting was extremely difficult. Brown, even in 1931, wrote that it was necessary to cut where there was a natural break in the sound, and the initial practice was certainly to direct the camera at the source of the sound and cut when this changed. In general, in a dialogue passage the film cut to a close or mid shot of the person speaking, or in the case of a duologue held the two people in mid shot. It is easy to see why. After all, in a theatre one naturally tends to look at the actor who is speaking unless attention is deliberately drawn to something else. A typical passage would cut to the speaker before he spoke, hold the shot while he delivered his lines carefully and slowly, hold it further to show him having finished and then cut away. *Atlantic* was shot like this, with whole conversations from start to finish, however trivial, recorded with slow and heavy emphasis. *Rookery Nook*, the first of the Aldwych farce adaptations, was a typical proscenium film. A large stage setting is seen, with noticeable cuts to closer camera angles for brief shots, and many lengthy conversations in mid shot during which the actors do not move about. The cuts are awkward and the film seems stilted.

In *Cape Forlorn*, made at the end of 1930, the film cuts to a close-up of a door handle rattling as we hear it rattle, and to the smoking barrel of a gun at the sound of a shot, remnants of silent technique and at the same time the literal use of synchronous sound. Yet in the same film Dupont uses a reaction shot, a much more sophisticated usage, showing the terrified heroine accompanied on the sound-track by the sounds of the two men struggling. The manifesto on sound by Eisenstein, Pudovkin and Alexandrov which had appeared in *Close Up* before British producers had even started sound film production, in October 1928, had already made a plea for sound to be used as a counterpoint to the visuals. Reaction shots are also to be found in the Aldwych farce *Plunder*, made in the late autumn of 1930. And in *The W Plan*, made even earlier, Saville sometimes refrained from showing the speaker. In *The Skin Game*, made at the end of 1930 and the beginning of 1931, Hitchcock continued to use sound with some freedom: the girl tosses her ball lightly again and again for the little dog as the boy's voice addresses her from off screen; a voice speaks over a vision of the factory superimposed over the countryside which it will spoil; elaborate cutting and movement in the auction scene reflect the bidding. Hitchcock later told Truffaut that he had four cameras and a single sound-track because 'we couldn't cut sound in those days'. But this is not strictly true. In November 1929, over a year earlier, *Kine Weekly* had carried an article by Thorold Dickinson on his return from America in which he wrote that although in theory sound-tracks were cut as little as possible in fact both RCA and Western Electric had solved the problem of cutting and that it was possible to 'graft' the sound from one take on to another; the cutting copy could be re-recorded at constant pitch. In the same article he wrote that it was possible to record the sound track in advance and film the visuals in synchrony to it. So, although some eighteen months later *Sunshine Susie* was shot in short takes with synchronous sound, a fact which is only too obvious in some of the songs, it would in fact have been possible to use playback. Birt wrote in September 1931:

> Since the sound is on a separate film the sound taken with one scene can be made to overlap another scene; mute, not taken with the sound, may be cut into a scene; sound may be cut to run with a mute with which it was not taken; dissolves and fades may be made in both sound and mute; where several angles have been taken on one scene simultaneously they can be cut on the synchroniser to one sound track.[12]

Thorold Dickinson himself, acting as editor for Wilcox on his return from America, put his advanced ideas into practice by selecting the best shots and the best sections of sound-track and overlapping them.[13]

During these first few years the story-telling technique built up over some thirty or more years changed completely. Vestiges of it lingered on for a while. Humorous or dialogue titles did not disappear immediately, and even Hitchcock had gag titles in *Rich and Strange*. The introductory or establishing title persisted throughout the decade as the long rolling title which set the scene, often historical, of many a heavyweight film. *Tell England*, conceived as a silent film, included narrative titles. Voice-over narration was slow to catch on, although it was used to revamp some silent films. The use of visual details for reference and association and the use of visual contrasts and analogies were translated into sound terms. *Sunshine Susie* cross-cuts the quarrelling lovers, each of them declaring 'I'm *going* to have my way!' In *The Flag Lieutenant* the hero and heroine are cross-cut, both listening, alone, to the same sentimental gramophone record. And in Korda's *Service For Ladies*, as the girl, the young man and the old father sleep on the train, their voices interweave to the rhythm of the wheels: 'I like him a lot' – 'Oh, isn't she sweet!' – 'Forgotten me pills.' Hitchcock, of course had led the way in the use of non-realistic sound in *Blackmail*. *The Skin Game*, often dismissed as literary and uninteresting, continued his exploration of sound in the flickering noise that accompanies the double-exposure face of the girl's pursuer from her past as it flickers towards the camera, and in the indistinguishable words of the conditions of sale as they are read out by the auctioneer. In *Murder* he showed Herbert Marshall thinking aloud as he shaved. In Saville's *Woman to Woman* the mother, thinking of her lost child, hears him cry 'Mommy! Mommy!', the sound-track doing what a flash or double exposure would have done in a silent film. In Korda's *Wedding Rehearsal* the racing printing presses are accompanied by a chorus chanting the news. A sequence in Asquith's *Tell England* shows the soldier's mother chatting to a woman friend, thinking of her son at the war. The conversation fades and is replaced by sounds of farewell. We see a big close up of the mother's eyes and, as Asquith wrote,

> a quick glimpse of the woman's hat, about six frames, cut very short, and the mother's face. And I had the sound of the faint on the track. It was what would now be called, *musique concrète*. A note on a string and then, as she falls, a very high note on a piccolo, and the sort of telephone bell ringing you get in your ears if you are feeling ill. It was, in fact a kind of sound metaphor of a faint.[14]

Rotha, whilst praising the use of natural sound in the battle and landing scenes, criticised this impressionist passage as being out of keeping with the rest of the film. Sound was central to the very theme of Walter Summers's *Suspense*. Soldiers are nerve-racked by the sound of German sappers mining their trench, knowing that when the noises stop the mines will be ready to go off. These random examples show film makers eager to find out what sound could do, but not everyone was so receptive. The actor Sir Seymour Hicks, who was to make a large number of films in the next few years, said, 'The new screen technique is 90 per cent theatre. When that is realised we shall get better pictures',[15] and proceeded to demonstrate how wrong he was with some extremely stagey and boring films. Indeed, many proscenium films appeared. Although Tom Walls in *Plunder* used reaction shots and small panning movements, he still made a most theatrical first entrance, held for effect in true stage tradition, and the story relies so much on the endless talk that a section of the National Film Archive copy with its sound missing is almost incomprehensible.

Unlike Hollywood, British studios had always relied heavily on stage actors who continued to work in the theatre, and the new need to memorise lines and rehearse comparatively long takes was less of a problem for them than it was for some film players. In some studios dialogue directors worked alongside the directors, almost as much of a nuisance as sound engineers in their devotion to a monotonous flow of clear, even speech. Accents, in class-ridden Britain, gave the uniform young West End actors and actresses what they thought was an advantage. For many years working-class and regional accents were to be considered suitable only for comedy. The touching belief of some people that talkies would favour British actors rather than American ones proved unfounded. It was quite a shock when the American magazine *Motion Picture News* remarked that in *Escape* the English accent was 'no obstacle to understanding'.[16] The writer St John Ervine complained in the *Observer* of 'horrible vulgarities such as "Oh, yea!" and "Sez you!" '[17] but filmgoers adopted the new idioms with enthusiasm, and were more likely to complain about 'Oxford accents' and the 'BBC voice'. The extreme refinement of most English leading men in the early thirties was a contrast to the many rugged American he-men, and in both *Suspense* and *Tell England* the grim realism of the war background is belied by the fancy speech of the young officers. 'A'me heppy, somehow,' says the youngster in *Suspense*, and in *Tell England* the young officer visiting his dying friend in hospital can think of nothing more moving to say than 'I say, A'me fratefully sorry'. Bathos crept in to many a well intentioned line. John Loder, the young officer on the sinking liner in *Atlantic*, turns away slightly with hunched shoulders and chokes out, 'The ship – has three hours to live.' In *The Outsider*, a strong drama about a crippled girl, her father delivers slowly and emphatically a line which may have sounded better in the original stage presentation, 'Thank God – she has – *her music.*' And in *White Cargo* the true-blue British hero repulses the advances of a sultry half-caste maiden in the steamy jungle with a strangled 'Now listen! – I'm white!' Clearly more attention to the quality of the dialogue was needed. Pitkin and Marston in 1930 suggested that dialogue should be brief, rapid and monosyllabic compared with that of the theatre, 'telegraphic' in order to convey a lot of information in few words. A credit for 'additional dialogue' began to appear on films. The fact that speech could be treated as just one more sound effect, too, was realised by Walter Forde and Sidney Gilliatt in *Rome Express*, where porters and railway staff of different nationalities speak only in their own languages.

The early staginess of dialogue and delivery did not last long, however. A mere three or four years after sound production began, mastery of the new techniques and improved equipment had changed the appearance and structure of films completely. Seized gratefully by film makers as a straightforward way of conveying information which they would previously have put across by mime, reference shots or titles, sometimes cumbersome and elaborate, dialogue gave films a new form of flexibility to replace the mobility of camera and editing which they had lost. What could not be replaced, of course, was the dreamlike quality of the silent film and its ability to appeal to people speaking many different languages.

Chapter 6
Language Barriers

A silent film could be understood in any country in the world, for narrative or dialogue titles could easily be translated. All the talkies shown in Britain in the first year of the sound film were in English. Most were from America, some from Britain and one, *The Crimson Circle*, was made silent in Germany by a German firm and fitted with a synchronised part talkie sound-track on BTP disc by Sinclair Hill. But before long, as other countries began sound production, films in other languages were being trade shown as before, without any special comment, and many in the trade seem to have expected them to be equally acceptable to the public. With ingenuity and perhaps a few explanatory titles the films could be made understandable. René Clair later explained that in order to retain his English-speaking audience he had used only a little dialogue in his early sound films,[1] and *Kine Weekly* described *Sous les Toits de Paris* as 'easily followed although in French'[2] and *Le Million* as 'so cleverly directed that a knowledge of French is not necessary for it to be appreciated'.[3] Josef von Sternberg wrote: 'In the German tongue, *The Blue Angel* played in one theatre in Paris for four years without an interruption, clearly showing that the international cinematic formula need not be abandoned.'[4] These were exceptional films, but many lesser productions were recommended by *Kine Weekly* for general showing throughout 1931 and 1932. The public did not like them, however, and, as film makers forgot the technique of visual story-telling and relied more and more heavily on a sound-track loaded with dialogue, foreign-language films virtually disappeared.

There were four ways of overcoming this difficulty: the simultaneous production of a film in different language versions; remaking foreign films in English; dubbing English voices; and subtitling. There were also a number of international co-productions which led to the production of films in English which did not qualify for registration as British, even though some of them were actually made in Britain. All of these methods had their drawbacks, and before long the majority of the British public saw only American and British films.

The simultaneous production of several versions in different languages, known at the time as multilingual production, began in 1929. Planned together from the start, the versions were made by overlapping units following the same scenario and using the same sets. Alternative stars or directors might be used, or in some cases different supporting players or key technicians. BIP, accustomed to employing foreign directors and stars, took up multilingual production in a big way and it has been claimed that their epic *Altantic*, the English version of which was trade shown in Britain on 15 November 1929 and the German one in January 1930, was the first multilingual film in the world.[*5] A French version followed. *Atlantic* was directed by the German director E. A. Dupont, already working at Elstree on silent films. It consisted of long static dialogue sequences, and some sensational crowd shots of the sinking liner and fleeing passengers and crew which could be used in all versions. In Hollywood, too, foreign language versions of many films were soon being made, often by nationals of the countries for which they were intended. Paramount built its studio at Joinville, near Paris, to make Continental versions of its Hollywood films, and from March 1930 had a large output of multilinguals in France. The French themselves were unprepared for the talkie revolution and the first French talkie, *La Route est Belle*, was made by Robert Florey, a French director already well established in Hollywood, at BIP's Elstree studio. Twickenham was also used by a few foreign directors and Hagen himself was responsible for a certain amount of multilingual production.

British cinemas showed not only the English versions of British multilinguals, but also many English language versions of Continental films. These provided employment and experience abroad for a number of British actors and some technicians, chiefly writers and dialogue directors, but were not, of course, British films. Two well-known examples, *Baroud* and *Don Quixote,* illustrate the disconcerting results of this form of production. Rex Ingram's *Baroud* was made in 1932 at his studio in Nice and on location in Morocco, and some territorial rights to the English-language version were bought by Ideal, as a result of which it was shown in England as an Ideal film.[6] Stunningly photographed, the English version has an international cast which includes Ingram himself and a Spanish actress playing the shy little Arab girl, whose duenna is played by the American Arabella Fields like a black mammy from the Southern states, all Lawks-a-mussy in the hot Sahara sand. G. W. Pabst's *Don Quixote* was made a little later in French and English.[†] The great singer Chaliapin starred in both, and George Robey played Sancho Panza in the English one. The sets by Andreiev and photography by Nicholas Farkas create the same powerful and haunting images in both versions, which were shot together scene by scene[7] at Nice and along the coast, a lengthy process which

---

* The German four-language *Melodie des Herzens* was premiered in December 1929.

† The Museum of Modern Art *Film Index*, George Robey's autobiography and the actress Lydia Sherwood, who was in it, speaking on BBC Radio 4 on 15 February 1983, all say it was made in two languages, not three as has sometimes been stated.

made damaging demands on Chaliapin's voice. The film, which was distributed by United Artists, cost £100,000 and was a financial disaster, and the English version, although treated with respect by the critics, ran only a few weeks in London.

Another method, and in the end a more successful one, was to remake a foreign film in your own language. Players and technicians might be borrowed, and modifications made to suit the home market or local stars. There is a certain ambiguity in the distinction between multilinguals and remakes. Even in the case of *Atlantic*, the classic multilingual, the French version was made several months after the English and German ones and some sets had to be reconstructed. A number of English versions of what are commonly referred to as multilinguals were in fact made not only later but by different companies, and are more accurately described as remakes. John Stafford, an independent English producer who had acquired general experience in Hollywood, made several of them. *Where is This Lady?* was his remake of a Marta Eggerth film directed by Billy Wilder for which Franz Lehar had composed a special score. Stafford's version was one of the only two films Marta Eggerth made in England, and the only one to be registered as a British film.

Dupont and other directors at Elstree followed *Atlantic* with several more multilinguals, mostly heavy dramas deriving emotionally from the German silent film, and with *Elstree Calling*, a musical revue film consisting of turns presented as a television show, linked by a compère and two subplots. Its director, Adrian Brunel, has said[8] that it was put out in eleven different languages, but as most multilinguals were only made in English, French and German, with a very occasional venture into Spanish or Italian, it seems unlikely that eleven full translations were made. The fact that several of these films did not qualify for registration as British was a disadvantage for a studio like BIP whose films relied on the home market, and F. W. Kraemer's English-language *Dreyfus* in 1931, made after the French and Germans versions, was the last BIP multilingual. Two other BIP films were remakes. *Let's Love and Laugh* was an Elstree remake of a Marta Eggerth film* made abroad, and starred Muriel Angelus in place of the popular Hungarian singer. *Happy* in 1933 was another. A lighthearted musical about three 'lads', played with gusto by the rather too mature comedians Stanley Lupino, Laddie Cliff and the Scottish music-hall comic Will Fyffe, a most improbable trio to be seeking their fortunes in the streets and bistros of Paris, it is a good example of the confused sense of national identity and locale to which this form of production was subject. Despite its cheap sets and perfunctory production it has a bizarre charm, but it is pervaded by an uneasy placeless feeling. From 1930 the company had also taken a lead in importing early German sound films, a number of them simply synchronised music and sound effects. Out of almost a dozen films, which included *The Blue Angel*, two were English-language versions of Lilian Harvey

* Die Bräutigamswitwe.

musicals made for the British market with English leading men, one of them Laurence Olivier in his first film part.

BIP was by far the largest producer of multilinguals in Britain. At Gainsborough, Michael Balcon did not favour this method of production. He already had considerable experience of co-production in Germany and Austria, and was caught by the arrival of the sound film with a stock of silent co-productions which had to be given synchronised sound tracks. According to him,[9] speaking in 1973, it was Isidore Ostrer who initiated the programme of multilingual co-productions to be made by Pommer at the UFA studio. *Happy Ever After*, *FP 1*, *The Only Girl* and *Early to Bed* followed, but none of them were registered as British, nor can they realistically be regarded as products of the British film industry. Far more successful was *Sunshine Susie*, (q.v.), which was a remake. Although a gay and delightful film it resembled other international productions in having a disembodied air, with no explanation for the presence of the two very English actors, Owen Nares and Jack Hulbert, in an obviously German setting. It was a great success, however, both critically and commercially and was followed by a second remake starring Renate Müller, *Marry Me*, made by German director William Thiele. Alexander Korda, who returned from Hollywood for Paramount's multilingual production at Joinville, returned to Paris after launching his own company in London and made both English and French versions of *The Girl from Maxim's* in 1933. He was responsible for several more multilinguals and remakes but none of them was a major production. The busiest independent in international production was Arnold Pressburger, a Hungarian from the German and Austrian film industries who had earlier been associated with Gaumont-British. His first British sound film, *City of Song*, was part of the ASFI bid to assert the ASFI-Tobis sound system as a rival to RCA and Western Electric (q.v.). Unlike others, this film did secure British registration. But four more, three of them with Jan Kiepura and two with Marta Eggerth, failed to qualify even though one of them was shot at Beaconsfield.

In the end this unwieldy form of production, upon which BIP had embarked with such high hopes, proved disappointing and it became less common in the mid-thirties. The fact that most of the films were not formally British was important, but possibly less so than the fact that they were usually not very good.* Remakes, on the other hand, were much more likely to succeed, and continued to be made throughout the decade. Two late examples, *Prison Without Bars* and *Hell's Cargo*, each starring the same leading lady in both versions, were available in London in both French and English at the same time.†

* To set the record straight, a number of films which are sometimes referred to as British multilinguals were English-language versions of foreign films. These include *Temptation*, *The Divine Spark*, *Koenigsmark*, *The Last Waltz*. *Did I Betray?* and *Thirteen Men and a Gun*.

† Other remakes included *The Tunnel*, *Emil and the Detectives*, *Moscow Nights*, *Dreaming Lips*, *Mademoiselle Docteur* and *Who's Your Lady Friend?*.

FIRST A GIRL

Sonnie Hale and Jessie Matthews. One of her most successful films, it was directed by Victor Saville at Shepherd's Bush in 1935. Art director Oscar Wendorff, costumes by Joe Strassner.

MURDER AT MONTE CARLO

One of approximately 120 Warner Brothers quota films made at Teddington in the decade. Molly Lamont, Peter Gawthorne, Eve Gray and newcomer Errol Flynn. The latter was immediately transferred to Hollywood and not wasted on another British production.

THINGS TO COME

Based on a Monard of Learned Classroom. In 1935 the Korda film of H. G. Wells' vision of the future gave a 1930s view of what clothes and houses would look

FOREVER ENGLAND
John Mills in a film of life in the Royal Navy, directed for Gaumont-British by Walter Forde in 1935.

FOREVER ENGLAND
Much of the film was shot on location. Walter Forde directing.

THE 39 STEPS

Rooted in the studio, Hitchcock and art director Oscar Werndorff recreate the hills for Madeleine Carroll and Robert Donat's famous escape, handcuffed together, in this successful film of 1935.

MIDSHIPMAN EASY

Desmond Tester, Hughie Green and Robert Adams. The first film for which Carol Reed received full credit as director, with sets by Edward Carrick. Made at Ealing in 1935.

Later in the decade dubbing and titling took over as ways of restoring some of the film's international viability. At first the terms 'dubbing' and 'post-synchronisation' were both used loosely to refer to the synchronisation of the sound-tracks, some of them simply music and effects but some part talking, which were added to many of the last silent films. Another contemporary meaning of the word 'dubbing' was the recording on set of the voice of an actor concealed from the camera, who spoke or sang while another actor mimed the actions. Well-known examples were that of Warner Oland, miming to the singing of an unseen Jewish cantor in *The Jazz Singer*, and Joan Barry providing the voice for the Czech actress Anny Ondra in *Blackmail*. English voices were being substituted for foreign ones in sound films made in foreign languages as early as October 1929. *Kine Weekly* noted efforts in Germany to 'superimpose English words on the lip movements of the German actors', and Douglas Fairbanks referred to 'Zelnik's wonderful lip-matching doubling in foreign tongues' in the same mouth.[10] During the next few years many imports were doubled, or 'dubbed' and, while some groups of actors were travelling to foreign studios to appear in full English-language versions, others were going to supply voices alone. Brunel, for example, took a team of minor actors to Italy for *Vally*, a Pittaluga film shown here with its Italian cast and what *Kine Weekly* called 'bad voice doubling'.[11] English dialogue for *M* was directed in Germany by Charles Barnett, and it is interesting that in 1933 Joe May's *Paris-Méditerranée*, made in France with a French cast, was shown in England at the same time both in its original French and in a version dubbed into English by May himself and called *Into the Blue*. In the early thirties many *Kine Weekly* reviews appraised the quality of synchronised lip movements, frequently finding the careful articulation and refined accents unsuitable. *The Woman he Scorned*, the film Czinner had shot silent in 1929 in Britain with Pola Negri, was shown in May 1930 in what the trade paper called a dubbed version, supplied with the hated BBC accents.* In 1932 Paramount gave up producing foreign-language versions and turned its Joinville studio over to dubbing their films for the Continental market. Before long the dubbing of American films was general. Despite improvements there were disadvantages to the system. Not only did sound effects and the sound perspective often suffer, but the substitute actors were unlikely to have the dramatic ability of the originals. But all the same dubbing did succeed in retaining the European market for Hollywood. The dubbing of Continental films for the English-speaking market, however, did not become widespread and before long European films could claim only a minority audience in Britain.

But this serious audience, at the specialist cinemas, was prepared to accept the fourth method of overcoming language barriers, the subtitle. Reading an abbreviated translation of the spoken dialogue printed at the bottom

---

* Other dubbed films include *Bride No. 68*, *The White Devil*, *The Last Company*, *The Immortal Vagabond*, *Fra Diavolo*, *Avalanche*, *The Love Duet*.

of the picture without losing track of the images was relatively demanding. But subtitles were artistically preferable to dubbing and made steady progress during the decade, as a new manifestation of the dialogue title used previously in the silent film.

Some of the films imported in their original language in the early years had, as we have seen, a few explanatory titles in English. Ambrose S. Dowling of the RKO export department took advertising space in *Kine Weekly* in December 1931 in which he proclaimed the need for more action and music in films, minimum dialogue, and 'the superimposing of explanatory titles in the language of the country'.[12] The old dialogue title also crept back, this time not as an insert but superimposed on the bottom of the picture. The art of compressing a great deal of talk into a few suitable words which could be picked up quickly by the eye without missing the action on the screen was difficult and, according to Brunel, very underpaid.[13] A key figure in the development of the subtitle was Elsie Cohen, who, at the Academy Cinema in London, had set about exhibiting there some of the unusual films from abroad which the growing number of serious film enthusiasts wanted to see. She has written that 'we always showed the films with subtitles'.[14] The first were *Kameradschaft,* with seventy or eighty titles, in January 1932 and *Mädchen in Uniform* in April with two hundred and thirty.[15] At first the titles were set up in the lab, photographed and combined with the negative. The results were low in contrast and hard to read, and re-photographing affected the quality of the picture. References in reviews to the quality of the titling became more frequent. From early 1933 Mai Harris did the translating and titling for Unity Films, of which Elsie Cohen was managing director. In 1937 a new method, using etching, was found to be cheaper and as it did not affect the photographic quality of the projection print it gave better results. The type was set up in metal and applied to the release print, cutting through the emulsion and giving a much brighter result. It was adopted by Julia Wolfe of Technique Films, a newcomer to the business.

By now very few foreign-language films were imported, and they were of interest only to an educated minority audience which preferred the subtitle, despite the small effort it entailed, to dubbing. Only the best foreign films were imported, the term 'specialised' began to creep into reviews, and before long the stars of Continental films were unknown to the majority of the British public. By dubbing their films for the Continent and being able to export them to Britain and the Commonwealth with no language barriers, the Hollywood companies were now the only ones with a truly international market.

Chapter 7
Colour Films

For many years inventors had sought a photographic method of reproducing natural colours on the screen. Various systems had been tried, some of them additive and some of them subtractive. Briefly, in additive systems separate pictures stained in the primary colours or various combinations of them, which had been taken through similarly coloured filters, were superimposed on the screen; in subtractive systems images in various pigments, taken with more than one negative, were superimposed on each other on the film itself. Additive systems were hampered by cumbersome and unreliable attachments to camera or projector or both, and often suffered from inaccurate registration on the screen. Subtractive systems were extremely complicated and expensive and two-colour subtractive ones, in particular, did not cover the full range of colours. Additive systems at first appeared more practicable, but work continued on both and in the mid-1930s a subtractive system, Technicolor, achieved the first really successful colour film.

The Technicolor Motion Picture Corporation was founded in America in 1915 by the inventors Daniel F. Comstock and Herbert T. Kalmus. Over the years they had experimented with several systems, the most recent of which, a subtractive process, was developed in the late twenties. Although it was not perfect they enjoyed considerable success with it after Warner Brothers, as part of their expansion in the late twenties, used it for *On With the Show* in 1929. This was a revue film, advertised as '100 per cent natural colour all-talking, all-singing, all-dancing'. Before long a number of Technicolor films were made in Hollywood and aroused interest on both sides of the Atlantic. Many believed that colour would take over completely, as sound had just done. Indeed, until half-way through 1931 the wide screen and stereoscopy were also believed to be imminent and there was much anxiety about the expense and technical confusion they would bring. During the next couple of years many systems with strange names appeared and disappeared. In December 1929 Kalmus journeyed to Europe to seek openings there. The big producers waited to see what would happen. However, the colour quality was obviously not yet perfect and there was little interest from either the public or the critics. There were even some protests from highbrows, to whom it seemed that the visual essence of the film, the composition of form in movement by the use of light in black-and-white images, was threatened. It seemed a desecration similar to the introduction of speech, destroying the essence of film art.

The most important British system was Raycol. The £300,000 Raycol British Corporation was formed in July 1929 with a board which included the Duke of Richmond and Gordon, J. S. Courtauld, C. A. Bolton and Maurice Elvey. Its aim was to exploit a system patented in February 1928 by Dr Anthony Bernardi, a two-colour additive system using black-and-white panchromatic stock in the camera and projector, but with an arrangement of prisms behind the lens to split the light.* Unlimited copies of the films could be made at the same price as black-and-white films, and could be projected on any projector after its lens had been replaced by a special fitting with two lenses. Colours were reported to be soft and pleasing, although with some fringing; red, black and white were very good; browns satisfactory; greens, oranges and blues 'a fair approximation'.[1] But four times the normal exposure was needed and, according to the colour expert Major Adrian Bernard Klein, adjustment of the lens for projection was difficult. Elvey went to America to promote it in October 1929, and on the ship coming home in December met and interested Basil Dean of ATP, who was later to feel that he had been somewhat glib.[2] As a result of this meeting ATP acquired an interest in Raycol; Stephen Courtauld joined the ATP board and was, incidentally, to play a crucial part in the further development of that company, and Dean joined the Raycol board. With plenty of financial backing there was talk of the Indian film maker Niranjan Pal making a coloured *Khyber Pass* film in India, but nothing seems to have come of this. Elvey made *The School for Scandal* at Elstree in Raycol that summer. When it eventually appeared in 1931, however, difficulties were encountered and it was shown in black and white. An effort was made to revive the system later but only one short feature film was made. This was the W. W. Jacobs story *Skipper of the 'Osprey'*, made at Ealing in the summer of 1933. *Kine Weekly* noted that the colour 'fluctuates a little in quality'. The paper's sober technical expert, R. H. Cricks, however, was much more critical and wrote that only pastel red, blue-green and white were present, with red fringing on the left of objects and blue on their right, and a lack of definition.[3] Little more was heard of Raycol.

Another system which seemed for a time to have a chance of success was the Keller-Dorian process, a three-colour additive system using panchromatic stock with embossed lenticulations in an ordinary camera with red, green

* It was described by the Society of Motion Picture Engineers thus: Light entering the camera is divided into two parts by means of a beam splitter and is then caused by a system of rhomboids to form two images one quarter normal size in opposite corners of the frame on standard size film, one through an orange filter and the other through a blue-green filter. A twin lens projector with the appropriate filters over the lens superimposes the two positive images on the screen.

and blue filters.* The lenticular process had been patented in France about 1909 by R. Berthon. A. Keller-Dorian had worked with him in Paris around 1914 and the Keller-Dorian Berthon process had been demonstrated in Paris in 1923. In 1928 an effort was made to exploit it commercially and it was adopted by Kodak for a substandard film for amateurs, Kodacolor. Ludwig Blattner in Elstree acquired the British film rights and much was expected from it, but his company failed and neither it nor his sound system was ever used. Moviecolour was formed later to exploit it but there were copyright difficulties and despite later attempts to improve it the projector adaptation was unsatisfactory.

Apart from Raycol and Keller-Dorian there was little attempt to make colour films in England during the short period of the early Technicolor system's success. A few hand-tinted films appeared, and British rights to the American bipack (doubled-coated) film Multicolor were acquired in March 1931 by Alan J. Williamson, who planned to produce at Worton Hall. But the system required much more lighting than usual and films from America showed that the system was prone to fringing, and plans were abandoned. Zoechrome was an English system invented by T. A. Mills in 1920. Very complex, it had a camera with four lenses and four consecutive printing operations from a double-length negative. It was demonstrated early in 1929, but the company was wound up late in 1934.

By 1932 it was clear that black-and-white films were not doomed as silent films had been. The technical problems continued to be of interest, however, and T. Thorne Baker addressed the Royal Society of Arts on colour cinematography in November of that year. Meanwhile, there was much theoretical and aesthetic discussion of the place of colour in films. Rudolf Arnheim, in his 1930 book *Film*, maintained that whereas the public had welcomed sound because it lessened the artificiality of the silent film they seemed in no hurry to give a similar welcome to realism in the guise of colour. Nothing, he argued, could exceed the visual artificiality of the black and white film, in which the world was presented in a one-dimensional grey series all the way from white to black and in which, moreover, even relative tonal values were distorted with, for example, red lips and green leaves both appearing black. Yet this apparently gave an acceptable and intelligible picture of the world. Writers in *Cinema Quarterly* saw it differently, suggesting that black-and-white film was actually more 'real' than colour:

> We can grasp form, and even form in motion, but it is extremely hard to enjoy the composition, as well as the literal content, of colour in motion . . . Our colour sense may be developing, our spectrum dividing, but until the retino-cerebral apparatus is far more advanced than it is at

---

* The SMPE described it as: A three-colour additive motion picture process. A banded tricolor filter is associated with the camera lens. The film support which faces the lens is embossed with small lens elements. Each lenticular element images the filter bands upon the emulsion surface. A filter of similar form is associated with the projection lens.

present, it is improbable that we shall sensually enjoy coloured films, except for their purely kaleidoscopic characteristics. . . . The manipulation of light and movement is, then, much better controlled in black and white, or any definite monochrome, than in imperfect if triumphant colours.[4]

Colour seems to be an entity in itself. It trespasses on the field of vision. It provides an abstract spectacle imposed over the spectacle concrete. Monochrome allows the eye to come closer, as it were, to concentrate more, and all the other rays afford our vision a means of deeper penetration, so black-and-white photography pierces a fog of light sensations.[5]

Whether there was a spontaneous demand for colour or not, when technical progress made it possible it was to be exploited with vigour. Work at Technicolor led to a breakthrough in the mid-thirties, with the development of a new and successful system using a special new camera. In some ways the process had something in common with that owned by British Colour Films, a company which had been registered with £6,000 capital in September 1933. An American working in England, Aaron Hamburger, who for some years had been experimenting with a system called Polychromide, had died in November 1932. The system used a beam splitter and a double-coated positive and was a four-colour subtractive one. After his death it was claimed that the system was ready for commercial exploitation and a company was formed, capital being obtained from an elderly colliery owner from Dudley. A demonstration was held to interest film makers, but little more was heard of it.

Technicolor had taken a decisive step in 1932 when it adopted a trichromate process, which overcame the inability of earlier two-colour subtractive methods to record the whole spectrum accurately. A new camera was devised, the famous three-strip camera, using a beam splitter and a bipack film as well as a single-coated film, giving three colour negatives; the former printing gave way to three printings, and later four.* Technicolor was now ready for full commercial development and, spurred on by it, several other processes also appeared on the market.

The major Hollywood producers were slow to take up the new Technicolor. But Walt Disney used it in 1932 in the cartoon *Flowers and Trees*, and found it so successful that from then on it was used for all Silly

---

* The system is described in the *Oxford Companion to Film*, p. 682, as follows: ' . . . three separate negatives replaced the single camera film, each recording one primary colour. A beam-splitter reflected light to an aperture to the left of the lens; over the prism was placed a magenta filter, which excluded green light from a panchromatic negative. Directly behind the aperture were two films: the front one, being orthochromatic, recorded only blue components and carried a red-orange dye which prevented blue light from reaching the back (panchromatic) film, which recorded the red components. An aperture in the normal position behind the lens and covered with a green filter, recorded the green components on the back film. The three films were then processed to make separate relief matrices from which prints were made as in the previous process.

Symphonies, and from 1936 for Mickey Mouse films as well. The first live-action film was a short two-reel story film made in 1934, *La Cucaracha*. It was a sensation. The first three-strip feature film, RKO's *Becky Sharp*, was trade shown in Britain in July 1935 and created even more of a stir. This film was to colour what *The Jazz Singer* was to sound, the indisputable proof of a viable commercial system. Graham Greene, writing in the *Spectator*, called it a triumph for colour:

> The colour is everything here; the process has at last got well away from blurred mauve wind-flowers and Killarney lakes, and admits some lovely gradations, from the bright dresses to the delicately suggested landscapes on the walls.

He qualified this by complaining that skin tones did not reproduce well, and added:

> But one must remember that colour has been tried out on the easiest kind of subject; the fancy dress.[6]

Before long all the big American companies plunged into colour production, all going for spectacular 'colourful' subjects. There was no question of making ordinary films in colour, for the system was expensive. According to a Fox executive it added from £20,000 to £25,000 to the cost of a picture in negative and printing costs.[7] It was realised that colour was not going to take over completely, after all. For the time being it was simply one option, which would be used for some films.

Meanwhile in Britain Alexander Korda had been toying with the idea of acquiring a system of his own, Hillman Colour. Developed by A. G. Hillman, this was a two-colour additive system with three colour-separation images on a single negative, which suffered from the usual disadvantage of a projector attachment. Gerrard Industries' subsidiary Colourgravure, formed to conduct research and perfect this system, was taken over by London Film Productions in October 1934, and Korda and Montagu Marks joined its board. But the system was not yet ready for commercial exploitation and once *Becky Sharp* had appeared Korda's interest shifted to Technicolor.

By this time Dr Kalmus was in Europe again, once more searching for associates. His method of exploiting Technicolor was not through franchise holders but by setting up labs, renting out cameras and keeping tight control of the actual production process through the presence of a Technicolor consultant on every picture. At the end of July 1935 a deal with Korda was announced. A private British company was registered with £160,000 capital owned half by Technicolor and half jointly by Korda, Gerrard Industries and the Prudential Assurance Company. The colour process was to be available to all producers. The new company was to build British Technicolor labs at Denham, alongside the new Korda studio which was being built there. Early the following year a £250,000 factory at Harmondsworth, Middlesex, was announced and the capital was increased to £325,000. The department at Denham was set up by Kalmus's wife Natalie, who stayed on and acted as Technicolor consultant on the nine British films which used Technicolor before the war. An art student when young, this determined and knowledgeable woman, described as Titian-haired and dynamic, had worked with her husband since the company started. She insisted on rigorous training and high standards, and made her wishes felt on the set.

Even before Denham studio or the labs were finished, work began at Denham and Epsom and in Ireland on the first Technicolor film produced in Britain, Twentieth Century-Fox's story about racing, *Wings of the Morning*. It was processed in America. Not only was it considered by many to be outstandingly beautiful and a triumph for colour, but it was romantic and exciting and was a world-wide box-office success. The praise was not unanimous, the lush green of Ireland and the rich colours of horse racing and gypsy life being too much for some people. The painter Paul Nash spoke of the 'vivid vulgarity of the picture postcard'.[8]

The Technicolor films made in Britain before the war included five from Korda and two from Herbert Wilcox. They were all major productions and handsome films, if rather overemphatic in their use of colour by later standards. Alongside Natalie Kalmus, whose presence on the set was not always welcome, they were shot by some of the best cameramen in England and designed with considerable imagination. Wilcox was the first British producer to embark on Technicolor, with some colour sequences in *Victoria the Great*. This was made a year after *Wings of the Morning* by the British cameraman Freddie Young with Bill Skall, the Technicolor lighting expert. The same team later made *Sixty Glorious Years* entirely in colour. The Korda films were two glamorous contemporary vehicles for Merle Oberon, *The Divorce of Lady X* and *Over the Moon*, two A. E. W. Mason adventure stories set in the Empire in the nineteenth century, *The Drum* and *The Four Feathers*, and the spectacular fantasy *The Thief of Bagdad*. The only other British Technicolor feature was *The Mikado*.

In July 1935, before he had seen *Becky Sharp*, Major Klein had written:

> The coming year is likely to be a decisive one in the history of the colour film. Whether there will be a prolonged struggle between additive and subtractive processes remains to be seen. On the whole the balance of advantage would seem to be on the side of the subtractive (colour-on-film) processes, but it is rash to prophesy the course of evolution in an industry which has seen so many technical revolutions during the last few years.[9]

Klein regarded the cost of the new Technicolor camera as a disadvantage and believed that the adjustment of focus and registration of multiple images would prove difficult. Working as technical director of another system, Gasparcolor, he thought its prospects as a rival to Technicolor were good. Developed by the Hungarian Dr Belá Gaspar at Geyer labs in Germany, it was a subtractive process with a triple-layered coloured-emulsion positive using acid dyes. These gave the films a characteristically rich glowing appearance which was very attractive although perhaps not very flexible. Gaspar came to Britain in 1934 and a group of advertising films were made, at first under the management of C. H. Dand and later under a younger brother, Imre Gaspar. Delightful films were also made by Len Lye, a highly articulate and original artist who wrote interestingly about the use of colour and whose views stimulated serious discussion among fellow artists and intellectuals. Another Hungarian, George Pal, who made puppet advertising films for Horlicks, used Gasparcolor for one of them in 1936, called *On Parade*. Gasparcolor seems to have been confined to advertising and animated films, although Klein did make a short film called *Colour on the Thames* in 1936.

The success of Technicolor stimulated the promoters of several other processes in the mid-thirties. Brewster-color, the system of an American, P. D. Brewster, was used in Britain for advertising by Revelation Films after a demonstration of *Let's Look at London* early in 1935. British Ondiacolor, also new in 1935, was a two-colour subtractive process for which a company was registered in June 1936 with a capital of £12,000. A lab was set up in Wardour Street and some travel films were made, including a *Beautiful Britain* series, with some success. Dunningcolor, also new in 1935, was an American three-colour system devised by C. H. Dunning, who had been with Prizma, and was soon being used in Britain by the animated cartoon maker Anson Dyer. In 1937 it was hoped to use it for a new newsreel, but this was not a success. Two other systems were used for some undistinguished entertainment films. Spectracolor, of which no details are available, was adopted by Publicity Picture Productions, and besides being used in a number of entertainment shorts in 1936 was used at Bushey for a four-reel *Faust* and another four-reel film called *Railroad Rhythm*. Finally there was British Chemicolour, a firm within the Schach group, using the German four-colour system Ufacolor. The company was formed by Max Schach's associates Major Procter and L. A. Neel with the film director Karl Grune and cameraman Otto Kanturek. It was used in the fantasy parts of the Tauber film *Pagliacci*, but was far from good. It was intended to shoot the finale of Cutts's and Kanturek's musical *Over She Goes* in Chemicolor. This was to be an ingenious production number with a black-and-white set and coloured lighting, and girls dressed in frills which were white on one side of their dresses and dark on the other. They were to dance in changing coloured light which would make coloured patterns with the dresses, swaying to illustrate the words of the title *Over She Goes*. This promising sequence, however, does not seem to have appeared in colour after all. It is black and white in the surviving copy held by the National

Film Archive and there is no mention of colour in the *Kine Weekly* review in 1937. By early 1939 the company was in the hands of the receivers.

There was only one real alternative to Technicolor in Britain, and that was Dufaycolor. This, based on the work in France by Louis Dufay on a screen-plate process* before the 1914 war, was developed as 'Spicer-Dufay' after the mid-twenties with generous backing from the paper firm of Spicer. In 1931 there were two successful demonstrations, one in May at the Royal Society and one in October at the British Kinematograph Society. It was a three-colour additive system, but with a difference, for it used the ordinary camera and projector without attachments. T. Thorne Baker, who was in charge of the technical development work, described it in his book. The film stock appeared to be ordinary, but there was a film of collodion between the emulsion and the celluloid; on this was printed a matrix of blue and green squares, one millionth of a square inch each, separated by red lines of corresponding area. It was noted that this system, like some others, needed a lot of light. By 1932 it was reported to be almost ready, although it was marginally more expensive than black and white and the need for extra lighting remained a problem.

In February 1933 Spicer-Dufay (British) was registered as a private company with a capital of £600,000, provided mainly by the photographic firm of Ilford, which was interested in perfecting a substandard colour film for the amateur market. A couple of months later Dufaycolor was expanded to acquire part of Colortone Holdings, registered a month previously as a private £88,750 company. The next year they held another demonstration, and announced that their output capacity of 250,000 feet a month was to be greatly increased by opening a new factory at Elstree. Another factory was planned in America, also, and Dufaycolor Inc. was formed in 1935. By now they were ready for business. Part of British Movietone's coverage of the royal jubilee procession in May 1935 was in soft and pleasing Dufaycolor and brought the process to the notice of a very large audience, but its use in BIP's musical feature *Radio Parade of 1935* was disappointing. The climax was shot in Dufaycolor by Claude Friese-Greene, but although the colour was satisfactory in close-up it was said to be very pale in long shot.

Dufay now expanded by joining with another company. Chromex was a holding company formed to take over British Cinecolor, a British two-colour additive system with a beam splitter somewhat like Raycol, evolved by Demetre Daponte and given the name Cinecolor in 1929. It could be traced back, through Cinechrome in 1914 and Colin Bennett's work in 1911, to the original Kinemacolor patents. It had been adopted briefly in 1933 by Pathé-Natan in Paris and film shot at Joinville was demonstrated here in October 1933, but proved of poor quality. Chromex now joined forces with Dufay and in January 1936 Dufay-Chromex was registered, with a capital of £750,000. Early in 1937 Dufay, with Daponte on the board, was

* A colour process using a surface bearing a mosaic, either regular or irregular, of minute, juxtaposed, transparent elements of the primary colors.

I GIVE MY HEART
Shooting crowd scenes in 1935 at
B.I.P., Elstree, for one of their
lighthearted operettas, this one about
the Dubarry. Cedric Dawe was their
prolific art director.

TURN OF THE TIDE
J. Fisher White and Derek Blomfield in British National's brave attempt in 1935 to make a realistic film about working people. Shot partly in Yorkshire.

THE EDGE OF THE WORLD
John Laurie with islanders in the Hebrides. In 1936 Michael Powell's first important film was acclaimed as a dramatic documentary.

DREAMING LIPS
Raymond Massey and Elisabeth Bergner in a glamorous love story with some music by William Walton. Produced at Denham by Max Schach and directed by Paul Czinner, it was a remake of the latter's German film of 1932. Art directors Andreiev and Tom Morahan, costume designer Joe Strassner.

CHICK
Sydney Howard, a mild and somewhat rueful comedian, with Betty Ann Davis in a B & D film of 1936.

SABOTAGE
Hitchcock's famous crime film of 1936. The London procession which delays the messenger carrying a time bomb set up on the Shepperton lot by art director Oscar Werndorff.

ready to promote Dufaycolor as the only practicable additive process. In May an issue of £270,000 was oversubscribed within minutes. Pathé's news film of the coronation was shot in Dufaycolor and reached a wide public, like the jubilee. By October the company had new labs at Thames Ditton and Major Klein, after leaving Gaspar, had joined it. A series of shorts by Humphrey Jennings, a documentary film maker and artist and a friend of Len Lye, was also planned, including one on fashion which featured couturier Norman Hartnell and was called *Design for Spring*. A new emulsion with four times the speed solved the lighting problem and by January 1939 they had made many short films. In 1938 the veteran director George Pearson made three short films in Dufaycolor, anecdotes rather than stories. At the same time, however, it was announced that the company had made a loss of £122,000, which was blamed on the production crisis in the industry as a whole. In 1939 their first long feature was finished as war began. This was a spy adventure, *Sons of the Sea*, directed by Elvey and shot largely on location at Dartmouth College, with Klein in charge of the colour. The National Film Archive copy* has worn badly, with a flicker that affects the sound and makes it difficult to assess the original colour, which certainly did not pose a challenge to Technicolor.

So the colour film had arrived. But it had not caused a revolution comparable to that brought about by the talkies, either commercially or artistically. After the first visit to a cinema especially to see what colour was like, people reverted to choosing their films largely because of star, story or local habit as before. The use of colour was a sign that a film was an important production, but many major films continued to be made in black and white. Box-office returns could only justify the greater expense if the film was a winner on grounds other than colour. Some people had supposed that colour would add to a film's realism as sound had done, and this would create such a public demand for it that all producers would have to adopt it. This begs the question whether it actually was realism that made sound so attractive. The distant shadows of the silent film had their own charm. But, although much loving care had been spent on developing the narrative technique of the silent film, ordinary audiences were apparently more comfortable when a spoken word here or there replaced passages of visual imagery or mime, and abandoned it without a backward glance. Colour was different. It did impose certain limitations on cutting and movement but gave rise to nothing like the changes in narrative structure brought by sound. Moreover it is questionable whether the use of colour in these early days added much to the realism of the films. Vibrant, exuberant they may have been, but not realistic. Paul Nash agreed with Graham Greene on the catastrophic effect on complexion when he wrote of the ethereal French actress Annabella in *Wings of the Morning*: 'I could not help feeling that the most significant achievement of Technicolor to date was in making Annabella look *swarthy*.'[10] Greene, as a novelist and

* Viewed in April 1974.

critic whose perceptive and intelligent film reviews from 1935 to 1940, reprinted in book form as *The Pleasure Dome* in 1972, form a useful commentary representing an intellectual's point of view, was vehement:

> To an artist, the appearance of the average colour photography picture is more or less of an abomination. It lacks everything he prizes – form, definition and subtlety. It emphasises everything he has striven to overcome – realism, banality, false values. He recognises in it potential beauty but is forced to realise that, at present, its whole apparatus is being used for stupid or venal ambitions.[11]

Nash despised *Wings of the Morning* and spoke of 'the inane pursuit of naturalism, colour for its own, or rather, for Technicolor's sake, and the naive attempts at colour harmony'.[12]

It was fashionable among highbrows at the time to find colour acceptable only in cartoon films, upon which, and especially upon Disney, they heaped extravagant praise. Its use in other films was often condemned as strident. Clearly the deliberate use of colour to draw attention to it was a natural desire of the company which controlled it. Klein's view that 'the first colour film to be received with universal acclamation will be that one in which we shall never have been conscious of colour as an achievement'[13] would hardly have been to the liking of the Technicolor consultants. It was they, now, who stood at the director's elbow, trying to ensure that the technical process was in charge of the imagination, and not the other way about, just as the sound engineer had done a few short years before. Nevertheless the colour of *The Four Feathers*, with lighting cameramen Georges Périnal and Osmond Borradaile, of *Sixty Glorious Years* by Freddie Young, and of *The Mikado* by Bernard Knowles were effective in totally different and imaginative ways.

Klein was critical. True, he was writing in 1936, which was rather soon to pass judgement. But he was to write in the same vein after the war.* Explaining that colour could be used to induce mood, concentrate attention, to emphasise depth, heighten reality or to act as a comment on a dramatic situation, he clearly felt that film people were such utter fools that it was almost hopeless 'to suppose that when colour comes to be generally used the producers will exhibit any restraint at all'. A man of strong views, he wrote passionately and picturesquely. Colour composition as a process in time seemed to him even more difficult than the painter's art, yet 'Vulgarity is invariably the outcome of the gift of self-expression which applied science has by various instruments given the lazy and shallow minds of entertainers'.[14]

---

* During the war he changed his name to Cornwell-Clyne.

Chapter 8

Production in the Early Thirties

In the early 1930s British film production was either quality or quota. The term 'quality' in the sense in which it was used by Maxwell and others referred to films made to a reasonable standard of production, films which would have been made even if there had been no quota, by producers who were genuinely interested in making as good as film as they could. But approximately half the enormous number of films turned out by British studios up to 1937 were produced at minimum cost simply to exploit the protected market or, at worst, to comply with the law. Maxwell himself only just managed to scrape into the category of quality producer; his costs were comparatively low and although many excellent people worked at Elstree the films did suffer from this. The word 'quality' here refers to the standard of production rather than to the merit of the film. Many were good but many were not. On the whole, however, the films of the quality producers were as good as their budgets permitted and the British public liked them. Why, then, did people come to believe that British films were rarely any good and why, when British films of the thirties are brought out of the archives for an occasional show, are people surprised to find that many of them are well made and enjoyable? Unfortunately British production was swamped by the boring, badly made and routine work of the quota producers. Of course, there were exceptions even here. Some of Michael Powell's quota films, one that Douglas Fairbanks made for Warners, the Old Mother Riley and Max Miller films and others are examples. But the flood of cheap pictures which was caused by the badly framed 1927 Act did, in fact, harm the reputation of the British film.

Even the quality producers had to operate on a scale of production far below that of their competitors in the British market, the Hollywood companies. Only Korda was rash enough to try to compete on equal terms. The size of the market to which the Americans had unquestioned access, not just for the occasional special picture but for all their films, made a very lavish scale of production economically viable. They were able to afford the best of everything, including a lot of talent from Britain. During the decade every British quality producer tried to break into this market, but circuit distribution and the terms upon which films were distributed were in the control of the big producers and they very naturally did not wish to encourage British competition. Basil Dean gave up early, Gaumont and BIP somewhat later; Korda and Wilcox both secured promising agreements just before the war. The story of the decade is the struggle of the quality producers to survive in this situation, with the dead weight of the quota producers creating an artificial expansion of the industry until it was abruptly chopped in half by the new legislation of 1938.

Of the five important production companies which spanned the decade, three dated from the silent days – British International Pictures, Gaumont-British with Gainsborough, and British and Dominion. They were joined by two important new firms, Ealing Studios and London Film Productions. The many smaller firms, headed by Twickenham Film Studios, British Lion and Sound City, however much they denied it, existed almost entirely to serve the quota, and this was, of course, also true of the various forms of production in which the American renters engaged before the Act of 1938. But during the mid-thirties two other groups appeared which did not conform to the usual pattern, and which in their different ways were to exert an important influence on British production. One, associated with Max Schach, was to start the unhealthy boom and subsequent collapse of the late thirties; and that associated with J. Arthur Rank and C. M. Woolf was still only taking shape as the decade ended, but was eventually to transform the British film industry.

During the earlier part of the decade, from 1929 to 1935 or 1936, adjustment to the new situation brought about by the quota legislation was thrown into further turmoil by the advent of the talkie. Both the protected market and the sound film seemed to offer easy profits and many new companies came and went, as they learnt the hard lesson that a small home market makes economic survival very difficult indeed.

BIP

Gaumont-British and British International Pictures, with their respective circuits, were the two biggest companies in the British film industry. By 1929 Associated British Cinemas was already a million-pound company. But John Maxwell, the former Scottish solicitor who headed it and the associated production and renting companies British International Pictures and Wardour Films, had little of the impresario about him and BIP's history is strangely impersonal compared with the companies run by Michael Balcon, Basil Dean and Alexander Korda. Less a producer than a manufacturer, he left production to Walter Mycroft, a bitter man with Fascist views who became scenario chief and later Director of Productions. He operated a policy of cut-price window dressing, trying to make cheap films which looked like expensive ones. After determined efforts in the early years to get their films into America had largely failed, costs were kept firmly down in order that the films, still ostensibly first features, might make a profit from the home market alone.

The studio at Boreham Wood, Elstree, which had been built in the twenties, remained the largest in England until Denham was built in 1936. It covered 40 acres and had over 60,000 square feet of floor space, in nine stages. Four of these had tanks, two with facilities for underwater filming. The studio used mains electricity and had two sound-recording systems, RCA and their own non-royalty system Ambiphone. A report in 1933 mentions seventeen cameras, eight of them on mobile trucks with modern blimps, and telescopic booms for the microphones. Elstree had other studios and was often called the British Hollywood, and some two hundred feature films and innumerable shorts were made at BIP during the decade. Besides the large permanent staff many other film makers, both British and foreign, and many visiting stars worked at the studio. BIP was at first reluctant to engage players on contract and although they gave way on this later the company did little to build stars of its own.

In May 1929 the authorised capital of ABC was put up to £2 million. A public issue was made in July but as it was a time of economic depression only 20 per cent of the issue was taken up, despite estimated profits of £280,000 for ABC and £194,651 for BIP. There was a pause in production while economies were made to recoup the expense of converting to sound.

For the studio had taken to sound with enthusiasm. Hitchcock's *Blackmail*, Harry Lachman's *Under the Greenwood Tree* and Thomas Bentley's *The American Prisoner* were turned into talkies at about the same time in mid-1929, and as we have seen *Blackmail* was the first British talkie to be shown commercially. The imagination with which Hitchcock used sound and the enormous success of the film have been written about exhaustively.

Like other studios, during the next two years BIP released a number of films which had been made silent and later fitted with synchronised sound-tracks, including one made by the German director Arthur Robison from the Irish novel *The Informer*. The studio also turned out a large number of short musical and comedy items. They embarked on the large-scale production of multilingual films (q.v.), but these proved less successful than had been hoped. The first of them, *Atlantic*, was a spectacular production about the sinking of a liner, but the impressive action sequences were slowed down by the stilted dialogue passages.

Atlantic was directed by a German, E. A. Dupont, and there followed several more dramas made by him and two other German directors, Richard Eichberg and F. W. Kraemer. BIP's large output at this time fell into several categories. As well as heavy dramas in the German manner there were music-hall comics, West End musicals, operettas, modern stage plays and some early films by Hitchcock. Will Kellino's 'typically British' comedy *Alf's Carpet*, actually shot silent with the Scandinavian comics Pat and Patachon, began a stream of comedies featuring music-hall stars and aimed at lower-class audiences, which became a BIP staple. The following year Monty Banks produced another of the many slapstick comedies he made at Elstree, *Not So Quiet on the Western Front*. This film, shot in four days, introduced the comedian Leslie Fuller, who was to make many films there. They were written by Syd Courtenay, a former concert party colleague who had been writing sketches for him since 1919, and always featured him as 'Bill'. Fuller was the sad sort of comedian with a large, lugubrious face, depending on mugging and catch phrases like his 'Aw dearr dearr *dearr!*' The films found no favour with *Kine Weekly*. which complained that both they and BIP's rather similar films of Ernie Lotinga, or 'Josser', were vulgar.

Musicals appeared from early 1930 onwards. *Elstree Calling*, a loose collection of acts from revue with connecting passages featuring comedian Tommy Handley, was made by Adrian Brunel with some of the sketches directed by Hitchcock. It was crisply described by the critic James Agate as unmitigated footle. A number of musical comedies were filmed, and an attempt made to promote Gene Gerrard, a musical comedy lead in the same mould as Jack Buchanan but shorter and less well known, as both director and star. His film *Out of the Blue* gave Jessie Matthews her first starring part. More successfully, Stanley Lupino in 1931 began a long series of adaptations of his stage musicals and later of original screenplays with *Love Lies*, directed by his cousin Lupino Lane. More serious music was also represented, and Dr Malcolm Sargent conducted the New Symphony Orchestra for a version of *Carmen* directed by Cecil Lewis.

Stanley Lupino and Lupino Lane, who also appeared in films for BIP, belonged to a famous theatrical family whose members had been on the British stage as dancers, acrobats and latterly music-hall performers since 1780. Lupino Lane, small and neat, had made short comedy films in Britain before 1920, and since then had acted in and directed small comedies in Hollywood. He returned to Britain and in 1930 appeared in a BIP film version of *The Yellow Mask*, a musical comedy by Edgar Wallace which had appeared at the Criterion Theatre in 1928. He made much of his Hollywood experience but some of the sound films he directed in Britain during the thirties show that as a director he did not adapt his style to the new demands of the sound film, but continued to employ the techniques of the stage and the silent film. Independently, he directed and starred in a film made at Cricklewood whose appeal was, in the words of *Kine Weekly*, 'limited to uncritical audiences'.[1] A film for Gaumont followed, the bad taste, crudity and slowness of which is mentioned elsewhere. He then became one of BIP's comedy directors, making among other films two which starred his cousin, and a version of the romantic musical show *The Maid of the Mountains*. This was slow and stagy, with jokes held interminably, using close-ups and illustrative reference shots in the manner of the silent film. A second film of the same type followed the next year, *A Southern Maid*. This time he did not direct the film but played a role in it, and his delicate and delighful mime revealed quite a different side of his talents.

His cousin Stanley Lupino had been in variety and his own very successful musical shows. Keen and eager, with slicked-down hair parted slightly off centre, he was bright, brisk and endlessly cheerful. Like other members of the family he could sing and dance and he excelled at acrobatic slapstick, and although neither handsome nor particularly young he was always the hero, surrounded by girls whose role was to look gorgeous rather than to sing or dance. At the advent of sound he was quick to see the possibilities of transferring his shows to film. After making six films for BIP and one for Gainsborough-British Lion he tried to produce on his own, making two independent films at Ealing in 1935. After making a further film for British Lion he returned to BIP, or Associated British Picture Corporation as it had by then become, and made three more films for them. Formula films, they could be great fun but their quality was variable and in their efforts to be sophisticated they could sometimes lapse into bad taste. He is seen at his best, breezy and enthusiastic, when he and one or two bachelor friends, his stage partner Laddie Cliff often one of them, brass their way in and out of amorous entanglements. House parties, resorts, boating parties, titled people and young men about town – the films shared many of the ingredients of the subtly different but equally unreal pictures of high society found in the films of both Jack Buchanan and Tom Walls. They were unusual for their energy and high spirits and usually included small but well staged production numbers, of which the enjoyable 'Side by Side' number in *Over She Goes*, with its long tracking shot, was a good example.

Hitchcock made several more films for BIP but left in 1932, feeling that his relations with Maxwell had been poisoned by Mycroft. After his innovative use of sound in *Blackmail* he made a literal, though moving, version of Sean O'Casey's stage play about an Irish informer, *Juno and the Paycock*, featuring players from the Abbey Theatre in Dublin. Nominally in charge of production the following year, he also managed to direct one film, in which he was able to experiment further with sound. *Murder* was about crime in a touring theatrical company and its solution by a member of the jury, and starred Herbert Marshall. The next year the highly cinematic adaptation of Galsworthy's play *The Skin Game*, about conflict between two families, one of them county and the other *nouveau riche*, was followed by a strange little film about the bizarre adventures of a suburban couple abroad, *Rich and Strange*. The film was not liked at the time and Hitchcock was next given a film he did not want to direct, *Number Seventeen*. According to Rodney Ackland, who collaborated with him on the script, they guyed the film and made it an incomprehensible and absurd but exciting pastiche of crime films, but it was taken seriously by the company. Whether this is so or not, in his talks with François Truffaut Hitchcock simply referred to it as a disaster, saying that it 'reflected a careless approach to my work'.[2] All he did the next year was to supervise the production of *Lord Camber's Ladies*, a filmed play directed by the stage playwright Benn Levy and notable only for the appearance in it of Sir Gerald du Maurier and Gertrude Lawrence. Increasingly unhappy, he then left BIP.

Needless to say, BIP relied heavily on stage plays, usually light contemporary ones. They also made two disastrous adaptations from George Bernard Shaw. The first, *How he Lied to Her Husband*, was a short play with only three characters, all the action taking place in one room. Cecil Lewis, a young writer, one of the founders of the BBC and a former air ace of the First World War, had become friendly with Shaw through his work at the BBC and now secured his permission to film it provided that it was performed exactly as on stage. The static and boring film which resulted was shown at the third Malvern Festival in 1931 and was a total failure. After making an unsuccessful but interesting little experimental film 'written, composed and directed' by himself, Lewis tried again and Shaw agreed to his filming a more popular play, *Arms and the Man*. It was made with slightly more flexibility of movement but the same rigid adherence to the dialogue. Much of it was shot on location in Wales, where difficulty was experienced in recording sound in the open air. Shown like the other at the next Malvern Festival, the film proved so loquacious that with Shaw's permission it was cut by 1,500 feet and re-edited. Shaw was pleased with the freedom of movement allowed by the cinema, but again the film failed. According to Mycroft it had cost £5,000, which was more or less the cost of a quota quickie at the time, and it is clear that he had little faith or interest in the project.

One of BIP's directors was Walter Summers, described by the actor Henry Kendall as a 'short, dark man with an overflowing enthusiasm for his work and a terrific energy'.[3] An interesting though uneven director who had been responsible for some of the silent war reconstructions made by British Instructional, he had good ideas which he did not always manage to put into practice. His film of trench warfare, *Suspense*, which used the tapping of approaching enemy sappers as the dramatic key, was technically inferior to its contemporary *Journey's End* but compares well with it for its greater realism and a more adult attitude to war. A man obsessed with the idea of bravery, Summers himself played in the air and motor stunts which he filmed, and examined courage under pressure in his re-creation of a recent submarine disaster, *Men Like These*, which was widely admired at the time despite its poor technical quality and jingoistic tone. He was rarely given congenial subjects and, when he was, was frequently unlucky. *Timbuctoo*, filmed early in 1932 on location in Africa, had to be largely remade at Elstree because of technical faults. The unit trekked from Algiers to Nigeria and filmed the Yakouba tribe's dance of the *'jongleurs des enfants'*.[4] The competitive dancing of the young men, the stamping, hovering, gliding dance of the little boys darting like humming birds beside and in front of the braves, and the sacramental climax in which the men flung to each other the little girls, hypnotised and stiff as poles, finally catching them on the flat of their outstretched swords, was rare stuff indeed. But after many months delay this was cobbled together at the studio as a tasteless comedy starring Kendall, who was yet another of the debonair West End light comedians with smoothly brilliantined hair, and was ignored by the public. *Kine Weekly* actually criticised it for including too much 'travel' footage.

British Instructional Films, the company for which Summers had made the wartime reconstructions, was absorbed by BIP in the early thirties and its serious and documentary style of production was discontinued. This company, founded by Harry Bruce Woolfe, had converted one small stage for sound production at its Welwyn studio by April 1929, but production was held up by long delays in receiving the Klangfilm equipment from Germany. The cost of conversion and the delay left them seriously short of working capital. Their first sound film, Anthony Asquith's *A Cottage on Dartmoor*, was in fact a silent film with music and one dialogue sequence added in Berlin. The second was the unusual and interesting semi-documentary *Windjammer*, mainly shot silent on fully rigged ships at sea. A larger sound stage built within a former silent stage was ready by August 1930. A few months later, however, it was announced that BIF was to be absorbed by BIP by means of an exchange of shares, although at first it was denied that this would be a complete take-over. At long last their big film of the battle of Gallipoli in the First World War, begun as a silent film in 1928, was finished. *Tell England* was from a novel about two young friends who joined the army and how one was fatally wounded. It was directed by Asquith with much of the location work on Malta being handled by Geoffrey Barkas, who had also made silent films for BIF and had a flair for big crowd scenes on location. Photography and editing of the battle sequence was magnificent, but the strangled patrician characterisation and dialogue and the true-blue patriotism seemed out of date. Finally, the first film planned from the start as a talkie was Asquith's *Dance, Pretty Lady*, a delicate and decorative version of a Compton Mackenzie novel, with the Marie Rambert *corps de ballet* and choreography by Frederick Ashton in a remarkable early ballet sequence filmed at the Metropolitan, Edgware Road. Outstanding sets, locations, camerawork and editing did not save the rather shallow characterisation and the film got a lukewarm critical reception and was a box-office failure. In both films Asquith showed an unusually imaginative approach to the possibilities of sound. A couple more films followed, one of them a short romantic feature by the woman director of BIF nature films, Mary Field. But Maxwell, who was now chairman, disapproved of what he disparagingly called 'films for the intelligentsia' and asserted that it 'was solely with the idea of making box office product that the association with BIP had been arranged'.[5] During the following year only advertising and documentary films were made. Early in 1933 Maxwell planned to revive Pathé Pictures, which had made no feature films since the sound film had arrived, and decided that they would make four a year at Welwyn under the Pathé Pictorial editor, Fred Watts.

Disappointed with Maxwell's brusque and commercial approach, Bruce Woolfe resigned in 1933. He later set up Gaumont-British Instructional, where his academic style was more appropriate. W. J. Gell joined Pathé, and took over the running of Welwyn later that year. BIP was formally amalgamated with ABPC in December. From time to time independent producers hired space there, but for the rest of the decade Welwyn was chiefly used as an overflow for the studios at Elstree.

BIP was profitable from the beginning, although at a declining rate. Profits of £170,000 in 1929/30 had fallen to £110,426 in 1932/3. ABC, which in August 1930 had 120 cinemas, 1,250,000 admissions a week and a labour force of 3,000, suffered an even more marked decline during the depression and profits fell from £221,241 in 1931/2 to £105,261 the following year. A public issue recently made by Gaumont-British had been unsuccessful and Maxwell accordingly decided to reorganise rather than to make a share issue, combining the boards of ABC and BIP as Associated British Picture Corporation. Despite much opposition the new £3,500,000 company was formed late in 1933, at the same time as the formal disappearance of BIF. The reorganisation was complete by July 1934. ABPC, with an issued capital of £2,933,557, was expected to make profits of £570,000, or more than twice the combined profits of the two companies. Its wholly owned subsidiaries were ABC, now with over 200 cinemas and 6,000 employees; BIP, owning Elstree studios; BIF (Proprietors), owning Welwyn studios; and the distributor Wardour Films. At the annual general meeting its assets in cinemas were put at £5.5 million and in studios, film stocks and distribution business at £1.5 million. The authorised capital was increased to £4 million.

During the next couple of years the studios continued to be busy. Leslie Fuller appeared in a number of routine comedies and Claude Hulbert, the agile little music-hall comedian Albert Burdon and the comic and female impersonator George Lacy also made films there. Will Hay, already famous on the halls for his schoolmaster sketch, at the age of forty-six made his first film, an adaptation of Pinero's *The Magistrate* called *Those Were the Days*. Musical comedies continued with several more from the exuberant Stanley Lupino and the dapper Gene Gerrard, and a new recruit from the same sort of show, Clifford Mollison. With his gentle ugly face and sprightly, throwaway manner Mollison had a most lovable quality but he lacked glamour and was usually wasted in feeble films. Walter Summers, now working at Welwyn, made several crime films there while at the main studio a very large number of directors were at work. Harry Hughes's *A Southern Maid* was so bad as to appear almost a parody of *The Maid of the Mountains*. Thomas Bentley made several, including the Will Hay film and one of his slow and literary Dickens adaptations, *The Old Curiosity Shop*. They were joined by two directors who came from the German film industry via Hollywood, Paul Stein and Friedrich Zelnik, and the Anglo-French Marcel Varnel, also from Hollywood. Arthur Woods, who had been an editor with British Instructional, directed his first film in 1933 and was considered a most promising director. Allan Dwan directed Ben Lyon and Sally Eilers, all three of them from Hollywood, in a desperately contrived zany spy comedy, and other American stars who appeared were Thelma Todd, Zelma O'Neal and Bebe Daniels. Raquel Torres and Charles Bickford, also, appeared in a big adaptation of Lady Eleanor Smith's circus novel *Red Wagon*, which lost its way in the long and shapeless story but had some pleasant road sequences. In the spring of 1933, reflecting the news that there were 5½ million radio licences in the country, BIP began an annual series of *Radio Parade* films featuring many acts widely known through the radio.

BIP's biggest celebrity, however, was the great Austrian tenor Richard Tauber. A fine singer of *lieder* and opera, Tauber also had a popular audience for his operettas and ballads. One of his favourite parts was that of Schubert in *Das Dreimädlerhaus*, which had been put on in London as *Lilac Time* several times in the twenties and thirties. Tauber himself appeared in the German original at the Aldwych Theatre in 1933. Shortly afterwards he left Nazi Germany for good and settled in England as a voluntary exile. He filmed *Blossom Time*, very loosely based on *Lilac Time*, for BIP in 1934.

The film was a major event for the company, costing far more than its other films, with crowd scenes and some large and decorative baroque sets. Despite anachronistic costumes and a story which strangely seemed to portray Schubert more as a singer than as a composer, the film was carried by its distinguished star, and was considered both artistic and box-office. It received a kind review even from the highbrow *Cinema Quarterly*. It was directed by Stein, who followed it with *My Song Goes Round the World*, featuring another tenor. This was Josef Schmidt, known as the Swiss Caruso, who was only four feet tall and had hitherto confined his singing to radio and records. BIP rashly devised a story of Bohemian life in Venice for 'the diminutive tenor', in which he played a singer struggling to establish a reputation despite his small stature. Romantic interest was difficult enough with the paunchy Tauber, but even a fine voice could not make a film star of this tiny man with his large heavy face.

The amalgamation had proved a success, and the year 1934/5 saw profits rising to £656,725. ABC now had 225 cinemas, and early the next year an issue of £1 million in debenture stock was fully subscribed in the first sixty-five minutes. But production was now not as profitable as the exhibition side of the business and output was curtailed in 1935. The following year, with the number of cinemas up to 283, a record gross profit of £926,042 was declared in August 1936. The company had an authorised capital of £3½ million with land and buildings now valued at £10,510,043 and films at £545,972. Maxwell himself, extensively backed by Scottish banking and other interests, was the largest single holder of ordinary shares.

Will Hay made a second Pinero film, *Dandy Dick*, an updated version of the old play directed by William Beaudine, an American who was to direct many British comedies during the next few years. In it Hay, playing a well-meaning, precise but slightly bumbling vicar, not without a touch of asperity at times, began to outline the screen character which was to become so familiar later when he moved to Gainsborough. More *Radio Parades* featured popular dance bands and many turns with very little connecting story. There was one more attempt to make something of the diminutive tenor. *Royal Cavalcade* in 1935 was intended as a celebratory production in time for George V's silver jubilee and was a long, pedestrian, episodic survey of the last twenty-five years made by no less than five directors and a huge cast. Of much better quality was *Abdul the Damned*, a rare collaboration with an outside producer, Max Schach. This was Schach's first incursion into British production. He and BIP produced it on a fifty-fifty basis, and it was much more ambitious and elaborate than most Elstree films. Directed by the middlebrow German director Karl Grune and starring the Austrian actor Fritz Kortner, now a refugee, it had music by the communist composer and musicologist Hanns Eisler, an ex-pupil of Schoenberg and now a refugee also. A long, ponderous film about the Young Turks' revolt against the Turkish despot in 1908, it had big sets and crowd scenes, including a production number with dancing girls, and a huge throne room lighted dramatically by wheeling searchlights outside the windows as the tyrant cowered in fear.

More characteristic of BIP, however, were two costume films made early in 1935, *Drake of England* and *Mimi.*Woods directed the former, a version of Louis Parker's 1912 play, but so many characters of roughly equal weight were crammed into it that it seemed more like a pageant than a drama. Much use was made of a set of the Plymouth waterfront, complete with quay and approaching boat, and of model work for the sea battles, but the film has a strange air of being a spectacular in miniature. The other film, *Mimi*, was based on the original play from which *La Bohème* had been taken and used some of Puccini's music only as background. The stars were that romantic pair Gertrude Lawrence and Douglas Fairbanks Jr, and the costumes had been specially designed by Doris Zinkeisen, not hired from an anonymous theatrical costumier as was more often the case at Elstree. A large set was built for the ball, with glittering gondolas gliding through the ballroom, and it was clearly intended to be a major production.

Stein, who had directed *Mimi*, now made a second Tauber film, *Heart's Desire.* Still trying to find a conventionally romantic role for their fat and none too good looking singer, this time they put him in a story about a humble tenor discovered in a Viennese beer garden and turned into a great star by a high society lady, eventually returning to his little Viennese sweetheart. Appearing first as clumsy rough diamond, indeed almost a buffoon, Tauber dieted drastically and was groomed, slick and much slimmer as the star. He sings a little Schumann and a lot of tuneful popular stuff, and the story plunges from absurdity to absurdity. Unfortunately none of Tauber's British films seem to have done him justice, and certainly BIP was not prepared to go to the expense of producing a true operetta, of the type for which he was so well known, or of providing him with adequate musical support. Other musical films followed, including a Heidelberg number with Continental singer Grete Natzler and another film with the Hungarian opera singer Gitta Alpar, *I Give My Heart.* Trilling loudly, harsh and clear, she flounced on as a little milliner who fell in love with Louis XV, went to court, learnt to be a lady and, as Madame Dubarry, became the king's mistress. The film, making entertaining nonsense of history, was based on a recent stage import from Germany. Once again big sets and elaborate rococo decor were featured and there were even a number of Watteau paintings which dissolved into tableaux and came to life. The same spirit of romantic impossibility was found in another film, *Invitation to the Waltz*, which was a lighthearted confection about the romance of a dancer at the time of Napoleon, based on a story by Holt Marvel. It portrayed the composer Weber as her accompanist, giving a fanciful account of how he 'discovered' the waltz. Lilian Harvey, the English girl who had become a star in German films, was slightly disappointing in this British film.

Other types of production continued alongside this cycle of operettas, including slapstick comedy and modern drama: *Living Dangerously*, Herbert Brenon's film featuring Otto Kruger in one of the many films he made for the company, was praised by Graham Greene for its rare social comment and bite. The same critic attacked the Irish director Brian Desmond Hurst for being arty, but many believed that he had outstanding talent. After working in Hollywood Hurst had made three independent productions, including a version of Edgar Allan Poe's *The Tell-Tale Heart*, and a short film of J. M. Synge's *Riders to the Sea* which featured players from the Abbey Theatre in Dublin and was made with welcome backing from Gracie Fields. Early in 1936 he was engaged by BIP and with Summers made a film about Sinn Fein, *Ourselves Alone*, a serious minor film about the tragedy of civil war. His third film for BIP, *Sensation*, was a crime reporter thriller in the Hollywood mould, and was fast and efficient although little more than a second feature.

An unusual independent film partly made at Elstree in 1935 was *The Robber Symphony*. Friedrich Feher, who had worked in the expressionist cinema in post-war Germany, was particularly interested in the use of music. Commenting on the music in an earlier film of his, *Le Loup Garou*, Paul Rotha had written: ' . . . 'its phrasing is admirably in sympathy with the changes of mood. It swells to a climax, cuts sharp to silence, builds slowly again and so on. It is essentially an accompaniment emphasising the action, and I found it singularly successful.'[6] The same might have been said of any of the scores composed specially to accompany silent films, but what Feher now wanted to do was to edit a film to fit a score that had already been recorded. He described the result, almost entirely without speech, as the first 'composed' film. It was produced, directed, composed and written by him and featured his twelve-year-old son. A story about a family of travelling musicians and their adventures in the mountains when a bag of stolen gold is hidden in their piano, it is bizarre, picturesque and at times hilarious. It was shot on location at Nice, in Austria and Switzerland with studio work and cutting at Elstree, and a large market set constructed on the Shepperton lot. Design was by Ernö Metzner, working at Gaumont-British since leaving Germany after the rise of Hitler. It took almost a year to make, nine months of that in editing, and was very expensive, for according to Graham Greene the fact that it was cut to the music had made it necessary to shoot 600,000 feet of film. An interesting idea and a highly individual film, it was extremely long. After a first trade show at no less than 12,600 feet, it was described as unsuitable for children because of some frightening passages and was not given a U certificate until it had been cut drastically twice, ending at 8,150 feet. *Kine Weekly* regarded it as too artistic and whimsical for any but the most high-class districts. When the idea was originally conceived in the early thirties the sound track of the ordinary commercial film was still fairly immature. But by 1937, when the cut version was finally available for showing, considerable progress had been made and in most films both speech and music were used with greater discrimination. The films of the late twenties, with constant musical accompaniment and no dialogue, had been more or less forgotten and the experiment would have seemed very strange to most audiences.

Early in 1936 a fire destroyed the older part of the studio at Elstree and production fell sharply. Leslie Fuller left the company, and the bid to promote Gene Gerrard and Clifford Mollison was abandoned. As films became fewer they became individually more important and the company tended to use outside stars of greater weight than hitherto, but the films they made at Elstree were never their best. The studio's output during the early thirties had been very large and varied, and efficient management ensured that it operated at a profit. Some excellent technicians worked at Elstree, cameramen like Claude Friese-Greene, Otto Kanturek and Jack Cox, editors like Leslie Norman and designers like Duncan Sutherland, but with budgets cut to the bone the films did not compare well with the Hollywood films they imitated.

Gaumont and Gainsborough

Far better films were being produced at Islington and Shepherd's Bush under the more imaginative management of Michael Balcon. Gainsborough Pictures (1928) at Islington was formally associated with, but not controlled by, Gaumont-British Picture Corporation, and C. M. Woolf and Maurice Ostrer of Gaumont-British were on the Gainsborough board. Balcon was comparatively slow to adopt the talkie and made several late silent features which had to be revamped later with synchronised sound tracks, and for the first couple of years the Gainsborough output was undistinguished. However, the technicians were being assembled and the environment created for a stable and creative production unit. Among the last silent films was *The Wrecker*, the first film shot in Britain by the Czech cameraman Otto Kanturek, which also marked the arrival of the Austrian art director Oscar Werndorff. Both were to make many films for Balcon. Angus MacPhail was to head his scenario department and was one of a group of young men from the universities, especially from Cambridge, whom he was to employ during the next few years. Adrian Brunel's thriller *The Crooked Billet* was the first to credit Ian Dalrymple as editor and Louis Levy as music director. Levy, who had started as a cinema violinist in 1910, had become a leading cinema conductor and had recently recorded a score for Elvey's first sound film, Gaumont's *High Treason*. As conductor and composer he was to contribute to an enormous number of Gainsborough and Gaumont films. Dalrymple, like MacPhail a product of the public schools and Cambridge, was to head the editing department. During the next few years Balcon was to produce a very large number of films of high quality, spending far more on them than BIP, and trying to break into the American market with them.

In 1929 Balcon visited America with his electrician George Gunn, another key member of his staff, to study sound techniques and to order equipment. While they were in the States the chairman of Gaumont-British, Isidore Ostrer, was also there on a mission which was to have many repercussions. Early in the year this company had increased its capital to £3,750,000 and the two Ostrers, who had backed the company for some years, joined the Bromhead brothers on the board. At this time the company controlled 287 cinemas and was one of the biggest film concerns in the country, with C. M. Woolf distributing its films through the associated company W & F.

Despite denials, it would seem that the Ostrers intended to sell a controlling interest in the company to the erratic American film tycoon William Fox, who wanted a British cinema chain as an outlet for both his films and the sound equipment in which he had an interest. It was rumoured that the Ostrers would sell shares in the Metropolis and Bradford Trust, a holding company formed early in 1929, which owned 65 per cent of the ordinary share capital of Gaumont-British. In his biography of Fox, Upton Sinclair later stated as a fact that Fox had bought 'the Gaumont theatres, paying $14m. in cash and giving notes for $6m. due in six months'.[7] Certainly Fox thought the deal concluded in the summer of 1929 gave him control. But there was an acrimonious struggle going on behind the scenes, with denials and accusations and public anxiety at the idea of an American firm taking over a big British company, which was to continue for several years.

The Bromheads promptly held an extraordinary general meeting at which the articles of association were changed in such a way that while foreign nationals could hold shares in Metropolis and Bradford, they could not hold a controlling interest. The Ostrers and Fox Film Corporation now held equal voting stock, but a casting vote was held by Lord Lee of Fareham. The latter was meant to represent the national interest, and was believed to have been introduced at the request of the Board of Trade.

Next the Bromheads resigned from the company they had founded over thirty years before. Isidore Ostrer became chairman and Mark vice-chairman; Woolf and Will Evans were joint managing directors. The five Ostrer brothers made the best of the situation. So did Fox, with a big shareholding which had failed to get him what he wanted. Isidore Ostrer, an intellectual who supported the Labour Party and was the author of a privately printed treatise called *The Conquest of Gold*, had considerable power in the entertainment industry; but this thin, delicate-featured man with wispy hair was a financier rather than a showman and was largely unknown to the public. Balcon has said little about him, but the Conservative MP and journalist Beverley Baxter described him as shy, sensitive and cultured, a 'financial genius who despised money except as an economic factor, a mystic who dreamed of a world made better for the worker and his wife'. It is doubtful whether Balcon, who liked to be his own master, got on well with the younger brother, Maurice, who exercised a more managerial function. From now on the Ostrers were to edge the old guard out. Evans, for one, resigned early in 1931 after many years in the industry, and was replaced by Mark Ostrer.

Doubts about the extent of Fox influence continued. In the *Financial Times* in June 1930 Woolf categorically denied American control of the company, and so did Lord Lee shortly afterwards. Woolf repeated this denial in January 1931, but when the Conservative MP J. R. Remer questioned the Labour President of the Board of Trade, William Graham, the latter explained the formal structure of the company but admitted that the reality of power was a difficult matter. Remer continued to badger him. Isidore then wrote to Graham offering a 'gift to the nation of the Ostrer voting shares in the Metropolis and Bradford Trust Co. Ltd, or by the creation of a special voting trust'.[8] The offer was discussed privately with lawyers, and turned down.

Gainsborough's Islington studios had been fitted with sound equipment in the summer of 1929 at a cost of £70,000. Wooden false walls were fitted inside the brick ones to ensure sound insulation. Balcon's first two big feature films in sound, however, were made in Hollywood.

The first of these was a new version of *Woman to Woman*. Balcon's old friend Victor Saville rejoined him in 1929 to make a talkie of their early success in collaboration with the American firm of Tiffany-Stahl. It was Saville's first sound film and suffered from slow diction, static filming and a dated story, but his delicate handling of the love scenes showed his skill with actors, and the dance numbers were ambitious. Betty Compson starred, as she had in the first version. The veteran English director George Pearson, also in Hollywood, wrote in his diary 'Saw *Woman to Woman* (Saville) DREADFUL!' but it was technically competent and promised well, and Saville was soon to become one of the most important directors in England.

Pearson was in Hollywood to supervise production of the other

Gainsborough film with Tiffany-Stahl, *Journey's End*. R. C. Sherriff's enormously popular play about a group of officers in a dugout during the recent war had been acquired jointly by Gainsborough and the old firm of Welsh-Pearson, Elder for £15,000, a large sum for British producers, and was made in the winter of 1929–30. Involved in films since before the 1914 war, Pearson had been quick to see the possibilities of sound and eager to adopt it. Despite his protests the board of his own company had insisted on a programme of silent films which, in the end, ruined the company. *Yellow Stockings*, a film directed in 1928 by Theodor Komisarjevsky, was fitted with a music track and issued in 1930. Komisarjevsky, the designer of Granada's atmospheric cinemas, was a distinguished theatrical producer-designer and wished to experiment with lighting and camera angles, and was scathing about the conditions under which he had to work. Given the scenario only a couple of days before shooting began and with only five weeks in which to complete it, he complained about the sets, designed and built without his approval, and of inadequate facilities or time for setting up interesting shots; furthermore, as sets were struck before the rushes, retakes were impossible.[9]

Journey's End was the first film to be directed by James Whale, who had produced it on the London stage and was already in Hollywood working as dialogue director for Howard Hughes. All the actors were British and Colin Clive, who was playing the lead on stage, went over to America to repeat it in the film. With a budget of £100,000 it was far more expensive than any British films. Artistic control was in Balcon's hands. When there was last-minute trouble over the script provided by V. Gareth Gundrey he sent Pearson, a gentle and avuncular man, to secure a better script and to supervise production. Fighting to ensure good casting, resisting the introduction of such vandalisms as a heroine or a theme song, this honest and idealistic man, somewhat out of his depth, was made wretched by Hollywood studio politics and demanding telegrams from Islington. The film, however, was a triumphant success both at the box office and with the critics. Less a war film than a picture of human relations under pressure, it launched both Whale and Clive on Hollywood careers. James Agate, normally no friend of the cinema, considered it even more moving than the play and described Clive's performance as stupendous.

It was hoped that *Journey's End* would restore the fortunes of Welsh-Pearson, Elder, but the large profits expected from the American market were not forthcoming despite good reviews, and after a little more desultory production the company became moribund. An attempt to reconstruct it with reduced capital in August 1932 had a poor response from the public and the company disappeared. Meanwhile Gainsborough production at Islington began in earnest with an Ivor Novello film based on one of his own plays. But before it was finished, on 18 January 1930, there was a serious fire in the wood-lined studio and production was moved to BIP at Elstree. Already late with its talkies, Gainsborough was unable to cope with these further expensive delays on its own and a month after the fire Simon Rowson of Ideal and W. J. Gell, managing director of Gaumont, joined the Gainsborough board. The phrase 'associated with but not controlled by' began to sound a little thin.

Production in 1930 continued to be disappointing. At the end of the year, however, the arrival of Walter Forde to make *Third Time Lucky* was a sign of better things to come. Forde had begun as a youngster in the music hall and now, at thirty-four, was already a veteran performer and director. He developed a fast, sure technique and a command of timing which made him a master of both comedy and suspense, and he was to make some of Gainsborough's most enjoyable films. An amiable, easy going man with a fund of comedy ideas and routines, he had a sense of fun which could make even an old gag seem fresh.

Among the films of 1931 there were two more by Forde, one of them, a film of Edgar Wallace's thriller *The Ringer*, being the first of a series made in collaboration with British Lion (q.v.). The third, *The Ghost Train*, was made on the initiative of Herman Fellner, who had met Balcon during the Anglo-German co-production of a few years before. It was at his suggestion, too, that it introduced stage comedians Jack Hulbert and his wife Cicely Courtneidge to British films. This also was successful and the company seemed to be on its way.

Several of the films of late 1931 were outstanding. Saville's *Hindle Wakes* was made at Shepherd's Bush from a popular play of 1912 about a modern and independent mill girl, who enjoys a holiday with the boss's son but then shocks her family by declining to marry him. It was a big production with crowd scenes and location work at seaside resorts and factories. It was also the first film shot for Balcon by the German cameraman Mutz Greenbaum, who was to stay with him and later, as Max Greene, to become one of Britains's leading cameramen. The next Gainsborough-British Lion film, Wallace's *The Calendar*, starred Herbert Marshall and his wife Edna Best, who were to appear in several more Gainsborough films. The first of these was Saville's best film to date, *Michael and Mary*. Both had been in the stage production. Marshall, already forty and a successful stage and film actor, had a slight limp and an air of quiet suffering which greatly appealed to women fans. From a sentimental A. A. Milne play about a young deserted wife befriended by a writer, whom she marries bigamously, it shows Saville at his best with a strong, although not too realistic, story concerned with tender feelings and relationships. He followed it with an even more sentimental and successful production, again starring Marshall and Edna Best, *The Faithful Heart*. Saville and the script writer Robert Stevenson transformed an unlikely and melodramatic story with a skilful use of detail and beautifully directed performances. Delightful sequences in Southampton harbour are full of movement and music.

The year ended in triumph with Saville's remake of the musical *Sunshine Susie*. This gay and enjoyable film was based on a story by the German writer Franz Schulz about a cheery little typist who marries her boss, and had already been filmed in Germany. Its remake was arranged by Fellner and the original Susie, the German actress Renate Müller, appeared in it. Her sparkle and an endearingly funny performance by Jack Hulbert made this small film an outstanding success. Susie's catchy song 'Today I Feel so Happy' became a popular hit. Cheaply made, the film was one of the most profitable of the period and although not the first British musical it was certainly the best so far.

However, the annual report at the end of the year admitted that the company was not yet prosperous. Complicated share exchanges were carried out to reorganise the capital on a better basis and finally gave Gaumont-British outright control of Gainsborough. As part of the rearrangement Balcon was put in charge of production at the Gaumont studios at Shepherd's Bush as well as at the Gainsborough studios at Islington. The combined output from the two studios for the next few years was very large and his capacity as a producer was stretched to the limit.

For the Ostrers had recently decided to expand Gaumont-British production. The old studios at Lime Grove, Shepherd's Bush, had their own sound system, British Acoustic, which they continued to use throughout the decade, and had early installed a soundproof shell of Masonite. Maurice Elvey, almost as quick off the mark as Hitchcock, had hurriedly remade his silent film *High Treason* as a sound film and it was shown in August 1929. It was from a play by the enthusiastic patriot and moral crusader Noel Pemberton-Billing, an Independent MP, and showed a future in which women get together to prevent war. Pearson, diligently watching the first talkies, wrote in his diary: 'A terrible film yet with money in it due to novelty.'

Gaumont had a small output in the next two years under its production manager L'Estrange Fawcett, a former journalist and film critic. The films were not important. Lupino Lane directed and starred in *No Lady*, giving a crude performance which showed little of his skill as a mime. This badly directed, under-rehearsed and distasteful film about a henpecked husband is unusual for the aggressive and hostile tone of its humour and the inordinate length of time for which shots expecting a laugh are held.

Fawcett left in July 1931 and the studio was altered, to be reopened under Balcon's management a year later. With four large stages one above the other, it was like Islington in being on a cramped London site without an exterior lot. The old studio beside it, built by the Bromheads, was also altered and a studio survey later in the decade gave the total floor space as 87,600 square feet in five stages, far larger than Islington with its 12,000 square feet in two stages. The biggest Gaumont stage, on the first floor, had galleries for lighting at two levels and a water tank. There were also large automatic labs. Between them the two studios had a capacity for thirty or forty films a year, but in such crowded and complicated premises that it was going to take skill and good management to make full use of them.

Until the studio was ready work continued at Islington, Elstree and Beaconsfield. At Islington early in 1932 Walter Forde had a major success with Jack Hulbert and Cicely Courtneidge in *Jack's the Boy*, a comedy with songs rather than a musical. It recognised that this tall, amiable performer with his long legs and long chin, and his ability to toss off a pleasing song and a casual-seeming dance, needed an image for the public to identify. A would-be detective in this film, he assumed an air of unquenchable optimism, chatting breezily as he bumbled along in the face of disaster. This was, in fact, rather like the character earlier played by Forde himself when he had starred in some silent features. In addition to slapstick and verbal humour, a firm story line was needed, or in Hulbert's own words 'tough adventure and a hero doing mad things, but coming out on top in the end'. A second film followed quickly, this time directed by Saville. In *Love on Wheels* Jack, still the cheerful muddler, was allowed to win the girl. It was from a story about a big department store by the same Franz Schulz who had written *Sunshine Susie*, and who seems to have been fascinated by modern urban life. At Beaconsfield, meanwhile, under the British Lion agreement, the young musical-comedy and revue star Jessie Matthews was making her first film for Balcon in a straight part in *There Goes the Bride*. This was directed by Albert de Courville, a successful revue producer who had been brought into the company by Woolf against Balcon's will. He never became a good director and this film, although pleasant, made little impression apart from securing Jessie Matthews a contract. In her autobiography she remembered him as a bullying and Svengali-like director.

The Ostrers were now firmly in command, but rumours about ownership continued. Early in 1932 the Fox Film Corporation and its associates issued writs against Isidore Ostrer and Metropolis and Bradford, to recover the £4 million it had invested in Gaumont-British and to upset the agreement which left control in the hands of others. The matter was settled out of court later in the year. As a result of this settlement the new president of Fox, Sidney Kent, and Richard W. Aldrich of the Chase National Bank joined the main board. The position of Lord Lee was altered slightly, although in public it was maintained that he still had a casting vote. All this led to more claims and denials, and to repeated questions in Parliament as to the true position of the American company.

It was at this time that Isidore Ostrer, much struck by the English-language version of the spectacular German musical *Congress Dances*, initiated a policy of Anglo-German co-production between UFA and Gaumont-British which was announced in May 1932. A contract was agreed with Erich Pommer of UFA whereby Gaumont would distribute in Britain the English versions of a number of films to be made in Germany in three languages, not necessarily at the same time, the basic version being the German one. Balcon was responsible for the casting and scenario adaptation of the English versions and sometimes for help with their direction and dialogue. The ebullient Polish tenor Jan Kiepura, Marta Eggerth, Lilian Harvey and the

Hulberts were among those featured in co-productions, which also gave Robert Stevenson an early chance to direct. But Pommer had final control and in later years Balcon was anxious to dissociate himself from these films. Having had some experience of producing in Germany before the talkies and the quota system had made it inexpedient he disapproved of co-production, which he later referred to as suicidal,[10] and much preferred the newer policy of buying rights to German films and remaking them in England. The result of mixing casts and accents, giving English names to characters in obviously foreign locales and situations, strong foreign accents unexplained by the exigencies of the story and other anachronisms made the films oddly unconvincing. Mostly musicals, on the whole they were commercially and artistically disappointing and, a matter of some practical importance, none were eligible for British quota. With the rise of Nazism the practice died out. Indeed, before long the traffic was reversed and many talented Continental film makers and actors arrived in Britain as refugees, some to stay and contribute to the British film industry, some to travel on to Hollywood. A number found a welcome at Islington and Shepherd's Bush.

The latter studio reopened in June 1932. The first production was the thriller *Rome Express*, the biggest film Balcon had so far made and a resounding success. It was directed by Walter Forde and had an outstanding cast headed by the German Conrad Veidt in his first film in England, where he was to settle. Forde chose the subject himself and the film was a personal triumph for him. With excellent performances from Cedric Hardwicke, Gordon Harker and others, it was also the first of many screen credits for Sidney Gilliat, who was already a mainstay of the scenario department, and the first film made for Balcon by the Austrian cameraman Gunther Krampf. It was set entirely on the train except for an introductory passage in the station, and used back projection extensively and with great skill, effectively conveying the impression of being on a moving train.

From now until late 1936 output was large, especially in 1934 and 1935. Balcon, the only producer in Britain of Hollywood calibre apart from Korda, had able lieutenants in his brother Chandos, Harold Boxall, Ivor Montagu and the studio manager Phil Samuel, a boyhood friend from Birmingham. Later he was to have the assistance of Edward Black, who also came from Birmingham and who first took over studio management at Islington and then became associate producer. Angus MacPhail, Ian Dalrymple, George Gunn and Louis Levy functioned as an effective associate production team under the title 'Production Personnel'. Some of the films, of course, were intended only as supporting features. Among his directors at this time in addition to Forde and Saville he employed veterans like Milton Rosmer, Sinclair Hill and the ever-buoyant Maurice Elvey. One film was made by Anthony Asquith and others by the American Tim Whelan. Balcon had an impressive team of editors and of cameramen from America and the Continent as well as from Britain, and the art department was greatly enhanced by the arrival of Alfred Junge from Germany in 1932. Even more important, perhaps, was the scenario department under MacPhail, which included a number of well-known dramatists and song writers as well as W. P. Lipscomb, Gilliat and Robert Stevenson.

Balcon was very aware of the importance of stars and star building, a difficult matter for British producers because of the welcome any successful British actor found in Hollywood, and also because of the British habit of using actors whose main occupation was in the London theatre. In Jessie Matthews he realised he had discovered a star. She made a second light comedy under the 'strange penetrating eyes' of de Courville, and one for Sinclair Hill. She was now to be given a part in the biggest production since *Rome Express*, Saville's very successful adaptation of J. B. Priestley's recent best seller *The Good Companions*. This story of a touring concert party had another large and excellent cast, including John Gielgud, who had been in the stage version, and it gave Jessie Matthews a chance to sing and dance.

From a working-class family, Jessie Matthews was talented and ambitious. Not conventionally beautiful, she had extremely large dark eyes, a *retroussé* nose and a pouting mouth with prominent teeth. At her best, when she was well photographed and felt confident, she had a piquant charm. A delightful singer with somewhat mannered elocution, she also had a willowy and individual style of dancing, combining her famous high kicks with elements of classical dance. She was to be Balcon's biggest property, and although she was a big international star he managed to keep her away from Hollywood. In *The Good Companions* she was directed for the first time by Saville, who she felt was a comforting, warm and honest person. 'Oh, Victor Saville was a lovely man,' she wrote many years later. The film, with its pleasant English scenery and English 'types' created by Priestley, gave British audiences an ordinary English girl with enough personality and talent to make her as popular at home as any Hollywood star.

Saville followed this with another important picture, *I Was A Spy*. This was based on a book by a Belgian woman about her espionage work in the 1914 war. It had important stars, ambitious crowd scenes and a huge outside set of a Belgian town built at Welwyn, but for a Saville film it was unusually devoid of feeling. The heroine was played by Madeline Carroll, back from Hollywood and groomed to brittle elegance whatever the age, date or condition of the character she was playing; although beautiful, she seemed cold. Veidt, all smouldering eyes and brooding presence in his second British film, played the wicked German officer and Herbert Marshall, returning briefly from Hollywood with many new mannerisms, played his last part for Balcon as the good German and fellow spy. Even-handedly showing both sides in acts of brutality, the film dared to show British planes bombing soldiers at prayer. It hovered between spy drama and moral statement, but many years later when a new generation of admirers saw it as an anti-war film Saville, while gratified, privately expressed surprise and Balcon dismissed the idea with a brisk 'Nonsense!'[11]

Cicely Courtneidge made *Soldiers of the King* with the visiting American comedian Edward Everett Horton. Cicely, as tall, awkward and long-chinned as her husband Jack Hulbert, was not chosen to play heroine to his hero. A warm personality, eager but coy, formal and polite and just a little arch, she accentuated her size and ungainliness and guyed herself, but retained her natural charm. She was a gifted comedian and with sympathetic material could be extremely funny, and became a much-loved aunty figure to British audiences. Early in 1933 she and Hulbert together made *Falling For You*, this time directed by Hulbert himself with Robert Stevenson. In this slapstick comedy set at a winter sports resort Jack Hulbert plays one of his less endearing roles as a smart journalist and, as always, wins the girl. Cicely, also as a journalist, is determinedly bright.

A film made by Anthony Asquith and shown after much delay was *The Lucky Number*. A comic fantasy about an ex-footballer and his girl in pursuit of a lost lottery ticket, it included some slight but charming songs and funny and delightful performances from Clifford Mollison and Gordon Harker. Credited to another story by Schulz, it was not unlike René Clair's *Le Million*. Asquith, suffering from a reputation for the artiness which Woolf disliked so much, was given no other films while he was under contract to Gaumont-British.

An important addition to the company early in 1933 was Tom Walls, bringing with him his fellow comedians and the Aldwych farces they had been filming for Herbert Wilcox (q.v.). Woolf, as a personal friend of Wilcox, had distributed these films through his firm W & F, but in the spring of 1933 Wilcox abruptly decided to distribute through United Artists. Woolf was upset, and at his request Balcon persuaded Tom Walls to leave Wilcox and join Gaumont. Walls got good terms for the move, with the right to approve story and cast and also to direct his own pictures. Balcon tolerated him because of Woolf but resented his autocratic manner.

Gaumont-British Picture Corporation now consisted of the two studios, over 300 cinemas, film printing works with a capacity of about a million feet a week and over 14,000 employees, as well as a newsreel and subidiary companies making school films and substandard equipment. A major reorganisation was carried out in 1933, increasing the share capital to £6,250,000 and issuing £5 million of new debenture stock, as well as getting rid of more old timers and strengthening the control of the Ostrers. The issue was not a success, however, and the underwriters took up much of the stock. The old regime was gradually eased out. W. J. Gell, who had been with the company since 1909 and was made managing director in 1929, resigned. So did Simon Rowson of Ideal. Later, Gaumont-Ideal and Woolf's W & F distribution agencies were merged to form Gaumont-British Distribution. An export organisation was set up in America. The Ostrers firmly believed that in order to make the films attractive to American audiences it was necessary to feature American stars, and Balcon was to make many sea voyages across the Atlantic to secure them, although in retrospect it is doubtful whether those engaged were sufficiently important to justify the extra cost of their contracts.

Woolf himself became deputy chairman as well as joint managing director of the corporation but some eighteen months later he, too, left to set up a new distribution company in association with J. Arthur Rank, leaving Mark Ostrer as chairman and sole managing director. Rumours were once more circulating about the American participation. Early in 1934 changes in the holding company left Fox still with its financial interest in the company but with the Ostrers now in full control, Lord Lee having discreetly disappeared. Rumours and denials of attempts to sell the Ostrer shares persisted.

In December 1933 Balcon had signed a new contract for five years, of which he was in fact to work only three.* The output of the two studios grew in volume and quality. Hitchcock rejoined Balcon and he, Saville and Forde made an impressive trio of directors. Robert Stevenson, soon to be recognised as one of the best directors in the country, joined their number. Several more film makers arrived from Europe and Basil Dean, also, made a film for Balcon in 1933. More cameramen, editors and writers joined, including Frank Launder. The art departments under Junge at Shepherd's Bush and Werndorff at Islington were joined by the distinguished Hungarian refugee from Germany, Ernö Metzner. More attention was given to costume design, not only for the historical films which now became popular, but with contemporary contributions from several fashionable couturiers.

Jessie Matthews continued to be a valuable asset. In the summer of 1933 she made *Friday the Thirteenth* with Saville. An ingenious story bringing the lives of a number of strangers together in a London bus crash, it contained a number of plots which were skilfully intercut and the large cast gave the good performances characteristic of Saville's films. Hitchcock, at a loose end after leaving BIP, came to Shepherd's Bush to make a film for the independent producer Tom Arnold, a musical extravaganza about Johann Strauss from the Alhambra Theatre called *Waltzes from Vienna*. It featured some decorative sets and a flight of fancy showing the 'Blue Danube' waltz being composed to the rhythm of culinary processes in a vast kitchen, but it had no interest for Hitchcock and was unlike the rest of his work. Jessie Matthews was the heroine and was photographed for the first time by Glen MacWilliams, who she later remembered as being tall, bespectacled and serious-looking, and who was to be her favourite cameraman. An Englishman with long experience in Hollywood, he was second only to Saville in the creation of Jessie the film star, for he changed her make up and lit her to stress her large, wistful eyes. At the end of the year she made her first big starring vehicle, *Evergreen*. This C. B. Cochrane stage show with music by Rodgers and Hart, in which she had appeared in 1930, was transferred to the screen with additional songs by Harry Woods. 'Over

* Despite conflicting dates given in the trade press and various memoirs, the contract of December 1933 was for five years, and Balcon was released from it in December 1936.

My Shoulder Goes One Care' and 'When You've Got a Little Springtime in Your Heart' were to become virtually her signature tunes. It was in *Evergreen* that Buddy Bradley, a black American dancer and dance director who had directed her dance numbers in several Cochrane stage shows and was to do so in a number of her films, introduced the infinitely extendable stage into British films, in which performers are seen on a realistic stage which then proceeds to lose its proscenium arch and expand at will. This show business story, beginning in the Edwardian music hall and ending with a modern musical, also starred her husband Sonnie Hale and at £60,000 was an expensive production for a British company. Feeling the strain despite the tactful Saville, she suffered a breakdown and had to rest. Over a year later she made one of her best films, *First a Girl*. A comedy about a girl pretending to be a female impersonator, it was based on a German film and again co-starred Sonnie Hale. It was glossy and well produced, with some of the most popular songs of the thirties in Britain and some spectacular dance numbers. One well-known number in a huge bird-cage with a chorus of feather-clad dancers had Jessie herself on a swing high above the ground. Whatever her problems, in the capable hands of Saville and MacWilliams she looked prettier than ever. Early in 1936 she began *It's Love Again*, once more with Saville, MacWilliams and Hale, this time co-starring the American Robert Young. In a glamorous society setting with Jessie as a hopeful young actress who impersonates a fake celebrity in order to gain publicity, it was gay and tuneful and with outstanding comedy sequences seemed even more successful than the previous film. But Saville, who was already considering the next step in his own career, was preparing Sonnie Hale to take over as her director. In mid-1936 things began to go wrong. She was still the biggest British star, with considerable popularity in America, and was to make important films for several more years. But the next one, *Head Over Heels*, was directed by her husband and, whether it was this relationship or that as a director he lacked Saville's experience and skill, there were quarrels and he failed to give her the confidence she so badly needed. She was ill again at the end of 1936 and the film was not finished until later.

The Hulberts were also under contract. Hulbert, like his fellow comedians George Formby and Will Hay, chose a different milieu for each film, with the character he played remaining more or less the same. In his next film, *Jack Ahoy!*, he played a sailor, once again with romantic interest. Next he made *The Camels Are Coming*, directed by the American Tim Whelan, who like Forde had a reputation for comedy direction, and it set Jack in Egypt in a story with suspense, slapstick, amusing dialogue and a good character to play. As an amiable and upright Englishman with absurdly optimistic staying power however woefully wrong things went, he was more likeable than in some of his parts. The nonchalant dance, the wry song, the lopsided smile and the touch of romance were seen at their best. In 1935 *Bulldog Jack* featured him and his brother Claude Hulbert in a spoof thriller, delightfully using the interplay of their different personalities, he eager and incompetent and Claude honourable, kind but very, very anxious. Directed by Forde, it was a skit on the novelist Sapper's tough detective Bulldog Drummond, with hilarious chases in the underground railway and the British Museum. Fast and funny, it was one of Hulbert's best films. Next, *Jack of All Trades* was directed jointly by Hulbert and Robert Stevenson and was a clever story about a young man who works himself into a job by means of an entirely fictitious financial plan, ending with a wild slapstick sequence involving a fire engine with ladders and turntable which seem to have a will of their own. Meanwhile Cicely Courtneidge's films were less important but retained their own following. Despite the variable quality of their work and its lack of appeal to highbrow audiences or critics, both Hulberts had a big British public for their wholesome, cheerful fooling, especially Jack, whose style of dancing was neither acrobatic nor elegant but casual, floppy and humorous.

In addition to the Hulbert films the versatile Forde made three more big features while with Balcon. *Chu Chin Chow* in 1934 was a long adaptation of the Oscar Asche musical spectacle which had a record run in London during and after the 1914 war. An Arabian Nights fantasy, it had the original songs with new additions, dance numbers and solos, some arranged by ballet dancer Anton Dolin, and was lavishly costumed. A very large cast was headed by the Chinese star from Hollywood, Anna May Wong, and the veteran music-hall comic George Robey. It was an expensive production with impressive sets by Metzner, but it remained heavy and theatrical and even Forde was unable to give it life. *Forever England* was a different matter. Made with Admiralty co-operation in the latter part of 1934 at Shepherd's Bush and on location at Portsmouth and Plymouth, it included a superb action sequence shot at Nare Head, Cornwall, by a second unit under Anthony Asquith. Based on a C. S. Forester book with the more intriguing title of *Brown on Resolution*, it was an exciting story of a heroic action by a young able seaman Brown who, unknown to both of them, was the illegitimate son of a senior naval officer. The combination of this idea, the inheritance of courage and leadership, with some almost documentary scenes of life in the navy, and the beautifully shot and edited action sequence, made it an outstanding production. Forde's last for Gaumont-British was clearly aimed at the American market. *King of the Damned* was expensive and ambitious but a box-office flop. Starring Veidt and two Hollywood stars in a torrid drama of mutiny on a tropical penal island, it was loaded with significance about freedom and tyranny, but lacked credibility. During 1935 Forde was working on some Kipling stories under the working title of *Soldiers Three*, with Geoffrey Barkas in India shooting many reels of background material for it. The project was abandoned, however, and in mid-1936 Forde joined Max Schach, whose lavish promises were drawing much talent away from the older British companies. Forde's work at Gaumont-British had differed from that of Saville in showing greater interest in events than in character and relationships, but like Saville he could charm the best out of actors and technicians, who warmed to his practical and natural approach.

As for Saville, his *Evensong* in 1934 was Balcon's third and last bid to turn Evelyn Laye, the beautiful English-rose singer, into a film star. Based loosely on the book by Beverley Nichols fictionalising the life of *prima donna* Nellie Melba, it softened and glamorised it without succeeding in making an effective romance. Large and ornamental sets, including a Venetian canal built in the studio, did not save it and this pretty, ladylike singer returned to the stage. Saville's large output at this time was very varied. Enthusiastic and full of vitality, he was extremely responsive both to ideas and to people. The high level of the acting and the neat bridging passages which were so characteristic of his films were the marks of an intelligent and practical person rather than of outstanding creative originality. Realistically, he saw himself as a practical commercial film maker. He always preferred to produce as well as to direct, and after making *It's Love Again* he left Balcon to set up his own production unit with Korda at Denham.

Hitchcock had lost his way after the brilliant start to his career under Balcon in the silent days and the early BIP films. Balcon now rescued him and gave him a second chance, seizing the opportunity afforded by his presence in the studio for *Waltzes from Vienna* to invite him back into the company. In June 1934 Hitchcock accordingly began work on a pet project, *The Man Who Knew Too Much*. Like Saville, he was to flourish under Balcon's regime, and he now embarked on the type of film that suited him best, the thriller. He was to make four outstanding films in the next few years, to the scenarios of which he, his wife Alma Reville and Ivor Montagu all contributed. This first one starred Leslie Banks and Edna Best as the parents of a kidnapped child who become involved in a political assassination plot, and featured Peter Lorre, en route from German films to Hollywood, as a divertingly sinister villain. It had a number of features soon to be recognised as characteristic of Hitchcock's work. The suspense, the understatement, the use of commonplace details to highlight drama, even the use of outrageously bad process shots in the confident belief that the audience would be too preoccupied to bother about technical matters, were all to become familiar before long. The film was an outstanding success in both popular and critical terms and Hitchcock's career was on course once more. In 1935 came *The Thirty-Nine Steps*, freely adapted from the John Buchan novel of pursuit. Written again with Ivor Montagu, Alma Reville and Charles Bennett, not only was it a sensational success in Britain but it also achieved some success in America. It starred Madeleine Carroll, Hitchcock's first cool blonde,* and Robert Donat with his beguiling voice and crooked smile, also back from Hollywood as a world star after *The Count of Monte Cristo*. This was followed in 1936 by *Secret Agent*, based on a Somerset Maugham character who is persuaded to search for a spy and at first kills an innocent

* Anny Ondra in *Blackmail*, though blonde, was not cool.

man in error. Not Hitchcock's own choice in this case, the story was marred by its moral ambiguity and imperfect characterisation, but although it was not a complete success his reputation for the gripping thriller was unassailable. With Madeleine Carroll and Peter Lorre, the hero this time was played by John Gielgud and the spy by the American star Robert Young. *Sabotage* was made in the summer of 1936, towards the end of Balcon's time with Gaumont-British, but was finished well before he left. It starred the Austrian, Oscar Homolka, as a saboteur who accidentally causes the death of his wife's little brother, and is murdered by her. She was played with great intensity by the American star Sylvia Sidney. Set against a homely London background, it was based on a novel by Joseph Conrad. The motives and characters had a social significance and an emotional depth unusual in thrillers and the fine acting of the two leads, as well as the sombre story, make this more moving than Hitchcock's other films. Another success, it confirmed his supremacy among British directors.

A number of films were also made by Tom Walls and another star with whom Balcon had as little to do as possible, George Arliss. Both had devoted fan followings of their own and considerable independence, but Balcon did not welcome such challenges to his authority. The first Gaumont-British film of a Ben Travers farce was *A Cuckoo in the Nest*. Eight more similar films followed, some from the stage but some written specially by Travers. They had a steady, if limited, market.

George Arliss, an English actor of the old school who had been in America since 1901, had been quick to move to Hollywood when the talkies arrived, and had made a dozen successful films there. He chose simple subjects with big central parts which suited him, and like the actor-managers of the past made no attempt to sink his identity in the roles. At sixty-six he was ready to return to England. Dignified, practical and taking his work very seriously, he considered Gaumont-British a company worthy of him. He demanded, and got, not only a large salary but the right to approve story and director. The board saw him not as an ageing actor possibly past his best but as a veritable capture from Hollywood. Maude Howell, who had been his stage manager since 1920, accompanied him as his script writer and associate director. Basically her function was to look after his interests and to promote him in every way, and she was much resented at the studios, although Arliss claimed that the films benefited from her knowledge of what his fans would like. In 1934 he made *The Iron Duke*, in which he played the Duke of Wellington. This was a respectful and totally inaccurate treatment of history with a number of tableaux based on well-known paintings. Directed by Saville, it had beautiful and elaborate sets and costumes and excellent camerawork, and with its expensive crowd scenes was meant to be a big production worthy of its star. Whether it was Arliss or Saville who was not happy, the three other films Arliss made during Balcon's time were slight affairs made by lesser directors. They seem, however, to have pleased his public.

The capacity of the two studios was so large that Balcon was under constant pressure to find more talent. Michael Powell, with his reputation for the economical and efficient production of story-behind-the-headlines crime films, was engaged to make four of them in 1933 and 1934. Comedies with Will Hay, which were to gather a large following of their own and became a staple of Gaumont-British production, began in 1935 and 1936 with three directed by the American director William Beaudine, *Boys Will Be Boys*, *Where There's a Will* and *Windbag the Sailor*. In the first, a combination of the 'Narkover' characters created by J. B. Morton in his 'Beachcomber' column in the *Daily Express* and Hay's own music-hall character, he played a headmaster. His fast, bright and crazy style, a contrast to the two Pinero films he had made at Elstree, proved extremely popular. Only this first film was made before Balcon's departure. *Where There's a Will*, made in February 1936, cast Hay as a seedy and pedantic lawyer. Sniffing lopsidedly, adjusting his pince-nez, shrugging to adjust the sit of his shabby jacket, he was joined in this film by the fat boy Graham Moffat, a studio clapper boy who had drifted into small film parts and now became his stooge. *Windbag the Sailor*, made in the late summer, shows Hay as the lying captain of a barge whose boast that he is a sea captain lands him in charge of a ship manned by a mutinous and crooked crew. For the first time Moore Marriott joined the other two, as an eager, sly and incompetent old shipmate. Although he was in countless films, Marriott is best remembered as a member of the trio.

Other ambitious films of this period include *The Constant Nymph*, the talkie remake by Basil Dean of his own earlier film. The silent original was based on a 1926 play by Dean and Margaret Kennedy from her sentimental novel about a schoolgirl's love affair with a famous musician. The girl, played by little Mabel Poulton in the silent version, was played in 1933 by the young stage actress Victoria Hopper, who was later to marry Dean. Like so many of his films, the treatment was said by *Kine Weekly* to be unimaginative. More important was *Man of Aran*, a beautiful but controversial film made in 1933–4 in Galway Bay off the west coast of Ireland by the great American documentary film maker Robert Flaherty. A notoriously slow and therefore expensive film maker, Flaherty received more forbearance from Balcon than from any other producer and far exceeded the modest £10,000 allotted to the film, known in the studio as Balcon's folly. After two years of waiting Balcon was rewarded with an outstanding film which won a first prize at the Venice Film Festival, and although there were arguments over the legitimacy of its picture of the islanders' struggle with the inhospitable sea it was remarkable for its visual beauty, and was a source of pride to Balcon. Also dear to his heart, but at £100,000 not surprisingly a financial disaster, was a film made by Lothar Mendes in 1934, *Jew Süss*. From a 1926 best seller about the rise and fall of an ambitious Jew in an eighteenth-century German court, the film was handsomely designed by Junge and acted by a large and distinguished cast, headed by

Veidt. Disliked by Nazi Germany and yet at the same time said to have caused offence to the Jewish community in New York, the film is loaded with obscure significance. Another massive production aimed at the American market was *The Tunnel*, directed in 1935 by Maurice Elvey with Leslie Banks and stars from Hollywood in an English copy of a film already made in French and German versions by Kurt Bernhardt. This forecast of the building of a transatlantic tunnel, with spectacular underground disasters, also failed to live up to expectations at the box office.

The Austrian director Berthold Viertel, who after working in the German theatre had been in Hollywood for some years, made three films for Balcon at this time. *Little Friend*, made in 1934, was about the unhappy daughter of a broken home and had a touching performance from the fourteen-year-old Nova Pilbeam. *Rhodes of Africa* in 1936 was an extremely long adulatory film with Walter Huston as Rhodes and Oscar Homolka as Kruger. Background material had been shot in Africa in 1934 by the unit under Geoffrey Barkas and the film, with its big crowd scenes, took many months to complete.

Lastly, Robert Stevenson came into his own in 1936 as one of the best young directors in Britain with a historical film from his own scenario, *Tudor Rose*. The fresh and girlish Nova Pilbeam played the tragic young queen Lady Jane Grey and the film, beautifully designed by Vetchinsky, had another of the large, excellent casts found in Gaumont and Gainsborough films at the time. Stevenson followed it with *The Man Who Changed his Mind* with Boris Karloff and his own blonde wife Anna Lee in a full-blooded mad-scientist film, and towards the end of 1936 was busy with *King Solomon's Mines,* with more African backgrounds from the itinerant Barkas. Featuring the Hollywood English star Roland Young and Paul Robeson, and with Cedric Hardwicke as Allan Quartermaine, the film had a coy and unsuitable heroine written in for Anna Lee. Despite its failings this version of Rider Haggard's popular adventure story, not finished until after Balcon had left the company, was liked by the public.

Both Gainsborough and Gaumont films were popular with British audiences, but overall they were not making money. Although not lavish, production was not cheap. The average cost was some £30,000 or £40,000, with the Jessie Matthews musicals somewhat higher at between £50,000 and £70,000. *Jew Süss*, as we have seen, cost £100,000. This compares with much lower figures at BIP, where the Leslie Fuller and Ernie Lotinga comedies were on a level with quota quickies and where the £50,000 budget for *Abdul the Damned* was considered enormous, and only possible because it was to be shared with Max Schach. Full circuit distribution in the American market was essential if films of this standard were to be really profitable. But even if they were well received by the critics and successful in New York they did not get national distribution on equitable terms, and Mark Ostrer finally acknowledged that the powerful American companies had no intention of promoting British films. The financial scales were loaded against them at home as well. Gaumont-British was a loose amalgamation built up of many early circuits and the distribution pattern was not adjusted to help the company's own productions. For example, at the behest of Woolf, notorious for his disparagement of Hitchcock films, *The Man Who Knew Too Much*, which was one of the most popular of them, was booked by the Gaumont-British cinemas at a modest fixed price as a second feature, instead of on a percentage of box-office takings. And according to Saville his own film *The Good Companions*, which followed the American *Cavalcade* on the Gaumont chain and broke its attendance records, was booked at a mere 25 per cent including an allowance for a second feature, whereas the American film had been booked at 50 per cent.[12] If such discrimination was practised even within the organisation, production could hardly be expected to pay. By 1936 rising costs and the expense of importing American stars were causing additional difficulties. Some of the films made in 1935 had not come up to expectation and a small profit of £12,000 in the 1935 financial year was followed by a loss of £97,000 the next. It was admitted that the policy of high-quality films aimed at the American market had failed.

Herbert Wilcox

The third important production company which survived the change to sound was that founded by Herbert Wilcox. His firm, the British and Dominion Film Corporation, had at the beginning of the period an authorised capital of £500,000 and the valuable distribution arrangement with C. M. Woolf. The new studio at Elstree, called Imperial Studios, had been acquired from BIP next door before the arrival of sound. It had 20,860 square feet of floor space in three stages, a 10-acre lot and mains electricity. Wilcox was quick to realise the importance of the talkie and early in 1929 hurried to Hollywood, where he hired the Christie sound studio at £1,000 a day for five days and produced a crime film called *Black Waters,* made entirely by American technicians. Coming home with a licence for Western Electric sound recording, he set about adapting his own studio.

Wilcox, like so many others, turned first to the stage for material. The revue producer Albert de Courville directed the first British B & D talkie, *Wolves,* adapted from a play and starring stage actor Charles Laughton with Dorothy Gish, who had already made silent films for Wilcox. Shooting began at the silent Blattner studio in July 1929 and the film seems to have been recorded on a Western Electric sound-track separately or in part at Wilcox's own studio, which acquired recording facilities in September. It was not trade shown until May 1930, and Wilcox's boast that it was the first British talkie must be treated with reserve, as indeed should many of his claims. In August he made an agreement with the gramophone recording company HMV to film some of their recording stars on a fifty-fifty basis but, although he was to refer grandly to the many famous singers and concert artists who were under contract to HMV as though they were under contract to him as well, only one singer was actually filmed under the agreement, which soon lapsed.

The first sound film made entirely at Imperial Studios was *Splinters,* directed by Jack Raymond, and starring the stage actor Nelson Keys and the variety and revue comedian Sydney Howard. The film, a rudimentary story about an army concert party, was slow and static and relied heavily on a number of variety acts but Howard, who was to make some fourteen films for Wilcox in the next ten years, came over appealingly as a mild, sad and hopeless little man. Then in his forties, he was a popular comic actor of considerable talent. Somewhat flabby and doleful in appearance, he portrayed a humble and timid person who nevertheless maintained a dignified patience in the face of much bad luck in an unreasonable world. He was endearing with his small tentative gestures, an occasional small hiccup followed by a polite 'Pardon' and a final ability to rally, when necessary with a surprising and almost apologetic burst of aggression. He needed good situation comedies but was often wasted in slow, cliché-laden scripts.

Even more important to the company than Sydney Howard was the team led by Tom Walls and Ralph Lynn, famous for the farces in which they had been appearing at the Aldwych Theatre in London since the early twenties, the same team that was later to work for Gaumont. Wilcox's next film was a straightforward transfer to the screen of Ben Travers's 1926 Aldwych success *Rookery Nook.* Using many lengthy mid shots of theatrical sets with little movement of camera or people, it had typical stage entrances held for effect, long pauses for laughs and obvious difficulties with the sound recording. It was directed by Walls himself. He had been producing and appearing in similar comedies on the stage since 1924, and saw little need to change his style for the cinema. In this he proved right, for however stagy these films were they succeeded at the box office. If we are to believe Wilcox's autobiography this first one, which cost £14,000, grossed £150,000 in Britain alone. The group were to turn out a series of similar films during the next few years, ringing the changes of plot and personnel only slightly. Written with the players in mind, the situations and dialogue were fairly thin in themselves but were carried by the personalities, timing and practised team work of the group. From plays by Travers or Frederick Lonsdale, and later from many original screenplays by the likeable and popular Travers, they were set in an imaginary upper-middle-class society in stockbroker Tudor surroundings, where gay bachelors and men about town in faultless English tailoring, pretty girls, horrible mothers-in-law and henpecked husbands were involved in frantic muddles over sex and property; foreigners and the lower classes were the objects of ridicule, pretty 'gels' were treated with patronising gallantry ('Oh! you are a little darling!') and older women with undisguised dislike. Tom Walls and Ralph Lynn, both fiftyish and rather mature for such gay dogs, excelled in relaxed by-play and cross-talk with each other. The dominating Walls, with his wry air, deep quiet voice and air of authority, left the funny lines to the well-meaning silly-ass Lynn, rather improbably cast as the romantic lead. Winifred Shotter was lightweight, pretty and refined as the girl; Mary Brough the stout lower-class character lady; and Robertson Hare, with his wail of 'Oh calamity', the timid, bald, bullied little man or 'put-upon-ee', as Travers has described him. All had been in the stage productions, as had Yvonne Arnaud, the luscious French 'older woman' who sometimes played opposite Walls. *On Approval, Canaries Sometimes Sing, Tons of Money* and *Plunder* followed in quick succession.

These farces and the Sydney Howard films were popular and profitable, but other B & D films in 1930 and 1931 were not distinguished. *The Blue Danube* was an interesting attempt to get away from the ceaseless talking of theatrical films and make music the centre of interest. This, a romance concocted by Wilcox and a stage designer who often worked with him, Doris Zinkeisen, was about a popular gypsy orchestra of the day which played, according to *Kine Weekly,* with 'hysterical abandon'. The experiment failed, but happily recovered its costs from a freakish popularity in Sydney.[13] Purchase of the new noiseless Western Electric recording was announced in March 1931 and Wilcox, directing little himself at this time, gathered a group of key technicians which included cameraman Freddie Young and art director L. P. Williams. A steady return was obtained from leasing part of the studio. One stage was rented to Paramount for quota production from May 1930, a long lease being signed later for £27,000 a year.

At the end of 1931 B & D acquired two stars who were to be of the utmost importance in Wilcox's career, Jack Buchanan and Anna Neagle, both of whom appeared in *Goodnight, Vienna.* Jack Buchanan, an extremely popular musical-comedy star, had been on the stage since 1912 and was a matinée idol in America as well as England . Tall, slim, dark and debonair, he had made a few silent films and had recently starred in a Lubitsch talkie made by Paramount in Hollywood. He came to Elstree to make a Paramount-British film on the hired floor, and was soon engaged by Wilcox. He was to make a number of films for the latter and also a few independent productions, some of which he also directed. Like Jessie Matthews he became an extremely popular film star and his films, like hers, included many of the song hits which swept the country in the thirties. Records, sheet music and radio performances of these helped publicise the films and like her, again, he was as popular with British audiences as any Hollywood star. With his rather sharp face and a bright and chirpy manner, he played the bachelor man about town beloved of the London theatre, typically in white tie and tails. At his best with flip banter and facetious chat in a rather throwaway style, cool and uninvolved, at his worst with a cackle that suggested a nudge in the ribs, he sang casually in a light nasal voice. The tight, remote smile seemed inward and private and the sexless gallantry to pretty girls, like that of Walls and Lynn, seemed hardly to regard them as people at all, but this pleased the female film fans of the thirties. His delightful dancing, limber and relaxed, appeared casual and spontaneous.

Goodnight, Vienna, in which he played an aristocratic Austrian officer who fell on hard times after the recent war, was based on a radio play and contained several tuneful songs by George Posford and Eric Maschwitz, above all the repetitive but haunting title song. Production was rushed through in three weeks and the film proved a huge box-office success. Even more important for Wilcox, it introduced him to Anna Neagle, a young dancer who at the time was playing in Buchanan's stage show *Stand Up and Sing*, and was cast as the humble flower shop girl who becomes a star. She had been working in the chorus for several years. Adequate, with her refined, slightly severe prettiness and small sweet voice, she became Wilcox's star and later his wife, and as a personal and professional partner was undoubtedly a major factor in his career. A perfectionist, hard working, restrained and level-headed, she provided stability to the restless Irish chancer who was ready to try anything in his search for the secret of success.

Anna Neagle was immediately put under contract and both she and Jack Buchanan made several more films for Wilcox in the next few years. *The Little Damozel* was a deliberate attempt to create a more sophisticated and glamorous image for her but she continued to look demure even decked out in a daring black lace negligee. The farces and the Sydney Howard films continued, but the most important film made in 1932 was another Jack Buchanan vehicle, directed by the star himself, *Yes, Mr Brown*. Once again the title song was a hit. The film co-starred Elsie Randolph, often his partner on the stage and a talented singer and dancer, but a comedian rather than a romantic partner. Like other female comics she accentuated the grotesque, ruling herself out of romance, although in her case she could just as well have presented an attractive and glamorous image. About this time Korda and Gaumont-British began the systematic promotion of their contract stars, especially the girls, and Wilcox did the same with Anna Neagle, Elsie Randolph, Winifred Shotter and Chili Bouchier. The latter, with good looks and intelligence, played in many films during the thirties but for some reason never achieved the popularity that might have been expected. Meanwhile Wilcox's activities extended when Korda, who had come to Elstree to make Paramount-British quota, branched out on his own and hired the third floor for £17,000 a year. B & D took over the production of Paramount's quota from him (q.v.).

Now firmly established with two real stars, Wilcox felt he was in a position to tackle the American market. To Woolf's annoyance he broke with W & F and joined United Artists as one of their associated producers. Richard Norton, working for United Artists after leaving Paramount, joined the board of B & D. One result of the change, already mentioned, was that Woolf persuaded the Aldwych team to leave Wilcox and join Gaumont-British. All the B & D films from April 1933 to the end of 1935, with a couple of late ones in 1936, were distributed by United Artists. These, with the Korda films which were soon under way, were the mainstay of the latter's quota. Not all were really of high enough calibre for United Artists and it would have been unrealistic to expect the Sydney Howard comedies, for example, to have been distributed in America. But Wilcox certainly hoped that he was to get American distribution on equal terms, and his bigger films were now designed with the American market in mind.

The first was Noel Coward's operette [*sic*] *Bitter Sweet*, to which Wilcox secured the film rights for Anna Neagle at the end of 1932. The art direction and costumes, and the camerawork of Freddie Young, combined to make a film which was lovely to look at. The slight, smooth Belgian actor Fernand Graavey played opposite Anna. *Kine Weekly* wrote that her voice was 'not powerful, but is sweet, and gets over thanks to cunning orchestration', but added that the treatment was very literal and lacked inspiration, a complaint often directed at the films Wilcox made himself. Another Anna Neagle film by the same production team, *The Queen's Affair*, was scripted by a sophisticated American writer under contract to Paramount, Samson Raphaelson, and based on an Oscar Straus musical play. Again Graavey partnered Anna, poised and glamorously dressed this time in a slight satirical comedy, a sparkling commercial film about a Ruritanian queen and a dictator who fell in love, each without realising the other's identity. Merrill White, a leading American editor who was to work on a number of Wilcox's best films, edited this and the other big film of the year, Jack Buchanan's *That's A Good Girl*. Buchanan, like Tom Walls, had been in the habit of producing his own stage shows and he now directed the film of this 1928 musical by Douglas Furber, with a number of the original players. Once more he had a hit with a simple, repetitive song, 'Fancy Our Meeting', which he had sung on stage in *Wake Up and Dream* with Jessie Matthews. Elsie Randolph partnered his dancing style perfectly but rather overdid the mugging and cavorting, and left romance to the pretty stage actress Dorothy Hyson. The basic plot, in which a debonair but penniless man about town can inherit a fortune only if he fulfils certain conditions, was a familiar standby and the film also conformed to a musical comedy convention whereby the second or third act transports everybody to a resort, the deck of a liner, a hotel or some other holiday setting – in this instance by moving the action to the Riviera. Buchanan, complete with top hat, carnation and white tie, was once more the gay bachelor.

By the end of 1933 profits were increasing. Nevertheless there was a persistent shortage of trading capital, which was blamed on the initial cost of the sound studio, put at £285,408, and the heavy losses on silent films. According to Richard Norton, however, there was another explanation, the clue to which lay in Wilcox's own temperament. He wrote:

> Wilcox was the quickest man to start making pictures you ever saw; if you took your eyes off him for a moment two or three more would be on the way; and of course if you used up all your working capital in too many films, and could not do anything till the returns on them came

in, in the meanwhile you had virtually to close down your studios and sack your technicians.[14]

It was proposed to reconstruct the company by a reduction of capital, writing off almost £250,000. A big new issue was made in December, but it was largely undersubscribed. All the same the company declared its first ordinary dividend in June 1934, and claimed to be profitable at last.

Norton sought to restrain Wilcox's profligacy and output decreased in 1934, with three important films that year and three in 1935, and fewer minor productions. Following Korda's lead with *The Private Life of Henry VIII*, Wilcox produced and directed a big historical film, *Nell Gwyn*. This was a glossy, handsome and entertaining picture boasting of its authenticity and aimed, like the Henry VIII film, at critical approval as well as box-office success. By now Anna Neagle was taking herself more seriously as an actress and studied the historical records, and Nell Gwyn's famous laugh was diligently reproduced. Although she looked pretty the abandoned merriment, carefully studied, and the cockney 'Not 'arf, yer Majesty!' and 'Bloimey!' did not sully her respectability. The *Cinema Quarterly* critic, describing it as a good honest film but factory-made, said she was only adequate although a good hard-working actress. Charles II was played with great authority by Cedric Hardwicke. The film was shown first in America, where it had censorship difficulties over cleavage, and where it was necessary to add a properly retributive ending showing Nelly dying in the gutter. As in the case of Wilcox's silent film about Nurse Cavell, the publicity value of censorship problems was exploited to the full. According to his autobiography the film was profitable in Britain, although not in America, and it confirmed Anna Neagle's popularity in Britain as second only to that of Jessie Matthews.

Later in the year, after considerable changes of plan, Jack Buchanan made *Brewster's Millions*, the first film directed in the United Kingdom by the American director Thornton Freeland. Wilcox was seeking Hollywood gloss and Lili Damita, the international star from Hollywood, co-starred. Costing over £100,000 according to Norton, it had dresses designed by a top couturier, large and lavish sets and unusually ambitious dance numbers, and once more it was hoped that the film would do well in America. Buddy Bradley directed a large fiesta scene. Songs by the English song writers Ray Noble and Douglas Furber included 'Never Forget that One Good Turn Deserves Another' and other extremely popular numbers. *Brewster's Millions* was fast and bright and full of bounce and very well produced but the script, by a large number of writers, was again full of clichés. It was based on yet another conditional inheritance story, from an Edwardian play about an heir who had to get rid of £500,000 before he could inherit a much bigger fortune.

Norton was responsible for setting up *Brewster's Millions* and another big film of 1935, *Escape Me Never*. The Austrian director Paul Czinner, with

United Artists backing, directed his wife Elisabeth Bergner in a version of the Margaret Kennedy play in which she had appeared in late 1933, after their arrival in London from Paris. The film was produced by B & D but the cameraman was Georges Périnal, who had been working for Korda, and it used back-projected material of the Dolomites shot by the German mountain cinematographer Sepp Allgeier. The production unit was more high-powered than most at B & D, and the film included a ballet performed by the Vic Wells, with special music by William Walton and choreography by Frederick Ashton. A weepy with a weak script,* it was a solo vehicle for this fine if mannered actress, beloved of the intellectuals, who had already appeared in Korda's *Catherine the Great* and who according to Norton was paid £20,000 for this film. Teasing, poignant, wistfully gay, she was always believable and appears more like a girl of several decades later with her straight silky hair, her plain trench coat and her boyish manner, than a star of the permed and fussy thirties. Wilcox described her as mercurial. The strangled uniformity of the two English leading men added little to the film but its artistic prestige was enormous and it covered its costs by one eight-week run in central London. It had some success in the rest of Britain, but in America its popularity was confined to New York.

Three more films followed, including *The Hope of His Side*, a Sydney Howard vehicle written this time by the playwright Walter Greenwood, champion of the underdog. Graham Greene described Howard as a real actor and a 'character of devasting pathos'. Wilcox, seeking to repeat the success of *Nell Gwyn*, then cast Anna Neagle as the eighteenth-century actress Peg Woffington in *Peg of Old Drury*, which he directed, Hardwicke this time playing David Garrick. Anna Neagle, pleased with the success of her first real acting part, applied herself once more to research and this time to the acquisition of an Irish brogue. Jack Buchanan then appeared in a determinedly mid-Atlantic film about an English aristocrat in America, *Come Out of the Pantry*, a disappointing film directed with uninspired flatness by Jack Raymond and using an American leading lady and songs by the American team of songwriters Maurice Sigler, Al Goodhart and Al Hoffman, including 'Everything Stops for Tea'. These three writers, separately or together, were to contribute songs to some sixteen British films in the next few years, while at the same time Ray Noble, the British writer of some extremely successful songs, left for Hollywood.

It was as useless for Wilcox as it was for Gaumont-British and BIP to devise films that would appeal to the American public if proper distribution was not forthcoming. Richard Norton has written that the promise of American distribution which Wilcox thought he had secured from United Artists was worthless, for 'the man out in the field did not want to sell them'. In the end, at the annual general meeting late in 1935 it had to be admitted that B & D was not profitable, and that the United Artists distribution contract was no good.

* Carl Zuckmayer worked on the script, but his name was not on the final film.

By now, however, the whole situation had changed. C. M. Woolf had parted company with Gaumont-British, and together with J. Arthur Rank had registered a new renting company in May 1935 called General Film Distributors. Three months later Pinewood Studios was registered, a £150,000 company owned by Rank and another industrialist, to build big new studios at Pinewood (q.v.). Wilcox was invited to join them. Always reluctant to commit himself too heavily, he was unwilling to accept. But in view of the difficulties being experienced by B & D he registered a small £100 company, Herbert Wilcox Productions, to lease space at the B & D studio. It was decided that economical 'popular' films were to replace the expensive ones they had been making, and *Limelight*, a routine show business story with Anna as a kind-hearted chorus girl, was the first of them. The venture was backed by Rank and the films were to be distributed by the new firm GFD. Woolf, associated with Wilcox once more, was now managing director of both B & D and Herbert Wilcox Productions.

Basil Dean

Meanwhile two new producers of quality films had appeared, Basil Dean and Alexander Korda. Dean, a well-known stage producer who had already made a silent film, saw a Vitaphone performance on a visit to New York in 1928 and was so impressed that he turned his serious attention to the cinema, feeling that now speech was possible the English theatre had much to contribute to it. He and his friend John Galsworthy, who had disliked the film in its silent days, were now prepared to consider an offer from Paramount to film the latter's play *Escape*. In May 1929 Dean floated a company, Associated Talking Pictures, with a nominal capital of £125,000. New to the film world and its pitfalls, he was left in a precarious position when the issue was undersubscribed and his backers let him down. He went ahead despite this, however, with himself as managing director and the distinguished actor Sir Gerald du Maurier on the board. Dean had many literary, theatrical and society contacts and he intended to make films of a high cultural standard.

After taking Clive Brook and a cameraman to Dartmoor and inexpertly shooting some film for *Escape*, later found to be unusable, Dean like Wilcox went to America, where he wrote and directed a full talking film for Paramount, *The Return of Sherlock Holmes,* learning something about film making in the process. In America RKO, or Radio-Keith-Orpheum Productions, had recently been formed by Radio Corporation of America as an outlet for RCA recording and reproduction equipment. They agreed to co-operate with Dean in the production and world distribution of ATP films. RKO were, in fact, simply looking for quota for their British renting subsidiary, Radio Pictures, but Dean believed that they intended a genuine partnership.

He outlined plans at an extraordinary general meeting in January 1930, to which many literary and theatrical friends sent messages of good will. He expected technical knowledge and access to world markets to be provided by RKO. He announced that super-features would be produced in England with British authors and artistes. RKO would advise at all stages, from the choice of subjects onwards, and send over technical staff and Hollywood stars. Costs and profits would be shared equally. Had Dean known more about the film world he might have felt uneasy that RKO established a clear distinction between his films and their own by giving the former a separate name, Associated Radio Pictures.

The Americans did not stint on equipment and expertise, and modern lighting and cameras were sent over during 1930. Among the technicians who arrived were the cameramen Bob Martin and Robert de Grasse and the editor Otto Ludwig. Meanwhile Galsworthy and Dean bought *Escape* back from Paramount, removed the love interest which had been introduced and set to work on it with du Maurier as the gentleman convict escaping from Dartmoor prison. There was a large cast of good stage and film actors in the supporting parts. Editor Jack Kitchin and musical director Ernest Irving, with designer Clifford Pember, formed the nucleus of Dean's future production team. The film was shot at Beaconsfield studios and on location on Dartmoor and at Hyde Park. Dean, although from the theatre, was keen on location filming even at this early stage despite the difficulties of sound recording, and later recalled his 'crusade on behalf of the English outdoors'. The film, according to his autobiography, cost £42,762 and was a financial failure. The public may have been put off, as the trade certainly was, by the high-class air of the film and its makers, especially of its star, for Sir Gerald was an evident toff. The very success of Dean's attempt to make a superior film meant that its appeal would be limited.

Only one more film was made at this time, and that was from a play by A. A. Milne. Meanwhile changes took place in the structure of the company. It is related elsewhere how a chance meeting with Maurice Elvey led to an association with the colour film company Raycol. In March 1931 Stephen Courtauld, one of its directors and brother of the chairman of Courtaulds Ltd, joined the board of ATP and Dean joined that of Raycol. There was little production in colour, and Elvey soon began to direct for ATP. The company was strengthened by two more additions. Stephen Courtauld, quiet and reserved, was joined by his brother Major Jack Courtauld, a more sociable and outgoing member of the family, in June 1931. The chartered accountant R. P. Baker, who had been with Balcon in the early twenties, also joined the board of ATP from Raycol in 1930 and carried out what Dean described as 'cross fertilization on bank guarantees with insurance policies'.[15] With the Courtaulds and Reg Baker on the Board Dean could concentrate on filming.

Producing at a hired studio was inconvenient and on a trip to the United States Dean and Baker acquired blueprints for one of their own. In due course this, the first in England designed specially for talkie production, was built at Ealing by the architect Robert Atkinson, who had also been involved in an earlier attempt by theatrical producers Clayton and Waller to alter the old Barker studio there. It cost double the expected £70,000.[16] Because the economic depression caused the cancellation of insurance company support by way of mortgages, the company relied heavily on the personal backing of the Courtaulds.

Meanwhile production continued at Beaconsfield. Despite his love of the serious theatre Dean's third film, *Sally in Our Alley*, featured a star of the music hall, Gracie Fields. Filming this gawky Lancashire comedian had been suggested to Dean by a former comic, Archie Pitt, who had been her manager and mentor for most of her career and latterly, in an increasingly unhappy marriage, her husband as well. Dean wrote of him as 'a sad, cautious little man with a commonplace mind and a shrewd idea of the commercial value of the wife he had acquired'.[17] But he was impressed by Gracie's warmth and vitality, the range and power of her voice, and a personality which 'bounced off the screen'.[18] A script was prepared by Alma Reville and Miles Malleson, Pitt also insisting on a screen credit, on the basis of Charles McEvoy's short play of 1923, *The Likes of 'Er*. It was directed by Elvey. A story about a north-country working lass parted from her sweetheart for years by the war but eventually reunited, the film showed her as a good-hearted, ordinary girl speaking not in the accents of the West End theatre but her own broad Lancashire. In this first film there was none of the slapstick clowning which later played so great a part in her performances, and the several songs she sang were part of the story, including the one by cockney song writer Bill Haines which became her signature tune, 'Sally'.

The picture is said the have taken £100,000 in Britain. Whilst not a critic's picture, it had a coherent story and was rather more than a vehicle, and despite some technical inadequacies was to prove one of her best films. Her hair, make-up and clothes were natural and inconspicuous and the mugging and raucous singing which were to be so marked in some of her films were not allowed to get out of hand and make the romantic ending appear incongruous. For there was always to be a problem in providing scripts for this gifted and much-loved comedian, known to her fans as 'our Gracie'. She could hardly be described as good looking, but at the time some sort of love interest was expected in a film. Each of her pictures tackled this question differently, but attempts to make her more glamorous, with hard lipstick and eye make-up, tightly waved hair and fussy clothes, were inconsistent with the slapstick, the grimaces and clowning and the caricatured delivery of the comic songs. She was very proud of the range of her voice, but its tone was harsh and the vocal mannerisms and trills which delighted her fans in the sentimental songs which were always included, seemed tasteless to those with a more educated ear. She did not enjoy making films, but she was to make eleven in eight years, seven of them for Basil Dean, who directed or partly directed four of them himself and had great admiration for his hard-working star. They were hardly the kind of film he had intended to make, but they were the mainstay of the company's finances and she was soon in a position to demand a very large salary and a percentage of the profits, and become one of the best paid British film stars. Most of the films were vehicles but this first one and a later one written by J. B. Priestley, both of which had genuine dramatic content, were probably the best. She herself later said that Sally was a *real* story, based on a *real* play but that the rest were just 'stitched around' her.[19]

Elvey made two more films at Beaconsfield in 1931, *A Honeymoon Adventure*, with Scottish and railway locations, a promising little thriller of the type later associated with Hitchcock, and *The Water Gipsies*. The latter was from a novel by A. P. Herbert about the daughters of a bargee, one virtuous and one bad, and like the other film was full of location sequences. Elvey's assistant was Carol Reed, who had left British Lion after the death of Edgar Wallace (q.v.). Meanwhile the studios were being built, and ARP Studios was registered as a private £5,000 company in March 1931. The latest sound equipment arrived from America and sound proofing was carried out with a shell construction and insulated wall bases. Finally a modern, well built studio was ready, occupying 2½ acres, with one sound stage of nearly 12,000 square feet of floor space. The studio was opened in December. At the opening lunch Dean, rather ominously, outlined plans for co-operative production with RKO of two classes of film, one for Britain and the Empire only and another, using American stars, for America as well. At the same time a loss of £52,979 was announced.

During 1932 they made a few minor films at the new studio, taking less than a month over each, and another successful Gracie Fields film, *Looking on the Bright Side*. In this she played a manicurist whose success as a singer causes a temporary rift with her boy friend, an aspiring songwriter. It was a very different film from *Sally in Our Alley*. In it, in the kind of cute part which did not suit her, Gracie was groomed and put in dressy clothes, and both the glamour and the slapstick seem somewhat forced. Although she was only thirty-four *Kine Weekly* found her a trifle too mature for the part. It was directed by Dean with Graham Cutts but the script owed much to Archie Pitts's desire to make a film musical in the grand manner, despite Dean's 'last minute revision of its worst banalities'.[20] No longer did the songs occur naturally. The sweethearts burst into song in a shop with full orchestral backing on the sound-track, and crowds dance down the street singing. A vast set of two tenement blocks is extensively used, from the windows of which the young people are in the habit of sending messages to each other, and in a creaking finale the buildings actually move towards each other as the sweethearts sing from their windows, and finally embrace.

The studio was hired during the course of 1932 by Gloria Swanson, one of the owner-producer members of United Artists, for the production of a sophisticated comedy called *Perfect Understanding*. Gloria Swanson British

Productions was registered in May 1932 as a private £5,000 company, with Richard Norton of United Artists on the board. She used an American director but four talented young Englishmen were also engaged on this £150,000 production. Thorold Dickinson was assistant director, Michael Powell wrote the script, Edward Carrick was the art director and Laurence Olivier played opposite Gloria Swanson.

All was not well with the agreement between ATP and RKO. Dean had believed that ATP would eventually supply a quarter of RKO's films, but he gradually realised that the American company had no such plans. They were tactless enough to tell him: 'Our function in Great Britain is to distribute the quota pictures which you make for us.' They insisted on treating the British pictures as second features and the American ones as first features, and were so slow to pay money due to ATP that legal threats were necessary. Solly Newman, the head of the British subsidiary Radio Pictures, had the right to approve or disapprove the stars of the films and had considerable power. Dean described him as 'illiterate, over-shrewd where money was concerned, he would fall into egregious error when asked to pass judgement on a film story'. Distribution terms in America and Australasia were so unfavourable that they hardly covered exploitation and distribution costs and none of the films was given a general release in America.[21] The agreement broke down in May 1932. It was cancelled, and ATP made plans to handle their own films. Their own renting company, Associated British Film Distributors, was registered with £100 capital in July 1932, and Dean and Baker became joint managing directors. Jack Courtauld joined them in November 1933.

The studio closed temporarily in the autumn, but reopened in March 1933 to make *Loyalties*, the first film handled by ABFD. In May the studio formally changed its name from Associated Radio Pictures to Associated Talking Pictures. *Loyalties* was based on another play by Galsworthy, who had recently died. Its theme was the pernicious effect of group loyalties, and Basil Rathbone played an arrogant and aristocratic Jew rejected by an exclusive club. Dean had originally produced the play in 1922 and took the screen credit for the film's direction, with Carol Reed as his assistant.

The screen credits of some of these films caused considerable resentment and a feeling that Dean took more than his fair share. *Loyalties* is a case in point. In it the cad died not by shooting himself, as in the play, but by a more cinematic fall down a lift shaft. This was filmed through his eyes by mounting the camera on a pulley which dived to a halt just short of the ground, when the screen went blank; the crash was not shown, on the grounds that the suicide would neither see nor hear it. Basil Dean later wrote that he 'managed to translate sufficient of the play's atmosphere into film terms'. But on this film Carol Reed, brilliant illegitimate son of Sir Herbert Beerbohm Tree, had his first credit as assistant director; Thorold Dickinson, a University graduate, had his first as editor; and Edward Carrick, son of stage designer Edward Gordon Craig, his second as art

EDUCATED EVANS
Max Miller, here with Nancy O'Neil, Hal Walters and Arthur Westpayne, plays a quick witted wide boy with a kind heart, in a Warner Brothers quota film made at Teddinton in 1936.

THE GHOST GOES WEST
The American Eugene Pallette and Robert Donat in a film made at Isleworth for Korda by René Clair in 1935. Sets by Vincent Korda and costumes by Rene Hubert and John Armstrong.

OH! MR. PORTER
Graham Moffatt, Moore Marriott and Will Hay in one of the funniest films of this perfectly matched trio. A Gainsborough film of 1937.

THE LAST ADVENTURERS
Niall MacGinnis with Tony Wild in a little known film set in the fishing industry, mixing documentary footage and location filming at Grimsby with studio work at Shepperton in 1937.

A YANK AT OXFORD
American director Jack Conway, producer Michael Balcon and star Robert Taylor on the set of this M-G-M British film in late 1937.

A YANK AT OXFORD
'Cardinal College' created at Denham by art director L. P. Williams.

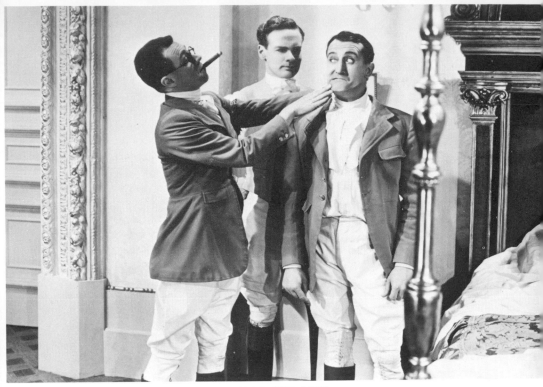

OVER SHE GOES
Laddie Cliffe and John Wood with Stanley Lupino in one of the latter's many adaptations of his own bright and popular stage musicals. Like most of them it was about frivolous young bachelors, gorgeous girls, country house parties and romantic complications. Made at Elstree in 1937.

ST. MARTIN'S LANE
Produced by Erich Pommer at Elstree in 1938. Charles Laughton as a London street entertainer on a large set by Tom Morahan.

director. The ingenious suicide might have come straight out of the kind of artistic silent film these gifted and privileged young men admired, and the idea is much more likely to have come from them than from Dean. They considered that he had no understanding of the cinema, and simply appropriated the ideas of those around him. This caused such lasting bitterness that in writing his own biographical entry for *Art and Design* some years later Carrick omitted Dean's name and stated that his work at Ealing between 1932 and 1935 was for RKO. As we have seen, from May 1932 RKO had nothing to do with the studio and *Loyalties* was made almost a year after this. There is no doubt that the high quality of many of the Ealing films of this period was due to the talent of these and other young film makers, like David Lean, who worked as an editor. It was as a producer rather than as a director that Dean was at his best, and it is no coincidence that four of the greatest talents in British films worked at his studio.

Loyalties and a Raycol short were the only films the company made during 1933. Space was rented by an independent producer, Bray Wyndham, and as we have seen Dean made *The Constant Nymph* for Gaumont-British. ATP itself was rescued by the Courtaulds, and at the annual general meeting in December it was hopefully predicted that the company was about to turn the corner.

In 1934 the studio spent £100,000 on changing over to High Fidelity RCA and building two new stages, each with tanks, so that by December the floor space had been doubled. A *Kine Weekly* item in January 1935 mentioned an advanced type of camera crane carrying the camera crew, and an organ control unit. The planned capacity of the studio was now twelve films a year, six of them to be made by ATP and six by other producers. But despite all the activity the company at this time had a debit balance of £120,000.

Autumn Crocus was adapted from a sentimental and extremely successful play by Dodie Smith, and directed by Dean, starring Ivor Novello and Fay Compton. Set in the Tyrol, this time it was not made on location but shot in the studio with large photographic backgrounds filmed by Bob Martin and Carol Reed at the same time as those for *The Constant Nymph*. These were an innovation at Ealing, and the film was very stagey in appearance, as it was in construction. About a spinster schoolteacher who has a brief love affair with a married inn keeper when on holiday in Austria, its treatment of sex was outspoken for the time yet at the same time coy, with stereotyped characters and pat solutions.

Gracie Fields, who had now parted with Archie Pitt, had recently made a film for RKO which, after the split with Dean, they had arranged to have produced at Twickenham by Julius Hagen. They paid her £20,000. She now returned to Ealing and made two more for Dean. *Love, Life and Laughter* marked the end of Elvey's contract with ATP. In it Fields again played a poor girl who becomes a star, indulging her taste for the shrill and bizarre. According to *Kine Weekly* 'her vocal acrobatics, too, are positively amazing'.[22] She falls in love with a prince, played by John Loder, who not surprisingly marries another girl. Loder was a large, good-looking and impassive young man from Eton and Sandhurst, with a hint of a smile which suggested wry resignation at the absurdity of the activities in which he was taking part. He was described by Dean as 'best described as an amiable Old Etonian determined to make a career in films, rather than an actor who happened to have been at Eton'.[23]

Her second film this year, *Sing as We Go*, was one of Gracie's best, and the first of four for which she was paid £40,000 each. Like *Sally* it had a good story, this time by J. B. Priestley, and a catchy title song. Restraining the trills for once, she was cast as a mill girl thrown out of work when the mill closes down, who cycles to Blackpool and meets with some hilarious adventures. The mild romantic interest was again supplied by John Loder, once more marrying the other girl. Male comedians like Jack Hulbert, Ralph Lynn and George Formby, however unattractive physically, usually had a pretty girl in attendance and frequently a romantic ending, but slapstick, it seems, robbed women comedians of their charm. With lots of location work and more realistic people, and with unemployment in the background, the film captures something of England in the thirties and is fast and often very funny. It owed a great deal to Thorold Dickinson, who was nominally editor but was also somewhat more than an assistant director.

In early 1934 space was rented to Bray Wyndham for two productions, including a jolly little film starring Loder as a rich young man masquerading as a poor artist in Paris. Wyndham was an independent producer who had already hired the studio and some of its staff for three films in 1933. The new one, *It Happened in Paris*, was Carol Reed's first chance to direct on his own, which he did with great success when a considerable amount of the original film by another director was reshot. There were also two ATP costume films. *Java Head* was nominally directed by an American whom Dean described as 'an uncouth Hollywood type', and was about a Bristol family shipping business in the nineteenth century, one of whose members brings home a Chinese bride. Although the film fell apart at its unlikely and melodramatic end it was full of sunlight and atmosphere, the appearance and pace owing much to the skills of Carrick, Thorold Dickinson, Carol Reed and David Lean. The other film, *Lorna Doone*, was particularly dear to Dean, who directed it, and starred stage actress Victoria Hopper, his third wife. Although he tried hard to promote her as a film star her delicate personality failed to make much impact on the cinema public. Much of the film was shot in the west country and it was beautiful to look at, with Loder seeming more at ease than usual as Jan Ridd, but it was too long and suffered from a fault which had earlier been found in many literary adaptations, that of trying to crowd too much of the book into the film. To Dean's distress it was derided at a charity première.

Not so many films were made at Ealing by outside producers as had been hoped, but between mid-1934 and September 1937 space was rented from time to time by Phoenix Films. This consisted of Reginald Denham as director, Hugh Perceval as producer and Basil Mason as scriptwriter. They made a handful of films which were meant to be rather sophisticated, and Graham Greene singled out one of them, *Brief Ecstasy*, dealing with a conflict between sexual desire and affection, as more adult than most films. Ealing technicians and several European cameramen were used, and casts were good. Two of the films were directed by an Anglo-French director of some artistic pretensions, Edmond T. Gréville. They were distributed by ABFD, as were most of the films made at Ealing by visiting companies, but they attracted from *Kine Weekly* such epithets as 'B.B.C. flavour', 'rather highbrow' and 'irritating toniness'.

Another tenant company was Toeplitz Productions. After parting from Korda (q.v.) Ludovico Toeplitz formed this private £100,000 company in June 1934. He planned to make two big films a year at Ealing, of a quality equal to that of Korda, importing stars and top directors. In the event he made only two. Both were glossy and important, although not comparable to the best Korda films. The first was *The Dictator*,* a fictitious and romantic account of the career of Dr Struensee at the eighteenth-century court of the mad King Christian VII of Denmark, and his love affair with the Queen. It starred Clive Brook and Madeleine Carroll, glamorous British re-imports from America. The American director Al Santell, according to an unpublished autobiography by Clive Brook, was sacked by the rich and eccentric Toeplitz after four days on the floor on the grounds that he was using too much film. Santell later successfully sued him. Victor Saville took over the film although according to Clive Brook he had little faith in it. However, it was lavishly and beautifully designed and photographed by the Russian art director Andrei Andreiev and the Czech cameraman Franz Planer. The great marble staircase outside the palace, constructed on the Ealing lot, was said at the time to be one of the biggest sets to be built in Europe. Andreiev was to remain in England for several years and work on some of the more important British films. *The Dictator*, which had its première in Paris, was favourably reviewed but not a big popular success.

The second Toeplitz film, *Beloved Vagabond*, was made by Kurt Bernhardt in French and English in early 1936. Freely adapted from the sentimental novel by W. J. Locke about a loquacious and philosophical architect, played by Maurice Chevalier, who took to the roads with two young companions, it had music by the French composer Darius Milhaud. Chevalier, in unaccustomed moustache, was more relaxed than usual and sang 'Loch Lomond' and 'Daisy, Daisy', as well as the more characteristic 'You look so sweet, Madame, I am at your feet, Madame!' Another handsome film, it was highly regarded despite the elaborate and unlikely story. Although both these films were treated respectfully by the critics, neither was successful and by late 1936 the company was in debt like so many others to the Aldgate Trustees, and produced no more.

* Produced, registered and released as *The Dictator*, but trade shown as *The Love Affair of the Dictator*.

For ATP itself 1935 was not a very productive year. Gracie Fields's *Look Up and Laugh* was directed by Dean from another Priestley screenplay, an unusual little story about an aspiring singer who becomes involved in a sit-in and an experiment in self-government by traders fighting to keep a covered market from being closed. This time there was no hero, but a number of variety comics took part in the film, including her brother Tommy Fields and her brother-in-law Douglas Wakefield. The story, with its rare social significance, stressed the warmth and resilience of its heroine and whereas *Kine Weekly* mentioned 'narratal shortcomings' Graham Greene spoke of its admirable provincial atmosphere. One of her more restrained films, it had several very funny sequences.

Carol Reed, this time fully in charge as director, made another literary costume adaptation, *Midshipman Easy*, from Captain Marryat's novel. This introduced a youth from whom much was expected, Hughie Green, excellent in the title part. Modestly made, the film was a solid, straightforward sea story, perfect in its way, and was greeted with enthusiasm. It compares well with the many classical adaptations expensively made in Hollywood, but without the established stars and the Hollywood exploitation machinery for promotion and world distribution it was soon forgotten.

The big event of 1935 for ATP, however, was the arrival of a second north-country comedian, George Formby, to be their other big money earner. Formby was the son of a Lancashire comic of the same name who had died comparatively young. George had become a jockey, incidentally appearing in this role in an early Broadwest racing picture. Since then he had taken after his father and with a similar act had become a successful comedian in the northern music halls, his career steered firmly by a possessive wife. Early in 1934 a Manchester cinema owner called John Blakely featured him in a short, crude film called *Boots! Boots!* It took only two weeks to make, in a room over a garage in London, and is said to have cost £3,000. It grossed £30,000, and it was clear that here was a comedian with an instant appeal to the less sophisticated majority of the cinema public. Formby's character, John Willie, was the overworked but irrepressible boots of a hotel, with thick stagey make-up, bowler hat and striped waistcoat, playing a ukulele and singing some cheerful, cheeky songs. With small sets and very few of them, elementary camera set-ups, slow dialogue and poor recording, the film was arbitrarily divided into sections to facilitate its issue as a series of shorts if desired. There were the familiar routines and patter of the music hall, and some of the young comic's clowning was somewhat aggressive, but the victim would be soothed with 'That was only my little joke, you see'. *Off the Dole* followed, made next year after Blakely had registered Mancunian Film Corporation. Neither was much to the liking of *Kine Weekly*, which found the song 'With My Little Ukulele in My Hand' gratuitously vulgar.

Basil Dean has written that one of his staff showed him *Boots! Boots!* and he immediately recognised 'another personality that seemed to bounce off

the screen'. Realising that a second popular comic would help to keep his more serious ventures afloat, Dean put Formby under contract and he started work at Ealing in June 1935. Dean left his films to other people. The two men were poles apart and disliked each other, but the association, like that with Gracie Fields, was to be of the greatest value to the company. The character Formby portrayed in the series of formula films he was to make at Ealing was less theatrical and less hostile than that of the first semi-amateur production. He played a suburban working-class lad, something of an oaf but perky, well-meaning and likeable despite his gaucheness. Once the setting had been chosen – motor bike racing, the Air Force, a recording company, a boxing competition – situations were devised whereby George messed things up but, like Jack Hulbert, came out on top in the end. Although the love interest was not stressed, a personable heroine was usually part of the picture. His songs, mild and mocking, were delivered crisply in a nasal voice and with a broad Lancashire accent, with an innocent stare as he accompanied himself with brisk toe-tapping rhythm on his ukulele. The simple effortless delivery, the huge grin and the clear direct gaze persuaded the audience that here was a wholesome fellow, good family entertainment, and were it not for an occasional wink the suggestiveness of some of the lyrics would seem to come more from the mind of the listener than from the beamish performer. Unlike Gracie Fields, his screen personality did not reflect his real character. Dean and others have described him as mean and selfish, and commented on the endless rows with his jealous and ambitious wife.

His first film for ATP was *No Limit*, in which, after a wild and dangerous ride, he won the Isle of Man TT motor bike race. Dean engaged the tiny Monty Banks, a comic himself and an experienced director of British comedies despite his Italian and American background, to direct. Songs were by Harry Parr-Davies, Harry Gifford and Fred Cliffe, who were to continue writing for Formby films. These were extremely successful except in London, where Formby was never to be popular. They were directed first by the tactful, fun-loving and breezy Banks and later by Anthony Kimmins. The next, *Keep Your Seats, Please*, was from a Russian play about the race to find a set of chairs one of which was known to be stuffed with banknotes, and was the only one of his films that did not conform to the pattern. Again directed by Banks and co-starring the comedian Florence Desmond, who had also been in *No Limit*, it included Formby's popular song 'When I'm Cleaning Windows'. A second film made late in 1936 was perhaps the best of all the Formby films made at Ealing, the delightful *Feather Your Nest*. In it an engaged young couple buying their dream house are blind to its gimcrack collapsibility, with handles falling off, windows breaking, doors falling down. A film of the times, with the jerry-built ribbon development house, the time payments, the dread of getting the sack or falling behind 'with me payments', it manages to be both funny and touching and the humour, soon to become so routine, was still fresh. It included another of his best known songs, the one about the lad waiting by the lamp post at the corner of the street 'until a certain little lady comes by'.

Gracie Fields now made two more films, her first with Monty Banks, to whom she was later to be happily married, and the last she made for Basil Dean. *Queen of Hearts* was about a seamstress who falls in love with a star of stage musicals, played with great *sang froid* by John Loder without singing a note or dancing a step. This time Gracie was given an adoring suitor and a romantic ending. In view of her very broad slapstick in a wild car ride and a grotesque apache dance this adoration is rather hard to believe, despite an apparent effort to make her look softer and more appealing. Basil Dean's film for her was the more sophisticated *The Show Goes On*. It was much criticised for its banal story of the heartbroken older man, a composer, left behind by the mill girl who makes good as a singer. This time the star became rather posh and was allowed another romantic ending. It was an expensive film, with big production numbers and an infinitely extendable stage, the designer of the crinoline finale even having a special screen credit. It was to be the last film Dean directed, and the last which Gracie Fields made for ATP. Twentieth Century now offered her better terms, and she and Monty Banks joined them to make several more films together (see under 'Twentieth Century').

Meanwhile two of Ealing's promising young men, Carol Reed and Thorold Dickinson, were coming to the fore. Reed directed a faithful adaptation of the neatly constructed Priestley play *Laburnum Grove*, about a respectable suburban householder who shocks his sponging relatives by telling them that the money they are so anxious to cadge was made by forgery. The part was played by Edmund Gwenn, who had played it on stage in both London and New York. Carrick's setting of a suburban home of the thirties was outstandingly good, the acting was excellent and the film was greatly admired. Carol Reed was ready to move on, and early in 1937 he directed an independent production of his own at Ealing, *Who's Your Lady Friend?*, which used Ealing technicians and was distributed by ABFD. After this he left Ealing. Thorold Dickinson also made an independent film there, which was his first actual screen credit as a director. He and the Chinese Australian scenarist Gordon Wong Wellesley, who had come to ATP from Hollywood, registered the £2,000 company Fanfare Pictures in August 1936 and made one film, *The High Command*. It was produced under the aegis of Reg Baker, and cost between £15,000 and £20,000. The story of murder and blackmail, much of it set in West Africa, was not remarkable. But the skill with which it was put together and the selection of detail to convey the atmosphere of British club life in an outpost of Empire were impressive.

Dean's penultimate film was *Whom the Gods Love*. He had long wanted to make a film about Mozart, which would reassert the high cultural ambitions with which he had founded the company, and provide an important part for Victoria Hopper as Mozart's wife. An extremely romantic script was prepared by Dean and Margaret Kennedy and the film was made during 1935, partly in Vienna and Salzburg. Originally budgeted at £60,000, production dragged on and on and the cost of the luxurious location and studio work in Austria soared. Crowd scenes, expensive top technicians and the London Philharmonic Orchestra conducted by Sir Thomas Beecham in operatic excerpts back at home all added to the cost. When the film finally came out in early 1936 it was a failure. It was said to be slow and Victoria Hopper and Stephen Haggard, promising young nephew of Rider Haggard, were too inexperienced and unknown to carry the film. It was a turning point in Dean's life. The production caused a rift between Dean and his friends and loyal supporters, Stephen Courtauld and his wife. According to Dean the latter 'went so far as to say that she regarded the expenditure on such a film as a betrayal of her husband's trust in my integrity'. In the course of his long career as a theatrical impresario, once Dean embarked on a favourite project in which he passionately believed he pursued it to the bitter end, regardless of financial considerations or the cost to others. In the theatre he could always look around for fresh backers next time. But a permanent film company was different and the Courtaulds, who had backed the company throughout, could not forgive such reckless spending. The breach was never healed.

Alexander Korda

The other big new company producing quality films in the first half of the thirties, and by far the most glamorous one, was Alexander Korda's London Film Productions. More has been written about Korda than about other producers in Britain, and he has been both praised for restoring British film production and blamed for ruining it. By the time he arrived in Britain in the early thirties many of the traits which were to be so characteristic of him were already marked. One in a remarkable exodus of creative talent from Hungary after the social upheavals first of Bela Kun and later of Horthy's White Army, he had early learnt how to get backing which would enable him to be his own boss, and shown the taste for a luxurious lifestyle, the close and protective relation with his two talented younger brothers and the ability to form lasting and friendly partnerships with people who worked on his films. Others* have written about his peasant childhood, his early days in journalism and in Hungarian, German and Hollywood film production. After the arrival of the talkie he returned to Europe in 1930, and he and the Hungarian writer Lajos Biro were engaged by Robert Kane, American head of Paramount production in Paris, to work on French and German versions of Paramount films at Joinville. Harold Young, an American editor with whom he had worked in Hollywood, joined them and his brother Vincent began his career as an art director there. Late in

* Notably Paul Tabori and Karol Kulik.

1931 Korda and Biro were sent to London with a contract for two pictures to improve Paramount's quota production, already begun at the B & D studio. They were followed by Vincent and the third brother, Zoltan, who had already worked in Hollywood. Harold Young was to rejoin Korda later. The team was taking shape. The importance of Biro, in particular, as a friend and collaborator for many years to come, should be stressed.

The great success of Korda's first British film, *Service for Ladies*, established that he was no mere quota producer (see under Paramount). He and Biro and a third Hungarian, Stephen Pallos, proceeded to plan independent production of their own and the second Paramount-British film, *Women Who Play*, was delegated to another director.

They registered London Film Productions in February 1932, as a private £100 company. Joint managing directors were Korda and the Conservative MP Captain A. C. N. Dixey; the chairman was an actor and writer with whom Korda had worked in America, George Grossmith, ageing member of a great English theatrical family and famous in his day as a fruity Edwardian entertainer. Backing came from the international banker Leopold Sutro, whose brilliant son from Rugby and Oxford, J. R. Sutro, represented him on the board, and from other highly placed contacts. Zoltan and Vincent were to work for the company as production supervisor and art director respectively.

The first production, *Wedding Rehearsal*, was made in May at the ASFI studio at Wembley for distribution by Ideal. It was a playful little film, unusually fast, funny and imaginative for a second feature, and though made cheaply it was cast with great care. It was from a story by Biro and Grossmith and one of the scriptwriters, the experienced stage writer Arthur Wimperis, was henceforth to be another Korda fixture. Roland Young, the English actor from Hollywood, played a confirmed bachelor who fell in love with his mother's mousy secretary, revealed as a beauty when she took off her glasses. This familiar part was played by one of Korda's attractive discoveries, Merle Oberon, whom he later married. Also in the cast were three other beautiful girls promoted by Korda to remedy the absence of glamorous film actresses in the British studios – Diana Napier who later married Richard Tauber, Joan Gardner who was to marry Zoltan, and Wendy Barrie, who was to have a long career in films in America as well as in Britain.

Between then and January 1933 five Paramount-British quota films were produced, though not directed, by Korda at the B & D studios. Directors included Zoltan, and Korda continued to find and encourage new young talent, including Robert Donat. Two things are noticeable even at this early stage, the care he took to find good players and match them with the right parts and the way that, with a few exceptions, people who worked with him were keen to stay. It is too easy to put this down to his legendary charm. With Pallos, Biro, Grossmith and his brothers as a nucleus, he seems to have had the rare ability to create the feeling of being at the centre of things.

By now he had discovered that quota films, however good, were distributed without enthusiasm. It was clear that he needed a better outlet if he was to become an important producer. Before the five Paramount films were finished he returned to Paris to make a lavish musical version of the Feydeau farce *The Girl from Maxim's*. This was made in French and English, the English version starring the young dizzy blonde Frances Day, whose brassy presence was somewhat out of tune with a lovely performance by Lady Tree, for example, and with the claustrophobic period atmosphere of Vincent Korda's design. The film did not qualify for British registration and remained on the shelf until after his next film, the phenomenal *The Private Life of Henry VIII*.

This went into production in May 1933 at B & D and was to prove a milestone not only for London Film Productions but for the British film industry itself, for it was so successful not only in Britain but internationally that it inspired new confidence in British production. The company's capital had been put up to £20,000 in November 1932. Richard Norton, who was a friend of Grossmith's, was at that time working for United Artists and he persuaded Nicholas Schenck and Sam Goldwyn of that company to put money into the film and to give Korda a distribution contract.[24] This distribution agreement was to be of key significance to London Films for United Artists did not treat Korda's films as other American companies did their British quota, but as important first features.

Casting Charles Laughton as the king, to whom he bore a strong physical resemblance, Korda built round him not a realistic historical study but a string of episodes in the marriage saga of Henry VIII as he is popularly imagined, and, although a historical adviser was employed, modern colloquial language and anachronistic hair styles were cheerfully allowed. Among the wives Merle Oberon looked enigmatic and exotic as Anne Boleyn and Laughton's wife Elsa Lanchester played the plain Anne of Cleves for comedy. Robert Donat was a gentle Culpeper, and the large cast wore their magnificent costumes with style. Stunning sets by Vincent Korda and photography by Georges Périnal, who came over from France to join London Films, made it an outstanding film.

The picture, which had its first show in November in New York two weeks before it appeared in London, was that rarity, a runaway success both with the critics and at the box office. It was fun, it was unusual and it was launched with a great deal of publicity. So successful was it that Laughton became identified with the part, Donat and Merle Oberon were launched on star careers, a wave of historical costume films followed, and it suddenly looked as if money could be made out of film production after all. Laughton won an Oscar as best actor of 1932–3, a most unusual achievement in a British picture.

Production had not been without its difficulties and estimates of the cost, which far exceeded the original backing, ranged according to Tabori from £50,000 to £80,000. Money to finish production had been provided by a rich Italian producer formerly with Pittaluga, Ludovico Toeplitz de Grand Ry, who was made joint managing director on a year's contract in the spring of 1933. In June the capital was put up once more, this time to £90,000. The partnership with Toeplitz came to an end in March 1934, by which time both *Henry VIII* and *The Girl from Maxim's* were on general release. The story is sometimes repeated that Toeplitz was offered one of the films as his share in the profits and unwisely chose *The Girl from Maxim's*. But it is clear from studio gossip in the trade and fan papers during production that *The Private Life of Henry VIII* was designed from the start as a sensational venture that would put Korda on the map, and it is quite impossible to believe that he would have been prepared to relinquish it. In the event it was highly profitable, and before it had finished its first world run it is said to have made £500,000.

The film transformed Korda's situation. The trade show in August was enough to convince United Artists that they had not made a mistake. The producer members of this company, who did not now make enough films to keep the renting organisation fully supplied, saw Korda as suitable new blood. He, never one to be afraid of committing himself, bounced into print with an announcement that he would make six to eight £100,000 films for United Artists.[25] Early in 1934 one of the founders of that company, Douglas Fairbanks, joined the board of London Films. During the course of the next few months Montagu Marks, an Australian who had had a successful business career in America, got the Prudential Assurance Company interested in investing in Korda and in July 1934 the capital was increased to £141,000. Sir Connop Guthrie was appointed to represent United Artists on the board and Marks became general manager. In October 1934 the capital went up yet again to £825,000, subscribed privately by the Prudential and other city interests, including another insurance firm, C. T. Bowring & Company, and the Midland and Lloyds banks. Much has been made of the fact that Korda raised capital from the City, with the implication that it was his extravagance and indebtedness which caused the crisis in confidence among City investors and the subsequent slump of 1937. This is an oversimplification, as we shall see. Julius Hagan of Twickenham raised £280,000 in debentures from the Westminster Bank and C. T. Bowring in 1935, and was the first company to crash, in January 1937. And the scandal which rocked the City concerned the reckless operations of the Aldgate Trustees, and of Max Schach, who was already raising short-term City loans in the summer of 1934 (see below).

Meanwhile London Films took a lease on the Worton Hall studios at Isleworth at £35,000 a year from the first of January 1935, and in November 1934 Douglas Fairbanks sold Korda a block of shares in United Artists. During the rest of 1933 and 1934 three big costume pictures had been made at Elstree and work had continued throughout the year on another production, later finished at Worton Hall. The first was *Catherine the Great*, made by Korda's technicians but directed by Paul Czinner and starring

Elisabeth Bergner as Catherine, Douglas Fairbanks Jr as a decadent and handsome Tsarevich and Flora Robson as the old Empress. Music direction was credited for the first of many times to the young Scot, Muir Mathieson, who was to become an important member of the staff at Denham, influential in securing many excellent scores by leading composers. Like *Henry VIII* it was a feast for the eye, theatrical and entertaining but this time more romantic and sophisticated. According to Tabori it grossed £350,000, an enormous sum for a British picture.[26]

Korda himself directed another costume picture, *The Private Life of Don Juan*, in the first half of 1934, using the private life formula to replace its unfortunate but prophetic working title of *Exit Don Juan*. In his last film its fading hero, Douglas Fairbanks Sr, looked the part of the ageing rake only too convincingly and the disenchanted, world-weary approach was not enlivened by his one obligatory leap. The story line was choppy and choked with moral philosophising. Music was by Mischa Spoliansky, who had come to England a few years earlier and was to compose for several more Korda films. Stage designer Oliver Messel joined the usual team to design the costumes and visually, again, the film was eye-catching, contrasting brilliant sunlight and deep shadow in an almost exaggeratedly picturesque way. Considered slow and arty, however, the film was an expensive failure.

During the second half of the year a fourth costume film, *The Scarlet Pimpernel*, was made from Baroness Orczy's popular adventure story about the fashionable English aristocrat who secretly and daringly helps French aristocrats escape from France during the Revolution. Just as the other three films had been built round their central actor, this one was built around Leslie Howard. Howard, whose father had actually been a Hungarian, seemed to personify the ideal fair-haired Englishman, cool, civilised, sensitive, with a hint of still waters running deep. He had starred in several important Hollywood films since the earlier one for Korda and was now a top star. By reimporting him for this part Korda again showed his flair for casting, for the fop in the underground movement has never been so elegantly portrayed as in this beautiful and spectacular version, directed by Korda's former editor Harold Young. It was the first of many Korda films to be edited by William Hornbeck, an American editor of great distinction. Merle Oberon played Lady Blakeney, her best part so far, with great elegance. Her original name had gone through several metamorphoses before Merle Oberon, an Anglo-Indian, settled on this one for her appearance in *Service for Ladies*. More than any of his starlets, she was publicised and groomed by Korda and lent abroad to build her reputation as a world star, and she responded with poise and style, if no great acting ability. A new arrival to the group who was to stay four years was the American expert in special photographic effects, Ned Mann. He set up a special effects department for London Films and his work, of which the company was very proud, received great publicity. It included a lot of rather obvious model work and was not universally admired, one critic referring to him as 'the egregious Mr Mann'. According to Tabori the film cost £81,000, expensive for Britain, but grossed £420,000, and was second only to *Henry VIII* as an earner.

The fourth film being made in 1934 was one planned as far back as August 1933 but not finished until early 1935. This was *Sanders of the River*, based on Edgar Wallace's story of a white district commissioner in West Africa, played by Leslie Banks, a popular stage actor not yet well known on the screen. The native Bosambo was played, with hit songs by Spoliansky and Wimperis based on traditional African music, by the famous American negro singer Paul Robeson. The refrain of one of the songs conveys the spirit of the film:

> Sandy the strong,
> Sandy the wise,
> Righter of wrongs,
> Hater of lies . . .

Robeson had recently made *Emperor Jones*, his first film, for United Artists in America. A big man, his gentle demeanour and a rich, velvety bass voice made him a great hit in *Sanders*, but he was criticised by some who saw the part of Bosambo as undignified and racially offensive. The Commissioner for Nigeria in London protested that it brought disgrace and disrepute to his country.[27] The general public was untroubled by such thoughts and simply enjoyed the adventure story and the songs, and the film was another box-office success. It was directed by Zoltan Korda, who had shot thousands of feet of tribal dancing and other background material on a protracted African location. Back home the cast was engaged and the riverside lot at Shepperton was hired for some action sequences. An African village was built and some three hundred black residents of Britain were engaged as extras.

These big productions cost far more than other British films, but they also took more at the box office. Indeed, they went far to justify Korda's view that if British films were to complete successfully with Hollywood in British cinemas they needed to be produced on a similar scale. Of the five made so far, one had been a failure but two had been extremely profitable. Korda had assembled an outstanding team and there was an air of creative momentum about the company. His habit of snapping up actors and technicians and putting them under contract but often keeping them idle for long periods, and of buying many more film rights than were actually used, was wasteful. Production times, too, were slow. But the promotion of new young talent and glamour, and the stress on good casting and actors of quality, seemed to be justified.

Before *Sanders* was finished they moved into the small and cramped Worton Hall studios, where they remained for nearly a year and a half, shooting exteriors on the Shepperton lot until a property at Denham, a country mansion and park in Buckinghamshire, was acquired early in 1935. The Fisheries at Denham was discovered by Marks and building began in the early summer of 1935, the studios being ready in May 1936. Further changes in the company had taken place by then. George Grossmith died in June 1935 and Korda became chairman as well as managing director. In September he joined the board of United Artists and became a full producing member of that company. Finally, in January 1936, Denham Laboratories was registered as a private £100,000 company, with capital from the Warburg family of international financiers and the Hamburg firm Grundwert AG. Korda also acquired an interest in Technicolor's British operations (q.v.). He had been interested in acquiring a colour system since 1934, and when Dr Kalmus was looking for a British partner they joined forces and British Technicolor laboratories were built at Denham alongside the studios. Five of the nine films using Technicolor which were made in Britain before the war were London films.

Four more big films were made in 1935 but only one was really profitable, and time was wasted on several projects which came to nothing. A couple of remakes of foreign films were disappointing. *Moscow Nights*, made at Worton Hall, starred the French actor Harry Baur in the part of a war profiteer which he had played in the French version. It was directed by Anthony Asquith, and was the only film he made while under contract to Korda. *Forget Me Not* was a remake of a German film starring the great Italian tenor Gigli and, made in association with an Italian firm, did not qualify for British registration. Time was spent on a partly documentary film, with re-enacted historical sequences, called *The Conquest of the Air*, which was to fit into a grand projected series on sea, land and air transport through the ages. This was put on the shelf for several years and later patched up by a documentary company. At the end of the year, too, there was much talk of a film starring Laughton as Cyrano de Bergerac, for which Humbert Wolfe was preparing a verse translation of Rostand's play, but this was abandoned. A plan for a film to celebrate King George V's silver jubilee in 1935, to be written by Winston Churchill, was also abandoned. Korda, who was now busy running the studio and less directly involved in production, was acquiring a reputation for grandiose and extravagant ways of working.

Of the major films, there were two much-vaunted adaptations from, and by, H. G. Wells. One of them was disappointing and the other, although a major success, was so expensive that it was not profitable. The same was true of a film made by Robert Flaherty, *Elephant Boy*, mostly shot during the tenure of Shepperton although on location in India and not at the studio.

The only real success in financial terms was René Clair's gentle and delicate comedy *The Ghost Goes West*. This starred Robert Donat, who played both a modern Scottish laird and the ghost of his kilted ancestor, who gets transported to America with the stones of his castle. It was Korda's last truly successful film until *The Four Feathers* in 1938, for although his productions continued to be big events and were popular with the public they were too expensive to make the enormous profits of the early days of *Henry VIII* and *The Scarlet Pimpernel.* Donat, who had made the American *Count of Monte Cristo* and Hitchcock's *The Thirty-Nine Steps* since working for Korda, was now a big star. Half Polish, like Leslie Howard he seemed 'very English', gentle and courteous, very romantic with his thick auburn hair, dark sad eyes, curling lip and beautiful if slightly rasping speech. With two Hollywood stars as the rich American buyer and his pretty daughter, the *Ghost* was tailored for the American market.

The first and most important Wells film was *Things to Come.* His book *The Shape of Things to Come*, not a novel but a long treatise or imaginary history supposedly written in the future, had come out in 1933. Wells, of course, had long flirted with the cinema. Korda, with his wealthy and cultivated image and his social connections, had no difficulty in persuading the great man to develop this into a treatment, promising him the sole writing credit and agreeing that nothing should be changed without his permission. As Wells later put it, he proceeded to invent a story to display the ideas contained in the book. It went through several treatments before it was finished. Work on the film began in 1934 in the hired Consolidated studio at Elstree, formerly the Whitehall studio. Later moving to Worton Hall, and using Denham for exteriors after May 1935, the film was directed by the Scottish-American William Cameron Menzies. He had spent many years in Hollywood as an art director, and the film was very much a designer's film, outstanding for stagecraft and spectacle rather than for emotional involvement. Wells in his sixties was a polemicist rather than a story-teller and the several generations of people he invented were types rather than individuals, vehicles for the great issues which he wished to discuss.

From the outbreak of war in the near future, 1940, the film passes through post-war collapse into anarchy and pestilence, the rough organisation of hostile gangs and eventual transition to a highly scientific society, classless and mechanised, culminating in the departure of a moon rocket. In the early thirties Wells was still optimistic about the benefits of scientific progress. Despite the highbrow content of the film and its length, 10,000 feet at its trade show, the film was extremely successful with both the critics and the public. The streamlined vision of future architecture, dress, homes, planes and rockets was so original that the film was news in itself and Vincent Korda, the designers and Wells himself, who gave definite instructions concerning the clothes, created the visual images of a new world. A beautiful passage in which machinery and people are intercut, representing the reorganisation of the world along scientific lines, and the final sequences in which huge crowds stream towards the rocket were as exciting to watch as the argumentation was tough. Not least important was the music specially composed by Arthur Bliss, which, as an orchestral suite, was one of the first serious film scores to be issued on records and which was to have an existence of its own. According to Tabori, the film took £350,000, but because of its cost it made a loss.[28]

Another Wells film was begun immediately at Worton Hall with Denham exteriors, directed by the German director Lothar Mendes. This was *The Man Who Could Work Miracles*, based on a short story about a mild little draper's assistant who receives the gift of omnipotence from a pair of heavenly spirits, curious to know what mankind would do with such power. He was played by Roland Young with his accustomed skill. As in the other film, Ned Mann's department was well to the fore, with appearances and disappearances, transformations and even an interference with gravity. The hero found that he was powerless to make the girl he loved return his affection. As usual with Wells at this period the moral lessons were rammed home. The mishmash of tricks, mild humour and moralising made a rather boring film, which depended heavily on its author's prestige.

During the same year another marathon film was being made not at Worton Hall but on location in India. *Elephant Boy* was not finally finished until after the new studio at Denham was opened in the summer of 1936. After Flaherty had made *Man of Aran* for Michael Balcon, Korda, seeing it as a prestige project, packed him off to India to make a film with Kipling's *Toomai of the Elephants* in mind. Flaherty, now in his fifties and with a reputation for costly filming which made it difficult for him to find a sponsor, proceeded to get the feel of his subject in his usual leisurely way and it was not until October that he even settled on Mysore as its setting. A suitable Toomai was found, a real mahout's orphan like the original. The twelve-year-old Sabu was a serious little boy with an enchanting smile. Becoming alarmed at the continued absence of a scenario, Korda sent the American director Monta Bell to hasten production, then further technicians arrived, and finally Zoltan. All were recalled in June 1936, by which time Korda was not too pleased to find that his original £30,000 had been stretched to an alarming £90,000 for some 300,000 feet of film still without a scenario. At the studio the film was taken out of Flaherty's hands, and a considerably altered story was concocted to use some of the background material and a few Flaherty sequences. Actors were engaged and shooting continued under Zoltan. When the film finally appeared in 1937 it was criticised on the one hand by those who considered Flaherty pretentious and arty, and on the other by those who considered it a commercial compromise and unworthy of his magnificent material. It is the most theatrical of his films and made a star of Sabu, and although it is not a true Flaherty film his power to conjure a lasting image can be discerned in many of the shots. Although very successful with the public it, too, had cost too much to be profitable.

Smaller Companies

So much for the big producers of first features during the early part of the decade. But what about the sector of the industry which made the films, usually shorter, used by importers and exhibitors as quota? There were three small studios, at Twickenham, Beaconsfield and Shepperton, and many small units and individual producers, busily turning out thousands and thousands of feet of film like so much ticker-tape, whilst several big American companies, Fox, Warners and Paramount, maintained production outfits of their own at Wembley, Teddington and Elstree. A nuisance to the Americans, the quota appeared to many British as an easy way to make money.

Trouble started as soon as the quota became law in 1928. A disagreeable example was the group of companies associated with G. W. Pearson and George Banfield. Both had been in the industry in various capacities since before the 1914 war, and both saw the new law as their big opportunity. Banfield had acquired the Walthamstow studio from Walter West in 1927 and formed British Filmcraft Productions with a capital of £200,000, which was increased in 1929. Pearson formed British Screen Productions, with £125,000 capital, and acquired the old studios at Worton Hall. Both made a handful of inferior silent films. The coming of sound made difficulties for both companies but Pearson launched an £850,000 scheme in 1929. The public, however, applied for only 3 per cent of the shares, and the underwriters repudiated the rest. 'It looks like a ramp,' said Mr Justice Eve at subsequent legal hearings.[29] In the spring of 1930 Pearson formed yet another scheme to save both Banfield's company and his own, but furious opposition from British Filmcraft shareholders led to that company being dissolved. Banfield then joined Pearson in an amalgamation of various remaining companies under the name of Audible Filmcraft, with a capital of £350,000, but legal and financial problems proved too much and they went into voluntary liquidation in August 1932. From all this activity and big talk just one feeble sound feature emerged.

Two other early studios, those at Twickenham and Beaconsfield, fared better. At Twickenham Julius Hagen ran a miniature mass production machine. Born in 1884, Hagen was an actor until he entered film renting at nearly thirty. He founded Strand Film Company in 1928, after the quota had started operation, in association with a young film director from Cambridge, Leslie Hiscott. Only a few Strand films were made. Early next year they bought the old Alliance studio at St Margaret's and founded Twickenham Film Studios, with a capital of £15,000. Hiscott was a major shareholder. Not typical of quota producers, Hagen remained an actor at heart and was a genuine film enthusiast.

The studio at this time consisted of a single stage of 8,400 square feet, with a further throwback of 50 feet, and an outside lot. There were three cameras and RCA sound recording was soon installed, with a mobile Visatone recording van as well. Hagen made several series of quota films under contract to various American firms, nominally renting the studio and staff to them as a unit. Hiscott did much of the directing but the volume of production soon became so great that many former directors of silent films, now out out of work, also came and went. Younger directors like Michael Powell, the American Bernard Vorhaus and John Baxter also made films for them, and Walter Forde made his first talkie there.

Starting with *At the Villa Rose* for Warner Brothers, the studio was soon bustling with activity by day and night, often with one film shot during the day and another at night, and in some cases French and English versions were being made side by side. With little location work, operations at the small studio were minutely planned. George Pearson has described how director and writers would spend a fortnight on the script, the duration of each shot being determined largely by the demands of the dialogue, and the film would then be shot in another fortnight. He refers to the films as 'pound-a-footers', a name often given to quota quickies, although according to Baynham Honri, who was in charge of Twickenham's sound department, the contracts would allow so much per foot up to a break figure after they had recovered their cost, so that Hagen would make more money if the film was successful.[30] Always a man to think well of others, Pearson wrote: 'Though the studio was more or less a film factory, there was a keen spirit amongst the staff to raise the quality of its product.'[31]

In January 1931 debentures of £15,000 were issued in favour of the Westminster Bank and Hagen's contract as managing director was signed at £7,250 a year and expenses. The figure is surprisingly high, for several years later even Michael Balcon was still only earning £10,000 for the much bigger job of running Gainsborough and Gaumont-British. A year later the capital was increased to £30,000. Two years of studio hire earned them some £65,000 and they now decided to go into production on their own account. The next four years saw an even higher output, but in view of subsequent events it seems that modest production on the earlier basis had been wiser.

In the early films there was little music, which was regarded as an unnecessary expense and used only at the beginning and end of a film. But after a while W. L. Trytel, who was later made a director of the company, became musical director and a rambling and irrelevant accompaniment, churning on regardless of changes of shot, sequence or mood, became a characteristic feature of Twickenham films. The cramped space, the simplicity demanded by the speed of production, and the theatrical-costumier appearance of any costume films suggest rigid economy but not all the films were pound-a-footers, and every now and then one would be advertised as a 'super'. Known as Twickenham Film Studios or Real Art productions, they were used for quota by all the American companies and by a number of British importers as well.

Films of every type poured from the studio. The casts are surprising. Many of the leading actors and actresses of the British theatre and film stars both from other studios and from Hollywood made the journey down to Twickenham for appearances which can hardly have been either well paid or prestigious. Hagen persuaded Sydney Howard to desert Herbert

Wilcox temporarily and Leslie Fuller came down from BIP. Sir John Martin Harvey filmed his favourite *The Lyons Mail*, Arthur Wontner made several appearances as Sherlock Holmes and Ivor Novello made two films. Gracie Fields made *This Week of Grace* there. Sir Seymour Hicks was filmed in a version of a part he had been playing on stage since 1901, *Scrooge;* Flanagan and Allen filmed a 'made-to-measure mirth-maker for the masses' and John Baxter made several films on his favourite themes of lower-class life and the music hall, featuring famous veterans of the halls. The American comedian Edward Everett Horton made a film for Hagen at the height of his career and Conrad Veidt, already famous in both German and English films, appeared in a slow mini-spectacular remake of *The Wandering Jew*. Pearson, after the collapse of his own company, made eight modest films in what he has called his 'years of quota seclusion', most of them thrillers and three of them made at night. His successful silent film *Squibs* was remade by Henry Edwards, with Betty Balfour playing her original part as an older and more suburban version of the cockney gamine; quaintly ambitious dance numbers staged in the tiny studio by Ralph Reader of Gang Show fame, Sigler-Goodhart-Hoffman songs and a monologue by Stanley Holloway were introduced to update and upmarket the old story.

Production outgrew the small studio, and by January 1934 the company was using another one at Merton Park for the overflow. They decided to build a second stage at Twickenham and this, 10,400 square feet, was opened in September. Ambitious plans were made. They needed to expand and, at a time when Korda's operations were mushrooming, Hagen may also have seen himself as an embryo tycoon, making and distributing his own films instead of producing for renters' quota. A capital of £240,000 was mentioned. No public issue was made, however, and instead a second debenture to the Westminster Bank was announced in January 1935. Twickenham Film Distributors was registered in May 1935 with a capital of £55,000, to rent their own films directly to exhibitors for quota. During the summer Hans Brahm, a German director who later worked in Hollywood as John Brahm, became his production supervisor. The main capital was increased to £33,000 – still a modest sum. More significantly, another large debenture was issued in May in favour of the City firm of C. T. Bowring (Insurance) Ltd, one of the firms which had invested in Korda the previous year.

After the summer of 1935 there seems to have been a lull in production. In October the old stage burned down, together with the sound-recording and stills department. The damage was at first said to amount to £100,000, although in the end the insurance company paid only £50,000. Instead of rebuilding, Hagen bought the old Whitehall studio at Elstree, raising another £110,000 from Bowring. At the end of 1935 he formed J. H. Productions, intending to make bigger films in future. Production resumed at Twickenham in February 1936. Next, Twickenham Film Distributors bought PDC-New Ideal, the firm which owned the Riverside Studios at

Hammersmith, so that now production was being carried on at three different places, with five stages in all, and with Elvey in charge at the recently acquired Elstree studio. The last Twickenham films came out, and then the more expensive J. H. Productions began. One of them, *Broken Blossoms*, shows how Hagen's ambitions had grown, for he brought D. W. Griffith over from America to remake his former film in sound. At sixty, Griffith had made no film for several years. Disagreements over the casting of the girl led to him walking out and Dolly Haas, the Austrian wife of Hans Brahm, played the part with Brahm directing the film himself as a lacklustre remake of the original. Dorothy Haas had a strong accent, and the combination of her Austrian cockney and Emlyn William's Welsh Chinaman struck a strange note in an effective, if old-fashioned, melodrama.

Very different were the films from two other studio companies – British Lion Film Corporation at Beaconsfield and Sound City (Films) at Shepperton. Neither of them showed the variety and liveliness imparted by Hagen's love of show business. Both exploited renters' quota by supplying the American firms, and exhibitors' quota by renting direct.

British Lion was the first of the two. It had been founded in 1927 to use the talents of Edgar Wallace, who had recently been very successful in adapting his crime stories to the stage and was now invited to try his hand at the screen. The capital was £210,000, and Wallace was made chairman. The managing director was Samuel Woolf Smith, who had been in film distribution since 1910. The little studio at Beaconsfield, north-west of London, was acquired, with its one stage of 6,235 square feet.

They began with a number of silent films, including *Red Aces*, the first to be directed personally by Wallace, who had already produced a number of his own plays in the theatre. The assistant director was Herbert Smith, but Wallace's personal assistant was the young Carol Reed, who had acted in one of his plays and become his assistant stage manager. Also at Beaconsfield was his son Bryan Wallace, who had spent some months in the scenario department of United Artists in Hollywood. With the arrival of the sound film at the end of 1929 RCA recording was installed and Wallace started on the only talkie he ever directed,* *The Squeaker*, starring Gordon Harker, who had already appeared in two of his plays and was to be in many more, and in the films based on them. Harker was a brusque, tough and competent cockney with a dry sense of humour, and the character he adopted was ideally suited to the London underworld of the Edgar Wallace stories.

From mid-1930 space was leased to Basil Dean and he made the first five ATP films there. British Lion's own films, all from Edgar Wallace stories, were few in number and not of a high enough standard to duplicate his success in the theatre. An arrangement was accordingly made with

---

* It was originally intended to use British Phototone for an earlier film, *The Clue of the New Pin*, but this proved impracticable and when the film was trade shown in March 1929 it turned out to be silent.

Michael Balcon to produce a series of joint Gainsborough-British Lion films which would be made at Beaconsfield by experienced directors with technicians from both studios, and which would be distributed by Gainsborough. Three were made in 1931, written by Angus MacPhail and other writers from Gainsborough together with Bryan Wallace. The first, *The Ringer*, again starring Gordon Harker, was directed by Walter Forde and received good reviews. *The Calendar* and *The Frightened Lady* followed. At the same time a renting subsidiary had been formed in 1930. From early 1931 British Lion imported films from abroad, at first only minor Westerns but later bigger films, including Harold Lloyd's *Safety Last* and many European films.

Although their own films had improved under the Gainsborough arrangement, between the arrival of the talkies and November 1931 the company lost £95,000. At the end of the month Edgar Wallace left for Hollywood on a well paid two-month contract with RKO, with an option for a further two months. Personally in debt, he intended both to earn money and to learn more about film making. It had been announced that British Lion would benefit from his experience of Hollywood methods, but from his letters home to his young second wife, later published, his motives seem to have been ambiguous. On 2 December he wrote: 'If I only had to do two pictures, I'd come back next week. My intention is to make myself more or less useful, not to say indispensable.' Much of his time in Hollywood was occupied with the script of what was later filmed as *King Kong*.* He was his usual busy, well organised self, working immensely hard and pushing out a stream of ideas, articles and stories in addition to his RKO work, arranging for publication and thinking of opportunities for members of his family. Experiencing the same Hollywood mixture of friendliness, energy and business toughness as George Pearson a year earlier, he allowed a note of fatigue and doubt to creep into his last letters. Whatever his intentions, he never did return to England, for at the beginning of February 1932, alone in Hollywood, he died suddenly of pneumonia at the age of fifty-seven.

It is doubtful if British Lion could have carried out its original plan to repeat Edgar Wallace's success in the theatre even if he had lived. The studio was too small, and S. W. Smith a producer of too little vision. Wallace, an industrious story teller and a generous and exuberant personality who enjoyed cutting a dash in theatrical and racing circles, had deserved a collaborator with more flourish. His stories were rapidly to become one

---

* There has been controversy about the extent of Wallace's contribution to *King Kong*, a fantasy completely unlike the rest of his work. It bore an introductory title which read 'Idea conceived by Merian C. Cooper, Edgar Wallace'. On 6 January Wallace wrote: 'If this big film gets over that Cooper is doing its going to make a big difference to me, for although I am not responsible for the success of the picture, and really can't be, since the ideas were mainly Cooper's, I shall get all the credit for authorship and invention which rightly belongs to him.' He died before it was shot and Cooper, who also had pneumonia but recovered, is quoted by Orville Goldner and George E. Turner in *The Making of King Kong*, published in the United States in 1975, as saying: 'Actually, Edgar Wallace didn't write any of Kong, not one bloody word . . . I'd promised him credit and so I gave it to him.'

of the staples of the cinema, used by many different companies. British Lion, however, was to develop in an entirely different way.

The character of the firm changed completely after Edgar Wallace's death. S. W. Smith remained in charge under the new chairman, Sir Robert John Lynn MP, but Herbert Smith became production supervisor in December 1932 and took an increasingly important part in production. Both British Lion and Gainsborough made one more Edgar Wallace film and then turned to other sources. Gainsborough finished its contract at Beaconsfield with the early Jessie Matthews film *There Goes the Bride* and a musical directed by Carmine Gallone. A new policy was evident in the British Lion films of 1933. Output expanded with small, safe, shortish light features, many of them comedies. Bryan Wallace remained with the company but no more Edgar Wallace stories were filmed except a version of his last play, *The Green Pack*. The company discovered an easy source of material in revue items, and for the next few years filmed the acts of singers, comedians, dancers and dance bands from variety, cabaret and radio. They put out many single-reelers and a number of long films composed entirely of revue items. Herbert Smith, beginning with the direction of single items for the short films and then for the longer collections of turns, finally graduated to ordinary features in 1935. Some of the short films were taken by M-G-M and Fox, but British Lion's imports continued to increase and it needed its films for its own quota. By mid-1934 it was showing a small profit.

Unlike Beaconsfield, where there had been a studio since before the 1914 war, Sound City at Shepperton was new. In 1930 Norman Loudon, a middle-class young Scot, had registered a company with a small capital of £3,500 called Flicker Productions, to make the flicker books so popular at the time. Adrian Brunel, who later made a number of films at Sound City, described these as 'little booklets of photos of sportsmen in action; these you flicked with your thumb and thereby saw the champions in movement'. Loudon, a keen sportsman himself, was said by Brunel to be 'a shrewd and resourceful beginner, tough, jolly and with undoubted charm'.[32] The venture succeeded and Loudon decided to go into films. For £5,000 he bought a 60-acre estate and mansion at Littleton Park, Shepperton, Middlesex, which had a magnificent river frontage and wooded islands on the River Ash. In February 1932 Sound City Film Producing and Recording Studios was announced. The capital was £20,950, much of it coming from people who wanted to try their own hands at film making.

Production began that summer in the conservatory and ballroom with a mobile Visatone recording van. Like other firms they started with short films, and then went into the production of cheap, medium-length features for the American renters to use as quota. After a few early films Loudon confined himself to management. Much of the writing was by a former member of Flicker Productions, W. Baring Pemberton. Ivar Campbell, a young recruit from Charterhouse public school and the Stock Exchange, both produced and directed. The chief cameraman, George Dudgeon

Stretton, was a Cambridge graduate who had been in the navy and two other directors were also former naval officers, Commander J. L. F. Hunt and Commander Kimmins. John Bryan, an assistant in the art department, was the son of a successful theatrical producer. According to Edward Carrick, Bryan was prepared to work for £7 10s 0d a week, considerably less than most art directors.[33] Sound City 'for the sons of gentlemen' as both Baynham Honri and Brunel say it was dubbed, afforded amateurs a chance to buy their way into production and the mansion, used as a residential hotel by the staff, had a country-house atmosphere.

There was nothing amateurish about the way Loudon ran the company, however. The excellent lot and river front were put to good use and rented out to other companies, and exteriors for some of the most important British films were shot there. The company prospered, and Sound City Films was registered in July 1933 with a capital of £175,000. Its films were pound-a-footers, with rare exceptions like *Colonel Blood* in 1934 which, at £60,000, was far over its budget and made a heavy loss. At the other extreme Brunel's *Sabotage*, made in 1934 for £5,000, was not even considered worthy of a trade show until the importer of foreign films for the Academy Cinema found himself short of quota two years later.

One director, however, was very different from the others. John Baxter, a Christian Socialist and a non-drinker and non-smoker, joined Sound City as casting director after some years as a theatrical touring manager. He acted as assistant on *Reunion*, an anecdotal film about comradeship among ex-servicemen. After this he made a film of his own, *Doss House*, in which a reporter and a detective pose as down-and-outs in order to observe life amongst 'human derelicts'. Shot with a minimum of sets and suffering from a banal story, it was nevertheless a remarkable attempt to get away from the falsity of most productions, and to import both realism and social meaning into a film about the underdogs of British society. This approach recurred in a number of later Baxter films, including *Song of the Plough* and *Lest We Forget*. The films, although cheap and artless, were most unusual in seeking to portray ordinary British people in a realistic way. Baxter also continued to be interested in the theatre and music hall, and made a number of show-business stories which enabled him to film many famous variety acts, not only at Sound City but also at Stoll's and Twickenham. He formed a partnership with John Barter and worked at Cricklewood for a while but they returned to Sound City in the spring of 1935 to make Baxter and Barter films there.

Other small studios, all grouped in and around London, saw the rise and fall of many hopeful ventures, attracted first by the quota and then coping, or failing to cope, with sound. Blattner Picture Corporation was registered in May 1928 with £200,000 capital. Ludwig Blattner was from Germany and according to Michael Powell, who joined him in 1928, was a promoter of genius. However, having bought the old Neptune studio at Elstree and the silent film rights to a number of works, including *Jew Süss*, he was slow to adopt the sound film and a public issue of his shares was heavily undersubscribed. The company acquired rights to the German Stille sound system and the Keller-Dorian colour process Moviecolour, neither of which proved a practical proposition. The tiny 2,000 square foot studio was put up for hire. Their one silent film was shown in a synchronised version the following year and Blattner tried to carry on production, but a receiver was appointed in December 1932. The studio was taken on a long lease by Joe Rock early in 1935 with Ludwig's son Gerry as manager, but Ludwig committed suicide later in the year.

Rock, a short, athletic American, had registered a company to make quota films in June 1934. He engaged Leslie Fuller, the former concert-party comic who had been making films at BIP since 1930. The first films were made at Cricklewood. During 1934 Rock met the sixty-year-old John Henry Iles, who had made a £200,000 fortune as an entertainment financier. Seeking to branch out as a film magnate, he backed Rock and they took over Blattner's studio, renaming it the Rock Studios. Production began there in January 1935 with a number of Fuller films and one starring the dance band leader Harry Roy and his wife Princess Pearl, daughter of the white British Rajah of Sarawak. Although they made a loss in the first year they bought the studio, and Rock Studios was registered in July 1936 as a £200,000 public company. Plans were announced to extend it to over 50,000 square feet at a cost of £500,000.

As so often happens, expansion led not to success but to failure. Production was kept just alive for a while by virtue of the company's involvement in the Dixey scheme for production financed by exhibitors (q.v.). But the only film of any interest, and one of a quality completely different from anything else from the studio, was Michael Powell's remarkable film *The Edge of the World*.

Powell's connection with Rock was somewhat fortuitous. By 1937 he had been making films for fifteen years and had a reputation for the efficient production of quota films which were often of an unusually high standard. Starting work at seventeen with Harry Lachman at Rex Ingram's studio at Nice, he had turned up at Walton in 1930 writing scripts for the United Artists quota films arranged by Richard Norton. He also wrote the Gloria Swanson film *Perfect Understanding* in 1932, which Norton set up at Ealing. He had met the American producer Jerome Jackson in 1929 and from 1931, as Film Engineering and later as Westminster Films, the two of them turned out short quota films for various firms, still at Walton and using the Walton staff. The first film he directed was *Two Crowded Hours*. There were also four films at Shepherd's Bush and Islington for Gaumont-British, one of which attracted the favourable attention of Graham Greene writing in the *Spectator*, and in early 1934 Powell was engaged by Asher to work for Warner Brothers at Teddington (q.v.). For Warners and others he made films which were usually crime stories or melodramas in contemporary settings, based on novels or recent news stories rather than on plays. He learnt economy the hard way with small sets, modern dress, library and background shots, and developed a taut style of direction, although some of the films were marred by bad scripts or far-fetched stories. A cold and external director he did not dwell on sentiment or romance. Rodney Ackland writes: ' "Micky", as I came to know him, has a small child-like face with a tiny mouth, thin-lipped instead of rose-buddish, a far-away voice and the pale blue eyes which are supposed to denote fanaticism. . . . It is difficult to guess what is going on behind Micky's ice-blue eyes.'[34]

Powell had long wanted to make a film showing the depopulation of the outer isles of Scotland.* He received encouragement and backing from Rock early in 1936 and in the summer and early autumn of that year he took a unit to the Shetlands where, under difficult conditions, they shot some 200,000 feet of film. With the help of Gaumont editor Derek Twist he turned this into an unusual seven-reel feature film called *The Edge of the World*. Less a story than a look at the lives of a group of islanders, played by actors with widely differing accents, the film meandered through a loose narrative with three climaxes, showing their attitudes to the new steam trawlers and their eventual departure from the island. The camera lingers on the faces of islanders, on the picturesque old church and on local customs. Interesting, intelligent and with an unusual authenticity, the film was very well received by critics, even being described as a documentary. A complete break with his former work, it established Powell as an outstanding director and got him a contract with Korda who, however, failed to find him a suitable film. It was to be two years before he made another one. This, *The Spy in Black* (see under Harefield), was the first of his many collaborations with Emeric Pressburger.

If the film was unlike the rest of his work, it was even more unlike the output of Rock Studios. It was clear before the film came out that both the company and the Dixey scheme were in trouble. Expansion of the studio to nearly 45,000 square feet had already cost £250,000, and was not yet finished. A receiver was appointed in March 1937 and Rock's backer J. H. Iles was declared bankrupt some time later. He ascribed the loss of his fortune to the general production slump, but in fact, although a number of films were put out in 1937, they had been made many months before and Rock Studios had virtually given up production before the slump began. Lack of working capital to support the studio expansion and above all the inferior quality of the films, with the single exception of Powell's, are enough to explain the company's collapse.

Another small studio was the one at Wembley Park, which was all that was left of the grand scheme to turn the site of the 1924 Wembley Exhibition

* Alasdair Alpin MacGregor, *The Times* special correspondent covering the 1930 evacuation of the Hebridean island St Kilda, or Hirta, published a book in 1931 called *A Last Voyage to St Kilda,* and in view of his knowledge of the locality and of the Gaelic language Powell had discussed with him a possible story, and the production of a film with him acting as adviser. Permission to film on the island had been refused by Lord Dumfries and, deciding to use the Shetland island of Foula instead, Powell had gone ahead without MacGregor. In March 1938 MacGregor unsuccessfully sued Powell for breach of copyright.

into a huge national studio. We have seen elsewhere that short films using Lee De Forest's sound system Phonofilm were made here. The international financier I. W. Schlesinger and Harold Holt had taken over the company in April 1927. In August 1928 they formed a new company, British Talking Pictures, with £500,000 capital, which was to handle the Phonofilm equipment business and operate the studio for hire. It had a £100,000 subsidiary, British Sound Film Productions, which was to produce films at the studio and rent them through British International Film Distributors. All the Phonofilm goodwill and patents were bought by BTP and the De Forest company was in liquidation by the end of 1930.

A couple of Phonofilm shorts emerged from Wembley in 1929 but the first BSFP feature, *The Crimson Circle*, was directed in Germany by Friedrich Zelnik, who had his own company. Both sound and silent versions appeared in March 1929. Their first feature film made in Britain was *Dark Red Roses*. The studio was formally opened in September 1929. It was a time when the holders of various patents for sound recording and reproducing equipment were struggling for monopoly of parts of the international market. Talks between Klangfilm and Western Electric had broken down, and GEC of America, which had a controlling interest in RCA, had acquired a holding in the group which controlled Klangfilm-Tobis, AEG and Siemens-Halske of Germany.

In October 1929 a £1 million company, Associated Sound Film Industries, was formed jointly by BTP, with a 45 per cent interest, and the International Tobis Company of Amsterdam with 55 per cent. Dr Rudolph Becker, previously director of foreign business at UFA, became general manager of ASFI and managing director of the production subsidiary. The company owned the Phonofilm and Klangfilm-Tobis patents, the studio and shares in BSFP, and had an agreement with Films Sonore Tobis in France and Società Anonima Films Sonori in Italy. The experienced Italian director Carmine Gallone was engaged, and the company intended to conduct large-scale international production of multilingual films, as a challenge to Western Electric. However, it was to make two ambitious films and then peter out. There was little activity at the studio during early 1930 except for a series of single-reel marionette skits made by John Grierson and others. But later in the year Gallone directed a big multilingual production, *City of Song*. It was produced by Arnold Pressburger, who had been in Austrian and German films since 1909 and had previously organised some joint production with Gaumont-British. He was one of the international wheeler-dealers whose itinerant activities were a feature of film production in the thirties, and the line-up of talents for this film was suitably cosmospolitan. It starred the bouncy young Polish tenor Jan Kiepura from La Scala, Milan, in his first film. The Hungarian cameraman Arpad Viragh died of peritonitis while on location and was replaced by another talented European cameraman, Curt Courant, who was to make a number of important films in Britain. One of the editors was the Danish-American Lars Moen, who had previously worked in Russia. *City of Song* was the first of a group of big international films, specially written for the screen, which were a cross between operetta and musical comedy, with light operatic singing in contemporary stories.

The following year the company made its only other big film, the trilingual *The Bells*. This time Sergei Nolbandov, a Russian who had worked with Brunel and Montagu on the adaptation of foreign silent films for the British market, was production supervisor. He was to have a long and distinguished career in British films. It was the first British production of the Austrian cameraman Gunther Krampf, who was also to remain in Britain. A distinguished and creative cameraman, he has been compared to Tissé and Toland.[35] Again editing was by Moen. An adaptation of the book upon which Henry Irving's famous melodrama was based, it had music specially composed by Gustav Holst. According to Holst's biographer later C. H. Dand, who had persuaded Holst to contribute to the production, had vague memories many years later of a march with two village bands coming from opposite directions and meeting, and scenes of a girl running down a mountain singing a wordless song. The production was not a happy one and Holst was displeased with the results,[36] although the *Bioscope* reviewer was complimentary about both music and recording. The film was a financial failure, however, and the venture was virtually at an end. Becker resigned and had returned to Europe by the end of 1931, and Dand also left. There was a little desultory production in 1932 and 1933 and the studio was hired by independents making quota films, especially for Fox. In the summer of 1934 this company decided to co-ordinate its quota operations and took a lease on the studio, which they bought in 1936.

The large ASFI operation had failed completely. Multilingual production itself, of course, had proved disappointing. And, although the company had engaged excellent players and technicians, it was run by people who were not primarily film men and took little day-to-day interest in production, who seem to have taken the quality of the script too much for granted and who probably did not realise that the studio was too small for such grandiose projects. The production of musical films like *City of Song* continued elsewhere.

The Wembley venture had failed on a grand scale, but there were a number of small British companies, relics of the twenties, which managed to survive on a very meagre scale. Stoll, Butcher's and Nettlefold, all of them run by men no longer young, were much diminished in size and importance. F. W. Baker, managing director of Butcher's Film Service, was a cinema pioneer who had joined the industry in 1897. His small private renting company backed low-budget pictures made for provincial audiences and was closely associated with Archibald Nettlefold Productions at Walton, and to a lesser extent with Stoll Picture Productions at Cricklewood. Their output was irregular until a series of short films was initiated for them by John Argyle, using the old Butcher's formula of basing a sentimental story on a ballad title, beginning with *Love's Old Sweet Song*, made at Cricklewood in 1933. In 1934 Butcher's announced a new brand called Butcher-Panther, to be made at Cricklewood by arrangement with Oswald Mitchell of Stolls. The enormous Stoll studio at Cricklewood, which had given up feature production some time before the arrival of sound, was slow to install sound equipment. One stage had been equipped with the British non-royalty system Visatone by August 1930 and a silent film was synchronised and shown in November, but never released. Some of the former staff remained at the studio but although it was hired by many small independent producers* there was little production except shorts, comic and educational films. In 1933 another sound stage was added, and after the 1934 deal Butcher's used the studio extensively under various brand names. But despite its vast size and the cheapness of its sound system the studio was out of date and the only producers who hired it were independents with few resources.

Nettlefold was another company closely associated with Butcher's, which had distributed their silent films in the late twenties. Archibald Nettlefold decided not to attempt sound production but to operate the studio for hire. The last silent films made by the company at the small Walton studio (called Nettlefold Studios from 1932) included two excellent comedies directed and acted by Walter Forde, but they could not compete with sound films. Their first and only talkie was made by Forde and the Walton technicians at Twickenham before Walton installed sound equipment. The studio was not ready until towards the end of 1930. Forde had left by then, and Nettlefold advertised it for hire along with its technicians. It had one small sound stage, RCA sound with travelling microphones, and modern cameras with silent travelling trucks, and late in 1932 it claimed to be the first British studio to install the new High Fidelity recording. It was widely used by independent producers for quota production for Fox, Paramount, Ideal, United Artists and others. During 1934 a second stage was added and back-projection equipment installed. But when Sound City expanded its superior facilities in 1935 the better quality units deserted Walton, although it continued to be busy with tenants even further down the scale. By far the most frequent visitor was George Smith. Smith had been in renting in various parts of the world since 1911. From late 1933 he was responsible for the production of a large number of quota quickies, mostly made at Walton and mostly directed by Peter Maclean Rogers. Used by all the American companies, the films were the cheapest of the cheap and were criticised by the trade press as 'a network of aimless inanities . . . boring and irritating', 'rubbish', 'dreadful' and other such descriptions.

Butcher's was responsible directly and indirectly for an increasing number of low-budget films rented to the poorest exhibitors for quota. They were treated with greater kindness than they deserved by the trade press for Baker, a powerful member of the industry through membership of the KRS, the Board of Trade Advisory Committee, the Consultative Committee of the

---

* Commander J. L. Freer Hunt used it to record an English language version of *Karma*, made in India by Himansu Rai.

British Board of Film Censors and later the Board of Governors of the British Film Institute, was a venerable and respected figure.

Comics popular with provincial audiences (like Will Fyffe and Ernie Lotinga) were well represented in Butcher's films. By far the best were the double act Lucan and McShane. They had already been in two ordinary variety films made at Walton and Cricklewood, but with *Old Mother Riley* in 1937 they translated their long-standing music-hall act to the films. Arthur Lucan, a slight, pale ugly man approaching fifty, with sparse hair and a large bulbous nose, was a comedian of genius who played a comic Irish washerwoman in pantomime dame's gear; his wife Kitty McShane played his 'daughter dear'. 'Mummy darling', with his wide acrobatic movements, tremendous but controlled waving of the arms, gesticulating with large, delicate and expressive hands, created a character of extreme subtlety. Servile yet aggressive, a little genteel but earthy when necessary, and occasionally exploding into unbridled fury, old Mother Riley was an eager, helpful and independent type of woman, ready to stand up for herself. Several more films followed, which acquired a large and delighted following. *Old Mother Riley* was directed by Mitchell at Cricklewood and written by an experienced writer of stage and film comedy, Con West, from a story by John Argyle. Taken at a terrific pace, it includes a bit of patter and a bit of slapstick, but is solidly based on the humour of character and situation. Old Mother Riley's anger with her defence counsel when she defends herself in court is both funny and understandable. Referring to herself as a poor, broken old woman, she shows blarney, cunning and aggression, darting malevolently and triumphantly about in the witness box.

In the middle of 1937 the Stoll studio was modernised and a third sound stage was added, giving a total of some 20,000 square feet. But the Nettlefold studio at Walton had also been enlarged, and units making films for Butcher's were henceforth to work there. A few independents used Cricklewood but 1938 was a bad year for production generally, and it was decided to sell it as a going concern. This failed, and the equipment, said to be worth £200,000, was sold off for some £6,000. Over two hundred silent films, relics of the twenties, were donated to the National Film Library.

American Quota Arrangements

The lower level of British production represented by these companies made only a small part of the quota footage needed by the American renters who, with their enormous imports, needed many thousands of feet of cheap British quota. None of them except United Artists was interested in handling good-quality British films. Each tackled the problem in a different way.

The Fox Film Company's record was an example. Fox needed a lot of British films. First acquiring and later producing many indifferent short second features made by a very large number of undistinguished directors at hired studios, they clearly did not expect the results to be taken seriously.

The trade press openly accepted that the films were only made to comply with the law. They began by acquiring very cheaply a random lot of late silent films. Then in 1930 it was announced that Fox would start production in Britain. Although a few films were made for them at Twickenham by one of the most prolific of the quota film makers, the former renter F. George King, things carried on much as before for a while. The first, *Too Many Crooks*, took less than a week to make. As a director and producer King was now to make over fifty quota films under contracts with various American companies, working at different times at all the hire studios in Britain. He quite often engaged good casts, but the films were never more than adequate and usually poor. He was later to film a number of old-fashioned melodramas played by Tod Slaughter, who specialised in rip-roaring productions that were almost burlesques, and for these King was to receive praise from some critics. But the routine and uninspired nature of his other films was typical of quota production. In 1931, as well as films made by King at Walton and Arthur Varney at Twickenham, Fox sponsored the first five films directed by Michael Powell.

Things changed in July 1932 when Fox British Pictures was registered as a £100 company to produce its own films. With Hugh Perceval as production manager it began work on *After Dark* at Walton in September, moving to Wembley in October. There they remained, taking a longer lease on the former ASFI studio in 1934 and finally buying it in 1936. The many directors employed there included the American Albert Parker, who later joined the Fox board. Another quota king, George Smith, continued the production of films for Fox at Walton, using Adrian Brunel as director, at the same time making quota for other American firms as 'G. S. Enterprises'. Peter Maclean Rogers, Manning Haynes and Hayes Hunter at Cricklewood and Anthony Kimmins at Sound City all contributed to the large Fox quota. Casts were reasonably good but little care was given to the scripts, and *Kine Weekly* commented often on the complicated and improbable stories and endless dialogue. Two which fared better than usual were *Late Extra* in 1935, a crime film with James Mason as a cub reporter in his first film part, and *Wedding Group* the following year, a fictionalised and romantic account of Florence Nightingale's career in the Crimea, starring Fay Compton, which was based on a radio play. It was claimed that the films at this time cost up to £10,000 each. Fox were thus spending up to £130,000 a year on their British output, and, although this might seem a lot to put into films which might well remain unbooked, it was little enough in comparison with the cost of one of their Hollywood films such as *The Little Colonel*.

Paramount Film Service was faced with the same problem. Their first reaction was to acquire films from the reputable British company of Welsh-Pearson, but the three silent films which ruined this company, and its laboriously synchronised Harry Lauder film described elsewhere, were disillusioning. So in 1930 they contracted for a handful of minor films from the Hollywood director Arthur Varney and two former directors of British films, Sidney Morgan and Carlyle Blackwell, and for some short musical films from Pat Heale.

Meanwhile the Paramount studio at Paris was humming with activity making foreign-language versions of Paramount films, and in the autumn of 1930 it was announced that similar production would be started at Herbert Wilcox's B & D studio at Elstree, where one of the stages would be hired for ten years at £27,000 a year. Paramount-British Productions was registered in July 1931, with £50,000 capital, under managing director J. C. Graham, the powerful London representative of Paramount, notorious for his intransigence towards British exhibitors. Walter Morosco, an executive from America, was made production manager. From now on they were to be responsible for a large volume of very perfunctory production.

Initially, however, the connection with Paris seemed to promise something better and their first film, *These Charming People*, was by the talented director Louis Mercanton. His next, *Man of Mayfair*, was Jack Buchanan's first British sound film. It was now that Alexander Korda and Lajos Biro, who were working at Joinville, were sent to Britain to make two Paramount films at the B & D studio. The first was *Service for Ladies*, and it was a remarkable success. The story had been written by Korda's Hungarian colleague Ernst Vajda for an earlier Adolph Menjou version and the film featured George Grossmith as a king travelling incognito. Leslie Howard, already a stage star in both England and America and having starred in the American film *Outward Bound*, played a head waiter masquerading as a prince. The combination of good casting, a good story, elegance and pretty girls was to prove characteristic of Korda films. The second of the two was handed over to an English director from Hollywood and Korda left Paramount to set up his own company on the basis of his success with the first.

The company used five of his first six independent films as quota (see under Korda), but their own British production faltered. Using capable directors like Harry Lachman, Arthur Rosson and Paul Stein and stars as well known as Owen Nares and Gertrude Lawrence, and relying heavily on stage plays, they nevertheless got only disappointing results. Made quickly and cheaply, the films failed to reach the remarkable standard set by Korda. In May 1932 it was announced that in future, although Paramount would continue to have a say in the stories and casting, the films would be produced for them on the hired floor by B & D itself.

For several years B & D were to turn out approximately one film a month for Paramount. The first was *Money Means Nothing*, produced in June 1932. From late 1934 production was under the supervision of Anthony Havelock-Allan. According to the debonair Richard Norton of B & D,[37] costs were kept down by adherence to 'the Norton formula', under which more than three takes required special permission from Havelock-Allan, and more than four from Norton himself. Many directors were engaged, each for a few films. Former directors of silent films like Henry Edwards, Sidney Morgan, G. A. Cooper and George Pearson were used, and younger ones who might have made better films if they had been given more scope, as well as some real quota merchants. Donovan Pedelty,* a young Irish film journalist who had been in Hollywood and from 1933 worked as a writer at the B & D studios, began to write and then to direct Paramount films. Adrian Brunel, whose once promising career seems to have petered out in the thirties, made three. The first, R. C. Sherriff's comedy of village life *Badger's Green*, had an early appearance by Valerie Hobson and according to Brunel himself was very successful, costing only £6,000 and grossing £60,000,[38] although this may be misleading as it played in London as supporting feature to *One Night of Love*. Since few of these quota quickies have survived it is not easy to tell what they were like. Certainly *Kine Weekly* disliked them, referring to Brunel's *Cross Currents* as 'a painfully childish affair',[39] and quickie after quickie was described as dull, boring and stupid. George Pearson, who made a number of quota pictures for Hagen and Paramount after the collapse of his own company, seemed modestly pleased with them many years later,[40] yet we find *Kine Weekly* describing his *Gentleman's Agreement*, with an early performance by Vivien Leigh, as feeble, crude, amateurish and novelettish.[41] But they were not all without merit. Brunel's *Love at Sea*, although bearing the marks of shoestring production and with a story full of coincidences, is a lighthearted and playful little film. Ringing the changes on three couples who ultimately find romance, it economically used library shots and the sound-track to establish its setting on an ocean liner.

Made in February 1936, it was the last Paramount-British film to be made at Wilcox's Elstree studio before it was burnt down. For some eight months after this Paramount quota was made by B & D in hired studios, and in addition the company backed a couple of Pedelty films and Gabriel Pascal's first film in Britain, *Cafe Mascot*, considered unusually good for a quota film. Then in October Paramount-British production, still under Havelock-Allan, moved like Wilcox himself to Pinewood, where it remained for just over a year. Output was bigger than ever, and far more independent productions were also used, many of them made by Pedelty. At Pinewood Havelock-Allan engaged some promising new young directors, including Harold French, David MacDonald and John Paddy Carstairs. The latter, son of the actor Nelson Keys, had been writing scripts since he returned from Hollywood. His second film as a director attracted favourable comment from *Kine Weekly*, while *The Fatal Hour* by Pearson, who at sixty-two was nearing the end of his career in feature films, also received good reviews.

* Pedelty and Victor Greene, as director and producer, formed Crusade Films and made a number of films at hired studios and in Belfast, some with Irish repertory players, including the singer, writer and comedian Richard Hayward. All were distributed by Paramount. Greene set up Admiral Films and in 1938 and 1939 made three slightly more ambitious films which seem, however, to have failed. Pedelty was associated with the first, but later joined the BBC.

Whilst Fox and Paramount thus combined some rough and ready production of their own with contract work from the growing army of quota producers, Warner Brothers by contrast went into regular production like a miniature, and inferior, copy of its Hollywood parent.

Like other companies, however, they began by acquiring films from independents. One of these, about a lighthouse keeper's wife, was directed by Paul Czinner in the summer of 1929 on location at Mevagissey in Cornwall and starred Pola Negri, under the working title *Leal of the Lost.* This was not distributed in its silent form, but was trade shown by Warners in May 1930 in a sound version called *The Woman he Scorned.* * According to June Head,[42] this was not released either, and the *Kine Weekly* review, describing it as a 'doubled' film, complained about the BBC accents.

Meanwhile Carlton Films, a small firm run by an Italian, G. G. Glavany, made a couple of films for Warner Brothers' renting subsidiary run by Max Milder, an executive from the parent company in the United States. They used the old Master Studio, built in the grounds of a mansion south of the Thames at Broom Road, Teddington, which was partly destroyed by fire in October 1929. Carlton failed, and Teddington Film Studios was registered in March 1931 as a private £15,000 company by Henry Edwards. He made one film there for Warners, and then in June sold the studio to them. In August Warner Brothers-First National Productions was registered as a £1,000 company, hoping to make French versions as well as quota at Teddington. At this time the studio consisted of just over 8,000 square feet in two stages with folding doors which enabled them to be combined, a tank, extensive grounds and the river bank.

From now on the studio was run with great professionalism by staff from Burbank. Irving Asher, the handsome young production chief, chairman and managing director, had been in films since he was sixteen. The director William McGann came over with him for a couple of years, and was joined by John Daumery. The latter, a Belgian, worked with Rex Ingram at Nice as well as in Hollywood, and was originally meant to make French-language versions. Behind the scenes was the highly efficient studio manager, Doc Salomon, who had worked for Warners since 1915. Sound, editing, design and camera sections were started and trained by American technicians, who went home as British staff took over, although American directors continued to come and go.

Like a well run factory, the small studio turned out medium-length features at breakneck speed, shot in as little as a week. Conventional contemporary settings were used which required little in the way of design or set dressing, and routine stories which made little demand on the actors and for which expensive royalties did not have to be paid. The key to speed and economy lay in the script. At first Asher visited Hollywood every year for consultation and returned with treatments from American scenarists. These were scripted by his British writers. The importance of the scenario

* This is referred to in some places as *The Street of Lost Souls* or *The Way of Lost Souls.*

department was continually stressed from November 1931, when the experienced British playwrights Roland Pertwee and John Hastings Turner were engaged, soon to be joined by the writers Randall Faye and W. Scott Darling, both of whom had some Hollywood experience. Before long most of the films were from original screenplays. For a while the American Russell Medcraft was story editor and John Meehan, also American, wrote several in 1937, but many of the best known British scriptwriters also worked for Warners from time to time, including Frank Launder, Sidney Gilliat, Guy Bolton, A. R. Rawlinson, Reginald Purdell, John Dighton and others, whilst Brock Williams started writing for them in 1932 and later became story editor.

Production began immediately. Jack Warner, over from America, asserted that the films would be of the same standard as those made in Hollywood and later Darryl Zanuck also visited Britain and made the same claim. It was routine for American companies to promise that their British films would be of the same quality as those from Hollywood, but experience invariably proved otherwise. Significantly, Warner was evasive on whether they would be shown in America on the same terms as their Hollywood product.

From now until the end of 1933 they turned out one or two rather short second features a month, cheap pictures which ranged from competent to bad. Few stand out. There were hardly any musicals and only one costume film. One after another the standardised and interchangeable young actors and actresses of the London stage travelled down to Teddington to appear in parts which differed little from one another. Many of them eventually became stars – indeed some were stars already – but their Warner films were small films which made little impact. Sally Blane and Asher's new wife Laura La Plante were two American stars who appeared but unlike other companies Warners did not bring players over from America. By late 1933 they seem to have reached a low point and even *Kine Weekly*, usually kind to this company, was using words like 'thin' and 'weak' to describe the films. There were some changes the following year. McGann returned to America and Daumery died after an illness in May 1934. George King, who had joined them the previous year, directed many of the films, including one which was intended to be rather more important than most, *The Blue Squadron*. This was an English version of an Italian film about the Italian air force, made by Ludovico Toeplitz, and King used spectacular air sequences from the original. It was refused British quota registration. Other directors were engaged, including Monty Banks, who was already established as a good comedy director. Michael Powell made the unusual and delightful *Something Always Happens*. Fast, neat and funny, it showed what he could do with a good story. Ralph Ince, brother of Thomas Ince and a veteran of the American industry, made many of them. Cyril Gardner, another American veteran, began with *Big Business*, starring Claude Hulbert, who made many films for Warners and developed an even more lovable characterisation than that of his more successful brother. And Harold Young, an American editor and director already in Britain working for Korda, moved to Warners in 1934. But many of the films were still only medium-length and some were still being described by *Kine Weekly* as banal, naive and even 'silly childish stuff'.[43]

Early in 1935 Asher engaged Jerome Jackson, who had been in production with Michael Powell, as his assistant. An American, Jackson had been in Britain since 1928. From now on there were fewer films but they had more important players. It is significant of Warner's attitude to their British production, however, that when they discovered real star quality in their own back yard in the handsome young adventurer from Tasmania Errol Flynn, he was whipped off to Hollywood after only one British film and put under contract there, not in England. *Widow's Might* featured Yvonne Arnaud with Laura La Plante, and Monty Banks's *Man of the Moment* was a funny light comedy about a rich young man's stag party and a beautiful girl disguised as a schoolboy trying to escape from the house.

Another experienced Hollywood director, William Beaudine, who had already made the two Will Hay films for Gainsborough, started a run of comedies with *So, You Won't Talk?* scripted by Launder. Later in the year they collaborated again on a Max Miller vehicle, *Get Off My Foot*, which began a series of his films. Miller, the cockney 'cheeky chappie' of the music halls, had already appeared, beguilingly irrepressible, in several small film parts, and during the next few years was to star in eight Warner Brothers features. A sharp and natty dresser, with eyes bright and hair slicked down, he would deliver a line of outrageous patter and quick repartee in a loud nasal monotone, with great clarity of diction. His character was one of surface brightness and hard-nosed kindness, unsentimental and practical. He would be at home on race-tracks and in street markets, as a bookie or a door-to-door salesman. His humour was verbal, with puns, ambiguities (although only clean ones for the cinema), catch phrases and much expostulation, protesting vigorously: 'Nah, *lissen* boys an' girls' or '*Do* me a favour, will yah!', 'Dahn' get excited!', and above all 'Dahn' get me wrong!' His personality dominated these Warner Brothers vehicles but, as always when full-length stories are needed to show off the talents of comics whose true medium is the comic turn, scripts presented problems. Less bound by formula than the Formby films, Miller's usually set him in some rather rough milieu and concocted a slender farce with a romantic ending. He played a butler in *Get Off My Foot*, a racing tipster in two films based on an Edgar Wallace character, *Educated Evans* and *Thank Evans*, a fairground entertainer in the extremely popular *Don't Get Me Wrong*, a boxing crook in *Take it from Me* and a cleaner salesman who gets mixed up in local politics in *Everything Happens to Me*. *The Good Old Days* was untypical in being a costume film and giving him no pretty co-star, but his last for the company, *Hoots, Mon!*, gave him a most suitable role as a cockney comic with an admirable partner in impersonator and comedian Florence Desmond. The films were all of second feature standard, more like the *Old Mother Riley* films than the more expensive vehicles of Gracie Fields, George Formby or Will Hay, but they were immensely popular steady, unexportable British fun.

Output continued at about the same level in 1936. Michael Powell made a couple of crime films but his next film was the independent production *The Edge of the World*, which lifted him out of the quickie ranks for good. Ince made four, one of which, *Twelve Good Men*, was the second script collaboration of Launder and Gilliat and was shown before their first, *Seven Sinners*, which had been made by Gaumont-British. In the summer the studio was reorganised and enlarged to over 21,000 square feet in three stages, and two new directors arrived. One was Arthur Woods, who came from BIP and whose first film for the company, *Where's Sally?*, was much admired. The other was Roy William Neill, an Irish American with a long career in Hollywood, including eighteen months with Thomas Ince.

RKO, as we have seen, hoped to secure British films from the deal with Basil Dean, but when Dean realised that he was not going to get distribution in America and that RKO regarded his films simply as quota he severed his connection with them. Radio Pictures* then turned to low-quality quota producers like George Smith and Widgey Newman. In early 1935 they became associated with John Stafford, a rather better independent with some Hollywood experience in the silent days and a particular interest in musical and operetta films. Working at various hire studios, he was to make some ten films for them during the next few years.

United Artists' approach reflected the nature of the parent company. A group of individual film makers whose output was small and irregular, its quota needs varied widely. As a result it did not at first engage in regular production or sponsorship in Britain, but sought to acquire a few films made by well-known individual film makers as the need arose. In the first couple of years its imports were so few that only two British films, both from Strand, were used. Imports increased in 1930 and they registered two British films produced and directed by Elinor Glyn and one made at the B & D studio by Louis Mercanton and starring Betty Balfour, *The Brat*. The latter was an English version of a multilingual already made in France.

The Glyn films throw some light on the controversial question of whether American companies acquired or made British films for registration purposes only. Elinor Glyn, the Edwardian novelist who had shocked Britain with a sensational best seller in 1907, had since then not only written novels but had also written and produced films in Hollywood. She returned to England in 1929. Promised distribution by United Artists, she hired space at BIP and rashly went into the production of *Knowing Men* with her own money. She engaged an American cameraman and directed the film herself. It was from an unused story she had written earlier and starred Elissa Landi in the part originally intended for Clara Bow. At its first showing it was received with great hostility, perhaps partly because it was considered *risqué*,

* It became RKO-Radio in 1937.

but also because Elinor Glyn herself, already sixty-five and sadly out of date, appeared in a prologue delivering a would-be shocking diatribe against men. Her co-writer, Edward Knoblock, secured an injunction to prevent the film from being shown and by the time this was lifted it had missed its release date and was never shown. Hoping to recover from the loss she borrowed money for a second film from one of her own novels, *The Price of Things*, this time with marital complications involving identical twins, played by real-life twins Alfred and Walter Tennyson. Despite the previous disaster United Artists had allowed her to believe that they would distribute the film, but although a trade show was held no effort was made to release it. The footage had been registered and that was that.

The number of films coming from Hollywood increased, and United Artists needed more British pictures. The American chairman and managing director, Murray Silverstone, was joined in October 1930 by Richard Norton, who set up a programme of production in the summer of 1931 at Walton and Worton Hall, neither of them prestigious studios. Captain the Hon. Richard Norton,* a former officer in the Brigade of Guards, with his monocle and a permanent stoop from a war injury, was an aristocrat with the very highest connections and a strange employee for the hard commercial Silverstone. Working largely behind the scenes in the film industry, gay, witty and influential, he continued to take part in the privileged life of high society as if he were still a man of private means. The six United Artists films only cost between £3,000 and £7,000 each, but according to Norton they 'had some box office value'.[44] However, as he seems to have put the best face on everything as a matter of good manners, it is possible to question this. Late in 1932 he was involved in the production at Ealing of a more important film by a producer member of United Artists, Gloria Swanson's *Perfect Understanding* (see under ATP). Other quota films followed, but United Artists was dissatisfied with their quality.

A turning point in United Artists' policy was the decision to handle Wilcox and Korda films in 1933. Norton joined the board of B & D, and for the next few years all Wilcox films were handled by United Artists. Norton, who numbered Korda's associate the actor George Grossmith among his many friends, was favourably impressed by Korda's first British films and because of his intervention United Artists helped Korda to finish *The Private Life of Henry VIII* when he was running out of money. After the success of this film all Korda films were distributed by United Artists. Although hopes that their films would get good distribution terms in America were not fully realised, both Korda and Wilcox did get bookings there for a number of them.

United Artists was the only American renter which did not make, sponsor or acquire quota quickies. Other companies found other solutions. Columbia discharged its legal obligations with great cynicism until the second quota prevented it. Columbia pictures, made in Hollywood by Harry and Jack

* He inherited the title of Lord Grantley in 1943.

Cohn, were at first distributed in Britain by Film Booking Offices, a British renter and one of the first to be prosecuted for not registering enough British quota. Columbia Pictures Corporation was registered in Britain in 1929 as a £100 company ostensibly to produce here, but early plans came to nothing. The company did not set up its own renting subsidiary until 1933, and then it was slow to acquire British quota. After a visit from Harry Cohn in June and the usual expansive talk about the production of films with British atmosphere and international appeal, a Columbia-British film went into production at B & D in July. But this, made by an American stage producer who happended to be in England at the time, seems to have been the only one made. During the year a collection of indifferent films was acquired from various sources, technically fulfilling their quota needs. When Paul Soskin was setting up his Amalgamated Studios (q.v.) in 1936 and 1937, there was talk of his making eight films for Columbia at a cost of over £500,000, but the venture failed and the films were never made. Meanwhile between 1935 and 1938 the only British films registered by Columbia were from Australia and Canada, especially the latter. It was known that some small American firms set up dummy 'British' companies in Canada, staffed by some of the less successful of the many British actors and technicians in Hollywood, and these made films in Canada which technically qualified for quota.[45] The trade reviews accepted frankly that these films were nothing but shelf fillers.

This was bad enough, but the company that abused the system more flagrantly than any other was M-G-M, although this was vehemently denied by the company's executives. The renting subsidiary of M-G-M* in Britain imported some fifty important and popular films a year. Its chairman and managing director Sam Eckman, who was President of the KRS from 1931 to 1934, was a powerful figure in the British film industry. After using two credible feature films by British Instructional and a series of revue shorts from Gainsborough for its quota, the company changed its policy abruptly and dredged the industry for the worst hack shorts and short features. Long, long silent Indian films made a gratifying contribution to their registered footage even if no one wanted to book them; golfing films, Australian films, short films of vaudeville turns from British Lion and British Sound Film Productions, Sound City films and the work of the industrious George King all played their part. They never acquired films from the bigger companies although on occasion they used films by Michael Powell and the owner of the Academy Cinema in London, Eric Hakim. But whereas the imports from Hollywood included films of the calibre of *Queen Christina*, *The Thin Man* and many others of the best known films of the thirties, the standard of the films from Britain was conspicuously bad. A lamentable example was *The Invader*, in which Adrian Brunel directed Buster Keaton when the latter was at perhaps the lowest point of his career. In this slow film with its tiny sets, made at Isleworth, Keaton walked sadly through a series of

---

* Jury-Metro-Goldwyn, until it changed to Metro-Goldwyn-Mayer in August 1930.

facetious gags typical of Brunel's own brand of humour, much of it verbal, and some aggressive slapstick entirely foreign to Keaton's style, with hardly any of his own identity left. Brunel later complained that the producer insisted on using every bit of film shot in order to maximise the footage, but there can be no excuse for the feeble comedy.

When L. B. Mayer himself was in Britain in 1934 he was said to have promised that M-G-M was going to produce in Britain, and of course that the films, which would be full of British atmosphere, would be no mere quota quickies but equal in quality to their Hollywood product. Eckman made a similar announcement in November, but nothing happened.

As we have seen, in his evidence before the Moyne Committee in 1936 Eckman maintained that M-G-M's imports were so great that if they had produced quota films in Britain themselves they would have had to maintain a studio almost as large as that of BIP, and that there were simply not enough technicians in the country for such an operation. But Warner Brothers had set up a studio and had given training and employment to many British technicians. In any case the volume of production needed was not as great as Eckman implied. M-G-M trade shows of their Hollywood films between December 1934 and November 1935 numbered 56, which they balanced with 21 British shorts and 12 miscellanous British features, many of them very short and tawdry. But in the same period Warners and First National had as many as 65 Hollywood imports, balanced by 12 features from Teddington. Eckman claimed that they had been unable to acquire quality British pictures because good British producers were afraid that the size and outstanding quality of the M-G-M output would put their own films in the shade. British producers had indeed become wary of arrangements with American renters because they had found that their films were not given fair distribution. In any case there were many better independents than those chosen by M-G-M, and no other big American company handled such a collection of mediocrities. The films, of no interest to audiences, cost M-G-M little and it hardly mattered whether they were ever booked. As an exhibitor, with its own large showcase cinema in London, the Empire, M-G-M was even accused of screening these films in the mornings when only the cleaners were in the building. But, although Michael Balcon many years later claimed that this was true,[46] it was vigorously denied by Eckman at the time. When asked by Sir Arnold Wilson at the Moyne hearings 'You do not admit American renters have been foremost in using the British quota quickie to fill up, and made rubbish for that purpose?' Eckman replied: 'I admit . . . I have discovered that the companies that are willing to make films for us and that spend £20,000 to make them can make no better films than other companies who spend £7,000 to £10,000. They lack the ability even though they have the money, and even though we take them. It is a question of brains and ability.'[47]

However, it seemed that production in Britain was contemplated after all, and Ben Goetz finally arrived from Hollywood to take charge in the spring of 1936. In November Metro-Goldwyn-Mayer British Studios was registered as a £250,000 company, and in December Michael Balcon left Gaumont-British and signed a two-year contract with M-G-M. Eckman had secured the necessary brains and ability. But it was to be some time before production began, and in the meantime M-G-M continued as before, scouring the market for bargains. In August 1937 they registered a real dud, a four-reel item made two years before by two radio cross-talk comedians with nothing visual to offer; it was described by *Kine Weekly* as five reels without a laugh.

Chapter 9

Production in the Late Thirties

During the early 1930s the new technology of the sound film had been absorbed and a clear distinction had emerged between quality producers and quota producers. The number of long films registered by renters in a year had increased from 96 in 1929–30, a low point during the change-over to sound, to 212 in 1935–6, and the number went on growing for another couple of years. Most of this growth was from the quota producers.

In 1934 two new people appeared in film circles who were both, in their very different ways, to have an important effect on the industry. They were J. Arthur Rank and Max Schach. Rank was eventually to take films into the world of high finance. But it was Schach, whose brief participation in the British film industry was to have such unfortunate consequences, who was of the more immediate importance. He and his associates borrowed a very large amount of short-term capital to finance production on a film-by-film basis from financial institutions in the City of London money market. These institutions, with no security and no control, did not wait to see if that money would be repaid but proceeded to make more available to a whole series of other new companies. The glamorous, extravagant and much publicised activities of these companies made it appear that there was a boom in British production, although their films were actually few in number compared with the quota films. In the middle of the decade, however, the whole scene changed. For one thing, from early 1936 until the new quota came into force in April 1938 there was considerable uncertainty as to what form it would take, and production tailed off as some producers decided to wait and see. Worse, the reckless overspending and inability to repay of these 'tramp' producers, none of whom had their own studios or permanent establishments, had its inevitable result. The City discovered its mistake, confidence in films plummeted and investment funds dried up. The ensuing scandal harmed the whole industry. It should be pointed out, however, that quota production was unaffected and the number of films continued to rise to 228 in 1937–8. It was not until the following year that production fell dramatically to 103 as a direct result of the new quota.

Max Schach and the Aldgate Trustees

Max Schach, a dapper little Central European in his forties who since 1920 had been a journalist, a film critic, a screen writer and an independent producer in Austria and Germany, came to England in 1934. He had been associated with Karl Grune on the production of *The Street* in 1923, and had become head of Universal's European operations. Fleeing Nazi Germany, he joined the British film industry just after it had been dazzled by Korda's success with *The Private Life of Henry VIII*. Capitol Film Productions was formed in July 1934. Besides Schach the directors were Grune, who was already in Britain working at Elstree, L. A. Neel, a company director, and Major Henry Procter. The latter had been the Conservative MP for Accrington since 1931 and was a self-made man who, in the forty years or so since he left school at twelve, had acquired degrees in law and political science in the United States and Australia and had become an expert in coal technology. They were joined next year by another Conservative MP, Beverley Baxter, a Canadian journalist who worked for the Beaverbrook press. As quiet and anonymous as Korda was showy and publicity-loving, Neel, Procter, Baxter and Schach were to form a number of film companies over the next two years and to trigger a speculative boom. Korda's glamour and success created a climate in which it was easy for them to raise several million pounds, which was largely squandered.

In August a Mr Austin of the City broking firm of Glanvill, Enthoven and Company, having been approached by Capitol, accompanied Neel to the Westminster Bank and obtained for them a loan of £12,500, later increased to £15,000, to make a film on the life of Abdul Hamid. It was to be produced by Schach jointly with BIP, a most unusual departure for Maxwell, each side providing £25,000 for what was intended to be a major production. The brokers had first been to see underwriters in the marine underwriting market and secured a guarantee policy. They asked the Westminster Bank for a loan on the security of this policy, which they lodged with the bank. The underwriters, it later transpired, expected the brokers to watch over their interests and supervise the financial management of the film company. The bank, one can only assume, thought the underwriters knew something about the film business. It all seemed so easy, and in the next couple of years many small companies were to borrow money for individual films in this way, from a number of banks. A lot of the money raised would go to companies formed by Schach, Neel, Procter and Baxter.

It was bound to be a long time before a loan which depended on the returns from a film could be repaid. It was also notoriously difficult to forecast with certainty what those returns would be. The great success of *Henry VIII* seems to have misled financial institutions in the City, especially when European film makers were involved. Although it was well known that even established British film companies found it difficult to survive, finance was made easily available on a film-by-film basis to many companies with hardly any capital of their own. There was a great air of prosperity, with companies running out of money before a film was finished and borrowing again, or using money already raised for another project.

Grune directed *Abdul the Damned* (see under BIP), which received much publicity during production and was well reviewed. The venture seemed to have started well. A few months later, in July 1935, two members of Glanvill, Enthoven and Company, F. C. Ells and L. H. Wilkins, founded Aldgate Trustees. The former was a member of Lloyd's and the latter an incorporated insurance broker; they were joined by Stanley Bayliss Smith, a chartered accountant from Casstelton, Elliott & Co. The company was a private £1,000 trustee company taking up debentures in trust for anonymous clients. Through it, a great deal of money was to be funnelled into the film industry during the next two years. A month after the formation of Aldgate Trustees, a larger company was registered by the Schach board, this time called Capitol Film Corporation, with £125,000 capital. It was to make films for distribution by C. M. Woolf's new firm General Film Distributors, of which Neel was a director, and which was to advance 37 per cent of production costs. In addition to these advances, during the next year and a half Capitol was to raise over £1 million in bank guarantees through Aldgate and another £160,000 in debentures from the Equity and Law Life Assurance Society.

Their opulent progress began the following month, at the B & D studio and on location at Warwick Castle, with a Jack Buchanan vehicle called *When Knights Were Bold.* This was an updated version of a popular Edwardian comedy about the heir to a castle and his battle with resentful relations who want the castle for themselves. It introduced songs by the American team of Sigler, Goodhart and Hoffman and an American leading lady, Fay Wray. A dream sequence of the days of chivalry and a relaxed performance from Buchanan pleased his fans but the film was slow and full of comedy clichés and in future Schach was to steer clear of middling British directors like Jack Raymond, who directed this one. The only other Capitol film in 1935 was *Koenigsmark*, a multilingual made jointly with a French producer at Joinville, which did not rank as a British picture.

Schach was looking for other openings, and for a while considered association with another Central European entrepreneur, Arnold Pressburger. British Cine Alliance was registered in August 1935 as a £25,000 company and initially Schach, Procter and Neel were on the board with the extreme right-wing Conservative MP Vice-Admiral Taylor. With idealistic naivety in a world of sharks, Taylor's interest in films was as a way of promoting the Empire. However, nothing came of the association and Pressburger went on to other things.

The next company was Cecil Films. Herman Fellner, greatly liked by all who knew him, was slightly older than other refugee film makers. Leaving Gaumont-British, where he had been under contract, he set out to produce independently as Cecil Films in late 1935, with Procter, Neel and Schach on the board. Aldgate money began to flow. Fellner made *Public Nuisance No. 1* at Beaconsfield. It starred Frances Day, who was suspended under contract to Gaumont-British at the time, and she eventually had to pay damages to them for having worked for Fellner. A month after the trade show of the film Fellner committed suicide, and only one more Cecil film was made, also by people who had been working for Balcon. Even so, by the end of 1936 this small company had charges of an impressive £150,000 outstanding to the Aldgate Trustees.

While *Public Nuisance No. 1* was being made Schach was looking for further opportunities and in January 1936 registered a £25,000 company called Trafalgar Film Productions to make big pictures at Denham, for distribution this time by United Artists. The directors were once again Schach, Neel, Procter and Baxter. In the spring there were plans for six films and prospects seemed good. Trafalgar was second only to Capitol in the amount of Aldgate money it obtained. The next month the same four directors registered Buckingham Film Productions, also with a capital of £25,000, with the intention of making three supers a year. These were also to be made at Denham but were to be distributed by GFD, in addition to the other GFD films already being made by Capitol at various other studios. In the event Buckingham made only one film, and that at Pinewood after Schach's empire had collapsed.

For there were signs of trouble. Aldgate money was now flowing into many other new companies not connected with Schach and his associates, and this attracted attention. As early as April 1936 *Kine Weekly* had an article under the heading 'Mystery Financiers' which mentioned speculation in City and film circles as to where the money was coming from to finance the current boom in production, and spotlighting the Aldgate Trustees, who were thought to have already advanced over £1½ million to independent producers. The documentary film maker Stuart Legg and a communist art historian, sociologist and writer, J. D. Klingender, in association with John Grierson's paper *World Film News*, began a study of film finance which later appeared in book form under the title *Money Behind the Screen*. They calculated from announcements published in the trade press that independent production units raised over £4,050,000 by these methods between 16 January and 30 October 1936, and that over two-thirds of this was through Aldgate Trustees. What they did not point out, however, was that 65 per cent of this Aldgate money went to four of the twenty-five companies concerned, and that these were the four Schach companies which had set the whole thing off in the first place.

Four Capitol films were made for GFD distribution at various studios in 1936. *Love in Exile* was from an American novel by an American director and scriptwriter, and starred Clive Brook and Helen Vinson, both from Hollywood. About a king and his mistress who strongly resembled King Carol of Rumania and Madame Lupescu, its showing coincided with the crisis involving Edward VIII and Mrs Simpson. The film was handsomely produced, with Schiapparelli gowns and considerable glamour. A thin story, it was saved by the stars and some brilliant dialogue by Herman Manciewitz. Karl Grune's *The Marriage of Corbal* was a spectacular and romantic film based on a Rafael Sabatini novel about the French Revolution. It starred Noah Beery, Nils Asther and the pretty but lifeless Hazel Terry, much publicised grand-niece of Ellen Terry. The influx of foreigners into the film industry was becoming conspicuous, and Graham Greene poured scorn on the idea that this was a British film. Richard Tauber, after several films for BIP, now joined Schach for *Land Without Music*, which was directed by Walter Forde, who also left Gaumont. It had music by Oscar Straus and was typical of the operettas with which Tauber was associated. June Clyde and Schnozzle Durante were meant to give it international appeal, but it was a disappointing production. *For Valour* was made by the Ben Travers and Tom Walls team, for once not a farce about marital complications but a flippant comment on crime and social class, with Tom Walls and Ralph Lynn both playing dual roles of contrasting age and class. A pleasantly wry story, like so many of their films it was rather slow and full of talk but beautifully acted by these past masters of comedy, with skilful use of matt shots.

Meanwhile things had begun to go wrong shortly after the 'Mystery Financiers' article. Ominously, the accountant Bayliss Smith of Aldgate was put on the board of Buckingham Film Productions in May 1936, three months after its formation and many months before it produced a film. Other firms began to run into difficulty. City Film Corporation, for example, which had been founded in 1934 by Harry Hughes and Basil Humphreys at Worton Hall, producing indifferent light entertainment films used as quota by various renters, was wound up after May 1936. It later transpired that this company, with a paid up capital of only £100, had obtained through Aldgate no less than £233,150.

At the other end of the social scale was Douglas Fairbanks Jr and his company Criterion. Fairbanks had come to England in the spring of 1933 with his father, whose Hollywood career had come to an end. The son had also had some years of a rather uneven career in Hollywood, despite the uneasy relation between father and son. Both were impressed by *The Private Life of Henry VIII*, and Fairbanks Sr offered Korda an owner-membership in United Artists while Fairbanks Jr agreed to appear in Korda's next film, *Catherine the Great*. Such was his father's fame that all doors were open to him. With his conservative and socially superior upbringing, his impeccable and tactful bearing, he gravitated to the rich, the famous, the powerful and socially desirable. He made *Mimi* for BIP (q.v.) a year later with Gertrude Lawrence, with whom he was friendly at the time. In need of money, he borrowed from a old friend from Hollywood, Irving Asher, and as repayment appeared in one of the best Warner Brothers quota films, *Man of the Moment*, with Asher's wife Laura La Plante. Finally he got backing and world-wide distribution from United Artists and registered Criterion Film Productions, a £10,000 company, in June 1935. Other directors were the recently arrived refugee Marcel Hellman, Paul Czinner and the Conservative MP Captain A. Cunningham-Reid, who was married to Lady Mountbatten's sister. They planned four £100,000 films and acquired the studios at Worton Hall in January 1936. The first film, *The Amateur Gentleman*, was made at BIP in the autumn of 1935. A picturesque version of a popular historical novel about the Regency period by Jeffrey Farnol, it was produced by Hellman and directed by Thornton Freeland, with James Laver of the Victoria and Albert Museum as costume adviser and with Fairbanks and Elissa Landi as tl 'scorative leads. The three other productions were modern crime films t!.: last, *Jump for Glory*, made at the end of 1936. By this time Czinner, who had played no part in the company, had resigned. The films were pleasant but undistinguished and by the end of the year the company was heavily in debt to Aldgate and to Cunningham-Reid. The directors fell out, and Fairbanks wrote to Cunningham-Reid: 'Our pictures, for what they are, have been disastrously expensive.'[1] Easy money and inadequate control, with wasted talent – it was a typical Aldgate story. The company made no more films and Fairbanks returned to America.

As for Schach, he extended his activities wherever he could. *Southern Roses*, the first film to be made at Denham, was a Capitol-Grafton film produced in May by yet another immigrant, Isadore Goldsmith, who had arrived from Vienna in 1931 and in the mid-thirties took over the small firm of Grafton. It was directed by Friedrich Zelnik, who had worked in German and American films and was now to settle in Britain, eventually being naturalised as Fred Zelnik. It was a musical with a complicated plot, and some of the music was by Johann Strauss. It had a lightweight cast with little singing or dancing talent, but contained an excellent if unpleasant characterisation by George Robey as an angry and bullying self-made man, the 'paint king'. The next Grafton film, this time produced by Schach for United Artists distribution and made at Welwyn by Zelnik, was *The Lilac Domino*. Based on an operetta of 1918, it was prettily staged and pleasantly sung by June Knight and the American tenor Michael Bartlett. All the usual ingredients were there – dancing peasants, brother officers, a masked ball, a lost fan, lovers' misunderstandings. The sets of Oscar Werndorff were ornate and the film, with many crowd scenes, was another expensive one.

Finally, Trafalgar at last embarked on what was to be the most extravagant programme of all, completing their only three films in the latter part of 1936. The first of the three was *Pagliacci*. Tauber, who had been making films since 1930, had long wanted to make a straight opera film. Schach paid £18,000 for the film rights, Tauber himself was paid £60,000 and no expense was spared on the music, which was arranged by Hanns Eisler. It was conducted by Albert Coates, assisted by Capitol's music director Boyd Neel. The film, however, was a costly disaster. Parts of it were shot in British Chemicolour, an expense not justified by the results. Many writers took a hand in adapting the opera for the screen, including Bertold Brecht, although his name did not appear in the credits. The result was slow and confused, padded with obviously studio-made sequences of the touring company on the move in the mountains, perfunctory acting and an uneasy combination of operatic convention and realism. Tauber, who dominated the film to such an extent that he was even given an aria transposed from another character, sang magnificently but the production was unworthy of him. *Pagliacci* was directed by Grune at Elstree. Meanwhile at Denham *Dreaming Lips* was produced jointly by Schach and Paul Czinner. Schach had agreed to pay £100,000 to Czinner and his wife Elisabeth Bergner for two films, of which this was the first and as it turned out the only one. The two had made their famous 1932 film *Der Träumende Mund* in Germany from an adaptation by Carl Mayer of the play *Melo*, about the love affair between a famous musician and the wife of a well-known conductor. The English version was sumptuous, glamorously set by Andreiev and Tom Morahan, and included part of an orchestral concert played straight through by the London Symphony Orchestra, with some incidental music to the rest of the film written by William Walton. The attention paid to music in Schach's films is their best feature. The early sequences – the concert and the conversation afterwards – were subtle in conception, acting and editing, and critics greeted the picture enthusiastically as adult and intelligent. A novelette for the intelligentsia, it appealed only to a minority audience. Even editing by David Lean, brilliantly effective in the early sequences, could not prevent the story collapsing into bathos as it wended its way to the heroine's suicide. Despite its prestige *Kine Weekly* condemned it as high-falutin, and once more box-office results far from justified the high cost of production.

Following it at Denham was the last of the three Trafalgar films, *Love from a Stranger*. This was from an Agatha Christie story, so it was British in origin at least, and the music was by Benjamin Britten. But the director, Rowland Lee, the scriptwriter, Frances Marion, and the stars, Basil Rathbone and Ann Harding – the latter at a salary of £12,000 – were all from Hollywood, as well as the costume designer and editor. Rathbone gave a hard, frightening performance as the man who marries rich women and kills them. The film, Schach's best and most successful, was famous for one terrifying moment as the heroine opens the door to escape and finds the killer waiting there for her, a shock cut which produced gasps in the cinemas.

In January 1937 *World Film News* carried a summary of the results of the investigation by Klingender and Legg. Their book *Money Behind the Screen*, which was published the same month, was largely concerned with listing publicly recorded details of the capital, directors, shareholders and indebtedness of companies in the film industry. Among other things it drew attention to the charges on the Schach companies outstanding to the Aldgate Trustees, already published in *Kine Weekly*, namely Capitol £1,100,000, Trafalgar £450,000 and Cecil and Buckingham £150,000 each.[2] Also listed were the many other smaller companies whose borrowing through Aldgate had been reported week by week in *Kine Weekly*. We have already described the collapse of City and Criterion. But many other companies had been formed or expanded in 1935 and 1936, each producing a few pictures, usually of poor quality. Grosvenor Sound Films was a typical case. It was registered in May 1935 with £15,000 capital. Its seven films were produced by Harcourt Templeman and directed by a former journeyman director from Stoll's, Sinclair Hill. The films rose in cost from £18,600 to £32,100 and every one lost from £7,000 to £9,000. By the time the Klingender and Legg report came out they had charges outstanding to Aldgate for £90,000. Other firms owed less, but as the films were of generally poor standard the chances of repayment were small. The only film of any worth was a modest but pleasant adaptation by John Clein of *The Mill on the Floss*. Budgeted at £30,000, thanks to Aldgate it had cost £60,000. There were others. The Anglo-French Edmond T. Gréville registered the £5,000 company British Artistic Films in June 1935; it was wound up in 1937 owing money to Aldgate after only one film, Lupe Velez's *Gypsy Melody*. Franco-London Films and the Garrick Film Company were others. Alexander Esway, a Hungarian who had worked as a director and writer in the German film industry and had been trying to get a foothold in British production for some time, registered Atlantic Film Productions in November 1935 with £1,000 capital and made *Thunder in the City* at Denham in 1936 for United Artists release. With a Hollywood director, writer, cameraman, editor and star, and a story by the American playwright Robert Sherwood about an American businessman in England, it was clearly designed as Esway's ticket to Hollywood. According to Graham Greene it was a strong contender for the title of worst 'English' film of the quarter. The company, with £58,750 outstanding to Aldgate, was heard of no more. There were even more unlikely recipients of Aldgate money, such as Tudor Films, consisting of the Marquis of Ely, a former news cameraman, and the celebrated airman T. Campbell Black. And L. C. Beaumont, son of the Dame of Sark, filmed Victor Hugo's *Toilers of the Sea* on the island with notable lack of success.

Both article and book had repercussions. It has been claimed that copies were read with surprise and alarm by banking and financial firms in the City and actually caused the ensuing crisis in production finance. Certainly money became much harder to raise and production declined, causing considerable unemployment. But two things should be remembered. From the formation of the Moyne Committee early in 1936 to discuss forthcoming changes in quota legislation there was growing uncertainty about the future of British production, and a tendency to wait and see. Secondly, by the end of 1936 sufficient time had elapsed for the poor box-office returns of many of the films concerned to have become known. Even if there had been no report the system would have collapsed as company after company failed to repay its loans. Unfortunately, because of the scandal, far wider interests than the Aldgate Trustees were affected and there was a general withdrawal of support for British production. Indeed, the whole film industry was under a cloud and the response to a share issue by Odeon Cinemas, although nothing to do with production, was so small that Deutsch returned the subscription and waited for a more favourable opportunity. Writing before the Aldgate structure collapsed and the true story became known, Klingender and Legg seem to have been more interested in Korda's heavy borrowing than in the reckless flow of money through Aldgate. His extravagant style and general indebtedness were more obvious targets than the squandering of smaller producers without studios or permanent staffs, and in the collapse of investment confidence which followed he suffered along with those whose output had been negligible, in both quantity and quality, in comparison with his. Many have blamed him for the slump, and strangely little interest has been shown in the part played by Schach and the Aldgate Trustees.

There were to be three more films from Schach's companies. Buckingham, of which he was no longer in control, made its only film in the spring of 1937, over a year after its formation. This was *Jericho*, a Paul Robeson film made with little fanfare by an American producer at Pinewood. In July Schach himself produced *Mademoiselle Docteur* for Grafton at Worton Hall. This was a remake by Gréville of a heavy spy story filmed by Pabst in France. As in the original, Dita Parlo starred, with Erich von Stroheim, fatter and somewhat Americanised, making a disappointing reappearance in Europe. Later in the year another Tom Walls film by Travers, *Second Best Bed*, was made at Shepperton, more or less the mixture as before.

Meanwhile an insurance solicitor, W. C. Crocker, acting on behalf of the Lloyd's underwriters and other insurance interests, conducted an investigation into the production companies in the summer of 1937. The resulting report showed a serious situation. As repayment of the three or four million pounds advanced by the banks for individual films became due it was discovered that many films had failed and some had not even been made. By August production finance had dried up.

At the end of 1937 Capitol owed £1,210,000 to Aldgate, and Bayliss Smith of Aldgate was made chairman of Capitol in place of Schach. The total indebtedness included three Westminster Bank overdrafts of £450,000, £460,000 and £150,000 respectively and £150,000 from the District Bank, all through Aldgate Trustees, and debentures and collateral mortgages of £160,000 from the Equity and Law Life Assurance Society.

By the beginning of 1938 the companies involved were refusing to pay any more on guarantee policies. There was no more production and Schach was finished, after two heady years in his big office in Regent Street. During the following year all the parties prepared their cases for a legal battle over who should bear the losses. Mr Willinck, for Guildhall Insurance Company, instituted proceedings over reinsurance claims against the syndicate of Lloyd's underwriters for whom Crocker acted. Suits involving £2 million and twenty-three companies were prepared. And in February 1939 the Westminster Bank was said to be preparing a £1 million suit against fifteen insurance companies. At the same time Paul Czinner and Elisabeth Bergner prepared to sue Trafalgar over their uncompleted contract.

In May 1939 the Westminster Bank case, which was expected to be sensational, began in the King's Bench Division. Sir Stafford Cripps, acting for the bank, opened a series of actions for £1 million losses out of some £1.5 million loans against the fifteen guarantor companies. These were in two groups. Liverpool Marine and General Insurance Company and Century Insurance were represented by Sir Walter Monckton, and the group under the leadership of the Union Insurance Society of Canton was represented by Willink. The point at issue was who should have been responsible for controlling what Cripps called the 'quite incompetent and inefficient management of the producing companies'. Reference was made to the report produced for the Equity and Law Life Assurance Society, which mentioned 'books in confusion' and an 'absence of effective organisation when finances were provided or of proper control over directors who were able to deal with the money with no apparent regard to the specific purpose for which the loans were made and to use it to pay towards the excessive cost of pictures for which the money had been exhausted'. Reckless over spending on budgets, enormous star contracts, inter-company payments without authority and other irregularities had continued unknown and unchecked until the spring of 1937. The bank seems to have considered that Glanvill's, acting as broker, should have been responsible for supervision. But the group of insurance companies represented by Willink was equally emphatic that the bank itself should have supervised the producing companies' accounts, and put in counter-claims for £382,000 against the bank.

Faced with many months of litigation, everyone involved was relieved when the case was settled out of court eight days later. Schach had already quietly disappeared from the British film industry but Grafton, under Goldsmith, escaped the disaster. As a postscript to the Schach affair, the two Grafton films made before the outbreak of war included one of the best known British films of the thirties, Carol Reed's first big film, *The Stars Look Down*. This had been planned as a Schach-Grune film for Capitol back in 1935, but was eventually made at Denham between March and June 1939, with location work in Cumberland. A bitter story with the message that private ownership of the mines valued profit more highly than men's lives, it was adapted from A. J. Cronin's novel by J. B. Williams and was comparatively sombre and realistic, with scenes down the mine, in the mining village during a lock-out and at the pit-head, ending with a mining disaster. Michael Redgrave and the excellent supporting cast give the good performances which were increasingly recognised as characteristic of Carol Reed's films, and it was his most important work so far.

Schach's impact on British production was as crucial in its way as that of Korda. But unlike Korda he contributed nothing to the industry. Preferring to use visiting European and Hollywood stars and top technicians, he hired established British studios and used their infrastructures, and such British talent as he did employ was taken away from other companies. With his fellow directors Neel, Procter and Baxter, he used the Aldgate system to finance many independent producers and directors whose expensive failures did far more to discredit British production as an investment than the picturesque extravagance of Korda.

J. Arthur Rank

Schach's presence in England had other repercussions. It was partly his films, and his contacts, that enabled C. M. Woolf to break away from Gaumont and set up General Film Distributors with J. Arthur Rank, who was to become a major force in British films. Rank was a millionaire industrialist managing a family business empire, mainly in flour milling. An unusual businessman, he was a Methodist with strong religious views, a teetotaller, and he took an active interest in the Sunday school movement. He was in his forties when, between 1933 and 1939, he was drawn into the film industry. After buying projectors for his own local Sunday school at Reigate, then for those of other churches, he found that the standard of religious film available for them was very poor. In an attempt to remedy this he became involved in the production of some religious films which he hoped would be of better quality.[3] Before long he was taking tentative steps into the feature film industry. Shrewd and cautious and already at home in high finance, within ten years he was to dominate the industry. The best known of all British film financiers, he was a big man with a quiet demeanour and was a contrast not only to the Hollywood moguls but to most others in the British film industry. Like the Ostrers he was a financier first and foremost. The first of the many features he was to back seemed to promise some concern for the moral and spiritual content of the films, but in fact, despite his own personal piety, his interest in films seems to have been simply as product and not to have extended to their subject matter.

He was introduced by John Corfield, whom he had met through the production of religious films, and who had hitherto been on the fringes of the film industry, to the multimillionairess widow of the Calcutta jute magnate Sir David Yule. Lady Yule, casual, patriotic and somewhat eccentric, saw in films a possible way of promoting the British way of life. In July 1934 the three of them formed a private £6,000 company, British National Films. Major Jack Courtauld of Ealing, where they originally thought of working, joined them briefly. Distribution by Gaumont-British was arranged through C. M. Woolf.

Early in 1935, at the B & D studios and on location at Whitby, in Yorkshire, the company made *Turn of the Tide*. Based on a novel, this was a wholesome story of reconciliation between two rival families in a fishing village. It was directed by Norman Walker, a useful if not distinguished director who had been in films for some years. Somewhat slow, the film was made with such unusual realism in its locations, beautifully filmed by Franz Planer, and in its attempt to depict British working people in authentic settings that it was greeted with delight as a film in the new documentary style. Graham Greene even compared it favourably with *Man of Aran*. It won third prize at the Venice Film Festival, and trade reviews suggested that here at last art and box office were one. At a cost of only £30,000 it should easily have made a profit.

It was not trade shown until October 1935, for release in April 1936, and was handled by Gaumont-British with a marked lack of enthusiasm. In fact Louis Levy in his autobiography maintains that it was hardly shown in Britain at all, and even then on very unfavourable terms. Legend has it that this experience led Rank to move into film distribution on his own account. But in fact Woolf had already left Gaumont-British as early as June 1935, long before *Turn of the Tide* was ready for distribution, when he and Rank had registered the private company which was to form the hub of their activities, General Film Distributors. For Max Schach's first British film *Abdul the Damned* had considerable success, and the output of Schach's numerous associates, and also that of Herbert Wilcox, promised a source of films which would enable Woolf to branch out on his own. It was Schach who introduced Woolf to big business and real money, in the shape of the international banker Paul Lindenburg, and GFD was registered with the large capital of £270,000 with Lindenburg, Rank and Schach's colleague from Capitol, L. A. Neel, on the board. It was two months later that Schach registered his second Capitol company, Capitol Corporation, to make films for distribution by GFD.

At the same time Rank took a further step into production by venturing into studio ownership. Charles Boot, of the large Sheffield engineering and building concern Henry Boot and Son, had long wanted to build a first-class studio in Britain, and indeed had been involved in an abortive £3 million plan in early 1928. In May 1935 he bought a large area of parkland with a country house called Heatherden Hall, later called Iver Hall, at Pinewood, Iver Heath, Buckinghamshire, not far from the estate at Denham bought a few months earlier by Korda. He also bought an old liner which was being broken up, the *Mauretania*, to use the interior furnishings in the mansion. The latter had been built in the early twenties. Richard Norton has described the huge indoor swimming pool as luxury in the worst possible taste. With comfortable accommodation and a restaurant, tennis and squash courts and gardens, the house was to become a 'country club' hotel of great style, and the best studio in the country was to be built in the grounds, with a 50-acre lot. In August Pinewood Studios was registered as a private £150,000 company, owned equally by Boot and Rank. British National, now a £100,000 company, planned to use one of the stages, leaving the others for hire to other people. Boot went to America for equipment and expertise, and construction began at the end of 1935. When the studio was finished it had 72,490 square feet of floor space in five stages, the three larger ones having tanks. It generated its own electricity and used Western Electric sound. A compact studio, it was carefully planned by studio manager James Sloan to be suitable for hire and had its dressing rooms, camera, cutting and projection facilities and offices designed as units, with good centralised property stores and workshops and a system of covered ways, in recognition of the British climate.

Herbert Wilcox was invited to come into the scheme but at first declined to do so (see under Wilcox). As related elsewhere, however, he registered a small company of his own with the intention of making films for GFD. The studio company was backed by Rank, and C. M. Woolf and the paper magnate Lord Portal, another big financier, were on the board. GFD began operations in November with the distribution of three rather indifferent British films.

In the course of the next few months the situation changed radically. Because Wilcox's studio was burnt down he decided to join Rank after all, and an important new grouping took shape through Woolf's involvement with the American company Universal Pictures. Universal's answer to the problem of acquiring British quota had been to buy Australian, Indian and Canadian films of no value to British exhibitors at all. After a visit from Carl Laemmle in 1930 the new managing director, S. F. Ditcham, had announced plans for production in Britain, but the only film made was *Lloyd of the C.I.D.*, a lurid thriller in twelve two-reel episodes directed at high speed at Cricklewood by a visiting Canadian executive from Universal. In Hollywood in due course the aged Carl Laemmle Sr was obliged to sell out. Woolf, seeing an opportunity to extend his renting operations to America, began negotiations with the American financier J. Cheever Cowdin, President of Standard Capital Corporation, who had an option on the company. In the spring of 1936 a new holding company was formed, Universal Corporation Inc., whose board included Cowdin and the American film financier Dr Giannini, and Rank and his associate L. W. Farrow, who was a chartered accountant and a director of many companies; Woolf and Wilcox represented B & D. The old Universal renting subsidiary in London disappeared and Ditcham joined the board of GFD. American Universal films were to be handled by GFD in this country, and some of the GFD films were to be distributed by Universal in America. Wilcox, now with a half share in the studio, as usual had his eye on distribution in America. In March General Cinema Finance Corporation was registered in Britain, a £1,225,000 company formed to take over 90 per cent of the issued share capital of GFD. It was backed by the group of powerful capitalists which now included Lord Luke, whose interests extended all over the world, as well as Lindenburg, Portal, Rank and Farrow. Similarly, the GFD board, under the chairmanship of Portal until it was taken over by Rank in April 1937, now included Lindenburg, Farrow, Woolf and his brother Maurice Woolf, Ditcham and L. A. Neel. Rank eventually succeeded Portal as chairman of GCFC, also, in April 1938.

In all these financial moves the question of what films were going to be made seems to have played very little part. The capital of Pinewood was increased to £300,000 and the studio was opened in September 1936 under the managing directorship of Richard Norton of B & D, which was now the largest shareholder. The directors included Rank, Boot and his son-in-law Spencer Reis, with Wilcox, Norton and others representing B & D, and John Corfield representing British National. The original plan for British National and Wilcox to provide most of the production at the new studio, however, was changed. British National soon parted company with the others, and the agreement with Wilcox lasted only until April 1937. He then split with Woolf for a second time and departed for Denham to make *Victoria the Great* for RKO release and, at last, success in America. It fell to Woolf, through backing and distribution agreements, and to Norton as managing director to keep the studio full. No greater contrast can be imagined than the single-minded money man from the Midlands and the elegant and amusing aristocrat, and they disliked each other intensely.

As for British National, its later history did not fulfil Lady Yule's high hopes. Its second film, a naive adaptation of a Sapper story, had been made in late 1935 at the B & D studio and on location in West Africa. Nothing else was produced for a year, but when Pinewood was opened *The Street Singer*, a routine show-business story, was made there as a vehicle for a popular ballad singer Arthur Tracy, who had adopted this as his stage name. Early in 1937 Rank resigned from British National, Corfield resigned from the Pinewood board and Lady Yule withdrew from Pinewood, selling out to Rank. The companies went their separate ways. British National had a small and unremarkable output under Corfield's management, produced with hired staff at Welwyn or Walton and handled by ABPC. A handful of thrillers included David Macdonald's creepy *Dead Men Tell No Tales*, a story full of amazing coincidences, which had some success. Towards the end of 1938 there were plans to hire the old Whitehall studios at Boreham Wood to make films of greater importance, although at just over 13,000 square feet the studio was rather small. A modest spy film, a vehicle for the popular BBC 'rag and bone man' Syd Walker (with his catch phrase 'Wot would *yew* do, chums?'), and Old Mother Riley and a Tommy Trinder film were made there by British National. More interesting, after the outbreak of war Michael Powell and Emeric Pressburger continued their Denham collaboration on the successful Columbia film *The Spy in Black* with another spy film starring Conrad Veidt and Valerie Hobson, *Contraband*, made under the aegis of British National.

Meanwhile Norton was busy finding tenants for the studios at Pinewood, and Woolf was busy expanding GFD, which was now the leading British independent renter. In addition to films from Pinewood, Woolf handled all the Capitol and Cecil films from Schach and several independent productions by Richard Wainwright,* a producer whose films were distinguished by good casts and greater sophistication than usual and, although not widely known, were greatly admired by a select few. Films made at Pinewood not for GFD, but Paramount quota, accounted for about a quarter of the films made there before the war. They were produced by Anthony Havelock-Allan, as they had previously been at the Elstree studio of B & D. In 1938 Norton, Rank and Paul Czinner also formed a small company, Orion Film Productions, to make a major film starring Elisabeth Bergner, *Stolen Life*. This weepy 'woman's picture' was made under an agreement with Paramount. An incredible story adapted from a novel, it gave Bergner a double role as the wicked twin who steals her sister's lover, marries him and betrays him, and the good twin who, when her sister is drowned, tries to assume her identity as his wife. Its appeal was to a wider audience than Bergner's other films and it was very successful, consolidating the reputation of Michael Redgrave, who had recently come to the fore in *The Lady Vanishes*. Like Leslie Howard and Robert Donat, Redgrave personified the quiet, kind, upper-middle-class Englishman with just a hint of sadness, and stood out from the many neat, stereotyped and slightly effeminate West End actors of the previous few years. The film was glamorously produced by first-class technicians and like the other three Czinner films had music by William Walton. The technical standard of production was far higher than that of the dozen or so other Paramount films.

Most of the other films made at Pinewood were specifically for GFD distribution. Wilcox made seven films there before he left to make *Victoria the Great*. Jack Buchanan made four in little over six months. His six early productions for Wilcox and one for Schach had made him one of the most popular British films stars of the early thirties, and in February 1937 he registered his own company, Jack Buchanan Productions, with a capital of £100,500 and backed by Rank and Woolf. He had now been on the stage for twenty-five years, and wished to turn his attention to production, planning to appear in only some of the films and then not always to sing and dance. *Smash and Grab* was a crime comedy in which he, as a detective, with Elsie Randolph as his wife, unmasks a jewel thief. It was strongly influenced by *The Thin Man* and was written and directed by Americans. *The Sky's the Limit* was made immediately afterwards and in it Buchanan returned to his former style of musical comedy with great success, sharing the direction with another American, Lee Garmes. *Sweet Devil* was, in fact, the only one in which he did not appear. Immediately after it *Break the News* completed the quartet, and Buchanan returned to Elstree and ABPC. This last film was an expensive production with an auspicious gathering of talents.

* Americans who had long been associated with renting and exhibition in Britain, Wainwright and his father had been connected with the production of Anatole Litvak's British film *Sleeping Car* in 1932, and a scene-by-scene remake of the German *Emil and the Detectives*. In 1936 Universal-Wainwright Studios was registered to make films for Universal. Independent productions followed, the last being *Kate Plus Ten* in 1938, made at Denham, in which Jack Hulbert played a straight part as a detective in an Edgar Wallace story.

Produced and directed by René Clair, elegantly set and dressed by Lazare Meerson and Rene Hubert, it co-starred Maurice Chevalier and Buchanan as two chorus boys (in their late forties surely a trifle mature) who stage a phoney murder in order to get some publicity. A remake of a French film, it had an ingenious plot and the two stars were both funny in their own ways, yet somehow neither they nor Clair were at their best. Perhaps Chevalier's imminent execution as a murderer when the trick misfires was rather a hollow laugh. On the whole Buchanan's venture into independent production had not been a success.

Several producers made single independent films at Pinewood. One was the Buckingham production, *Jericho*. Another was *Kicking the Moon Around*, a bright show-business story with a line-up of variety stars by Walter Forde. Vogue Film Productions had been formed in 1934 to make pictures for Pathé at Walton, but little was done until it was resuscitated in 1937 for this production by Forde, whose second film for Schach had fallen through and who had not yet rejoined Balcon at Ealing. A more important film was *The Mikado*, made by Josef Somlo.* The latter was a Hungarian, somewhat older than the Kordas, who had worked in films since about 1907 and since 1919 in Germany, where he and Herman Fellner had started their own company, Felsom. Coming to Britain as a refugee in 1935, Somlo joined Victor Saville as the latter was beginning independent production with Korda. In 1937 he joined Rank and Woolf. An agreement to film Gilbert and Sullivan operas was signed in September 1937 between Rank's General Cinema Finance Corporation, the D'Oyly Carte Opera Company and Geoffrey Toye, a Gilbert and Sullivan expert and the conductor and former managing director of Covent Garden opera house. The latter was to be in charge of production. G & S Films was registered in February 1938 with a capital of £1,000, and Somlo and Norton were on the board with Woolf, Rank, Ditcham and Barrington Gain. *The Mikado* was the opera chosen, and Toye went to Hollywood to engage Victor Schertzinger, the director of Grace Moore's operatic film *One Night of Love*, and the American tenor Kenny Baker. The film was made in the summer. Yum-Yum was played by the British musical star Jean Colin, but the rest of the cast were D'Oyly Carte regulars. There were some song changes and bridging narrative titles were introduced, but the performances were traditional and much of the familiar stage business treasured by Gilbert and Sullivan fans was retained. Shot in Technicolor, it was a designer's film and the spare, clean art deco lines of sets and costumes, with stylised flowers, trees and clouds, were dazzlingly pretty in gold, pink and orange. The film was yet another expensive failure. Although a visual *tour de force*, it seemed slow and lacking in shape and the humour was less effective without the interplay of actors and devotees in the living theatre. The plan to film Gilbert and

---

* See under Korda. Somlo was also connected, through his associate J. G. Saunders, with Fanfare Pictures, registered in August 1936 with £2,000 capital, for which Thorold Dickinson directed his first film, *The High Command*.

Sullivan operas had been a policy decision in accordance with the new style of management, and the film had been set up very much in this spirit. It seemed to have been the wrong decision, and no more operas were filmed. Three modestly priced G & S films followed quickly. Turning its back on the exotic, the company adopted the motto 'Bring Britain to the Screen'. Produced by Somlo for GFD after Pinewood was closed, the films were made at Denham in the spring and early summer of 1939. The second, by Brian Desmond Hurst, who had been under contract at Denham with nothing to do, was *On the Night of the Fire*, which hovered between realism and Grand Guignol. Its unlikely story and characterisation were extravagantly attacked by Graham Greene, who hounded this very uneven director as vigorously as he promoted Carol Reed and Thorold Dickinson. The latter, who had been unit director on *The Mikado* after his return from filming the Spanish Civil War, directed the last and best G & S film, *The Arsenal Stadium Mystery*. This turned a routine newspaper serial into a lively and imaginative whodunit with a footballing background.

The most picturesque of the producers who used Pinewood was another Hungarian, Gabriel Pascal. He has been described by Lawrence Langner, an American, as a smallish man with a roly-poly body and a vivid imagination[4] and by the American playwright S. N. Behrman as mesmeric, an optimistic liar but one with a real love of art – 'short, thick-set . . . what he looked like and talked like was a gypsy'.[5] Yet another itinerant film maker from Europe, Pascal romanced vividly about his youth. He also liked to repeat a story of how he had met George Bernard Shaw when swimming at Antibes in the twenties, and how Shaw had promised that one day he would allow him to film one of his plays. In May 1935 Pascal arrived in London with no money but lots of cheek and took Shaw up on the offer.*

Shaw's original disinclination to allow a word of his plays to be changed during filming had been slightly modified by the failure of the two early BIP films, but he was not keen on the medium and had turned down many requests for film rights. *Pygmalion*, which was to be Pascal's triumph, had already been filmed twice† on the Continent but Shaw had nothing to do with these productions. Pascal's achievement was to introduce changes, and to persuade Shaw himself to make changes, which would preserve both spirit and letter of the play and yet translate it to the screen. The association of the great man of letters and the film maker with his funny English and wild enthusiasms was a strange and puzzling one, but Norton affirms Pascal's genuine admiration for Shaw's work and both Valerie Pascal and Shaw's secretary Blanche Patch have written that Shaw considered Pascal a genius. He tried in vain to teach his impetuous friend some of his own business acumen.

* According to Valerie Pascal's biography, he had previously been in England for the production of the Pola Negri film *Street of Lost Souls*, a title sometimes given to *The Woman he Scorned* (q.v.), but his name did not appear in connection with it.

† By Erich Engel in Germany in 1934 and by Ludwig Berger in Holland in 1937.

It was some time before Pascal could raise the money for production, and in the meanwhile he made two quota films for American companies. Finally, in the spring of 1937, he secured the support of Richard Norton. The financier Nicholas Davenport formed a syndicate which raised £10,000, Norton joined the board of Pascal Productions, whose capital was increased to £25,000, and the film went into production at Pinewood for GFD distribution early in 1938, directed by Anthony Asquith. Shaw stipulated that Pascal should have complete artistic and production control. Originally put on in 1914, the play was performed in modern dress for the film. As usual, many people contributed to the adaptation and scenario although the finished film credited only Shaw, Cecil Lewis and W. P. Lipscomb, but Pascal himself was the one who was able to persuade Shaw to accept the many changes which turned the play into a brilliantly successful film. Fourteen new scenes were introduced, half of them with new dialogue and half of them with no dialogue. These included the important bath scene with its delightful music and the big reception, with a completely new character, the diplomat Karpathy. Shots of the characters in the London streets gave the film an agreeable sense of place. Most important of all, the happy ending, which was not altogether to Shaw's liking, effectively turned it into a romance and was undoubtedly a major factor in its success. Settings, camerawork, editing, supporting cast and the score by Arthur Honegger combined to make it an outstanding film and certainly one of the best from a British studio during the thirties, a success with both critics and public. Eliza was played by Wendy Hiller, who had become a star on the stage with her performance in *Love on the Dole* and had already played Eliza at the Malvern Shaw festival in 1936. Professor Higgins was played by Leslie Howard, who also co-directed with Asquith. Woolf had already contemplated backing films which Howard would produce and registered United Players Productions with him in 1935, but direction was a new departure for Howard. *Pygmalion* also marked a turning point in the hitherto halting career of Anthony Asquith, who after a brilliant start in silent films had been assigned to one unsatisfactory project after another. A shy, self-effacing and cultivated man, he seems to have had no strong sense of direction in the early thirties and neither Balcon, Korda nor Schach, to all of whom he had been under contract, had realised his potential, perhaps misled by his upper-class manner.

Pascal, also, had found his vocation. Clearly more Shaw films would be a good idea, and lengthy negotiations went on in Hollywood over *The Devil's Disciple*, possibly starring Clark Gable. In the end Pascal went ahead with *Major Barbara*, again with Wendy Hiller, this time cast opposite Rex Harrison. It was in production when war broke out and was not shown until 1941. Pascal developed an extravagant habit of getting details right at any cost, even if the audience would not notice or even see them. This, like his statement that adapting Shaw's plays for a world-wide audience was a task given to him by God,[6] suggests a fervent and not entirely rational person very different from his compatriot, the self-controlled and responsible Korda.

After Gaumont-British Distributors closed down early in 1937 Woolf was reconciled with Gaumont and took over the distribution of the whole of the Gaumont-British and Gainsborough output. When Shepherd's Bush itself closed in April 1937 its production moved to Pinewood. Only four Gaumont films were made there, however, and the new studio itself closed down at the end of 1938. Badly timed, it had been difficult to keep it fully occupied during the slump of 1937 and 1938, and only about forty feature films had been made there, less than ten of them of top rank. One of Norton's stratagems for survival was a production co-operative, Pinebrook, which was registered with £100 capital in January 1938. The plan was to make six fairly cheap films for Paramount and GFD. Later in the year a similar arrangement was set up in association with Ealing (q.v.) called CAPAD, or Co-operative Association of Producers and Distributors. The directors were Michael Balcon, Reg Baker and Stephen Courtauld for Ealing and Norton, Havelock-Allan and Rank for Pinewood. Meanwhile the general situation continued to be difficult. The financial problems of Korda and his studio at Denham were making his principal backers, the Prudential company, increasingly anxious. At the end of 1938 a company called Denham and Pinewood Studios was formed to take Denham over from him, leaving him free to produce. The board included Norton, Rank, Boot, Reis and Crammond from the Rank side and Sir Connop Guthrie and E. H. George of London Film Productions and a representative of the Prudential. Pinewood was closed and production, including the end of the Pinewood programme, moved to a Denham no longer controlled by Korda.

Notwithstanding the closure of Pinewood, Rank acquired yet another studio early in 1939, not because he needed the space but to prevent either Maxwell or one of the American companies from having it. He bought it for a rumoured £200,000, and let it to the government as a store on a 21-year lease at £10,000 a year. This was Amalgamated Studios at Elstree. Paul Soskin and his uncle Simon Soskin, originally from Russia, had formed the Niksos Trust in October 1935 with £2,000, and acquired land at Elstree for what they announced would be a £500,000 studio. Amalgamated Studios was formed with £50,000 capital in November and plans were made, reputedly for 140,000 square feet of floor space. A studio was built, compact and well designed in units, mortgaged to the builder Robert McAlpine and Sons to raise the cost of construction, but the Soskins were unable to finish equipping it. It seems to have cost far more than expected, and by the time it was finished film production was in decline. The builders foreclosed and a receiver was appointed in the summer of 1938. Estimates of the size varied, but when it eventually opened after the war it had 80,000 square feet in seven stages, two of them new.

The Rank interests now owned three of the largest studios in Britain. Production continued at Denham and in July 1939 Legeran Films was registered as a £1,000 company. On the board, Zoltan Korda came together with Rank, Woolf, Barrington Gain and Harold Boxall. It was intended that Boxall and Josef Somlo should be in charge of production at Denham, making films for GFD. However, war broke out and plans were suspended.

The various activities and interests of Max Schach, now vanished from the scene; of Herbert Wilcox, now moving on to RKO's sphere of operation and a foothold in Hollywood; of the Hon. Captain Richard Norton, coming by way of the B & D commitment to manage Pinewood; and of C. M. Woolf and the American Universal company – all had played their part in forming a conglomerate of great potential power. The last of the moves which were eventually to make Rank the dominating force in the British film industry was the appointment of him and Farrow to the board of Odeon Theatres in January 1939. Rank's interest in exhibition was not new. In the last few months of 1936 plans for a circuit of about a hundred cinemas had led to the registration of Cinema Theatres (GCFC) Ltd, as a £150,000 holding company associated with GFD, Lord Portal being chairman and Woolf managing director. The venture came to nothing at the time but, when Odeon was looking for additional finance in 1938 for further expansion, GCFC subscribed heavily to a debenture issue and Rank and Farrow joined Deutsch's board. The Odeon headquarters moved from Birmingham to London in July 1939 and the transformation of a small provincial business into an important national institution was complete, and Rank found himself with interests in all three branches of the industry.

Whether Rank would have dominated the British film world as he later did had circumstances not conspired to remove any possible rival during the early years of the war is not easy to say. Maxwell was to die in 1940, Deutsch in 1941 and Woolf in 1942, and Isidore Ostrer retired from the film industry in 1941. Rank's progress in the industry in the thirties was not so much a deliberate attempt to take it by storm as a step by step response to changing events, drawing him further and further along the road to power. Woolf was almost as unlikely a partner for Rank as he was for Norton, but the partnership was important. For, if Woolf provided the knowledge of the film world which Rank at first lacked, it was Rank's business background which determined the new approach to film making. These high-powered financial magnates approached film from a different standpoint from that of someone like Korda, for example. The latter raised money because he wanted to make films. They, on the other hand, looked around for people to make films because they had the money. They treated films as they would any other commodity; they organised the backing and took it for granted that the talent would be there when required. In his biography of Rank, Alan Wood quotes John Davis, the Rank executive, as saying: '. . . all businesses are fundamentally the same. The engineers, technicians and creative workers look after the product. The accountant co-ordinates the whole on sound lines.'[7] But sound business is not necessarily synonymous with artistic excellence and, although the films made in connection with the Rank and Woolf interests at this time were very varied, from an artistic point of view they did not generally justify this attitude.

Alexander Korda

Korda's new studio at Denham opened in May 1936 and for a brief period it looked as if London Films could do no wrong. At the time it was the biggest studio in England, with seven stages, in grounds of 165 acres through which ran the River Colne. It had 118,800 square feet of floor space, with eighteen cutting rooms. Designed by the American art director and designer Jack Okey, who had been brought over from Hollywood as technical consultant, it was modern and well equipped with its own labs, film vaults and special process department. It used Western Electric wide-range sound, generated its own electricity and employed some 2,000 people. According to a later survey it was very spread out, haphazard and inconvenient, with long communications between offices, dressing rooms, workshops and stages.[8] Nevertheless the grand Korda manner flowered here with the mansion at the heart of it, and there seemed to be a general feeling that nothing was too good for the people making films. Such a large studio needed outside producers as well as London Films to keep it occupied and Korda was to spend more and more of his time in administration and finding tenants. By the end of the year thirteen films had been made, or at least started, only three of them Korda films. All except two from Schach and two from Twentieth Century were distributed by United Artists and its new head, Dr Giannini, was reported to be much in favour of British production. A number of the independent films made at the studio had Aldgate backing.

The first film on the floor was the Schach musical comedy *Southern Roses*, but Korda began London Films production himself by personally directing a major prestige picture, the last he was to direct in the thirties. This was *Rembrandt*, again starring Laughton.

Laughton, who had made four important Hollywood films since *The Private Life of Henry VIII*, in most of which he played unsympathetic roles, required careful casting. A powerful personality, his obesity limited the parts he could play and he had many mannerisms – the mutter, the jerkily averted head, the side-squinting eye, the closed mouth in the pudgy face as the audience waits and waits for the words to come. Korda was one of the only producers in the British film industry of sufficient stature to build stars and control images, and in this film he secured a performance of great dignity as the ageing genius from his temperamental and difficult star. Written by the eminent German playwright Carl Zuckmayer, like the Henry VIII film it was episodic, but slow and reverent where the other was frivolous, with a number of big speeches expressing Rembrandt's philosophy. Great trouble was taken to recreate the look of seventeenth-century Holland, and the sets and camerawork provide many memorable images. The sumptuous and beautiful appearance of Korda films was due to his cameramen, here Georges Périnal and Robert Krasker, to his designers and costume designers and above all to his brother Vincent. The critics were respectful and according to Tabori the film made a small profit, but it was more a *succès d'estime* than a money earner.

Although the next production, *Men Are Not Gods*, was a comparatively minor affair with a novelettish story, directed by the Austrian film writer Walter Reisch on his way to Hollywood after fleeing Nazi Europe, it was in fact a good box-office picture which made money. Much more important to the company, however, was *Knight Without Armour*, one of their most expensive and extravagant films of all. So expensive was it that once again, although extremely successful both with the critics and the public, it was not profitable.

This film was the high-water for Korda since arriving in England in 1931, a sensational production made in his own fine studio. Planned and largely finished before the financial crisis of 1937, it was characteristic of Korda at the height of his success and optimism. It had become fashionable to visit Denham, and society people, diplomats and celebrities of all kinds came to see and be seen. Trouble lay ahead, but during the second half of 1936 all seemed well. Korda assembled talent from far and wide for this film, which was in production by September 1936. Marlene Dietrich, one of the biggest stars in the world at the time, was paid £80,000. She played a Russian countess escaping after the Russian Revolution with the help of a young Englishman, played by Robert Donat, in an adaptation by the important American scenarist Frances Marion of James Hilton's novel. Dietrich, and the production as a whole, received enormous publicity. The outstanding director Jacques Feyder was accompanied by cameraman Harry Stradling and art director Lazare Meerson, who had both been with him on *La Kermesse Héroïque*, and together they conveyed the chaotic atmosphere of revolutionary Russia. Miklos Rozsa, a newly arrived Hungarian composer, joined the Korda entourage. The story of escape and romantic love, its politics ambiguous, gave Donat a perfect part. Handsome in his furs, chivalrous and protective, he was even admired by the critic Graham Greene, who was usually obsessively critical of Korda films. Dietrich, posing rather than acting, her beautiful thin face too worldly and invulnerable to bring out the intimacy and tenderness of the romantic escape, gave a performance which was not so much understated as expressionless, but her presence invested the production with great glamour.

Outsiders using the studio at this time included Max Schach, who followed his musical comedy with the Tauber film *Land Without Music*, the important Bergner film *Dreaming Lips* and then *Love from a Stranger*. Twentieth Century-Fox finished *Wings of the Morning* there and at the end of the year began *Under the Red Robe*. Four independent films made in close association with Korda were the two produced by Erich Pommer and two by Victor Saville. Film makers were flocking to the studio.

Erich Pommer had left UFA in 1934 and gone to Hollywood. He came to Britain in 1935 and together with Korda set up Pendennis Production Company, which was registered as a £10,000 company in March 1936, to make films for United Artists release at Denham. The first, *Fire Over England*, was set up by Korda himself as a big international production but produced by Pommer, with the Hollywood director William K. Howard and the important Chinese-American cameraman James Wong Howe. A spirited swashbuckling adventure story about the Armada, it starred Flora Robson as a regal and lonely Queen Elizabeth and Laurence Olivier and Vivien Leigh, both idle under their Korda contracts, as the young lovers. It was a glossy and professional picture in the Hollywood manner, with dramatic sets and magnificent costumes, glamorous highlighting of close shots and some carefully composed 'art' shots like the one with sunlight streaming through four long thin windows and falling fan-shaped on the lovers. Long introductory titles sought to give it an appearance of historical seriousness and even contemporary relevance, with its references to freedom, although in fact it was criticised in some quarters for falsifying history. Extensive model work by Ned Mann's department was used in the Armada sequences and a panorama of Lisbon.

Later in the year another American director, Tim Whelan, who had already made several films in Britain, embarked on the second Pendennis film, *Farewell Again*, once more with James Wong Howe. A story by Wolfgang Wilhelm based on a recent newspaper item, it told the stories of some of the people on board a troopship when, arriving on leave after a tour of duty abroad, it is ordered to turn round and return after only a few hours in port. Flora Robson and Leslie Banks headed a large cast in a long, fragmentary 'interwoven lives' film which the multinational unit managed to make true-blue and class-conscious, full of British clichés and sentimental patriotism.

The association with Victor Saville was slightly different. Saville's last film for Balcon had been made at the beginning of 1936. The Hungarian producer Josef Somlo, who had known Korda in the early days, had arrived in England as a refugee in 1935. Somlo Films was registered in December as a £10,000 company, and in April 1936 Victor Saville Productions was registered, also with a capital of £10,000 and with Saville, Somlo and J. G. Saunders on the board. The films were made at Denham and distributed through United Artists. Backing, staff and studio space was provided by Korda, but not active participation in production.

The first film, *Dark Journey*, was made between July and November 1936. Although directed by Saville himself it was the most influenced by Korda for it had been concocted by the studio as a vehicle for one of their contract stars, Conrad Veidt. An obsure plot about a German spy in the First World War, with Vivien Leigh as a double agent masquerading as a couturier in Stockholm, it was made by Korda writers and technicians but was disappointing technically and in every other way. The next film, however, made with a writer, a cameraman and a designer who had all been at Islington with him, was a true Saville film. Begun immediately after the other one in November, it was a mild comedy poking fun at the little hypocrisies of small-town politics. *Storm in a Teacup* was from a play which James Barrie had based on a German original, and had transformed into an affectionate look at a real issue in ordinary everyday Scotland. The rather stock theatrical characters played by Vivien Leigh, Rex Harrison and Cecil Parker were made believable by polished acting and direction. Modest and unassuming in comparison with Korda's films, it was highly successful.

Two other outside productions were made at Denham in the late summer of 1936. One was *Thunder in the City*, produced by Alexander Esway with Aldgate money (q.v.). *Moonlight Sonata*, made at the same time by Lothar Mendes operating as Pall Mall, registered in March 1936 as a £10,000 company, was little more than an excuse for the aged pianist and statesman Paderewski, looking a noble ruin of a great man, to play the piano a few times and walk through a part, making a few ponderous philosophic pronouncements.

By now Korda's status as a producer of world-class films was different from that of any other producer in Britain. The more European film makers arrived at Denham, the more eagerly his films embraced English subjects, English history and literature, traditions and even prejudices. He was naturalised in late 1936. He had always insisted that if a film were to succeed it had to be produced to a standard that would satisfy an international audience, and this was expensive. By May 1936 the company had losses of £330,842. His way of running the company, like own lifestyle, was lavish. But the resulting films and razzmatazz had got him a better foothold in the difficult American market than any other British company. In August 1936 Dr Giannini was reported as saying that Korda's latest films had been booked by 10,000 cinemas in America, although the figure given by Murray Silverstone early in 1937 is actually considerably lower than this. But Korda was still not satisfied with the terms of distribution and had some way to go. With the opening of Denham things looked up and in October 1937 a small profit of £35,839 was announced. Had he been able to get the more favourable terms he needed earlier, Korda might well have succeeded where others had failed, and obtained a market big enough to sustain top-class production.

But it was too late. The company was heavily in debt when the Aldgate scandal broke and in the ensuing collapse of investment confidence in British production the essential difference between him and the Aldgate producers counted for little. In December 1936 the board of London Film Productions consisted of himself as chairman and managing director, Sir Connop Guthrie of United Artists, J. R. Sutro, E. Stevinson of C. T. Bowring & Co. (Insurance), and H. A. Holmes. £428,700 of the authorised capital of £825,000 had been issued. £333,549 of this was in 6 per cent cumulative participating preference ordinary shares, of which £250,000 were held by the Prudential Assurance Company, and £95,250 in deferred ordinary shares of which £1,250 were held by the same company. £50,000 of the deferred ordinary shares were held by Lloyds Bank and £16,250 by the Midland Bank. Other major shareholders were the Sutro family and C. T. Bowring. Big debenture issues and loans had been made, and the company's total registered indebtedness at 31 December 1936 was £1,794,222.

While Korda was persuading insurance and banking firms to make conventional investments and loans, Schach was, as we have seen, operating in quite a different way. The money went to producers with little share capital of their own and little in the way of assets. Korda's assets were put at £2,229,973 at the end of 1936, and although he was notoriously overoptimistic about the value of completed and uncompleted films – a hopelessly bad film could stay on the shelf for ever as a book asset – London Films had a large capital and owned studios, equipment and the whole structure of a very large company. In the general alarm, however, his backers saw the debts, listened to tales of wastefulness and became restive.

The Aldgate collapse harmed the company in another way, too. With the disappearance of Aldgate money most of the tenant producers vanished. After the defection of Pommer to Elstree later in the year only Saville and Twentieth Century remained to help London Films make use of the studio. The company itself was busy in 1937, although most of the films were comparatively minor ones apart from *I, Claudius*, which was abandoned early in the year, and nothing on the scale of *Knight Without Armour* was attempted.

The Squeaker, from an Edgar Wallace play which was on in London at the time, was directed by William K. Howard and featured Alastair Sim in his stage part as a journalist, and the American star Edmund Lowe. *The Return of the Scarlet Pimpernel* was in production by May. Adrian Brunel's version is that Korda wanted to use the title for a sequel to the earlier Pimpernel film, but that there was no story until Brunel and Arthur Wimperis wrote one.[9] It is true that Baroness Orczy did not write a novel under this title, but the story is essentially that of her novel *The Triumph of the Scarlet Pimpernel*, and had already been filmed by Wilcox under that name. The director Hans Schwartz, a refugee from Germany to whom Korda rashly offered the hospitality of his studio, had at one time been highly thought of but in this case needed tactful guidance from Brunel as associate producer. Produced by Arnold Pressburger, the film was extremely decorative but had neither the romance nor the suspense of the earlier film. Sophie Stewart and Barry K. Barnes lacked the exotic grace of Merle Oberon as the Pimpernel's French wife and the aristocratic authority of Leslie Howard, and Francis Lister was a far cry from the snarling villainy of Raymond Massey's Chauvelin. The next film, *Paradise for Two*, a rare musical, was produced by Gunther Stapenhorst, a former U-boat commander and a voluntary exile from Germany recently engaged by Korda as an associate producer. Later in the year he started work on *The Challenge*, which had been in preparation since the summer of 1936. This was a new version, written by the recently arrived Hungarian Emeric Pressburger, of Luis Trenker's silent film about Whymper's ascent of the Matterhorn in 1865. Whymper was played by Robert Douglas. Trenker, who had specialised in German mountain films, directed the magnificent Alpine sequences but the film was spoilt by Milton Rosmer's pedestrian direction of sequences shot in the studio and the film was criticised for the liberties it took with history.

The two most important productions of 1937 were produced by Korda himself. *The Divorce of Lady X*, started in July, was in Technicolor and was planned as a glamorous production to mark the return of Merle Oberon, who had made several important Hollywood pictures on loan since appearing in *The Scarlet Pimpernel* three years before, and was now a top international star. Not the usual 'fancy dress' colour film of the time, it was a sophisticated comedy in a rich contemporary setting, but it lacked the sparkle it should have had. Ralph Richardson's wry performance as her husband stole the show from Merle Oberon and her co-star Laurence Olivier. *The Drum*, also in colour, was from an adventure story about a young Indian Prince and an uprising on the North-West Frontier of India in the nineteenth century. This was specially written by the novelist A. E. W. Mason for Sabu.[10] Directed by Zoltan Korda and designed by Vincent Korda, it was a popular and artistic success, winning the City of Venice Cup at the Film Festival in September 1938 and grossing £170,000 in America alone. This film, *Sanders of the River* and *The Four Feathers* (see below), all directed by Zoltan Korda, have latterly been called Korda's 'imperial' films. He was, of course, not the only producer to realise that the history of the British Empire, like the history of the Wild West, offered scope for films with magnificent scenery, picturesque costumes, mass action scenes and high drama. Hollywood films like *Clive of India* and *Wee Willie Winkie* exploited the same vein, as did Balcon's uncritical *Rhodes of Africa*. In the thirties the cinema public as a whole accepted such films as drama, not as expressions of approval for illiberal attitudes or racial exploitation, and the three Korda films owed more to Zoltan's love of vast exotic locations than to social or political attitudes.

A lot of time had been wasted in 1937 with projects which either hung fire or were eventually abandoned. *Twenty-One Days*, made to promote Vivien Leigh, was made by Basil Dean (see under ATP) but was shelved for two years before its inglorious appearance at a trade show and was not released until 1940. More work was done on *The Conquest of the Air*, and on a planned film about Lawrence of Arabia called *Revolt in the Desert*, which was never finished. One of the best known unfinished films in the world is *I, Cluadius*, an adaptation by Carl Zuckmayer of the two books by Robert Graves. This, and not *The Divorce of Lady X*, was in fact to have been Merle Oberon's return performance and was planned as a big production starring Laughton as Claudius and Emlyn Williams as the evil Caligula. Shooting began in

February under the Hollywood director Josef von Sternberg, with magnificent Roman sets by Vincent Korda. A large part of the film was made, and shows Laughton investing the part of the despised and stuttering future emperor with dignity and pathos in what could have been a fine performance, but personalities clashed and the atmosphere was explosive with temperament and quarrels. In a spiteful autobiography von Sternberg, who had a low opinion of actors, portrays Laughton as vain, 'difficult' and proud of it, causing endless delays and problems. Referring to him as 'a comparatively minor actor', he even suggests that Korda had found him too difficult to direct any more. The matter settled itself at the beginning of March when Merle Oberon was injured in a car accident, and Korda took the opportunity to abandon the production.

Victor Saville continued his independent production in association with Korda with *Action for Slander*. This, starring Clive Brook, was a stilted and unlikely story about country house parties, cheating at poker, the honour of the regiment and stiff upper lips. Directed by Tim Whelan, the film was well made and acted but the behaviour of the characters was too far-fetched to carry conviction. In the summer Saville himself directed by far the most important of his four films, *South Riding* . Based on a novel by Winifred Holtby, it was about a country gentleman and a lady schoolteacher and their involvement in local politics, raising social issues like housing, schools and local government corruption. Ralph Richardson and Edna Best played with the subtlety and restraint characteristic of Saville's direction and a fine cast portrayed such slightly stock figures as the county lady, the corrupt tradesman and the idealistic young socialist. The American cameraman Harry Stradling caught the quiet beauty of the English countryside and he and Lazare Meerson gave the film a visual realism – at the county show, in the council chamber, the great houses or the dales – which was as unusual as the social significance of the theme. Ultimately complacent about the reconciliation of opposing interests, the priviliged gentry, trade and the honest workers, the film sentimentalised what had been a hard and bitter novel, giving it a happy and romantic ending. In a long final sequence the ceremonial opening of the Coronation Housing Estate was made the occasion of patriotic scenes quite foreign to Winifred Holtby's work. Saville knew his audience, however, and was probably right in thinking that this comfortable middle-class picture of England would attract people who would find even this sequence acceptable in the mood of coronation year. Apart from this ending, about which considerable doubt was expressed at the time, it is certainly one of the most enjoyable and durable of Saville's films.

Thus the studio was busy in 1937, but according to Tabori the new policy was for 'good entertaining pictures of comparatively little expense'.[11] Apart from *The Drum* and *South Riding* they were unremarkable, and the exhilarating days of *Knight Without Armour* were over. The Prudential was less willing to provide finance and set about reducing its commitment. In February London Films made a gesture in the direction of economy and announced some salary cuts, partly restored later in the year when a profit was announced. At the same time, however, it was announced that the studio had expanded by the acquisition of Denham Court.

Korda continued to believe in the expensive picture of world calibre, however, and still pursued better terms for distribution in America. In June a 'stupendous deal' with United Artists was announced. This gave Korda and Sam Goldwyn the option, to remain open until the end of the year, of buying the rest of the share capital of the company on a fifty-fifty basis by paying Mary Pickford, Douglas Fairbanks and Charles Chaplin £400,000 each (eventually Mary Pickford and Douglas Fairbanks decided to retain a £300,000 interest). Much was made of the fact that Korda would be the first British producer to put real money into an American firm.

As a distributor, United Artists needed more films than the original founder members could now provide, and, whilst Korda wanted greater control over distribution terms, they wanted his films. Negotiations continued through the second half of 1937. Korda, who always raised his capital by private subscription, looked around for backers for his share of the purchase price. According to Tabori, Oscar Deutsch was prepared to put up some money and in mid 1937 Korda joined the board of Odeon. Cinema Holdings, already associated with United Artists (q.v.). One matter which caused disagreement in the negotiations with United Artists was Korda's desire to be allowed to make films for other distributors as well in order to keep his big studio occupied. This was looked on with disfavour by the others.

In November the *Financial Times* prematurely announced that the deal had been concluded, but in fact it collapsed shortly before Christmas and the option ran out. There was face-saving talk of legal difficulties and changes in the international situation and Korda, who retained his 20 per cent share in United Artists, was tactful and optimistic in public. Like many British studios Denham was empty for a time during the early months of 1938 because of the coming quota. But meanwhile there were changes at United Artists which gave Korda much of what he would have got by buying into the company, in the way of cheaper distribution and a fairer share of the profits. The owner members decided to reduce overheads and the cost of distribution, and for the first time to allow producers to participate in the profits in accordance with what they contributed, with special consideration for British production and distribution. Dr Giannini was to be succeeded as president and chairman by Murray Silverstone from the London office and distribution was to be centred in New York, in the control of Goldwyn and Korda.

Denham reopened, but London Films produced little in 1938. Brian Desmond Hurst finished *Prison Without Bars,* a remake of a French film set in a girls' reform school. It had been assigned to Maxwell Wray, a stage actor and producer and a friend of Basil Dean who had been under contract to Korda for some time, but he proved unequal to the task. Irving Asher joined Korda as an associate producer in May 1938, during the making of this film. Even worse was *Rebel Son,* a feeble rehash of some English-language footage shot in France in 1935, when Korda had been making *Moscow Nights.* Starring Harry Baur as the Cossack leader Tarass Bulba, it was taken off the shelves and doctored by Adrian Brunel, who reshot parts of it at minimal cost. The results, by all accounts, were farcical.

Strangely enough, *The Four Feathers,* the only film other than these spiritless items to be made in 1938, was one of the best of all Korda films. Production began in July on a Technicolor version of the exciting and romantic novel about the Sudan War of the 1880s by A. E. W. Mason. John Clements starred as the sensitive scion of a military family who regard his dislike of war as cowardice. Disguised as an Arab, he saves the lives of three brother officers who had sent him symbolic white feathers on his refusal to fight, redeeming himself in their eyes with quiet courage. Made by all the old Korda team, better than ever after their fallow period, it was directed by Zoltan and included magnificent location sequences shot in the Sudan, with huge crowd scenes of soldiers and natives, whilst at home Vincent created gorgeous and opulent scenes of upper-class life in Victorian England. The colour was particularly fine, the rich colours and dark panelling and leather of the English country house contrasting with the parched dun colour of the earth and the delicate duck egg blue skies of Sudan. Script, acting and music all lived up to this high standard and Graham Greene, reconciled to Denham at last, wrote that 'it cannot fail to be one of the best films of the year'.

Four big films were made at Denham by tenants during 1938, *The Citadel* and *Goodbye, Mr Chips* by M-G-M and *Q Planes* and *The Spy in Black* produced by Asher for Columbia. But the Prudential, chief creditor as well as chief shareholder in London Film Productions, was increasingly unhappy about the company's financial situation and determined to do something about it. A possible reorganisation of the company was discussed with other financial interests in the industry and, as mentioned earlier, at the end of the year the two studios of Denham and Pinewood were combined by the Rank and B & D interests on the one hand and Sir Connop Guthrie, E. H. Lever and P. C. Stapleton of Denham on the other as Denham and Pinewood Studios Ltd. Established in January 1939 with a capital of £750,000, it was an amalgamation of the two private companies, London Film Productions, with its capital of £428,540 and backing from the Prudential, and Pinewood Studios with £300,000 capital and backing from the Equity and Law Life Association. The executive directors were Richard Norton, E. H. George of United Artists, and W. S. and P. C. Stapleton, and the board also included Crammond, Guthrie, Rank, Lever and Reis.

Korda remained chairman and managing director of London Film Productions, and retained his controlling interest in Denham Laboratories and his United Artists partnership. But he lost his majority shareholding in London Film Productions Trust and, above all, control of the studio.

The Prudential kept the studio, its preference shareholding in London Film Productions and the income from the films, as well as a substantial holding in British Technicolor. In late 1938 Korda publicly announced that he had given up the management of Denham and in future would confine himself to production. Thus, like Michael Balcon and Basil Dean, he lost control of the studio he had created. He made the change sound as if it were his choice, and indeed running the studio had taken up too much of his time, but it ended a chapter in the history of the industry and Korda felt the rebuff keenly.

Early the next year, however, he announced plans for six films to be made for United Artists, three at Denham and three in Hollywood. In March he registered a new company, Alexander Korda Productions, with a capital of £200,000,[12] and in May started shooting a spectacular fantasy, *The Thief of Bagdad*. Korda now found himself a tenant in the studio he had built only three years before. The film had been planned before the reorganisation, with Marc Allégret as director. Instead, Ludwig Berger was engaged. But Berger's style, meticulous concentration on the actors, did not suit Korda's conception of the film as a spectacle. He put two other directors, Michael Powell and Tim Whelan, to work on the film as well and even took a hand himself, eventually freezing Berger out. The credit titles included all three directors, but it seems that little of Berger's work survived in the finished film, which contains many good things but not surprisingly lacks unity.[13] It starred Conrad Veidt as a wicked magician and Sabu, no longer an enchanting child but a strong, stolid little youth, as an urchin in a fantastic Arabian Nights story about spells and curses, a beautiful princess and a blind beggar. Desert sequences which they had intended to shoot in the Middle East were shot by Zoltan Korda in Arizona after the outbreak of war in July 1940. A stunning series of pictorial and magical effects, it had sumptuous sets by Vincent Korda and special effects which included a flying horse, a magic carpet, a genie emerging from a bottle and growing to giant size, a vertiginous flight with him over craggy ravines and a series of spectacular mechanical models. Colour was used in many different ways, in the sugary pastels of the palace, the rich realism of the flight over the ravine, and shots of the Princess and her father in a garden which might have been taken from a Persian miniature. It received Academy Awards for photography, art, special effects and sound effects, and was indeed an entertainment full of lovely and astonishing effects rather than an integrated film. Great fun rather than great art, it was an appropriate finale to pre-war Denham.

Meanwhile the studio had also been used in 1939 for Carol Reed's *The Stars Look Down* (q.v.) and for the three modest productions by Somlo (see under Rank). A postscript as war broke out was Korda's rapidly assembled propaganda film *The Lion Has Wings*. Work on *The Thief of Bagdad* was put aside for the time being. Raising money on his own life insurance, Korda made a film which had Ministry of Information blessing but no official backing. It was directed by Michael Powell, Brian Desmond Hurst and Brunel. Made in six weeks at a cost of some £30,000, it began with a sequence of edited actuality shots from newsreels and documentaries, including shots from a Gaumont-British Instructional film of 1937 called *The Gap*, made to recruit Territorials to London's defences against air attack. Shots of peaceful, tolerant Britain were contrasted with shots of regimented Germany preparing for war: goose-stepping soldiers cut into crowds watching football, rowing, racing; massed Nazi salutes accompanied on the sound track by the bleating of sheep; huge German crowds intercut with the British royal family performing 'Underneath the Spreading Chestnut Tree' with the Boy Scouts. Lyrical and satirical juxtapositions made their points largely without commentary but E. V. Emmett insisted heavily: 'This is Britain, where we believe in freedom.' With shots of Britain arming, reality merges with acted sequences in which Ralph Richardson as an RAF officer, Merle Oberon and June Duprez express patriotic thoughts such as 'We must keep our land, darling – we must keep our freedom.' The air raid on the Kiel Canal was re-enacted for the film, and a sequence from *Fire Over England* of Queen Elizabeth exhorting her troops made a rather surprising appearance. The propaganda was hardly subtle, but the speed with which it was made was enterprising.

Korda was one of a number of European film producers and directors who moved about the world making films wherever they could until they struck lucky and settled. Many would have liked to end up in Hollywood, and a number of them did. Korda found a niche in Britain, and quickly sank himself into a British identity, proclaimed by the very name of his company and its emblem, Big Ben. Of all the producers in Britain, he was the only one who thought and acted in the grand Hollywood manner, and he had considerable charisma as well as both creative and administrative ability. It is interesting to compare him with another Hungarian wanderer, Gabriel Pascal. Both had creative talent, both succeeded in Britain rather than America, and both captured literary giants of the day, the former H. G. Wells and the latter George Bernard Shaw. But, whereas Korda had a close family unit with his two brilliant brothers, was lavish rather than careless with money and had a large output of films, Pascal's youth was shrouded in stories of picturesque insecurity; he was a loner, lacking Korda's judgement, responsibility and gift for human relations, an emotional and flamboyant producer who made comparatively few films.

Leslie Howard's daughter, in a book about her father, wrote that Korda appeared a slightly pretentious fraud to his enemies, a genius to his supporters.[14] His charm and generosity were legendary, as was his love of the arts and of good living. At first he was given much credit for revitalising British production. But, as the flow of Hitler's refugees increased and many talented film makers from Europe found work in Britain, resentment grew. Elstree, Shepherd's Bush and Islington all welcomed them, but nowhere were they more in evidence than at ostentatious Denham, with its large

Hungarian contingent. Korda's detractors criticised him for nepotism, extravagance and snobbery. After the investment crisis it became fashionable to ascribe the City's loss of confidence in film production to Korda's extravagance and to that of his 'imitators', and to hold him responsible not for revitalising British production, but for ruining it. But the recipients of City money after *Henry VIII's* success were the Aldgate companies. Schach was far from being an imitator of Korda. Not for him a large studio employing a big workforce, or conventional methods of raising capital. Korda's success with *The Private Life of Henry VIII* may indeed have misled the companies behind the Aldgate Trustees into thinking that film production was a good field for speculation, and even that European film makers had some special secret of success. But the panic that ensued when they realised they had no hope of recouping the money they had so blindly poured into fly-by-night companies damaged confidence in all producers, including Korda, at a critical time in the development of his company. He had not yet solved the central problem of British production, that to make films of a standard which could compete with the best American films in the British home market was expensive, and that unless they had a regular and assured circuit distribution in America on fair percentage terms they could not possibly afford it. Korda had deliberately produced on this scale and his big enjoyable films had box-office takings which were enormous by British standards, but he had not yet achieved what he wanted. After the crisis his output was reduced in size, and most of it in scale as well, only *The Drum, The Four Feathers* and *The Thief of Bagdad* approaching the glamour of *Knight Without Armour*. The idea that somehow Korda's profligate ways were responsible for the slump has lingered on in some quarters while Schach, who slid silently out of sight, has been forgotten.

ABPC

Of the other big companies, most gave up the struggle to get into the American market. In the discussions about new quota legislation, in which John Maxwell took a prominent part, he continued to assert BIP's position as a quality producer. Elstree films* before the 1938 Act occupied an ambiguous place. Although not quota quickies, they were only of medium quality and certainly did benefit from the exhibitors' need for British films. Nevertheless, by and large they were acceptable to the British public and were certainly not made as a cynical exploitation of the law, so Maxwell's claim to be on a footing with Balcon, Wilcox and Korda must be allowed. It is significant, however, that his evidence to the Moyne Committee was given in his capacity as a member of the Kinematograph Renters' Society, not as a producer. It is also clear that the exhibition side of the business was of more interest to him and that he would have liked to expand the circuit. As far back as 1934 there had been rumours that he was interested

* Called ABPC from February 1937.

in acquiring the Gaumont-British shares held by Fox. The subject came up again in the second half of the decade and in October 1936 it was announced that he had paid £620,000 to Gaumont-British, and allotted 300,000 ordinary shares in BIP to the Ostrer brothers, in return for which he received the 250,000 non-voting shares in Metropolis and Bradford held by the Ostrers, a seat on the Gaumont-British board and an option on the voting A shares. In the end the deal fell through (see below, under Gaumont), but the arguments took two years and led to much bitterness. By the time the matter was finally settled, however, ABC had grown to nearly 500 cinemas by acquiring a large holding in the Union circuit, with its 168 cinemas.

Union Cinema Company, which had been formed with seven cinemas in 1928 by C. F. Bernhard, had grown to sixty by early 1935. At this time Gaumont-British acquired an interest in the company and appointed a member to its board, as with H & G Kinemas, in an attempt to secure the advantages of large-scale booking for these two circuits (see Chapter 1). We have seen how the plan failed because of KRS opposition, but Union continued to grow on its own. In August it registered a subsidiary, National Provincial Cinemas, a public company with £100,000 capital. Bernhard continued to work through a system of loose groupings, with a policy of controlling all or at least the chief cinemas in particular towns. By the end of 1935, 128 cinemas were listed in *Kine Year Book* as being in Union and associated companies, and its share rose sensationally in value. National Provincial, now with an authorised capital of £750,000, made an issue of £325,000 in December for which as much as £8 million was offered. By January 1936 Bernhard was claiming control of over 200 cinemas, and by September of 250, although the exact identity of all of them is difficult to ascertain. If true, the group was now similar in size to Gaumont-British and ABC. In December the three companies Union Cinema Company, National Provincial Cinemas and Oxford and Berkshire Cinemas, with a combined capital of £1,450,000, nearly all of it issued, merged to form a new public company Union Cinemas, which was registered in December with a capital of £6½ million. The directors were the same as those of the original company, Fred Bernhard and his father David, who although chairman remained in the background, and L. J. Clements. All seemed well until, in September 1937, at the age of seventy-seven David Bernhard died.

Things suddenly fell apart. ABPC acquired a large holding and in November Maxwell joined the board as chairman. The first annual general meeting was held in December and, mentioning legal proceedings, Maxwell freely accused the previous directors of keeping unsatisfactory accounts and of writing up the assets and inflating the capital without the justification of either earning capacity or capital value. Mention was also made of enormous salaries, expenses and allowances to directors, and transfers of shares and assets which resulted in large profits to individuals to the detriment of the company. The meeting was adjourned and an investigation was held. Affairs were gradually untangled and the cinemas remained under ABC control from then on. As a result of the scandal Maxwell was in a much stronger position.

Changes had been made at the old British Instructional studios at Welwyn. A new company, Welwyn Studios, was registered in December 1935 with £1,000 capital and a board of its own, and with the actor and producer Warwick Ward as production supervisor. During the next few years films were made there not only by ABPC but also by Stafford, Grafton, Paramount and British National. In addition, Welwyn Studios produced some seventeen second features of its own, which were distributed by Pathé. (The directors Summers, Bentley and Norman Lee worked there, continuing to make films at Elstree as well. At the same time John Argyle also made films for Pathé at Welwyn. The last two of these, directed by Summers, were *The Dark Eyes of London*, the horror film with Bela Lugosi which was the first British film to be given an H certificate, and *Traitor Spy,* a slight but timely thriller about Nazi espionage.

Meanwhile ABPC itself continued to expand during 1937 and 1938. The merger in the early thirties had been justified and combined profits rose year by year. Gross profits of £1,265,829 were announced in July 1937, with total assets of £14,750,000, and in August next year profits were up again to £1,302,000. During this time Maxwell was scrapping furiously with other producers, especially with Basil Dean, over the new quota proposals. He had tried and failed to get an American market which would enable him to spend more on production, and his policy now was to make medium-priced films which would satisfy a protected and not very demanding home market. He therefore consistently opposed any measures which would favour high-priced films.

By 1937 declining profits and the current uncertainty about the new quota meant a drastic reduction in output, and only eight films were trade shown in that year. Operetta and costume films became less frequent and the company fell back on stage comedy and contemporary drama. *Aren't Men Beasts,* directed by Cutts, was taken from a current stage farce with Robertson Hare and Alfred Drayton. A sex-war comedy which was considered 'rather near the knuckle', it raised laughs with marital hostility and unkindness – 'You've probably been unfaithful!' '*Probably*! You flatter yourself!' The presence of Robertson Hare, worried and plaintive with his little cries of 'Oh! Botheration!' or 'Oh! What does it *mean*?' was a redeeming feature. *Let's Make a Night of it*, also directed by Cutts, was this year's mishmash of radio turns with no less than six dance bands and with the Americans Buddy Rogers and June Clyde, often in BIP pictures, providing a connecting story. Like so many films of its type it was a backstage story of a struggle to put on a show, which finally turns out to be a great success. Fred Emney, a large, fat middle-aged comedian who specialised in drunks, gives a good performance with his sad jowelly face, his peppery and cutting manner as he strives to keep his dignity intact, and a high-pitched giggle when it slips a little. Brian Desmond Hurst was rashly entrusted with *Glamorous Night*, Ivor Novello's long-running Drury Lane musical show about a Ruritanian king, played here by Otto Kruger, and his struggle with a villainous dictator. Mary Ellis played her original part as his platonic lover, a gypsy queen who is the power behind the throne. In Mary Ellis BIP had at last found a singing star of real quality, but the bathos of the long-drawn-out sexless love affair, the stagy sets and behaviour, the slow and emphatic dialogue and a general air of economy made the film a disaster and it was heavily cut after the trade show. One of the best of Stanley Lupino's films, *Over She Goes*, was made by Cutts after Lupino's return to the company. Laddie Cliff, Sally Gray and others appeared in their original parts. Fast, brightly lit, with three glamorous girls and the usual story of bachelor friends and a country house party, it had bright catchy tunes and for once some lavish sets even if it, also, reeked of the stage. The three young men kiss their girls, the first murmuring 'My lamb!', the second 'My sweet!' and the third 'My joint! My two veg!'

Production picked up in late 1937 and a large number of trade shows were held in 1938, with films by Brenon, Stein, Lee, Albert de Courville, Bentley and Summers. With lots of contemporary plays, musicals and crime stories, ABPC appeared anxious to get up to date and away from romantic costume and musical films and, although the films were not memorable, they were generally of better quality than before. Brenon's *The Housemaster* with Kruger and Diana Churchill, although it remains a stage play and never establishes the school outside the housemaster's drawing room, was a pleasant enough film. Several domestic and romantic comedies, two more with Albert Burdon, appeared during the year. Another enjoyable film from Brenon was *Yellow Sands*, from Eden Phillpotts's play about a revolutionary-minded young fisherman and his inheritance from his Aunt Jennifer. Shot mostly on location in Devon and Cornwall, it shows many local places and people and although slow and wordy is refreshingly authentic, with a lovely quiet performance from Marie Tempest as Aunt Jennifer and with Wilfrid Lawson, another frequent performer at Elstree, as a boozy old fellow, scruffy and benevolently sly. There were two musicals. *Hold My Hand* was yet another from Stanley Lupino, directed this time by the American Thornton Freeland. Despite all the usual people, for once it seemed a slow and tasteless production, with Fred Emney less a funny drunk than an actual alcoholic. *Yes, Madam?* was the popular conditional inheritance story, this time the heir having to act as a servant for a month in order to qualify for his legacy. Prolonged set pieces from the stage production include a sloshed Emney again, blundering but harmless. The star, Bobby Howes, was yet another of the young men about town and was very popular on the stage, but the mannerisms of this little leading man, wiggling coyly, shrugging, smirking, biting his lip and mugging heavily, did not appear to advantage on the screen. Rather different was *The Terror*, a workable thriller full of Edgar Wallace characters including the excellent Lawson as a mad master criminal, all cackling laughs, with owl hoots, hooded figures and Linden Travers in one of her high-intensity performances. Bentley's *Marigold*, a late costume film from a stage play, was set in Edinburgh at the time of Queen Victoria's visit in 1842. The queen was written into the story and played by Pamela Stanley, who had recently played her in Laurence Housman's *Victoria Regina* on the London stage. Trade shown in the same month as Wilcox's *Sixty Glorious Years*, it was gently amusing and romantic, with agreeable Edinburgh backgrounds.

By now the new quota was in existence and clearly efforts were being made to improve the standard of production, although as none of these films were registered for double quota it would appear that costs were still being kept down. The only double quota before the war was a Jack Buchanan film. Buchanan, after his independent productions in association with GFD, joined ABPC again and produced and starred in *The Gang's All Here* in the winter of 1938. This was not a musical comedy but gave him a straight part as a detective, again in wisecracking Thin Man style. It was directed by Thornton Freeland, who had directed Buchanan once before, and the cast included Googie Withers as his wife and the Americans Edward Everett Horton, Otto Kruger, Jack La Rue and Walter Rilla. Somehow, perhaps partly because even this film managed to look slightly mean, partly because Buchanan's perky and not very sympathetic performance was not quite right, the result was disappointing. He later starred in a routine remake of Commander King-Hall's comedy *The Middle Watch*. There were other remakes between now and the war, including A. E. W. Mason's perennials *At the Villa Rose* and *The House of the Arrow*, and three French films. Stanley Lupino's last was *Lucky to Me*, in his familiar world of peers and house parties, lovely girls and romantic entanglements hilariously sorted out. *Just William* was Cutts's competent and popular film of several of the Richmal Crompton stories starring yet another Lupino as William, Wallace Lupino's ten-year-old son Dicky, a delightful serious fat little boy with just the right look of disarming innocence. The most important of these last pre-war films, well reviewed at the time, was *Poison Pen*, directed by Stein. From a recent play about how anonymous letters from the repressed sister of the local vicar wreak havoc in a village community, like other Elstree films it took little advantage of the film's ability to establish locality and ambience and remained too close to its stage origin, with lighting which emphasised its studio nature. But the large and excellent cast with many characters and cross-currents, although theatrical, made it an interesting production and the central performance by Flora Robson, changing from the gracious lady of early scenes to the charged venom of the end, with the final grotesque and blundering suicide, was a step in her typecasting as a neurotic woman.

Apart from *Abdul the Damned* and *The Robber Symphony* the films made at Elstree had been the company's own.* However, towards the end of the period the studio was used by Mayflower Pictures. This was formed by Erich Pommer and Charles Laughton in January 1937, when they were both working at Denham. In the first two months of 1937 the disastrous *I, Claudius* episode ended Laughton's association with Korda and when in September Mayflower began preparation for their first film, *Vessel of Wrath*, it was at Elstree and not at Denham. The three films they were to make with the participation of Maxwell, their capital having been increased to £50,000, were made by their own technicians and were of a quality and scale otherwise unknown at Elstree. They were distributed by ABPC and all were successful.

Vessel of Wrath, directed by Pommer, was from a Somerset Maugham story about the reformation of an outrageous, roistering beachcomber living on a tropical island, when he copes responsibly with an epidemic among the islanders. He masterfully subdues the prudish and disapproving woman missionary teacher, played by Laughton's wife Elsa Lanchester, and they end in domestic bliss back home keeping a pub. It was a virtuoso comedy part for Laughton, who was on screen almost all the time, and both he and Elsa Lanchester caricatured their parts, she indeed almost to the point of hysteria. The film was well made and highly successful.

The next Mayflower film, begun in January 1938, was written for Laughton by the novelist Clemence Dane but so altered during the course of production that she refused a screen credit. It was directed by Tim Whelan. *St Martin's Lane* is about a London busker who lends a helping hand to a cockney gamine, played by Vivien Leigh, and who declines into hopelessness as she rises to stardom and forgets all about him. After the male chauvinist ending of the previous film Laughton portrayed unspoken adoration in this one, his love ignored, with unintentional cruelty, by the girl. The production included musical numbers and was more ambitious, expensive and polished than anything previously made at Elstree. For the crowded scenes in and around St Martin's Lane and the Holborn Empire, with their theatre queues, buskers and traffic, Mayflower art director Tom Morahan designed some spectacular sets with both actual and scaled-down London buses.

The third and last film was *Jamaica Inn,* from Daphne du Maurier's colourful novel about Cornish smugglers in the late eighteenth century. The secret head of the gang, it is revealed at the end, is the respectable squire played by Laughton. It was directed by Hitchcock, who had known Pommer in the early twenties in Germany and had time to fill between making *The Lady Vanishes* and the beginning of his Hollywood contract. He agreed to do the film before he realised what it was going to be like.

---

* Maxwell had learnt from experience, when in 1929 he had agreed to finance two films to be made on a stage hired by C. Clayton Hutton for £150 a day. The films were to cost £10,000 each. Eventually made in 1931 for £16,000 and £22,000 respectively, they were complete failures, and afterwards the company avoided such arrangements.

OWD BOB

John Loder, a usefully rugged leading man who made over thirty British films during the decade, in a Gainsborough film of 1938 about an old shepherd and his beloved sheepdog. Much of the film was shot on location on Exmoor.

I'VE GOT A HORSE
A modest British Lion comedy made at Beaconsfield in 1938 by trouble-prone music hall comic Sandy Powell.

HOLD MY HAND
Another Stanley Lupino musical, made at Elstree in 1938. In this finale, in which three runaway couples are married at the famous forge at Gretna Green, he and Barbara Blair are flanked by Jack Melford with Sally Gray, and John Wood with Polly Ward.

ALF'S BUTTON
AFLOAT
Chaos created by the Crazy Gang
in a Gainsborough film of 1938.
Left to right standing are
Chesney Allen, Teddy Knox,
Jimmy Nervo and Bud Flanagan,
and sitting Charlie Naughton and
Jimmy Gold.

THE DRUM
A Korda Technicolor film set in the North West Frontier of India during the nineteenth century. It was directed in 1938 by Zoltan Korda, who several times used the Empire as a British equivalent to the American West. Art director Vincent Korda.

OLD MOTHER RILEY, M.P.
The expressive gestures of Arthur Lucan in his music hall character of Old Mother Riley in a 1939 film.

FRENCH WITHOUT TEARS
David Tree, Roland Culver and Ray
Milland in a glossy and popular film
version of Terence Rattigan's stage
comedy, directed by Anthony Asquith
for Two Cities at Shepperton in 1939.
Art director Paul Sherriff, with
Carmen Dillon.

He disapproved of the incredible and melodramatic plot and felt that the identity of the villain would be guessed from the fact that he was being played by the star. Hitchcock, like Korda and von Sternberg, found Laughton's approach to acting affected and unprofessional, but the public loved the film and it was a big success. Another expensive production, with large sets, it marked the first starring part for an eighteen-year-old Irish girl, Maureen O'Hara, who had had a small part in Forde's *Kicking the Moon Around* a year before. She was to make a film for Argyle later in the year and was put under contract by Mayflower. Laughton now left for Hollywood to make *The Hunchback of Notre Dame*, in which she also appeared, and Pommer followed. Mayflower was no more.

During the last ten years Elstree had turned out some 200 films of every description. To keep the large studio fully occupied the company needed enormous numbers of stories, actors and directors. Many people, British, American and Continental, passed through it but few were of top rank and those who were did not usually do their best work there. Many cameramen, too, worked there, from the lowly Horace Wheddon to more talented and modern cameramen such as Otto Kanturek, Phil Tannura and Ronald Neame. Many British writers took a turn, from the slapstick comedy writers of the Leslie Fuller and Ernie Lotinga films to Launder and Gilliat and Wolfgang Wilhelm. A constant influence on the characteristic look of the films was that of the art department under Clarence Elder, who became studio director in 1939. From Maxwell's point of view it was a well managed business, which remained profitable in a way no other production company did for any length of time. During the last two years, after the new quota came into operation, some attempt at greater sophistication could be discerned, but film after film demonstrated that real quality required more money than ABPC would, or could, spend.

Gaumont and Gainsborough

Gaumont-British had tried even harder and longer than ABPC to get into the American market, spending large sums on American stars in order to make its films attractive, but the policy had failed. Big changes took place at Islington and Shepherd's Bush in 1936, well before the shape of the future quota could be seen. Ominously declaring in June 1936 that in future they would aim at a steady output of 'marketable product', Maurice Ostrer, who was senior to Balcon, moved into the office next door to his to take a more active part in production. Balcon has written stiffly that 'the arrangement had its complications'. During the second half of 1936, although Balcon was still formally in charge of the studios, his capable associate producer, Edward Black, took more and more of the burden.

Both the Ostrers and the Fox interests were increasingly worried. In July 1936 Isidore Ostrer was in America to discuss the possibility of selling out to Joe Schenck, President of Twentieth Century-Fox, as it had become.

There were renewed rumours during the next few months involving the Ostrers selling part or all of their holding but retaining operational control, with Balcon as head of production working closely with the American end. This caused fresh anxiety in Parliament and there were hints that the idea of so many British cinemas being under American control was not liked by the government. In the end it fell through, whether over money or, as Mark Ostrer subsequently maintained, over the issue of foreign control.

It was at this point that Maxwell stepped in with his offer, and in the autumn of 1936 ABPC acquired the Ostrer's non-voting B shares in Metropolis and Bradford, with a seat on the board and a five-year option on their voting A shares. The Ostrers were allotted shares in ABPC. The Government was relieved but the Fox interests, which of course still had a veto on the sale of voting shares, were displeased at the prospect of Maxwell eventually being in control of the best fifth of all the cinemas in Britain, and Sidney Kent vetoed the deal. Maxwell was said at the time to have paid £620,000 for the B shares, and the disputed A shares were believed to be worth £800,000, which would have meant a total of nearly £1½ million for the Ostrers. Maxwell now found himself left with a large block of shares and no hope of gaining control.

The Gaumont annual general meeting in late 1936 was an angry one. A vocal minority were resentful that the Ostrer family should be in a position to sell control of a large public company. They succeeded in forcing an adjournment on the grounds that a consolidated balance sheet showing the position of over a hundred associated and subsidiary companies should have been prepared. This was published a month later and the adjourned meeting promptly held, but during the delay the situation had changed. Staff cuts were announced and it was declared that Balcon had been released from what was called the last year of his contract,* in order to join M-G-M. Others went with him, including his brother Chandos, Ivor Montagu, who had resigned, and his scenario editor Angus MacPhail, who was reported in *Kine Weekly* to have been sacked.

Balcon left the company in December 1936 and on the 16th signed a two-year contract with M-G-M at a much higher salary. What was his true reason for leaving Gainsborough, the company he had created twelve years before, and Gaumont-British? Publicly, the reason was his quest for genuine Anglo-American co-operation. But George Arliss, who was working for the company at the time, unequivocally wrote in his autobiography that Balcon left because 'control of the Gaumont-British had passed into somebody else's hands'.[15] The Ostrers, who had already stopped Balcon making the films he wanted, were in favour of getting out of production altogether, but at the time Balcon left the company so precipitately Maxwell had just acquired his holding and the right to sit on the board. He would certainly have wanted to continue production. Balcon, like the Ostrers a Jew and a man of liberal sympathies, detested both Maxwell and his style of film making, and can

---

* See the footnote on p. 136

hardly have liked Maxwell's associate Mycroft, and it is unlikely that he would have considered working with them.

Production was now to be much reduced in volume. After Balcon left, the company was reorganised under Edward Black, who turned out to be a most successful producer. The last few films made while Balcon was still nominally in charge came out early in 1937 without any screen credit for production. The first Gainsborough film on which Black's name appeared formally as producer was a Will Fyffe comedy started by Beaudine early in 1937, after Balcon's departure. At Shepherd's Bush one more film was made and then the studio was closed in April 1937, although the labs and the Gaumont-British Instructional studio remained open. Four more important Gaumont-British films were produced, three Jessie Matthews musicals and Hitchcock's *Young and Innocent*, but they were made at Pinewood. *Climbing High*, made in July 1938, was the last Gaumont-British production for the time being. Pinewood itself closed down later in the year. But production continued at Islington under the chairmanship of Mark Ostrer, with Maurice Ostrer as director of production, Black as producer and most of the films directed by Marcel Varnel, with isolated films by Hitchcock, Stevenson and Carol Reed. The best of the George Arliss films, *Dr Syn*, was directed by Roy William Neill. A number of star contracts, including those of Jessie Matthews, Anna Lee, Nova Pilbeam, Lilli Palmer and Oscar Homolka as well as directors Hitchcock, Stevenson, Sonnie Hale and Herbert Mason, in fact much of the team so carefully assembled by Balcon, were worked out and not renewed. The strong scenario department under Launder included Val Guest, G. Marriott Edgar, Michael Pertwee and J. O. C. Orton. Two Tom Walls films were made at Pinewood and from late 1938, when Pinewood was closed, five films were made at Islington for Twentieth Century (q.v.) alongside the Gainsborough ones. Later, after two and a half years, Shepherd's Bush was opened again and some Arthur Askey films were made there at the beginning of the war.

The new regime began badly with Maxwell, a notoriously quarrelsome man, issuing a writ against the Ostrers in the spring of 1937. Charging them with fraudulent misrepresentation that the annual profits of the company were £700,000, he claimed £600,000 damages. The unrest among the dissident shareholders continued. Sir Arnold Wilson questioned Walter Runciman in Parliament about the closure of Shepherd's Bush and asked him to dissolve Metropolis and Bradford, which he said enabled a large public company to be controlled by three people 'one of whom was an unnaturalised alien'. It should be remembered that Wilson supported Nazism, and that the Ostrers were Jews. Runciman replied, however, that the three in question were all British.[16]

The most important of the remaining contracts was that of Hitchcock, and before it was finished he made two classic thrillers. *Young and Innocent*, an enjoyable light film in which Nova Pilbeam plays the girl who helps the young suspect, Derrick de Marney, to track down a murderer, has fun with novel settings like a children's party and a *thé dansant*. The latter has a famous two-minute shot tracking from a 145-foot long shot taken from the ballroom roof to a 4-inch close up of the nervously twitching eye of the guilty man, the drummer in the dance band. The *Lady Vanishes* was Hitchcock's last British thriller for many years. It shows Margaret Lockwood and Michael Redgrave as a young couple drawn together in the search for an old lady who mysteriously disappears on a train travelling across a politically troubled Europe. Mostly taking place on the train, it was made at Islington with one coach and the extensive use of transparencies and models. From a novel, it had a brilliant script by Launder and Gilliat and was packed with characters who intrigued or amused the audience, especially Basil Radford and Naunton Wayne as a pair of cricket-mad Englishmen. The spy dénouement was topical, as the film opened just before the Munich crisis of 1938, and it was an enormous success.

Jessie Matthews made three more films. *Gangway* was the second musical to be directed by Sonnie Hale, and was a mistaken identity romance between a girl reporter and an aristocratic detective in an involved search for a jewel thief. Production values were high, with elegant sets, but the songs on the whole were not memorable, the complicated plot was shapeless and unsatisfactory and Sonnie Hale's direction lacked the emotional involvement of Saville. *Sailing Along* was the last made by Hale, and was a Galatea story about a bargee's daughter who was turned into a star. For the third time Matthews's leading man was Barry Mackay, a pleasant young actor, with some excellent comedy from Alastair Sim and Athene Seyler. The film had several big production numbers, including a modern ballet in the manner of *Slaughter on Tenth Avenue*, one of the ballets in the outstanding recent stage show *On Your Toes*. It included a seven-minute take as the infinitely extendable stage, using two studios, stretched along a riverbank landscape. Her dancing partner, indeed, was Jack Whiting, who had been in *On Your Toes*, and whose top-hat-and-cane style of dancing in the film is deliciously guyed by Jessie Matthews in one of the funniest sequences. The film was an important one, but even MacWilliams could not entirely conceal the star's signs of strain and overweight, and it proved to be her last big musical. The company procrastinated until Sonnie Hale's contract ran out, and her next film, *Climbing High*, was rewritten as a straight comedy. It was directed in July 1938 by Carol Reed, who had just consolidated his position as a director with a film of unexpected realism and credible characters, *Bank Holiday*, another tangled-lives story set firmly in ordinary British life with lots of location work. Not regarded with much favour by the Ostrers, this had however been a decided critical success. Michael Redgrave, who had reached stardom with his recent films *The Lady Vanishes* and *Stolen Life*, played opposite her in *Climbing High*. But despite the contributions of these two talented young men the film was not a success. At thirty, time and the pressures of life were destroying the essentially girlish nature of her charm and it was her last film as a big star.

Of the other films during this period, Stevenson's *Owd Bob* was a quiet rural film about an old Border sheep farmer and his beloved dog, and included some lovely location filming, including sheep dog trials. But much of the company's emphasis under the new regime was on comedy. Joining towards the end of 1936, Marcel Varnel was to prove a talented and efficient comedy director in a string of Will Hay and Crazy Gang pictures.

The Crazy Gang consisted of three pairs of stand-up comics from the music hall, Flanagan and Allen, Nervo and Knox, and Naughton and Gold. They had been working together for years, appearing in George Black shows at the London Palladium, and had a tremendous following which included many highbrows, who tended at this time to despise the British regional comics but who appreciated the chaotic and uproarious style of this metropolitan group. Each pair had made several films already, but they now appeared together for the first time in three feature films, *O-Kay for Sound*, *Alf's Button Afloat* and *The Frozen Limits*.* With the help of writers G. Marriott Edgar and Val Guest, the wildly improbable stories were used as pretexts for rough knockabout, rapid cross-talk and set pieces like their skit on Snow White's seven dwarfs in *Frozen Limits*, undressing in chorus in an Alaskan bunkhouse. Loud, unhibited and non-stop, with verbal acrobatics and mad non sequiturs, their anarchic behaviour had something in common with that of the Marx brothers, although they made little effort to establish separate individualities.

But the most popular comedy came from Will Hay, who had by now settled into the character of a slightly sleazy and incompetent person in a position of some responsibility, bumbling through his duties with an unconvincingly confident and businesslike air, briskly misapplying common sense. Unlike other comedians he eschewed romantic interest. His first film with Varnel, who was to prove a more congenial director than Beaudine, was *Good Morning, Boys*, suggested by the schoolmaster sketch he had perfected over many years in the halls. Confined largely to the classroom, much of the humour is verbal and involves a great deal of misunderstanding. Will Hay was a comedian who needed stooges, and in Moore Marriott and Graham Moffatt he had the ideal foils. It was clear that this was what the public wanted and the next, *Oh! Mr Porter*, making more use of comic situations, was a box-office winner and perhaps the best of all his films. The three are in charge of a run-down country railway station and become involved with a gang of crooks. Moore Marriott was an experienced supporting player who here developed an unforgettable character, shambling and almost toothless but sharp and brightly malevolent, opening the flap of the ticket office to snap 'Next train's gorn!' and slam it shut again. The film is a mixture of hilarious ineptitude and eerie mystery, with verbal mix-ups and slapstick sequences like the three of them trying to reach the ground from the top of a windmill by clambering about its uncontrollable sails. As an out-of-work schoolmaster in *Convict 99* Hay accidentally becomes

* *Gasbags* followed during the war.

the governor of a prison, which he runs on exaggeratedly reformed lines, treating the inmates like honoured guests. This incidentally provoked an attack by E. W. and M. M. Robson in *The Film Answers Back*, claiming that he was supporting authoritarianism by mocking liberal views, an interesting early example of the earnest interpretation of film as a text. Once more Moore Marriott nearly stole the show, this time as an aged convict trying to tunnel his way to freedom, only to surface in the Governor's study. A hard man who had shown little consideration to his stooges during his long music-hall career, Hay was not pleased with Marriott's success and for his next film, *Hey! Hey! USA*, he dispensed with both of his colleagues. Taking the American slow-burn comedian Edgar Kennedy as a partner instead, he made a mid-Atlantic film about crooks on an ocean liner as a bid to get into the American market, but it pleased nobody. The relationship between the three characters was the essence of the comedy, and the trio was reassembled for *Old Bones of the River*, more a reference to the Edgar Wallace stories than a skit. Here Hay plays a well-meaning missionary trying to stand in for a district commissioner. Once more Marriott excelled with a wildly funny slapstick sequence with a ladder. *Ask a Policeman* and *Where's That Fire?*, the latter made by the same team but for Twentieth Century, repeated the formula in different milieus, and then Hay broke up the team. An autocratic and remote man, Will Hay was unlike other comedians in having interests outside show business. Self-educated, he was interested in science and was well known as an amateur astronomer. He had given up touring the halls when his success in films enabled him to do so, but he continued to perform his schoolmaster sketch on the radio from time to time.

Maxwell's legal action against the Ostrers and the shareholders' revolt continued to trouble the company whilst these films were being made. The apparent leader of the shareholders' protests was a Mr W. H. J. Drown, the owner of only 700 10/- shares. He and his shareholders' committee decided in May 1937 to ask the Board of Trade to instigate an inquiry. To be entitled to do this they had to represent 10 per cent of the shares. By early the next year they had mustered over 3,000 shareholders with more than 11 per cent of the total shares, and the application went ahead. The inquiry was to investigate how reserves of £2½ million in 1931 had fallen to £85,000 in 1937, what the directors had been paid and what was the extent of foreign control since Sidney Kent of Fox had joined the board in 1932.

It was suspected that there were interested parties behind the shareholders' committee and that the whole agitation was an attempt to oust the Ostrers. These suspicions led in March to a parliamentary question to the President of the Board of Trade as to whether the committee which had asked for the investigation had been financed by the petitioning shareholders, or 'mainly by the head of an opposition company who desires to extend his control',[17] clearly pointing a finger at Maxwell. An inspector was finally appointed a full year after the original fuss. Just before the war the new President of the Board of Trade, Oliver Stanley, replying to a question in the House from Vice-Admiral Taylor, said that the Gaumont directors had been slow in producing books and accounts, and 'not as helpful to my inspector as I should have expected them to be'. Meanwhile the Labour MP Tom Williams tried, on behalf of the vast majority of the shareholders who had not signed the petition, to discover the names of those who had, alleging malicious intent. Maxwell had certainly wished to wrest control of Gaumont from the Ostrers, who he seems to have felt would defer to their American partners without protecting British interests. His case against them was due to come before the Lord Chief Justice in July 1938, the formidable array of lawyers including Sir Patrick Hastings, Sir William Jowitt and Norman Birkett for the Ostrers and Sir Stafford Cripps for ABPC. According to Hastings there was very bitter feeling between the two sides. However, before the case came to court Maxwell resigned from Gaumont-British, after acute differences over the accounts, which he considered inaccurate. The action was subsequently withdrawn and judgement was given with costs in favour of the Ostrers.

After Maxwell's attempt to take over the company failed, the link between Gaumont-British and Twentieth Century-Fox became closer. Between November 1938 and the war the latter's British films were made for them by Edward Black at Islington under the management of Maurice Ostrer. Meanwhile tentative talks were held in July 1938 between Isidore Ostrer and J. Arthur Rank. There were rumours of a new grouping, to include Odeon Theatres and Gaumont-British, which together would control some 600 cinemas. Oscar Deutsch of Odeon was said to be interested in acquiring the Ostrer holdings, including voting control, and to have had reason to believe that the Fox side would, at last, raise no objections. War broke out at this point, however, and the talks were dropped.

Herbert Wilcox

1936 was an important year of change for Herbert Wilcox, as it had been for Gaumont-British and Balcon. In February the B & D studio at Elstree burned down. A Sydney Howard comedy called *Fame* was the last to be completed there, Wilcox's own film *The Three Maxims* being finished at other studios hired after the fire. Some minor films, produced at various studios, carried out the policy previously announced of making economical popular pictures for the home market. But both Wilcox and Buchanan continued to make big prestige pictures also, still with an eye on America. *The Three Maxims* (not registered as a British film) was a circus story scripted by Herman Mankiewicz and starred the Hollywood star Tullio Carminati opposite Anna Neagle. Jack Buchanan's *This'll Make You Whistle*, also directed by Wilcox, was transferred from a stage musical which had appeared out of town with an almost identical cast in 1935, and was filmed before the London opening in September 1936. The usual story of high jinks in high society, it had the usual playboy hero and the usual shift to the South of France. There were a number of hit songs like the title number and 'I'm in a Dancing Mood', written by the same American team who wrote so many of the songs in British films, and ambitious dance numbers staged by Buddy Bradley, as well as one of the biggest sets made in a British studio until then, a courtyard at fiesta time. Wilcox's production unit was much as before and it seems that his own determination to break into the American market was as great as ever, whatever B & D might decide.

According to Norton the company had been at a low ebb financially at the time of the fire, and as the vaults and cutting rooms were unharmed and the films intact the insurance on the rest of the studio was very welcome. It was a new start for Wilcox. The recent company changes involving Rank, Woolf and Universal provided him with an opening. Carl Laemmle in America had disposed of his company Universal, and as related above Universal Corporation was formed in the spring of 1936 by Dr Giannini and J. Cheever Cowdin in association with Rank and L. W. Farrow, C. M. Woolf, and Wilcox himself. The new group would make it possible for GFD pictures to be distributed in America. It was decided that B & D would not rebuild at Elstree, but would join the others on a fifty-fifty basis in building and operating the new studio at Pinewood. In May the capital of the studio owning company, hitherto owned by Rank and Boot, was increased to £300,000 with the addition of a half-share owned by B & D, which thus became the biggest single shareholder. The studio opened in September with Richard Norton as managing director, Rank as chairman, and with Ronald Crammond and Wilcox representing B & D on the board and John Corfield representing British National.

The films were in future to be called Herbert Wilcox Productions, and the first to be made at the new studio in September 1936 was also the last B & D film. This was *Talk of the Devil*. Although intended as a modest production it was a slick, tense and well acted melodrama, outstandingly well directed by Carol Reed, and although not his first film it attracted more favourable comment from the critics than earlier ones. A number of minor films were made by lesser directors but like this first one all boasted Hollywood stars, and both *Talk of the Devil* and Wilcox's own *London Melody* were distributed by United Artists, not by GFD as planned. The latter film, which had begun production at Hagen's small studio at Elstree, was finished at Pinewood and once again used songs by Sigler, Goodhart and Hoffman. The American star Tulio Carminati and Robert Douglas played opposite Anna Neagle.

Although Wilcox had been drawn into part ownership and management of one of the largest and best studios in Britain, this was not really his style and the arrangement did not last long. Laurence Housman's play *Victoria Regina* had been put on with great success in New York in 1935 and 1936, permission to represent the queen on the stage for the first time having been granted by Edward VIII, and it was due to be put on in London in the summer of 1937. As early as January Wilcox was planning to star Anna Neagle in a film about the queen, although not one based on the play. Instead of making it at Pinewood for GFD distribution he made it at Denham, where Korda gave him a studio credit of £50,000,[18] and it was distributed by RKO-Radio. According to Wilcox the break with GFD was due to Woolf's opposition to the casting of Anna Neagle as the queen. Admittedly Woolf's judgement was sometimes faulty, as in the lack of confidence in Hitchcock and Asquith, but Wilcox had already turned to United Artists for the distribution of his last two films, and RKO distribution for this one was a real breakthrough to the American market at last, and seems likely to have been a more important reason.

He registered a small but suitably imperial-sounding company to produce it, the £100 Imperator Film Productions, in March 1937. He took five weeks to shoot it and overspent his £150,000 budget. His usual production team was joined by the historical adviser from his earlier costume films, and once more Anna plunged into research. The final sequence, that of the jubilee, was shot in the newly arrived Technicolor under the advice of Bill Skall from RKO. The score by Anthony Collins, conducted by Korda's music director Muir Mathieson, incorporated music used at the 1838 coronation. Anton Walbrook, an actor from Austria who had already made a Hollywood film, played Prince Albert, to whom he bore a strong resemblance, and Anna endured hours of elaborate make-up for the sequences of Victoria's old age.

The result was a beautifully produced, long and respectful series of scenes from the queen's life, *Victoria the Great*. It was both a box-office and a critical success, even if James Agate carped at the star's accent, 'overlaid by layer after layer of suburban refinement', and described her portrayal of the queen when young as arch and uppish.[19] Others found the romance of the young queen and her consort charming, but the personal interest in her long life was difficult to sustain after Albert's early death and the film hardly touched on social and political matters. The latter part of it was little more than a pageant of public occasions. It opened first in America, where it had a great success, and it was awarded the Gold Cup of All Nations at the Venice Film Festival, as well as awards from various film papers.

In his autobiography Wilcox is very free with the costs and profits of his early films, but more reticent over these later ones. There are no glowing claims of enormous profits from *Victoria the Great*, and it is noticeable that both Imperator and Herbert Wilcox Productions were bankrupt two years later. Like Korda, he probably found that a high-budget film was not always a big profit maker even if it was a popular success. Nevertheless, the film was important and both he and Anna Neagle gained considerable prestige from it. His position in the industry was transformed. In August 1937 he secured a ten-year contract to make three Imperator films a year for RKO-Radio, a contract said at the time to be worth £6 million. A remake of *The Rat* starring Walbrook was made at Denham by Jack Raymond, whilst less important pictures, called Herbert Wilcox Productions, were made at Beaconsfield and handled by British Lion. As for B & D, now engaged in managing Pinewood, it made further losses and eventually merged with Denham in the new studio company Denham and Pinewood Ltd.

Meanwhile Wilcox, once again trying to repeat a popular success, planned another film about Victoria called *Sixty Glorious Years*. With the ingenuous excuse that 'in the vast canvas of Queen Victoria's life . . . there were several films to be made – all different in theme and period',[20] he proceeded to cover her whole life episodically once more. Working at Denham in the summer of 1938 he used the same expert team, with the addition of Sir Robert Vansittart's help on the script. This time they were given facilities at the royal palaces and were able to shoot exteriors at Windsor, Balmoral and Buckingham Palace. Interiors were carefully copied, with special process work by Percy Day, and this time the whole film was shot in Technicolor by Freddie Young, with nominal supervision by the Americans. The result was an outstandingly handsome and authentic evocation of Victorian upper-class surroundings. The script gave little opportunity to glimpse anything else for, like the other film, it included only public and political snapshots and a private life lacking in drama after Albert's death. Once more Anna Neagle threw herself into the part. Both she and Wilcox seem to have felt sincere respect for the queen and to have had no interest in the England or the Empire behind the pomp, or the real people behind the royal facade. Graham Greene said unkindly that 'Both the director and the star seem to labour under the impression that they are producing something important', but it is only fair to add that the public agreed with them.

The two Victoria films aroused great interest in America, and late in 1938 Wilcox and his star toured the United States to publicise the second one. Recognised in America at last, on their return they triumphantly announced a partnership deal with RKO-Radio. They were to make three or four £150,000 films a year, Anna Neagle would make one film a year in Hollywood, Wilcox would have access to major Hollywood stars and, best of all, nine to ten thousand bookings in America would be guaranteed for all his films. The importance of this contract should not be underestimated. Had the war not intervened Wilcox, like Korda, might have achieved what all the big British producers had been aiming at, a real market in America. In May he registered yet another £100 company called Imperadio, its name incorporating both the royal image and his new collaborator. The chairman was Dr Giannini, and Wilcox was managing director with two RKO-Radio executives on the board.

For Anna's first Hollywood film Wilcox chose to repeat yet another of his successes, the silent *Dawn*, with a new version called *Nurse Edith Cavell*, about the British nurse who helped refugees escape from the Germans in Belgium in the First World War. The writer Michael Hogan and Wilcox's associates Freddie Young, art director L. P. Williams and composer Anthony Collins were joined in Hollywood by his old colleague Merrill White as associate producer. Production was smooth and efficient. The patriotic note must have seemed timely when production began, but by the time the film was released just after war had broken out the issues of the 1914 war seemed remote and irrelevant. Anna Neagle gave a starchy, pure and determined portrayal, suggesting crisp efficiency rather than the humanity and magnanimity conveyed by Sybil Thorndike in the earlier version. Wilcox's single-minded pursuit of American distribution had got thus far, but this was an American film and RKO-Radio had still to honour their promise of wide distribution for his British productions.

Norton wrote of Wilcox, 'Herbert is not an easy man to work with', although he praised his showmanship, his Irish charm, his enthusiastic way of making every film sound important, and his 'infinitely quick and tremendously tidy mind'. Another contemporary later described him as a charming Irish liar, and certainly he made a number of claims in his autobiography which were quite wrong – the first British talkie, the first sound studio built in Europe, the first British film made by Elisabeth Bergner, the first British-Hollywood co-production. He spoke as a showman, exaggerating hopefully. Some of his films were among the most important British productions of the time, although as a director he was competent rather than imaginative. Searching for what the public would like next, he was always looking for a formula he could repeat. Thus he made two films about Nell Gwyn and followed with one about another actress, Peg Woffington; he remade both *The Rat* and the film about Nurse Cavell and shamelessly made a second, rather similar, film about Queen Victoria. Wary of big commitments, he wisely tried not to get too involved in management, leasing two of his three B & D stages and getting out of the Pinewood arrangement as soon as he could, whereas Korda all but sank under the weight of his studio responsibilities. His production team was small but good and extremely constant, and in Freddie Young he had one of the best lighting cameramen in the world. An important factor in his success was that in Anna Neagle he had been lucky enough to form a lifetime's partnership with a woman of some talent, great popularity and remarkable character. By 1940 it was clear that despite bankruptcies he was a survivor, and that he would continue to provide the public with plenty of well made musicals, with an occasional film about a famous woman giving Anna Neagle an opportunity to do some serious acting.

Ealing

The studio at Ealing, with its private backing and a policy of first-class pictures, was affected by neither the investment famine nor the new quota. After the failure of his Mozart film and the disagreement with the Courtaulds, however, Basil Dean did comparatively little in the studio and spent much of his time negotiating the new quota legislation. He also directed a film for Korda at Denham in May 1937, which was not a happy experience.

Scripted by Dean and Graham Greene from the Galsworthy play *The First and the Last*, it had all the advantages of Korda's studio, Vincent Korda's design and a cast which included Vivien Leigh and Laurence Olivier. But the autocratic and precise Dean could not bear Korda's interference, the profligate and chaotic atmosphere at Denham, or the passionate and all-absorbing love affair between his two leading players. The film, *Twenty-One-Days*, was one that nobody wished to remember afterwards. Although it was trade shown two years later it was not released until 1940, by which time Vivien Leigh was so famous because of her appearance in *Gone with the Wind* that it was hoped that its imperfections might be forgiven. Graham Greene, repenting of his own contribution, reviewed it as 'slow, wordy, unbearably sentimental'.

Things were quiet at Ealing.* Jack Kitchin had become a very able associate producer and the Formby films did not need Dean's attention. There were three of them in 1937 and 1938, all written and directed by Kimmins and all sticking closely to the formula. Gormless George gets himself into a situation where he has to attempt something he can't really do, and manages to make a triumphant success of it. In *Keep Fit* he wins a boxing contest, in *I See Ice* he is roped into a game of ice hockey and in *It's in the Air,* made in the early summer of 1938 and his last film under Dean's management, he gets accidentally airborne and flies a plane not over but through a hangar. At the same time Carol Reed came back to direct an excellent small film about a Liverpool tugboat captain who mistakenly thinks he has won the football pools, *Penny Paradise.* Surprisingly realistic in its atmosphere and with the usual good acting, it starred north-country girl Betty Driver, a milder version of Gracie Fields, and an attractive little Irish comedian called Jimmy O'Dea.

The company was losing money, £97,679 in the year ending in June 1937 and £35,443 the following year. Dean was drifting apart from his colleagues on the board, who sought to control his spending. Early in 1938 Stephen Courtauld and Reg Baker tried to introduce a rule that directors whose budgets were about to be exceeded should discuss with the board whether to go on or to abandon the film. This was intolerable to Dean and he refused to comply. In April Courtauld, claiming that Dean was doing too much stage work and that Formby's dislike of him made difficulties for the company, said that he should not be both a producer and a member of the board. Furious, Dean resigned as a producer. He was next asked to resign his chairmanship and joint managing directorship.

Squeezed out, he was bitter. 'The ship was home at last,' he wrote later,

---

* There do not seem to have been any tenant companies at this time. Toeplitz made no more films at Ealing after *Beloved Vagabond*, but had gone on to found Two Cities. Kurt Bernhardt, who specialised in multilingual films, formed a £10,000 company in October 1936, British Unity Pictures, and made *The Girl in the Taxi* in English and French with another European film maker, Eugene Tuscherer. It proved a stepping stone to Hollywood for him, and he was to have a long career there as Curtis Bernhardt.

'but without its first captain; he had not abandoned it in a moment of crisis; he had been politely invited to walk the plank.'[21]

The new quota just introduced was a disappointment to Dean and he now turned his back on the film world, which had seemed to promise a new dimension to his career, and confined himself to the theatre once more. A self-contained and fastidious man, he was intelligent and impatient of fools, outspokenly autocratic and with a sharp tongue and a short temper which made him many enemies. His style was different from that of other producers, and his stage interests and social contacts set him apart so that he never quite seemed to be a film man. Good stories and good casts were his strong points, and his unusual liking for location work makes some of the early films a fascinating glimpse of Britain in the early thirties. The film technique of the comparatively few films he directed himself showed little insight into the medium, but they represented a sincere attempt to make films not so much for the masses as for the type of well educated person for whom he catered in the theatre. His contribution to the film industry, in founding Ealing studios and in employing there some of Britain's best young film makers and two of Britain's most popular comedians, was considerable.

As Dean was being pushed out of Ealing, Michael Balcon moved in. After leaving Gaumont-British he had a distressing period with M-G-M (q.v.) and for some months after completing *A Yank at Oxford*, at loggerheads with the American executives in London, had been kept inactive. He was legally unable to work for anyone else until June 1938. He had therefore examined the possibility of producing on his own with Walter Forde, independent since his one film for Schach, as director. At first he looked around for some way of financing it. But immediately he secured his release from M-G-M *Kine Weekly* carried the announcement that Balcon, with his brother Chandos, Forde, Sidney Gilliat and Robert Stevenson, former members of Gaumont-British, were joining ATP. At this time a number of people* were considering co-operative production as a way to overcome the slump, and Balcon decided to adopt a form of co-operative finance. In August Ealing joined Pinebrook in founding the Co-operative Association of Producers and Distributors, or CAPAD. This was registered as a £100,000 company by Norton, Anthony Havelock-Allan and J. Arthur Rank representing Pinewood, and Balcon, Baker, now managing director, and Stephen Courtauld, now chairman, representing ATP. It was intended to make economical but good-quality films at Ealing, which would be distributed by ABFD. Balcon's first film there, and the first CAPAD film, was Forde's *The Gaunt Stranger*. An Edgar Wallace thriller, it was made largely by technicians who had worked with Balcon at Gaumont-British. It set the tone of good middle-of-the-road films for which the studio was to become known.

Basil Dean's resignation was not officially made public until September,

* Cameraman-director Roy Kellino, his wife Pamela Ostrer and James Mason, whom she was later to marry, made *I Met a Murderer* as a co-operative venture in the summer of 1938, and at the same time Tom Walls and Ben Travers made *Old Iron* at Shepperton on a similar basis.

when a face-saving announcement was made that he wished to concentrate on the theatre in future. The name of the production company was changed from ATP to Ealing Studios and later, when D & P Studios was formed as part of a major realignment, Ealing reverted to its customary seclusion. Behind Balcon, as formerly behind Dean, was the discreet, reliable, likeable but to the outside world unknown figure of Reg Baker. A business head of great skill, he played an important part in the survival of the company. During the next year twelve films were made at Ealing, all CAPAD films* except for three more Formby comedies and one more with Jimmy O'Dea.

The Formby team at first remained much the same. Kitchin, who had been called associate producer under Dean, now received the full credit as producer. *Trouble Brewing* was about crime reporting and detection; *Come on, George!*, about horse racing, was the last from Kimmins. *Let George Do It*, made at the end of 1939, was a spy story which followed the same formula but was written by Angus MacPhail and directed by Marcel Varnel, both previously with Balcon at Gaumont.

Balcon's lighting cameraman at this time was Ronald Neame, and most of the design was by Oscar Werndorff, with whom he had also worked before. Many familiar faces turned up at the studio, especially in the script department, including Ian Dalrymple, Roland Pertwee, Michael Hogan, Roger MacDougall and Allan MacKinnon. Direction was by Basil Dearden, Forde, Robert Stevenson and a young protégé, Pen Tennyson, great-grandson of the poet.

The Ware Case, faultlessly directed by Stevenson, was from a 1915 play about a charming cad and his eventual downfall. It was made on the initiative of Clive Brook, who took part on a percentage basis and played the main part. Films from now on were modest in scale but there were interesting signs of future developments. *Cheer, Boys, Cheer*, for example, starring Jimmy O'Dea and Nova Pilbeam, foreshadowed the ingenious and gently ironic post-war Ealing comedies, and Pen Tennyson's first film, *There Ain't No Justice*, was a remarkable small film which anticipated another post-war style. Moderately priced but not cheap and shoddy, it was a fairly realistic, if slightly cosy, treatment of ordinary British working people. The advertisement ran: 'Real people – Real problems – a human document'. It was about the attraction the crooked fight game had for underprivileged youngsters, and starred young Jimmy Hanley. Unusual at the time both for its degree of realism and for the serious theme, it was a critical success. Balcon showed his faith in Pen Tennyson in a more ambitious film, again with a social slant. This was *Proud Valley*, set in a Welsh mining community. In the finale the miners, after the closure of the pit, break in on the board of directors and reach an amicable agreement about opening it again. The intention of its left-wing writers, Herbert Marshall and his wife Fredda Brilliant, had been to show the miners taking over the mine and running

* The only other CAPAD film was *The Lambeth Walk*, made at Pinewood and put out as a Pinebrook-CAPAD film. See under M-G-M.

it as a co-operative. War broke out during production, however, and a patriotic note was hurriedly introduced with them all getting together to provide the country with coal. The film was rather a mixture with two pit disasters, an Eisteddfod and a choir, and a secondary theme with Paul Robeson as a black man reluctantly accepted by his fellow miners because his voice was an asset to the choir, and dying nobly to save others. His kindly smile never wavering, he was described by Graham Greene as a big black Pollyanna. Partly a vehicle for Robeson, partly a trouble-down-the-pit film, partly an unusually outspoken political film, it was technically uneven and not up to the standard of Tennyson's first production, although it was received with delight by *Kine Weekly*. Tennyson's promising career was cut short, however, for he was killed during the war after making one more film.

Dean's regime was over and Balcon, with some twenty years' experience of the problems of British film production, was at last in a position to develop entirely on his own lines. The characteristics of post-war Ealing production, a small and congenial team and good but modest films for the home market, with a bias towards British life and work and a growing interest in social questions, were already discernible.

Smaller Companies

Among smaller companies, the three with studios at Twickenham, Beaconsfield and Shepperton were all badly hit during the second half of the decade.* Hagen, at Twickenham, was the first to be affected. The expansion of 1935 with its heavy borrowing from C. T. Bowring (Insurance) continued, but his transformation into a quality producer did not go well and late in 1936 when the company issued more debentures in favour of Bowring, E. Stevinson of that company joined the board. They had now received a massive £430,000. JH Productions began to appear with *Spy of Napoleon* in September, starring Richard Barthelmess; *Juggernaut* with Boris Karloff and *The Man in the Mirror* with Edward Everett Horton followed. Seven JH films were made, at a cost of £195,000, but although an average cost of some £28,000 was high for Hagen it was no longer enough to make a top-class film with expensive American stars, and although the last was a very funny film they continued to look like minor productions, with small sets and an air of frugality. It was not easy to overcome the limitations of the old studios and the old production team, trained in the ways of economy. Very few bookings were secured.

Bowring, with by far the largest stake, wished to carry on production, but at the instigation of the Westminster Bank a receiver was appointed for JH Productions and Twickenham Film Distributors in January 1937.

* The late years of the thirties were not a good time for new companies to start, but one small new firm which appeared with three minor but promising films in 1938 and 1939 was Charter Film Productions, founded by the Boulting brothers, 25-year-old twins John and Roy.

Hagen struggled to stay in business while bankruptcy proceedings, which did not start until the spring, dragged on. The studio at Twickenham with its equipment was sold immediately and very cheaply to a small private company formed to hire it back to Hagen. This was Studio Holdings Trust, of which James Carter of the Twickenham board was joint managing director. In April St Margaret's Film Studios was registered, owned by Studio Holdings Trust, with a capital of £10,000 and with all the former personnel, including Hagen as managing director. Work was in progress by April, but most of the few films they managed to produce were inferior. The Riverside and Elstree studios were disposed of and by mid-1938, with the new quota in force, Twickenham also closed down. The Receiver's report on the studios disclosed that the deficiency of assets to meet liabilities as regards creditors was fairly small. But it was severely critical of the board's failure to make provision for the necessary amount of capital for production, of Hagen's excessive optimism about the value of the films, and of heavy salaries paid to the directors, especially to him. He sought help from moneylenders but was declared bankrupt with unsecured liabilities of £416,947. He was ruined, and died the following year aged only fifty-six.

He had met the demand for British films with engaging verve. Like Irving Asher and Norman Loudon he worked his small studio hard and efficiently. The disciplines of speed and economy contrasted with the extravagance and delay of producers backed by Aldgate money. Unlike Asher with his anonymous modern sets and unlike Loudon, to whom films were so much merchandise, Hagen flung himself into the most varied types of production with a genuine love of drama. Everything from costume melodrama to modern farce, music hall, Dickens, Sherlock Holmes, Agatha Christie detective stories, musicals, stage adaptations, remakes and multilinguals was pushed through the studios and, despite the small stages, with nerve and ingenuity even spectacle films were tackled. The lack of space, the lighting, costumes and decor which were somewhat less than lavish, as well as Trytel's irritating musical scores, were handicaps and there was little time for imagination or subtlety in either continuity or dialogue. Yet the approach was remarkably varied and lively and the films seem to have been conceived as small first features rather than as second features. The writer Peter Cotes later described Hagen as a philistine and a tough businessman[22] but Michael Balcon said that he was rather nice, likeable but somewhat irresponsible and careless about money.[23] Walter Forde has endearingly described him as 'a beautiful man, very sweet',[24] and he must indeed have been a charmer to get stars like Lupe Velez, Cedric Hardwicke and all the others to appear in his films at the height of their careers, when he could certainly not have afforded to pay them properly.

At Beaconsfield, British Lion muddled on through the mid-thirties under Sam Smith. The renting of low-quality American imports had become an important part of their activities even before Edgar Wallace's death, and their own films, many of them short revue items or collections of such items, served as their own quota as well as providing M-G-M with footage. By the middle of 1935 British Lion was doing well enough to expand its capital to £750,000. An agreement was signed with Republic Pictures Corporation of America. Imports increased and, with them, their own production. Some sixty undistinguished films were made during the decade.

During 1936, the year of their biggest output, Tom Arnold hired the studio to make *It's a Grand Old World*, a vehicle for the Yorkshire music-hall and radio comic Sandy Powell. In the same year British Lion also had several joint productions with Hammer Productions. Hammer had been founded in November 1934 as a £1,000 company by joint managing directors Henry Fraser Passmore and G. A. Gillings. The chairman was Will Hammer,* who had for years been a producer and performer in music hall, revue and summer shows. Passmore, who had been in the navy before entering films as an art director and assistant director, was producer. At Beaconsfield he now made two films starring Paul Robeson, who wished to redeem his reputation after being criticised for playing Bosambo in *Sanders of the River*. *Song of Freedom* shows him as a black British docker who becomes famous as an opera singer and seeks to bring the benefits of Western civilisation to the land of his forefathers. This misguided attempt to re-establish the left-wing Robeson as an intelligent and concerned person mixed his singing and some fairly realistic scenes of racial harmony in dockland with an egregious caricature of African life which was unintentionally far from flattering. It was certainly unusual, and was treated with cautious respect by some critics, not knowing quite what to make of it. Later in the year a second Robeson film was made, *Big Fella*.

Passmore, an interesting producer although he made few feature films, later produced an unusual film about trawlermen and their families which has been somewhat overlooked, *The Last Adventurers*. It may be mentioned here, in passing, although made at Shepperton not Beaconsfield. A film with some beautiful passages, if rather slow, it included much actuality material shot at sea and at Grimsby, on the quays and at fish auctions. It was the first film to be directed by cameraman Roy Kellino, and was well photographed and edited, with an excellent score by Eric Ansell. Unfortunately the refined accents and glamorous clothes of the two leading ladies and the idealised homes struck a false note in what would otherwise have been quite a realistic film about British working people.

By early 1937 British Lion was in difficulties. Only two films were made that year, a second Sandy Powell film written and produced by Tom Arnold, *Leave it to Me*, and a film directed by Elvey exploiting the talents of the teenage Hughie Green and his Gang. Wilcox hired the studio for a short while in the autumn of 1937 for three minor productions, one an echo of the early owner, Edgar Wallace's *Return of the Frog*. But British Lion itself produced nothing for a year after May 1937. Their production had been

---

* Will Hammer re-entered films in 1947 at the age of sixty, starting the later Hammer Films with the Carreras family.

far below the minimum cost clauses of the new quota legislation, and the studio stood empty. In May 1938, however, Herbert Smith started the first of three more Sandy Powell films. This plump, flabby and plaintive Yorkshire comic with his sandy hair and eyelashes and his familiar cry of 'Can you hear me, mother?', yet another of the great British regional comics, had a wide and enduring popularity but the films were minor ones compared with the Formby of Will Hay vehicles. Finally, in 1939 George King occupied the studio to make some juicy melodramas for British Lion release as Pennant Pictures.

The third studio, that of Sound City at Shepperton, was a direct casualty of the cost clause of the new Quota Act. In the mid-thirties Norman Loudon moved out of direct participation in film production apart from John Baxter's films, and Sound City became solely a studio-owning company, leasing space to various independent producers, including City, George King, Randall Faye, John Clein and Gabriel Pascal. Loudon and general manager L. Grandfield Hill expanded the company, which became public in June 1935 with an authorised capital of £350,000, although no issue took place at the time. In December it was announced that they were to acquire a renting company and that expansion would be facilitated by an advance of £100,000 from the Equity Law Life Assurance Company.

Sound City was reorganised in 1936. It acquired the small importing and renting firm of Gilbert Church and Frederick White, called AP&D. (Associated Producing and Distribution Company), and its associated firm Gilbert Films, together forming a renting operation under the new title Sound City Distributors. A new production subsidiary, UK Films, was formed to take over Baxter and Barter Productions. Its board included Hill, Loudon and Frederick White as well as joint managing directors Baxter and Barter.

In February 1936 a public issue of £291,263 was made. It was heavily undersubscribed, but they went ahead with the planned expansion of the studio, which was ready by June. There were now seven stages with a total floor space of 73,000 square feet. The four big new stages were in units that could easily be converted into two double-sized stages, and all four had tanks and were air-conditioned. With the large lot, and with both RCA and Visatone sound recording, Sound City was ready for hire. Contracts were signed with two of the more sophisticated independent producers, John Stafford and Richard Wainwright, each of them making a series of films for an American renter and leasing stages at Sound City for several years. The company enjoyed a brief heyday before the 1938 Act destroyed most of their customers.

Until the end of 1937 the reorganised studio was very busy. Baxter and Barter made a series of films, one of them the mild and episodic *Song of the Road* with Bransby Williams as an old labourer travelling the country with his horse. Baxter's last two, made late in 1937 and early in 1938, tried to present the eight-year-old Hazel Ascot as an English Shirley Temple.

Considered homely and very British, the films were all second features. Wainwright and Stafford continued to make their more ambitious films at the studio, the American James Fitzpatrick made a number of four-reel quota films for M-G-M based on popular ballads and the lives of famous composers, and others hired space for various cheap productions. The only first features made here were the two Capitol films starring Tom Walls.

The annual report in September 1937 claimed that the company was doing well, but Loudon had miscalculated the future of the quota and its days were numbered. At this time he was taking a prominent part in the discussions, doing his best to preserve the market for low-cost production. His scheme for a protected market for films eligible for exhibitors' quota was designed to save the type of film made at his studio. By early 1938, however, production there had petered out and it was closed. Loudon later ascribed its closure to the 1937 crisis in confidence and the withdrawal of insurance finance for production, as well as to the long-drawn-out uncertainty about the terms of the new quota. It is true that a number of the units using Sound City had been financed with Aldgate money, which had now dried up. But the ending of uncertainty when the new quota became known did nothing to restore the studio's fortunes and it remained shut for some time. Loudon did not welcome the term 'quota quickie', preferring to talk instead of 'modest second features'. But the differences of opinion between him and other producers were due to the fact that a large volume of cheap films, upon which hire studios thrived, was exactly what the quality producers wanted to stop.

American Quota Arrangements

The big American importers, too, were profoundly affected by the new quota regulations. As before, different companies reacted in different ways. While some were ready for the change, others paused in the production or acquisition of their British quota to see what would happen.

The first to anticipate the new situation was Twentieth Century-Fox. They had already taken a step into production in Britain when in 1935 they backed Interallied Film Productions, a £2,000 company registered in July. A year earlier it had been reported that George Bernard Shaw had agreed to let C. B. Cochrane produce a film of *St Joan* starring Elisabeth Bergner. In fact this fell through, partly because they feared censorship troubles over possible offence to Catholics, partly because Shaw did not like her performance of St Joan at the Malvern Festival. Instead, the company turned its attention to *As You Like It*, which was produced and directed by Czinner and handled by Twentieth Century-Fox. The aged James Barrie, who was fascinated by her little-boy charm, wrote his last play *The Boy David* for her at about the same time, and *As You Like It* bears the credit 'Treatment suggested by J. M. Barrie'. Carl Mayer was nominally the literary editor of the company but the scenario credit was R. J. Cullen. Fewer liberties were taken with the text than in Max Reinhardt's Hollywood production of *A Midsummer Night's Dream* which just preceded it, and the acting of the large cast of stage actors, which included Henry Ainley, Leon Quartermaine and Laurence Olivier, was traditional. Bergner herself, although an experienced Shakespearean actress, gave a high-spirited tomboy performance in her charming but incongruous Austrian accent which retained all the mannerisms and whimsy of her other films, including one of her favourite somersaults, but was somewhat lacking in poetry. Even more surprising was the design by Lazare Meerson, in his first British film. The ornate palace with its turrets, pools, grand staircase and mirror-like floor might have come from a German fairy-tale filmed by Hollywood, and the crowded silvan scenes, with everything from mossy banks to flocks of sheep present in profusion, was unlike the solitude of more traditional Ardens.

Meanwhile Fox-British films continued to be made at Wembley on the same low level as before, right up to the introduction of the new quota. One by Maurice Elvey, a sad little romance about escaping prisoners of war called *Who Goes Next?*, was of better quality than usual. With the arrival of the new quota the studio closed down, but by this time Twentieth Century-Fox had already made a number of big films in Britain under the name of New World.

The parent company in America had undergone great changes. William Fox had been ousted some years before and Joseph Schenck, who had founded Twentieth Century in 1933 with Darryl Zanuck, resigned from United Artists in 1935 and joined Fox, bringing Twentieth Century with him. Early in 1936 it was announced that Robert T. Kane, an American who had been in films some twenty years and had been in charge of the Paramount venture at Joinville during the early years of sound, was going to make New World pictures for Twentieth Century-Fox in Britain. In May production started at Denham, and on Epsom and Irish locations, of *Wings of the Morning*, the first Technicolor film to be made in Britain. The film was loosely based on racing stories by the Irish writer Donn Byrne in his book *Destiny Bay** and gypsies, racing and the Irish scenery were the background to a pleasantly improbable romance between Henry Fonda and the beautiful French actress Annabella, unbelievably masquerading as a stable lad, with guest appearances from the jockey, Steve Donaghue, and a song or two from the Irish tenor, John McCormack. It was directed by the American ex-editor Harold Schuster and photographed by Technicolor cameraman Ray Rennahan, who had been with Kalmus since 1921. With him worked the British cameraman Jack Cardiff, with ample supervision from Natalie Kalmus, and the film was processed in America. Beautiful location scenes and the colourful world of gypsies and racing made it a visually exciting production, done with Hollywood polish, and it was extremely successful all over the world.

* One more or less self-contained chapter of this is called *Tale of the Gypsy Horse.*

Kane then engaged the great Swedish director Victor Sjöstrom, known in Britain and America as Victor Seastrom, to direct a belated last film, *Under the Red Robe*, with Korda technicians and writers. After some years in Hollywood Seastrom devoted the latter part of his career to acting in Sweden, but made this last film, a swashbuckling Stanley J. Weyman historical romance of the time of Cardinal Richelieu, with great brio and style. It starred Annabella again and Conrad Veidt, a hero for once, bitter and tender, in a story of suspense and courage in a dark mysterious castle and its enfolding forest.

Three less successful films were made at Denham in 1937. A story by Graham Greene was filmed in January by an American, William Cameron Menzies, as *Four Dark Hours*, but not shown until 1940, when it appeared under the title *The Green Cockatoo*. Schuster again directed Annabella, this time opposite David Niven, in *Dinner at the Ritz*, a complicated and unlikely story about swindling and jewel thieves saved by glamorous production and the delightful leading players. But glossy international films were abandoned in favour of a vehicle for the very local talents of Gracie Fields who, with Monty Banks, was enticed away from Basil Dean by an offer she could not resist, despite her dislike of film making. An ambitious costume picture set in South Africa in the 1880s, *We're Going to be Rich* co-starred Victor McLaglen and Brian Donlevy, and was intended to establish Fields's reputation in America. But, as in the case of Will Hay, her humour was strictly for local consumption and teaming her with American stars in an unfamiliar format dismayed her British fans without attracting an American following. The film, like Hay's film with Edgar Kennedy, was not a success. The new legislation was in operation by the time this expensive production was ready and it was registered for triple quota.

The plan to make films which would be equally acceptable in Britain and the United States was now abandoned and the rest of the Twentieth Century films made in Britain before the war were considerably cheaper and aimed solely at British audiences. Moving to Pinewood when Denham was closed in 1938, Kane and Monty Banks made a second Gracie Fields film, *Keep Smiling*, which reverted to her earlier style. The story, about a struggling concert party and their attempts to stage a show, needed a light romantic touch like *The Good Companions* but there was little supporting talent for the star. Her mugging and cavorting was this time confined to the show-within-a-show, and as the leader of the troupe she had a more becoming role. *Jerusalem*, sung in church for all it was worth, and a blues number enlivened by characteristic trills, gave her opportunities for serious singing, as well as comedy numbers such as 'I Never Cried So Much In All Me Life'.

Even more English was the modest but successful *Inspector Hornleigh*, with Gordon Harker and Alastair Sim in a story based on a popular BBC series. Although both its producer and director were American, Graham Greene singled it out as an example of how British films had improved and acquired an English identity. Late in 1938 Pinewood in turn closed down and

Twentieth Century moved to Islington, and between then and the outbreak of war five Twentieth Century productions were made for them by the Islington staff. Building on the reputation of *Inspector Hornleigh*, they continued the unpretentious but distinctively British style of production.

A Girl Must Live was an intriguing, fast and funny film set backstage and in a theatrical boarding house, with rival chorus girls and a host of characters, its lively and realistic early scenes falling away to an unlikely end as romance took over. Directed by Carol Reed, it had good performances from two players often wasted, Renee Houston and George Robey, as well as many others. As was so often the case, many people worked on the script, which was credited on the film to Frank Launder. *Where's that Fire?* continued the comedies that Gainsborough had been making with Will Hay, this time in the fire brigade. *Shipyard Sally*, made in March 1939 after she had visited Hollywood, was the last film Gracie Fields was to make in the United Kingdom and was again directed by Monty Banks, whom she was shortly to marry.* She had been awarded the CBE the previous year and was conscious that her popularity gave her a certain social responsibility and in this film the working-class image was enhanced with a touch of social significance and patriotism. She plays a good-hearted working lass who averts unemployment in a Clydeside shipyard by charming the authorities in London into keeping it open. The film opens with a section of newsreel showing the launch of the *Queen Mary* and closes with a montage of work in progress again on the Clyde, with double exposure of the Union Jack and of Gracie singing 'Land of Hope and Glory'. One of her best known songs, 'Wish Me Luck as You Wave Me Goodbye', occurs as she leaves the shipyard on her mission to London. Like two of her other greatest successes, 'Sing as We Go' and 'Smile When You Say Goodbye', it struck a note of cheery fortitude. No attempt was made this time to introduce romantic interest. Her co-star Sydney Howard played her father, but the part was a disaster for this comedian, whose touching and wistful quality was missing from what was meant to be a lovable old reprobate but came across as an unlikeable fraud. Various Islington writers worked on the script but the only credits on the film itself go to two Americans. Gracie herself, whose comedy routines were now noticeably less grotesque, at forty-one was blonder, softer, better dressed and better made up than in earlier films. Banks, with whom she felt happy and secure, and the Hollywood skill in shaping images had changed her considerably.

Like Fox, Paramount realised that things would have to change when the new quota came into force. Speaking to the Moyne Committee, Maxwell had quoted J. C. Graham as saying that Paramount had been making a loss of £100,000 a year on their quota productions.[25] Whether this was true or not, John Paddy Carstairs's *Incident in Shanghai*, made in December

---

* In Hollywood she made two films for Fox in 1943 and 1945 and one for United Artists in 1954. Banks died in 1950.

1937, was the last. From now on Paramount looked for quota from other sources. There was a pause, followed by the production, still by Havelock-Allan, of three more important Paramount-British films, still fairly low-cost but made with much greater care. *This Man is News* was made at Pinewood in the Pinebrook co-operative scheme by David MacDonald. It featured Barry K. Barnes and Valerie Hobson as a crime reporter and his wife, yet another Thin Man couple. Fast and witty, it was a box-office hit, and became a byword for what a British film should be. Another from the same team, *This Man in Paris*, repeated the formula. Like the third, *The Silent Battle*, it was made at Denham the following year after Pinewood had closed. The latter was a topical spy story again starring Valerie Hobson. In addition to these three films Paramount made distribution agreements with Wilcox for *A Royal Divorce* and with Czinner for *Stolen Life*. Finally, they distributed two films made in the summer of 1939 by the new British firm of Two Cities.

The name Two Cities had originally been used by Ludovico Toeplitz in 1937 for a firm linked with the Italian company Pisorno, but by August 1938 Two Cities had an entirely new board, including the Italian banker Filippo Del Giudice. The capital was £40,000. The intention was to make Anglo-Italian multilinguals at Shepperton and Rome but the first film, *13 Men and a Gun*, was made in Italy and although the English-language version had a British cast it was not registered as a British film. Mario Zampi, who had joined the Italian film industry years before and since 1930 had worked as an editor at Warner's Teddington studio, was to direct and produce in Britain and Anatole de Grunwald, Russian-born but educated at Cambridge, was the unit's scenario writer. In May 1939 a recent stage success by the young Terence Rattigan, who worked on the script with de Grunwald and Ian Dalrymple, was made into one of the most successful British films of the thirties, *French Without Tears*, and this was distributed by Paramount. About a group of boisterous young Englishmen staying at a pension in France to learn French, its theatrical stereotypes and rather schoolboy humour were made gay and enjoyable by Anthony Asquith's direction and funny performances from Roland Culver, David Tree and Ray Milland. Mostly rather stagy, it had some ambitious camerawork in a long take accompanying the streams of dancers at carnival time, and another scene on bicycles with some complicated timing as the characters weave in and out of frame, a tracking shot filmed on a road at Shepperton without the aid of back projection or post-synchronisation.[26] The film was extremely popular, passing into the language as a hilarious and characteristically British comedy.

Thus by the time war broke out both Fox and Paramount were using good-quality British films as quota. At Teddington Warner Brothers' films continued to be made until the end of 1937 by Woods and others, but Ince was killed in a car crash in April, at the age of fifty. The studio was shut during the final quota discussions. When the new legislation came into force production was adapted to make fewer but rather more expensive and ambitious films. By the time it reopened for Woods's drama *The Return of Carol Deane*, Irving Asher had left and it was under the management of Jerry Jackson. Production continued with films directed by Woods and Roy W. Neill, including more Max Miller films. *They Drive by Night*, probably the best of the Teddington films, was directed by Woods. It was a thriller set among the lorry drivers of the Great North Road, with a chilling climax in which a sex maniac sets out to strangle the heroine. Unlike earlier films made by the same people, it showed considerable attention to atmosphere and detail, with excellent London location material and a more realistic treatment of English low life than usual. Graham Greene went so far as to claim that dialogue, acting and direction were on a level with the French films so much admired by highbrows at the time. Whether Woods would have proved as outstanding as many people expected is hard to say. After making three more films he, like Pen Tennyson, was killed in the war.

Jackson left the company in March 1939 and the general production manager of Warner's eastern studios in America, Sam Sax, came over to take temporary charge as executive producer. *The Midas Touch* was made by another young director of whom much was expected, David MacDonald, who had recently had considerable success with the two Paramount crime reporter films. A Scot who had spent some years in Hollywood, MacDonald again starred Barry K. Barnes in this adaptation of a novel by Margaret Kennedy, but as its completion coincided with the outbreak of war it received little attention. The studio was closed for the first few months of the war but reopened in December under the management of Doc Salomon.

During the eight years of Warner Brothers' English operation it had produced about 140 films. Run with streamlined efficiency, the company achieved its aim of registering the necessary footage at a minimal cost of some £100,000 to £150,000 a year. This was considered more economical than acquiring or sponsoring the work of independent producers. If the films were good second features, which some of them were, that was a bonus. Many had been extremely poor, but it hardly mattered. The technicians, cameramen, writers, directors and art directors, as well as the casts, on the whole were good but they could not be expected to make outstanding pictures on budgets of less than £8,000.

RKO-Radio, apart from handling the Wilcox pictures *Victoria the Great* and *The Rat* in 1937 and *Sixty Glorious Years* in 1938, continued to make as little use as possible of British films, successfully registering many shorts and films from quota king George Smith as late as 1939. But even this company eventually found it necessary to come to terms with the new situation, and brought its producer William Sistrom over from America early in 1939. Two crime films were made at the Rock studios, directed by John Paddy Carstairs.

United Artists, which had lost the B & D films after the Elstree fire of 1936 and Wilcox's move to Pinewood, continued to handle Korda's films and in addition those of a number of independent producers, most of them made at Denham. These included Victor Saville's four films, the Douglas Fairbanks Jr films and others made by a number of emigrants from Europe including Max Schach, Paul Soskin, Erich Pommer, Alexander Esway, Lothar Mendes and Garrett-Klement.* There were few United Artists imports from America, and the company was not in need of quota. On the contrary, in 1937 as many as two-thirds of their offerings in Britain were from British studios. A number of these expensive and not always successful films were backed by Aldgate money, and United Artists was deeply involved in the production crisis. But in the last two years before the war its own output in America declined so much that the Korda films alone were more than enough to satisfy its quota needs.† As they had always handled expensive British films they were unaffected by the new cost clause.

When United Artists went into the large-scale exploitation of good-quality British films with the output of Korda, Wilcox and others, they needed a circuit outlet. There had been rumours as early as 1929 that they wanted a cinema circuit, although this was denied by Joe Schenck. But a company registered in November 1930 with a capital of £110,000, Entertainments and General Investment Corporation, acquired a controlling interest in County Cinemas, and although nothing was said in the trade press at the time it later transpired that there were two representatives of United Artists on the EGIC board, including Murray Silverstone. County had been founded in 1927 by C. F. Donada. By 1935 it had forty-three cinemas, organised somewhat like Odeon in many small companies. At this time more rumours were heard, this time of links not only with County but also with Deutsch. It would be convenient for Odeon, which unlike ABC and Gaumont-British had no production organisation, to have access to good British pictures for its quota. So an agreement between Odeon and United Artists was announced in January 1936. After some months, according to the 1952 report of Political and Economic Planning, United Artists duly acquired 50 per cent of Odeon's ordinary shares and a third of the preference shares; they also had the right to nominate three directors, although Deutsch retained his casting vote. Then the rationalisation of County was announced. A new issue of shares was made but subsequently withdrawn, and instead the company was integrated further with United Artists.

Big developments were to take place in 1937. In January a bid to turn Odeon into a £5 million company by a large capital issue failed because

---

* Garrett-Klement Pictures was a £1,000 company registered in March 1935 by Robert Garrett, whose background was Cambridge and the diplomatic service, and Otto Klement, a Czech who had been a theatrical producer and arrived in Britain via Austria and America. They made two ambitious films, *A Woman Alone* and *The Amazing Quest of Ernest Bliss*. But these, with foreign stars, directors and others in the unit, were not eligible for quota and the company closed down.

† On the outbreak of war they screened *An Englishman's Home*, produced by a patriotic commercial magnate from a play written in 1909 by 'a patriot'. It had also been filmed at the outbreak of the First World War.

it coincided with the crisis in confidence in British films, and although Deutsch did not intend to go into production the reluctance to invest in films temporarily extended to anything to do with the cinema. The subscription was so small that it was returned. Instead, Odeon merged with County Cinemas. Odeon Theatres Holding Company was registered with £10,000 capital in February, and in May Odeon acquired control of the body controlling County, EGIC. Deutsch joined its board, on which United Artists was already well represented, and R. S. Bromhead of County became general manager of the new group. This now numbered about 250 cinemas, most of them new and superior, and rivalled the other two big circuits.

Deutsch next reorganised his many small individual cinema companies into a new £6 million company, Odeon Theatres. The share issue in July was a great success, for this time the prospectus made it clear that the company would not engage in production. It was to be controlled by Odeon Cinema Holdings, in which United Artists had a 50 per cent interest. Murray Silverstone and George Archibald were on the board although Deutsch, who now joined the board of United Artists, still had his casting vote.

At the other end of the scale from the prestigious producers distributed by United Artists was Columbia, whose former policy had been to use cheap Empire films as quota. These no longer qualified and Columbia changed its approach completely, entering British production itself and making some excellent films. Irving Asher, who had been working for Korda as an associate producer since leaving Warners at the end of 1937, was engaged as executive producer and Harefield Productions was launched at Denham in the autumn of 1938. Made under a Korda contract, the films were expensive enough to register as double or triple quota and were to be distributed in America as well as Britain. *Q Planes*, from a script by Ian Dalrymple, was a fast and exciting spy story with a romantic angle and a light humorous touch. About the mysterious disappearance of secret experimental planes, it starred Ralph Richardson as a delightfully debonair secret service chief, Laurence Olivier as a test pilot and Valerie Hobson as a girl reporter. It was directed by the American Tim Whelan and made by Korda technicians, and its première was held in New York. Next *The Spy in Black* was directed by Michael Powell, who had been under contract to Korda but unoccupied since making *The Edge of the World*. From a novel about a U-boat commander in the First World War who landed in the Orkneys but was foiled by a beautiful British spy posing as a schoolmistress, it was a vehicle for Conrad Veidt, who was also under contract to Korda, and once more the cool and statuesque Valerie Hobson. Emeric Pressburger, a Hungarian scriptwriter who had worked at UFA and then gone to Paris after the rise of Hitler, came to Britain in September 1935 and joined Korda; he collaborated with Roland Pertwee on this script. The partnership with Powell gave the latter's career a new direction and was to last for many years. Fast and exciting, the film was full of tension and mystery and gave a powerful feeling of the sea, the island at night and the submarine. No attempt was made to reproduce the clothes and appearance of the 1914 war and the film seemed up to date, shown as it was in London the month before war broke out, and was a great success. Once Columbia decided to take the quota seriously they contributed good quality films, made with Asher's usual competence but on budgets which gave him greater scope than he had had at Teddington.

Both *Q Planes* and *The Spy in Black* were filmed in the autumn of 1938. In April the next year Asher registered his own £500 company, Irving Asher Productions, with J. R. Sutro and J. G. Saunders, and announced a large programme of films to be made independently at Denham for Columbia and others. Jerry Jackson, who had left Warners and rejoined him early in the year, was to produce. Only the first of these films was made, a spy film called *Ten Days in Paris* directed by Whelan and starring Rex Harrison. Its first screening coincided with the outbreak of war and Asher returned to America.*

By far the biggest changes were to be found at M-G-M. It had been the least co-operative under the previous quota but once it decided to produce in Britain it did so with greater panache than any other American company. At first, even after announcing plans to produce, the company continued to put out their Fitzpatrick travelogues, George King productions and Australian films until the very end of the old quota, and even offered an old Hagen film derided by *Kine Weekly* as 'a childish travesty'. But it embarked on the new quota with a flourish with its first British film, *A Yank at Oxford*, ready for showing as the new legislation came into force. An expensive film, it was registered as a treble, or the equivalent of 25,413 feet. Henceforth, although it occasionally fell back on short actualities and revue items, M-G-M's demand for rubbish disappeared and some of the worst film makers in the country found themselves without a customer. The three films shown before the war, all with an angle on Britain which would appeal to American audiences, were oustandingly successful.

After much discussion, with Michael Balcon and the M-G-M executives crossing and recrossing the Atlantic for consultations, it had been decided to go ahead with a story about a brash young American discovering a new way of life at Oxford University, an idea originally conceived several years before by J. Monk Saunders, a well-known American film writer who had himself been to Oxford. Many writers took a hand before it was finished, and the film is yet another example of the inadequacy of screen credits for scriptwriting. Robert Taylor, already a big star, was mobbed by fans on his arrival in Britain in September 1937. Production began at Denham with Jack Conway, a Hollywood director of long standing, and an American cameraman and editor. The fictitious Oxford college was created by a British art director, L. P. Williams. Production was marked by friction and

---

* In addition Columbia distributed *Twenty-One Days*, the 1937 flop made by Basil Dean with Korda – see under ATP.

frustration, both for writers Sidney Gilliat and Michael Hogan and for Balcon himself. Personalities clashed and Balcon, used to being his own boss as far as production went, found head office interference from Ben Goetz and the dictatorial L. B. Mayer intolerable. The film, however, with its rather strange American version of life at Oxford, was entertaining and technically worthy of M-G-M's Hollywood standards, and was extremely successful both in Britain and in America. It made an international star of Vivien Leigh.

Big plans were immediately announced in April for further films but Balcon, ostracised by the executives but legally unable to work for anyone else, finally sued M-G-M successfully for damages and in June 1938 formally parted company with them. In the meantime Victor Saville, after his four independent productions at Denham, had thoughtfully acquired for £14,000 the film rights to Dr A. J. Cronin's recent best seller about an idealistic young doctor from a Welsh mining town temporarily seduced by the temptations of a wealthy society practice. Before *Yank* was finished M-G-M already had plans to film it. Saville later claimed[27] that he let M-G-M have the rights for the same sum that he paid for them. He slipped into Balcon's place as producer in May. Unlike Balcon, and indeed many other people, he had no difficulty in getting along with 'LB', whom he later described as 'terrific'.[28] After this he and his old friend Balcon, with whom relations were already strained, were not on speaking terms for many years.

The Citadel was directed by King Vidor. His wife, the American scriptwriter Elizabeth Hill, was nominated for an Oscar for her work on it, but again, in true Hollywood style, this film was the product of many writers. The unit included many former members of Balcon's team. It starred the American Rosalind Russell and Robert Donat, already well known in America for *The Count of Monte Cristo*, backed by an outstanding cast which included Ralph Richardson as a doctor colleague from Wales. Combining a little picturesque poverty, some glamorous society settings, a mild sentimental denouement and a bit of social significance, the film was well made and beautifully acted and was another box-office and critical success. For Saville, it was a step towards Hollywood.

In July 1938 M-G-M announced that in addition to their own films they would in future distribute certain Gainsborough and Gaumont-British productions as well. Under this agreement *The Lady Vanishes*, *Climbing High* and *Ask a Policeman* were handled by them. So, also, was the Pinebrook film *The Lambeth Walk*, made at Pinewood in September. This version of the successful 1937 musical *Me and My Girl*, containing a dance called the Lambeth Walk which had swept the dance halls of the country, starred Lupino Lane, who had been in the stage production. Directed by Albert de Courville, it seems to have been corny and overplayed, trading on the popularity of the original.

The next of M-G-M's own productions, *Goodbye, Mr Chips*, was an adaptation by R. C. Sherriff of a popular novel by James Hilton. Like both the previous films it exploited an English subject in a way that would appeal to the American public, and its première was held in America. Like *The Citadel* it starred Donat, who portrayed the shy and gentle master at a public school through a long career from nervous beginner to final much-loved, white-haired retirement. Greer Garson, an Irish actress sadly ignored by British producers, entered films as his young wife who dies in childbirth, making a brief and gracious appearance and then departing for Hollywood. Using Repton school as its background, the film gave a sentimental picture of the British public school from the 1870s to the 1920s. It was directed by another Hollywood director, Sam Wood, and photographed by Freddie Young, and was made with the same technical excellence and assurance as the other M-G-M films. It was another resounding success, and the character of Mr Chips became synonymous with the benign old schoolmaster. Donat won an Oscar for his performance.

Goodbye, Mr Chips proved to be another stepping stone for Saville, who now left for Hollywood and was not to make another film in Britain for ten years. The last of the four planned, *Busman's Honeymoon*, which he was originally going to produce, starred Robert Montgomery as Dorothy L. Sayers's amateur sleuth Lord Peter Wimsey and was eventually produced by Harold Huth after war broke out.

It has been suggested that M-G-M had no intention of making more than a few films in Britain, but made them on an impressive scale to disarm criticism during the quota discussions. This cannot be true. Only the first was in production in time to have any such effect, and meanwhile tawdry quota films continued to be registered until the last possible date. Sam Eckman showed complete contempt for his critics throughout. Once the new legislation had disqualified the rubbish, this extremely business-like company produced and handled only triple- and double-quota films, thus considerably reducing the footage they required. And these three expensive and lavish productions were among the most successful and best remembered films made in Britain during the thirties.

Had there been no war the new legislation would certainly have succeeded in raising the average quality of British films whilst reducing their number, by the mere fact that quota quickies were not made any more. The doubling and trebling clauses also encouraged a reduction in numbers, as well as a more lavish scale of production. We have seen elsewhere that the drop in output was regarded in some quarters as proof of the Act's failure, for studios closed and many were unemployed. But, remembering what the quota films had been like, their disappearance can hardly be regarded as a bad thing. Safeguarding the employment of those producing quota films had not been one of the objectives of the Act, but in the discussions preceding it the fact that many of those working in the industry were making just the kind of films it was proposed to abolish does not seem to have been faced. The Act did succeed in revolutionising the activities of the American companies, which now either distributed good quality British films or produced such films themselves. Whether in time this might have led to an opening up of the American market not only to their own British films but to those of other British producers as well is an open question. The reciprocity proposals were a practical encouragement of this, but, whereas an occasional import might be all very well, there was no reason why Hollywood should welcome large-scale invasion of its own market. The three M-G-M films were proof of the British producer's continuing dilemma. M-G-M intended to distribute them in America, and therefore could afford to produce them on a similar scale to their Hollywood films. It has been argued in this study that although it is sometimes possible, with a lot of talent, to make good films on modest budgets in general a constant level of high quality is expensive and needs to be sure of a big market not just for isolated films but as a matter of course. The Americans had one and the British did not, and underlying the history of the British film industry is its struggle to come to terms with that fact.

Notes

Chapter 1 Exploitation

1 *Kine Weekly*, 15 March 1934, p. 21.
2 ibid., 7 August 1930, pp. 19 and 39.
3 ibid., 26 March 1931, p. 55.
4 S. L. Bernstein, 'A Memorandum on the Scarcity of the Film Supply together with a Scheme to Assist British Film Production'.
5 *Kine Weekly*, 17 January 1935, p. 4.
6 ibid., 25 July 1935, p. 4.
7 ibid., 17 September 1937, p. 37.
8 ibid., 29 November 1934, p. 5.
9 Charles Davy (ed.), *Footnotes to the Film*, p. 275.

Chapter 2 The Organisation of Labour

1 G. H. Elvin, 'Trade Unionism and the British Film Industry' in *Penguin Film Review*, No. 3, 1947.
2 *Kine Year Book*, 1931, p. 137.
3 G. H. Elvin, op. cit.
4 *Kine Weekly*, 15 February 1934, p. 3.
5 ibid., 24 October 1935, p. 5.
6 ibid., 21 July 1938, pp. 3 and 15.
7 ibid., 30 July 1936, pp. 4 and 15.
8 ibid., 28 July 1938, p. 36.
9 ibid., 9 February 1939, p. 11.
10 ibid., 23 February 1939, p. 12.
11 *Kine Year Book*, 1932, p. 128.
12 R. J. Minney, *Puffin Asquith.*
13 *Kine Weekly*, 8 February 1934, p. 55.
14 ibid., 19 January 1939.
15 Alan and Mary Wood, *Silver Spoon.*
16 ibid.
17 Proposed studio standard agreement presented by the ACT (Basil Dean papers).

Chapter 3 The Quota

1 *Kine Weekly*, 31 July 1930, p. 19.
2 *Minutes of Evidence taken before the Departmental Committee on Cinematograph Films* (Moyne Committee), para. 1045.
3 Basil Dean papers.
4 ibid.
5 Moyne Report (op. cit.) para. 1008.
6 Memorandum to the FBI by Simon Rowson, 8 February 1937.
7 Basil Dean papers.
8 ibid.
9 *Proposals for Legislation on Cinematograph Films.*
10 *Kine Weekly*, 10 December 1936, p. 4.
11 Basil Dean papers.

12 *Kine Weekly*, 24 February 1938.
13 *Daily Telegraph* 2 January 1939.
14 Letter of 6 January 1939 to Christopher Powell (Basil Dean papers).
15 Report of the annual general meeting of the AC-T, April 1939.

Chapter 4   The Censorship of Feature Films

1   Canon Hall, *Kine Weekly*, 19 May 1932, p. 15.
2   *Kine Weekly*, 14 August 1930, p. 60.
3   Dorothy Knowles, *The Censor, the Drama and the Film, 1900–1934*.
4   British Board of Film Censors, *Report*, 1930 p. 10.
5   *Kine Weekly*, 21 April 1932, p. 25.
6   ibid. 22 January 1931, p. 51.
7   Dorothy Knowles, op. cit.
8   ibid.
9   *Listener*, 27 December 1934, 16 January 1935.
10 *The Times*, 29 October 1934.
11 British Board of Film Censors, *Report*, 1932, p. 16.
12 Dorothy Knowles, op. cit., p. 193.
13 *Kine Weekly*, 12 September 1935, p. 36.
14 British Board of Film Censors, *Report*, 1932, p. 6.
15 *Kine Weekly*, 11 November 1933, p. 38.
16 ibid., 21 March 1935, p. 16.
17 *Spectator*, 18 December 1936.
18 Dorothy Knowles, op. cit., p. 226.
19 *The Oxford Companion to Film*.
20 B. Causton and G. G. Young, *Keeping it Dark* p. 45.
21 Dorothy Knowles, op. cit., p. 260.
22 British Board of Film Censors, *Report*, 1929, p. 2.
23 *Kine Weekly*, 24 January 1935, p. 5.
24 B. Causton and G. G. Young, op. cit., p. 49.

Chapter 5   The Arrival of the Talkie

1   *Kine Weekly*, 18 June 1931, p. 65.
2   John Scotland, *The Talkies*.
3   Bernard Brown, *Talking Pictures*.
4   *Close Up*, September 1931, p. 205.
5   Bernard Brown, op. cit., p. 276.
6   *Kine Year Book*, 1932, p. 204.
7   *Films and Players*, item 532.
8   W. Pitkin and W. M. Marston, *The Art of Sound Pictures*.
9   *Films and Players*, item 634.
10 W. Pitkin and W. M. Marston, op. cit. pp. 228–9.
11 *Close Up*, September 1931, pp. 203–4.
12 ibid., p. 205.
13 Interview with the author, June 1971.
14 R. J. Minney, op. cit., p. 63.
15 *Kine Weekly*, 4 June 1931, p. 46.
16 ibid., 25 September 1930, p. 25.
17 ibid., 30 June 1932, p. 43.

Chapter 6 Language Barriers

1 *Life and Letters*, September 1935, pp. 199–200.
2 *Kine Weekly*, 11 December 1930.
3 ibid. 30 April 1931, p. 46.
4 Josef von Sternberg, *Fun in a Chinese Laundry*, p. 221.
5 *World Film Encyclopedia*, p. 351.
6 Interview with the author, June 1973.
7 *Close Up*, December 1932.
8 Adrian Brunel, *Nice Work*.
9 Interview with the author.
10 *Kine Weekly* 31 October 1929.
11 ibid., 3 November 1932.
12 ibid., 10 December 1931.
13 Adrian Brunel, op. cit., p. 162.
14 *The Silent Picture*, No. 11/12, summer/autumn 1971.
15 J. M. Harvey in *Life and Letters Today*, Autumn 1936, pp. 166–70.

Chapter 7 Colour Films

1 Lucien Egrot in *Kine Weekly*, 10 October 1929, p. 63.
2 Basil Dean, *Mind's Eye*, p. 108.
3 *Kine Weekly*, 9 November 1933.
4 Pennethorne Hughes in *Cinema Quarterly*, Vol. 2, No. 1, p. 17.
5 Eric Elliott in *Cinema Quarterly*, Vol. 2, No. 3, p. 163.
6 *Spectator*, 19 July 1935.
7 *Kine Year Book*, 1935, p. 258.
8 Charles Davy, op. cit., p. 121.
9 Major Adrian Klein, 'Three-Colour Cinematography' in *Discovery*, July 1935.
10 Charles Davy, op. cit.
11 Graham Greene, *The Pleasure Dome*.
12 Charles Davy, op. cit.
13 Major Adrian Klein, *Colour Cinematography*.
14 ibid.

Chapter 8 Production in the Early Thirties

1 *Kine Weekly*, 19 March 1931, p. 53.
2 François Truffaut, *Hitchcock*, pp. 65 and 67.
3 Henry Kendall, *I Remember Romano's*, p. 111.
4 ibid., pp. 118–35.
5 *Kine Weekly*, 3 December 1931, p. 36.
6 *Cinema Quarterly*, Vol. 2, No. 2.
7 Upton Sinclair, *Upton Sinclair Presents William Fox*, pp. 78–9.
8 *Hansard*, 16 March 1937, col. 1885.
9 Theodore Komisarjevsky, *Myself and the Theatre*, pp. 166–7.
10 Interview with the author, June 1973.
11 Interview with the author, December 1972.
12 Interview with the author, June 1973.
13 Herbert Wilcox, *25,000 Sunsets*, p. 139.
14 Alan and Mary Wood, op. cit., p. 172.
15 Basil Dean, op. cit., p. 145.
16 Michael Balcon, *Michael Balcon Presents . . . A Lifetime of Films*, p. 117.
17 Basil Dean, op. cit. p. 134.
18 ibid., p. 138.

19   Michael Parkinson Show, BBC TV, 5 November 1977.
20   Basil Dean, op. cit., p. 165.
21   ibid.
22   *Kine Weekly*, 15 March 1934, p. 37.
23   Basil Dean, op. cit., p. 203.
24   Alan and Mary Wood, op. cit., p. 164.
25   *Kine Weekly*, 24 August 1933.
26   Paul Tabori, *Alexander Korda*, p. 178.
27   *Cinema Quarterly*, Vol. 3, No. 3.
28   Paul Tabori, op. cit., pp. 162 and 178.
29   *Kine Weekly*, 5 June 1930, p. 24.
30   Interview with the author, July 1972.
31   George Pearson, *Flashback*, pp. 193–5.
32   Adrian Brunel, op. cit., pp. 173–4.
33   Edward Carrick, *Art and Design in the British Film*, p. 42.
34   Rodney Ackland and Elspeth Grant, *The Celluloid Mistress*, p. 87.
35   Edward Carrick, *Designing for Films*, p. 27.
36   Letter to the author from Janet Jacomb-Hood dated October 1971.
37   Alan and Mary Wood, op.cit.
38   Adrian Brunel, op. cit., p. 170.
39   *Kine Weekly*, 18 July 1935, p. 33.
40   Interview with the author, 1950.
41   *Kine Weekly*, 2 May 1935, p. 20.
42   June Head, *Star Gazing*, p. 110.
43   *Kine Weekly*, 27 September 1934, p. 20.
44   Alan and Mary Wood, op. cit., p. 162.
45   Peter Morris, *Embattled Shadows*.
46   Interview with the author, June 1973.
47   Moyne Report (op. cit.), para. 1084.

Chapter 9   Production in the Late Thirties

1   Brian Connell, *Knight Errant*, p. 80.
2   F. D. Klingender and Stuart Legg, *Money Behind the Screen* p. 49.
3   See *Films of Comment and Persuasion of the 1930s* by the author.
4   Lawrence Langer, *GBS and the Lunatic*, p. 226.
5   S. N. Behrman, *The Suspended Drawing Room*, pp. 69–70.
6   Gabriel Pascal, 'Shaw as Scenario Writer', in *GBS 90*.
7   Alan Wood, *Mr Rank*, p. 102.
8   Helmut Junge, *Plan for Film Studios*.
9   Adrian Brunel, op. cit., p. 180.
10   Jack Whittingham, *Sabu and the Elephants*, p. 99.
11   Paul Tabori, op. cit. p. 181.
12   See *Kine Year Book*, 1940, p. 196.
13   See Karol Kulik, *Alexander Korda*; and 'Powell and Pressburger: The War Years', report of an interview by David Badder in *Sight and Sound*, winter 1978–9.
14   Leslie Ruth Howard, *A Quite Remarkable Father*, p. 176.
15   George Arliss, *George Arliss by Himself*, p. 241.
16   *Hansard*, 9 March 1937, col. 962; 16 March 1937, col 1884–6.
17   *Hansard*, 8 March 1938, col. 1705.
18   Herbert Wilcox, op. cit., p. 113.
19   James Agate, *Around Cinemas*, pp. 185–8.
20   Herbert Wilcox, op. cit., p. 121.
21   Basil Dean, op. cit., p. 256.
22   Letter to the author, September 1981.
23   Interview with the author, June 1973.

24   Unedited transcript of an interview with Anthony Slide on 1 October 1976.
25   Moyne Report (op. cit.), para. 1045.
26   R. J. Minney, op. cit., p. 100.
27   Interview with the author, December 1972.
28   ibid.

Appendix: Quota Registrations

Table 1   *Number of Long Films Registered by Renters*

Quota Year (1 April–31 March)	British Long Films	Foreign Long Films	All Long Films
1928–9	131	550	681
1929–30	96	506	602
1930–1	125	556	681
1931–2	154	464	618
1932–3	162	481	643
1933–4	195	484	679
1934–5	189	477	667
1935–6	212	506	718
1936–7	225	521	746
1937–8	228	614	842
1938–9	103	535	638
1939–40	108	399	507

(Based on *Kine Year Book* registration lists).

Table 2 Renters' Quota

Footage of films registered by renters (in thousand feet)

Quota Year (1 April–31 March)	Long Films			Short Films			All Films		
	British	Foreign	Total	British	Foreign	Total	British	Foreign	Total
1928–9	904	3,400	4,304	170	922	1,092	1,074	4,322	5,396
1929–30	624	3,331	3,955	150	1,204	1,354	774	4,535	5,309
1930–1	789	3,649	4,438	60	1,160	1,220	849	4,809	5,658
1931–2	928	2,962	3,890	59	1,071	1,130	987	4,033	5,020
1932–3	961	3,057	4,018	47	893	940	1.008	3,950	4,958
1933–4	1,180	3,115	4,295	60	769	829	1,240	3,884	5,124
1934–5	1,183	3,116	4,299	68	891	959	1,251	4,007	5,258
1935–6	1,379	3,316	4,695	96	756	852	1,475	4,072	5,547
(Based on figures supplied by the Board of Trade to the Moyne Committee)									
1938–9	871	3,214	4,085	335	892	1,227	1,206	4,106	5,312
1939–40	818	2,355	3,173	273	522	795	1,091	2,877	3,968

(Figures from the *Board of Trade Journal*)

Table 3 *Renters' Quota 1 April 1938 – 31 March 1939*

Long Films – British

Registration		Number of Films	Reg. Length (ft)	Renters' Quota (ft)
Br/E	Exhibitors' only	25	137,494	—
Br/R (single)	Renters' quota	47	321,176	321,176
Br/DR (double)	Renters' × 2	21	158,979	317,958
Br/TR (treble)	Renters' × 3	10*	80,093	231,770
	Total	103	697,742	870,904

Long Films – Foreign

Number of Films			Registered Length (ft)	
Renters' quota		501	Renters' quota	3,214,347
Exempt under Section 4†		34	Exempt under Section 4	274,475
	Total	535	Total	3,488,822

Short Films – British

Registration	Number of Films	Reg. Length (ft)	Renters' Quota (ft)
Exhibitors' quota only	3	5,084	—
Renters' quota	272	335,437	335,437
Total	275	340,521	335,437

Short Films – Foreign

Number of Films			Reg. Length (ft)	Renters' Quota (ft)
	Total	776	891,840	891,840

* includes 1 which counts as double under Section 3.

† In addition 12 films of an aggregate length of 93,260 feet which were registered under the 1927 Act were exempt from the Renters' Quota under Section 4.

(Figures from *Board of Trade Journal*).

Table 4   *Renters' Quota 1 April 1939 – 31 March 1940*

Long Films – British

Registration		Number of Films	Reg. Length (ft)	Renters' Quota (ft)
Br/E	Exhibitors' only	25	131,753	—
Br/R (single)	Renters' quota	57	383,611	383,611
Br/DR (double)	Renters' × 2	20	148,506	287,623
Br/TR (treble)	Renters' × 3	6	52,114	146,799
	Total	108	715,984	818,033

Long Films – Foreign

Number of Films			Registered Length (ft)	
Renters' quota		368	Renters' quota	2,354,920
Exempt under Section* 4		31	Exempt under Section 4	260,883
	Total	399	Total	2,615,803

Short Films – British

Registration		Number of Films	Reg. Length (ft)	Renters' Quota (ft)
Exhibitors' quota only		2	1,747	—
Renters' quota		205	272,804	272,804
	Total	207	274,551	272,804

Short Films – Foreign

Number of Films			Reg. Length (ft)	Renters' Quota (ft)
	Total	508	521,925	521,925

* Directions cancelled in respect of one film.
(Figures from *Board of Trade Journal*).

Table 5 *Films Registered by Renters, Comparing Statutory and Actual Quota*

Quota Year (1 April–31 March)	Renters' Quota Obligation	All Films Registered (000 ft)		Approximate Quota actually Registered*
		British	Total	
1928–9	7·5 %	1,074	5,396	19·9 %
1929–30	10	774	5,309	14·5
1930–1	10	849	5,658	15·0
1931–2	12·5	987	5,020	19·6
1932–3	15	1,008	4,958	20·3
1933–4	17·5	1,240	5,234	24·1
1934–5	17·5	1,251	5,258	23·8
1935–6	20	1,475	5,547	26·6

Quota Year (1 April–31 March)	Renters' Quota (Short) Obligation	All Short Films Registered (000 ft)		Approximate Quota actually Registered*
		British	Total	
1938–9	15 %	335	1,227	27·3 %
1939–40	15	273	795	34·3

Quota Year (1 April–31 March)	Renters' Quota (Long) Obligation	All Films Registered (000 ft)		Approximate Quota actually Registered*
		British	Total	
1938–9	15 %	871	4,085	21·3 %
1939–40	20	818	3,172	25·8

(Figures for 1928–36 are based on evidence given to the Moyne Committee by the Board of Trade, those for 1938–40 from the *Board of Trade Journal*.)

* Although the Board of Trade figures treat all registered films as eligible for quota there were in fact some exceptions, especially among short films.

Table 6 *Films Registered by Exhibitors,*
Comparing Statutory and Actual Quota

Quota Year (1 April–31 March)	Exhibitors' Quota Obligation	Aggregate Length of Film Registered (Million Feet)		Quota Actually Shown
		British	Total	
1931–2	10 %	7,130	32,980	21·6 %
1932–3	12·5	8,100	34,100	23·7
1933–4	15	9,460	36,256	26·1
1934–5	15	9,575	37,520	25·5
1935–6	20	10,896	39,735	27·4
1936–7	20	11,939	42,726	27·9
1937–8	15*	11,555	44,999	25·7
1938–9	12·5†	10,618	45,776	23·2

Quota Year (1 April–31 March)	Aggregate Length of Long Films Registered (Million Feet)			Aggregate Length of Short Films Registered (Million Feet)		
	Total	British	Percentage of Total Long Films	Total	British	Percentage of Total Short Films
1931–2	28,380	6,890	(24·3)	4,600	240	(5·2)
1932–3	30,100	7,900	(26·2)	4,000	200	(5·0)
1933–4	32,433	9,219	(28·4)	3,823	241	(6·3)
1934–5	33,498	9,406	(28·1)	4,022	169	(4·2)
1935–6	35,900	10,571	(29·4)	3,835	325	(8·5)
1936–7	39,099	11,447	(29·3)	3,627	492	(13·6)
1937–8	41,435	10,949	(26·4)	3,564	606	(17·0)
1938–9†	41,616	9,475	(22·8)	4,160	1,143	(27·5)

Aggregate lengths include repeated performances. News, travel and educational films are not included. Years from 1928 to 1931 not published in the *Board of Trade Journal.*

* Quota was reduced from original figure.
† In the first year of the second Quota Act there were separate quotas for long and short films, in both cases of 12%.

Bibliography

Ackland, Rodney, and Grant, Elspeth, *The Celluloid Mistress* (Allan Wingate, 1954).

Agate, James, *Around Cinemas* (Home and Van Thal, 1946).

Aldgate, Tony, 'The British Cinema in the 1930s', in *Popular Culture* (Open University, 1981).

Aldgate, Tony, 'Ideological Consensus in British Feature Films, 1935–1947', in K. R. M. Short (ed.), *Feature Films as History* (Croom Helm, 1981)

Arliss, George, *George Arliss by Himself* (John Murray, 1940).

Arnold, J. E., and Enid Jones, M., *Over Fifteen Hundred Things You Want to Know About Films and Players* (English Newspapers Ltd, 1933).

Atwell, David, *Cathedrals of the Movies* (Architectural Press, 1980).

Baker, Thomas Thorne, *The Kingdom of the Camera* (G. Bell, 1934).

Balbi, C. M. R., *Talking Pictures and Acoustics* (Pitman, 1931).

Balcon, Michael, *Michael Balcon Presents . . . A Lifetime of Films* (Hutchinson, 1969).

Barkas, Natalie, *Behind the Camera* (Geoffrey Bles, 1934).

Barkas, Natalie, *Thirty Thousand Miles for the Films* (Blackie and Son, 1937).

Baxter, Beverley, *Strange Street* (Hutchinson, 1935).

Behrman, S. N., *The Suspended Drawing Room* (Hamish Hamilton, 1966).

Bennett, Alfred Gordon, *Cinemania: Aspects of Filmic Creation* (Jarrolds, 1937).

Bernstein, S. L., 'A Memorandum on the Scarcity of the Film Supply Together with a Scheme to Assist British Film Production' (privately printed, November 1939).

Betts, Ernest (ed.), *Jew Süss*, script of the film (Methuen, 1935).

Betts, Ernest (ed.), *The Private Life of Henry VIII*, story and dialogue of the film (Methuen, 1934).

BKSTS Journal, The, Volume 63, Number 1, January 1981, fiftieth anniversary issue (British Kinematograph Sound and Television Society).

Board of Trade, *Minutes of Evidence taken before the Departmental Committee on Cinematograph Films* under the Chairmanship of Lord Moyne (HMSO 1936).

Board of Trade Journal 13 June 1935, 28 May 1936, 26 August 1937, 7 July 1938, 25 May 1939, 13 June 1940.

Bond, Ralph, *Film Business is Big Business* (Association of Cine-Technicians, 1939).

Bower, Dallas, *Plan for Cinema* (Dent, 1936).

British Board of Film Censors, Annual Reports.

Brook, Clive, 'The Eighty-Four Ages of Clive Brook' (unpublished manuscript).

Brown, Bernard, *Talking Pictures* (Pitman, 1931).

Brown, Geoff, *Launder and Gilliat* (British Film Institute, 1977).

Brown, Geoff, *Walter Forde* (British Film Institute, 1977).

Brunel, Adrian, *Nice Work* (Forbes Robertson, 1949).

Burnett, R. G. and Martell, E. D., *The Devil's Camera*, (The Epworth Press, 1932).

Calder-Marshall, Arthur, *The Innocent Eye* (W. H. Allen, 1963).

Carrick, Edward, *Designing for Films* (Studio Publications, 1949).

Carrick, Edward, *Designing for Moving Pictures* (Studio Publications, 1941).

Carstairs, John Paddy, *Honest Injun!* (Hurst and Blackett, 1943).

Carstairs, John Paddy, *Movie Merry-go-round* (Newnes, 1937).

Castle, Charles, in collaboration with Diana Napier Tauber, *This Was Richard Tauber* (W. H. Allen, 1971)

Causton, Bernard and Young, G. G., *Keeping it Dark* (Mandrake Press, 1930).

Chesmore, Stuart, *Behind the Cinema Screen* (Nelson, 1934).

Cinema Quarterly 1932–1935.

Clarence, O. B., *No Complaints* (Jonathan Cape, 1943).

Close Up 1928–1933.

Cochrane, Charles B., *Cock-a-Doodle-Do* (Dent, 1941).

Coe, Brian, 'Colour Systems of the Thirties', in *The BKSTS Journal* (Vol. 63, No. 1, January 1981).

Connell, Brian, *Knight Errant* (Hodder & Stoughton, 1955).

Coster, Ian, *Friends in Aspic* (John Miles, 1939).

Cotes, Peter, *George Robey* (Cassell, 1972).

Courtneidge, Cicely, *Cicely* (Hutchinson, 1953).

Cousins, E. G., *Filmland in Ferment* (Denis Archer, 1932).

Cousins, E. G., *How to Enter the Film World* (Allen & Unwin, 1935).

Cowan, Lester (ed.), *Recording Sound for Motion Pictures* (McGraw-Hill, 1931).

Crowther, Bosley, *The Lion's Share* (E. P. Dutton and Company, New York, 1957).

Davies, Brenda (ed.), *Carol Reed* (British Film Institute, 1978).

Davy, Charles (ed.), *Footnotes to the Film* (Lovat Dickson, 1938).

Dean, Basil, *Mind's Eye* (Hutchinson, 1973).

Dean, Basil, correspondence and related papers.

Dickinson, Thorold, *A Discovery of Cinema* (Oxford University Press, 1971).

Donaldson, Frances, *Freddy Lonsdale* (Heinemann, 1957).

Dunbar, Janet, *Flora Robson* (Harrap, 1961).

Economist, The, 15 April 1939, 'First Year of the Film Act'; 23 January 1937 'Notes of the Week'; 6 February 1937, leading article; 13 February 1937, leading article.

Eisler, Hanns, *Composing for the Films* (Dennis Dobson, 1951).

Elliott, W. F., *Sound Recording for Films* (Pitman, 1937).

Ellis, Vivian, *I'm on a See-Saw* (Michael Joseph, 1953).

Elvin, G. H., 'Trade Unionism in the British Film Industry', in *Penguin Film Review*, No. 3, 1947.

Fairfax-Jones, Martin, 'The Everyman in the Thirties', in *Hampstead in the Thirties* 1934.

Fawcett, L'Estrange, *Writing for the Films* (Pitman, 1932).

Federation of British Industries, *Cinematograph Films Bill. A Summary of the Present Position showing the Defects of the Measure from the Point of View of the British Film Producers* (Film Producers' Group, 21 February 1938).

Federation of British Industries, *The Case for British Films* (Film Producers' Group, February 1938).

Fields, Gracie, *Sing as we Go* (Frederick Muller, 1960).

Film Art, 1933–1937.

Film Quarterly, The, Spring and Summer 1937.

Film Society, The, Programmes for Season 5 (1929–30) to Season 14 (1938–9).

Financial Times, 7 June 1930, 'Gaumont Denial'; 7 January 1939, item about merger; 10 January 1939, interview with Oscar Deutsch.

Flaherty, Frances Hubbard, *Elephant Dance* (Faber, 1937).

Flynn, Errol, *My Wicked, Wicked Ways* (Heinemann, 1959).

Fisher, John, *George Formby* (The Woburn Press, 1975).

Gifford, Denis, *The British Film Catalogue 1895–1970* (David & Charles 1973).

Glyn, Anthony, *Elinor Glyn* (Hutchinson, 1955).

Green, Roger Lancelyn, *A. E. W. Mason* (Parrish, 1952).

Greene, Graham, *The Pleasure Dome* (Secker & Warburg, 1972).

Griffith, Richard, *The World of Robert Flaherty* (Gollancz, 1953).

Hardwicke, Sir Cedric, *A Victorian in Orbit* (Methuen, 1961).

Hare, Robertson, *Yours Indubitably* (Robert Hale, 1956).

Head, June, *Star Gazing* (Peter Davies, 1931).

Hicks, Sir Seymour, *Hail Fellow Well Met* (Staples Press, 1949).

Higham, Charles, *Charles Laughton* (W. H. Allen, 1976)

Honri, Baynham, 'Sixty Years in the Show Business', in *Cine Trade News,* May/June 1970.

Honri, Baynham, 'Photographic Sound Recording', in *British Journal of Photography,* 23 April 1971, 15 May 1971 and 21 May 1971.

Howard, Leslie Ruth, *A Quite Remarkable Father* (Longmans, 1959).

Hulbert, Jack, *The Little Woman's Always Right* (W. H. Allen, 1975).

Junge, Helmut, *Plan for Film Studios* (Focal Press, 1945).

Kendall, Henry, *I Remember Romano's* (Macdonald, 1960).

Kiesling, Barrett C., *Talking Pictures* (E. & F. N. Spon, 1937).

Kinematograph Weekly 1929–1939 (Odhams).

Kine Year Book 1929–40 (Odhams).

Klein, Major Adrian, *Colour Cinematography* (Chapman & Hall, 1936; revised and enlarged, 1939).

Klein, Major Adrian, 'Three-Colour cinematography', in *Discovery,* July 1939.

Klingender, F. D., and Legg, Stuart, *Money Behind the Screen* (Lawrence & Wishart, 1937).

Knight, Esmond, *Seeking the Bubble* (Hutchinson, 1943).

Knowles, Dorothy, *The Censor, the Drama and the Film, 1900–1934* (Allen & Unwin, 1934).

Komisarjevsky, Theodore, *Myself and the Theatre* (Dutton, 1930).

Korda, Michael, *Charmed Lives* (Allen Lane, 1980).

Kulik, Karol, *Alexander Korda – The Man Who Could Work Miracles* (W. H. Allen, 1975).

Lambert, R. S. (ed.), *For Film Goers Only* (Faber, for British Institute of Adult Education, 1934).

Lanchester, Elsa, *Charles Laughton and I* (Faber, 1938).

Langner, Lawrence, *GBS and the Lunatic* (Hutchinson, 1964).

Lee, Norman, *Money for Film Stories* (Pitman, 1937).

Lejeune, C. A., *Chestnuts in her Lap, 1936–1946* (Phoenix House, 1947).

Lejeune, C. A., *Cinema* (Maclehose, 1931).

Lejeune, C. A., *Thank You for Having Me* (Hutchinson, 1964).

Leprohon, Pierre, *Le Cinéma et la Montagne* (Editions J. Susse, 1944).

Levy, Louis, *Music for the Movies* (Sampson Low, Marston, 1948).

Life and Letters, 1928–35.

Life and Letters Today 1935–39.

London, Kurt, *Film Music* (Faber, 1936).

Lupino, Stanley, *From the Stocks to the Stars* (Hutchinson, 1934).

MacGregor, Alasdair Alpin, *A Last Voyage to St Kilda* (Cassell, 1931).

Macqueen-Pope, W., *Ivor* (W. H. Allen, 1951).

Maltby, H. F., *Ring up the Curtain* (Hutchinson, 1950).

Mason, A. E. W., 'The Artistic Future of the Film', in the *Journal of the Royal Society of Arts,* 22 July 1938.

Matthews, A. E., *Matty* (Hutchinson, 1952).

Matthews, Jessie, *Over My Shoulder* (W. H. Allen, 1974).

Milton, Billy, *Milton's Paradise Mislaid* (Jupiter, 1976).

Minney, R. J., *Puffin Asquith* (Leslie Frewin, 1973).

Montagu, Ivor, *The Youngest Son* (Lawrence & Wishart, 1970).

Morris, Peter, *Embattled Shadows* (McGill-Queen's University Press, 1978).

Moyne Committee, The, *Cinematograph Films Act 1927: Report of a Committee appointed by the Board of Trade* (HMSO, 1937).

Mullen, Pat, *Man of Aran* (Faber, 1934).

Myerscough-Walker, R., in *The Artist* Vol. XIV, September 1937–February 1938. pp. 22, 54, 86, 118, 150, 190.

Napier-Tauber, Diana, *Richard Tauber* (Art and Educational Publishers, 1949).

Nathan, Archie, *Costumes by Nathan* (Newnes,1960).

Neagle, Anna, *An Autobiography* (W. H. Allen, 1974).

Parker, John (ed.), *Who's Who in the Theatre* (Pitman, ninth edition, 1939).

Pascal, Valerie, *The Disciple and his Devil* (Michael Joseph, 1971).

Patch, Blanche, *Thirty Years with GBS* (Gollancz, 1951).

Patterson, Lindsay, (ed.), *Black Films and Film Makers* (Dodd, Mead & Co., USA, 1975).

Pearson, George, *Flashback* (George Allen and Unwin, 1957).

Pearson, George, Unpublished diary of visit to Hollywood between September 1929 and March 1930, and notes on the filming of *Journey's End.*

Pitkin, Walter and Marston, William M. *The Art of Sound Pictures* (Appleton & Company, 1930).

Political and Economic Planning, *The British Film Industry* (PEP, 1952).

Powell, Michael, *200,000 Feet on Foula* (Faber, 1938).

Randall, Alan and Seaton, Ray, *George Formby* (W. H. Allen, 1974).

Reader, Ralph, *Ralph Reader Remembers* (Bailey Brothers & Swinfen 1974).

Richards, Jeffrey, 'The British Board of Film Censors and Content Control in the 1930's: Images of Britain, in *Historical Journal of Film, Radio and Television*, Vol. 1, No. 2, 1981.

Robeson, Eslanda C., *Paul Robeson, Negro* (Gollancz, 1930).

Robey, George, *Looking Back on Life* (Constable, 1933).

Robinson, Martha, *Continuity Girl* (Robert Hale, 1937).

Robson, E. W., and Robson M. M., *The Film Answers Back* (John Lane, 1939).

Rotha, Paul, *Celluloid – The Film Today* (Longmans, Green, 1931).

Rowson, Simon, Address to the Royal Statistical Society on 17 December 1935, in the *Journal of the Royal Statistical Society*, Vol. XCIX, 1936.

Sabaneev, Leonid, *Music for the Films* (Pitman, 1935).

Scenario, March–August 1934.

Scotland, John, *The Talkies* (Crosby Lockwood & Son, 1930).

Screenwriters' Association, *The Case for British Films* (SA, 1938).

Seaton, Ray, and Martin, Roy, *Good Morning Boys: Will Hay* (Barrie & Jenkins, 1978).

Seton, Marie, *Paul Robeson* (Dennis Dobson, 1958).

Sharp, Dennis, *The Picture Palace and Other Buildings for the Movies* (Hugh Evelyn, 1969).

Sherriff, R. C., *No Leading Lady* (Gollancz, 1968).

Sight and Sound, 1932–1939.

Sinclair, Upton, *Upton Sinclair Presents William Fox* (published by the author, 1933).

Singer, Kurt, *The Charles Laughton Story* (Robert Hale, 1954).

Slide, Anthony, unedited transcript of an interview with Walter Forde, October 1976.

Sternberg, Josef von, *Fun in a Chinese Laundry* (Macmillan, New York, 1965).

Stuart, John, *Caught in the Act* (The Silent Picture, 1971).

Symons, Julian, *The Thirties* (Faber, 1960).

Tabori, Paul, *Alexander Korda* (Oldbourne, 1959).

Thomas, D. B., *The First Colour Motion Pictures* (HMSO, The Science Museum, 1969).

Thornton, Michael, *Jessie Matthews* (Hart-Davis, MacGibbon, 1974).

Travers, Ben, *Vale of Laughter* (Geoffrey Bles, 1957).

Trenker, Luis, *Brothers of the Snow* (Routledge, 1933).

Trewin, J. C., *Robert Donat* (Heinemann, 1968).

Truffaut, Francois, *Hitchcock* (Secker & Warburg, 1968).

Waley, H. D. and Spencer, D. A., *The Cinema Today* (Oxford University Press, 1939).

Wallace, Edgar, *My Hollywood Diary* (Hutchinson, 1932).

Wallace, Mrs Ethel, *Edgar Wallace* (Hutchinson, 1932).

Wells, H. G., *The Shape of Things to Come* (Hutchinson, 1933).
Wells, H. G., *Things to Come* (Cresset Press, 1935).
White, James Dillon, *Born to Star: the Lupino Lane Story* (Heinemann, 1957).
Whittingham, Jack, *Sabu of the Elephants* (Hurst & Blackett, 1938).
Wilcox, Herbert, *25,000 Sunsets* (The Bodley Head, 1967).
Winsten, S. (ed.), *GBS 90* (Hutchinson, 1946).
Wood, Alan, *Mr Rank* (Hodder & Stoughton, 1952).
Wood, Alan, and Wood, Mary, *Silver Spoon* (Hutchinson, 1954).
Wood, Leslie, *The Romance of the Movies* (Heinemann, 1937).
World Film News, 1936–1938.

Film List

The following Film List broadly includes mainstream feature films (i.e. films of 3,000 feet or more) made in Britain between midsummer 1929 and the outbreak of war in September 1939. Certain three- or four-reel films consisting almost entirely of variety acts have been excluded. So have some two dozen films which, although using some British players and technicians, were simply English-language versions of Continental films, made abroad by foreign companies and registered here as foreign films. On the other hand a number of films registered as foreign although made in England, and several made abroad and indisputably not British films, but of particular interest to the British production industry, have been included with a note about their origin. A few films made in Ireland and distributed here have also been included.

The Film List records the names of many of the technicians and players responsible for the films of the thirties, but is should be pointed out that no attempt has been made to compile a complete and comprehensive register of production. The reader's attention is drawn to the Introduction, where it is explained that the material was gathered as a basis for a historical account rather than as an end in itself.

The material is arranged as follows:

Title[1]

Production company,[2] studio[3] and some locations. Censorship category. Distribution company,[2] month and year of first show[4] and length in feet at registration. Sound details are given for the first few years, that is to say whether the film was Full Talking (FT), Part Talking (PT) or silent, and the sound recording equipment used. Colour details are given where appropriate.

p:	producer, and some executive and associate producers
d:	director
c:	camera
sc:	general heading for scenario department, including adapt: – adaptation, add. dial: – additional dialogue, etc.,[5] and source
des:	design
cost:	costume design
ed:	editing
sd:	sound recording
sp: effects	special effects
MD:	musical direction, and in some cases conductor, composer, song and lyric writers and dance directors
	Leading players[6]

Notes:

1 The titles given are those under which the films were first distributed in the UK. Many working titles are included, with cross references.
2 In many cases the names of production and distribution companies have been abbreviated. Full names will be found in the Index.
3 In the case of Elstree studios, the word Elstree alone refers to the large BIP-ABPC studio, and the others are distinguished by company.
4 Unless otherwise stated this is the London trade show.
5 Writing credits are frequently complex and debateable, but as a rule I have followed the official attribution.
6 Space forbids the inclusion of more than a few leading players for each film. Those seeking greater detail are directed to Denis Gifford's *The British Film Catalogue 1895–1970*.

Abdul Hamid See **Abdul the Damned**

Abdul the Damned BIP-Capitol at Elstree, Istanbul (A). Wardour, 2.35 (9,899). p: Max Schach, d: Karl Grune, c: Otto Kanturek, sc: Warren Chetham-Strode, Roger Burford, Ashley Dukes from story of Robert Neumann, des: Clarence Elder, John Mead, cost: Joe Strassner, ed: A. C. Hammond, Walter Stokvis, sd: S. Attkins, MD: Idris Lewis, Music: Hanns Eisler. With Fritz Kortner, Nils Asther, Walter Rilla, John Stuart.

Abide with Me See **Hearts of Humanity**

Above Rubies Ralph J. Pugh (U). UA, 1.32 (3,921). p: Ralph J. Pugh, d: Frank A. Richardson, sc: Eliot Stannard from story by Douglas Hoare. With Zoe Palmer, Robin Irvine.

Academy Decides, The UK Films at Shepperton (A). M-G-M, 3.37 (4,536). p: John Barter, d: John Baxter, c: Jack Parker, sc: from story by Stuart Jackson. With Henry Oscar.

Account Rendered PDC at Cricklewood (A). PDC 3.32 (3,257). With Reginald Bach, Cecil Ramage.

Accused Criterion at Isleworth (A). UA, 7.36 (7,866). p: Marcel Hellman, d: Thornton Freeland, c: Victor Armenise, Jack Parker, sc: Zoe Akins, George Barraud and Harold Frend from story by Zoe Akins, des: Edward Carrick, ed: Conrad von Molo, MD: Percival Mackey, lyrics: Clifford Grey, dances: Philip Buchel. With Douglas Fairbanks Jr, Dolores Del Rio.

Ace of Spades, The Real Art at Twickenham (U). Radio, 2.35 (5,934). p: Julius Hagen, d: George Pearson, c: Ernest Palmer, sc: Gerard Fairlie from novel by John Crawford Fraser, des: James Carter, ed: Michael Chorlton, sd: Eric Clennell, MD: W. L. Trytel. With Jane Carr, Dorothy Boyd, Michael Hogan.

Action for Slander Victor Saville-LFP at Denham (A). UA, 7.37 (7,530). ex.p: Alexander Korda, p: Victor Saville, assoc. p: Stanley Haynes, d: Tim Whelan, c: Harry Stradling, sc: Miles Malleson, add:dial: Ian Dalrymple, from novel by Mary Borden, des: Vincent Korda, Frederick Pusey, cost: Joe Strassner, ed: Jack Dennis, Hugh Stewart, sd: A. W. Watkins, MD: Muir Mathieson. With Clive Brook, Ann Todd, Ronald Squire.

Admirals All John Stafford at Beaconsfield (U). Radio, 6.35 (6,939). p: John Stafford, d: W. Victor Hanbury, sc: from play by Stephen King-Hall and Ian Hay (1934). With Gordon Harker, Anthony Bushell.

Admiral's Secret, The Real Art at Twickenham and Merton Park (U). Radio, 2.34 (5,753). p: Julius Hagen, d: Guy Newall, sc: H. Fowler Mear from play by Cyril Campion and Edward Dignon (1928). With Edmund Gwenn.

Adventure Limited B & D-Para-Brit: at B & D Elstree (A). Paramt, 10.34 (6,256). d: George King, sc: George Dewhurst from play by Cyril Campion, *Trust Berkely* (1933). With Harry Milton, Pearl Argyle, Hugh E. Wright.

After Dark Fox Brit. at Walton (U). Fox, 10.32 (4,104). prod.-man: Hugh Perceval, d: Albert Parker, sc: John Barrow from play by J. Jefferson Farjeon (1926). With Grethe Hansen, Hugh Williams.

After Many Years Savana Films (U). J-M-G, 2.30 (6,321) Silent. p: Alvin Saxon, d.sc: Lawrence Huntington. With Harry Thompson, Nancy Kenyon.

After Office Hours BIP at Elstree, Highgate (U). Wardour, 6.32 (7,100). d: Thomas Bentley, c: H. E. Palmer, Arthur Crabtree, sc: Frank Launder, Thomas Bentley from play by John Van Druten, *London Wall* (1931), des: Duncan Sutherland, John Mead, ed: John Neill-Brown, sd: A. E. Rudolph, MD: music: John Greenwood. With Heather Angel, Frank Lawton.

After the Ball G-B at Shepherd's Bush (A). Gaumont, 11.32 (6,389). p: Michael Balcon, d: Milton Rosmer, c: Percy Strong, sc: J. O. C. Orton, H.

M. Harwood from story by Max Neufeldt, des: Alfred Junge, cost: Gordon Conway, ed: Derek Twist. With Esther Ralston, Basil Rathbone, Marie Burke.

Against the Tide Fox Brit. at Cricklewood (U). Fox, 3.37 (6,021). p: Victor M. Greene, d: Alex Bryce, c: Ronald Neame, sc: David Evans and Alex Bryce from story by Reginald Pound, des: William Hemsley, ed: Challis Sanderson, sd: Charles E. Knott. With Robert Cochran, Cathleen Nesbitt, Linden Travers.

Agony Column See **Villiers Diamond, The**

Alf's Button G-B at Shepherd's Bush (U). Gaumont, 3.30 (8,606). FT & songs, Brit. Ac. Part colour, Pathé. p: L'Estrange Fawcett, d: W. P. Kellino, c: Percy Strong, William Shenton, sc: L'Estrange Fawcett from play by W. A. Darlington (1924), des: A. L. Mazzei. With Tubby Edlin, Alf Goddard, Nora Swinburne, Anton Dolin.

Alf's Button Afloat Gainsborough at Islington (U). GFD, 6.38 (8,062). p: Edward Black, d: Marcel Varnel, c: Arthur Crabtree, sc: George Marriott Edgar and Val Guest, Ralph Smart, from farce by W. A. Darlington (1924), des: Vetchinsky, ed: R. E. Dearing, Alfred Roome, sd: S. Wiles, MD: Louis Levy. With Crazy Gang, Alastair Sim.

Alf's Carpet BIP at Elstree (U). Wardour, 11.29 (5,892). PT, RCA d: W. P. Kellino, c: Theodor Sparkuhl, sc: Val Valentine, Arthur Le Clerq and Blanche Metcalfe from novel by W. A. Darlingon (1928), des: J. Elder Wills, ed: Emile de Ruelle, sd: B. Ross, MD: John Reynders. With Long and Short (Pat and Patachon).

Alias Bulldog Drummond See **Bulldog Jack**

Alias the Bulldog See **Bulldog Sees It Through**

Alibi Twick: at Twickenham (A). W & F, 4.31 (6.710). p: Julius Hagen, d: Leslie Hiscott, c: Sydney Blythe, sc: H. Fowler Mear from play by Michael Morton (1928) based on story by Agatha Christie, *The Murder of Roger Ackroyd.* With Austin Trevor, Franklin Dyall, Elizabeth Allan.

Alibi Inn Central (A). M-G-M, 7.35 (4,980). p:d: Walter Tennyson, sc: Sydney and Muriel Box. With Molly Lamont.

All At Sea Fox Brit. at Wembley (U). Fox, 10.35 (5,463). d: Anthony Kimmins, c: Alex Bryce, sc: Charles Bennett and Anthony Kimmins from play by Ian Hay, *Mr. Faintheart* (1931), des: Ralph Brinton, ed: Sam Simmonds, sd: John Cox. With Googie Withers, Rex Harrison.

All At Sea Brit. Lion (U). Brit. Lion, 10.39 (6,700). p.d: Herbert Smith, c: Hone Glendinning, sc: Gerald Elliott. With Sandy Powell, Kay Walsh.

All In Gainsborough at Islington (A). G-BD, 10.36 (6,438). p: Michael Balcon, d: Marcel Varnel, c: Arthur Crabtree, sc: Leslie Arliss and Val Guest from play by Philip Merivale and Brandon Fleming, *Tattenham Corner.* With Ralph Lynn, Gina Malo.

All that Glitters G.S.Ent. (U). Radio, 12.36 (6,437). p: A. George Smith, d: P. Maclean Rogers, sc: Denison Clift. With Jack Hobbs.

Almost a Divorce B & D (A). W & F, 8.31 (5,456). FT, WE. p: Herbert Wilcox, d: Arthur Varney, sc: Brock Williams from story by Arthur Varney. With Nelson Keys, Sydney Howard.

Almost a Gentleman Butcher's at Walton (U). Butcher's, 5.38 (7,043). p: Sidney Morgan, d: Oswald Mitchell, c: Geoffrey Faithfull, sc: Sidney Morgan, Oswald Mitchell from story by Willie Singer, des: Holmes Paul, MD: Percival Mackey. With Billy Bennett, Kathleen Harrison.

Almost a Honeymoon BIP at Elstree (U). Wardour, 9.30 (9,016). FT, RCA d: Monty Banks, c: J. J. Cox, sc: Walter Mycroft, Val Valentine, Monty Banks from play by Walter Ellis (1930), ed: A. C. Hammond, Emile de Ruelle, sd: A. S. Ross. With Clifford Mollison, Dodo

Watts.

Almost a Honeymoon Welwyn at Welwyn (A). Pathé, 4.38 (7,286). d: Norman Lee, c: Bryan Langley, sc: Ralph Neale and Kenneth Horne from play by Walter Ellis (1930), des: Duncan Sutherland, cost: Paquin, ed: E. Richards, sd: H. Benson, MD: John Reynders. With Tommy Trinder, Linden Travers.

Almost a Husband See **Honeymoon for Three**

Alone At Last See **Her Night Out**

Amateur Night in London Bostock at Elstree (U). PDC, 2.30 (3,154). FT. songs. p: Gordon Bostock, d: Monty Banks, c: J. J. Cox. With Tubby Phillips, Billy Caryll.

Amateur Gentleman, The Criterion at Elstree (A). UA, 1.36 (9,118). p: Marcel Hellman, d: Thornton Freeland, c: Gunther Krampf, sc: Clemence Dane, Sergei Nolbandov from novel by Jeffrey Farnol, des: Edward Carrick, historical adviser James Laver, music: Richard Addinsell. With Douglas Fairbanks Jr, Elissa Landi. Gordon Harker, Hugh Williams.

Amazing Quest of Ernest Bliss, The Garrett-Klement (U). UA, 8.36 (7,138). Registered as foreign film. p:d: Alfred Zeisler, c: Otto Heller, sc: John L. Balderston from novel by E. Phillips Oppenheim, des: David Rawnsley, ed: Merrill White. With Cary Grant, Mary Brian.

Amazing Quest of Mr. Ernest Bliss, The See **Amazing Quest of Ernest Bliss, The**

American Prisoner, The BIP at Elstree (U). Wardour, 9.29 (6,666). FT, songs. d: Thomas Bentley, c: René Guissart, sc: Eliot Stannard from play by Eden Phillpotts, des: T. H. R. Gibbings, ed: Sam Simmonds, sd: C. Thornton, MD: John Reynders, music: John Reynders and Jules Sylvain. With Carl Brisson, Madeleine Carroll.

Angelus, The St. Marg. at Twickenham (A). Ambassador, 6.37 (6,840). p: Julius Hagen, d: Thomas Bentley, c: Sydney Blythe, William Luff, sc: Michael Barringer from his own story, des: James Carter, ed: Jack Harris. With Anthony Bushell, Nancy O'Neil.

Anne One Hundred B & D-Para-Brit: (U). Paramt, 6.33 (5,998). d: Henry Edwards, sc: from play by Sewell Collins, *Anne – One Hundred Per Cent* (1927). With Betty Stockfield, Gyles Isham.

Annie Laurie Mondover at Cricklewood (U). Butcher's 7.36 (7,444). p: Wilfred Noy, d: Walter Tennyson, c: Jack Parker, sc: Frank Miller. With Will Fyffe, Polly Ward.

Annie, Leave The Room! Twick. at Twickenham (A). Universal, 2.35 (6,927). p: Julius Hagen, d: Leslie Hiscott, c: William Luff, sc: Michael Barringer from play by Norman Cannon, *Spendlove Hall.* With Jane Carr, Morton Selten, Eva Moore.

Antoinette See **Love Contract, The**

Anything Might Happen Real Art at Twickenham (A). Radio, 9.34 (5,949). p: Julius Hagen, d: G. A. Cooper, c: Ernest Palmer, sc: H. Fowler Mear from novel by Lady Evelyn Balfour. With John Garrick, Judy Kelly.

Anything to Declare? Rembrandt at Walton (U). Butcher's 11.38 (6,865). p: Ralph C. Wells, Neville Carter, d: Redd Davis, c: Geoffrey Faithfull, sc: from story by W. E. Hayter Preston, des: R. Holmes Paul, MD: Percival Mackey. With John Loder, Belle Chrystall, Leonora Corbett.

Apron Fools Marks (U). Radio, 7.36 (3,102). p: Harry S. Marks, d: Widgey Newman, sc: John Quin. With Hal Walters, Wally Patch.

Archer Plus Twenty See **Meet Maxwell Archer**

Aren't Men Beasts! BIP at Elstree (A). ABPC, 1.37 (6,066). p: Walter Mycroft, d: Graham Cutts, c: Roy Kellino, sc: Marjorie Deans, William Freshman from play by Vernon Sylvaine (1936), des: John Mead, ed: Monica Kimmick, sd: B. Cook. With Robertson Hare, Alfred Drayton, June Clyde, Billy

Milton.

Aren't We All? Para-Brit. at Elstree B & D (U). Paramt, 3.32 (7,139). d: Harry Lachman, c: Jack Whitehead, sc: Basil Mason, Gilbert Wakefield from play by Frederick Lonsdale (1923), song by Ord Hamilton. With Gertrude Lawrence, Owen Nares.

Are You a Mason? Twick. at Twickenham (U). Universal, 8.34 (7,690). p: Julius Hagen, d: Henry Edwards, c: Sydney Blythe, sc: H. Fowler Mear from German play by Leo Dietrichstein (1901) translated by E. Lederer. With Sonnie Hale, Robertson Hare.

Arms and the Man BIP at Elstree and in Wales (U). Wardour, 1) Malvern 6.32 (9,073), 2) Trade Show 9.32 (7,746). d: Cecil Lewis, c: J. J. Cox, Jimmy Wilson, Bryan Langley, sc: Cecil Lewis and George Bernard Shaw from the latter's play (1894), des: John Mead, cost: W. Chappell, ed: Walter Stokvis, C. H. Frend, sd: Alec Murray. With Anne Grey, Maurice Colbourne, Barry Jones.

Aroma of the South Seas Gainsborough (U). Ideal, 4.31 (3,375). FT. p: Michael Balcon, d: W. P. Kellino, sc: Angus MacPhail. With Wallace Lupino.

Around the Town Brit. Lion (U). Brit. Lion, 5.38 (6,115). d: Herbert Smith c: George Stretton, sc: from story by Fenn Sheric, Ingram d'Abbes. With Vic Oliver.

Arsenal Stadium Mystery, The G & S at Denham (A). GFD, 10.39 (7,775). p: Josef Somlo, assoc. p: Richard Norton, d: Thorold Dickinson, c: Desmond Dickinson, sc: adapt: Thorold Dickinson and Alan Hyman, screenplay Patrick Kirwan and Donald Bull from *Daily Express* serial by Leonard Reginald Gribble, des: Ralph Brinton, football adviser George Allison, ed: Sidney Stone, sd: A. W. Watkins. With Leslie Banks, Greta Gynt, George Allison.

As Good As New WB-FN at Teddington (A). WB, 3.33 (4,391). p: Irving Asher, d: Graham Cutts, sc: Randall Faye from play by Thompson Buchanan. With.

Winna Winfried, John Batten.

Ask a Policeman Gainsborough at Islington, Shepperton lot (U). M-G-M, 4.39 (7,492). p: Edward Black, d: Marcel Varnel, c: Derick Williams, sc: J. O. C. Orton, Val Guest, George Marriott Edgar from story by Sidney Gilliat, ed: R. E. Dearing, Alfred Roome, sd: S. Wiles. With Will Hay, Moore Marriott, Graham Moffatt.

Ask Beccles B & D-Para-Brit. at Elstree B & D (A). Paramt, 12.33 (6,107). d: Redd Davis, sc: Cyril Campion from play by Cyril Campion and Edward Dignon (1926). With Garry Marsh, Mary Newland.

Asking for Trouble See **Me and My Pal**

As You Like It Interallied (U). 20th Cent.-Fox, 9.36 (8,674). p.d: Paul Czinner, assoc. p: Dallas Bower, prod. man: R. J. Cullen, c: Hal Rosson, Jack Cardiff, sc: R. J. Cullen from play by Shakespeare, 'treatment suggested by J. M. Barrie', des: Lazare Meerson, cost: John Armstrong, Joe Strassner, ed: David Lean, sd: L. E. Overton, C. C. Stevens, MD: William Walton, music by William Walton and Dr Arne, conductor Efrem Kurtz. With Elisabeth Bergner, Laurence Olivier, Henry Ainley, Leon Quartermaine.

Atlantic BIP at Elstree (A). Wardour, 11.29 (8,213). FT, RCA p.d: E. A. Dupont, c: Charles Rosher, sc: Victor Kendall from play by Ernest Raymond, *The Berg*, des: Hugh Gee, ed: Emile de Ruelle, sd: Alec Murray, MD: John Reynders. With John Stuart, John Longden, Madeleine Carrol, Ellaline Terriss.

At the Villa Rose Twick. at Twickenham (U). WB, 2.30 (9,010). FT, RCA p: Julius Hagen, d: Leslie Hiscott, c: Sydney Blythe, sc: Cyril Twyford from novel by A. E. W. Mason, des: James Carter. With Austin Trevor, Norah Baring, Richard Cooper.

At the Villa Rose ABPC at Elstree (A). ABPC, 8.39 (6,656). p: Walter Mycroft, d: Walter Summers, c: Claude Friese-Greene, sc: Doreen Montgomery from the novel by A. E. W. Mason, des: John Mead, ed: Lionel Tomlinson. With Judy Kelly, Keneth Kent.

Auld Lang Syne W-P-E (U). Famous-Lasky, 4.29 (silent version 6,000, sound version 6,871). Songs, RCA. d: George Pearson, c: Bernard Knowles, sc: P. L. Mannock, Hugh E. Wright, des: Walter Murton, co-ed: Thorold Dickinson. With Sir Harry Lauder, Dorothy Boyd, Pat Aherne.

Auld Lang Syne Fitzpatrick at Shepperton and in Scotland (A). M-G-M, 2.37 (6,437). p: d: James A. Fitzpatrick, c: Hone Glendinning. With Andrew Cruikshank.

Aunt Sally Gainsborough at Islington (U). G-B D, 12.33 (7,620). p: Michael Balcon, d: Tim Whelan, c: Charles Van Enger, sc: Guy Bolton, A. R. Rawlinson, Austin Melford from story by Tim Whelan, des: Vetchinsky, cost: Gordon Conway, Norman Hartnell, ed: Derek Twist, sd: H. Hand, conductor: Debroy Somers and his Band, music by Harry Woods, dances by Edward Royce. With Cicely Courtneidge.

Autumn Crocus ATP at Ealing and in Austrian Tyrol (A). ABFD, 1.34 (7,495). p.d: Basil Dean, asst. d: Carol Reed, c: Robert Martin, sc: Dorothy Farnum from play by 'C. L. Anthony' (Dodie Smith) (1931), des: Edward Carrick, ed: Walther Stern, sd: A. D. Valentine, MD: Ernest Irving. With Ivor Novello, Fay Compton.

Avenging Hand, The John Stafford (A). Radio, 4.36 (5,974). p: John Stafford, d: W. Victor Hanbury, sc: Reginald Long, Akos Tolnay. With Noah Beery, Louis Borell.

Awakening, The Cosmopolitan (A). Cosmopolitan FD, 3.38 (5,850). d: A. Frenguelli.

Bachelor's Baby, The BIP at Elstree (U). Pathé 5.32 (5,181). d: Harry Hughes, c: Jimmy Wilson, sc: Harry Hughes from novel by Rolphe Bennett. With William Freshman, Alma Taylor.

Bad Boy Radius at Cricklewood (A).

Radius 3.38 (6,200). d: Lawrence Huntington, c: Stanley Grant, sc: Lawrence Huntington. With John Warwick, Kathleen Kelly, John Longden.

Bad Companions, The BIP-BIF at Welwyn (U). Pathé, 4.32 (3,917). d: John Orton, sc: Con West from story by Fred Karno. With Wallace Lupino, Nor Kiddie, Renee Gadd.

Badger's Green B & D-Para-Brit. (U). Paramt, 9.34 (6,111). p: Anthony Havelock-Allan, d: Adrian Brunel, c: Henry Harris, sc: Violet Powell from play by R. C. Sherriff (1930). With Valerie Hobson, Bruce Lister.

Bagged BIP (U). (Wardour) Pathé, 6.34 (3,592). d: John Harlow, sc: Wallace Lupino. With Wallace and Barry Lupino.

Bailiffs, The ATP (U). Ideal, 9.32 (2,2971). p: Clayton Hutton, d: Frank Cadman, sc: based on Fred Karno sketch. With Flanagan and Allen.

Balaclava Gainsborough at Beaconsfield (U). W & F, 4.30 (10,000 at Trade Show, 8,500 registered). FT RCA, silent version not shown. p: Michael Balcon, d: Maurice Elvey, dialogue d: Milton Rosmer, c: Jimmy Wilson, sc: W. P. Lipscomb, Angus MacPhail, Robert Stevenson, V. Gareth Gundrey, Milton Rosmer from story by Boyd Cable, based on poem by Lord Tennyson, *'Charge of the Light Brigade'*, MD: Louis Levy. With Benita Hume, Cyril McLaglen, Miles Mander.

Ball At Savoy John Stafford at Elstree (U). Radio, 1.36 (6,553). p: John Stafford, d: W. Victor Hanbury, sc: Akos Tolnay from musical by Oscar Hammerstein *Ball at the Savoy* (1933) based on operetta by Alfred Grunewald and Fritz Löhner-Beder *Bal im Savoy*, music: Paul Abraham. With Conrad Nagel, Marta Labarr, Lu-Anne Meredith.

Band Wagon Gainsborough/GFD, in production at Shepherd's Bush 8.39. p: Edward Black, d: Marcel Varnel, c: Henry Harris, sc: Marriott Edgar, Val Guest from radio series by Harry S. Pepper, Gordon Crier. With Arthur

Askey, Jack Hylton, Richard Murdoch.
Bank Holiday Gainsborough at Islington, Hastings (A). GFD, 1.38 (7,744). p: Edward Black, d: Carol Reed, c: Arthur Crabtree, sc: Rodney Ackland and Roger Burford from story by Rodney Ackland and Hans Wilhelm, des: Vetchinsky, ed: R. E. Dearing, Alfred Roome, sd: S. Wiles, MD: Louis Levy. With Margaret Lockwood, Hugh Williams, John Lodge.

Bargain Basement See **Department Store**

Barnacle Bill City at Cricklewood (U). Butcher's 1.35 (8,135). p: Basil Humphreys, d: Harry Hughes, c: Desmond Dickinson, sc: Aveling Ginever from story by Archie Pitt. With Archie Pitt, Joan Gardner, Gus McNaughton.

Barton Mystery, The Para-Brit. at B & D Elstree (A). Paramt, 11.32 (6,974). d: Henry Edwards c: Stanley Rodwell, sc: from play by Walter Hackett (1916), des: Wilfred Arnold. With Wendy Barrie, Ursula Jeans, Ellis Jeffreys, Lyn Harding.

Bats in the Belfry See **Joy Ride**

Beauty and the Barge Twick. at Twickenham, Hammersmith (U). Wardour, 2.37 (6,493). p: Julius Hagen, d: Henry Edwards, c: Sydney Blythe, William Luff, sc: Edwin Greenwood from play by W. W. Jacobs and Louis N. Parker (1904), des: James Carter, ed: Jack Harris, Michael Chorlton, sd: Carlisle Mountenay, MD and music: W. L. Trytel. With Gordon Harker, Judy Gunn, Jack Hawkins, George Carney,

Be Careful, Mr. Smith Union at Elstree BIP (U). Apex, 5.35 (6,573). d: Max Mack, sc: Ernest Longstaffe, Frank Atkinson. With Bobbie Comber, Bertha Belmore.

Because of Love See **Everything in Life**

Bed and Breakfast G-B at Shepherd's Bush (U). Gaumont, 12.30 (6,239). FT Brit. Ac. p: L'Estrange Fawcett, d: Walter Forde, c: William Shenton, sc: H. Fowler Mear from play by Frederick Witney, des: A. L. Mazzei. With Richard Cooper, Jane Baxter.

Bed and Breakfast Walter West (A). Coronel, 12.37 (5,300 at Trade Show, 4,300 registered). d: Walter West, sc: Frank Miller. With Barry Lupino, Mabel Poulton.

Bedrock Piccadilly at Twickenham (A). Paramt, 6.30 (3,686). FT. p.d: Carlyle Blackwell, sc: Noel Shannon from screen story by Michael Arabian. With Sunday Wilshin, Jane Baxter, Carlyle Blackwell.

Bedtime Story Admiral at Cricklewood (U). Admiral, 3.38 (6,800); Grand Nat., 11.39 (6,458). p: Victor M. Greene, d: Donovan Pedelty, c: Ernest Palmer, sc: Donovan Pedelty from play by Walter Ellis (1937), des: George Provis. With Lesley Wareing, Jack Livesey.

Bees and Honey See **His Lordship Regrets**

Beggar Student, The Amalgamated at Beaconsfield (U). Brit. Lion, 12.31 (5,900). FT RCA. p: John Harvel, prod. man: John Stafford, d: John Harvel and W. Victor Hanbury, c: Jimmy Rogers, Alex Bryce, sc: John Stafford from operetta by Carl Millöcker *Der Bettelstudent* (English version by W. Beatty Kingston, 1884), des: Norman Arnold, sd: Harold King, MD: Horace Shepherd. With Shirley Dale, Lance Fairfax.

Behind the Mask See **Four Masked Men**

Behind the Tabs Ace, 3.38 (4,400). d: R. A. Hopwood. Variety from Windmill Theatre.

Behind Your Back Crusade at Wembley (U). Paramt, 4.37 (6.345) p: Victor M. Greene, d: Donovan Pedelty, sc: from play by Charles Landstone. With Dinah Sheridan, Jack Livesey.

Bella Donna Twick. at Twickenham (A). Gaumont, 8.34 (8,243). p: Julius Hagen, d: Robert Milton, c: Sydney Blythe, William Luff, sc: H. Fowler Mear from novel by Robert Hichens and play by J. B. Fagan (1911), des: James Carter, sd: Baynham Honri. With Mary Ellis, Conrad Veidt, Sir Cedric Hardwicke, John Stuart.

Belles of St. Clements, The B & D-Para-Brit: (A). Paramt, 1.36 (6,170). d: Ivar Campbell, sc: from story by Ivar and

Sheila Campbell. With Evelyn Foster, Meriel Forbes.

Bells, The BSFP at Wembley (A). PDC, 10.31 (6,756). FT ASFI-Tobis. p: Sergei Nolbandov, d: Oscar Werndorff and Harcourt Templeman, c: Gunther Krampf, Eric Cross, sc: C. H. Dand from story by Erckmann and Chatrian, *Le Juif Polonais*, des: Oscar Werndorff, ed: Lars Moen, Michael Hankinson, sd: F. J. G. Cox, music by Gustav Holst. With Donald Calthrop, Jane Welsh.

Bells of St. Mary's, The GP (U). J-M-G, 1.30 (5,500). Silent. p: Arthur Phillips, d: Redd Davis, sc: Arrar Jackson from story by Redd Davis and Claude Gill. With Tubby Phillips.

Bells of St. Mary's, The Fitzpatrick at Shepperton (U). M-G-M, 10.37 (4,106). d: James A. Fitzpatrick, sc: W. K. Williamson based on the song by A. Emmett Adams. With John Garrick, Kathleen Gibson.

Beloved Imposter John Stafford at Welwyn (A). Radio, 2.36 (7,769). p: John Stafford, d: W. Victor Hanbury, sc: from novel by Ethel Mannin *Dancing Boy*. With Rene Ray, Fred Conyngham.

Beloved Vagabond, The Toeplitz at Ealing (A). ABFD, 8.36 (6,803). p: Ludovico Toeplitz, d: Kurt Bernhardt, dialogue supervisor Owen Nares, c: Franz Planer, sc: Hugh Mills, Arthur Wimperis and Walter Creighton freely adapted from novel by W. J. Locke, des: Andre Andreiev, cost: Schiaparelli, ed: Dug Myers, sd: Eric Williams, MD: Leslie Bridgewater, music by Darius Milhaud, songs by Mireille Heimann. With Maurice Chevalier, Betty Stockfield, Desmond Tester, Margaret Lockwood.

Bermondsey Kid, The WB-FN at Teddington (A). FN, 11.33 (6,802). p: Irving Asher, d: Ralph Dawson, sc: W. Scott Darling from screen story by Bill Evans. With Esmond Knight, Pat Paterson, Len Harvey.

Betrayal Fogwell at Blattner Elstree (A). Universal, 4.32 (5,966). d: Reginald Fogwell, c: D. P. Cooper, sc: Reginald Fogwell and Hubert Griffith from play by Hubert Griffith. With Stewart Rome, Marjorie Hume, Leslie Perrins.

Betty in Mayfair See **Lilies of the Field**

Beware of Women WB-FN at Teddington (U). FN, 5.33 (4,643) p: Irving Asher, d: George King. With Pat Paterson, Jack Hobbs.

Beyond Our Horizon GHW at Pinewood (U). Unity, 4.39 (3,851). d: Norman Walter. With Milton Rosmer.

Beyond the Cities Piccadilly (A). Paramt, 11.30 (6,309). FT. p:d: Carlyle Blackwell, sc: Noel Shannon. With Carlyle Blackwell, Edna Best.

Big Business Sheridan at Twickenham (U). Fox, 9.30 (6,871). FT, songs Movietone. p: d: sc: Oscar Sheridan, music: Oscar Sheridan and H. W. David. With Frances Day, Jimmie Godden.

Big Business WB-FN at Teddington (U). WB, 10.34 (4,876). p: Irving Asher, d: Cyril Gardner. With Claude Hulbert, Eve Gray.

Big Fella Fortune at Beaconsfield (U). Brit. Lion, 6.37 (6,414) p: H. Fraser Passmore, d: J. Elder Wills, c: Cyril Bristow, sc: Fenn Sherie and Ingram d'Abbes, music: Eric Ansell, lyrics: Henrik Ege. With Paul Robeson, Elizabeth Welch.

Big-Hearted Bill See **Boys Will Be Girls**

Big Noise, The Fox Brit. at Wembley (U). Fox, 3.36 (5,855). p: John Findlay, d: Alex Bryce, c: Stanley Grant, sc: Gerard Fairlie from story by Gene Markey and Harry Ruskin. With Alastair Sim, Norah Howard.

Big Splash, The Brit. Lion at Beaconsfield (U). M-G-M, 5.35 (6,034). p: supervisor Herbert Smith, d: Leslie Hiscott, c: Alex Bryce, sc: Michael Barringer. With Frank Pettingell, Marguerite Allan.

Big Sweep, The See **Lucky Loser**

Bill and Coo BIP at Elstree (U). Wardour, 7.31 (3,918). FT RCA. d: John Orton, c: Walter Harvey, Horace Wheddon, sc: J. O. C. Orton, Billy Merson, des: Clarence Elder, ed: Winifred Cooper, sd: A. C. O'Donoghue. With Billy Merson.

Bill in the Legion See **Lost in the Legion**

Bill's Legacy Twick. at Twickenham (A). Ideal, 11.31 (5,169) p: Julius Hagen, d: Harry J. Revier, sc: Leslie Fuller, Syd Courtenay from story by Syd Courtenay. With Leslie Fuller, Mary Clare.

Bill Takes a Holiday See **Tonight's the Night**

Birds of a Feather Macnamara at Isleworth (U). G & L, 6.31 (4,600). FT, songs Fidelytone. d: Ben R. Hart. With Haddon Mason, Dorothy Bartlam.

Birds of a Feather Baxter & Barter at Shepperton (U). Universal, 10.35 (6,234). p: John Barter, d: John Baxter, c: Ernest Palmer, sc: Con West, Gerald Elliott from novel by George Cecil Foster, *The Rift in the Loot*, music and songs: Arthur Stanley, Kennedy Russell. With Sir George Robey, Horace Hodges, Diana Beaumont.

Birds of Prey APT at Beaconsfield, Dunmow (A). Radio, 11.30 (8,832). FT RCA. p: d: Basil Dean, c: Alex Bryce, Robert Martin, sc: Basil Dean from play by A. A. Milne, *The Fourth Wall* (1928). With Robert Loraine, Frank Lawton, C. Aubrey Smith.

Biter Bit, The Fox Brit. at Wembley (A). Fox, 3.37 (4,514). p: Ivor McLaren, d: Redd Davis, c: Roy Kellino. With Billy Caryll, Hilda Mundy.

Bitter Sweet B & D (A). UA, 7.33 (8,458). p: d: Herbert Wilcox, c: Freddie Young, sc: Herbert Wilcox, Lydia Hayward, add. d: Monckton Hoffe from operette by Noel Coward (1929), des: L. P. Williams, cost: Doris Zinkeisen, MD: Lew Stone, music by Noel Coward. With Anna Neagle, Fernand Graavey, Miles Mander.

Black Abbot, The Real Art at Twickenham (A). Radio, 1.34 (5,047). p: Julius Hagen, d: G. A. Cooper, sc: H. Fowler Mear from novel by Philip Godfrey, *The Grange Mystery*. With John Stuart, Judy Kelly.

Black Coffee Twick. at Twickenham (U). W & F, 8.31 (7,189). p: Julius Hagen, d: Leslie Hiscott, c: Sydney Blythe, sc: H. Fowler Mear and Brock Williams from play by Agatha Christie (1930), ed: Jack Harris, sd: Baynham Honri. With Austin Trevor, Adrianne Allen, Richard Cooper, Elizabeth Allan.

Black Eyes ABPC at Elstree (A). ABPC, 4.39 (6,419). p: Walter Mycroft, d: Herbert Brenon, c: Gunther Krampf, sc: Dudley Leslie, remake of French film *Les Yeux Noirs* by W. Tourzhanski, des: Ian White, ed: Lionel Tomlinson, music: Walford Hyden, Bela Bizoni. With Otto Kruger, Mary Maguire, Walter Rilla.

Black Hand Gang, The BIP (U). Wardour, 10.30 (4,758). FT RCA. d: Monty Banks, c: Walter Blakeley, H. E. Palmer, sc: Victor Kendall from music-hall sketch by Bert Lee and R. P. Weston, des: John Mead, ed: Emile de Ruelle, A. C. Hammond, sd: C. V. Thornton. With Wee Georgie Wood, Dolly Harmer.

Black Limelight ABPC at Elstree (A). ABPC, 6.38 (6,200). p: Walter Mycroft, d: Paul L. Stein, c: Claude Friese-Greene, sc: D. Leslie, Walter Summers from play by Gordon Sherry (1937), des: Cedric Dawe. With Raymond Massey, Walter Hudd, Joan Marion.

Blackmail BIP at Elstree (A). Wardour, 6.29 sound version, 8.29 silent version (7,000) FT RCA. p: John Maxwell, d: Alfred Hitchcock, c: J. J. Cox, sc: Alfred Hitchcock, Benn Levy, Charles Bennett from play by Charles Bennett, des; Wilfred and Norman Arnold, ed: Emile de Ruelle, sd: Harold King, music: Campbell and Connelly, arranged Hubert Bath, Henry Stafford, MD: John Reynders. With Anny Ondra, John Longden, Donald Calthrop, Sara Allgood, Cyril Ritchard.

Black Mask, The WB-FN at Teddington (A). WB, 12.35 (6,066). p: Irving Asher, d: Ralph Ince, c: Basil Emmott, sc: Paul Gangelin, Frank Launder, Michael Barringer from novel by Bruce Graeme, *Blackshirt*, des: Peter Proud, sd: Leslie Murray. With Wylie Watson,

Aileen Marson.

Black Trunk, The See **Passenger to London**

Black Tulip, The Fox Brit. at Wembley (A). Fox, 2.37 (5,154). d: Alex Bryce, sc: from novel by Alexandre Dumas. With Ann Soreen, Patrick Waddington.

Black Waters B & D-Sono Art World Wide in Hollywood (A). W & F, 5.29 (7,182). FT. Registered as foreign film. p: Herbert Wilcox, d: Marshall Neilan, sc: from play by John Willard. With Mary Brian, James Kirkwood, John Loder.

Blarney O'D in Ireland (U). ABFD, 4.38 (5,902). p: Harry O'Donovan, Jimmy O'Dea, d: Harry O'Donovan, sc: Jimmy O'Dea, Harry O'Donovan. With Jimmy O'Dea.

Blarney Stone, The B & D at Elstree (U). W & F, 3.33 (7,218). p: Herbert Wilcox, d: Tom Walls, c: Stanley Rodwell, sc: A. R. Rawlinson, Lennox Robinson from screen story by A. R. Rawlinson, cost: A. L. Mazzei. With Tom Walls, Anne Grey.

Blind Folly George Smith at Walton (U). RKO-Radio, 11.39 (7,028). p: George Smith, d: Reginald Denham, c: Geoffrey Faithfull, sc: H. F. Maltby from story of John Hunter. With Clifford Mollison, Lilli Palmer.

Blind Justice Twick. at Twickenham (A). Universal, 10.34 (6,602). p: Julius Hagen, d: Bernard Vorhaus, sc: Vera Allinson from play by Arnold Ridley, *Recipe for a Murder* (1932). With Frank Vosper, John Stuart, Eva Moore.

Blind Man's Buff Fox Brit. at Wembley (A). Fox, 3.36 (6,429). d: Albert Parker, c: Roy Kellino. With Basil Sydney, Enid Stamp-Taylor, James Mason.

Blind Spot, The WB-FN at Teddington (A). WB, 9.32 (9,796). p: Irving Asher, d: John Daumery, sc: Roland Pertwee. With Percy Marmont, Muriel Angelus, Warwick Ward.

Blondes for Danger Herbert Wilcox at Beaconsfield (A). Brit. Lion, 3.38 (6,176). p: Herbert Wilcox, d: Jack Raymond, sc: W. G. Elliott from novel by Evadne Price, *Red for Danger*. With

Gordon Harker, Enid Stamp-Taylor.

Blossom Time BIP at Elstree (U). Wardour, 7.34 (8,193). p: Walter Mycroft, d: Paul L. Stein, c: Otto Kanturek, Bryan Langley, sc: Franz Schulz, John Drinkwater, Roger Burford, G. H. Clutsam from story by Franz Schulz, des: David Rawnsley, Clarence Elder, ed: Leslie Norman, sd: B. Cook and A. E. Rudolph, MD: Idris Lewis, music by Franz Schubert, lyrics: John Drinkwater and G. H. Clutsam. With Richard Tauber, Jane Baxter, Carl Esmond, Paul Graetz.

Blue Army, The See **Blue Squadron, The**

Blue Danube, The B & D at Elstree (A). W & F, 1.32 (6,510). p: d: Herbert Wilcox, sc: Herbert Wilcox, Miles Malleson from story by Doris Zinkeisen, music: Alfred Rode and Royal Tzigane band. With Brigitte Helm, Joseph Schildkraut, Massine and Nikitina.

Blue Smoke Fox Brit. at Wembley (U). Fox, 12.35 (6,791). p: John Barrow, d: Ralph Ince, c: Alex Bryce, sc: Charles Bennett from story by Fenn Sherie and Ingram d'Abbes. With Tamara Desni, Ralph Ince.

Blue Squadron, The WB-FN with Pittaluga at Teddington (U). FN, 5.34 (8,700). Registered as foreign film. p: Irving Asher, d: George King, sc: Brock Williams, based on Italian film by Ludovico Toeplitz, *L'Armata Azzura*. With Esmond Knight, John Stuart, Greta Hansen.

Bluff See **Little Bit of Bluff, A**

Blunder in the Air See **Live Wire, The**

Bohème See under **Mimi**

Bone of Contention See **There Was a Young Man**

Boomerang Arthur Maude at Walton (A). Columbia, 3.34 (7,331). d: Arthur Maude, sc: John Paddy Carstairs from play by David Evans. With Lester Matthews, Nora Swinburne.

Boots! Boots! Blakeley at Albany studios (U). Butcher's, 2.34 (7,246 reduced to 6,352 and to 5,194 in 1936). Visatone. p: John E. Blakeley, d: Bert Tracey, c:

James S. Hodgson, sc: George Formby and Arthur Mertz from revue by Arthur Mertz, des: Thomas Fleetwood, sd: Vaughan S. Sawyer, MD: Harry Hudson, songs: Jack Cotterill. With George Formby, Beryl.

Born Lucky Westminster (U). M-G-M, 12.32 (7,005). p: Jerome Jackson, d: Michael Powell, sc: Ralph Smart from novel by Oliver Sandys, *Mops*, des: Ian Campbell-Gray. With Rene Ray, John Longden

Born That Way Randall Faye at Walton (U). Radio, 7.36 (5,804). p: d: Randall Faye, c: Geoffrey Faithfull, sc: Randall Faye from story by V. C. Clinton-Baddeley, Diana Bourbon. With Terence de Marney, Kathleen Gibson.

Borrow a Million Fox Brit. at Wembley (U). Fox, 11.34 (4,445). d: Reginald Denham, sc: from screen story by Margaret McDonnell. With Reginald Gardiner, Vera Boggetti.

Borrowed Clothes Arthur Maude (A). Columbia, 2.34 (6,213). d: Arthur Maude, sc: from play by Aimée and Philip Stuart, *Borrowed Clothes* (1929). With Anne Grey, Lester Matthews.

Bosambo See under **Sanders of the River**

Bottle Party Ace, 11.36 (4,156). R. A. Hopwood. Variety from Windmill Theatre.

Boys Will Be Boys Gainsborough at Islington (A). G-BD, 7.35 (6,867). p: Michael Balcon, d: William Beaudine, c: Charles Van Enger, sc: Will Hay and Robert Edmunds based on 'Narkover' characters by 'Beachcomber' (J. B. Morton) in *Daily Express*, des: Vetchinsky, ed: A. Roome, sd: W. Salter, MD: Louis Levy, song by 'the two Leslies' (Leslie Sarony and Leslie Holmes). With Will Hay, Gordon Harker.

Boys Will Be Girls Fuller at Elstree, Rock studio (U). BIED, 7.37 (6,000, later 6,262). p: Joe Rock, d: Gilbert Pratt, c: Cyril Bristow, sc: Georgie Harris, Syd Courtenay, Jack Byrd from a story by Evelyn Barrie. With Leslie Fuller, Nellie Wallace.

Bracelets G-B at Shepherd's Bush (U). Gaumont, 1.31 (4,600). p: L'Estrange Fawcett, d: Sewell Collins, c: Percy Strong, sc: Sewell Collins, des: A. L. Mazzei. With Bert Coote.

Brat, The Betty Balfour at B & D, Elstree (U). UA, 5.30 (7,589). FT, songs WE. d: Louis Mercanton, c: René Guissart, Bernard Knowles, sc: Donovan Parsons, Reginald Berkeley from play by Michel Carré and E. Acrement, *La Mome*. With Betty Balfour, John Stuart.

Breakers Ahead Anglo-Cosmopolitan (U). Reunion, 1.35 (5,200). p: Fraser Foulsham, d. sc: Anthony Gilkison. With Barrie Livesey, April Vivian.

Break the News Jack Buchanan at Pinewood (U). GFD, 3.38 (7,037). p: d: René Clair, c: Phil Tannura, sc: Geoffrey Kerr from French film *Le Mort en Fuite*, des: Lazare Meerson, cost: Rene Hubert, ed: Francis Lyon, Fred Wilson, sd: John Dennis, MD: Van Phillips, incidental music: Theo Mackeben, songs: Cole Porter. With Jack Buchanan, Maurice Chevalier, Marta Labarr.

Brewster's Millions B & D at Elstree B & D (U). UA, 1.35 (7,538). p: Herbert Wilcox, d: Thornton Freeland, c: Henry Harris, sc: Donovan Pedelty, Clifford Grey, Wolfgang Wilhelm, add. d: Douglas Furber, from screen story by Arthur Wimperis based on play (1907) by G. B. McCutcheon and Winchell Smith, des: L. P. Williams, cost: Schiaparelli, Motley, Norman Hartnell, ed: Merrill White, sd: L. E. Overton, J. S. Dennis, MD: Geraldo, Harry Perritt, music: Ray Noble, lyrics: Douglas Furber, dances: Buddy Bradley. With Jack Buchanan, Lili Damita.

Bridegroom's Widow, The See **Let's Love and Laugh**

Brides To Be B & D-Para-Brit. (A). Paramt, 5.34 (6,095). d: Reginald Denham, sc: Basil Mason from his screen story. With Betty Stockfield, Constance Shotter.

Brief Ecstasy Phoenix-IFP at Ealing (A).

ABFD, 8.37 (6,447). p: Hugh Perceval, d: Edmond T. Gréville, c: Henry Harris, Ronald Neame, sc: Basil Mason. With Paul Lukas, Linden Travers, Hugh Williams, Marie Ney.

Bright Lights of London See **That Night in London**

Brighton Trunk Mystery, The See **Dead Men Tell No Tales**

Britannia of Billingsgate G-B at Shepherd's Bush (U). Gaumont-Ideal, 6.33 (7,125). p: Michael Balcon, d: Sinclair Hill, c: Mutz Greenbaum, sc: Ralph Stock from play by Christine Jope-Slade and Sewell Stokes, des: Alfred Junge, cost: Gordon Conway, music by George Posford, lyrics: Holt Marvel. With Violet Loraine.

Broken Blossoms Twick. at Twickenham (A). Twick. FD, 5.36 (7,725) Visatone. p: Julius Hagen, technical supervision: Bernard Vorhaus, d: Hans Brahm, c: Curt Courant, Hal Young, sc: Emlyn Williams from book by Thomas Burke, *The Chink and the Child,* and film by D. W. Griffith, des: James Carter, special settings Paul Minine, ed: Jack Harris, Ralph Kemplen, sd: Baynham Honri, C. Mountenay, MD: W. L. Trytel, music: Karol Rathaus. With Dolly Haas, Emlyn Williams, Arthur Margetson.

Broken Melody, The W-P-E at Cricklewood (A). Paramt, 10.29 (6,441) synchronised. d: Fred Paul, c: Bernard Knowles, Fred Ford, sc: Fred Paul, T. C. Elder from play by Herbert Keith and James Leader, des: Edward Carrick. With Georges Galli, Audrée Sayre.

Broken Melody, The Twick. at Twickenham (A). AP & D., 5.34 (7,500). p: Julius Hagen, d: Bernard Vorhaus, c: Sydney Blythe, William Luff, sc: H. Fowler Mear, Vera Allinson, Michael Hankinson from story by Bernard Vorhaus, des: James Carter, ed: Jack Harris, sd: Baynham Honri, MD: W. L. Trytel. With Margot Grahame, John Garrick, Merle Oberon.

Broken Romance. A Harry B. Parkinson

(A). Fox, 10.29 (6,854) Silent. p: Harry B. Parkinson, d: J. Stevens Edwards. With William Freshman, Blanche Adele.

Broken Rosary, The Butcher's (U). Butcher's 10.34 (7,768). p: Wilfred Noy, d: Harry Hughes. With Derek Oldham, Jean Adrienne, Vesta Victoria.

Brother Alfred BIP at Elstree (U). Wardour, 4.32 (6,633). d: Henry Edwards, c: Walter Harvey, Horace Wheddon, sc: Henry Edwards, Claude Gurney from story by P. G. Wodehouse and Herbert Westbrook, des: David Rawnsley, ed: A. S. Bates, MD: Idris Lewis, music: Vivian Ellis. With Gene Gerrard, Molly Lamont, Elsie Randolph.

Brown On Resolution See **Forever England**

Brown Sugar Twick. at Twickenham (A). WB, 4.31 (6,326). p: Julius Hagen, d: Leslie Hiscott, c: Sydney Blythe, sc: Cyril Twyford from play by Lady (Arther) Lever (1920), des: James Carter, sd: Baynham Honri. With Francis Lister, Constance Carpenter.

Brown Wallet, The WB-FN at Teddington (A). FN, 2.36 (6,086). p: Irving Asher, d: Michael Powell, c: Basil Emmott, sc: Ian Dalrymple from story by Stacy Aumonier. With Patric Knowles, Nancy O'Neil.

Bulldog Drummond at Bay BIP-ABPC at Elstree (U). Wardour, 3.37 (7,166). p: Walter Mycroft, d: Norman Lee, c: Walter Harvey, sc: James Parrish, Patrick Kirwan from novel by 'Sapper' (H. C. McNeile), des: John Mead, ed: J. Corbett, sd: A. G. Ambler. With John Lodge, Dorothy Mackaill, Victor Jory.

Bulldog Jack G-B at Shepherd's Bush (U). G-B D, 4.35 (6,581). p: Michael Balcon, d: Walter Forde, c: Mutz Greenbaum, sc: J. O. C. Orton, Sidney Gilliat, Gerard Fairlie based on character by 'Sapper' (H. C. McNeile), idea and dialogue: Jack Hulbert, des: Alfred Junge, cost: Joe Strassner, ed: Otto

Ludwig, sd: A. C. O'Donoghue, MD: Louis Levy. With Jack Hulbert, Claude Hulbert, Fay Wray.

Bull Rushes Gainsborough (U). Ideal, 2.31 (3,368) FT, songs. p: Michael Balcon, d: W. P. Kellino, sc: Angus MacPhail. With Wallace Lupino.

Busman's Holiday GS Ent.-Bow Bell (U). Radio, 11.36 (6.122). p: A. George Smith, d: P. Maclean Rogers, c: Geoffrey Faithfull, sc: H. F. Maltby, Kathleen Butler from story by Wally Patch. With Wally Patch, Gus Mc-Naughton, Muriel George.

Butler's Millions, The See **Money Means Nothing**

Butter and Egg Man, The See **Hello, Sweetheart**

By-Pass to Happiness Sound City at Shepperton (A). Fox, 3.34 (6,652). p: Ivar Campbell, d: Anthony Kimmins, c: Hone Glendinning, sc: Anthony Kimmins. With Tamara Desni, Maurice Evans, Kay Hammond.

Café Colette Garrick at Wembley (A). ABFD, 1.37 (6,532). p: W. Devenport Hackney, d: Paul L. Stein, c: Ronald Neame, sc: Eric Maschwitz, Val Gielgud, Walford Hyden from BBC feature by Eric Maschwitz and Walford Hyden, music by George Posford, Walford Hyden. With Paul Cavanagh, Greta Nissen.

Café Mascot Pascal at Wembley (U). Paramt, 7.36 (6,910). p: Gabriel Pascal, d: Lawrence Hungtington, sc: Gerald Elliott from story by Cecil Lewis. With Geraldine Fitzgerald, Derrick de Marney, George Mozart.

Calendar, The Gainsborough-Brit. Lion at Beaconsfield (A). W & F, 10.31 (7,015) FT RCA p: Michael Balcon, d: T. Hayes Hunter, c: Bernard Knowles, Alex Bryce, sc: Angus MacPhail, Robert Stevenson, Bryan Wallace from play by Edgar Wallace (1929), s: Harold King. With Herbert Marshall, Edna Best.

Callbox Mystery, The Westminster (A). UA, 3.32 (6,547). p: Gordon Craig, d:

G. B. Samuelson, sc: Joan Wentworth Wood. With Harold French. Warwick Ward, Wendy Barrie.

Called Back Real Art at Twickenham (A). Radio, 2.33 (4,527). p: Julius Hagen, d: Reginald Denham, Jack Harris, sc: from novel by Hugh Conway. With Franklin Dyall, Dorothy Boyd.

Calling All Crooks Mancunian at Cricklewood (A). Mancunian, 7.38 (7,763). p: John E. Blakeley, d: George Black Jr, c: Desmond Dickinson, sc: Arthur Mertz. With Douglas Wakefield and his Gang.

Calling All Ma's See **Biter Bit, The**

Calling All Stars Brit. Lion at Beaconsfield (U). Brit. Lion, 3.37 (7,100). p: d: Herbert Smith, c: George Stretton. With Ambrose and his Orchestra.

Calling the Tune Phoenix-IFP at Ealing (U). ABFD, 7.36 (7,203, later 6,467). p: Hugh Perceval, d: Reginald Denham, c: Franz Weihmayr, sc: Basil Mason, des: R. Holmes Paul, cost: Norman Hartnell, ed: Thorold Dickinson, Ray Pitt, sd: Eric Williams. With Sally Gray, Adele Dixon, Sam Livesey, Sir George Robey.

Call Me Mame WB-FN at Teddington (A). WB, 6.33 (5,434). p: Irving Asher, d: John Daumery, sc: Randall Faye. With Ethel Levey, John Batten, Dorothy Bartlam, Carroll Gibbons and his Savoy Orpheans.

Call of the Sea, The Twick. at Twickenham (U). WB, 11.30 (5,961). FT RCA. p: Julius Hagen, exec. p: Henry Edwards, d: Leslie Hiscott, c: Jimmy Rogers, Sydney Blythe, sc: Harry Fowler Mear from screen story by Frank Shaw, des: James Carter. With Henry Edwards, Chrissie White.

Camels Are Coming, The Gainsborough at Islington, Egypt (U). G-B D, 10.34 (7,154). p: Michael Balcon, assoc. p: Robert Stevenson, d: Tim Whelan, c: Glen MacWilliams, Bernard Knowles, sc: Guy Bolton, W. P. Lipscomb, add. d: Jack Hulbert, from story by Russell Medcraft and Tim Whelan, des: Oscar Werndorff, ed: Frederick Y. Smith, commentary E. V. H. Emmett, sd: H. Hand, MD: Louis Levy, music Ray Noble, Max Kester, Noel Gay. With Jack Hulbert, Anna Lee.

Canaries Sometimes Sing B & D at Elstree B & D (A). W & F, 9.30 (7,225). FT WE. p: Herbert Wilcox, d: Tom Walls, c: Bernard Knowles, sc: W. P. Lipsomb, add. d: Frederick Lonsdale from his play (1929), ed: Duncan Mansfield, des: L. P. Williams. With Yvonne Arnaud, Tom Walls, Athole Stewart, Cathleen Nesbitt.

Can You Hear Me, Mother? New Ideal at Hammersmith (U). PDC, 12.35 (7,706). p: Geoffrey Rowson, d: Leslie Pearce, c: Leslie Rowson, sc: Sandy Powell, Paul Thompson from story by Sandy Powell. With Sandy Powell.

Cape Forlorn BIP at Elstree (A). Wardour, 1.31 (7,781) FT RCA. p: d: E. A. Dupont, c: Claude Friese-Greene, Walter Blakeley, Hal Young, sc: Victor Kendall from play by Frank Harvey, des: Alfred Junge, ed: A. C. Hammond, sd: Alex Murray, MD: John Reynders. With Ian Hunter, Fay Compton, Frank Harvey.

Captain Bill Leslie Fuller at Elstree Rock (U). ABFD, 11.35 (7,362). p: Joe Rock, d: Ralph Ceder, sc: from story by Val Valentine, Georgie Harris and Syd Courtenay. With Leslie Fuller, Georgie Harris, Judy Kelly.

Captain's Orders Liberty at Isleworth (U). Liberty, 11.37 (6,714). d: Ivar Campbell, c: George Stretton, W. G. Duncalf, sc: from story by Frank Shaw, des: Clifford Pember. With Henry Edwards, Jane Carr.

Captain's Table, The Fitzpatrick at Shepperton (A). M-G-M, 11.36 (4,962). p: James A. Fitzpatrick, d: Percy Marmont, sc: John Paddy Carstairs. With Percy Marmont, Hugh McDermott.

Captivation John Harvel at Beaconsfield (A). Ideal, 5.31 (6,816) FT RCA. d: John Harvel, c: Alex Bryce, sc: from play by Edgar C. Middleton, MD: W. L. Trytel. With Conway Tearle, Betty Stockfield, Violet Vanbrugh.

Cardinal, The Grosvenor (A). Pathé, 3.36 (6,800). p: Harcourt Templeman, d: Sincair Hill, sc: D. B. Wyndham-Lewis from play by Louis N. Parker (1903), des: Aubrey Hammond, ed: Dr Max Brenner. With Matheson Lang, June Duprez.

Carnival (1931) See **Dance, Pretty Lady**

Carnival B & D at Elstree B & D (A). W & F, gala 11.31 (7,959). p: d: Herbert Wilcox, c: Freddie Young, sc: Donald Macardle from play by Matheson Lang and H. C. M. Hardinge (1920), des: Doris Zinkeisen. With Matheson Lang, Joseph Schildkraut, Dorothy Bouchier.

Car of Dreams G-B at Shepherd's Bush (U). G-B D, 9.35 (6,510). p: Michael Balcon, d: Graham Cutts and Austin Melford, c: Mutz Greenbaum, sc: Austin Melford, des: Alfred Junge, music Mischa Spoliansky. With John Mills, Grete Mosheim.

Carroll Levis and his Discoveries See **Discoveries**

Carry On London Ace, 2.37 (4,188). d: R. A. Hopwood. Variety from Windmill Theatre.

Case for the Crown, The B & D-Para-Brit: at Elstree B & D (U). Paramt, 11.34 (6,359). d: G. A. Cooper, sc: Sherard Powell from story by Anthony Gittins, *An Error of Judgement.* With Miles Mander, Whitmore Humphries, Meriel Forbes.

Case of Gabriel Perry, The Brit. Lion at Beaconsfield (A). Brit. Lion, 4.35 (7,043). p: supervisor Herbert Smith, d: Albert de Courville, c: Charles Van Enger, sc: L. du Garde Peach from play by James Dale, *Wild Justice* (1933). des: A. L. Mazzei. With Henry Oscar, Olga Lindo, Margaret Lockwood.

Case of Lady Camber, The See **Lord Camber's Ladies**

Case of the Frightened Lady, The See **Frightened Lady, The**

Cash LFP at Elstree B & D (U). Paramt, 5.33 (6,611). p: Alexander Korda, d: Zoltan Korda, sc: Dorothy Greenhill and Arthur Wimperis from story by

Anthony Gibbs, ed: Stephen Harrison. With Edmund Gwenn, Wendy Barrie, Robert Donat.

Caste Harry Rowson at Walton (U). UA, 9.30 (6,421) FT RCA. p: Harry Rowson, exec. p: Jerome Jackson, d: Campbell Gullan, sc: Michael Powell from play by T. W. Robertson (1867). With Nora Swinburne. Hermione Baddeley.

Castle Sinister Delta (A). Filmophone, 4.32 (4,410). d: Widgey Newman. With Haddon Mason, Wally Patch.

Catch As Catch Can Fox Brit. at Wembley (A). Fox, 6.37 (6,428). d: Roy Kellino, c: Ronald Neame, sc: Richard Llewellyn from story by Alexander George, des: William Hemsley, ed: Reginald Beck, Fergus McDonell, sd: John Cox, Cecil Mason, MD: Colin Wark. With James Mason, John Warwick, Eddie Pola.

Catherine the Great LFP (A). UA, 1.34 (8,792). p: Alexander Korda, d: Paul Czinner, c: Georges Périnal, Robert Lapresle, sc: Lajos Biro, Arthur Wimperis, Melchior Lengyel from play by Melchior Lengyel and Lajos Biro *The Czarina*, des: Vincent Korda, cost: John Armstrong, ed: Harold Young, sd: A. W. Watkins, MD: Muir Mathieson, music: Ernst Toch. With Douglas Fairbanks Jr, Elisabeth Bergner, Flora Robson, Sir Gerald du Maurier. (Registered, trade shown and usually known as **Catherine the Great**, it was also known as **The Rise of Catherine the Great**).

Cat's Whiskers, The See **Annie, Leave the Room!**

Cavalier of the Streets, The B & D-Para-Brit. at Pinewood (A). Paramt, 3.37 (6,340). p: Anthony Havelock-Allan, d: Harold French, c: Francis Carver, sc: George Barraud, Ralph Neale from story by Michael Arlen. With Carl Harbord, Margaret Vyner, Patrick Barr.

Challenge, The LFP-Denham Films at Denham, Matterhorn (U). UA, 5.38 (6,946). p: Alexander Korda, Gunther Stapenhorst, d: Milton Rosmer, d: (on Matterhorn) Luis Trenker, c: Georges Périnal, c: (on Matterhorn) Albert Benitz, sc: Patrick Kirwan, Milton Rosmer from screenplay by Emeric Pressburger, des: Vincent Korda, Frederick Pusey, ed: E. B. Jarvis, sd: A. W. Watkins. With Robert Douglas, Luis Trenker, Joan Gardner.

Chance of a Night-time, The B & D (U). W & F, 5.31 (6,700). FT WE. p: Herbert Wilcox, d: Herbert Wilcox and Ralph Lynn, c: Freddie Young, sc: Ben Travers. With Ralph Lynn, Winifred Shotter.

Change for a Sovereign WB-FN at Teddington (A). FN, 9.37 (6,517). p: Irving Asher, d: Maurice Elvey, c: Basil Emmott, sc: from stage play by Sir Seymour Hicks, *Sand in the Sugar*. With Sir Seymour Hicks, Bruce Lister, Chili Bouchier.

Channel Crossing G-B at Shepherd's Bush (A). W & F, 10.33 (6,237). p: Angus MacPhail, Ian Dalrymple, d: Milton Rosmer, c: Phil Tannura, sc: W. P. Lipscombe, Cyril Campion from story by W. P. Lipscombe and Angus MacPhail, des: Alfred Junge, ed: Dan Birt. With Matheson Lang, Constance Cummings.

Charing Cross Road Brit. Lion at Beaconsfield (U). Brit. Lion, 7.35 (6,575). p. supervisor: Herbert Smith, d: Albert de Courville, c: Phil Tannura, sc: Con West, Clifford Grey from radio play by Gladys and Clay Keyes, des: Norman Arnold, sd: Harold King, music: Percival Mackey and his orchestra, Arthur Young and the Tzigane band. With June Clyde, John Mills, Derek Oldham, Jean Colin.

Charley's Big-Hearted Aunt Gainsborough, in production in 10.39 at Shepherd's Bush. GFD. p: Edward Black, d: Walter Forde, c: J. J. Cox, Arthur Crabtree, sc: Val Guest, J. O. C. Orton, G. Marriott Edgar from play by Brandon Thomas (1892), *Charley's Aunt*, des: Vetchinsky, ed: R. E. Dearing, sd: S. Wiles, MD: Louis Levy. With Arthur Askey, Richard Murdoch,

Moore Marriott, Graham Moffatt.

Chauffeur Antoinette See **Love Contract, The**

Checkmate B & D-Para-Brit. (A). Paramt, 10.35 (6,045). d: George Pearson, sc: Basil Mason from story by Amy Kennedy Gould. With Felix Aylmer, Maurice Evans.

Cheer, Boys, Cheer ATP. at Ealing (U). ABFD, 7.39 (7,642). p: Michael Balcon, assoc. p: S. C. Balcon, d: Walter Forde, c: Ronald Neame, Gordon Dines, sc: Roger MacDougall, Allan MacKinnon from story by Ian Dalrymple and Donald Bull, des: Wilfred Shingleton, ed: Ray Pitt, sd: Eric Williams, MD: Ernest Irving. With Jimmy O'Dea, Nova Pilbeam.

Cheer Up Stanley Lupino (U). ABFD, 1.36 (6,174). p: Stanley Lupino, d: Leo Mittler, c: John Boyle, sc: Michael Barringer from story by Stanley Lupino. With Stanley Lupino, Sally Gray.

Chelsea Life B & D-Para-Brit. (A). Paramt, 11.33 (6,238). d: Sidney Morgan, sc: Joan Wentworth Wood from story by Sidney Morgan. With Louis Hayward, Molly Johnson, Anna Lee.

Chick B & D at Elstree JH Studios (U). UA, 9.36 (6,446). p: Jack Raymond, d: Michael Hankinson, c: Francis Carver, sc: D. B. Wyndham-Lewis, dial: R. P. Weston, Bert Lee, Jack Marks, from story by Edgar Wallace, des: Wilfred Arnold, ed: John Morris, sd: C. C. Stevens, MD: Percival Mackey. With Sydney Howard, Betty Ann Davies.

Child in their Midst, A See **Man of Mayfair**

Children of Chance BIP at Elstree (A). FN-Pathé, 11.30 (7.279) FT RCA. d: Alexander Esway, c: H. E. Palmer, sc: Miles Malleson, Frank Launder, ed: E. B. Jarvis, sd: C. V. Thornton. With John Stuart, Elissa Landi, Mabel Poulton, John Longden (bilingual).

Children of the Fog Jesba Films at Southall (A). NPFD, 2.37 (5,564). d: Prof. Leopold Jessner, John Quin, c: Eugen Schüfftan, sc: John Cousins.

With Barbara Gott.

Chinatown Nights Victory (U). Columbia, 3.38 (6,414). d: A. Frenguelli, sc: Nigel Byass. With Nell Emerald, H. Agar Lyons, Anne Grey.

Chin, Chin, Chinaman Real Art at Twickenham (U). M-G-M, 8.31 (4,339). p: Julius Hagen, d: Guy Newall, c: Basil Emmott, sc: Brock Williams, Guy Newall from play by Percy Walsh. With Leon M. Lion, George Curzon, Elizabeth Allan.

Chinese Bungalow, The WP at Elstree (A). WP, 9.30 (6,790). d: J. B. Williams, c: Claude McDonnell, sc: from play by Marion Osmond and James Corbet (1925), des: Norman Arnold. With Matheson Lang, Jill Esmond Moore, Anna Neagle.

Chinese Bungalow, The Pennant, in production at Beaconsfield, Sound City exteriors, in 6.39. Brit. Lion. p: d: George King, c: Hone Glendinning, sc: A. R. Rawlinson, Gordon Wellesley from play by James Corbet, Marion Osmond, des: Philip Bawcombe. With Paul Lukas, Robert Douglas, Jane Baxter.

Chinese Puzzle, The Twick. at Twickenham (A). W & F, 3.32 (7,359). p: Julius Hagen, d: Guy Newall, sc: Harry Fowler Mear from play by Leon M. Lion and Marian Bower (1918). With Leon M. Lion, Lilian Braithwaite, Austin Trevor, Elizabeth Allan.

Chips BFAP at Cricklewood, Poole Harbour (U). BFAP, 2.38 (7,491 reduced finally to 5,532). For Sea Scouts. p: d: Edwin Godal, c: Desmond Dickinson, sc: Vivian Tidmarsh, ed: Charles Barnett. With Tony Wickham, Robb Wilton, etc.

Chu Chin Chow Gainsborough at Islington (U). G-B D, 5.34 (9.304). p: Michael Balcon, assoc. p: Philip Samuel, d: Walter Forde, c: Mutz Greenbaum, sc: Edward Knoblock, Sidney Gilliat, L. du Garde Peach from musical play by Oscar Asche, *Chu-Chin-Chow* (1916), des: Ernö Metzner, cost: Cathleen Mann, ed: Derek Twist, sd:

A. C. O'Donoghue, MD: Louis Levy, conductor Hubert Bath, songs and music Frederic Norton, add. songs Sidney Gilliat, dances Anton Dolin. With Sir George Robey, Anna May Wong, Fritz Kortner.

Church Mouse WB-FN at Teddington (A). FN, 5.34 (6,841). p: Irving Asher, d: Monty Banks, c: Basil Emmot, sc: W. Scott Darling, Tom Geraghty from play by Ladislas Fodor, Paul Frank, cost: Norman Hartnell. With Laura La Plante, Ian Hunter, Monty Banks.

Citadel, The M-G-M Brit. at Denham (A). M-G-M, 12.38 (9,970). p: Victor Saville, d: King Vidor, c: Harry Stradling, sc: Ian Dalrymple, Cmdr Frank Weed, Elizabeth Hill, add.d: Emlyn Williams from novel by A. J. Cronin, des: Lazare Meerson, Alfred Junge, ed: Charles Frend, sd: A. W. Watkins, MD: and music Louis Levy. With Robert Donat, Rosalind Russell, Ralph Richardson.

City of Beautiful Nonsense, The Butcher's at Cricklewood (U). Butcher's 5.35 (7,974). p: Wilfred Noy, d: Adrian Brunel, c: Desmond Dickinson, sc: Donovan Pedelty from novel by E. Temple Thurston. With Emlyn Williams, Sophie Stewart.

City of Play Gainsborough (A). W & F, 7.29 silent (6,383), 11.29 sound (6,760) PT RCA. p: Michael Balcon, d: Denison Clift, c: Claude McDonnell, sc: Angus MacPhail. With Chili Bouchier, Pat Aherne.

City of Song BSFP at Wembley, Naples (U). Sterling, 1.31 (8,910) Tobis. p: Arnold Pressburger, prod. supervison: Bernard Vorhaus, d: Carmine Gallone, assoc: Harcourt Templeman, c: Arpad Viragh, Curt Courant, sc: Miles Malleson, Hans Szekcly from story by C. H. Dand, des: Oscar Werndorff, ed: Carmine Gallone with Lars Moen and L. B. T. Chown, sd: George Burgess. With Jan Kiepura, Betty Stockfield, Heather Angel. (English version).

Clairvoyant, The Gainsborough at Islington (A). G-B D, 6.35 (7,254). p:

Michael Balcon, d: Maurice Elvey, c: Glen MacWilliams, sc: Bryan Wallace, Charles Bennett and Robert Edmunds from novel by Ernst Lothar, des: Alfred Junge, cost: Joe Strassner. With Jane Baxter, Claude Rains, Fay Wray.

Claydon Treasure Mystery, The Fox Brit. at Wembley (A). 20th-Cent.-Fox, 3.38 (5,775). d: Manning Haynes, c: Jimmy Wilson, sc: Edward Dryhurst from story by Neil Gordon, *The Shakespeare Murders*; des: Carmen Dillon. With Annie Esmond, Garry Marsh, John Stuart, Evelyn Ankers.

Cleaning Up Brit. Lion at Beaconsfield (U). Brit. Lion 5.33 (6,314). prod. supervison: Herbert Smith, d: Leslie Hiscott, c: Alex Bryce, sc: Michael Barringer, des: Norman Arnold, sd: Harold King. With George Gee, Davy Burnaby, Betty Astell.

Clean Sweep, A See **Lucky Sweep, A**

Climbing High G-B at Pinewood (U). M-G-M, 11.38 (7,096). d: Carol Reed, c: Mutz Greenbaum, sc: Stephen Clarkson from story by Lesser Samuels and Marion Dix, des: Alfred Junge, cost: Norman Hartnell, ed: Michael Gordon, sd: Alex Fisher, MD: Louis Levy. With Jessie Matthews, Michael Redgrave.

Clock, The See **Fatal Hour, The**

Clothes and the Woman JH Prod. at Estree (A). ABPC, 7.37 (6,294). p: Julius Hagen, d: Albert de Courville, c: Curt Courant, sc: F. McGrew Willis from story by Franz Schulz, des: A. L. Mazzei. With Rod La Rocque, Constance Collier, Tucker McGuire.

Clue of the New Pin, The Brit. Lion (A). PDC, 3.29 (7,292). p: S. W. Smith, d: Arthur Maude, c: Horace Wheddon, sc: Kathleen Hayden from novel by Edgar Wallace. With Benita Hume, Kim Peacock, John Gielgud.

Cock o' the North Panther-Oswald Mitchell at Cricklewood (U). Butcher's 7.35 (7,563). p: Oswald Mitchell, d: Oswald Mitchell, Challis Sanderson, c: Desmond Dickinson, sc: Oswald Mitchell. With George Carney, Marie

Lohr, Ronnie Hepworth.

C.O.D. Westminster (A). U.A., 3.32 (5,967). p: Jerome Jackson, d: Michael Powell, c: Geoffrey Faithfull, sc: Ralph Smart from story by Philip MacDonald, des: Frank Wells. With Garry Marsh, Roland Culver.

Code, The See **Heat Wave**

Collision New Era-G. B. Samuelson (A). UA 1.32 (8,000). p: Gordon Craig, d: G. B. Samuelson, sc: from play by E. C. Pollard. With Sunday Wilshin, Wendy Barrie, Gerald Rawlinson.

Colonel Blood Sound City at Shepperton (A). M-G-M, 1.34 (8,815). p: Norman Loudon, d: W. P. Lipscomb, c: George Stretton, sc: W. P. Lipscomb, historical adviser Arthur Bryant, des: Laurence Irving, John Bryan, sd: J. K. Byers. With Frank Cellier, Anne Grey, Allan Jeayes.

Come into my Parlour GEM at Elstree Blattner (U). M-G-M, 3.32 (4,214). d: John Longden, c: William Shenton, sc: John Longden, Jean Jay. With Renee Houston, Pat Aherne.

Come on, George! ATP at Ealing (U). ABFD, 10.39 (7,981). p: Jack Kitchin, d: Anthony Kimmins, c: Ronald Neame, Gordon Dines, sc: Anthony Kimmins, Leslie Arliss, Val Valentine from story by Anthony Kimmins, des: Wilfred Shingleton, ed: Ray Pitt, MD: Ernest Irving, music and lyrics George Formby, Fred E. Cliffe, Harry Gifford, Alan Nicholson. With George Formby, Pat Kirkwood.

Come out of the Pantry B & D at Elstree B & D (U). UA, 11.35 (6,477). p: Herbert Wilcox, d: Jack Raymond, c: Freddie Young, Henry Harris, sc: Austin Parker, Douglas Furber from novel by Alice Duer Miller, des: L. P. Williams, ed: Frederick Wilson, sd: John S. Dennis, Harry Perritt's orchestra, songs and music Maurice Sigler, Al Goodhart, Al Hoffman. With Jack Buchanan, Fay Wray.

Comets Alpha at Twickenham (U). J-M-G, 1.30 (5,600, later 4,459) FT, songs RCA. p: Maurice J. Wilson, d:

Sasha Geneen. With Heather Thatcher, Charles Laughton, Billy Merson, etc.

Coming of Age G. S. Ent. (U). Columbia 3.38 (6,192). p: George Smith, d: Manning Haynes, c: Sydney Blythe, sc: from story by Paul White, Rowan Kennedy. With Eliot Makeham, Joyce Bland.

Command Performance Grosvenor at Pinewood (U). GFD, 8.37 (7,547). p: Harcourt Templeman, d: Sinclair Hill, c: Cyril Bristow, sc: Michael Hankinson, George Pearson, Sinclair Hill from play by Stafford Dickens (1928). With Arthur Tracy, Lilli Palmer.

Commissionaire Granville at Cricklewood (U). M-G-M, 10.33 (6,555). p: Edward G. Whiting, d: Edward Dryhurst, c: Desmond Dickinson, sc: Herbert Ayres. With Sam Livesey, Barrie Livesey.

Compromising Daphne BIP at Elstree (A). Wardour, 10.30 (7,242) FT RCA. d: Thomas Bentley, c: Claude Friese-Greene, sc: Val Valentine, from play. With Jean Colin, Phyllis Konstam.

Compulsory Husband, The BIP at Elstree (A). Wardour, 2.30 (7,546) PT RCA. p: Harry Lachman, d: Monty Banks, c: René Guissart, Jimmy Rogers, sc: Val Valentine, Rex Taylor from novel by John Glyder, des: Hugh Gee. With Monty Banks.

Compulsory Wife, The WB-FN at Teddington (A). FN, 3.37 (5,138). p: Irving Asher, d: Arthur Woods, c: Robert Lapresle, sc: Reginald Purdell, John Dighton from novel by John Glyder. With Joyce Kirby, Henry Kendall, Margaret Yarde.

Concerning Mr. Martin Fox Brit. at Wembley (A). Fox, 3.37 (5,322). d: Roy Kellino, c: Stanley Grant, sc: Ernest Dudley. With Wilson Barrett, William Devlin.

Concert Party 5.37 (4,142). d: R. A. Hopwood. Variety from Windmill Theatre.

Condemned to Death Twick. at Twickenham (A). W & F, 1.32 (6,972). p: Julius Hagen, d: Walter Forde, c: Sydney Blythe, sc: Harry Fowler Mear from

play by George Goodchild, *Jack o'
Lantern*, des: James Carter, ed: Jack
Harris, sd: Baynham Honri. With
Arthur Wontner, Edmund Gwenn,
Gordon Harker.

Confidential Lady WB-FN at Teddington
(U). FN, 7.39 (6,708). exec. p: Sam
Sax, d: Arthur Woods, c: Basil Emmott,
sc: Brock Williams, Derek Twist. With
Ben Lyon, Jane Baxter.

Conflict See **Woman Between, The**

Congo Raid See **Sanders of the River**

Consider your Verdict Charter at
Highbury (A). Anglo-Am., 11.38
(3,400). p: John Boulting, d: Roy
Boulting, c: D. P. Cooper, sc: Francis
Miller from play by Laurence Hous-
man. With Marius Goring.

Constant Nymph, The G-B at Shepherd's
Bush, Austrian Tyrol (A). G-B D, 12.33
(8,388). p: Michael Balcon, d: Basil
Dean, c: Mutz Greenbaum, sc: Basil
Dean, Margaret Kennedy, Dorothy
Farnum from play by Basil Dean and
Margaret Kennedy (1926) based on
novel by Margaret Kennedy, des: Alfred
Junge, cost: Gordon Conway, Music:
Eugene Goosens, John Greenwood.
With Victoria Hopper, Brian Aherne.

Contraband (1934) See **Luck of a Sailor,
The**

Contraband Brit. Nat., in production
12.39. Anglo-Am. p: John Corfield, d:
Michael Powell, c: Freddie Young,
Skeets Kelly, sc: Brock Williams,
Michael Powell from story by Emeric
Pressburger, des: Alfred Junge, ed: John
Seaborne, sd; C. C. Stevens, MD: Muir
Mathieson, music: Richard Addinsell.
With Conrad Veidt, Valerie Hobson.

Contraband Love London Screen Plays
(A). Paramt, 3.31 (6,954) FT, songs
WE. p: d: Sidney Morgan, sc: Joan
Wentworth Wood. With C. Aubrey
Smith, Janice Adair.

Convict 99 Gainsborough at Islington (A).
GFD, 5.38 (7,874). p: Edward Black, d:
Marcel Varnel, c: Arthur Crabtree,
Philip Grindrod, sc: G. Marriott
Edgar, Val Guest, Ralph Smart, adapt:
Jack Davies Jr from story by Cyril

Campion, des: Vetchinsky, ed: R. E.
Dearing, sd. W. Salter, MD: Louis
Levy. With Will Hay, Moore Marriott,
Graham Moffatt.

Convoy Ealing Studios. In production at
Ealing in 11.39 ABFD. p: Michael
Balcon, assoc. p: Sergei Nolbandov, d:
Pen Tennyson, c: Wilkie Cooper,
Gordon Dines, sc: Pen Tennyson,
Patrick Kirwan, des: Wilfred Shingle-
ton, ed: Ray Pitt, MD: Ernest Irving.
With Clive Brook, John Clements.

Co-optimists, The New Era at Twicken-
ham (U). New Era, 11.29 (7,269). FT,
songs. RCA. p: Edwin Greenwood, d:
Edwin Greenwood, Laddie Cliff, c:
Sydney Blythe, Basil Emmott, sc: from
revue by Melville Gideon, Laddie Cliff.
With Davy Burnaby, Laddie Cliff,
Phyllis Monkman.

Copper-Proof See **Perfect Crime, The**

Cottage on Dartmoor, A BIF at Welwyn,
recorded in Berlin (A). Pro Patria, 1.30
(7,528) Part T, Klangfilm disc, also
silent version. p: Harry Bruce Woolfe,
d: Anthony Asquith, c: Stanley
Rodwell, M. Lindblom, sc: Anthony
Asquith from story by Herbert Price,
des: Ian Campbell-Gray, sd: Victor
Peers, technical supervision Max Stern,
MD: William Hodgson. with Norah
Baring, Uno Henning, Hans Schlettow.

Cotton Queen Rock Studios at Elstree
Rock and Manchester, Blackpool (U).
BIED, 5.37 (7,300). p: Joe Rock, d:
Bernard Vorhaus, c: Eric Cross, sc:
Scott Pembroke, dial: Louis Golding,
from story by Syd Courtenay, Barry
Peake, des: George Provis. With Stanley
Holloway, Will Fyffe, Jimmy Hanley,
Mary Lawson.

Counsel's Opinion LFP at Elstree B & D
(A). Paramt, 3.33 (6,806). p: Alexander
Korda, d: Allan Dwan, c: Bernard
Browne, sc: Dorothy Greenhill, Arthur
Wimperis from play by Gilbert Wake-
field (1931). With Cyril Maude, Henry
Kendall, Binnie Barnes, Lawrence
Grossmith, Francis Lister.

Count's Livery, The See **Take My Tip**

Crackerjack Gainsborough at Pinewood

(A). GFD, 10.38 (7,134). p: Edward Black, d: Albert de Courville, c: J. J. Cox, sc: A. R. Rawlinson, Michael Pertwee from novel by W. B. Ferguson. With Tom Walls, Lilli Palmer, Noel Madison.

Crazy People Brit. Lion at Beaconsfield (U). M-G-M, 9.34 (6,053). d: Leslie Hiscott, sc: Michael Barringer from story by Margot Neville, *Safety First.* With Henry Kendall, Nancy O'Neil.

Creeping Shadows BIP at Welwyn (A). Wardour, 8.31 9.31 (7,078). d: J. O. C. Orton, sc: J. O. C. Orton from play by Will Scott, *The Limping Man* (1930). With Franklin Dyall, Margot Grahame.

Crime at Blossoms, The B & D-Para-Brit. at Elstree B & D (A). Parmt. 3.33 (6,921). p: Henry Edwards, d: Maclean Rogers, sc: from play by Mordaunt Shairp (1931). With Hugh Wakefield, Joyce Bland.

Crime on the Hill BIP at Welwyn (A). Wardour, 12.33 (6,190). d: Bernard Vorhaus, c: Claude Friese-Greene, sc: Bernard Vorhaus, Michael Hankinson from play by Jack Celestin and Jack de Leon (1932). With Judy Kelly, Anthony Bushell, Sally Blane, Nigel Playfair.

Crime over London Criterion at Isleworth (A). UA, 10.36 (7,143). p: Marcel Hellman, Douglas Fairbanks Jr, d: Alfred Zeisler, c: Victor Armenise, Claude Friese-Greene, sc: Norman Alexander from novel by Louis de Wohl, *House of a Thousand Windows,* des: Edward Carrick, ed: Conrad von Molo. With Margot Grahame, Paul Cavanagh, Joseph Cawthorne.

Crime Reporter See **Warren Case, The**

Crimes at the Dark House Pennant at Beaconsfield, in production 11.39. Brit. Lion. p: d: George King, c: Hone Glendinning, sc: Frederick Hayward, Edward Dryhurst, add: H. F. Maltby, from novel by Wilkie Collins, *The Woman in White,* des: Bernard Robinson, ed: Jack Harris. With Tod Slaughter, Hilary Eaves.

Crimes of Stephen Hawke, The George King at Shepperton (A). M-G-M, 5.36

(6,203). p: d: George King, c: Ronald Neame, sc: H. F. Maltby from story by Jack Celestin. With Tod Slaughter, Marjorie Taylor.

Crime Unlimited WB-FN at Teddington (A). FN, 8.35 (6,571). p: Irving Asher, d: Ralph Ince, c: Basil Emmott, sc; Brock Williams, Ralph Smart from novel by David Hume. With Esmond Knight, Lilli Palmer.

Crimson Candle, The Bernerd Mainwaring at Wembley (A). M-G-M, 2.34 (6,020). p: d: sc: Bernerd Mainwaring. With Eve Gray, Eliot Makeham.

Crimson Circle, The Wainwright at Shepperton (U). Universal, 3.36 (6,881). p: Richard Wainwright, d: Reginald Denham, c: Phil Tannura, sc: Howard Irving Young from story by Edgar Wallace. With June Duprez, Niall MacGinnis, Alfred Drayton, Noah Beery.

Crooked Billet, The Gainsborough (A). Ideal, (1) 5.29 silent, (2) 3.30 sound (7,002) PT RCA. p: Michael Balcon, d: Adrian Brunel, Robert Atkins, c: Claude McDonnell, sc: Angus MacPhail from play by Dion Titheradge (1927), ed: Ian Dalrymple, MD: Louis Levy. With Carlyle Blackwell, Madeleine Carroll, Miles Mander, Gordon Harker.

Crooked Gentleman, The See **Concerning Mr. Martin**

Crooked Lady, The Real Art at Twickenham (U). M-G-M, 3.32 (6,956). p: Julius Hagen, d: Leslie Hiscott, sc: Harry Fowler Mear from story by William Stone. With Ursula Jeans, George Graves, Isobel Elsom, Austin Trevor.

Cross Currents B & D-Para-Brit. at Elstree B & D, Budleigh Salterton in Devon (U). Paramt, 7.35 (6,007). d: Adrian Brunel, sc: Adrian Brunel, Pelham Leigh Aman from novel by W. G. Elliott, *Nine Days Blunder.* With Marjorie Hume, Ian Colin, Evelyn Foster.

Cross My Heart B & D-Para-Brit. (A). Paramt, 1.37 (5,901). p: Anthony

Havelock-Allan, d: Bernerd Mainwaring, c: Francis Carver, sc: Basil N. Keyes from story by Robert Skinner. With Kathleen Gibson, Ken Duncan.

Cross Roads, The (1939) See **Dead Man's Shoes**

Cross Roads Sound version (FT Klangfilm) of **Warning, The** q.v.

Crouching Beast, The John Stafford at Welwyn (A). Radio, 8.35 (6,992). p: John Stafford, d: W. Victor Hanbury, sc: Valentine Williams from his own story. With Fritz Kortner, Wynne Gibson, Andrews Englemann.

Crown Trial AIP (U). Exclusive, 4.38 (3,150). p: Widgey Newman, d: sc: John N. Ruffin. With John Nathaniel.

Crown V Stevens WB-FN at Teddington (A). WB, 3.36 (5,997). p: Irving Asher, d: Michael Powell, c: Basil Emmott, sc: Brock Williams from novel by Laurence Meynell, *Third Time Unlucky*, des: Peter Proud, ed: A. Bates, sd: Leslie Murray, H. C. Pearson. With Beatrix Thompson, Patric Knowles, Googie Withers.

Crucifix, The New Era (A). Universal, 3.34 (4,301). p: Gordon Craig, d: G. B. Samuelson, sc: G. B. Samuelson, Roland Pertwee. With Nancy Price, Sydney Fairbrother.

Cuckoo in the Nest, A G-B at Shepherd's Bush (A). W & F, 10.33 (7,782). p: production personnel: Angus MacPhail, Ian Dalrymple, George Gunn, Louis Levy, d: Tom Walls, c: Glen MacWilliams, sc: A. R. Rawlinson, adapt. and dial: Ben Travers from his play (1925), des: Alfred Junge, cost: Gordon Conway, ed: Helen Lewis, sd: A. C. O'Donoghue. With Tom Walls, Ralph Lynn, Robertson Hare, Yvonne Arnaud.

Cup of Kindness, A G-B at Shepherd's Bush (A). G-B D, 4.34 (7,121). p: Michael Balcon, d: Tom Walls, c: Phil Tannura, sc: Ben Travers from his play (1929), des: Alfred Junge, cost: Berleo, ed: A. W. Roome, sd: P. Dorté. With Tom Walls, Ralph Lynn, Robertson Hare, Dorothy Hyson.

Dance Band BIP at Elstree (U). Wardour, 6.35 (6,860). p: Walter Mycroft, d: Marcel Varnel, c: Bryan Langley, sc: Roger Burford, Jack Davies, Denis Waldock, des: David Rawnsley, ed: Sidney Cole, MD: Harry Acres, songs Mabel Wayne, Desmond Carter, Arthur Young, Sonny Miller, Jack Shirley. With Buddy Rogers, June Clyde.

Dance of Death, The Glenrose at Cricklewood (A). Fidelity, 3.38 (5,827). d: Gerald Black, c: Desmond Dickinson, sc: Ralph Dawson. With Vesta Victoria, Stewart Rome, Julie Suedo.

Dance of the Witches See **Strange Evidence**

Dance, Pretty Lady BIF at Welwyn (A). Wardour, 12.31 (5,786) FT Klangfilm. p: Harry Bruce Woolfe, d: Anthony Asquith, c: Jack Parker, sc: Anthony Asquith from novel by Compton McKenzie, *Carnival*, des: Ian Campbell-Gray, sd: Victor Peers, A. F. Birch, MD: John Reynders, Marie Rambert Corps de Ballet, ballet adviser and choreographer Frederick Ashton. With Ann Casson, Carl Harbord.

Dancing Boy See **Beloved Imposter**

Dandy Dick BIP at Elstree (U). Wardour, 2.35 (6,534). p: Walter Mycroft, d: William Beaudine, c: Jack Parker, sc: Clifford Grey, Will Hay, Frank Miller, William Beaudine from play by Arthur Wing Pinero (1887), des: Duncan Sutherland, ed: A. C. Hammond, sd: Stanley Attkins. With Will Hay, Esmond Knight, Nancy Burne.

Dangerous Companions A. N. C. Macklin (U). Beacon, 3.34 (4,192). d:sc: A. N. C. Macklin. With A. N. C. Macklin.

Dangerous Fingers Rialto at Welwyn (A). Pathé, 12.37 (7,271). p: John Argyle, d: Norman Lee, sc: Vernon Clancey from his novel *Manhunt*. With James Stephenson, Betty Lynne.

Dangerous Ground B & D-Para-Brit. at Elstree B & D (A). Paramt, 4.34 (6,026). d: Norman Walker, c: Cyril Bristow, sc: Dion Titheradge, Dorothy Rowan from story by Dion Titheradge, des: G. S.

Stegmann, ed: David Lean. With Malcolm Keen, Joyce Kennedy, Jack Raine.

Dangerous Medicine WB-FN at Teddington (A). FN, 7.38 (6,450). p: Jerome Jackson, d: Arthur Woods, c: Basil Emmott, sc: Paul Gangelin, Paul England from story by Edmond Deland. With Cyril Ritchard, Elizabeth Allan.

Dangerous Seas E. G. Whiting (U). Filmophone, 3.31 (4,850) FT. d: sc: Edward Dryhurst. With Julie Suedo, Charles Garrey.

Danny Boy Panther Pictures at Cricklewood (U). Butcher's 6.34 (7,775). p: d: Oswald Mitchell, Challis Sanderson, c: Desmond Dickinson, sc: Oswald Mitchell, Archie Pitt, H. Barr-Carson. With Frank Forbes-Robertson, Dorothy Dickson, Archie Pitt.

Darby and Joan Rock Studios at Elstree Rock (A). M-G-M, 2.37 (6,867). p: Nat Ross, d: Syd Courtenay, c: John Silver, sc: Syd Courtenay from novel by Rita. With Peggy Simpson, Ian Fleming, Tod Slaughter.

Dark Eyes of London Argyle at Welwyn (H). Pathé, 10.39 (6,853). p: John Argyle, d: Walter Summers, c: Bryan Langley, sc: Patrick Kirwan, Walter Summers, dial: John Argyle, from novel by Edgar Wallace, des: Duncan Sutherland, ed: E. G. Richards, sd: A. E. Rudolph, music by Guy Jones, organ music by C. King Palmer. With Bela Lugosi, Greta Gynt, Hugh Williams.

Dark Journey Victor Saville at Denham (U). UA, 1.37 (7,238). p: d: Victor Saville, exec. p: Alexander Korda, c: Henry Stradling, Georges Périnal, sc: Arthur Wimperis from film play by Lajos Biro, des: Andre Andreiev, cost: Rene Hubert, ed: William Hornbeck, Hugh Stewart, sd: A. W. Watkins, sp: effects Ned Mann, MD: Muir Mathieson, music Richard Addinsell. With Conrad Veidt, Vivien Leigh.

Dark Red Roses BSFP (A). BIFD, 10.29 FT, songs BTP. d: Sinclair Hill, c: Arpad Viragh, sc: L. H. Gordon, Harcourt Templeman from story by

Stacy Aumonier, des: Oscar Werndorff, sd: John Ree. With Stewart Rome, Frances Doble.

Dark Stairway, The WB-FN at Teddington (A). WB, 1.38 (6,523). p: Irving Asher, d: Arthur Woods, c: Robert Lapresle, sc: Brock Williams, Basil Dillon from novel by Mignon G. Eberhart, *From What Dark Stairway*. With Hugh Williams, Chili Bouchier, Garry Marsh.

Dark World Fox Brit. at Wembley (A). Fox, 12.35 (6,620). p: Leslie Landau, d: Bernard Vorhaus, sc: Hugh Brooke from story by Leslie Landau and Selwyn Jepson, ballet Hedley Briggs. With Tamara Desni, Leon Quartermaine.

Darts Are Trumps George Smith Productions (U). RKO-Radio, 3.38 (6,588). d: P. Maclean Rogers, sc: from story by Gordon Bushell. With Eliot Makeham, Nancy O'Neil.

Daughters of Today FWK Productions at Cricklewood (U). UA, 2.33 (6,694). p: d: F. W. Kraemer, c: Desmond Dickinson, sc: Michael Barringer, des: Oscar Werndorff. With Betty Amann, George Barraud, Marguerite Allan.

David Livingstone Fitzpatrick at Shepperton (U). M-G-M, 11.36 (6,570). d: James A. Fitzpatrick, c: Hone Glendinning, sc: W. K. Williamson, des: John Bryan. With Percy Marmont, Hugh McDermott.

Dawn, The Thomas G. Cooper at Hibernia Film Studios Killarney (A). International Productions, 1.37 (7,900). p: d: c: Tom Cooper. With Tom Cooper.

Deadlock George King at Walton (A). Butcher's, 9.31 (7,632) FT. d: George King, c: Geoffrey Faithfull, sc: H. Fowler Mear from story by Charles Bennett and Billie Bristow. With Stewart Rome, Warwick Ward, Marjorie Hume.

Dead Man's Shoes ABPC at Elstree (A). ABPC, 7.39 (6,153). p: Walter Mycroft, d: Thomas Bentley, c: Gunther Krampf, sc: Nina Jarvis, Hans Kafka from French film *Carrefour*, des: Ian White, ed: Monica Kimmick. With Leslie Banks, Judy Kelly, Wilfrid Lawson.

Dead Men Are Dangerous Welwyn at Welwyn (A). Pathé, 3.39 (6,162). p: Warwick Ward, d: Harold French, sc: Victor Kendall, Harry Hughes, Vernon Clancey from novel by H. C. Armstrong, *Hidden*. With Robert Newton, John Warwick, Betty Lynne.

Dead Men Tell No Tales Brit. Nat. at Welwyn (A). ABPC, 2.38 (7,217). p: John Corfield, d: David MacDonald, c: Bryan Langley, sc: Walter Summers, Stafford Dickens, add:dial: Emlyn Williams, from novel by Francis Beeding, *The Norwich Victims*. ed: James Corbett, MD: W. L. Trytel. With Emlyn Williams, Hugh Williams, Lesley Brook.

Deadwater See **I Met a Murderer**

Death Adds Up See **Mr. Smith Carries On**

Death at Broadcasting House Phoenix at Wembley (A). ABFD, 10.34 (6,724). p: Hugh Perceval, d: Reginald Denham, c: Gunther Krampf, sc: Basil Mason from novel by Val Gielgud and Holt Marvel, des: R. Holmes Paul. With Ian Hunter.

Death Croons The Blues St Margaret's at Twickenham (A). M-G-M, 10.37 (6,636). p: Julius Hagen, d: David MacDonald, c: Sydney Blythe, sc: H. Fowler Mear from story by James Ronald. With Hugh Wakefield, Antoinette Cellier, George Hayes.

Death Drives Through Clifford Taylor Productions at Ealing (U). ABFD, 2.35 (5,585). p: Clifford Taylor, p: supervisor Bernerd Mainwaring, d: Edward L. Cahn, sc: from story by John Huston and Katherine Strueby. With Robert Douglas, Miles Mander, Dorothy Bouchier.

Death on the Set Twick. at Twickenham (A). Universal, 3.35 (6,502). p: Julius Hagen, d: Leslie Hiscott, c: Ernest Palmer, sc: Michael Barringer from novel by Victor McClure. With Henry Kendall, Eve Gray.

Debt of Honour Brit. Nat. at Elstree B & D, West Africa (A). GFD, 3.36 (7,465). p: John Corfield, d: Norman Walker, c: Robert Martin, sc: Tom Geraghty, Cyril Campion from story by 'Sapper' (H. C. McNeile). With Leslie Banks, Will Fyffe, Geraldine Fitzgerald, Niall MacGinnis.

Department Store Real Art at Twickenham (A). Radio, 5.35 (6,004). p: Julius Hagen, d: Leslie Hiscott, c: William Luff, sc: H. Fowler Mear from screen story by H. F. Maltby, *Johnston's Stores*, des: James Carter. With Eve Gray, Sebastian Shaw.

Deputy Drummer, The St. George's Pictures (U). Columbia, 9.35 (6,443). d: H. W. George, c: Alex Bryce, sc: Reginald Long, Arthur Rigby, des: A. L. Mazzei, music and lyrics Billy Mayerl, Frank Eyton. With Lupino Lane, Jean Denis.

Derelict, The M. V. Gover (U). Ind. F.D., 11.37 (5,150). p: Victor Gover, Joe Rosenthal, d: Harold Simpson, sc: Harold Simpson from story by Ralph Spence.

Designing Women Sound City at Shepperton (A). M-G-M, 3.34 (6,428). p: Norman Loudon, d: Ivar Campbell, sc: N. W. B. Pemberton from story by George Robinson. With Stewart Rome, Valerie Taylor.

Devil's Maze, The G-B at Shepherd's Bush (A). Gaumont, (1) 10.29 sound (7,517), (2) 11.29 silent (7,754) FT Brit. Ac. p: d: Gareth Gundrey, sc: Sewell Collins from play by G. R. Mallock, *Mostly Fools*. With Renee Clama, Trilby Clark, Hayford Hobbs.

Devil's Rock G. G. Burger in Ireland (U). Columbia, 3.38 (4,915). d: Germain Burger and Richard Hayward, sc: Richard Hayward. With Richard Hayward, Geraldine Mitchell.

Dial 999 Fox-Brit. at Wembley (A). 20th Cent.-Fox, 1.38 (4,058). p: man: Edward Dryhurst, d: Lawrence Huntington, c: Stanley Grant, sc: Ernest Dudley from story by Lawrence Huntington, W. Gerald Elliott, des: W. J. Hemsley, ed: Fergus McDonell, sd: John Cox.

With John Longden, Elizabeth Kent.

Diamond Cut Diamond Cinema House at Elstree (A). M-G-M, 8.32 (6,385). p: Eric Hakim, d: Fred Niblo, Maurice Elvey, sc: based on idea by Viscount Castelrosse, des: Laurence Irving. With Claud Allister, Adolphe Menjou, Benita Hume.

Dick Turpin John Stafford at Cricklewood (U). G-B D, 11.33 (7,058). p: John Stafford, d: John Stafford, W. Victor Hanbury, c: Walter Blakeley, Desmond Dickinson, sc: Victor Kendall from novel by Harrison Ainsworth, *Rookwood*, des: Wilfred Arnold. With Victor McLaglen, Jane Carr, Frank Vosper.

Dictator, The See **Love Affair of the Dictator, The**

Digging Deep See **Man I Want, The.**

Dinner at the Ritz New World at Denham (U). 20th Cent.-Fox,10.37 (6,963). p: Robert T. Kane, d: Harold D. Schuster, c: Phil Tannura, sc: Roland Pertwee, Romney Brent, des: Frank Wells, cost: Rene Hubert, ed: James B. Clark, sd: A. W. Watkins, sp. effects: Ned Mann, MD: Muir Mathieson, music and songs Lee Sims. With Annabella, Paul Lukas, David Niven.

Dirty Work G-B at Shepherd's Bush (A). G-B D, 12.34 (6,546). p: Michael Balcon, d: Tom Walls, c: Philip Tannura, sc: Ben Travers from his own play (1932), des: Alfred Junge, cost: Berleo, ed: Alfred Roome, sd: A. Birch, MD: Louis Levy. With Ralph Lynn, Robertson Hare, Gordon Harker.

Digging for Gold Ace, 9.36 (4,066). d: R. A. Hopwood. Variety from Windmill Theatre.

Discord B & D-Para-Brit. at Elstree B & D (A). Paramt. 1.33 (7,235). d: Henry Edwards, sc: from play by Ernest Temple Thurston, *A Roof and Four Walls* (1923). With Owen Nares, Benita Hume, Harold Huth.

Discoveries Grand Nat. at Highbury (U). Grant Nat., 8.39 (6,100). d: Redd Davis, c: Bryan Langley, sc: Anatole de Grunwald, Redd Davis, Cyril Campion based on Carroll Levis's BBC series,

des: James Carter, ed: John Seabourne, sd: Norman Daines, Leo Wilkins, Conductor Lew Stone and his band, music arranged Peter Akister.

Dishonour Bright Cecil at Beaconsfield (A). GFD, 9.36 (7,394). p: Max Schach, d: Tom Walls, c: Phil Tannura, sc: Ben Travers from his own story. With Tom Walls, Eugene Pallette, Betty Stockfield.

Divorce of Lady X, The LFP-Denham at Denham (A). UA, 1.38 (8,337). Technicolor (colour direction Natalie Kalmus). p: Alexander Korda, d: Tim Whelan, c: H. Stradling, Tech: c: W. V. Skall, sc: Ian Dalrymple, Lajos Biro, Arthur Wimperis from play by Gilbert Wakefield, *Counsel's Opinion* (1931), des: Lazare Meerson, Paul Sheriff, cost: Rene Hubert, ed: William Hornbeck, Walter Stokvis, sd: A. W. Watkins, sp. effects: Ned Mann, MD: Muir Mathieson, music Miklos Rozsa. With Merle Oberon, Lawrence Olivier, Ralph Richardson, Binnie Barnes.

Dizzy Limit, The Edward G. Whiting (U). PDC (1) 2.30 (5,722) silent, (2) 12.30 as **Kidnapped** (5,801) sound RCA. d: sc: Edward Dryhurst. With Jasper Maskelyne, Joy Windsor, Dino Galvani.

Doctor O'Dowd WB-FN, in production at Teddington 8.39. exec. p: Sam Sax, d: Herbert Mason, c: Basil Emmott, sc: Austin Melford, Derek Twist from novel by L. A. G. Strong. With Shaun Glenville, Peggy Cummins.

Doctor's Orders BIP at Elstree (U). Wardour, 10.34 (6,142). p: Walter Mycroft, d: Norman Lee, c: Bryan Langley, sc: Clifford Grey, R. P. Weston, Bert Lee from story by Lola Harvey and Syd Courtenay. With Leslie Fuller, John Mills.

Dodging the Dole Mancunian at Southall (U). Mancunian FC, 6.36 (8,128). p: John Blakeley, d: Arthur Mertz. With Roy Barbour, Jenny Howard.

Dominant Sex, The BIP at Elstree (A). ABPC, 2.37 (6,680). p: Walter Mycroft, d: Herbert Brenon, c: J. J. Cox, Roy Clark, sc: Vina de Vesci, John Fernald from play by Michael Egan (1935), des: Cedric Dawe. With Diana Churchill, Phillips Holmes, Romney Brent, Carol Goodner.

Don't be a Dummy WB-FN at Teddington (A). FN, 12.32 (4,531). p: Irving Asher, d: Frank A. Richardson, sc: Brock Williams. With George Harris, Muriel Angelus.

Don't Get Me Wrong WB-FN at Teddington (U). FN, 3.37 (7,276). p: Irving Asher, d: Arthur Woods, Reginald Purdell, c: Robert Lapresle, sc: John Dighton and Brock Williams, des: Peter Proud, ed: Arthur Ridout, sd: W. S. Nunn. With Max Miller, George E. Stone, Olive Blakeney.

Don't Rush Me Karno at Hammersmith (U). PDC, 1.36 (6,404). p: Fred Karno, d: Norman Lee, sc: Con West, Michael Barringer from Fred Karno sketch *When we are Married*. With Robb Wilton.

Dora H & S (U). H & S, 5.33 (3,650). d: sc: St John L. Clowes. With Moore Marriott, Sydney Fairbrother.

Doss House Sound City at Shepperton (A). M-G-M, 6.33 (4,760). p: Ivar Campbell, d: John Baxter, c: George Stretton, sc: from story by Herbert Ayres, des: D. W. L. Daniels, ed: R. Gardener, R. Swan, sd: J. Kilburn Byers, MD: Colin Wark. With Frank Cellier, Mark Daly.

Double Alibi Fox Brit. (A). Fox, 2.37 (3,611). p: Edward Dryhurst, d: David MacDonald, c: Stanley Grant, sc: Edward Dryhurst from story by Harold Weston, des: W. A. Hemsley, ed: Peter Tanner. With Ernest Sefton, John Warwick.

Double Dealing Real Art at Twickenham (A). Fox, 5.32 (4,373). p: Julius Hagen, d: Leslie Hiscott, sc: Harry Fowler Mear. With Frank Pettingell, Richard Cooper.

Double Error See **Price of Folly, The**

Double Event, The Triumph (A). PDC, 3.34 (6,132). d: L. H. Gordon, sc: from play by Sydney Blow, Douglas Hoare. With Jane Baxter, O. B. Clarence.

Double Exposures Triangle at Shepperton

(U). Paramt, 5.37 (6,032). p: George King, d: John Paddy Carstairs, sc: W. G. Elliott. With Julian Mitchell, Ruby Miller.

Double or Quits WB-FN at Teddington (A). WB, 3.38 (6,535). p: Irving Asher, d: Roy W. Neill, c: Basil Emmott, sc: Michael Barringer. With Patricia Medina, Frank Fox.

Double Trouble See **His Wife's Mother**

Double Wedding WB-FN at Teddington (U). WB, 3.33 (4,547). p: Irving Asher, Frank A. Richardson. With Joan Marion, Jack Hobbs.

Down Our Alley BSS at Highbury (U). BSS, 7.39 (5,075). d: G. A. Cooper, c: Germain Burger. With Hughie Green and his Gang, Wally Patch.

Down Our Street Para-Brit. (A). Paramt, 6.32 (6,795). d: Harry Lachman, sc: Harry Lachman from play of E. H. George (1930). With Nancy Price, Elizabeth Allan, Hugh Williams.

Down River G-B at Shepherd's Bush (A). Gaumont, 5.31 (6,610). p: L'Estrange Fawcett, d: Peter Godfrey, sc: Ralph Bettinson from novel by 'Seamark' (Austin Small), des: A. L. Mazzei. With Charles Laughton, Jane Baxter, Harold Huth.

Downstream G. G. Glavany at Isleworth (U). Carlton Films, 12.29 (6,058) silent. d: G. Glavany, c: Baron Ventimiglia, sc: G. Glavany, Jane Tarlo, Richard de Keyser. Registered as foreign film. With Chili Bouchier, Harold Huth.

Drake of England BIP at Elstree, Plymouth Hoe (U). Wardour, 5.35 (8,890). p: Walter Mycroft, d: Arthur Woods, c: Ronald Neame, Jack Parker, Claude Friese-Greene, sc: Marjorie Deans, Akos Tolnay, Norman Watson, add.: Clifford Grey, from play by Louis N. Parker *Drake* (1912), des: Duncan Sutherland, Clarence Elder, ed: E. B. Jarvis, MD: Idris Lewis, music G.H. Clutsam, dances Espinosa. With Matheson Lang, Athene Seyler, Jane Baxter.

Dream Doctor, The Bernard Smith and Widgey Newman (A). M-G-M, 9.36

(3,671). p: Bernard Smith and Widgey Newman, d: R. W. Lotinga. With Julie Suedo, Sidney Monckton.

Dreamers, The GBPC (U). Gaumont-Ideal, registered 6.33 (1,864). p: man: Clayton Hutton, d: Frank Cadman, c: Stanley Rodwell. With Flanagan and Allen.

Dreaming Lips Trafalgar at Denham (A). UA, 2.37 (7,611). p: Max Schach, Paul Czinner, d: Paul Czinner, Lee Garmes, c: Roy Clark, sc: adapt: Carl Mayer, R. J. Cullen from play by Henri Bernstein, *Melo*, and film, *Der Träumende Mund* made by Czinner in 1932, des: A. Andreiev, Tom Morahan, cost: Joe Strassner, ed: David Lean, sd: L. E. Overton, C. C. Stevens, concert music played by Brosa and London Symphony Orchestra conducted by Boyd Neel, incidental music by William Walton. With Elisabeth Bergner, Raymond Massey, Romney Brent.

Dream of Love, A Fitzpatrick at Shepperton (U). M-G-M, 1.38 (3,360). p: d: James A. Fitzpatrick, c: Hone Glendinning, sc: W. K. Williamson. With Ian Colin, Cathleen Nesbitt.

Dreams Come True London & Cont. at Ealing (A). Reunion Films, 10.36 (6,939). p Ilya Salkind, John Gossage, d: Reginald Denham, c: Otto Heller, sc: Donald Bull, dial: Bruce Sievier, from Austrian film *Liebesmelodie*, based on operetta by Franz Lehar, *Clo-Clo*, lyrics Bruce Sievier. With Frances Day, Hugh Wakefield, Nelson Keys.

Dressed to Kill See **His Brother's Keeper**

Dreyfus BIP at Elstree (U). Wardour, 4.31 (7,816) FT RCA. p: F. W. Kraemer, d: F. W. Kraemer and Milton Rosmer, c: W. Winterstein, W. Harvey, Horace Wheddon, sc: Walter Mycroft, Reginald Berkeley from play by Herzog and Rehfisch, *The Dreyfus Case*, des: W. Reimann, ed: John Harlow, sd: Alec Murray, MD: John Reynders. With Sir Cedric Hardwicke. (Made after German and French productions.)

Driven See **One Precious Year**

Dr. Josser, K. C. BIP (U). Pathé, 11.31 (6,495). d: Norman Lee, sc: Norman Lee, Ernie Lotinga from their sketch. With Ernie Lotinga, Jack Hobbs.

Dr. Sin Fang Victory at Elstree, former Whitehall (A). M-G-M, 9.37 (5,633). d: A. Frenguelli, c: Roy Fogwell, sc: F. T. Reynolds, Nigel Byass from novel by Kaye Mason. With Harry Agar Lyons, Nell Emerald, Anne Grey.

Dr. Syn G-B at Islington (A). GFD, 8.37 (7,299). d: Roy William Neill, assoc. d: Maude Howell, c: J. J. Cox, Jack Parry, sc: Roger Burford, add.: Michael Hogan from novel by Russell Thorndike, des: Vetchinsky, ed: R. E. Dearing, Alfred Roome, sd: A. Cameron, MD: Louis Levy. With George Arliss, Margaret Lockwood, John Loder.

Drum, The LFP-Denham Films at Denham, North Wales, India (U). UA, 4.38 (8,726). Technicolour (colour direction Natalie Kalmus). p: Alexander Korda, d: Zoltan Korda, c: Osmond Borradaile (India), Georges Périnal, sc: Lajos Biro, Arthur Wimperis, Patrick Kirwan, Hugh Gray from story by A. E. W. Mason, des: Vincent Korda, cost: Rene Hubert, ed: William Hornbeck, Henry Cornelius, sd: A. W. Watkins, MD: Muir Mathieson, music John Greenwood. With Sabu, Raymond Massey, Valerie Hobson, Roger Livesey.

Dubarry See **I Give My Heart**

Duchess, The See **Irish For Luck**

Dusty Ermine J. H. Productions at Elstree, Austria (A). Twick. F. D., 9.36 (7,666). p: Julius Hagen, d: Bernard Vorhaus, c: Curt Courant (studio), Otto Martini (location), sc: L. du Garde Peach, Arthur Macrae from play by Neil Grant (1935), des: A. L. Mazzei, ed: Jack Harris, Ralph Kemplen, sd: Baynham Honri, Leo Wilkins, MD: W. L. Trytel. With Ronald Squire, Anthony Bushell, Jane Baxter.

D'Ye Ken John Peel? Twick. at Twickenham (A). AP & D, 1.35 (7,950). p: Julius Hagen, d: Henry Edwards, c: Sydney Blythe, William Luff, sc: H.

Fowler Mear, from story by Charles Cullum, des: James Carter, ed: Jack Harris, Lister Laurence, sd: Baynham Honri, MD: and music W. L. Trytel. With John Stuart, Winifred Shotter, Stanley Holloway.

Early Bird, The Crusade at Highbury and in Ulster (U). Paramt, 8.36 (6,287). p: Victor M. Greene, d: Donovan Pedelty, sc: D. Pedelty from play by J. McGregor Douglas. With Richard Hayward.

East Lynne on the Western Front Welsh-Pearson at Shepherd's Bush (U). Gaumont, 7.31 (7,402) FT Brit. Ac. p: T. A. Welsh, d: George Pearson, c: Percy Strong, sc: Donovan and Mary Parsons from story by George Pearson. With Herbert Mundin, Alf Goddard, Hugh E. Wright.

East Meets West G-B at Shepherd's Bush (A). G-B D, 8.36 (6,695). d: Herbert Mason, assoc. d: Maude Howell, c: Bernard Knowles, sc: Maude Howell from play by Edwin Greenwood, *The Lake of Life*, des: Oscar Werndorff, cost: Joe Strassner, music John Greenwood. With George Arliss, Lucie Mannheim, Godfrey Tearle.

East of Ludgate Hill Fox Brit. at Wembley (U). 20th Cent.-Fox, 12.37 (4,269). d: Manning Haynes, c: Stanley Grant, sc: Edward Dryhurst from story by Arnold Ridley. With Nancy O'Neil, Robert Cochran.

Easy Money (1933) See **Forging Ahead**

Easy Money B & D-Para-Brit. (U). Paramt, 8.34 (6,180). d: Redd Davis, sc: Basil Mason from his play *The Ghost of Mr. Pim*. With George Carney, Mary Newland, Gerald Rawlinson.

Easy Riches G. S. Ent. (U). RKO-Radio, 1.38 (6,006). p: George Smith, d: P. Maclean Rogers, c: Geoffrey Faithfull, sc: from story by John Hunter. With George Carney, Gus McNaughton.

Ebb Tide Paramt-Brit. at Elstree B & D (A). Paramt, 2.32 (6,700). d: Arthur Rosson, sc: Basil Mason, Reginald

Denham from earlier American film *God Gave Me Twenty Cents*. With Joan Barry, George Barraud.

Edge of the World, The Joe Rock at Elstree Rock and Foula (A). BIED, 7.37 (7,300, later 7,247). p: Joe Rock, d: Michael Powell, c: Monty Berman, Skeets Kelly, Ernest Palmer, sc: Michael Powell, ed: Derek Twist, sd: L. K. Tregellas, MD: Cyril Ray, music W. L. Williamson, women of the Glasgow Orpheus Choir conducted by Sir Hugh S. Roberton. With Niall MacGinnis, Belle Chrystall, John Laurie, Finlay Currie.

Educated Evans WB-FN at Teddington (U). FN, 8.36 (7,736). p: Irving Asher, d: William Beaudine, c: Basil Emmott, sc: Frank Launder, Robert Edmunds from story by Edgar Wallace, des: Peter Proud. With Max Miller, Nancy O'Neil.

Eight Cylinder Love Tribune (U). Columbia, 12.34 (3,837). p: c: Peter Saunders. With Pat Aherne, Dodo Watts.

18 Minutes Allied Film Productions at Walton, Paris (A). Pathé, 4.35 (7,670). d: Monty Banks, c: Geoffrey Faithfull, J. J. Cox, sc: Fred Thompson from story by Gregory Ratoff, des: Andre Andreiev, ed: Émile de Ruelle, sd: Michael Rose, sp. effects: Lloyd Knechtel, music Alexis Archangelsky. With Gregory Ratoff, John Loder, Benita Hume.

Elder Brother, The Triangle at Shepperton (A). Paramt, 2.37 (6,030). p: George King, d: Frederick Hayward, c: Jack Parker, sc: Dorothy Greenhill from novel by Anthony Gibbs. With John Stuart, Marjorie Taylor.

Elephant Boy LFP at Denham, India (U). UA, 2.37 (7,587 registered, later 7,373). p: Alexander Korda, assoc. p: Zoltan Korda, Robert Flaherty, Zoltan Korda, c: Osmond Borradaile, sc: John Collier, with Akos Tolnay, Marcia de Silva, from story by Rudyard Kipling, *Toomai of the Elephants*, ed: William Hornbeck, Charles Crichton, sd: A. W. Watkins, MD: Muir Mathieson, music

John Greenwood. With Sabu, Walter Hudd, Allan Jeayes.

Eliza Comes to Stay Twick. at Hammersmith (A). Twick. FD., 4.36 (6,500). p: Julius Hagen, d: Henry Edwards, c: Sydney Blythe, William Luff, sc: H. Fowler Mear from play by H. V. Esmond (1913), des: James Carter, ed: Jack Harris, Michael Chorlton, sd: G. E. Burgess, Charles Poulten, MD: W. L. Trytel, musical number Ray Moreton and Horatio Nicholls, dances Howard Deighton. With Betty Balfour, Sir Seymour Hicks.

Elstree Calling BIP at Elstree (U). Wardour, 2.30 (7,767) FT, songs RCA. Part Pathécolour. d: Adrian Brunel (supervisor), Alfred Hitchcock (sketches), c: Claude Friese-Greene, sc: Val Valentine, Adrian Brunel, ed: Émile de Ruelle, A. C. Hammond, sd: Alex Murray, music Reg Casson, Vivian Ellis, Chick Endor, Ivor Novello, Jack Strachey, lyrics Douglas Furber, Rowland Leigh, Donovan Parsons, ensembles Jack Hulbert, Paul Murray, Andre Charlot, conductors Teddy Brown, John Reynders, Sydney Baynes. With Tommy Handley, Gordon Harker, Jack Hulbert, Cicely Courtneidge, etc. (Multilingual).

Emil and the Detectives Wainwright at Shepperton (U). G-B-D, 2.35 (6,399). p: Richard Wainwright, d: Milton Rosmer, c: Mutz Greenbaum, sc: Cyrus Brooks, Frank Launder from novel by Erich Kästner and sc: by Billy Wilder for earlier German version, des: D. W. L. Daniels, ed: Cyril Heck, music Allan Gray. With John Williams, George Hayes, Mary Glynne.

End of the Road, The Fox Brit. at Wembley (U). Fox,10.36 (6,472). d: Alex Bryce, c: Stanley Grant, sc: Edward Dryhurst. With Sir Harry Lauder.

Enemy of the Police WB-FN (A). FN, 10.33 (4,676). p: Irving Asher, d: George King. With John Stuart, Viola Keats.

Englishman's Home An Aldwych Film Productions at Denham (A). UA,10.39 (6,900). p: Neville E. Neville, Sidney Harrison, d: Albert de Courville, c: Mutz Greenbaum, Henry Harris, sc: Albert de Courville from play by Major Guy du Maurier (1909), ed: Lister Laurence. With Edmund Gwenn, Mary Maguire, Paul Henried.

Enter Sir John See **Murder**

Enter the Queen Starcraft at Twickenham (U). Fox, 11.30 (3,838). p: Harry Cohen, d: Arthur Varney, sc: Brock Williams. With Herbert Mundin, Richard Cooper, Chili Bouchier.

Escape ATP at Beaconsfield, Dartmoor, Hyde Park (A). Radio, 8.30 (6,725) FT RCA. p: d: Basil Dean, c: John MacKenzie, Robert Martin, sc: Basil Dean from play by John Galsworthy, des: Clifford Pember, ed: Jack Kitchin, sd: J. G. Eisenberg, MD: Ernest Irving. With Sir Gerald du Maurier, Edna Best, Gordon Harker.

Escape Me Never B & D at Elstree B & D, Dolomites, Venice, Drury Lane (A). UA, 4.35 (9,158, later 8,584). p: Herbert Wilcox, assoc.: Dallas Bower, d: Paul Czinner, c: Georges Périnal (studio), Sepp Allgeier (location), sc: Margaret Kennedy, R. J. Cullen from play by Margaret Kennedy (1933), des: Andre Andreiev, Wilfred Arnold, cost: Joe Strassner, ed: Merrill White, David Lean, sd: L. E. Overton, C. C. Stevens, Vic Wells ballet, ballet music William Walton, choreography Frederick Ashton. With Elisabeth Bergner, Hugh Sinclair, Irene Vanbrugh, Griffith Jones.

Eternal Feminine, The Starcraft at Twickenham (U). Paramt, 2.31 (7,313). p: d: Arthur Varney, sc: Brock Williams, Hugh Broadbridge from story by Arthur Varney, music and songs Doria March. With Guy Newall, Doria March, Jill Esmond Moore, Terence de Marney.

Eunuch of Stamboul, The See **Secret of Stamboul, The**

Evensong G-B at Shepherd's Bush (U). G-B D, 9.34 (7,666). p: Michael Balcon, d: Victor Saville, c: Mutz Greenbaum, sc: adapted Dorothy Farnum, sc: and dial: Edward Knoblock from play by Beverley Nichols and Edward Knoblock (1932) based on novel by Beverley Nichols, des: Alfred Junge, cost: Cathleen Mann, ed. Otto Ludwig, sd: A. C. O'Donogue, MD: Louis Levy, songs Mischa Spoliansky, lyrics Edward Knoblock. With Evelyn Laye, Emlyn Williams, Fritz Kortner.

Evergreen G-B at Shepherd's Bush (A). G-B D, 4.34 (8,489). p: Michael Balcon, d: Victor Saville, c: Glen MacWilliams, sc: adapt: and dial: Emlyn Williams, sc: Marjorie Gaffney from C. B. Cochrane musical play by Benn Levy, *Ever Green* (1930), des: Alfred Junge, Peter Proud, cost:Berleo, ed: Ian Dalrymple, sd: A. F. Birch, MD: Louis Levy, music and lyrics from show by Richard Rodgers and Lorenz Hart, additional numbers Harry M. Woods, dances Buddy Bradley. With Jessie Matthews, Sonnie Hale, Betty Balfour.

Everybody Dance Gainsborough at Islington (A). G-B D, 9.36 (6,793). p: Michael Balcon, d: Charles Reisner, c: J. J. Cox, sc: Leslie Arliss, Ralph Spence from story by Leslie Arliss, Stafford Dickens, des: Vetchinsky, cost: Paula Newman, ed: R. E. Dearing, sd: G. E. Burgess, MD: Louis Levy, songs Mack Gordon and Harry Revel. With Cicely Courtneidge, Charles Reisner Jr.

Everything Happens to Me WB-FN at Teddington (A). WB, 12.38 (7,453). p: Jerome Jackson, d: Roy William Neill, c: Basil Emmott, sc: Austin Melford, John Dighton, from their own story, des: Peter Proud, Michael Relph, ed: Leslie Norman sd: H.C. Pearson, MD: Louis Levy, songs Max Miller, Fred Godfrey, Harry Gifford, Fred E. Cliffe, dances Jack Donohue, Winifred Izard. With Max Miller, H. F. Maltby, Chili Bouchier.

Everything in Life Tudor Films at Highbury (U). Columbia, 11.36 (6,376). p: Marquis of Ely, d: J. Elder Wills, sc: Courtney Terrett, ed: Julia Wolfe, music Hans May. With Gitta Alpar, Neil Hamilton.

Everything Is Rhythm Joe Rock at Elstree Rock (U). ABFD, 6.36 (6,607). p: Joe Rock, d: Alf Goulding, c: Ernest Palmer, sc: Syd Courtenay, Jack Byrd, Stanley Haynes from story by Tom Geraghty, des: A. L. Mazzei, George Provis: Harry Roy and his Band, songs Cyril Ray, Jack Meskill, Harry Roy, dances Joan Davis. With Harry Roy, Princess Pearl.

Everything Is Thunder G-B at Shepherd's Bush (A). G-B D, 7.36 (6,938). assoc. p: S. C. Balcon, d: Milton Rosmer, c: Gunther Krampf, sc: J. O. C. Orton, Marion Dix from novel by Jocelyn L. Hardy, des: Alfred Junge, cost: Joe Strassner. With Constance Bennett, Douglass Montgomery, Oscar Homolka.

Eve's Fall Gordon Bostock at Elstree BIP (U). PDC 2.30 (3,158) FT. p: Gordon Bostock, d: Monty Banks. With John Stuart, Muriel Angelus, Donald Stuart.

Excess Baggage Real Art at Twickenham (U). Radio, 3.33 (5,358). p: Julius Hagen, d: Redd Davis, sc: H. Fowler Mear from novel by Capt. H. M. Raleigh. With Frank Pettingell, Claude Allister.

Excuse My Glove Alexander Film Productions at Elstree Rock (A). ABFD, 1.36 (6,815). p: R. H. Alexander, Joe Rock, d: Redd Davis, c: Jack Wilson, sc: Katherine Strueby, Val Valentine from story by R. Howard Alexander. With Len Harvey, Betty Ann Davies.

Exit Don Juan See **Private Life of Don Juan, The**

Expert's Opinion B & D-Para-Brit.(A). Paramt, 10.35 (6,476). d: Ivar Campbell, sc: Ivar and Sheila Campbell from story by Guillan Hopper. With Leslie Perrins, Lucille Lisle.

Eyes of Fate Sound City at Shepperton (A). Universal, 12.33 (6,136). p: Norman Loudon, d: Ivar Campbell, sc: from story by Holloway Horn. With Allan Jeayes, Valerie Hobson, Terence de Marney.

Face At The Window, The Real Art at Twickenham (A). Radio,10.32 (4,717). p: Julius Hagen, d: Leslie Hiscott, c: Sydney Blythe, sc: H. Fowler Mear from play by F. Brooke Warren. With Raymond Massey, Isla Bevan, Eric Maturin.

Face at the Window, The Pennant at Beaconsfield (A). Brit. Lion, 4.39 (5,911). p: d: George King, c: Hone Glendinning, sc: A. R. Rawlinson from play by F. Brooke Warren, des: Philip Bawcombe. With Tod Slaughter.

Faces B & D-Para-Brit, (A). Paramt, 1.34 (6,197). d: Sidney Morgan. With Anna Lee, Harold French.

Facing The Music BIP at Elstree (U). Wardour, 6.33 (6,207). p: Walter Mycroft, d: Harry Hughes, c: Walter Harvey, Bryan Langley, sc: Clifford Grey, Stanley Lupino, Frank Launder from story by Clifford Grey, Sidney Gilliat, des: David Rawnsley, ed: Leslie Norman, sd: A. E. Rudolph, MD: Harry Acres, music and lyrics Noel Gay, Stanley Lupino. With Stanley Lupino, Jose Collins.

Fair Exchange WB-FN at Teddington (U). FN, 7.36 (5,710). p: Irving Asher, d: Ralph Ince, c: Basil Emmott, sc: Brock Williams, Russell Medcraft. With Roscoe Ates, Patric Knowles.

Faithful WB-FN at Teddington (U). WB, 3.36 (7,067). p: Irving Asher, d: Paul L. Stein. With Jean Muir, Gene Gerrard, Hans Sonker.

Faithful Heart, The Gainsborough at Islington (A). Ideal, 5.32 (7,504). p: Michael Balcon, d: Victor Saville, c: Mutz Greenbaum, sc: Victor Saville, Robert Stevenson from play by Monckton Hoffe (1921), add. dial: W. P. Lipscomb, des: Vetchinsky, cost: Gordon Conway, ed: Ian Dalrymple, sd: George Gunn, MD: Louis Levy. With Herbert Marshall, Edna Best.

Falling for You Gainsborough at Islington (U). W & F, 6.33 (7,930 registered, later 7,391). p: Michael Balcon, p.personnel: Angus MacPhail, Ian Dalrymple, George Gunn, Louis Levy, d: Jack Hulbert, Robert Stevenson, c: Bernard Knowles, sc: Jack Hulbert, Douglas Furber, Robert Stevenson from story by Sidney Gilliat, add. dial: Claude Hulbert, des: Vetchinsky, cost: Gordon Conway, ed: R. E. Dearing, sd: A. L. M. Douglas, MD: Louis Levy, music Vivian Ellis, lyrics Douglas Furber. With Jack Hulbert, Cicely Courtneidge.

Falling in Love Vogue Film Productions at Walton (U). Pathé, 9.34 (7,300). p: Howard Welsch d: Monty Banks, c: Geoffrey Faithfull, sc: John Paddy Carstairs. With Charles Farrell, Gregory Ratoff, Margot Grahame.

Fall of an Empire See **Spy of Napoleon**

False Evidence Crusade at Wembley (A). Paramt, 9.37 (6,396). p: Victor M. Greene, d: Donovan Pedelty, sc: from novel by Roy Vickers, *I'll Never Tell*. With Gwenllian Gill.

Fame Herbert Wilcox at Elstree B & D (U). GFD. 3.36 (6,373). p: Herbert Wilcox, d: Leslie Hiscott, c: Henry Harris, sc: Michael Barringer from story by John Harding and W. Hargreaves. With Sydney Howard, Muriel Aked.

Farewell Again Pendennis Pictures-LFP at Denham, HMT 'Somersetshire'. UA, 5.37 (7,539). p: Erich Pommer, presented by Alexander Korda, d: Tim Whelan, c: James Wong Howe (interiors), Hans Schneeburger (exteriors) sc: Clemence Dane, Patrick Kirwan from story by Wolfgang Wilhelm, des: Frederick Pusey, cost: Rene Hubert, ed: Jack Dennis, sd: A. W. Watkins, music Richard Addinsell. With Leslie Banks, Flora Robson.

Farewell to Cinderella G.S.Ent. (U). Radio, 4.37 (5,819). p: George Smith, d: P. Maclean Rogers c: Geoffrey Faithfull, sc: Kathleen Butler, P. Maclean Rogers from story by Arthur Richardson. With Anne Pichon, John Robinson.

Farewell to Yesterday see **Return to Yesterday.**

Fascination Regina Films at Elstree (A). Wardour, 7.31 (6,381). p: Clayton Hutton, d: Miles Mander, sc: Victor Kendall from play by Eliot Crawshay Williams *This Marriage*. With Madeleine Carroll, Carl Harbord, Dorothy Bartlam.

The Fatal Hour B & D-Para-Brit. at Pinewood (A). Paramt, 5.37 (5,828). p: Anthony Havelock-Allan, d: George Pearson, sc: from story by Cicely Fraser-Simson, *The Clock*. With Edward Rigby.

Father and Son WB-FN at Teddington (A). WB, 9.34 (4,348). p: Irving Asher, d: Monty Banks, sc: Randall Faye from story by Ben Ames Williams. With Edmund Gwenn, Esmond Knight.

Father O'Flynn Butcher's at Shepperton (U). Butcher's,11.35 (7,500). p: Wilfred Noy, d: Wilfred Noy, Walter Tennyson, c: Stanley Rodwell. With Tom Burke, Jean Adrienne.

Father O'Nine Fox Brit. at Wembley (U). 20th Cent.-Fox, 3.38 (4,292). prod. man: Ivor McLaren, d: Roy Kellino, c: Robert Lapresle, sc: from story by Harold G. Brown, des: Carmen Dillon, ed: Reginald Beck. With Hal Gordon, Dorothy Dewhurst.

Father Steps Out George Smith Productions at Walton (U). Radio, 6.37 (5,776). d: P. Maclean Rogers, c: Geoffrey Faithfull, sc: Kathleen Butler from story by Henry Holt, Irving Leroy. With George Carney, Dinah Sheridan.

Faust Publicity Picture Productions at Bushey (A). Reunion, 2.36 (4,063). Spectra colour. p. supervisor: Fred Swann, d: A. E. C. Hopkins, sc: from opera by Gounod. With Webster Booth, Anne Zeigler.

Fear Ship, The ASFI-J. Stevens Edwards at Wembley (A). Paramt, 10.33 (5,921). ASFI mobile sound vans. d: James Stevens Edwards, c: Eric Cross, Frank Grainger, sc: James Stevens Edwards from novel by R. F. W. Rees, *The Second Mate,* sd: G. E. Burgess. With Edmund Willard, Dorothy Bartlam, Cyril McLaglen.

Feather, The Strand at Twickenham, songs recorded at Islington (A). UA, 11.29 (8,223). Synch RCA, songs. d: Leslie Hiscott, c: Basil Emmott, sc: Leslie Hiscott from novel by C. M. Matheson. With Jameson Thomas, Vera Flory.

Feathered Serpent, The G.S.Ent. at Walton (A). Columbia, 12.34 (6,494). p: George Smith, d: P. Maclean Rogers, c: Geoffrey Faithfull, sc: P. Maclean Rogers, Kathleen Butler from story by Edgar Wallace. With Enid Stamp-Taylor, D. A. Clarke-Smith.

Feather Your Nest ATP at Ealing (U). ABFD, 2.37 (7,296). p: Basil Dean, d: William Beaudine, c: Ronald Neame, sc: Austin Melford, Val Valentine from story by Ivar and Sheila Campbell, des: R. Holmes Paul, ed: Ernest Aldridge, sd: Paul F. Wiser, music and songs Leslie Sarony and Leslie Holmes, Noel Gay, Harry Gifford and Fred E. Cliffe. With George Formby, Polly Ward.

Fifty-Fifty See **Just My Luck**

Fifty-Shilling Boxer, The George Smith Productions at Walton (U). Radio, 5.37 (6,631). p: George Smith, d: P. Maclean Rogers, sc: Guy Fletcher. With Bruce Seton, Nancy O'Neil.

Fighting Stock Gainsborough at Islington (A). G-B D, 3.35 (6,541). p: Michael Balcon, d: Tom Walls, c: P. Tannura, sc: Ben Travers from his own story. With Tom Walls, Ralph Lynn, Robertson Hare.

Final Reckoning, The Equity British (A). Equity British, 3.32 (5,825) silent with synchronised music. d: sc: John Argyle. With James Benton, Margaret Delane.

Find the Lady Fox Brit. at Wembley (A). Fox, 3.36 (6,363). d: Roland Gillett, c: Stanley Grant, sc: Roland Gillett, Edward Dryhurst from story by E. L. Waller. With Jack Melford, Althea Henley, George Sanders.

Flames of Fear John F. Argyle (U). Equity British, 9.30 (5,655) silent. p: sc: John Argyle, d: Charles Barnett. With John Argyle, Ernest Bakewell.

Fine Feathers Brit. Lion at Beaconsfield (U). Brit. Lion, 5.37 (6,168). p: Herbert

Smith, d: Leslie Hiscott, c: George Stretton, sc: Michael Barringer from his own story. With Renee Houston, Donald Stewart, Francis L. Sullivan.

Fire Has Been Arranged, A Twick. at Twickenham (U). Twick. FD, 10.35 (6,300). p: Julius Hagen, d: Leslie Hiscott, c: Sydney Blythe, sc: H. Fowler Mear, Michael Barringer from screen story by H. Fowler Mear and James Carter. With Flanagan and Allen.

Fire Over England Pendennis Productions-LFP at Denham (U). UA, 1.37 (7,750). p: Erich Pommer, presented by Alexander Korda, d: William K. Howard, c: James Wong Howe, sc: Clemence Dane, Sergei Nolbandov from novel by A. E. W. Mason, des: Lazare Meerson, Frank Wells, ed: Jack Dennis, cost: Rene Hubert, sd: A. W. Watkins, sp. effects. Ned Mann, MD: Muir Mathieson, music Richard Addinsell. With Raymond Massey, Laurence Olivier, Vivien Leigh, Leslie Banks, Flora Robson.

Fire Raisers, The G-B at Shepherd's Bush (A). W & F, 9.33 (6,998). assoc. p: Jerome Jackson, d: Michael Powell, c: Leslie Rowson, sc: Michael Powell and Jerome Jackson from their own story, des: Alfred Junge, cost: Gordon Conway, ed: Derek Twist, sd: A. F. Birch. With Leslie Banks, Carol Goodner, Anne Grey.

Fires of Fate BIP (U). Wardour, 9.32 (6,650). d: Norman Walker, c: Claude Friese-Greene, sc: Dion Titheradge from novel by Sir Arthur Conan Doyle, *The Tragedy of the Korosko* and play, *Fires of Fate* (1909). With Jack Raine, Kathleen O'Regan.

First a Girl G-B at Shepherd's Bush, Riviera (A). G-B D, 11.35 (8,273). p: Michael Balcon, assoc. p: S. C. Balcon, d: Victor Saville, c: Glen MacWilliams, sc: Marjorie Gaffney from Alfred Zeisler's film *Viktor and Viktoria*, des: Oscar Werndorff, cost: Joe Strassner, ed: Al Barnes, sd: A. C. O'Donoghue, MD: Louis Levy, songs Sigler,

Goodhart and Hoffman, dances Ralph Reader. With Jessie Matthews, Sonnie Hale, Griffith Jones, Anna Lee.

First and the Last, The See **Twenty-One days**

First Mrs. Fraser, The Sterling at Wembley ASFI (A). Sterling, 4.32 (8,462). p: Louis Zimmerman, d: Sinclair Hill, c: Gunther Krampf, sc: L. H. Gordon from play by St John Ervine (1929), des: Oscar Werndorff, music Billy Cotton and his Band, Gaucho Tango Orchestra. With Henry Ainley, Joan Barry, Harold Huth, Dorothy Dix.

First Night Crusade at Wembley (U). Paramt, 6.37 (6,290). p: Victor M. Greene, d: Donovan Pedelty, sc: Donovan Pedelty from play by Sheila Donisthorpe. With Jack Livesey, Rani Waller.

First Offence Gainsborough at Islington, French locations (A). G-B D 2.36 (5,994). d: Herbert Mason, c: Arthur Crabtree, sc: Stafford Dickens, Austin Melford based on French film by Billy Wilder des: Walter Murton, ed: Michael Gordon, sd: Michael Rose, MD: Louis Levy, music F. Waxman and Gray. With John Mills, Lilli Palmer.

£5 Man, The Fox-Brit at Wembley (A). Fox, 3.37 (6,862). d: Albert Parker, c: Stanley Grant, sc: David Evans. With Judy Gunn, Edwin Styles.

Flag Lieutenant, The B & D (U). W & F, 10.32 (7,748). p: Herbert Wilcox, d: Henry Edwards, c: Stanly Rodwell, sc: Joan Wentworth Wood from play by Lt Col. W. P. Drury and Major Lee Trevor (1908), des: Wilfred Arnold, Naval adviser Cmdr. F. W. Gleed, ed: Michael Hankinson, sd: J. S. Dennis MD: Lew Stone, music Harris Weston, lyrics, R. P. Weston, Bert Lee. With Henry Edwards, Anna Neagle.

Flame in the Heather Crusade (A). Paramt, 9.35 (5,936). p: Victor M. Greene, d: Donovan Pedelty, sc: Donovan Pedelty from novel by Esson Maule. With Gwenllian Gill, Barry

Clifton.

Flame of Love, The BIP-Richard Eichberg Production at Elstree (A). Wardour, 3.30 (7,100) FT, songs RCA. p: d: Richard Eichberg, c: Henry Gartner, sc: Monckton Hoffe, Ludwig Wolff, des: Clarence Elder, W. A. Hermann, ed: Sam Simmonds, Émile de Ruelle, sd: Harold King, MD: John Reynders, music Hans May, dances A. Oumansky. With Anna May Wong, John Longden. (Bilingual, made in UK but registered as foreign film.)

Flashback Charles B. Cochrane (U). Anglo-American,11.38 (6,300). d: R. E. Jeffrey.

Flat No.9 V. Deuchar (U). Fox, 5.32 (4,456). d: Frank A. Richardson, sc: Brock Williams from story by Patricia Bach. With Reginald Gardiner, Jane Baxter.

Flat No. 3 Brit Lion (A). M-G-M, 2.34 (4,228). p: supervisor: Herbert Smith, d: Leslie Hiscott, sc: from story by Michael Barringer. With Mary Glynne, D. A. Clarke-Smith, Betty Astell.

Flaw, The Patrick K. Heale at Wembley (A). Paramt, 9.33 (6,001). p: Pat Heale, d: Norman Walker, sc: Brandon Fleming with Henry Kendall, Eve Gray.

Fledermaus, Die See under **Waltz Time**

Fleet Street Murder See **Warren Case, The**

Flood Tide Real Art at Twick. (U). Radio, 11.34 (5,768). p: Julius Hagen, d: John Baxter, c: Walter Blakeley, sc: from story by Ernest Anson Dyer. With George Carney.

Flowery Walk, The See **Primrose Path, The**

Flying Doctor, The G-B and National Productions in Australia (Pagewood) (U). GFD, 9.37 (6,100). d: Miles Mander, c: Derick Williams, sc: J. O. C. Orton from story by Robert Waldron. With Charles Farrell, Mary Maguire, Margaret Vyner.

Flying Fifty-Five Admiral Films at Welwyn (U). RKO-Radio, 5.39 (6,439). p: Victor M. Greene, d: Reginald Denham, c: Ernest Palmer, sc: Victor M. Greene from story by Edgar Wallace. With Derrick de Marney, Nancy Burne, Marius Goring.

Flying Fool, The BIP at Elstree (U). Wardour, 7.31 (6,991). d: Walter Summers, c: Claude Friese-Greene, Stanley Rodwell, Jimmy Wilson, Joe Rosenthal, A. Fisher, sc: Walter Summers from play by Arnold Ridley and Philip Merivale (1929), des: Clarence Elder, John Mead, ed: Walter Stokvis, sd: A. E. Rudolph, MD: John Reynders. With Henry Kendall, Benita Hume, Ursula Jeans.

Flying Scotsman, The BIP at Elstree (U). Warner Brothers, 5.29 silent, 2.30 sound (5,502) PT RCA. d: Castleton Knight, c: Theodor Sparkuhl, sc: Garnett Weston, Victor Kendall from story by Joe Grossman, des: T. H. Gibbings, ed: A. C. Hammond, MD: John Reynders, musical theme Idris Lewis and John Reynders. With Moore Marriott, Pauline Johnson, Raymond Milland, Alec Hurley.

Flying Squad, The Brit. Lion at Beaconsfield (A). Brit. Lion, 7.32 (7,140). p: S. W. Smith, d: F. W. Kraemer, c: Alex Bryce, sc: Bryan Edgar Wallace from *Daily Mail* serial and play (1928) by Edgar Wallace, des: Norman Arnold, sd: Harold King. With Harold Huth, Carol Goodner.

Flying Squad, The ABPC. In production at Elstree in summer 1939. p: Walter Mycroft, d: Herbert Brenon, c: Walter Harvey, sc: Doreen Montgomery from '*Daily Mail*' serial and play (1928) by Edgar Wallace. With Phyllis Brooks, Sebastian Shaw, Jack Hawkins.

Follow the Lady George Smith (A). Fox, 6.33 (4,484). p: George Smith, d: sc: Adrian Brunel. With William Hartnell.

Follow the Sun See **Dinner at the Ritz**

Follow Your Star Belgrave Films at Pinewood (U). GFD, 5.38 (7,198). p: Harcourt Templeman, d: Sinclair Hill, c: Cyril Bristow, sc: George Pearson, Stafford Dickens from story by Sinclair Hill and Arthur Tracy, songs Jimmy Kennedy and Michael Carr. With Arthur Tracy and Belle Chrystall

Footlights 6.37 (4,082). d: R. A. Hopwood. Variety from Windmill Theatre.

Forbidden Territory Progress Pictures at Shepherd's Bush (U). G-B D, 10.34 (7,588). p: Richard Wainwright, d: Phil Rosen, c: C Van Enger, sc: Dorothy Farnum from novel by Dennis Wheatley. With Gregory Ratoff, Tamara Desni, Barry Mackay.

Foreign Affairs Gainsborough at Islington (U). G-B D, 11.35 (6,492). p: Michael Balcon, Tom Walls, c: Roy Kellino, sc: Ben Travers from his own story, des: Vetchinsky, ed: Alfred Roome, sd: Philip Dorté, MD: Louis Levy. With Tom Walls, Ralph Lynn, Robertson Hare.

For Ever And Ever See **Jump for Glory**

Forever England G-B at Shepherd's Bush, Portsmouth, Plymouth, etc (A). G-B D, 5.35 (7,264). p: Michael Balcon, d: Walter Forde, island sequence Anthony Asquith, c: Bernard Knowles, sc: J. O. C. Orton, dial: Michael Hogan, Gerard Fairlie, from novel by C. S. Forester, *Brown on Resolution*, des: Alfred Junge, ed: Otto Ludwig, sd: Philip Dorte. With Betty Balfour, John Mills.

Forget Me Not LFP and Itala GmbH (U). UA, 3.36 (6,555). p: Alberto Giacolone, Alexander Korda, d: Zoltan Korda, c: Hans Schneeberger, sc: Hugh Gray, Arthur Wimperis. With Beniamino Gigli, Joan Gardner. (International remake in English of German film, registered as foreign film).

Forging Ahead Harry Cohen at Wembley (A). Fox, 3.33 (4,349). p: Harry Cohen, d: Norman Walker, sc: from novel by K. R. G. Browne and play by Brandon Fleming and S. W. Carroll, *Easy Money* (1926). With Margot Grahame, Garry Marsh.

For Love of You Windsor at Elstree, Venice (U). p: Frank A. Richardson, d: Carmine Gallone, c: Wilhelm Goldberger, sc: Selwyn Jepson, des: R. Holmes Paul. With Arthur Riscoe, Naunton Wayne, Franco Foresta.

For the Love of Mike BIP at Elstree (U). Wardour, 12.32 (7,725). d: Monty Banks, c: Claude Friese-Greene, sc: Frank Launder, Clifford Grey from musical play by Clifford Grey and H. F. Maltby (1931) des: David Rawnsley, sd: C. V. Thornton, music Jack Waller and Joseph Tunbridge. With Bobby Howes, Arthur Riscoe, Wylie Watson.

Fortunate Fool, The ABFD at Ealing (A). ABFD, 11.33 (6,474). p: Jack Eppel, d: Norman Walker, c: Alan Lawson, sc: from play by Dion Titheradge. With Hugh Wakefield, Joan Wyndham.

For Valour Capitol at Shepperton (A). GFD, 3.37 (8,464). p: Max Schach, d: Tom Walls, c: Phil Tannura, sc: Ben Travers from his own story, des: Oscar Werndorff, ed: E. B. Jarvis, sd: A. C. Geary, MD: Van Phillips. With Tom Walls, Ralph Lynn, Veronica Rose.

Four Dark Hours See **Green Cockatoo, The**

Four Feathers, The LFP at Denham, Sudan (A). UA, 4.39 (11,318, later 10,381). Technicolor – colour director Natalie Kalmus. p: Alexander Korda, assoc. p: Irving Asher, assoc. p: (Sudan) Charles David, d: Zoltan Korda, c: Georges Périnal (Sudan), Osmond Borradaile, Jack Cardiff (studio), sc: R. C. Sherriff, Lajos Biro, Arthur Wimperis, from novel by A. E. W. Mason, des: Vincent Korda, cost: Rene Hubert, Godfrey Brennan, ed: William Hornbeck, Henry Cornelius, sd: A. W. Watkins, Geoffrey Boothby, MD: Muir Mathieson, music Miklos Rozsa. With John Clements, Ralph Richardson, June Duprez, C. Aubrey Smith.

Four Just Men, The Ealing Studios (CAPAD) at Ealing (A). ABFD, 6.39 (7,628). p: Michael Balcon, assoc. p: S. C. Balcon, d: Walter Forde, c: Ronald Neame, sc: Angus MacPhail, Sergei Nolbandov, dial: Ronald Pertwee, from novel by Edgar Wallace, des: Wilfred Shingleton, ed: Charles Saunders, sd: Eric Williams, MD: Ernest Irving. With Anna Lee, Hugh

Sinclair, Griffith Jones, Frank Lawton, Francis L. Sullivan.

Four Masked Men, The Twick. at Twickenham and Merton Park (A). Universal, 2.34 (7,317). p: Julius Hagen, d: George Pearson, sc: H. Fowler Mear, Cyril Campion from play by Cyril Campion *The Masqueraders*. With John Stuart, Judy Kelly.

Fourth Wife of Henry VIII, The See **Private Life of Henry VIII, The**

Frail Women Real Art at Twickenham (A). Radio, 1.32 (6,519). p: Julius Hagen, d: Maurice Elvey, c: Basil Emmott, William Luff, sc: Michael Barringer from his screen story, des: James Carter, ed: Jack Harris, Lister Laurence, sd: Baynham Horni. With Mary Newcomb, Owen Nares, Edmund Gwenn.

Freedom of the Seas BIP at Elstree (U). Wardour, 4.34 (6,698). p: Walter Mycroft, d: Marcel Varnel, c: Otto Kanturek, sc: Roger Burford from play by Walter Hackett (1918), des: Cedric Dawe, technical adviser Lt. Com. de Burgh, ed: Sidney Cole, sd: A. E. Rudolph. With Clifford Mollison, Zelma O'Neal, Wendy Barrie.

French Leave D & H Productions at Elstree B & D (U). Sterling, 8.30 (8,361) FT W.E. p: Louis Zimmerman, d: Jack Raymond, c: Bernard Knowles, sc: W. P. Lipscomb, Reginald Berkeley from play by Reginald Berkeley (1920), des: G. T. Stoneham. With Madeleine Carroll, Sydney Howard, Arthur Chesney.

French Leave Welwyn Studios at Welwyn (A). Pathé, 6.37 (7,556). p. supervisor: Warwick Ward, d: Norman Lee, c: Bryan Langley, sc: Vernon Clancey from play by Reginald Berkeley (1920), ed: E. R. Richards. With John Longden, Betty Lynne, Edmond Breon.

French Salad See **Happy Family, The**

French Without Tears Two Cities at Shepperton (A). Paramt, 10.39 (7,757). p: David E. Rose, exec. p: Mario Zampi, d: Anthony Asquith, c: Bernard Knowles, Jack Hildyard, sc: Anatole de Grunwald, Ian Dalrymple from play by Terence Rattigan (1936), des: Paul Sheriff, Carmen Dillon, ed: David Lean, cost: Worth, sd: Alex Fisher, music Nicholas Brodsky. With Ray Milland, Ellen Drew, David Tree, Roland Culver, Guy Middleton.

Friday The Thirteenth Gainsborough at Islington (A). G-B D, 11.33 (7,796). p: Michael Balcon, p: personnel Angus MacPhail, Ian Dalrymple, George Gunn, Louis Levy, d: Victor Saville, c: C. Van Enger, sc: G. H. Moresby-White from story by Sidney Gilliat and G. H. Moresby-White, dial: Emlyn Williams, des: Alfred Junge, Vetchinsky, cost: Gordon Conway, ed: R. E. Dearing, sd: H. Hand. With Jessie Matthews, Sonnie Hale, Emlyn Williams, Edmund Gwenn, Gordon Harker, Max Miller etc.

Frightened Lady, The Gainsborough-Brit. Lion at Beaconsfield (A). Ideal, 3.32 (7,848) FT RCA. p: Michael Balcon, d: T. Hayes Hunter, c: Bernard Knowles, Alex Bryce, sc: Angus MacPhail, Bryan Wallace from play by Edgar Wallace, *The Case of the Frightened Lady* (1931), des: Norman Arnold, ed: Ralph Kemplen, sd: Harold King. With Gordon Harker, Cathleen Nesbitt, Emlyn Williams.

Frog, The Herbert Wilcox at Pinewood (A). GFD, 3.37 (6,747). p: Herbert Wilcox, d: Jack Raymond, c: Freddie Young, sc: Ian Hay, W. G. Elliott from play by Ian Hay (1936) based on novel by Edgar Wallace, *The Fellowship of the Frog*. With Gordon Harker, Noah Beery, Carol Goodner, Jack Hawkins.

From a Dark Stairway See **Dark Stairway, The**

Frozen Fate BSP in Lapland (U). J-M-G, registered 5.29 (5,080) silent. p: d: sc: Ben R. Hart, St John L. Clowes.

Frozen Limits, The Gainsborough at Islington (U). GFD, 10.39 (7,587). p: Edward Black, d: Marcel Varnel, c: Arthur Crabtree, sc: J. O. C. Orton, dial: Val Guest, G. Marriott Edgar, des: Vetchinsky, ed: R. E. Dearing, Alfred Roome, sd: William Salter, MD: Louis

Levy. With the Crazy Gang, Moore Marriott.

Full Circle WB-FN at Teddington (A). WB, 4.35 (4,915). p: Irving Asher, d: George King, sc: George King from screen story by Michael Barringer. With Garry Marsh, Rene Ray.

Full Sail See **Sailing Along**

Full Speed Ahead Lawrence Huntington at Wembley (U). Paramt., 11.36 (6,377). d: Lawrence Huntington, c: Stanley Grant, sc: W. Gerald Elliott from story by Lawrence Huntington and W. Gerald Elliott. With Moira Lynd, Richard Norris, Paul Neville.

Full Speed Ahead Trading Corp. for Educational and General services (U). GFD, 4.39 (5,430). d: Commander John L. F. Hunt, sc: 'Bartimeus'. With Michael Osler, Frederick Peisley, Dinah Sheridan.

Full Steam 10.36 (4,266). d: R. A. Hopwood. Variety from Windmill Theatre.

Funny Face See **She Couldn't Say No**

Gables Mystery, The Welwyn Studios (A). M-G-M, 3.38 (5.928). p: Warwick Ward, d: Harry Hughes, sc: Victor Kendall, Harry Hughes from play by Jack de Leon and Jack Celestin, *The Man at Six* (1928). With Frances L. Sullivan, Antoinette Cellier.

Gainsborough Burlesques Gainsborough, 1931 (3 reels each), Ideal: **Bull Rushes, Aroma of the South Seas, Who Killed Doc Robin? My Old China, Hot Heir.**

Game of Chance, The Delta Pictures at Dryden Studios Tamworth (U). Equity British, 2.32 (5,970) silent with synchronised music. p: John Argyle, d: Charles Barnett, sc: from story by John Argyle. With John Argyle, Margaret Delane.

Gang See **Crime over London**

Gang's All Here, The ABPC – Jack Buchanan at Elstree and Welwyn (A). ABPC, 2.39 (6,877). p: Walter Mycroft, d: Thornton Freeland, c: Claude Friese-Greene, sc: Ralph Spence, des: John Mead, Cedric Dawe, ed: E. B. Jarvis.

With Jack Buchanan, Edward Everett Horton, Otto Kruger, Jack La Rue, Walter Rilla, Googie Withers.

Gang Show, The Herbert Wilcox at Pinewood (U). GFD, 4.37 (6,448). p: Herbert Wilcox, d: Alfred Goulding, c: Ernest Palmer, sc: Marjorie Gaffney from story by Ralph Reader. With Ralph Reader, Gino Malo.

Gangway G-B at Pinewood (A). GFD, 8.37 (8,097). d: Sonnie Hale, c: Glen MacWilliams, sc: Sonnie Hale, Lesser Samuels from story by Dwight Taylor, des: Alfred Junge, ed: Arthur Barnes, sd: A. C. O'Donoghue, MD: Louis Levy, songs Lerner, Goodhart and Hoffman, dances Buddy Bradley, with Jessie Matthews, Barry Mackay.

Gaolbreak WB-FN at Teddington (A). FN, 3.36 (5,797). p: Irving Asher, d: Ralph Ince, c: Basil Emmott, sc: Michael Barringer. With Ralph Ince.

Gaunt Stranger, The Northwood Enterprises (CAPAD) at Ealing (A). ABFD, 10.38 (6,631). p: Michael Balcon, assoc. p: S. C. Balcon, d: Walter Forde, c: Ronald Neame, sc: Sidney Gilliat from play by Edgar Wallace *The Ringer* (1926) and novel *The Gaunt Stranger,* des: Oscar Werndorff, ed: Charles Saunders, sd: Eric Williams. With Sonnie Hale, John Longden, Wilfrid Lawson.

Gay Adventure, The Grosvenor Sound Films at Welwyn (A). Pathé, 7.36 (6,710). p: Harcourt Templeman, d: Sinclair Hill, c: Cyril Bristow, sc: D. B. Wyndham-Lewis from play by Walter Hackett, des: Aubrey Hammond, ed: Dr. Max Brenner. With Yvonne Arnaud, Barry Jones, Nora Swinburne.

Gay Lord Strathpeffer, The See **Guest of Honour**

Gay Love Brit. Lion at Beaconsfield (A). Brit. Lion, 8.34 (6,898). d: Leslie Hiscott, c: Alex Bryce, sc: Charles Bennett from play by Audrey and Waveney Carter (1933), des: Norman Arnold, sd: Harold King. With Florence Desmond, Sophie Tucker.

Gay Old Dog Embassy (A). Radio, 11.35

(5,681). p: d: George King, sc: Randall Faye from story by Enid Fabia. With Edward Rigby, Moore Marriott, Ruby Miller.

General Goes Too Far, The See **High Command, The**

General John Regan B & D at Elstree B & D and N. Ireland (U). UA, 10.33 (6,713). d: Henry Edwards, c: Cyril Bristow, sc: Lennox Robinson from play by George A. Birmingham (1913), des; G. S. Stegman, ed: C. C. Stevens. With Henry Edwards, Chrissie White.

Gentleman of Paris, A Gaumont at Cricklewood, Paris (A). Gaumont, 12.31 (6,997) FT Visatone. d: Sinclair Hill, c: Mutz Greenbaum, sc: Sinclair Hill, Sewell Collins, Sidney Gilliat from story by Niranjan Pal, *His Honour the Judge*, des: A. L. Mazzei, cost: Patou, Schiaparelli. With Arthur Wontner, Phyllis Konstam, Hugh Williams.

Gentleman's Agreement B & D-Para.-Brit. at Elstree B & D (A). Paramt, 4.35 (6,312). d: George Pearson, sc: Basil Mason from story by Jennifer Howard. With Antony Holles, David Horne, Vivien Leigh.

Gentleman's Gentleman, A WB-FN at Teddington (U). WB, 4.39 (6,338). p: Jerome Jackson, d: Roy William Neill, c: Basil Emmott, sc: Austin Melford, Elizabeth Meehan from play by Philip MacDonald. With Eric Blore, Peter Coke, Marie Lohr.

Georges Bizet, Composer of Carmen Fitzpatrick Pictures at Shepperton (U). M-G-M, 1.38 (3,075). p: d: James A. Fitzpatrick, sc: W. K. Williamson. With Dino Galvani, Madeleine Gibson.

Get Off My Foot WB-FN at Teddington (A). FN, 10.35 (7,460). p: Irving Asher, d: William Beaudine, c: Basil Emmott, sc: Frank Launder, Robert Edmunds from play by Edward A. Paulton. *Money by Wire*, des: Peter Proud, sd: Leslie Murray. With Max Miller, Jane Carr, Chili Bouchier.

Get Your Man B & D-Para-Brit. (A). Paramt, 8.34 (6,049). d: George King, sc: George Dewhurst from play by Louis Verneuil. With Dorothy Boyd, Sebastian Shaw.

Ghost Camera, The Real Art at Twickenham (A). Radio, 7.33 (6,139, later 6,061). p: Julius Hagen, d: Bernard Vorhaus, sc: H. Fowler. Mear, Bernard Vorhaus from screen story by J. Jefferson Farjeon. With Ida Lupino, Henry Kendall, John Mills.

Ghost Goes West, The LFP at Isleworth, Denham exteriors (A). UA, 12.35 (7,400). p: Alexander Korda, d: René Clair, c: Harold Rosson, sc: Geoffrey Kerr, film play by Robert Sherwood from short story by Eric Keown, *Sir Tristram Goes West.* des: Vincent Korda, cost: Rene Hubert, John Armstrong, ed: W. Hornbeck, Harold Earle-Fischbacher, sc: A. W. Watkins, sp. effects. Ned Mann, MD: Muir Mathieson, music Mischa Spoliansky. With Robert Donat, Jean Parker, Eugene Pallete.

Ghost Train, The Gainsborough at Islington (U). W & F, 9.31 (6,425) FT. p: Michael Balcon, assoc. p: Philip Samuel, d: Walter Forde, c: Leslie Rowson, sc: Angus MacPhail, Lajos Biro from play by Arnold Ridley (1925), add. dial: Sidney Gilliat, des: Walter Murton, ed: Ian Dalrymple, sd: George Gunn.

Ghoul, The G-B at Shepherd's Bush (A). W & F, 7.33 (7,217). p: Michael Balcon, d: T. Hayes Hunter, c: Gunther Krampf, sc: Roland Pertwee, John Hastings Turner from story by Frank King and Leonard J. Hines, des: Alfred Junge. With Boris Karloff, Cedric Hardwicke.

Gipsy Blood BIP at Elstree (U). Wardour, 11.31 (7.183) d: Cecil Lewis, c: Jimmy Wilson, sc: Cecil Lewis, Walter Mycroft from novel by Prosper Merimée and opera of Bizet, *Carmen*, MD: D. Malcolm Sargent, New Symphony Orchestra. With Marguerite Namara, Thomas Burke, Lance Fairfax.

Girl in Possession, The WB-FN at Teddington (U). WB, 2.34 (6,440). p: Irving Asher, d: Monty Banks. With

Laura La Plante, Henry Kendall, Claude Hulbert, Monty Banks.

Girl in the Crowd, The WB-FN at Teddington (U). FN, 12.34 (4,683). p: Irving Asher, d: Michael Powell, c: Basil Emmott, sc: Brock Williams. With Barry Clifton, Patricia Hilliard.

Girl in the Flat, The B & D-Para-Brit. at Elstree B & D (A). Paramt, 6.34 (5,976). d: Redd Davis, c: Percy Strong, sc: Violet Powell from story by Evelyn Winch, des: Fred Pusey. With Stewart Rome, Belle Chrystall.

Girl in the Night, The Henry Edwards Films at Elstree BIP (U). Wardour, 7.31 (7,893) FT RCA d: Henry Edwards, c: Walter Blakeley, sc: Edwin Greenwood from story by Henry Edwards. With Henry Edwards, Dorothy Boyd.

Girl in the Taxi, The British Unity Pictures at Ealing (A). ABFD, 8.37 (6,530). p: Eugene Tuscherer, Kurt Bernhardt, d: André Berthomieu, c: Roy Clark, sc: Austin Melford, Val Valentine from operetta by Georg Okonowsky translated by Arthur Wimperis and F. Fenn (1912), des: d'Eaubonne, ed: Ray Pitt, MD: Jean Gilbert. With Henri Garat, Frances Day, Lawrence Grossmith. (Bilingual.)

Girl Must Live, A Gainsborough-20th Century at Islington (A). 20th Century-Fox, 4.39 (8,349). p: Edward Black, d: Carol Reed, c: J. J. Cox, sc: Frank Launder from novel by Emery Bonett, des: Vetchinsky, ed: R. E. Dearing, sd: W. Salter, MD: Louis Levy, songs Eddie Pola, Manning Sherwin. With Margaret Lockwood, Lilli Palmer, Renee Houston, Sir George Robey.

Girls Please! B & D (A). UA, 7.34 (6,466). p: Herbert Wilcox, d: Jack Raymond, sc: R. P. Weston, Bert Lee, Jack Marks from story by Michael Hankinson, Basil Mason. With Sydney Howard, Jane Baxter.

Girls Will Be Boys BIP (U). Wardour, 9.34 (6,322). p: Walter Mycroft, d: Marcel Varnel, c: Claude Friese-Greene, Ronald Neame, sc: Clifford Grey, Roger Burford, Kurt Siodmak

from play by Kurt Siodmak, *The Last Lord*, des: Cedric Dawe, ed: A. S. Bates, sd: C. V. Thornton, song by Franz Vienna and Michael Carr. With Dolly Haas, Cyril Maude, Esmond Knight.

Girl Was Young, The See **Young and Innocent**

Girl Who Forgot, The Dan Birt-Butcher's at Walton (U). Butcher's, 10.39 (7,190). p: Dan Birt, d: Adrian Brunel, c: Geoffrey Faithfull, sc: Adrian Brunel and D. L. Harden (Mrs Dan Birt) from play by Gertrude M. Jennings, *The Young Person in Pink* (1920). With Elizabeth Allan, Ralph Michael, Basil Radford.

Give Her a Ring BIP at Elstree (U). Pathé, 6.34 (7,120). p: Walter Mycroft, d: Arthur Woods, c: Claude Friese-Greene, Ronald Neame, sc: Clifford Grey, Marjorie Deans, Wolfgang Wilhelm from story by Clifford Grey based on play by H. Rosenfeld, des: Duncan Sutherland, cost: Norman Hartnell, ed: E. B. Jarvis, sd: C. V. Thornton, MD: Harry Acres, lyrics and music Clifford Grey and Hans May. With Clifford Mollison, Zelma O'Neal.

Give Me a Ring See **Give Her a Ring**

Giving You the Stars See **Give Her a Ring**

Glamour BIP at Elstree (A) Wardour, (1) 5.31 (6,419), (2) 8.31 (5,421). d: Sir Seymour Hicks, Harry Hughes, sc: Sir Seymour Hicks. With Sir Seymour Hicks, Ellaline Terriss, Margot Grahame.

Glamour Girl WB-FN at Teddington (U). WB, 2.38 (6,071). d: Arthur Woods, c: Basil Emmott, sc: John Meehan Jr, Tom Phipps. With Gene Gerrard, Lesley Brook.

Glamorous Night BIP-ABPC at Elstree (U). ABPC, 4.37 (6,703). p: Walter Mycroft, d: Brian Desmond Hurst, c: Fritz Arno Wagner, sc: Dudley Leslie, Hugh Brooke and William Freshman from play by Ivor Novello (1935), des: Cedric Dawe, ed: Flora Newton, sd: C. V. Thornton, MD: Harry Acres, music Ivor Novello, lyrics Christopher Hassall, dances Keith Lester. With

Mary Ellis, Otto Kruger, Barry Mackay, Victor Jory.

Glimpse of Paradise, A WB-FN (U). FN 10.34 (5,018). p: Irving Asher, d: Ralph Ince, sc: Michael Barringer from story by Sam Mintz. With Eve Lister, George Carney.

Going Gay Windsor Films at Elstree (U). Sterling, 9.33 (7,057). p: Frank A. Richardson, d: Carmine Gallone, sc: Selwyn Jepson, Jack Marks. K. R. G. Browne from story by Selwyn Jepson, des: R. Holmes Paul, MD: W. L. Trytel. With Arthur Riscoe, Naunton Wayne, Magda Schneider, Grete Natzler.

Going Straight WB-FN at Teddington (U). WB, 3.33 (4,568). p: Irving Asher, d: John Rawlins, c: Willard Van Enger. With Moira Lynd.

Golden Cage, The Sound City at Shepperton (A). M-G-M, 4.33 (5,600). p: Norman Loudon, d: Ivar Campbell, sc: D. B. Wyndham-Lewis, Pamela Frankau from story by Lady Troubridge. With Anthony Kimmins, Anne Grey.

Goodbye, Mr. Chips M-G-M-British at Denham, Repton (U). M-G-M, 6.39 (10,227). p: Victor Saville, d: Sam Wood, c: Freddie Young, sc: R. C. Sherriff, Claudine West, Eric Maschwitz from novel by James Hilton, des: Alfred Junge, ed: Charles Frend, sd: A. W. Watkins, C. C. Stevens, MD: Louis Levy, music Richard Addinsell. With Robert Donat, Greer Garson, Paul von Henreid.

Good Companions, The G-B Welsh-Pearson at Shepherd's Bush (U). Ideal, 2.33 (10,146). p: Michael Balcon, assoc. p: George Pearson, p. personnel: Angus MacPhail, Louis Levy, Ian Dalrymple, George Gunn, d: Victor Saville, c: Bernard Knowles, sc: W. P. Lipscomb from novel by J. B. Priestley and play (1931) by J. B. Priestley and Edward Knoblock, des: Alfred Junge, cost: Gordon Conway, ed: Frederick Y. Smith, sd: W. Salter, music George Posford, lyrics Douglas Furber. With

Jessie Matthews, Edmund Gwenn, Mary Glynne, John Gielgud.

Good Luck See **Lucky Number, The**

Good Morning, Boys Gainsborough at Islington (A). G-B D, 1.37 (7,018). assoc. p: Edward Black, d: Marcel Varnel, c: Arthur Crabtree, sc: Val Guest, Leslie Arliss, George Marriott Edgar from story by Anthony Kimmins (suggested by Will Hay's music-hall sketch), des: Vetchinsky, ed: R. E. Dearing, Alfred Roome, sd: W. Salter, MD: Louis Levy. With Will Hay, Graham Moffatt, Martita Hunt, Lilli Palmer.

Goodness, How Sad See **Return to Yesterday**

Goodnight, Vienna B & D (U). W & F, 3.32 (6,833). p: d: Herbert Wilcox, c: Freddie Young, sc: Holt Marvel, George Posford, Eric Maschwitz, des: L. P. Williams, ed: E. Aldridge, music George Posford, Eric Maschwitz, lyrics Holt Marvel. With Jack Buchanan, Anna Neagle, Gina Malo.

Good Old Days, The WB-FN at Teddington (U). FN, 6.39 (7,129). p: Jerome Jackson, d: Roy William Neill, c: Basil Emmott, sc: Austin Melford, John Dighton from story by Ralph Smart, sd: Baynham Honri. With Max Miller.

Goodwin Sands See **Lady from the Sea, The**

Governor Bradford AIP at Marylebone (U). Columbia, 3.38 (3,016). p: Widgey Newman, d: Hugh Parry, sc: John N. Ruffin, Hugh Parry. With Hetty Sawyer.

Grand Finale B & D-Para-Brit. at Shepperton (A). Paramt, 9.36 (6,443). d: Ivar Campbell, c: Ernest Palmer, sc: Vera Allinson from story by Paul Hervey Fox. With Guy Newall, Mary Glynne.

Grand Prix St John L. Clowes and L. Stock at Cricklewood (U). Columbia, 3.34 (6,473). d: St John L. Clowes, c: Desmond Dickinson, sc: St John L. Clowes, ed: Challis Sanderson. With John Stuart, Gillian Sands, Milton

Rosmer.

Great Barrier, The G-B at Shepherd's Bush, Canada, S. Africa, Khyber Pass; Welwyn (U). G-B D, 2.37 (7,500, later 7,590). assoc. p: Gunther Stapenhorst, d: Milton Rosmer, Geoffrey Barkas (S. Africa and Khyber), c: Glen MacWilliams (studio), Robert Martin and Sidney Bonnett (exteriors), sc: Ralph Spence, Michael Barringer, Milton Rosmer from story *C.P.R.*, and novel, *The Great Divide,* by Alan Sullivan, des: Walter Murton, ed: Charles Frend, sd: Philip Dorté, MD: Louis Levy, music Hubert Bath. With Richard Arlen, Lilli Palmer, Barry Mackay.

Great Defender, The BIP at Welwyn (A). Wardour, 7.34 (6,300). p: Walter Mycroft, d: Thomas Bentley, c: J. J. Cox, Phil Grindrod, sc: John Hastings Turner, Marjorie Deans, Paul Perez, des: John Mead, ed: Walter Stokvis, sd: David Howells. With Matheson Lang.

Great Divide, The See **Great Barrier, The**

Great Game, The G-B at Shepherd's Bush (U). Gaumont, 8.30 (7,036) FT Brit. Ac. p: L'Estrange Fawcett, d: Jack Raymond c: Percy Strong, sc: W. P. Lipscomb, Ralph Bettinson from story by William Hunter, John Lees. With Renee Clama, John Batten.

Great Gay Road, The Butcher's at Cricklewood and in Kent (U). Butcher's, 10.31 (7,676) FT Visatone. d: Sinclair Hill, sc: L. H. Gordon from play by Tom Gallon. With Stewart Rome, Pat Paterson.

Great Stuff Brit. Lion at Beaconsfield (U). Fox, 6.33 (4,514). assoc. p: Herbert Smith, d: Leslie Hiscott, c: Alex Bryce, sc: Michael Barringer from story by Brandon Fleming, des: Norman Arnold. With Henry Kendall, Betty Astell.

Greek Street G-B at Shepherd's Bush (A). Gaumont, 5.30 (7,646) FT, songs Brit. Ac. p: L'Estrange Fawcett, d: Sinclair Hill, c: Percy Strong, James Rogers, sc: Ralph Bettinson, L. H. Gordon from story by Robert Stevenson, des: A. L. Mazzei, music W. L. Trytel, Stanelli.

With Sari Maritza, William Freshman, Renee Clama.

Green Cockatoo, The New World at Denham (A). 20th Century Fox in 1938, not shown until 1940 – cut to 5,852. p: Robert Kane, d: William Cameron Menzies, c: Osmond Borradaile, sc: Edward O. Berkman, Arthur Wimperis from story by Graham Greene, music Miklos Rozsa. With John Mills, Rene Ray, Robert Newton.

Green Pack, The Brit. Lion (A). Brit. Lion, 10.34 (6,182). p: supervisor Herbert Smith, d: T. Hayes Hunter, c: Alex Bryce, sc: John Hunter from play by Edgar Wallace (1932), des: Norman Arnold, sd: Harold King. With John Stuart, Aileen Marson.

Green Spot Mystery, The see **Lloyd of the C.I.D.**

Guest of Honour WB-FN at Teddington (A). FN, 3.34 (4,838). p: Irving Asher, d: George King, sc: W. Scott Darling from play by F. Anstey, *The Man from Blankley's* (1901). With Henry Kendall, Miki Hood.

Guest Reporter, The See **Hot News**

Guilt Reginald Fogwell at Isleworth (A). Paramt, 1.31 (5,841) FT Fidelity. d: Reginald Fogwell, c: Joe Rosenthal Jr, sc: Reginald Fogwell, des: Norman Arnold. With James Carew, Anne Grey, Harold Huth.

Guilty Melody Franco-London Films at Ealing (A). ABFD, 7.36 (6,587). d: Richard Poitier, c: Jan Stallich, sc: G. F. Salmony from novel by Hans Rehfisch. With Gitta Alpar, Nils Asther, John Loder. (English version of French multilingual, **Disque 413.**)

Gypsy WB-FN at Teddington (new studio) (A). WB, 12.36 (7,171). p: Irving Asher, d: Roy W. Neill, sc: Brock Williams, Terence Rattigan from novel by Lady Eleanor Smith, *Tzigane.* With Roland Young, Chili Bouchier, Hugh Williams.

Gypsy Melody British Artistic Films at Elstree BIP (A). Wardour, 7.36 (6,925 later 6,615). p: Emile Reinert, assoc. p: Leon Hepner, d: Edmond T. Gréville, c: Claude Friese-Greene, sc: Irving

Leroy, Dan Weldon from story by Alfred Rode. With Alfred Rode, Lupe Velez.

Hail and Farewill WB-FM at Teddington (A). FN, 9.36 (6,612). p: Irving Asher, assoc. p: Jerome Jackson, d: Ralph Ince, c: Basil Emmott, sc: Reginald Purdell, John Dighton from story by Paul Merzbach. With Claude Hulbert, Reginald Purdell.

Half-Day Excursion, The Q Film Studios (U). Universal, 9.35 (3,034). d: A. L. Dean. With Wally Patch, Moore Marriott.

Handle With Care Embassy Pictures at Walton (U). Radio, 3.35 (5,410). p: George King, d: Redd Davis, sc: from story by Randall Faye. With Molly Lamont, Jack Hobbs.

Hands Off See **East Meets West**

Happy BIP at Elstree (U). Wardour, 12.33 (7,409). p: d: Fred Zelnik, c: Claude Friese-Greene, Ronald Neame, Bryan Langley, sc: Austin Melford, Frank Launder, Stanley Lupino from German and French films by Jacques Bachrach, Alfred Halm, Karl Noti; des: Clarence Elder, Cedric Dawe, ed: A. S. Bates, sd: A. E. Rudolph, MD: Harry Acres, songs and music Noel Gay, Stanley Lupino and others. With Stanley Lupino, Will Fyffe, Laddie Cliff.

Happy Days Are Here Again Argyle Talking Pictures at Shepperton (U). AP & D, 3.36 (7,950). p: John Argyle, d: Norman Lee, c: Jimmy Wilson, sc: Dan Birt, F. H. Bickerton, Alan Rennie from story by Alan Rennie. With Renee and Billie Houston.

Happy Ending, The G-B at Shepherd's Bush (A). Gaumont, 9.31 (6,480). p: L'Estrange Fawcett, d: Millard Webb, c: Percy Strong, sc: H. Fowler Mear from play by Ian Hay, des: A. L. Mazzei. With Benita Hume, Anne Grey, George Barraud;

Happy Event Anglo-French Films at Highbury (U). Grand Nat., 12.39 (3,250). Dufaycolour. p: Leon Hepner,

d: Patrick Brunner, c: Leslie Murray, sc: commentary by D. B. Wyndham-Lewis, spoken by E. V. H. Emmett. With Diana Magwood.

Happy Family, The Brit. Lion at Beaconsfield (A). Brit. Lion, 8.36 (6,076). p: supervison Herbert Smith, d: P. Maclean Rogers, c: George Stretton, sc: Max Catto, Kathleen Butler from play by Max Catto, *French Salad,* sd: Harold King. With Leonora Corbett, Hugh Williams.

Happy Husband, The See **Uneasy Virtue**

Harmony Heaven BIP at Elstree (U). Wardour, 3.30 (5,500) FT, songs RCA Part colour. d: Thomas Bentley, c: T. Sparkuhl. sc: Arthur Wimperis, Randall Faye, des: John Mead, ed: Sam Simmonds, sd: A. Ross, MD: John Reynders, musical numbers Eddie Pola, Edward Brandt, dances Alexander Oumansky. With Polly Ward.

Hate in Paradise Chesterfields Films (A). BSS, 11.38 (5,637). p: Neville Clarke, d: Ward Wing, c: Billy Williams, sc: Loni Bara. With Eve Shelley, Nils Asther, Gibson Gowland.

Hate Ship, The BIP at Elstree (A). FN-Pathé, 12.29 (6,775) FT, songs RCA. d: Norman Walker, c: René Guissart, sc: Monckton Hoffe, Eliot Stannard from novel by Bruce Graeme, sc: Harold King, songs John Reynders, Idris Lewis. With Jameson Thomas, Jean Colin, Jack Raine. (Bilingual.)

Have You Come for Me? See **You Live and Learn**

Hawleys of High Street BIP at Elstree (U). Wardour, 5.33 (6,137). d: Thomas Bentley, c: J. J. Cox, sc: Frank Launder, Charles Bennett, Syd Courtenay from play by Walter Ellis, *What Woman Wants* (1932), based on his play, *Hawley's of the High Street* (1922), des: John Mead, sd: A. Ross. With Leslie Fuller, Moore Marriott, Judy Kelly.

Head Office WB-FN at Teddington (A). WB, 11.36 (6,070). p: Irving Asher, d: Melville Brown, sc: from novel by Hugh

Preston. With Owen Nares, Arthur Margetson, Nancy O'Neil.

Head of the Family, The WB-FN at Teddington (U). FN, 8.33 (5,910). p: Irving Asher, d: John Daumery, sc: Brock Williams. With Irene Vanbrugh, Roland Culver, Arthur Maude, John Stuart.

Head Over Heels G-B at Shepherd's Bush (U). G-B D, 2.37 (7,377). assoc. p: S. C. Balcon, d: Sonnie Hale, c: Glen MacWilliams, sc: Fred Thompson, Dwight Taylor, Marjorie Gaffney from play by François de Croisset, *Pierre ou Jack*, des: Alfred Junge, songs by Harry Revel and Mack Gordon, dances Buddy Bradley. With Jessie Matthews, Robert Flemyng.

Heads We Go BIP (A). Wardour, 7.33 (6,874). d: Monty Banks, sc: Victor Kendall, Fred Thompson from story by Fred Thompson. With Constance Cummings, Frank Lawton.

Head Waiter, The See **Service for Ladies**

Heart's Desire BIP at Elstree (U). Wardour, 8.35 (7,437). p: Walter Mycroft, d: Paul L. Stein, c: J. J. Cox, sc: Bruno Frank, L. du Garde Peach, Roger Burford, Jack Davies from story by Lioni Pickard, des: Clarence Elder, Cedric Dawe, ed: Leslie Norman, sd: Benjamin Cook, conductors Idris Lewis, Stanford Robinson, two songs by Robert Schumann, songs by Richard Tauber, one song by Edward Lockton and Rudolf Sieczynski, musical arrangement by G. H. Clutsam, lyrics by Clifford Grey. With Richard Tauber, Leonora Corbett, Diana Napier.

Hearts of Humanity UK Films at Shepperton (U). AP & D, 11.36 (6,750). p: John Barter, d: John Baxter, c: Jack Carter, des: John Bryan. With Eric Portman, Hay Petrie.

Hearts of Oak (1931) See **Men Like These**

Hearts of Oak International Productions (U). International Productions, 7.33 (4,500). d: M. A. Wetherell, Graham Hewett. With Frank Cellier, Hilda Sims.

Heat Wave Gainsborough at Islington (U). G-B D, 5.35 (6,877). p: Michael Balcon, assoc. p: Jerome Jackson, d: Maurice Elvey, c: Glen MacWilliams, sc: Jerome Jackson, Leslie Arliss, Austin Melford from story by Austin Melford, songs by Sigler, Goodhart and Hoffman. With Albert Burdon, Anna Lee.

Heavily Married Gerald Hobbs at Highbury (A). M-G-M, 5.37 (3,213). d: Clayton Hutton, sc: Mai Bacon, Will Collinson. With Mai Bacon, Collinson and Dean.

Heidelberg See **Student's Romance, The**

Heirloom Mystery, The G.S.Ent. (A). Radio, 11.36 (6,181).; p: George Smith, d: P. Maclean Rogers, sc: Kathleen Butler from story by G. H. Moresby-White. With Edward Rigby, Mary Glynne, Gus McNaughton.

Hello, Sweetheart WB-FN at Teddington (U). FN, 5.35 (6,390). p: Irving Asher, d: Monty Banks, sc: Brock Williams from play by George M. Cohan, *The Butter and Egg Man*, songs James Dyrenforth, dances Ralph Reader. With Claude Hulbert, Gregory Ratoff.

Hell's Cargo ABPC at Elstree (A). ABPC, 11.39 (7,317). p: Walter Mycroft, d: Harold Huth, c: Philip Tannura, sc: Dudley Leslie from French film by Leo Joannon, *Alerte en Méditerranée,* des: John Mead, ed: Lionel Tomlinson. With Robert Newton, Walter Rilla, Penelope Dudley Ward, Kim Peacock.

Help! See **Leave It to Me** (1933).

Help Yourself WB-FN at Teddington (U). WB-FN, 3.32 (6,637). p: Irving Asher, d: John Daumery, c: C. Van Enger, sc: Roland Pertwee, John Hastings Turner from novel by Jerome Kingston. With Benita Hume, Martin Walker. (Bilingual.)

Here's George Thomas Charles Arnold at Cricklewood (U). PDC, 9.32 (5,793). p: Tom Arnold, d: Redd Davis, c: Desmond Dickinson, sc: from sketch by G. Marriott Edgar, *The Service Flat*, des: Edward Delaney, sd: Dallas Bower. With George Clarke, G. Marriott

Edgar, Pat Paterson.

Her First Affaire St George's Productions-Sterling (A). Sterling, 12.32 (6,456). d: Allan Dwan, c: Geoffrey Faithfull, sc: Dion Titheradge, Brock Williams from story by Merrill Rogers and Frederick Jackson (1930), des: J. Elder Wills. With Diana Napier, Ida Lupino, George Curzon.

Her Imaginary Lover WB-FN at Teddington (U). FN, 10.33 (5,965). p: Irving Asher, d: George King, sc: Randall Faye from novel by A. E. W. Mason. With Laura La Plante, Percy Marmont, Lady Tree.

Her Last Affaire New Ideal Pictures at Hammersmith (A). PDC, 10.35 (6,502). p: Geoffrey Rowson, d: Michael Powell, c: Leslie Rowson, sc: Ian Dalrymple from play by Walter Ellis, *S.O.S.* With Francis L. Sullivan, Hugh Williams, Viola Keats.

Her Man of Destiny See **Little Napoleon**

Her Master's Voice See **Two Hearts in Harmony**

Her Night Out WB-FN at Teddington (A). WB, 10.32 (4,083). p: Irving Asher, d: William McGann, sc: W. Scott Darling. With Lester Matthews, Dorothy Bartlam.

Heroes of the Law See **Lloyd of the C.I.D.**

Heroes of the Mine Delta Pictures (U). Butcher's, 8.32 (4,375). p: Geoffrey Clarke, d: Widgey Newman. With Moore Marriott, Wally Patch.

Her Reputation London Screen Plays at Elstree B & D (A). Paramt, 7.31 (6,119) FT WE p: d: Sidney Morgan, c: William Shenton, sc: Sidney Morgan from play by Jevan Brandon-Thomas, *Passing Brompton Road* (1928). With Iris Hoey, Frank Cellier.

He Was Her Man See **We're Going to be Rich**

Hey! Hey! U.S.A. Gainsborough at Islington (U). GFD, 9.38 (8,198) p: Edward Black, d: Marcel Varnel, c: Arthur Crabtree, sc: J. O. C. Orton, dial: Val Guest and G. Marriott Edgar, from story by 'Jack Swain' (Howard Irving Young and Ralph Spence), des: Vetchinsky, ed: R. E. Dearing, sd: W. Salter, MD: Louis Levy, music Cecil Milner. With Will Hay, Edgar Kennedy.

Hide and I'll Find You See **It's a Bet**

High Command, The Fanfare Pictures at Ealing, West Africa (A). ABFD, 3.37 (7,990). p: Gordon Wong Wellesley, d: Thorold Dickinson, c: Otto Heller (studio), James Rogers (location), sc: Katherine Strueby, dial: Walter Meade, Val Valentine from novel by Col. Lewis Robinson, *The General Goes Too Far,* des: R. Holmes Paul, ed: Sidney Cole, sd: Paul F. Wiser, MD: Ernest Irving. With Lionel Atwill, Lucie Mannheim, James Mason, Steve Geray.

High Explosives See **I'm an Explosive**

High Finance WB-FN at Teddington (A). FN, 6.33 (6,101). p: Irving Asher, d: George King. With Gibb McLaughlin, Ida Lupino, John Batten.

High Treason G-B at Shepherd's Bush (A). Gaumont, (1) 8.29 sound (8,263), (2) 10.29 silent (7,046) FT Brit. Ac. p: L'Estrange Fawcett, d: Maurice Elvey, sc: L'Estrange Fawcett from play by Noel Pemberton-Billing, des: A. L. Mazzei, MD: Louis Levy. With Benita Hume, Jameson Thomas.

Highland Fling Fox Brit. at Wembley (U). Fox, 6.36 (5,960). p: John Findlay, d: Manning Haynes, c: Roy Kellino, sc: Ralph Stock, Alan d'Egville from story by Alan d'Egville. With Naughton and Gold.

High Seas BIP at Elstree (A). FN-Pathé, (1) 5.29 silent, (2) 3.30 sound (6,355) synchronised RCA. d: Denison Clift, c: René Guissart, sc: Denison Clift, Victor Kendall from story by Monckton Hoffe, des: J. Elder Wills, ed: Émile de Ruelle, MD: John Reynders. With Lillian Rich, Randle Ayrton, John Stuart.

High Society WB-FN at Teddington (U). FN, 7.32 (4,573). p: Irving Asher, d: Jack Rawlins, c: C. W. Van Enger, sc: W. Scott Darling, Randall Faye. With Florence Desmond, William Austin.

Hiking with Mademoiselle International

Productions (U). International Productions, 3.33 (3,650). d: Edward Nakhimoff. With Nina Bucknall, Dennis Clive.

Hindle Wakes Gainsborough at Shepherd's Bush, Llandudno, Blackpool, Preston (A). Gaumont, 9.31 (7,000) FT Brit. Ac. p: Michael Balcon, d: Victor Saville, c: Mutz Greenbaum, sc: Victor Saville, Angus MacPhail from play by Stanley Houghton (1912), des: A. L. Mazzei, ed: R. E. Dearing, sd: S. A. Jolly, MD: W. L. Trytel. With Sybil Thorndike, Edmund Gwenn, John Stuart, Belle Chrystall.

His Brother's Keeper WB-FN at Teddington (A). WB, 8.39 (6,333) exec. p: Sam Sax, d: Roy William Neill, c: Basil Emmott, sc: Austin Melford, Brock Williams from story by Roy W. Neill. With Tamara Desni, Clifford Evans.

His First Car PDC (U). PDC, 5.30 (3,288). FT RCA d: Monty Banks, sc: Brock Williams. With George Clarke, Mamie Watson.

His Grace Gives Notice Real Art at Twickenham (A). Radio, 7.33 (5,131). p: Julius Hagen, d: G. A. Cooper, c: Ernest Palmer, sc: H. Fowler Mear from novel by Lady Troubridge.

His Honour the Judge See **Gentleman of Paris, A**

His Lordship Westminster Films (U). UA, 6.32 (6,892). p: Jerome Jackson, d: Michael Powell, c: Geoffrey Faithfull, sc: Ralph Smart from novel by Oliver Madox Hueffer, *The Right Honourable,* des: Frank Wells, music Walter Leigh, Ronald Hill, Richard Addinsell, Leslie Holmes, lyrics V. C. Clinton-Baddeley, Clay Keyes. With Jerry Verno, Janet McGrew.

His Lordship G-B (U). G-B D, 11.36 (6,445). assoc. p: S. C. Balcon, d: Herbert Mason, c: Gunther Krampf, sc: L. du Garde Peach, Maude Howell and Edwin Greenwood from play by Neil Grant, *The Nelson Touch* (1931) des: Alfred Junge, cost: Joe Strassner. With George Arliss, Rene Ray.

His Lordship Goes to Press A. George Smith Production-Canterbury at Walton (U). RKO-Radio, 10.38 (7,274). p: George Smith, d: P. Maclean Rogers, c: Geoffrey Faithfull, sc: Kathleen Butler, H. F. Maltby from story by Margaret and Gordon McDonnell. With June Clyde, Romney Brent, Hugh Williams.

His Lordship Regrets A. George Smith Productions-Canterbury at Walton (U). RKO-Radio, 7.38 (7,066). p: George Smith, d: P. Maclean Rogers, c: Geoffrey Faithfull, sc: Kathleen Butler, H. F. Maltby from play by H. F. Maltby *Bees and Honey* (1928). With Claude Hulbert, Gina Malo, Winifred Shotter.

His Lucky Day See **It's a Grand Old World**

His Majesty and Co. Fox Brit. at Wembley (U). Fox, 1.35 (5,977). d: Anthony Kimmins, c: Alex Bryce, sc: from screen story by Sally Sutherland, Alfredo Campoli and the Tzigane Orchestra, music Ord Hamilton and Wilhelm Grosz.

His Majesty's Pyjamas See **Love in Exile**

His Night Out See **Their Night Out**

His Wife's Mother BIP at Elstree (U). Wardour, 10.32 (6,298). d: Harry Hughes, c: Walter Harvey, sc: Harry Hughes from story by Will Scott. With Gus McNaughton, Jerry Verno, Molly Lamont.

Hobson's Choice BIP (U). Wardour, 10.31 (5,822). d: Thomas Bentley, c: Horace Wheddon, sc: Frank Launder from play by Harold Brighouse (1916). With Viola Lyel, James Harcourt, Frank Pettingell, Belle Chrystall.

Hold My Hand ABPC at Elstree (U). ABPC, 7.38 (6,709). p: Walter Mycroft, d: Thornton Freeland, c: Otto Kanturek, sc: Clifford Grey, Bert Lee, William Freshman from musical comedy by Stanley Lupino (1931), des: Ian White, ed: E. B. Jarvis, MD: Harry Acres, songs from show by Noel Gay and Desmond Carter, new one by Grey, Lee and Harris Weston, new one by

Sigler, Goodhart and Hoffman, dances Philip Buchel. With Stanley Lupino, Polly Ward, Sally Gray, Barbara Blair, Jack Melford.

Holiday Lovers Harry Cohen at Wembley (A). Fox, 11.32 (4,390). p: Harry Cohen, d: Jack Harrison, c: Horace Wheddon, sc: Leslie Arliss, des: J. Elder Wills. With George Vollaire, Marjorie Pickard.

Holidays End B & D-Para-Brit. at Pinewood (A). Parmt, 3.37 (6,303). p: Anthony Havelock-Allan, d: John Paddy Carstairs, c: Desmond Dickinson, sc: from story by W. G. Elliott. With Wally Patch, Sally Stewart.

Home Broken See **House Broken**

Home from Home Brit. Lion at Beaconsfield (U). Brit. Lion, 4.39 (6,593). p: d: Herbert Smith c: George Stretton, sc: from story by Ingram d'Abbes and Fenn Sherie, des: Norman Arnold, ed: Jack Harris, sd: Harold King. With Sandy Powell, Rene Ray.

Home, Sweet Home Real Art at Twickenham (A). Radio, 9.33 (6,502, later 6,465). p: Julius Hagen, d: G. A. Cooper, c: Ernest Palmer, sc: H. Fowler Mear. With John Stuart, Marie Ney.

Honeymoon Adventure, A ATP at Beaconsfield, Inverness, the Royal Scot (U). Radio, 9.31 (6,084) FT RCA. p: Basil Dean, d: Maurice Elvey, c: Robert Martin, Alex Bryce, sc: Rupert Downing and John Paddy Carstairs from novel by Mrs Cicely Fraser-Simson, *Footsteps in the Night*, des: Norman Arnold, ed: Otto Ludwig, sd: Marcus Cooper, MD: Ernest Irving, waltz by Harold Fraser-Simson. With Benita Hume, Harold Huth, Nicholas Hannen.

Honeymoon for Three Gaiety Films at Ealing (A). ABFD, 9.35 (7,283). p: Stanley Lupino, d: Leo Mittler, c: Henry Harris, sc: Frank Miller from story by Stanley Lupino, des: J. Elder Wills, ed: Dan Birt, MD: Percival Mackey, music and lyrics Billy Mayerl and Frank Eyton, dances Carl Hyson, Leslie Roberts. With Stanley Lupino.

Honeymoon Merrygoround London Screenplays-Fanfare at Ealing (U). Made in 1936. p: Sidney Morgan, d: Alfred Goulding, c: Ernest Palmer, sc: Alfred Goulding, Monty Banks, Joan Morgan. With Claude Hulbert, Monty Banks, Princess Pearl, Sally Gray.

Honours Easy BIP at Welwyn (A). Wardour, 7.35 (5,637). p: Walter Mycroft, d: Herbert Brenon, c: Ronald Neame, sc: from play by Roland Pertwee (1930). With Greta Nissen, Patric Knowles, Margaret Lockwood.

Hoots, Mon! WB-FN at Teddington (A). WB, 11.39 (6,966). exec. p: Sam Sax, d: Roy William Neill, c: Basil Emmott, sc: Roy William Neill, Jack Henley, John Dighton, des: Norman Arnold, ed: Leslie Norman, sd: Baynham Honri, MD: Bretton Byrd. Florence Desmond, Max Miller.

Hope of his Side, The final title of **Where's George?**, q.v.

Horse Sense AIP (U). Columbia, 3.38 (3,540). d: Widgey Newman. With 'Buttercup'.

Hotel Splendide Film Engineering (U). Ideal, 3.32 (4,724). p: Jerome Jackson, d: Michael Powell, c: Geoffrey Faithfull, sc: Ralph Smart from novel by Philip MacDonald, des: W. G. Saunders. With Jerry Verno.

Hot Heir Gainsborough (U). Ideal, 2.31 (3,540) FT songs, p: Michael Balcon, d: W. P. Kellino, sc: Angus MacPhail. With Charles Austin, Bobbie Comber, Fred Kitchen Jnr.

Hot News St. George's Pictures at Cricklewood (U). Columbia, 3.36 (6,950). p: Ian Sutherland, d: W. P. Kellino, c: Jack Parker. With Lupino Lane, Wallace Lupino.

Hound of the Baskervilles, The Gainsborough at Islington, Devon. Ideal, 7.31 (6,761) FT RCA. p: Michael Balcon, d: V. Gareth Gundrey, c: Bernard Knowles, William Shenton, sc: Angus MacPhail, dial: Edgar Wallace, from novel by Sir Arthur Conan Doyle, des: Tom Heslewood. With John Stuart, Heather Angel.

Hours of Loneliness Carlton at

Teddington (A). WB, 2.31 (5,892) FT Edison Bell disc. p: d: G. G. Glavany. With Sunday Wilshin, Walter Sondes, Harold Huth, Carl Harbord.

House Broken B & D-Para-Brit. at Elstree BIP (A). Paramt 6.36 (6,627). d: Michael Hankinson, sc: Vera Allinson from story by Paul Hervey Fox. With Mary Lawson, Louis Borell.

Housemaster, The ABPC at Elstree (U). ABPC 1.38 (8,600). p: Walter Mycroft, d: Herbert Brenon, c: Otto Kanturek, sc: Dudley Leslie, Elizabeth Meehan from play by Ian Hay (1935) based on his novel, des: Cedric Dawe, ed: Flora Newton. With Otto Kruger, Phillips Holmes, Rene Ray, Diana Churchill.

House of Silence, The George King at Shepperton (A). M-G-M, 3.37 (4,067). p: George King, d: R. K. Neilson Baxter, sc: from story by Paul White. With Tom Helmore, Jennie Laird, Terence de Marney.

House of the Arrow, The Twick. at Twickenham (A). WB, 3.30 (6,881) FT RCA. p: Julius Hagen, exec. p: Henry Edwards, d: Leslie Hiscott, c: Sydney Blythe, sc: Cyril Twyford from novel by A. E. W. Mason. With Dennis Neilson-Terry, Benita Hume, Richard Cooper. (Bilingual.)

House of the Arrow, The ABPC, in production 7.39 at Elstree. p: Walter Mycroft, d: Harold French, c: Walter Harvey, sc: Doreen Montgomery from novel by A. E. W. Mason. With Kenneth Kent, Diana Churchill.

House of Trent, The Ensign Productions at Ealing (U). Butcher's, 11.33 (6,760). d: Norman Walker, c: Robert Martin, sc: Charles Bennett and Billie Bristow. With John Stuart, Anne Grey, Wendy Barrie.

House of the Spaniard, The Phoenix Films, IFP at Ealing (U). ABFD, 10.36 (6,264). p: Hugh Perceval, d: Reginald Denham, c: Franz Weihmayr, sc: Basil Mason from novel by Arthur Behrend, des: R. Holmes Paul. With Brigitte Horney, Peter Haddon.

House of Unrest, The Associated Picture Productions at Cricklewood (U). PDC, 3.31 (5,319) FT Visatone p: Sinclair Hill, d: L. H. Gordon, sc: L. H. Gordon from his own play. With Dorothy Boyd, Malcolm Keen.

House Opposite, The BIP at Elstree (U). Pathé, 3.32 (6,065). d: Walter Summers, c: Bert Ford, Jimmy Wilson, sc: Walter Summers from novel by J. Jefferson Farjeon. With Henry Kendall.

Howard Case, The Sovereign Films (A). Universal, 3.36 (5,881). p: Fraser Foulsham, d: Frank A. Richardson, sc: from play by H. F. Maltby, *Fraud.* With Jack Livesey, Olive Sloane.

How He Lied to her Husband BIP at Elstree (U). Wardour, 1.31 (3,341) FT RCA. d: Cecil Lewis, c: J. J. Cox, sc: Cecil Lewis, Frank Launder from play by George Bernard Shaw, des: Gladys Calthrop, ed: Sam Simmonds, sd: Alec Murray. With Edmund Gwenn, Robert Harris, Vera Lennox.

How's Chances? Sound City at Shepperton (A). Fox, 5.34 (6,667). d: Anthony Kimmins, sc: Ivar Campbell from German film *Der Frauendiplomat,* music arranged Hans May. With Tamara Desni, Harold French, Davy Burnaby.

Humpty-Dumpty See **If I Were Rich**

Hundred to One Twick. at Wembley (U). Fox, 1.33 (4,081). p: Julius Hagen, Harry Cohen, d: Walter West, sc: Basil Mason. With Arthur Sinclair, Dodo Watts.

Husband in Law See **Law and Disorder**

Hyde Park WB-FN at Teddington (U). FN, 11.34 (4,336). p: Irving Asher, d: sc: Randall Faye. With George Carney, Eve Lister.

Hyde Park Corner Grosvenor at Welwyn (A). Pathé, 11.35 (7,670). p: Harcourt Templeman, d: Sinclair Hill, c: Cyril Bristow, sc: D. B. Wyndham-Lewis from play by Walter Hackett (1934), des: Aubrey Hammond. With Gordon Harker, Binnie Hale.

I Adore You WB-FN at Teddington (U).

WB, 11.33 (6,651). p: Irving Asher, d: George King, c: Basil Emmott, sc: Paul England from story by W. Scott Darling, Carroll Gibbons and his Savoy Hotel Orpheans, lyrics by Paul England, dances Ralph Reader. With Margot Grahame, Clifford Heatherly, Harold French.

I, Claudius LFP at Denham, early 1937 – abandoned 3.37. p: Alexander Korda, d: Josef von Sternberg, c: Georges Périnal, sc: Carl Zuckmayer from books by Robert Graves, *I, Claudius* and *Claudius the God*, des: Vincent Korda, cost: John Armstrong. With Charles Laughton, Emlyn Williams, Merle Oberon, Flora Robson.

Idol of Moolah, The See **Kiss Me, Sergeant**

If I Were Boss G. S. Ent. at Walton (A). Columbia, 3.38 (6,509). p: George Smith, d: P. Maclean Rogers, c: Geoffrey Faithfull, sc: Basil Mason. With Bruce Seton, Googie Withers.

If I Were Rich Randall Faye at Walton (U). Radio 5.36 (5,367). p: d: Randall Faye, sc: Brandon Fleming from play by Horace Annesley Vachell, *Humpty-Dumpty*. With Jack Melford, Kay Walsh.

If You Had a Million See **Second Mr. Bush, The**

I Give My Heart BIP at Elstree (A). Wardour, 10.35 (8,200). p: Walter Mycroft, d: Marcel Varnel, c: Claude Friese-Greene, sc: Frank Launder, adapt: Kurt Siodmak from operetta by Paul Knepler and J. M. Welleminsky, *The Dubarry* (1932), des: Clarence Elder, David Rawnsley, ed: E. B. Jarvis, MD: Harry Acres, music Carl Millöcker, arr: Theo Mackeben, songs Desmond Carter, Rowland Leigh. With Gitta Alpar, Patrick Waddington, Owen Nares.

I Killed the Count Grafton Films at Highbury (A). Grand Nat., 5.39 (8,024). p: Isadore Goldsmith, d: Fred Zelnik, c: Bryan Langley, sc: Lawrence Huntington, Alec Coppel from play by Alec Coppel (1937), ed: Sam Simmonds. With Syd Walker, Terence

de Marney, Ben Lyon, Antoinette Cellier.

I Lived with You Twick. at Twickenham (A). W & F, 6.33 (8,800). p: Julius Hagen, d: Maurice Elvey, c: Sydney Blythe, Ernest Palmer, William Luff, sc: Ivor Novello, G. A. Cooper, H. Fowler Mear play by Ivor Novello (1932), des: James Carter, ed: Jack Harris, sd: Baynham Horni, MD: W. L. Trytel. With Ivor Novello, Ursula Jeans, Ida Lupino.

Illegal WB-FN at Teddington (A). FN, 4.32 (7,468). p: Irving Asher, d: William McGann, sc: Roland Pertwee. With Isobel Elsom, Margot Grahame.

I'll Never Tell See **False Evidence**

I'll Stick to You Brit. Lion at Beaconsfield (A). Brit. Lion, 7.33 (6,176). assoc. p: Herbert Smith, d: Leslie Hiscott, sc: Michael Barringer. With Jay Laurier, Betty Astell, Louis Hayward.

I Lost my Heart in Heidelberg See **Student's Romance, The**

I'm an Explosive George Smith at Walton (U). Fox, 3.33 (4,458). p: George Smith, d: Adrian Brunel, c: Geoffrey Faithfull, sc: Adrian Brunel from novel by Gordon Phillips. With Billy Hartnell, Gladys Jennings.

I Met a Murderer Gamma Films on location. Grand Nat., 2.39 (7,089). p: d: c: Roy Kellino, sc: Roy and Pamela Kellino, James Mason from their own story, cost: Motley, ed: Fergus McDonell, sd: A. Birch, MD: and music Eric Ansell. With James Mason, Pamela Kellino.

Immediate Possession Starcraft at Twickenham (U). Fox, 2.31 (3,994). p: Harry Cohen, d: Arthur Varney, sc: Brock Williams. With Herbert Mundin, Dorothy Bartlam.

Immortal Gentleman, The Bernard Smith (U). Equity British, 3.35 (5,400). d: Widgey Newman, sc: John Quin from story by Widgey Newman. With Basil Gill.

I'm Not Rich See **Mistaken Identity**

Impassive Footman, The ATP at Ealing (A). Radio, 6.32 (6,233). p: Basil Dean, d: Basil Dean, Graham Cutts, c: Bob de Grasse, sc: John Paddy Carstairs, John Farrow, Harold Dearden from story by 'Sapper' (H. C. McNeile). With Owen Nares, Betty Stockfield, George Curzon.

Important People G. S. Ent. at Wembley (A). M-G-M, 2.34 (4,449). p: George Smith, d: Adrian Brunel, sc: from play by F. Wyndham Mallock. With Stewart Rome, Dorothy Boyd.

Improper Duchess, The City Film Corp. at Elstree (A). GFD, 1.36 (7,013). p: Maurice Browne, d: Harry Hughes, sc: Harry Hughes, Vernon Harris from play by J. B. Fagan. With Yvonne Arnaud, Hugh Wakefield.

In a Lotus Garden Patrick K. Heale (U). Paramt, 2.31 (4,300) FT, songs Fidelytone. p: Patrick K. Heale, d: Fred Paul.

In a Monastery Garden Twick. at Twickenham (A). AP & D, 3.32 (7,260). p: Julius Hagen, d: Maurice Elvey, sc: H. Fowler Mear, Michael Barringer from screen story by Michael Barringer. With John Stuart, Joan Maude.

Incident in Shanghai B & D-Para-Brit. at Pinewood (A). Paramt, 1.38 (6,038). p: Anthony Havelock-Allan, d: John Paddy Carstairs, c: Francis Carver, sc: A. R. Rawlinson from screen story by John Paddy Carstairs. With Patrick Barr, Margaret Vyner.

Indiscretions of Eve, The BIP (A). Wardour, 5.32 (5,702). d: Cecil Lewis, c: Jimmy Wilson, Philip Grindrod, sc: Cecil Lewis, des: Clarence Elder, ed: Walter Stokvis, sd: A. C. O'Donoghue, MD: Francis Strange, Peggy Cochrane, Marius B. Winter's Orchestra, music Cecil Lewis. With Steffi Duna, Fred Conyngham, Teddy Brown (xylophone).

Infatuation Alpha Film Corp. at Twickenham (A). Alpha Film Corp., 1.30 (3,580) FT RCA. p: Maurice J. Wilson, d: Sascha Geneen, sc: from play by Julian Franke, *The Call*. With Jeanne de Casalis, Godfrey Tearle.

Informer, The BIP at Elstree (A). Wardour, 10.29 (7,688) PT RCA. d:

Arthur Robison, c: Werner Brandes, Theodor Sparkuhl, sc: Benn Levy from story by Liam O'Flaherty, des: Norman Arnold, J. Elder Wills, ed: Emile de Ruelle. With Lya de Putti, Lars Hanson, Warwick Ward, Carl Harbord.

Innocents of Chicago BIP at Elstree (A). Wardour, 4.32 (6,139). d: Lupino Lane, sc: Leslie Arliss, Lupino Lane from play by James Wedgewood Drawbell and Reginald Simpson, *The Milky Way*. With Henry Kendall, Margot Grahame, Bernard Nedell, Binnie Barnes.

Inquest Majestic Films and New Era at Isleworth (A). FN, 12.31 (8,547) FT RCA. p: Gordon Craig, d: G. B. Samuelson, sc: Michael Barringer from his own play. With Mary Glynne, Haddon Mason.

Inquest Charter Film Productions (A). Grand. Nat., 12.39 (5,432). p: John Boulting, d: Roy Boulting, c: D. P. Cooper, sc: Francis Miller, Michael Barringer from play by Michael Barringer, des: John Maxted, ed: Roy Boulting, sd: Carlisle Mountenay, MD: Charles Brill. With Elizabeth Allan, Herbert Lomas, Hay Petrie, Philip Friend.

Inside the Room Twick. at Twickenham (A). Universal, 3.35 (5,989). p: Julius Hagen, d: Leslie Hiscott, c: William Luff, sc: H. Fowler Mear from play by Marten Cumberland. With Austin Trevor, Dorothy Boyd.

Inspector, The Ace Films (U). WB, 1.37 (3,239). d: sc: Widgey Newman. With Stan Paskin, Roma Beaumont.

Inspector Hornleigh 20th Cent. Productions at Pinewood (A). 20th Cent. – Fox, 3.39 (7,648). p: Robert T. Kane, d: Eugene Forde, c: Derick Williams, sc: Bryan Wallace from radio series. With Gordon Harker, Alastair Sim, Hugh Williams.

Inspector Hornleigh on Holiday 20th Cent. Productions at Islington (A). 20th Cent. – Fox, 10.39 (7,872). p: Edward Black, d: Walter Forde, c: J. J. Cox, sc: Frank Launder, Sidney Gilliat from radio series, des: Vetchinsky, ed: R. E. Dearing, sd: S. Wiles, MD: Louis Levy. With Gordon Harker, Alastair Sim, Linden Travers.

Insult Para-Brit. (A). Paramt, 7.32 (7,162). d: Harry Lachman, sc: Basil Mason from play by J. Fabricius. With Elizabeth Allan, Hugh Williams, John Gielgud.

Interrupted Honeymoon, The Brit. Lion at Beaconsfield (A). Brit. Lion, 6.36 (6,607). p: Herbert Smith, d: Leslie Hiscott, c: George Stretton, sc: Michael Barringer from play by Franz Arnold and Ernst Bach. With Claude Hulbert, Jane Carr, Hugh Wakefield.

Interrupted Rehearsal, The Ace Films, 3.38 (3,672). d: R. A. Hopwood, variety from Windmill Theatre.

Interval for Romance See **Street Singer, The**

In the Blood See **Dusty Ermine**

In the Soup Twick. at Twickenham (U). Twick. F. D., 4.36 (6,600). p: Julius Hagen, d: Henry Edwards, c: Sydney Blythe, William Luff, sc: H. Fowler Mear from play by Ralph R. Lumley (1900), des: James Carter, ed: Jack Harris, Michael Chorlton, sd: Baynham Honri, MD: W. L. Trytel. With Morton Selten, Ralph Lynn, Judy Gunn.

Intimate Relations Tudor Films at Highbury (A). ABFD, 11.37 (6,019). d: Clayton Hutton, c: Jan Stumar, sc: Frank Atkinson from play by Stafford Dickens (1932), Lew Stone and his Band, songs by Bernard Francis. With June Clyde, Garry Marsh.

In Town Tonight Brit. Lion (U). Brit. Lion, 1.35 (7,036). d: Herbert Smith, c: Charles Van Enger, des: A. L. Mazzei. With Jack Barty.

Intruder, The see **Invader, The**

Invader, The British and Continental Film Productions at Isleworth (U). M-G-M, 1.36 (5,500). p: Sam Spiegel, Harold Richman, d: Adrian Brunel, c: Eugen Schufftan, Eric Cross, sc: Edwin Greenwood, ed: Dan Birt. With Buster Keaton, Lupita Towar, Esme Percy. (Multilingual.)

Invitation to the Waltz BIP at Elstree (A). Wardour, 10.35 (7,105). p: Walter Mycroft, d: Paul Merzbach, c: Ronald Neame, sc: Clifford Grey, Roger Burford, adapt: Paul Merzbach from story by Holt Marvel, des: Clarence Elder, John Mead, ed: J. Neill Brown, cost: Michael Wright, sd: C. V. Thornton, MD: Idris Lewis, music George Posford, arranged G. Walter Goehr. With Lilian Harvey, Carl Esmond.

Irish and Proud of it Crusade at Wembley (U). Paramt, 10.36 (6,585). p: Victor M. Greene, d: Donovan Pedelty, c: Jimmy Burger, sc: Donovan Pedelty from story by Dorothea Donn Byrne. With Richard Hayward, Dinah Sheridan.

Irish for Luck WB-FN at Teddington (U). FN, 12.36 (6,141). p: Irving Asher, d: Arthur Woods, c: Basil Emmott, sc: from story by L. A. G. Strong. With Athene Seyler, Margaret Lockwood, Patric Knowles.

Irish Hearts Clifton-Hurst Productions at Cricklewood, Ireland (A). M-G-M, 10.34 (6,392). p: H. Clifton, d: Brian Desmond Hurst, c: Eugen Schufftan, sc: from novel by Dr Johnson Abrahams, *Night Nurse*. With Nancy Burne, Lester Matthews, Patric Knowles, Molly Lamont.

Iron Duke, The G-B at Shepherd's Bush and Shepperton lot (U). G-B D, 12.34 (7,967). p: Michael Balcon, d: Victor Saville, c: Curt Courant, Leslie Rowson (exteriors), sc: H. M. Harwood, Bess Meredyth from story by H. M. Harwood, des: Alfred Junge, cost: Cathleen Mann, period adviser Herbert Norris, ed: Ian Dalrymple, sd: W. Salter, MD: Louis Levy, With George Arliss, Gladys Cooper, Emlyn Williams.

Iron Stair, The Real Art at Twickenham (A). Radio, 1.33 (4,575). p: Julius Hagen, d: Leslie Hiscott, c: Ernest Palmer, sc: H. Fowler Mear from novel by Rita. With Henry Kendall, Dorothy Boyd.

Iron Woman, The See **That's My Uncle**

Irresistible Marmaduke, The See **Oh, What a Night!**

I See Ice ATP at Ealing, (U). ABFD, 2.38 (7,348). p: Basil Dean, d: Anthony Kimmins, dial: d: Austin Melford, c: Ronald Neame, Gordon Dines, sc: Anthony Kimmins and Austin Melford, from their own story, des: Wilfred Shingleton, ed: Jack Kitchin, Ernest Aldridge, sd: Eric Williams, music and lyrics George Formby, Fred E. Cliffe. Harry Parr-Davies, James Harber, R. Campbell Hunter, W. Haines. With George Formby, Kay Walsh, Cyril Ritchard, Betty Stockfield.

I Serve See **Fire over England**

Island Fling See Tropical Trouble

I Spy BIP at Elstree (U). Wardour, 8.33 (6,196). p: Walter Mycroft, d: Allan Dwan, c: Jimmy Wilson, sc: Allan Dwan, Arthur Woods from story by Fred Thompson, des: Wilfred Arnold, ed: Leslie Norman, sd: George Adams, MD: Sydney Baynes and his Broadcasting Orchestra. With Sally Eilers, Ben Lyon, Harry Tate.

It Happened in Paris Wyndham Productions at Ealing, Paris (U). ABFD, 6.35 (6,163). p: Bray Wyndham, d: Robert Wyler, Carol Reed, c: Robert Martin, sc: H. F. Maltby, Katherine Strueby and John Huston from play by Yves Mirande, des: J. Elder Wills, music Monia Liter, lyrics Sonny Miller. With John Loder, Nancy Burne, (Bilingual?)

It's a Bet BIP (U). Wardour, 2.35 (6,230). p: Walter Mycroft, d: Alexander Esway, c: Bryan Langley, sc: L. du Garde Peach, Frank Miller, Kurt Siodmak from novel by Marcus McGill, *Hide and I'll Find You*. With Gene Gerrard, Helen Chandler, Judy Kelly.

It's a Boy Gainsborough at Islington (A). W & F, 6.33 (7,282). p: Michael Balcon, p: personnel Angus MacPhail, Louis Levy, Ian Dalrymple, George Gunn, d: Tim Whelan, c: Mutz Greenbaum, sc: L. H. Gordon, John Paddy Carstairs from German play by Franz Arnold and Ernst Bach adapted by Austin Melford

(1930), des: Vetchinsky, cost: Gordon Conway, ed: Harold M. Young, sd: H. Hand. With Leslie Henson, Edward Everett Horton, Albert Burdon, Wendy Barrie.

It's a Cop B & D (A). UA, 3.34 (6,904). p: Herbert Wilcox, d: P. Maclean Rogers, c: Cyril Bristow, sc: Charles Austin, R. J. Cullen, des: G. S. Stegman. With Sydney Howard, Dorothy Bouchier.

It's a Fair Cop See **Leave it to Me** (1937)

It's a Grand Old World Tom Arnold at Beaconsfield (U). Brit. Lion, 1.37 (6,438). p: Tom Arnold, d: Herbert Smith, c: George Stretton, sc: Fenn Sherie and Ingram d'Abbes from story by Tom Arnold. With Sandy Powell, Gina Malo, Cyril Ritchard.

It's a King B & D at Elstree B & D (U). W & F, 12.32 (6,037). p: Herbert Wilcox, d: Jack Raymond, c: Freddie Young, sc: R. P: Weston, Bert Lee, Jack Marks from story by Claude Hulbert and Paul England. With Sydney Howard, Joan Maude.

It's in the Air ATP. – Eltham Enterprises at Ealing (U). ABFD, 9.38 (7,882). p: Basil Dean, assoc. p: Jack Kitchin, d: Anthony Kimmins, c: Ronald Neame, Gordon Dines, sc: Anthony Kimmins from his own story, des: Wilfred Shingleton, ed: Ernest Aldridge, sd: Eric Williams, MD: Ernest Irving, songs George Formby, Harry Parr-Davies, Fred E. Cliffe, Harry Gifford. With George Formby, Polly Ward.

It's in the Bag WB-FN at Teddington (U). WB, 9.36 (7,256, later 6,531). p: Irving Asher, d: William Beaudine, c: Basil Emmott, sc: Brock Williams, Russell Medcraft, des: Peter Proud, ed: A. Bates sd: H. C. Pearson, A. R. Straughan. With Nervo and Knox, George Carney.

It's in the Blood WB-FN at Teddington (U). FN, 3.38 (5,046). p: Irving Asher, d: Gene Gerrard, c: Robert Lapresle, sc: Reginald Purdell from novel by David Whitelaw, *The Big Picture*. With Claude Hulbert, Lesley Brook.

It's Love Again G-B at Shepherd's Bush (U). G-B D, 5.36 (7,600, later 7,395). p: Michael Balcon, d: Victor Saville, c: Glen MacWilliams, sc: Marion Dix, Lesser Samuels, des: Alfred Junge, cost: Joe Strassner, ed: A. L. Barnes, sd: A. C. O'Donogue, MD: Louis Levy, music Louis Levy, Bretton Byrd, song Sam Coslow, Harry Woods, dances: Buddy Bradley. With Jessie Matthews, Robert Young, Sonnie Hale.

It's Never Too Late to Mend George King at Shepperton (A). M-G-M, 3.37 (6,007). p: George King, d: David MacDonald, c: Hone Glendinning, sc: H. F. Maltby from play by Charles Reade (1865). With Tod Slaughter, Marjorie Taylor, Jack Livesey.

It's Not Cricket WB-FN at Teddington (A). WB, 3.37 (5,767). p: Irving Asher, d: Ralph Ince, c: Basil Emmott, sc: from story by Henry Kendall. With Henry Kendall, Claude Hulbert.

It's No Use Crying See **Miracles Do Happen**

It's Turned Out Nice Again See **Leave It to Me** (1937)

It's You I Want Brit. Lion at Beaconsfield (A). Brit. Lion, 10.36 (6,625). p: Herbert Smith, d: Ralph Ince, c: George Stretton, sc: Cyril Campion from play by Maurice Braddell (1933), des: Norman Arnold. With Sir Seymour Hicks, Marie Lohr, Jane Carr, Hugh Wakefield.

I've Got A Horse Brit. Lion at Beaconsfield (U). Brit. Lion, 8.38 (6,988). p: d: Herbert Smith, c: George Stretton, sc: from story by Fenn Sherie and Ingram d'Abbes, sd: Harold King, songs Noel Gay. With Sandy Powell, Norah Howard.

I Was a Spy G-B at Sheperd's Bush, Welwyn exteriors (A). W & F, 7.33 (8,193). p: Michael Balcon, p: personnel Angus MacPhail, Ian Dalrymple, Louis Levy, George Gunn, d: Victor Saville, c: Charles Van Enger, sc: W. P. Lipscomb, add. dial: Ian Hay, from story by Marthe McKenna, des: Alfred Junge, cost: Gordon Conway, ed: Frederick Y. Smith, sd: William Salter. With Madeleine Carroll, Herbert Marshall, Conrad Veidt.

Jack Ahoy! G-B at Shepherd's Bush, Weymouth (U). G-B D, 1.34 (7,450). p: Michael Balcon, d: Walter Forde, c: Bernard Knowles, sc: Sidney Gilliat, J. O. C. Orton, dial: Jack Hulbert, Leslie Arliss, Gerard Fairlie, Austin Melford, des: Alfred Junge, ed: Ralph Kemplen, music Bretton Bryd. With Jack Hulbert, Tamara Desni.

Jack of All Trades Gainsborough at Islington, Shredded Wheat factory at Welwyn (U). G-B D, 2.36 (6,868). p: Michael Balcon, d: Robert Stevenson, Jack Hulbert, c: Charles Van Enger, sc: J. O. C. Orton, dial: Jack Hulbert and Austin Melford, from play by Hubert Griffith, *Youth at the Helm* (1934), based on French play by Paul Vulpius, des: Vetchinsky, cost: Joe Strassner, ed: T. R. Fisher, sd: W. Salter, MD: Louis Levy, music Sigler, Goodhart and Hoffman, dances Philip Buchel, Johnny Boyle. With Jack Hulbert, Gina Malo, Robertson Hare.

Jack O'Lantern See **Condemned to Death**

Jack's the Boy Gainsborough at Islington, Welwyn (U). W & F, 6.32 (8,004). p: Michael Balcon, d: Walter Forde, c: Leslie Rowson, sd: W. P. Lipscomb from story by Jack Hulbert, Douglas Furber, ed: Ian Dalrymple, John Goldman, des: Vetchinsky, sd: George Gunn, MD: Louis Levy, music Vivian Ellis, songs Douglas Furber, dances Jack Hulbert, Philip Buchel. With Jack Hulbert, Cicely Courtneidge.

Jailbirds Butcher's at Walton (U). Butcher's, 12.39 (6,670). d: Oswald Mitchell, c: Geoffrey Faithfull, sc: Con West from Fred Karno sketch, des: R. Holmes Paul. With Albert Burdon.

Jamaica Inn Mayflower Pictures at Elstree ABPC, Cornwall (A). ABPC, 5.39 (9,543). p: Erich Pommer (Charles Laughton), d: Alfred Hitchcock, c: Harry Stradling, Bernard Knowles, sc: Sidney Gilliat, Joan Harrison, dial:

Sidney Gilliat, J. B. Priestley, from novel by Daphne du Maurier, des: Tom Morahan, cost: Molly McArthur, ed: Robert Hamer, sd: Jack Rogerson, sp: effects: Harry Watt, MD: Frederic Lewis, music Eric Fenby. With Leslie Banks, Charles Laughton, Robert Newton, Maureen O'Hara.

Jane Steps Out ABPC at Elstree (A). ABPC 4.38 (6,372). p: Walter Mycroft, d: Paul L. Stein, c: Claude Friese-Greene, sc: Dudley Leslie, William Freshman from play by Kenneth Horne (1934), des: Cedric Dawe. With Diana Churchill, Peter Murray-Hill.

Java Head ATP at Ealing (A). ABFD, 7.34 (7,744). p: Basil Dean, d: J. Walter Ruben, asst. d: Carol Reed, c: Robert Martin, sc: Gordon Wellesley, Martin Brown from novel by Joseph Hergesheimer, des: Edward Carrick, ed: Thorold Dickinson, David Lean, MD: Ernest Irving. With Anna May Wong, John Loder, Elizabeth Allan.

Jealousy Majestic Films and New Era at Isleworth (A). WB, 8.31 (7,187) FT. p: Gordon Craig, d: G. B. Samuelson, sc: from play by John McNally, *The Green Eye*. With Mary Newland, Malcolm Keen.

Jennifer Hale Fox Brit. at Wembley (A). 20th Cent.–Fox, 10.37 (5,987). d: Bernerd Mainwaring, c: Stanley Grant, sc: Edward Dryhurst, Bernerd Mainwaring, Ralph Stock from novel by Rob Eden. With Ballard Berkeley, Rene Ray, John Longden.

Jericho Buckingham Film Productions at Pinewood (U). GFD, 8.37 (6,756). p: Walter Futter, d: Thornton Freeland, c: John Boyle, Jack Hildyard, sc: Frances Marion, George Barraud, R. N. Lee, Peter Ruric from story by Walter Futter, des: Oscar Werndorff, Edward Carrick. With Paul Robeson, Princess Kouka, Wallace Ford, Henry Wilcoxon.

Jerry Builders, The PDC (U). PDC, 5.30 (3,413). p: Gordon Bostock, d: Monty Banks, sc: from play. With George Graves.

Jewel, The Venture Films (U). Paramt,

10.33 (6,003) p: Hugh Perceval, d: Reginald Denham, sc: Basil Mason from novel by Edgar Wallace. With Hugh Williams, Frances Dean, Jack Hawkins.

Jew Süss G-B at Shepherd's Bush and Islington (A). G-B D, 10.34 (9,740). p: Michael Balcon, d: Lothar Mendes, unit p. man: Graham Cutts, c: Bernard Knowles, Roy Kellino, sc. adapt: Dorothy Farnum, sc: and dial: A. R. Rawlinson from novel by Lion Feuchtwanger, des: Alfred Junge, cost. and period adviser: Herbert Norris, ed: Otto Ludwig, sd: W. Salter, MD: Louis Levy. With Conrad Veidt, Benita Hume, Frank Vosper, Sir Cedric Hardwicke, Pamela Ostrer.

Jimmy Boy Baxter and Barter at Cricklewood and Ireland (U). Universal, 8.35 (6,462). p: John Barter, d: John Baxter, c: George Stretton, sc: from story by Harry O'Donovan and Con West. With Jimmy O'Dea.

John Halifax, Gentleman George King at Shepperton (U). M-G-M, 3.38 (6,200). d: George King, Hone Glendinning, sc: A. R. Rawlinson from novel by Mrs Craik, des: Philip Bawcombe. With John Warwick, Nancy Burne.

Johnson's Stores See **Department Store**

Josiah Steps Out See **That's My Wife**

Josser at Sea See **Josser Joins the Navy**

Josser in Camera See **Josser on the River**

Josser in the Army BIP (U). Wardour, 10.32 (7,200). d: Norman Lee, c: Walter Harvey, sc: Frank Launder from story by Con West and Herbert Sargent. With Ernie Lotinga.

Josser Joins the Navy BIP (U). Wardour, 3.32 (6,215). d: Norman Lee, sc: Con West and Herbert Sargent. With Ernie Lotinga.

Josser on the Farm Fox-Brit. at Cricklewood (A). Fox, 11.34 (5,712). d: T. Hayes Hunter, c: Alex Bryce, sc: Con West and Herbert Sargent. With Ernie Lotinga, Betty Astell.

Josser on the River BIP-BIF (A). Wardour, 8.32 (6,868). d: Norman Lee, sc; Norman Lee, Leslie Arliss. With Ernie

Lotinga.

Josser, P.C. see **P.C. Josser**

Journey's End Gainsborough and Welsh-Pearson-Elder, joint Anglo-American production with Tiffany-Stahl, in Hollywood (A). W & F, preview in USA 3.30, premier in UK 4.30 (11,539) FT RCA. Registered as foreign film. p: Michael Balcon, supervised George Pearson, d: James Whale, c: Benjamin Kline, sc: Joseph Moncure March from play by R. C. Sherriff (1928), des: Harvey Libbert, ed: Claude Berkeley, sd: Buddy Meyers. With Colin Clive, Anthony Bushell, David Manners.

Joy Ride City Film Corp. at Walton (A). ABFD, 6.35 (6,975). p: Basil Humph - reys, d: Harry Hughes, sc: from story by Vernon Harris. With Gene Gerrard, Zelma O'Neal.

Jubilee Window B & D-Para-Brit. (A). Paramt, 6.35 (5,544). d: George Pearson, sc: George Pearson and W. G. Elliott from story by W. G. Elliott. With Frank Birch, Margaret Yarde.

Juggernaut J. H. Productions at Twickenham (A). Twick. FD., 9.36 (6,518). p: Julius Hagen, d: Henry Edwards, c: Sydney Blythe, William Luff, sc: H. Fowler Mear, Cyril Campion, Heinrich Fraenkel from novel by Alice Campbell, des: James Carter, ed: Jack Harris, Michael Chorlton, sd: Baynham Honri, MD: and music W. L. Trytel. With Boris Karloff, Mona Goya.

Jump for Glory Criterion Film Productions at Isleworth (A). UA, 3.37 (8,038). p: Marcel Hellman, d: Raoul Walsh, c: Victor Armenise, sc: John Meehan, Harold French, Tom Geraghty from novel by Gordon McDonnell, des: Edward Carrick, cost: Schiaparelli. With Douglas Fairbanks Jnr, Alan Hale, Valerie Hobson.

Juno and the Paycock BIP at Elstree (A). Wardour, 12.29 (8,751) FT RCA. d: Alfred Hitchcock, c: J. J. Cox, sc: Alma Reville and Alfred Hitchcock from play by Sean O'Casey (1924), des: Norman Arnold, ed: Émile de Ruelle, sd: C. Thornton, Harold King. With Edward Chapman, Sidney Morgan, Sara Allgood, Maire O'Neill, John Longden.

Jury's Evidence Brit. Lion at Beaconsfield (A). Brit. Lion, 1.36 (6,656). p: Herbert Smith, d: Ralph Ince, c: George Stretton, sc: Ian Dalrymple from play by Jack de Leon and Jack Celestin. With Hartley Power, Margaret Lockwood, Nora Swinburne.

Just for a Song Gainsborough (A). Ideal, 3.30 (8,422) FT, songs, Part colour. p: Michael Balcon, d: V. Gareth Gundrey, c: Jimmy Wilson, sc: V. Gareth Gundrey from story by Desmond Carter. With Roy Royston, Lilian Davies.

Just Like a Woman ABPC at Elstree (A). ABPC, 2.38 (7,009). p: Walter Mycroft, d: Paul L. Stein, c: Claude Friese-Greene, sc: Alec Coppel. With John Lodge, Gertrude Michael.

Just My Luck B & D (U). W & F, 1.33 (6,931). p: Herbert Wilcox, d: Jack Raymond, sc: Ben Travers from play by H. F. Maltby, *Fifty-Fifty* (1932) and from French play. With Ralph Lynn, Robertson Hare, Winifred Shotter.

Just Smith G-B at Shepherd's Bush (A). W & F, 9.33 (6,863). p: Michael Balcon, d: Tom Walls, sc: J. O. C. Orton from play by Frederick Lonsdale, *Never Come Back* (1932), des: Alfred Junge, cost: Gordon Conway. With Tom Walls, Hartley Power, Carol Goodner.

Just William ABPC at Welwyn (U). ABPC, 7.39 (6,505). p: Walter Mycroft, d: Graham Cutts, c: Walter Harvey, sc: Graham Cutts, Doreen Montgomery, add. dial: Ireland Wood, from stories by Richmal Crompton, des: Cedric Dawe, ed: E. B. Jarvis. With Dicky Lupino, Fred Emney.

Karma Himansu Rai Indo-International Talkies and Indian and British Productions, at Stolls and in India (U). Gaumont-Ideal, 5.33 (6,220). p: sc: Himansu Rai, John L. F. Hunt, d: John L. F. Hunt. With Devika Rani, Himansu Rai, Abraham Sofaer. (Multilingual.)

Karno Comedies: The Bailiffs, They're

Off, The Dreamers, Sign Please, Post Haste, Tooth Will Out.

Kate Plus Ten Wainwright Productions at Shepperton (U). GFD, 3.38 (7,250). p: Richard Wainwright, d: Reginald Denham, c: Roy Kellino, sc: Jeffrey Dell from novel by Edgar Wallace, dial: Jeffrey Dell and Jack Hulbert, des: D. W. L. Daniels, ed: E. M. Hunter, sd: M. R. Cruickshank, music Allan Gray. With Jack Hulbert, Genevieve Tobin.

Kathleen Mavourneen Argyle-British Productions at Welwyn (U). Wardour, 2.37 (6,940). p: John Argyle, d: Norman Lee, c: Bryan Langley, sc: Marjorie Deans from story by John Glen based on song, des: David Rawnsley, ed: F. H. Bickerton, Irish adviser W. G. Fay, sd: Frank Midgley, MD: Guy Jones. With Sally O'Neil, Tom Burke, Sara Allgood, Lucan and McShane.

Keepers of Youth BIP at Elstree (A). Wardour, 6.31 (6,395) FT RCA. d: Thomas Bentley, c: Jimmy Wilson, sc: Thomas Bentley, Frank Launder, Walter Mycroft from play by Arnold Ridley (1929), sd: A. E. Rudolph. With Ann Todd, Robin Irvine.

Keep Fit ATP at Ealing (U). ABFD, 8.37 (7,393). p: Basil Dean, assoc. p: Jack Kitchin, d: Anthony Kimmins, dial: d: Austin Melford, c: John Boyle, sc: Austin Melford and Anthony Kimmins from story by Anthony Kimmins, des: Wilfred Shingleton, ed: Ernest Aldridge, sd: Paul F. Wiser, music and lyrics Harry Gifford and Fred E. Cliffe. With George Formby, Kay Walsh.

Keep it Quiet Brit. Lion at Beaconsfield (U). M-G-M, 3.34 (5,980). p: supervisor Herbert Smith, d: Leslie Hiscott, sc: from screen story by Michael Barringer. With Frank Pettingell, Davy Burnaby, Jane Carr.

Keep Smiling 20th-Cent. Productions at Pinewood (U). 20th Cent.-Fox, 10.38 (8,278). p: Robert T. Kane, d: Monty Banks, c: Mutz Greenbaum, sc: Val Valentine, dial: Rodney Ackland from screenplay by William Conselman from story by Sandor Farago and Alexander

G. Kemedi, des: Oscar Werndorff, ed: James B. Clark, sd: M. Paggi, MD: Bretton Byrd, dances Jack Donohue. With Gracie Fields, Mary Maguire, Roger Livesey.

Keep Your Seats, Please! ATP at Ealing (U). ABFD, 8.36 (7,670). p: Basil Dean, d: Monty Banks, c: John Boyle, sc: Anthony Kimmins and Tom Geraghty from Russian novel and play by Ilf and Petroff, *Twelve Chairs*, des: R. Holmes Paul, ed: Jack Kitchin, sd: Paul F. Wiser, Debroy Somers and his band, songs Harry Parr-Davies, Harry Gifford and Fred E. Cliffe. With George Formby, Florence Desmond, Binkie Stuart.

Kentucky Minstrels Twick. at Twickenham, Walton exteriors (U). Universal, 11.34 (7,671). p: Julius Hagen, d: John Baxter, c: Sydney Blythe, sc: from radio series by C. Denier Warren, John Watt and Harry S. Pepper, MD: Harry S. Pepper. With Scott and Whaley, Nina Mae McKinney etc.

Key to Harmony B & D-Para.-Brit. at Elstree B & D (A). Paramt, 3.35 (6,199). d: Norman Walker, sc: Basil Mason from novel by J. B. Wilson, *Suburban Retreat,* des: Hyton R. Oxley. With Belle Chrystall, Reginald Purdell.

Kicking the Moon Around Vogue Film Productions at Pinewood (U). GFD, 3.38 (7,038). p: Howard Welsch, exec. p: Herbert Wynne, d: Walter Forde, c: Francis Carver, sc: Angus MacPhail, Roland Pertwee, Michael Hogan, H. Fowler Mear from story by Tom Geraghty, des: John Bryan, ed: Derek Twist, sd: C. V. Thornton, songs Kennedy and Carr. With Evelyn Dall, Harry Richman, Ambrose and his Band.

Kidnapped See **Dizzy Limit, The**

Kingdom for Five & Six, A See **Lucky Number, The**

Kingdom of Twilight, The Seven Seas Screen Productions (U). Universal, 1.30 (8,360) silent and synchronised versions, WE. p: d: Alexander Macdonald. With Wendy Osborne, David Wallace, Laurel

Macdonald.

King of Cloves See **Millions**

King of Hearts Butcher's at Cricklewood (U). Butcher's, 3.36 (7,452). p: d: Oswald Mitchell, Walter Tennyson, c: Desmond Dickinson, sc: Oswald Mitchell from story by Matthew Boulton. With Will Fyffe.

King of Paris, The B & D (A). UA, 11.34 (6,733). p: Herbert Wilcox, d: Jack Raymond, c: Freddie Young, sc: Paul Gangelin from English adapt. by John Van Druten of play be Alfred Savoir, *La Voie Lactée*, des: L. P. Williams. With Sir Cedric Hardwicke, Marie Glory, Ralph Richardson.

King of the Castle City Film Corp. at Shepperton (U). GFD, 2.36 (6,270). p: Eric Donaldson, Basil Humphreys, d: Redd Davis, c: Ronald Neame, sc: George Dewhurst from story by Frank Atkinson. With June Clyde, Claude Dampier, Billy Milton.

King of the Damned G-B at Shepherd's Bush (A). G-B D, 12.35 (6,835). p: Michael Balcon, d: Walter Forde, c: Bernard Knowles, sc: Charles Bennett, Sidney Gilliat from play by John Chancellor, adapt. A. R. Rawlinson, addit. dial: Noel Langley, des: Oscar Werndorff, cost: Schiaparelli, ed: C. Randell, sd: A. F. Birch, MD: Louis Levy. With Conrad Veidt, Noah Beery, Helen Vinson.

King of the Ritz Gainsborough-Brit. Lion at Beaconsfield (U). G-B D, 3.33 (7,395). d: Carmine Gallone, c: Leslie Rowson, Alex Bryce, sc: Ivor Montagu from play by Henri Kistemaeckers, *Le Roi de Palace*, des: Norman Arnold, ed: Arthur Tavares, sd: Harold King, music Raoul Moretti, lyrics Clifford Grey. With Stanley Lupino, Betty Stockfield, Gina Malo, Henry Kendall.

King of Whales, The Argonaut Films (U). M-G-M, 6.34 (3,906). d: Challis Sanderson. With Barrie Livesey, Esmond Knight.

King's Cup, The B & D at Elstree B & D, Hanworth and Shoreham (U). W & F, 1.33 (6,881). p: Herbert Wilcox, d:

Sir Alan Cobham, Donald Macardle, Herbert Wilcox, sc: Sir Alan Cobham. With Dorothy Bouchier, Harry Milton.

King Solomon's Mines G-B at Shepherd's Bush and in Africa (U). GFD, 6.37 (7,283). d: Robert Stevenson, African exteriors Geoffrey Barkas, c: Glen MacWilliams, sc: Roland Pertwee and Michael Hogan from novel by H. Rider Haggard, des: Alfred Junge, ed: Michael Gordon, music Mischa Spoliansky, lyrics Eric Maschwitz. With Roland Young, Paul Robeson, Sir Cedric Hardwicke, John Loder, Anna Lee.

Kissing Cup's Race Butcher's at Walton, in Windsor (A). Butcher's 11.30 (6,755) FT RCA. d: Castleton Knight, sc: Castleton Knight from poem by Campbell Rae Brown. With Stewart Rome, John Stuart, Madeleine Carroll.

Kiss Me Goodnight See **Paradise for Two**

Kiss Me, Sergeant BIP (U). Wardour, 8.30 (5,100) FT RCA. d: Monty Banks, sc: Val Valentine from play by Lola Harvey and Syd Courtenay, *The Idol of Moolah*. With Leslie Fuller, Lola Harvey, Syd Courtenay.

Kitty BIP-Burlington at Elstree (U). Wardour, (1) 1.29 silent (8,100), (2) 6.29 PT (8,280), both registered 1.29. p: d: Victor Saville, c: Karl Püth, sc: V. Powell from novel by Warwick Deeping, des: Hugh Gee, music Hubert Bath. With Estelle Brody, John Stuart.

Knight Errant, The See **Girl in the Night, The**

Knight in London, A Ludwig Blattner Picture Corp. (A). WB, 2.30 synch. version (6,675). – silent version trade shown by Blattner 3.30. p: Ludwig Blattner, d: Lupu Pick, c: Karl Freund, sc: Charles Lincoln from story by Mrs Horace Tremlett, des: Mrs Wilfred Ashley, music Eduard Kunnecke. With Lilian Harvey, Ivy Duke, Robert Irvine.

Knights for a Day Pearl Productions at Welwyn (U). Pathé, 3.37 (6,231). p: Aveling Ginever, d: Norman Lee,

Aveling Ginever, sc: Aveling Ginever, Frank Atkinson, Charles Bray. With Nelson Keys, Nancy Burne, John Garrick.

Knight Without Armour LFP at Denham (A). UA, 6.37 (9,836, later 9,211). p: Alexander Korda, d: Jacques Feyder, c: Harry Stradling, Bernard Browne, Jack Cardiff, sc: adapt: Frances Marion from novel by James Hilton, sc: and dial: Lajos Biro and Arthur Wimperis, des: Lazare Meerson, cost: Georges Benda, ed: William Hornbeck, Francis Lyon, sd: A. W. Watkins, sp. effects: Ned Mann, MD: Muir Mathieson, music Miklos Rozsa. With Robert Donat, Marlene Dietrich.

Knowing Men Talkicolor at Elstree (A). UA, 2.30 (7,939) FT. p: d: Elinor Glyn, c: Charles Rosher, sc: Elinor Glyn and Edward Knoblock from story by Elinor Glyn, song by Harold Fraser-Simson. With Carl Brisson, Elissa Landi.

Kongo Raid See **Sanders of the River**

Labour Exchange See **Dodging the Dole**

Laburnum Grove ATP at Ealing (A). ABFD, 5.36 (6,622). p: Basil Dean, d: Carol Reed, c: John Boyle, sc: Gordon Wong Wellesley, Anthony Kimmins from play by J. B. Priestley (1933), des: Edward Carrick, Denis Wreford, ed: Jack Kitchin, sd: Paul F. Wiser, MD: Ernest Irving. With Edmund Gwenn, Sir Cedric Hardwicke, Victoria Hopper.

Lad, The Twick. at Twickenham (A). Universal, 2.35 (6,736). p: Julius Hagen, d: Henry Edwards, c: Sydney Blythe, sc: Gerard Fairlie from story by Edgar Wallace, sd: Baynham Honri. With Gordon Harker, Betty Stockfield, Jane Carr.

Lady from the Sea, The BIP at Elstree Kent (U). Paramt, (1) 5.29 silent, (2) 3.30 sound (5,540) FT RCA. d: Castleton Knight, c: Theodor Sparkuhl, sc: Victor Kendall, Garnett Weston from story by Joe Grossman, MD: John Reynders. With Moore Marriott, Raymond Milland, Mona Goya.

Lady In Danger G-B (A). G-B D, 11.34

(6,107). p: Michael Balcon, d: Tom Walls, c: Philip Tannura, sc: Ben Travers, des: Alfred Junge. With Tom Walls, Yvonne Arnaud.

Lady is Willing, The Columbia Brit. at Elstree B & D (A). Columbia, 1.34 (6,764). d: Gilbert Miller, c: George Seid, Joseph Walker, sc: Guy Bolton from play by Louis Verneuil, des: Oscar Werndorff, ed: Otto Ludwig, sd: Edward Bernds. With Cedric Hardwicke, Leslie Howard, Binnie Barnes.

Lady Jane Grey See **Tudor Rose**

Lady of the Lake, The Gainsborough at Islington (U). Select Films, 5.31 (5,168). Synch. version of 1928 film. p: Michael Balcon, d: James A. Fitzpatrick, sc: James A. Fitzpatrick and Angus MacPhail from poem by Sir Walter Scott. With Percy Marmont, Benita Hume.

Lady Vanishes, The Gainsborough-Gaumont-British at Islington (A). M-G-M, 8.38 (8,650). p: Edward Black, d: Alfred Hitchcock, c: J. J. Cox, sc: Frank Launder and Sidney Gilliat, add. dial: Alma Reville from novel by Ethel Lina White, *The Wheel Spins*. des: Vetchinsky, Maurice Carter, Albert Jullion, ed: R. E. Dearing, Alfred Roome, sd: S. Wiles, MD: Louis Levy, music Cecil Milner. With Michael Redgrave, Margaret Lockwood, Paul Lukas, Dame May Whitty.

Lambeth Walk, The Pinebrook (CAP-AD) at Pinewood (U). M-G-M, 4.39 (7,521). p: Anthony Havelock-Allan, d: Albert de Courville, c: Francis Carver, sc: John Paddy Carstairs from musical, *Me and My Girl* by L. Arthur Rose and Douglas Furber (1937), des: John Bryan, MD: Louis Levy, songs Noel Gay. With Lupino Lane, Sally Gray, Wallace Lupino, Sir Seymour Hicks.

Lancashire Luck B & D-Para.-Brit. at Pinewood (U). Paramt, 11.37 (6,767). p: Anthony Havelock-Allan, d: Henry Cass, c: Francis Carver, sc: A. R. Rawlinson from story by Ronald Gow. With Wendy Hiller, George Carney, Muriel George.

Landlady, The Charter Film Productions

(U). Fidelity Dist., 6.38 (3,200). p: John Boulting, d: Roy Boulting, c: D. P. Cooper, sc: Francis Miller. With Vi Kaley.

Landslide Crusade at Wembley (A). Paramt, 1.37 (6,002). p: Victor M. Greene, d: sc: Donovan Pedelty. With Dinah Sheridan, Jimmy Hanley.

Land Without Music Capitol at Denham (U). GFD, 10.36 (7,289). p: Max Schach, d: Walter Forde, c: John Boyle, sc: Marion Dix, L. du Garde Peach from story by Fritz Koselka, Armin Robinson (Rudolph Bernaur, Eric Maschwitz, Ernest Betts), des: Fred Pusey, cost: Cathleen Mann, sd: A. W. Watkins, music Oscar Straus. With Richard Tauber, Diana Napier, June Clyde, Jimmy Durante.

Lash, The Real Art at Twickenham (A). Radio, 5.34 (5,766). p: Julius Hagen, d: Henry Edwards, sc: H. Fowler Mear and Vera Allinson from play by Cyril Campion (1926), des: James Carter. With Lyn Harding, John Mills, Joan Maude.

Lassie from Lancashire Brit. Nat. at Welwyn (U). ABPC, 7.38 (7,364). p: John Corfield, d: John Paddy Carstairs, c: Bryan Langley, sc: Doreen Montgomery, Ernest Dudley from their own story. With Marjorie Browne, Hal Thompson.

Last Adventurers, The Conway Productions at Shepperton, Grimsby (U). Sound City Dist., 10.37 (6,976). p: H. Fraser Passmore, d: Roy Kellino, c: Eric Cross, sc: from story by Dennison Clift, des: Ralph Brinton, ed: David Lean, sd: John K. Byers, MD: and music Eric Ansell. With Niall MacGinnis, Linden Travers, Kay Walsh, Roy Emerton.

Last Barricade, The Fox Brit. at Wembley (U). 20th Cent.-Fox, 3.38 (5,279). d: Alex Bryce, c: Jimmy Wilson, sc: Alex Bryce from story by R. F. Gore-Brown, Lawrence Green, des: Carmen Dillon. With Greta Gynt, Frank Fox, Meinhart Maur.

Last Chance, The Welwyn Studio at Welwyn (U). Pathé, 11.37 (6,800). p:

Warwick Ward, d: Thomas Bentley, sc: Harry Hughes from story by Frank Stayton. With Judy Kelly, Frank Leighton, Billy Milton.

Last Coupon, The BIP (U). Wardour, 7.32 (7,553). d: Thomas Bentley, c: J. J. Cox, Bryan Langley, sc: Frank Launder, Syd Courtenay from play by Ernest Bryan, des: Duncan Sutherland, ed: Walter Stokvis, ed: A. S. Ross, MD: Idris Lewis. With Leslie Fuller, Molly Lamont.

Last Curtain, The B & D-Para-Brit. at Pinewood (U). Paramt, 7.37 (6,056). p: Anthony Havelock-Allan, d: David MacDonald, sc: A. R. Rawlinson from story by Derek Mayne. With Greta Gynt, Campbell Gullan.

Last Hour, The Nettlefold at Twickenham (U). Butcher's, 6.30 (6,998) FT RCA. p: Archibald Nettlefold, d: Walter Forde, c: Geoffrey Faithfull, sc: H. Fowler Mear from play by Charles Bennett (1928), des: W. G. Saunders, ed: Walter Forde. With Stewart Rome, Kathleen Vaughan, Richard Cooper.

Last Journey, The Twick. at Twickenham (A). Twick. FD, 10.35 (6,000) FT Visatone. p: Julius Hagen, p: supervisor Hans Brahm, d: Bernard Vorhaus, c: William Luff, Percy Strong, sc: H. Fowler Mear, John Soutar from story by J. Jefferson Farjeon, des: James Carter, ed: Jack Harris, Lister Laurence, sd: Baynham Honri, MD: W. L. Trytel. Hugh Williams, Godfrey Tearle, Judy Gunn.

Last Lord, The See **Girls Will be Boys**

Last Post, The Britannia (A). (1) Gaumont 1.29, silent (8,000), (2) Showman 1.30, PT RCA. (9,000). p: d: Dinah Shurey, c: D. P. Cooper, sc: Lydia Hayward from story by Dinah Shurey. With Trilby Clark, John Longden.

Last Rose of Summer, The Fitzpatrick Pictures at Shepperton (U). M-G-M, 9.37 (5,436). p: James A. Fitzpatrick, c: Hone Glendinning, sc: W. K. Williamson. With John Garrick, Kathleen Gibson.

Last Tide, The John F. Argyle (A). Equity British, 2.31 (5,200). Silent. p: d: sc: John Argyle. With Margaret Delane, Grace Johnson, James Benton.

Late Extra Fox Brit. at Wembley (A). Fox, 11.35 (6,255). d: Albert Parker, sc: Fenn Sherie and Ingram d'Abbes from story by Anthony Richardson. With Virginia Cherrill, James Mason, Alastair Sim.

Laugh It Off Brit. Nat. In production at Walton, 10.39. p: John Corfield, d: John Baxter, sc: Bridget Boland, Austin Melford from story by Bridget Boland. With Tommy Trinder, Jean Colin.

Laughter of Fools, The George Smith (U). Fox, 10.33 (4,277). p: George Smith, d: Adrian Brunel, sc: Adrian Brunel from play by H. F. Maltby. With Pat Paterson, Derrick de Marney.

Law and Disorder British Consolidated, in production at Highbury, 10.39. p: K. C. Alexander, d: David MacDonald, sc: from story by Roger MacDougall. With Barry K. Barnes, Alastair Sim, Diana Churchill.

Laying of the Glourie Ghost, The See **Ghost Goes West, The**

Lazybones Real Art at Twickenham (U). Radio, 1.35 (5,811). p: Julius Hagen, d: Michael Powell, c: Ernest Palmer, sc: Gerard Fairlie from play by Ernest Denny, des: James Carter, cd: Ralph Kemplen, sd: Leo Wilkins, MD: W. L. Trytel. With Ian Hunter, Claire Luce, Bernard Nedell.

Leal of the Lost See **Woman He Scorned, The**

Leap Year B & D at Elstree B & D (A). W & F, 9.32 (8,106). p: Herbert Wilcox, d: Tom Walls, sc: From screen story by A. R. Rawlinson. With Tom Walls, Anne Grey.

Leave It to Blanche WB-FN at Teddington (U). FN, 8.34 (4,602). p: Irving Asher, d: Harold Young, sc: Brock Williams from story by Rowland Brown. With Henry Kendall, Olive Blakeney, Miki Hood.

Leave it to Me George King at Twickenham (U). Fox, 10.30 (3,744). d: George King, sc: P. L. Mannock from story by

Billie Bristow. With Robin Irvine, Dorothy Seacombe.

Leave It to Me BIP (U). Wardour, 4.33 (6,884). d: Monty Banks, sc: Gene Gerrard, Cecil Lewis, Frank Miller from novel by P. G. Wodehouse, *Leave it to Psmith,* and play by P. G. Wodehouse and Ian Hay (1930). With Gene Gerrard, Olive Borden.

Leave It to Me Tom Arnold at Beaconsfield (A). Brit. Lion, 9.37 (6,493). p: Tom Arnold, d: Herbert Smith, c: George Stretton, sc: Fenn Sherie and Ingram d'Abbes from story by Tom Arnold, songs Jimmy Kennedy and Michael Carr. With Sandy Powell.

Lend Me Your Husband Embassy Pictures (A). Radio, 6.35 (5,449). p: George King, d: Frederick Hayward, sc: Randall Faye from story by Michael Trevellyan. With John Stuart, Nora Swinburne.

Lend Me Your Wife Grafton Films at Elstree BIP (A). M-G-M, 10.35 (5,648). p: F. Browett, d: W. P. Kellino, c: Jack Parker, sc: from play by Fred Duprez and Edmund Dalby. With Henry Kendall, Kathleen Kelly.

Lest We Forget Sound City at Shepperton (U). M-G-M, 8.34 (5,478). p: Norman Loudon, d: John Baxter, c: George Stretton, sc: Herbert Ayres. With Stewart Rome, George Carney, Tony Quinn, Esmond Knight.

Let George Do It Ealing Studios, in production at Ealing 11.39. p: Michael Balcon, assoc. p: Basil Dearden, d: Marcel Varnel, c: Ronald Neame, Gordon Dines, sc: Angus MacPhail, Basil Dearden, Austin Melford, John Dighton, des: Wilfred Shingleton, ed: Ray Pitt, MD: Ernest Irving. With George Formby, Phyllis Calvert.

Let Me Explain, Dear BIP (A). Wardour, 11.32 (7,000). d: Gene Gerrard, sc: Gene Gerrard, Frank Miller from play by Walter Ellis, *A Little Bit of Fluff* (1915). With Gene Gerrard, Viola Lyel.

Let's Be Famous ATP at Ealing (U). ABFD, 2.39 (7,316). p: Michael Balcon, assoc. p: S. C. Balcon, d: Walter Forde, c: Ronald Neame, Gordon Dines, sc: Roger MacDougall, Allan MacKinnon from their own story, des: Oscar Werndorff, ed:. Ray Pitt, sd: Eric Williams, MD: Ernest Irving, music Van Phillips, songs Noel Gay. With Jimmy O'Dea, Betty Driver, Sonnie Hale.

Let's Love and Laugh BIP at Elstree (A). Wardour, 5.31 (7,640) FT RCA. p: d: Richard Eichberg, sc; Walter Mycroft from German film *Die Bräutigamswitwe*, music Hans May. With Muriel Angelus, Gene Gerrard.

Let's Make a Night of It BIP-ABPC (U). ABPC, 6.37 (8,415). p: Walter Mycroft, d: Graham Cutts, c: Otto Kanturek, sc: Hugh Brooke from radio play by Henrik N. Ege, *The Silver Spoon*, adapt. F. McGrew Willis, des: Clarence Elder, Cedric Dawe, ed: A. C. Hammond, Flora Newton, sd: C. V. Thornton, MD: Harry Acres, Eddie Carol, Joe Loss, Rudy Starita, Jack Jackson, Jack Harris, Sydney Lipton and their Bands, songs Kennedy and Carr, Ray Noble, Allan Murray. With Charles Buddy Rogers, June Clyde, Fred Emney.

Letting in the Sunshine BIP (U). Wardour, 2.33 (6,680). d: Lupino Lane, c: J. J. Cox, Bryan Langley, sc; Frank Miller, adapt: Con West and Herbert Sargent from story by Anthony Asquith, des: David Rawnsley, ed: E. B. Jarvis, sd: A. E. Rudolph, MD: Idris Lewis, song Noel Gay. With Albert Burdon.

Lie Detector, The See **Who Killed John Savage?**

Lieutenant Daring, R.N. Butcher's at Cricklewood (U). Butcher's, 10.35 (7,636). p: Lawrence Huntington, d: Reginald Denham, sc; W. G. Elliott from story by Captain Frank H. Shaw. With Hugh Williams, Frederick Lloyd, Geraldine Fitzgerald.

Life Goes On B & D-Para-Brit. (U). Paramt, 3.22 (7,021). d: Jack Raymond, sc: from play by Walter Hackett, *Sorry You've Been Troubled* (1929). With Elsie Randolph, Hugh Wakefield, Betty Stockfield.

Life of Cecil Rhodes, The See **Rhodes of Africa**

Life of Chopin, The Fitzpatrick Pictures at Shepperton (A). M-G-M, 1.38 (3,289). p: d: James A. Fitzpatrick, c: Hone Glendinning, sc: W. K. Williamson. With Frank Henderson, Julie Suedo.

Life of Liszt, The See **Dream of Love, A**

Life of the Party, The WB-FN at Teddington (A). FN, 4.34 (4,847). p: Irving Asher, d: Ralph Dawson, sc: Brock William from play by Margaret Mayo, Salisbury Field. With Betty Astell, Jerry Verno.

Life's a Stage Encore Films (A). Argosy Films, 3.30 (5,885) silent. p: d: Arthur Phillips, sc: Arrar Jackson from story by Frank Gibbs. With Frank Stanmore, Joy Windsor.

Lightning Conductor Pinebrook at Pinewood (A). GFD, 11.38 (7,131). p: Anthony Havelock-Allan, d: Maurice Elvey, c: Francis Carver, sc: J. Jefferson Farjeon, Lawrence Green from story by Evadne Price. With Gordon Harker, John Lodge, Sally Gray.

Lilac Domino, The Grafton Films at Welwyn (U). UA, 7.37 (7,695). p: Max Schach, assoc. p: Isadore Goldsmith, d: Fred Zelnik, c: Roy Clark, Bryan Langley, sc: and dial: Basil Mason, Neil Gow from story by R. Bernauer based on operetta of 1918 by E. Gatti and B. Jenbach, adapt. R. Hutter, des: Oscar Werndorff, cost: Beatrice Evans, ed: Lynn Harrison, sd: A. S. Ross, MD: Harry Acres, music Charles Cuvillier, Hans May, lyrics Clifford Grey, dances Derra de Moroda. With June Knight, Michael Bartlett, Szoke Szakall.

Lilies of the Field B & D at Elstree B & D (U). UA, 7.34 (7,368). d: Norman Walker, c: Cyril Bristow, sc; Dion Titheradge from play by John Hastings Turner (1923), des: G. S. Stegman, music Philip Braham. With Winifred Shotter, Judy Gunn, Anthony Bushell.

Lily Christine Para-Brit. at Elstree B & D (A). Paramt, 5.32 (7,452). d: Paul L. Stein, sc: Robert Gore-Brown from novel by Michael Arlen. With Corinne Griffith, Colin Clive, Anne Grey.

Lily of Killarney Twick. at Twickenham, in Ireland (U). AP & D, 1.34 (7,850). p: Julius Hagen, d: Maurice Elvey, c: Sydney Blythe, William Luff, sc: H. Fowler Mear from play by Dion Boucicault, *The Colleen Bawn* (1860), des: James Carter, ed: Jack Harris, sd: Baynham Honri, MD: W. L. Trytel. With Gina Malo, John Garrick, Stanley Holloway.

Lily of Laguna Butcher's at Walton (A). Butcher's, 1.38 (7,123). p: Sidney Morgan, d: Oswald Mitchell, c: Geoffrey Faithfull, sc: Oswald Mitchell, Ian Walker from story by Joan Wentworth Wood, des: R. Holmes Paul, MD: Percival Mackey. With Nora Swinburne, Jenny Laird, Richard Ainley.

Limelight Herbert Wilcox at Elstree B & D, Lyceum Theatre (U). GFD, 1.36 (7,041). p: d: Herbert Wilcox, c: Henry Harris, sc: from story by Laura Whetter, des: L. P. Williams, music Geraldo and his Orchestra, dances Ralph Reader. With Ann Neagle, Arthur Tracy.

Limping Man, The (1931) See under **Creeping Shadows**

Limping Man, The Welwyn Studios at Welwyn (A). Pathé, 10.36 (6,550). d: Walter Summers, c: Bryan Langley, sc: Walter Summers from play by Will Scott (1931). With Hugh Wakefield, Francis L. Sullivan, Patricia Hilliard.

Line Engaged Brit. Lion at Beaconsfield (A). Brit. Lion, 11.35 (6,180). p: supervisor Herbert Smith, d: Bernerd Mainwaring, c: George Stretton, sc: from play by Jack de Leon and Jack Celestin (1934). With Jane Baxter, Arthur Wontner, Bramwell Fletcher, Mary Clare.

Lion and Lamb See **River Wolves, The**

Lion has Wings, The Alexander Korda Film Productions-LFP (U). UA, 10.39 (6,287). p: Alexander Korda, assoc. p: Ian Dalrymple, d: Michael Powell, Brian Desmond Hurst, Adrian Brunel from story by Ian Dalrymple, commentary E. V. H. Emmett, des: Vincent Korda, ed: William Hornbeck, Charles Frend, Henry Cornelius, sd: A. W. Watkins, MD: Muir Mathieson, music Richard Addinsell. With Ralph Richardson, Merle Oberon, June Duprez, Flora Robson, Robert Douglas.

Little Bit of Bluff, A G. S. Ent. at Walton (U). M-G-M, 3.35 (5,699). p: George Smith, d: P. Maclean Rogers, sc: H. F. Maltby, Kathleen Butler. With Reginald Gardiner, Marjorie Shotter.

Little Damozel B & D at Elstree B & D (A). W & F, 2.33 (6,639). p: d: Herbert Wilcox, sc: Donovan Pedelty from play by Monckton Hoffe (1909), music Ray Noble, Noel Coward. With Anna Neagle, James Rennie.

Little Dolly Daydream Argyle British Productions and Butcher's (U). Butcher's 4.38 (6,900). p: John Argyle, d: Oswald Mitchell, c: Geoffrey Faithfull, sc: Oswald Mitchell and Ian Walker, des: R. Holmes Paul, ed: F. H. Bickerton. With Binkie Stuart, Talbot O'Farrell, Jane Welsh.

Little Fella WB-FN at Teddington (U). FN, 10.32 (4,017). p: Irving Asher, d: William McGann, c: Bernard Knowles, sc: W. Scott Darling. With John Stuart, Joan Marion, Dodo Watts.

Little Friend G-B (A). G-B D, 7.34 (7,652). p: Michael Balcon, assoc. p: Robert Stevenson, d: Berthold Viertel, c: Gunther Krampf, sc: Margaret Kennedy, Berthold Viertel, Christopher Isherwood from novel by Ernst Lothar, des: Alfred Junge, ed: Ian Dalrymple, cost: Schiaparelli, sd: A. Birch, music Ernst Toch. With Nora Pilbeam, Matheson Lang, Fritz Kortner.

Little Miss Nobody WB-FN (U). WB, 2.33 (4,796). p: Irving Asher, d: John

Daumery. With Winna Winfried, Sebastian Shaw.

Little Miss Somebody Mondover Film Productions at Walton (U). Butcher's, 10.37 (7,030). p: Alfred D'Eyncourt, d: Walter Tennyson, c: Geoffrey Faithfull, sc: Harry Fowler Mear from story idea by Walter Tennyson, des: R. Holmes Paul, MD: John Reynders. With Binkie Stuart, John Longden, Kathleen Kelly.

Little Napoleon George Smith at Walton (U). Fox, 7.33 (4,000). d: Adrian Brunel, sc: Adrian Brunel from story by Marshall Reade. With Nancy Burne, Terence de Marney.

Little Stranger George King (A). M-G-M, 3.34 (4,605). d: George King. With Sir Nigel Playfair, Eva Moore, Nora Baring.

Little Waitress Delta Pictures (U). Ace Films, 11.32 (4,365). p: Geoffrey Clarke, d: Widgey Newman. With Moore Marriott.

Live Again Morgan Productions at Elstree Rock (A). NPFD, 11.36 (7,666). p: d: Arthur Maude, c: Horace Wheddon, sc: from story by John Quin. With Noah Beery, Bessie Love, John Garrick.

Live and Let Live See **Spy for a Day**

Live Wire, The Tudor-Olympic at Beaconsfield (U). Brit. Lion, 10.37 (6,248). p: Marquis of Ely, d: Herbert Brenon, c: George Stretton, sc: Stafford Dickens from his own play *Plunder in the Air*, des: Norman Arnold. With Bernard Nedell, Jean Gillie.

Living Dangerously BIP at Elstree (A). Wardour, 3.36 (6,446). p: Walter Mycroft, d: Herbert Brenon, c: Bryan Langley, sc: Marjorie Deans, Dudley Leslie, Geoffrey Kerr from play by Reginald Simpson and Frank Gregory (1934) des: Cedric Dawe. With Otto Kruger, Leonora Corbett.

Lloyd of the C.I.D. Mutual Pictures at Cricklewood (U). Universal, (1), 2.32 12 2-reelers, (2) 8.32 condensed version

The Green Spot Mystery, 6 reels. p: d: Henry McRae, sc: Henry McRae, Ella O'Neill. With 'Jack Lloyd' (Claude Saunders), Muriel Angelus, Wallace Geoffrey.

Lodger, The Twick. at Twickenham (A). W & F, 9.32 (7,685). p: Julius Hagen, d: Maurice Elvey, c: Basil Emmott, sc: H. Fowler Mear, Ivor Novello, Miles Mander from novel by Mrs Belloc Lowndes. With Ivor Novello, Elizabeth Allan, Jack Hawkins.

Londonderry Air, The Fox Brit. at Wembley (U). 20th Cent.-Fox, 12.37 (4,205). p: Victor M. Greene, d: Alex Bryce, c: Ronald Neame, sc: David Evans, Alex Bryce from play by Rachel Field. With Liam Gaffney, Sara Allgood.

London Melody British Screen Productions at Isleworth (U). Audible Filmcraft, 8.30 (5,269) FT, songs BTP. d: Geoffrey Malins, c: D. P. Cooper, sc: Geoffrey Malins from story by Donald Stuart. With Lorraine La Fosse, Haddon Mason.

London Melody Herbert Wilcox at Elstree BIP, Pinewood (A). GFD, 2.37 (6,736). p: d: Herbert Wilcox, c: Freddie Young, sc: Monckton Hoffe from story by Ray Lewis, des: L. P. Williams, music Sigler, Goodhart and Hoffman, dances Ralph Reader. With Anna Neagle, Tullio Carminati, Robert Douglas.

London Wall See **After Office Hours**

Lonely Road, The ATP at Ealing (A). ABFD, 8.36 (6,517). p: Basil Dean, d: James Flood, c: Jan Stallich, sc: James Flood, Gerard Fairlie, Anthony Kimmins from story by Neville Shute. With Clive Brook, Nora Swinburne, Victoria Hopper.

Long Live The King WB-FN at Teddington (U). FN, 4.33 (3,988). p: Irving Asher, d: William McGann, sc: W. Scott Darling. With Florence Desmond.

Looking on the Bright Side ATP at Ealing (U). Radio, 9.32 (7,398). p: Basil Dean, assoc. p: Archie Pitt, d: Basil Dean, Graham Cutts, c: Robert Martin, sc: Archie Pitt, Brock Williams from story by Basil Dean and Archie Pitt, dial: Reginald Purdell, des: Clifford Pember, ed: Otto Ludwig, sd: A. D. Valentine, music Carroll Gibbons and Savoy Hotel Band. With Gracie Fields, Julian Rose.

Look Up and Laugh ATP at Ealing (U). ABFD, 6.35 (6,944). p: d: Basil Dean, c: Robert Martin, sc: Gordon Wellesley from story by J. B. Priestley, des: J. Elder Wills, ed: Jack Kitchin, MD: Ernest Irving, songs Harry Parr-Davies. With Gracie Fields, Tommy Fields, Douglas Wakefield.

Loose Ends BIP at Elstree (A). Wardour, 5.30 (8,567) FT RCA. d: Norman Walker, c: Claude Friese-Greene, sc: Norman Walker and Dion Titheradge from play by Dion Titheradge (as 'Geoffrey Warren', 1926), des: A. J. Thompson, ed: Émile de Ruelle, Sam Simmonds, sd: A. S. Ross, MD: John Reynders, songs William Helmore, dances Fred Lord. With Owen Nares, Edna Best, Adrianne Allen, Miles Mander.

Lord Babs Gainsborough at Islington (U). Ideal, 2.32 (6,934) FT RCA. p: Michael Balcon, d: Walter Forde, c: Leslie Rowson, sc: Angus MacPhail, Clifford Grey from play by Keble Howard (1928), des: Vetchinsky, ed: Ian Dalrymple, sd: George Gunn, songs Vivian Ellis, Clifford Grey. With Bobby Howes, Jean Colin.

Lord Camber's Ladies BIP (A). Wardour, 11.32 (8.624). p: Alfred Hitchcock, d: Benn Levy, c: Jimmy Wilson, sc: Benn Levy, Edwin Greenwood, Gilbert Wakefield from play by H. A. Vachell, *The Case of Lady Camber* (1915), des: David Rawnsley, sd: Alec Murray. With Sir Gerald du Maurier, Gertrude Lawrence, Nigel Bruce, Benita Hume.

Lord Edgware Dies Real Art at Twickenham (A). Radio, 8.34 (7,344). p: Julius Hagen, d: Henry Edwards, sc: H. Fowler Mear from story by Agatha Christie. With Austin Trevor, Jane Carr.

Lord of the Manor, The B & D-Para-Brit. at Elstree B & D (U). Paramt, 5.33 (6,367). d: Henry Edwards, c: Henry Harris, sc: Dorothy Rowan from play by John Hastings Turner, sd: C. C. Stevens. With Fred Kerr, Betty Stockfield, Harry Wilcoxon.

Lord Richard in the Pantry Twick. at Twickenham (U). WB, 7.30 (7,981) FT, songs RCA. p: Julius Hagen, exec. p: Henry Edwards, d: Walter Forde, c: Sydney Blythe, William Luff, sc: H. Fowler Mear from play by Sydney Blow and Douglas Hoare (1919) from novel by Martin Swayne, des: James Carter, ed: Jack Harris, sd: Baynham Honri. With Richard Cooper, Dorothy Seacombe. (Bilingual film.)

Lorna Doone ATP at Ealing, Lynton, Exmoor (A). ABFD, 12.34 (8,023). p: d: Basil Dean, c: Robert Martin, sc: Dorothy Farnum, Gordon Wellesley, dial: Miles Malleson, from novel by R. D. Blackmore, des: Edward Carrick, ed: Jack Kitchin, sd: A. D. Valentine, MD: Ernest Irving, music Dr. C. Armstrong, one song by Rutland Boughton. With Victoria Hopper, John Loder, Margaret Lockwood.

Lost Chord, The Twick. at Twickenham (A). AP & D, 4.33 (8,274). p: Julius Hagen, d: Maurice Elvey, sc: H. Fowler Mear from story by Reuben Gilmer based on music by Sir Arthur Sullivan, MD: W. L. Trytel. With Elizabeth Allan, John Stuart.

Lost in the Legion BIP at Welwyn (U). Wardour, 7.34 (6,456). p: Walter Mycroft, p: man: John Harlow, d: Fred Newmeyer, c: Jack Parker, sc: John Paddy Carstairs, Syd Courtenay, Lola Harvey, sd: A. S. Ross. With Leslie Fuller, Renee Houston, Betty Fields.

Lost Lady, The See **Lady Vanishes, The**
Love Affair of the Dictator, The Released as **Dictator, The** Toeplitz Productions at Ealing, Copenhagen (A).

G-B D, 2.35 (7,760). p: Ludovico Toeplitz, d: Al Santell, Victor Saville, c: Franz Planer, sc: Benn Levy from story by H. G. Lustig, Michael Hogan and Hans Wilhelm, des: Andre Andreiev, cost: Joe Strassner, ed: Paul Weatherwax, sd: Eric Williams, music Karol Rathaus. With Clive Brook, Madeleine Carroll, Emlyn Williams.

Love and Let Love See **Sleeping Car**

Love at Sea B & D-Para-Brit. at Elstree B & D (U). Paramt, 4.36 (6,362). p: Anthony Havelock-Allan, d: Adrian Brunel, c: Francis Carver, sc: Beaufoy Milton from story by Jane Browne, des: Hylton R. Oxley, ed: Richard Wootton, sd: W. H. Lindop. With Rosalyn Boulter, Carl Harbord.

Love at Second Sight BIP-Radius at Elstree (U). Wardour, 3.34 (6,400). p: Julius Haimann, d: Dr Paul Merzbach, c: J. J. Cox, Philip Grindrod, sc: Harold Simpson, Frank Miller, Jack Davies from story by Paul Merzbach and Harold Simpson, des: David Rawnsley, ed: John Neill Brown, music and lyrics Mischa Spoliansky and Clifford Grey. With Marian Marsh, Anthony Bushell.

The Love Contract B & D (A). W & F, 7.32 (7,233). p: Herbert Wilcox, d: Herbert Selpin, c: Cyril Bristow, sc: from play by Letraz, Desty and Blum, *Chauffeur Antoinette,* music by Ralph Benatzky. With Winifred Shotter, Owen Narcs.

Love from a Stranger Trafalgar Film Productions at Denham (A). UA, 1.37 (8,310). p: Max Schach, d: Rowland V. Lee, c: Phil Tannura, sc: Frances Marion from play by Frank Vosper (1936) based on short story by Agatha Christie, des: Fred Pusey, cost: S. Lange, ed: Howard O'Neil, sd: A. W. Watkins, MD: Boyd Neel, music Benjamin Britten. With Ann Harding, Basil Rathbone, Binnie Hale.

Love Habit, The BIP at Elstree (A). Wardour, 1.31 (8,064) FT RCA. d: Harry Lachman c: J. J. Cox, sc: Val Valentine from play by Louis Verneuil, adapt. by Sir Seymour Hicks. With Sir

Seymour Hicks, Margot Grahame, Ursula Jeans, Elsa Lanchester.

Love in Exile Capitol at Elstree and Isleworth (A). GFD, 5.36 (7,023). p: Max Schach, d: Alfred L. Werker, c: Otto Kanturek, sc: Roger Burford, Ernest Betts, add. dial: Herman Mankiewitcz, from novel by Gene Markey, *His Majesty's Pyjamas,* des: John Mead, cost: Schiaparelli, ed: E. B. Jarvis, sd: F. Fisher, MD: Benjamin Frankel. With Clive Brook, Helen Vinson, Will Fyffe, Ronald Squire.

Love Insurance See **Glamour Girl**

Love Lies BIP at Elstree (U). Wardour, 8.31 (6,324). d: Lupino Lane, c: Walter Harvey, Horace Wheddon, sc: Frank Miller, adapt: Stanley Lupino and Arthur Rigby from their musical comedy (1929), des: D. M. Sutherland, ed: E. B. Jarvis, sd: A. S. Ross, music Hal Brody and others, lyrics Desmond Carter. With Stanley Lupino, Jack Hobbs, Binnie Barnes, Dorothy Boyd.

Love, Life and Laughter ATP at Ealing (U). ABFD, 3.34 (7,641). p: Basil Dean, d: Maurice Elvey, c: Robert Martin, sc: Maurice Braddell, Gordon Wellesley from story by Eric Dunstan and John Sterndale Bennett. With Gracie Fields, John Loder.

Love, Mirth and Melody Mancunian Film Corp: (U). Universal, 9.34 (5,856). p: John Blakeley, d: Bert Tracey.

Love Nest, The BIP (A). Wardour, 7.33 (5,658). d: Thomas Bentley, c: Walter Harvey, sc: Gene Gerrard, H. F. Maltby, Frank Miller from story by H. F. Maltby. With Gene Gerrard, Camilla Horn.

Love on the Spot ATP at Ealing (A). Radio, 6.32 (5,866). p: Basil Dean, d: Graham Cutts, c: Hal Young, sc: John Paddy Carstairs, dial: Reginald Purdell, from novel by 'Sapper' (H. C. McNeile). With Richard Dolman, Rosemary Ames.

Love on Wheels Gainsborough at Elstree, Selfridges department store (U). W & F, 7.32 (7,831). p: Michael Balcon, d: Victor Saville, c: Mutz Greenbaum, sc:

Angus MacPhail, Robert Stevenson, add. dial: Douglas Furber, story by Franz Schulz and Ernst Angel, des: Vetchinsky, cost: Gordon Conway, ed: Ian Dalrymple, Derek Twist, sd: George Gunn, MD: Louis Levy, music Jean Gilbert, lyrics Douglas Furber, dances Jack Hulbert. With Jack Hulbert, Leonora Corbett, Gordon Harker.

Love Race, The BIP at Elstree (U). Pathé, 12.31 (7,243). d: Lupino Lane, c: J. Williams, sc: Edwin Greenwood from musical play by Stanley Lupino (1930), music Jack Clarke. With Stanley Lupino, Dorothy Boyd.

Lover's Knot See **Jane Steps Out**

Loves of Robert Burns B & D-HMV at Elstree B & D (A). Ideal, 3.30 (8,656) FT, songs WE. p: d: Herbert Wilcox, c: Dave Kesson, Jimmy Rogers, sc: Herbert Wilcox, Reginald Berkeley, des: Clifford Pember. With Joseph Hislop.

Love's Old Sweet Song Argyle Talking Pictures at Cricklewood (A). Butcher's, 7.33 (7,187). p: John Argyle, d: Manning Haynes, c: Desmond Dickinson, sc: Lydia Hayward from song by J. L. Molloy, des: Hugh Gee, sd: Lance Comfort. With William Freshman, John Stuart, Joan Wyndham.

Love Test, The Fox Brit. at Wembley (U). Fox, 1.35 (5,772). p: Leslie Landau, d: Michael Powell, c: Arthur Crabtree, sc: Selwyn Jepson from story by Jack Celestin. With Judy Gunn, Louis Hayward.

Love up the Pole Hope-Bell Productions, British Comedies and Butcher's Film Service at Cricklewood (A). Butcher's, 9.36 (7,450). p: Oswald Mitchell, d: Clifford Gulliver, c: Jack Parker, sc: Oswald Mitchell from story by Con West, Herbert Sargent, ed: Challis Sanderson. With Ernie Lotinga, Vivienne Chatterton, Wallace Lupino.

Love Wager, The Anglo-European Pictures (U). Paramt, 6.33 (5,802). p: E. A. Fell, d: A. Cyran, sc: Moira Dale. With Frank Stanmore, Pat Paterson.

Loyalties ATP at Ealing (A). ABFD, 5.33

(6,610). p: d: Basil Dean, assist. d: Carol Reed, c: Robert Martin, sc: W. P. Lipscomb from play by John Galsworthy (1922), des: Edward Carrick, ed: Thorold Dickinson, sd: A. D. Valentine. With Basil Rathbone, Miles Mander.

Luck of a Sailor, The BIP at Elstree (U). Wardour, 5.34 (6,000). p: Walter Mycroft, d: Robert Milton, c: Claude Friese-Greene, sc: Wolfgang Wilhelm, Clifford Grey, Robert Milton from play by Cmdr Horton Giddy, *Contraband*, sd: A. E. Rudolph. With David Manners, Camilla Horn, Greta Nissen, Clifford Mollison.

Luck of the Irish, The Crusade Films at Elstree Rock and in Ulster (U). Paramt, 12.35 (7,330). p: Victor M. Greene, Richard Hayward, d: Donovan Pedelty, sc: Donovan Pedelty from play by Col. Victor Haddick. With Richard Hayward, Kay Walsh.

Luck of the Navy ABPC (U). ABPC, 10.38 (6,386). p: Walter Mycroft, d: Norman Lee, c: Walter Harvey, sc: Clifford Grey from play by Mrs Clifford Mills (1918), des: Ian White. With Albert Burdon, Judy Kelly, Geoffrey Toone, Keneth Kent.

Luck of the Turf Randall Faye (A). Radio, 9.36 (5,755). p: d: Randall Faye, sc: John Hunter. With Jack Melford, Moira Lynd.

Lucky Blaze Ace Films (U). Ace Films, 8.33 (4,403). d: sc: Widgey Newman. With Moore Marriott.

Lucky Days B & D-Para-Brit. at Elstree B & D (U). Paramt, 8.35 (6,028). d: Reginald Denham, sc: Margaret McDonnell from screen story by Gordon and Margaret McDonnell. With Chili Bouchier, Whitmore Humphries.

Lucky Girl BIP (U). Wardour, 6.32 (6,700). d: Gene Gerrard, Frank Miller, c: J. J. Cox, Bryan Langley, sc: Gene Gerrard, Frank Miller from musical play *Lucky Girl* (1928) by Douglas Furber, R. P. Weston and Bert Lee, and from play by Reginald Berkeley, *Mr. Abdulla*, des: John Mead, ed: Leslie

Norman, sd: C. V. Thornton, music and lyrics Arthur Margetson, piano Raie de Costa. With Gene Gerrard, Molly Lamont.

Lucky Jade Welwyn Studios at Welwyn (A). Paramt, 3.37 (6,272). p: F. Browett, d: Walter Summers, c: Horace Wheddon, sc: Walter Summers from story by Jane Browne. Betty Ann Davies, John Warwick.

Lucky Ladies WB-FN at Teddington (U). FN, 9.32 (6,734). p: Irving Asher, d: John Rawlins, c: Bernard Knowles, sc: Randall Faye from story by W. Scott Darling. With Sydney Fairbrother, Emily Fitzroy.

Lucky Loser B & D-Para-Brit. at Elstree B & D (A). Paramt, 3.34 (6,200). d: Reginald Denham, sc: Basil Mason from play by Matthew M. Brennan, *The Big Sweep*. With Anna Lee, Richard Dolman.

Lucky Number, The Gainsborough at Islington, Highbury (Arsenal football ground), Welwyn (U). Gaumont-Ideal, 5.33 (6,535). p: Michael Balcon, p: personnel Ian Dalrymple, Angus Mac-Phail, George Gunn, Louis Levy, d: Anthony Asquith, c: Gunther Krampf, Derick Williams, sc: Anthony Asquith from story by Franz Schulz, add. dial: Douglas Furber, des: Vetchinsky, cost: Gordon Conway, ed: Dan Birt, sd: A. Douglas, MD: Louis Levy, music Mischa Spoliansky, lyrics Douglas Furber. With Clifford Mollison, Gordon Harker, Joan Wyndham, Joe Hayman.

Lucky Star See **Once in a New Moon**

Lucky Sweep, A National Talkies at Elstree Blattner (U). PDC, 3.32 (5,103). p: Harry Rowson, d: A. V. Bramble. With John Longden, Diana Beaumont.

Lucky to Me ABPC at Elstree (A). ABPC, 11.39 (6,267). p: Walter Mycroft, d: Thomas Bentley, c: Derick Williams, sc: Clifford Grey from play by Stanley Lupino and Arthur Rigby, *So This is Love* (1928), des: Cedric Dawe, ed: Monica Kimmick, MD: Harry Acres, music and lyrics Noel Gay, dance Joan Davis. With Stanley Lupino, Barbara Blair, David Hutcheson.

Lure, The Maude Productions at Wembley (A). Paramt, 8.33 (5,979). d: Arthur Maude, c: Eric Cross, sc: from play by J. Sabben Clare, des: J. Elder Wills, sd: George Burgess. With Anne Grey, Cyril Raymond.

Lure of the Atlantic, The H. B. Parkinson (A). Fox, 10.29 (4,550) silent. p: H. B. Parkinson, d: Norman Lee. With Eric Hales, Iris Derbyshire.

Lyons Mail, The Twick. at Twickenham (A). W & F, 4.31 (6,839). p: Julius Hagen, d: Arthur Maude, c: Sydney Blythe, sc: H. Fowler Mear from play by Charles Reade (1877). With Sir John Martin-Harvey, Norah Baring.

Mac See **Rolling Home**

Machine-Made Troubador See **Mayfair Melody**

Macushla Fox Brit. at Wembley (U). 20th Cent.-Fox, 12.37 (5,359). p: Victor M. Greene, d: Alex Bryce, sc: David Evans. With Liam Gaffney, Pamela Wood.

Mad About Money Morgan Productions at Elstree Rock (U). Brit. Lion, 11.38 (6,760), 2 years delay. p: William Rowland, d: Melville Brown, c: John Stumar, sc: John Meehan Jnr from story by John Harding, music and lyrics James Dyrenforth and Kenneth Leslie-Smith, dances Larry Ceballos. With Lupe Velez, Wallace Ford, Ben Lyon, Harry Langdon.

Madame Guillotine Reginald Fogwell at Isleworth (A). W & F, 2.31 (6,694) FT Fidelity. p: Reginald Fogwell, Mansfield Markham, d: Reginald Fogwell, c: Joe Rosenthal Jr, sc: Harold Huth from story by Reginald Fogwell. With Madeleine Carroll, Brian Aherne.

Mademoiselle Docteur Grafton Films at Isleworth (A). UA, 11.37 (7,563). p: Max Schach, assoc. p: Isadore Goldsmith, d: Edmond T. Gréville, c: Otto Heller, sc: Ernest Betts, Rudolph Bernaur, dial: Basil Mason, from story by George Nevely, I. Cube. Remake of French film d: Pabst. des: Oscar Werndorff, ed: Ray Pitt, sd: S. A. Jolly, music Hans May. With Dita Parlo,

Erich von Stroheim, John Loder, Claire Luce.

Mad Hatters, The B & D-Para-Brit. at Elstree B & D (U). Paramt, 7.35 (6,203). d: Ivar Campbell, c: Francis Carver, sc: Christine Jope-Slade from screen story by James Stewart, des: Wilfred Arnold. With Sidney King, Chili Bouchier.

Magenta Street See **Money Talks**

Magistrate, The See **Those Were the Days**

Maid Happy Bendar Films at Elstree BIP (A). WP, 6.33 (6,728). p: d: Mansfield Markham, c: Emil Schunemann, Jimmy Wilson, sc: Jack King from story by Garrett Graham, des: Walther Reimann, music Jack King. With Charlotte Cinders, Johannes Reimann, Denis Hoey.

Maid of the Mountains BIP at Elstree (U). Wardour, 9.32 (7,228). d: Lupino Lane, c: Claude Friese-Greene, Arthur Crabtree, sc: Edwin Greenwood, Victor Kendall, Frank Miller; adapt: Douglas Furber, Lupino Lane from musical play by Frederick Lonsdale (1917), des: Clarence Elder, David Rawnsley, ed: Leslie Norman, sd: A. E. Rudolph, MD: Idris Lewis, music Harold Fraser-Simson, lyrics Harry Graham. With Harry Welchman, Betty Stockfield, Albert Burdon.

Maid to Order See **Maid Happy**

Major Barbara Pascal Productions, in production at Pinewood from 8.39. p: Gabriel Pascal, d: Gabriel Pascal, Harold French, David Lean, c: Ronald Neame, sc: Anatole de Grunwald, George Bernard Shaw from play by George Bernard Shaw (1905), des: Vincent Korda, John Bryan, ed: Charles Frend, music Sir William Walton. With Wendy Hiller, Rex Harrison, Sybil Thorndike, Ralph Richardson.

Make it Three St Margaret's Film Studio at Twickenham (U). M-G-M, 2.38 (7,003). p: Julius Hagen, d: David MacDonald, sc: Vernon Sylvaine. With Hugh Wakefield, Edmund Willard, Diana Beaumont.

Make-Up Standard International Productions at Shepperton (U). ABFD, 6.37 (6,473). p: K. C. Alexander and C. M. Origo, d: Alfred Zeisler, c: Eric Cross, sc: Reginald Long, Jeffrey Dell from novel by Hans Passendorf, *Bux,* des: David Rawnsley, ed: George Grace, With Nils Asther, June Clyde. (Bilingual film.)

Man at Six, The BIP (U). Wardour, 7.31 (6,415). d: Harry Hughes, c: Ernest Palmer, sc: Harry Hughes and Val Valentine from play by Jack Celestin and Jack de Leon (1928). With Anne Grey, Lester Matthews.

Man Behind the Mask, The Joe Rock at Elstree Rock (A). M-G-M, 3.36 (7,131). p: Joe Rock, d: Michael Powell, c: Ernest Palmer, sc: Sid Courtenay, Jack Byrd, add. dial: Ian Hay, from novel by Jacques Futrelle, *The Chase of the Golden Plate.* With Jane Baxter, Hugh Williams.

Man Eater, The See **Peace and Quiet**

Man from Chicago, The BIP (U). Wardour, 10.30 (7,598) FT RCA. d: Walter Summers, c: Jimmy Wilson, sc: Walter Summers from play by Reginald Berkeley, *Speed.* With Bernard Nedell, Dodo Watts.

Man from M.I.5., The See **Secret Journey**

Man from Toronto, The Gainsborough at Islington, Amberley (U). Ideal, 1.33 (6,921). p: Michael Balcon, d: Sinclair Hill, c: L. Rowson, sc: W. P. Lipscomb from play by Douglas Murray (1918), des: Vetchinsky. With Jessie Matthews, Ian Hunter.

Man in the Mirror, The J. H. Productions at Elstree (former Whitehall) (A). Twick. F. D., 10.36 (7,362). p: Julius Hagen, d: Maurice Elvey, c: Curt Courant, sc: F. McGrew Willis, Hugh Mills from novel by William Garrett, des: A. L. Mazzei, ed: Jack Harris, Ralph Kemplen, sd: Baynham Honri, Leo Wilkins, MD: W. L. Trytel. With Edward Everett Horton, Genevieve Tobin, Ursula Jeans.

Man I Want, The Brit. Lion at

Beaconsfield (A). M-G-M, 3.34 (6,162). p: Supervisor Herbert Smith, d: Leslie Hiscott, sc: from story by Michael Barringer. With Henry Kendall, Wendy Barrie, Betty Astell, Davy Burnaby.

Mannequin Real Art at Twickenham (A). Radio, 12.33 (4,855). p: Julius Hagen, d: G. A. Cooper, sc: from story by Charles Bennett, des: James Carter. With Harold French, Judy Kelly.

Man of Aran Gainsborough in Galway Bay, Ireland, recorded at Shepherd's Bush. G-B D, 4.34 (6,832). p: Michael Balcon, d: c: Robert Flaherty, field laboratory John Taylor, sc: Robert and Frances Flaherty, John Goldman, ed: John Goldman, sd: H. Hand, MD Louis Levy, Music John Greenwood. With Tiger King, Maggie Dirrane, Michael Dillane.

Man of Mayfair Para-Brit. at Elstree B & D (U). Paramt, 11.31 (7,500). d: Louis Mercanton, dial: d: Reginald Denham, sc: Eliot Crawshay Williams from novel by May Edginton, *A Child in their Midst*, des: R. Holmes Paul. With Jack Buchanan, Joan Barry, Warwick Ward, Nora Swinburne.

Man of the Moment WB-FN at Teddington (A). FN, 9.35 (7,371). p: Irving Asher, d: Monty Banks, c: Basil Emmott, Leslie Rowson, sc: Guy Bolton, Roland Pertwee, A. R. Rawlinson from story by Yves Mirande, *Water Nymph*, des: Peter Proud, ed: A. Bates, sd: Leslie Murray, H. C. Pearson. With Douglas Fairbanks Jr, Laura La Plante, Claude Hulbert, Margaret Lockwood.

Man Outside, The Real Art at Twickenham (A). Radio, 5.33 (4,781). p: Julius Hagen, d: G. A. Cooper, sc: H. Fowler Mear from story by Donald Stuart. With Henry Kendall, Joan Gardner.

Man Save The Queen See **Lady in Danger**

Man They Couldn't Arrest, The Gainsborough (U). Ideal, 7.31 (6,657) FT RCA. p: Michael Balcon, d: T. Hayes Hunter, c: Leslie Rowson, sc:

Angus MacPhail, Arthur Wimperis, T. Hayes Hunter from novel by 'Seamark' (Austin J. Small). With Nicholas Hannen, Gordon Harker.

Man Who Changed his Mind, The Gainsborough at Islington (A). G-B D, 9.36 (5,914). p: Michael Balcon, d: Robert Stevenson, c: J. J. Cox, sc: L. du Garde Peach, Sidney Gilliat from story by John Balderston, *The Devil Goes Calling*, des: Vetchinsky, cost: Molyneux, ed: R. E. Dearing, Alfred Roome, sd: W. Salter, MD: Louis Levy. With Boris Karloff, Anna Lee, John Loder.

Man Who Changed his Name, The Brit. Lion at Beaconsfield, 6.30 (7,134) silent. p: S. W. Smith, d: A. V. Bramble, sc: Kathleen Hayden from play by Edgar Wallace. With Stewart Rome, Betty Faire.

Man who Changed his Name, The Twick. at Twickenham (A). Universal, 3.34 (7,203). p: Julius Hagen, d: Henry Edwards, sc: H. Fowler Mear from play by Edgar Wallace. With Lyn Harding, Betty Stockfield.

Man Who Could not Forget, The See **Debt of Honour**

Man Who Could Work Miracles, The LFP at Isleworth, exteriors at Denham (U). UA, 7.36 (7,384). p: Alexander Korda, d: Lothar Mendes, c: Hal Rosson, sc: H. G. Wells from his own novel, des: Vincent Korda, cost: John Armstrong, ed: William Hornbeck, Philip Charlot, sd: A. W. Watkins, sp. effects: Ned Mann, Harry Zech, MD: Muir Mathieson, music Mischa Spoliansky. With Roland Young, Ralph Richardson, Joan Gardner.

Man Who Knew Too Much, The G-B at Shepherd's Bush (A). G-B D, 12.34 (6,764). p: Michael Balcon, assoc. p: Ivor Montagu, d: Alfred Hitchcock, c: Curt Courant, sc: A. R. Rawlinson and Edwin Greenwood, add. dial: Emlyn Williams, from story by Charles Bennett and D. B. Wyndham-Lewis, des: Alfred Junge, Peter Proud, ed: H. St C. Stewart, sd: F. McNally, MD: Louis

Levy, music Arthur Benjamin. With Edna Best, Leslie Banks, Peter Lorre, Nova Pilbeam.

Man Who Made Diamonds, The WB-FN at Teddington (A). FN, 6.37 (6,609). p: Irving Asher, d: Ralph Ince, sc: Michael Barringer, Anthony Hankey from story by Frank A. Richardson. With Noel Madison, James Stephenson.

Man with a Million, The See **Smithy**

Man without a Face, The Embassy Pictures at Walton (A). Radio, 9.35 (5,555, later 5,500). p: d: George King, c: Geoffrey Faithfull, sc: Randall Faye from story by St John Irvine. With Cyril Chosack, Carol Coombes.

Man with your Voice, A See under **Talk of the Devil**

Many Tanks, Mr. Atkins WB-FN at Teddington (U). FN, 12.38 (6,145). p: Jerome Jackson, d: Roy William Neill, c: Basil Emmott, sc: Reginald Purdell, Austin Melford, John Dighton, J. O. C. Orton. des: Peter Proud, Michael Relph, ed: B. Rule, sd: H. C. Pearson. With Claude Hulbert, Reginald Purdell.

Many Waters Associated Metropolitan Pictures at Elstree BIP (A). Pathé, 11.31 (6,884) FT RCA. p: J. A. Thorpe, d: Milton Rosmer, c: Hal Young, Henry Gerrard, sc: Monckton Hoffe from his own play (1928), des: Marcel Courrou, ed: A. S. Bates, sd: A. C. O'Donoghue, MD: John Reynders, With Lilian Hall Davis, Arthur Margetson, Elizabeth Allan.

Maria Marten, or The Murder in the Red Barn George King at Shepperton (A). M-G-M, 4.35 (6,015). p: d: George King, sc: Randall Faye. With Tod Slaughter, Sophie Stewart.

Marigold ABPC at Elstree, Edinburgh (U). ABPC, 10.38 (6,666). p: Walter Mycroft, d: Thomas Bentley, c: Gunther Krampf, sc: Dudley Leslie from play by Allen Harker and F. R. Pryor (1927), des: John Mead, cost: Motley, ed: Monica Kimmick, music Anthony Collier. With Sophie Stewart, Patrick Barr, Pamela Stanley.

Marooned Brit. Lion at Beaconsfield (U).

Fox, 11.33 (6,022). p: supervisor Herbert Smith, d: Leslie Hiscott, sc: from screen story by Michael Barringer. With Edmund Gwenn, Viola Lyel.

Marriage Bond, The Twick. at Twickenham (A). Radio, 3.32 (7,392). p: Julius Hagen, d: Maurice Elvey, c: Basil Emmott, sc: H. Fowler Mear. With Mary Newcomb, Guy Newall, Elizabeth Allan.

Marriage of Corbal, The Capitol at Elstree B & D, France, Madeira (U). GFD, 5.36 (8,329). p. Max Schach, d: Karl Grune, c: Otto Kanturek, sc: S. Fullman from novel by Rafael Sabatini, *The Nuptials of Corbal*, des: John Mead, ed: Walter Stokvis. With Nils Asther, Hazel Terry, Noah Beery, Hugh Sinclair.

Marry Me Gainsborough at Islington (U). Ideal, 10.32 (7,800). p: Michael Balcon, d: William Thiele, c: Bernard Knowles, sc: Angus MacPhail, Anthony Asquith from story by Franz Schulz, Ernst Angel, Stephen Zador in German film, music Michael Krausz, lyrics Desmond Carter, Frank Eyton. With Rene Müller, Sir George Robey, Ian Hunter.

Marry the Girl Brit. Lion (A). Brit. Lion, 4.35 (6,190). P. supervisor Herbert Smith, d: P. Maclean Rogers, c: Cyril Bristow, sc: Kathleen Butler, P. Maclean Rogers from play by George Arthurs and Arthur Miller (1930). With Sonnie Hale, Winifred Shotter.

Master and Man BIP at Welwyn (U). Pathé, 3.34 (4,023). p: Walter Mycroft, d: John Harlow, sc: Wallace Lupino. With Wallace and Barry Lupino.

Matinee Idol Wyndham Films at Wembley (A). UA, 3.33 (6,864). p: Bray Wyndham, d: George King, c: Eric Cross, sc: from story by Charles Bennett. With Camilla Horn, Miles Mander, Marguerite Allan.

Mayfair Girl WB-FN at Teddington (A). WB, 8.33 (6,076). p: Irving Asher, d: George King. With Sally Blane, John Stuart.

Mayfair Melody WB-FN at Teddington

(U). FN, 3.37 (7,582). p: Irving Asher, d: Arthur Woods, sc: from screen story by James Dyrenforth, music Kenneth Leslie-Smith, lyrics James Dyrenforth. With Keith Falkner, Joyce Kirby, Chili Bouchier.

Mayor's Nest, The B & D at Elstree B & D (U). W & F, 6.32 (6,684). p: Herbert Wilcox, d: P. Maclean Rogers, sc: P. Maclean Rogers from story by R. P. Weston, Bert Lee, Jack Marks. With Sydney Howard, Claude Hulbert, Miles Malleson.

McGlusky the Sea Rover BIP at Elstree and in Devon (A). Wardour, 7.35 (5,300). p: Walter Mycroft, d: Walter Summers, c: Horace Wheddon, sc: Walter Summers from novel by A. G. Nales, des: Donald Wilson. With Jack Doyle, Tamara Desni.

Me and Marlborough G-B at Shepherd's Bush (U). G-B D, 7.35 (7,617). p: Michael Balcon, d: Victor Saville, c: Curt Courant, sc: W. P. Lipscomb and Marjorie Gaffney from story by W. P. Lipscomb and Reginald Pound, des: Alfred Junge, sd: Philip Dorté, song by Noel Gay. With Cicely Courtneidge, Tom Walls.

Me and my Pal Welwyn Studios at Welwyn (U). Pathé, 1.39 (6,626). p: Warwick Ward, d: Thomas Bentley. With Dave Willis, Pat Kirkwood.

Medicine Man, The Real Art at Twickenham (A). Radio, 2.33 (4,704). p: Julius Hagen, d: Redd Davis, c: Ernest Palmer, sc: Michael Barringer. With Claude Allister, Frank Pettingell.

Medicine Man, The (1934) See **Doctor's Orders**

Medium, The Film Tests (A). M-G-M, 9.34 (3,432). d: Vernon Sewell, sc: from Grand Guignol play. With Shayle Gardner, Nancy O'Neil.

Meet Maxwell Archer RKO-Radio at Elstree Rock (A). RKO-Radio, screened 9.39 (6,655). p: William Sistrom, d: John Paddy Carstairs, c: Claude Friese-Greene, sc: Katherine Strueby and Hugh Clevely from novel by Hugh Clevely, *Archer Plus Twenty*. With John

Loder, Marta Labarr, Lueen MacGrath.

Meet Mr. Penny Brit. Nat. at Welwyn (U). ABPC, 4.38 (6,355). p: John Corfield, d: David MacDonald, c: Bryan Langley, sc: Doreen Montgomery and Victor Kendall from BBC Series by Maurice Moiseivitch. With Richard Goolden, Vic Oliver.

Meet my Sister Pathé at Welwyn (A). Pathé, 7.33 (6,200). p: supervisor Freddie Watts, d: John Daumery, c: Jack Parker, des: Ian Campbell-Gray. With Clifford Mollison, Constance Shotter.

Meet the Duchess See **Irish for Luck**

Melody and Romance Brit. Lion at Beaconsfield (U). Brit. Lion, 12.37 (6,390). d: Maurice Elvey, c: George Stretton, sc: L. du Garde Peach, Maurice Elvey from story by L. H. Gordon, ed: Charles Saunders. With Hughie Green and his Gang, Margaret Lockwood.

Melody Maker, The WB-FN at Teddington (U). FN, 3.33 (5,098). p: Irving Asher, d: Leslie Hiscott. With Joan Marion, Lester Matthews.

Melody of Fate See **Hate Ship, The**

Melody of my Heart Incorporated Talking Films at Cricklewood (A). Butcher's, 4.36 (7,456). p: Brandon Fleming, d: Wilfred Noy, c: Jack Parker, sc; from story by Brandon Fleming, London Philharmonic Orchestra, Convent Garden Chorus. With Derek Oldham, Lorraine La Fosse.

Member of the Jury Fox Brit. at Wembley (A). Fox, 3.37 (5,597). d: Bernard Mainwaring, c: Ronald Neame, sc: David Evans from novel by John Millard. With Ellis Irving, Marjorie Hume.

Menace See **Sabotage**

Men Are Not Gods LFP at Denham (A). UA, 11.36 (8,105). p: Alexander Korda, d: Walter Reisch, c: Charles Rosher, Robert Krasker, sc: Iris Wright, G. B. Stern from story by Walter Reisch, des: Vincent Korda, cost: Rene Hubert, ed: William Hornbeck, Henry Cornelius, sd: A. W. Watkins, sp. effects: Ned Mann, MD: Muir Mathieson, music based on 'Othello' suite by Samuel Coleridge-Taylor. With Miriam Hopkins, Gertrude Lawrence, Rex Harrison, Sebastian Shaw.

Men Like These BIP (U). Wardour, 11.31 (4,000). d: Walter Summers, c: Jack Parker, Horace Wheddon, sc: Walter Summers, Walter Mycroft from their own story, des: John Mead, James A. Marchant, ed: Leslie Norman, sd: Alex Murray, RN. advisers: Capt. K. Bruce, Lt-Com. John L. F. Hunt, Lt-Com. E. V. Hume-Spry. With John Batten, Syd Crossley.

Men of Steel Langham Productions at Walton (U). UA, 9.32 (6,449). p: Bray Wyndham, d: George King, c: Geoffrey Faithfull, sc: Edward Knoblock, Billie Bristow from story by Douglas Newton, des: W. G. Saunders. With Franklin Dyall, John Stuart, Heather Angel, Benita Hume.

Men of Tomorrow LFP at Elstree B & D, Oxford (U). Paramt, 10.32 (8,000). p: Alexander Korda, d: Leontine Sagan, Zoltan Korda, c: Phil Tannura, Bernard Browne, sc: Anthony Gibbs, Arthur Wimperis, Leontine Sagan from novel by Anthony Gibbs, *Young Apollo,* des: Vincent Korda, ed: Stephen Harrison. With Maurice Braddell, Emlyn Williams, Joan Gardner, Merle Oberon.

Men of Yesterday UK Films at Shepperton (U). AP & D, 5.36 (7,350). p: John Barter, d: John Baxter, sc: W. G. Elliott, Jack Francis. With Stewart Rome, Sir George Robey, Will Fyffe, Ella Shields.

Men without Honour Bernard Smith and Widgey Newman (A). Equity British, 3.39 (5.225). p: Bernard Smith, d: Widgey Newman, sc: G. A. Cooper. With Ian Fleming.

Merely Mr. Hawkins George Smith Productions (U). RKO-Radio, 1.38 (6,589). d: P. Maclean Rogers, sc: from story by John Hunter. With Eliot Makeham, Sybil Grove.

Merry Comes to Town Embassy Pictures at Shepperton (U). Sound City Dist. 5.37 (7,127, later 6,309). p: d: George King, c: Hone Glendinning, sc: Brock Williams from story by Evadne Price, des: Jack Hallward. With ZaSu Pitts, Guy Newall, Betty Ann Davies.

Merry Men of Sherwood, The Delta Pictures at Bushey (U). (1) Filmophone, 9.32, (2) Universal, 3.34 (3,369). d: Widgey Newman, c: D. P. Cooper. With John Thompson, Aileen Marson.

Michael and Mary Gainsborough at Islington (A). Ideal, 10.31 (7,619) FT RCA. p: Michael Balcon, d: Victor Saville, c: Leslie Rowson, sc: Victor Saville, Angus MacPhail, Robert Stevenson from play by A. A. Milne (1930), dial: Monckton Hoffe, des: Vetchinsky, cost: Gordon Conway, ed: Ian Dalrymple, John Goldman, sd: George Gunn, MD: Louis Levy. With Edna Best, Herbert Marshall.

Midas Touch, The WB-FN at Teddington (A). FN, Screened 9.39 (6,174). exec. p: Sam Sax, d: David MacDonald, c: Basil Emmott, sc: from novel by Margaret Kennedy, des: Norman Arnold. With Barry K. Barnes, Judy Kelly.

Middle Watch, The BIP at Elstree (U). Wardour, 10.30 (10,235) FT RCA. d: Norman Walker, c: J. J. Cox, sc: Norman Walker, Frank Launder from play by Ian Hay and Stephen King-Hall (1929), des: John Mead, ed: Sam Simmonds, Émile de Ruelle, sc: C. V. Thornton, Naval adviser Lt-Commander E. Donaldson. With Owen Nares, Dodo Watts, Jacqueline Logan, Fred Volpe.

Middle Watch, The ABPC at Welwyn (U). ABPC, 12.39 (7,038). p: Walter Mycroft, d: Thomas Bentley, sc: Lee Thompson, Clifford Grey from play by Ian Hay and Stephen King-Hall (1929), des: Charles Gilbert. With Jack Buchanan, Greta Gynt.

Midnight George King at Walton (U). Fox, 1.31 (3,986). p: Harry Cohen, d: George King, sc: Harry Fowler Mear. With John Stuart, Eve Gray.

Midnight at Madame Tussaud's Premier Sound Film Productions at Highbury (A). Paramt, 12.36 (6,008). p: James Edwards, d: George Pearson, sc: Roger MacDougall from screen story by James Edwards and Roger MacDougall. With James Carew, Lydia Sherwood, Lucille Lisle.

Midnight Mail See **Spider, The**

Midnight Menace Grosvenor Sound Films at Pinewood, exteriors at Elstree B & D (A). ABFD, 1.37 (7,042). p: Harcourt Templeman, d: Sinclair Hill, c: Cyril Bristow, sc: G. H. Moresby-White, dial: D. B. Wyndham-Lewis from story by Roger MacDougall, Alexander Mackendrick, ed: Michael Hankinson. With Charles Farrell, Fritz Kortner, Margaret Vyner.

Midshipmaid, The G-B at Shepherd's Bush (U). W & F, 12.32 (7,552). p: Michael Balcon, d: Albert de Courville, sc: Stafford Dickens from play by Ian Hay and Stephen King-Hall (1931). With Jessie Matthews, Nigel Bruce, John Mills.

Midshipman Easy ATP at Ealing (U). ABFD, 10.35 (6,897). p: Basil Dean, assoc. p: Thorold Dickinson, d: Carol Reed, dial. d: Tyrone Guthrie, c: John Boyle, sc: Anthony Kimmins from novel by Captain Marryat, *Mr. Midshipman Easy*, des: Edward Carrick, ed: Sidney Cole, sd: Eric Williams, MD: Ernest Irving, music Frederick Austin. With Hughie Green, Roger Livesey, Margaret Lockwood, Desmond Tester.

Mikado, The G & S Films at Pinewood (U). GFD, 1.39 (8,154 later, 8,767, 7,900, 8,932, 8,065). Technicolor (colour direction Natalie Kalmus). p: Geoffrey Toye, assoc. p: Josef Somlo, d: Victor Schertzinger, unit d: Thorold Dickinson, c: Bernard Knowles, Jack Hildyard, Cyril Knowles, Tech. lighting expert: W. Skall, sc: Geoffrey Toye from opera by Gilbert and Sullivan, des: Ralph Brinton, designer Marcel Vertes, ed: Philip Charlot, sd: Leslie Murray, conductor Geoffrey Toye with London Symphony Orchestra, chorus of the D'Oyly Carte Opera Company. With Jean Colin, Kenny Baker, Martyn Green.

Milky Way, The See **King of Paris, The**

Millionaire Pauper, The See **Mr. Quincy of Monte Carlo**

Millions Herbert Wilcox (U). GFD, 9.36 (6,340). p: Herbert Wilcox, d: Leslie Hiscott, c: Freddie Young, sc: from screen story by Michael Barringer, des: L. P. Williams. With Gordon Harker, Frank Pettingell, Richard Hearne, Jane Carr.

Mill on the Floss, The Morgan Productions at Shepperton (A). NPFD, 12.36 (8,581). p: John Clein, d: Tim Whelan, c: John Stumar, Hone Glendinning, sc: Garnett Weston, Austin Melford, Tim Whelan, dial: John Drinkwater from novel by George Eliot, des: D. W. L. Daniels, cost: Mlle Segalla and Bermans, Ltd, ed: C. Williamson, sd: M. R. Cruickshank, MD: Colin Wark. With Frank Lawton, Victoria Hopper, James Mason, Geraldine Fitzgerald.

Mimi BIP at Elstree (A). Wardour, 3.35 (8,600). p: Walter Mycroft, d: Paul L. Stein, c: J. J. Cox, sc: Clifford Grey, Jack Davies, Denis Waldock, adapt: Paul Merzbach from play by Henri Murger, *La Vie de Bohème* (1849) based on his sketches of 1848, des: Cedric Dawe, ed: Leslie Norman, sd: B. Cook, MD: Idris Lewis, music Puccini, G. H. Clutsam. With Douglas Fairbanks Jr, Gertrude Lawrence.

Mind of Mr. Reeder, The Jack Raymond Productions at Highbury (U). Grand. Nat., 2.39 (6,817). p: Charles Q. Steel, d: Jack Raymond, c: George Stretton, sc: Bryan Wallace, Marjorie Gaffney, Michael Hogan from *Mr. Reeder* stories by Edgar Wallace, des: James Carter. With Will Fyffe, John Warwick, Kay Walsh.

Minstrel Boy, The Dreadnought Films at Elstree former Whitehall (A). Butcher's, 8.37 (7,185). p: d: Sidney Morgan, sc:

Joan Wentworth Wood. With Fred Conyngham, Chili Bouchier.

Miracles Do Happen G. S. Ent. at Worton Hall between 29.12.38 and 7.1.39, also called **No More Cows** and **It's No Use Crying.** Not registered at the time. p: George Smith, d: P. Maclean Rogers, c: Geoffrey Faithfull, s: Kathleen Butler from story by Con West, Jack Marks, *No More Cows,* des: R. Holmes Paul. With Jack Hobbs, Bruce Seton, Marjorie Taylor.

Mischief B & D at Elstree B & D (A). W & F, 12.31 (6,121). p: Herbert Wilcox, d: Jack Raymond, sc: W. P. Lipscomb, P. Maclean Rogers from play by Ben Travers (1928). With Ralph Lynn, Winifred Shotter.

Missing – Believed Married B & D-Para-Brit. at Pinewood (A). Paramt, 9.37 (5,938). p: Anthony Havelock-Allan, d: John Paddy Carstairs, c: Francis Carver, sc: from screen story by A. R. Rawlinson. With Wally Patch, Julien Vedey, Hazel Terry.

Missing from Home See **Missing – Believed Married**

Missing People, The Jack Raymond Productions at Highbury (A). Grand. Nat., 5.39 (6,322). p: Charles Q. Steel, d: Jack Raymond, c: George Stretton, sc: Lydia Hayward from *Mr. Reeder* stories by Edgar Wallace. With Will Fyffe, Kay Walsh, Lyn Harding.

Missing Rembrandt, The Twick. at Twickenham (U). PDC, 2.32 (7,586). p: Julius Hagen, d: Leslie Hiscott, c: Basil Emmott, sc: H. Fowler Mear and Cyril Twyford from story by Sir Arthur Conan Doyle, *The Adventure of Charles Augustus Milverton.* With Arthur Wontner, Ian Fleming, Miles Mander.

Mistaken Identity Venture Films, in production at Isleworth 7.39. p: Alfred d'Eyncourt, Desmond Tew, d: Walter Tennyson, c: Gerald Gibbs, sc: Ian Walker. With Richard Goolden.

Mitey Man, A See **Where's George?**

Mixed Doubles B & D-Para-Brit. at Elstree B & D (A). Paramt, 9.33 (6,208). d: Sidney Morgan, sc: Joan Wentworth Wood from play by Frank Stayton (1925). With Jeanne de Casalis, Frederick Lloyd.

Monday at Ten See **Money Mad**

Money by Wire See **Get off my Foot**

Money for Nothing BIP at Elstree (U). Pathé 1.32 (6,569). d: Monty Banks, c: J. J. Cox, sc: Victor Kendall from story by Sir Seymour Hicks. With Sir Seymour Hicks, Betty Stockfield, Edmund Gwenn.

Money for Nothing (1939) See **Blind Folly**

Money for Speed Hall Mark at Wembley (A). UA, 3.33 (6,639). d: Bernard Vorhaus, c: Eric Cross, sc: Vera Allinson, Lionel Hale, Monica Ewer from story by Bernard Vorhaus. With John Loder, Ida Lupino.

Money in the Air See **Radio Pirates**

Money Mad Champion Productions at Isleworth (A). M-G-M, 9.34 (6,052). p: Basil Humphreys, d: Frank A. Richardson, sc; Frank A. Richardson, Selwyn Jepson from story by Selwyn Jepson, des: J. Elder Wills. With Virginia Cherrill, Garry Marsh.

Money Means Nothing B & D-Para-Brit. at Elstree B & D (U). Paramt, 8.32 (6,314). p: Herbert Wilcox, d: Harcourt Templeman, c: C. Van Enger, sc: Miles Malleson, Harcourt Templeman from story by Douglas Furber. With John Loder.

Money Talks BIP (U). Wardour, 11.32 (6,553). d: Norman Lee, c: Walter Harvey, sc: Norman Lee, Frank Miller, Edwin Greenwood, MD: Idris Lewis. With Julian Rose, Kid Berg, Judy Kelly.

Moonlight Sonata Pall Mall at Denham (U). UA, 2.37 (8,114 later 7,795). p: d: Lothar Mendes, c: Jan Stallich, sc: Edward Knoblock, add. dial: E. M. Delafield from story by Hans Rameau, des: Laurence Irving, ed: Philip Charlot, sd: C. M. Medlen. With Jan Paderewski, Marie Tempest, Charles Farrell.

Moorland Terror, The See **Road to Fortune, The**

Moorland Tragedy, A GEM Productions at Shepperton (U). Equity British, 3.33 (3,625). p: Hayford Hobbs, d: M. A. Wetherell, c: Sidney Eaton, sc: Allen Francis from *Man in the Corner* stories by Baroness Orczy. With Haddon Mason, Barbara Coombes.

Morals of Marcus, The Real Art at Twickenham (A). G-B D, 3.35 (6,902). p: Julius Hagen, d: Miss Mander, c: Sydney Blythe, sc: H. Fowler Mear, Miles Mander from play by W. J. Locke (1906) based on his novel *The Morals of Marcus Ordeyne*. With Ian Hunter, Lupe Velez.

Morita Patrick K. Heale (U). Britivox, 1.31, 3 reels. p: sc: Patrick K. Heale, d: Fred Paul.

Moscow Nights LFP and Capitol at Isleworth, exteriors at Denham (A). GFD, 11.35 (6,746). p: Alexis Granowsky, exec. p: Alexander Korda, d: Anthony Asquith, c: Philip Tannura, sc: Eric Siepmann and Anthony Asquith from unpublished novel by Pierrre Benoit and French film *Les Nuits Muscovites,* des: Vincent Korda, cost: John Armstrong, ed: William Hornbeck, Francis Lyon. With Harry Baur, Penelope Dudley Ward, Laurence Olivier.

Mountain, The Jackatoon Productions in Morecambe (U). Equity British, registered 3.35 (7,350). d: Travis Jackson. With Maurice Jones.

Mountains o' Mourne Rembrandt Film Productions and Butcher's at Walton (U). Butcher's, 4.38 (7,500). d: Harry Hughes, c: Geoffrey Faithfull, sc: Gerald Brosnan from story by Daisy L. Fielding, des: R. Holmes Paul, ed: Cecil Williamson. With Niall MacGinnis, Rene Ray.

Mr. Bill The Conqueror BIP at Elstree, Sussex (U). Pathé, 5.32 (7,855). d: Norman Walker, c: Claude Friese-Greene, sc: Dion Titheradge from his own book, des: John Mead, ed: Sam Simmonds, sd: C. V. Thornton, A. D. Valentine, MD: Idris Lewis. With Heather Angel, Henry Kendall, Nora Swinburne.

Mr. Cinders BIP at Elstree (U). Wardour, 10.34 (6,440). p: Walter Mycroft, d: Fred Zelnik, c: Otto Kanturek, sc: Clifford Grey, Frank Miller from play by Frank Miller and Greatrex Newman (1929), add. dial: the Western Brothers, des: Duncan Sutherland, ed: Sidney Cole, sd: A. Ross, MD: Harry Acres, music and lyrics Vivian Ellis, Clifford Grey. With Clifford Mollison, Zelma O'Neal, Western Brothers.

Mr. Cohen Takes a Walk WB-FN at Teddington (U). FN, 12.35 (7,300). p: Irving Asher, d: William Beaudine, c: Basil Emmott, sc: Brock Williams from novel by Mary Roberts Rinehart, des: Peter Proud. With Paul Graetz, Chili Bouchier, Violet Farebrother.

Mr. Quincy of Monte Carlo WB-FN at Teddington (U). FN, 1.33 (4,856). p: Irving Asher, d: John Daumery, sc: Brock Williams. With John Stuart, Rosemary Ames.

Mr. Nobody British Screen Classics (U). Fox, 1.30 (4,941) silent. d: Frank Miller, sc: Eric Strang. With Frank Stanmore, Pauline Johnson.

Mr. Penny takes the Air See **Meet Mr. Penny**

Mr. Reeder in Room 13 Brit. Nat. at Welwyn (A). ABPC, 1.38 (7,023). p: John Corfield, d: Norman Lee, sc: Doreen Montgomery, Victor Kendall, Elizabeth Meehan from novel by Edgar Wallace. With Gibb McLaughlin, Peter Murray-Hill, Sally Gray.

Mr. Satan WB-FN at Teddington (A). FN, 1.38 (7,192). d: Arthur Woods, c: Robert Lapresle, sc: J. O. C. Orton, John Meehan Jr, des: Peter Proud, Michael Relph, ed: Terence Fisher, sd: W. S. Nunn. With Chili Bouchier, Skeets Gallagher.

Mrs. Dane's Defence National Talkies at Wembley (A). Paramt. 11.33 (6,005). p: Harry Rowson, d: A. V. Bramble, sc: Lydia Hayward from play by Henry Arthur Jones (1900). With Joan Barry, Basil Gill.

Mr. Smith Carries On B & D-Para-Brit.

at Pinewood (U). Paramt, 9.37 (6,186). p: Anthony Havelock-Allan, d: Lister Laurence, c: Ernest Palmer, sc: Ronald Gow from story by John Cousins, Stephen Clarkson. With Edward Rigby.

Mrs. Pym of Scotland Yard Hurley Productions at Highbury (A). Grand. Nat., 11.39 (5,850). p: Victor Katona, d: Fred Elles, c: Bryan Langley, sc: Fred Elles and Peggy Barwell from novel by Nigel Morland. With Mary Clare, Nigel Patrick, Anthony Ireland.

Mr. Stringfellow Says 'No' Incorporated Talking Films at Shepperton (U). NPFD, 4.37 (6,790). p: Brandon Fleming, d: Randall Faye, c: Ernest Palmer, sc: from story by Brandon Fleming and Randall Faye. With Neil Hamilton, Claude Dampier.

Mr. Walker Wants to Know See **What Would You Do, Chums?**

Mr. What's His Name WB-FN at Teddington (A). FN, 4.35 (6,057). p: Irving Asher, d: Ralph Ince, c: Basil Emmott, sc: Frank Launder, Tom Geraghty from play by Sir Seymour Hicks (1927) adapted from French play by Yves Mirande, des: Peter Proud, sd: Leslie Murray. With Sir Seymour Hicks, Olive Blakeney, Enid Stamp-Taylor.

Mummers, The See **Oh, What a Duchess!**

Murder BIP at Elstree (A). Wardour, 8.30 (9,700) FT RCA. p: John Maxwell, d: Alfred Hitchcock, c: J. J. Cox, sc: Alfred Hitchcock, Walter Mycroft, Alma Reville from novel by Clemence Dane and play by Clemence Dane and Helen Simpson, *Enter Sir John,* des: John Mead, Peter Proud, ed: Émile de Ruelle, René Harrison, sd: C. V. Thornton, MD: John Reynders. With Herbert Marshall, Esme Percy, Norah Baring, Phyllis Konstam, Edward Chapman. (Bilingual.)

Murder at Covent Garden Twick. at Twickenham (A). W & F, 2.32 (6,000). p: Julius Hagen, d: Leslie Hiscott, Michael Barringer, sc: H. Fowler Mear, Michael Barringer from play by W. J. Makin. With Anne Grey, Dennis Neilson-Terry.

Murder at Monte Carlo WB-FN at Teddington (A). FN, 1.35 (6,331). p: Irving Asher, d: Ralph Ince, sc: Michael Barringer, John Hastings Turner from novel by Tom van Dyke. With Errol Flynn, Eve Gray, Paul Graetz.

Murder at the Cabaret MB Productions (A). Paramt, 12.36 (6,003). p: Reginald Fogwell, Nell Emerald, d: sc: Reginald Fogwell. With Phyllis Robins.

Murder at the Inn WB-FN at Teddington (A). WB, 2.34 (5,015). p: Irving Asher, d: George King, sc: Randall Faye.

Murder Auction, The See **Body Vanishes, The**

Murder by Rope B & D-Para-Brit. at Shepperton (A). Paramt, 8.36 (5,862). d: George Pearson, c: Ernest Palmer, sc: from story by Ralph Neale. With Constance Godridge, D. A. Clarke-Smith.

Murder in the Stalls See **Not Wanted on Voyage**

Murder in Soho ABPC at Elstree (A). ABPC, 2.39 (6,346). p: Walter Mycroft, d: Norman Lee, c: Claude Friese-Greene, sc: F. McGrew Willis, des: John Mead. With Jack La Rue, Sandra Storme, Bernard Lee, Googie Withers.

Murder in the Family Fox Brit. at Wembley (A). 20th Century-Fox, 2.38 (6,823). d: Al Parker, c: Ronald Neame, sc: David Evans from story by James Ronald, des: Carmen Dillon, ed: Peter Tanner. With Jessica Tandy, Barry Jones.

Murder on the Second Floor WB-FN at Teddington (A). FN, 1.32 (6,266). p: Irving Asher, d: William McGann, c: W. Van Enger, sc: Roland Pertwee, from play by Frank Vosper (1929), sd: George Groves. With Pat Paterson, John Longden.

Murder Pact See **Riverside Murder**

Murder Party See **Night of the Party**

Murder Tomorrow Crusade at Cricklewood (A). Paramt, 2.38 (6,254). p: Victor M. Greene, d: Donovan Pedelty, c: Ernest Palmer, sc: Frank Harvey from his own play (1937). Jack Livesey, Gwenllian Gill.

Murder Will Out WB-FN at Teddington (A). FN, 7.39 (5,926). exec. p: Sam Sax, d: Roy William Neill, c: Basil Emmott, sc: Austin Melford, Brock Williams, Derek Twist. With John Loder, Jane Baxter, Jack Hawkins.

Museum Mystery B & D-Para-Brit. at Pinewood (U). Paramt, 4.37 (6,226). p: Anthony Havelock-Allan, d: Clifford Gulliver, c: Francis Carver, sc: W. G. Elliott from his own story, des: Wilfred Arnold. With Jock McKay, Elizabeth Inglis.

Museum Peace See **Museum Mystery**

Musical Beauty Shop, The PDC (U). PDC, 3.30 (3,126). p: Andre Charlot, d: Monty Banks. With Leonard Henry.

Music and Mystery See **Singing Cop, The**

Music Hall Real Art at Twickenham (U). Radio, 6.34 (6,715, later 6,568) p: Julius Hagen, d: John Baxter, c: Sydney Blythe, Ernest Palmer, sc: Wallace Orton, H. Fowler Mear from story by John Baxter, des: James Carter, ed: Michael Chorlton, Lister Laurence, sd: Baynham Honri, MD: W. L. Trytel. With George Carney.

Music Hall Parade Butcher's at Walton (U). Butcher's 6.39 (7,300). d: Oswald Mitchell, c: Geoffrey Faithfull, sc: Con West, des: R. Holmes Paul, ed: Dan Birt, sd: Hal Fuller. With Glen Raynham, Richard Norris.

Music Hath Charms BIP at Welwyn (U). Wardour, 10.35 (6,350). p: Walter Mycroft, d: Alexander Esway, Walter Summers, c: Horace Wheddon, J. J. Cox, Otto Kanturek, Bryan Langley, sc: L. du Garde Peach, Jack Davies, des: Clarence Elder, Duncan Sutherland, Cedric Dawe, ed: J. Corbett, music arranged Benjamin Frankel, BBC Dance Orchestra, music Henry Hall, Mabel Wayne, Desmond Carter, Collie Knox. With Henry Hall.

Music Maker, The Inspiration Films (U). M-G-M, 3.36 (4,840). p: d: sc: Horace Shepherd ('Hugh Kaus'). London Philharmonic Orchestra. With Arthur Young, Violet Loxley.

Mutiny of the Elsinore, The Argyle-British Productions at Welwyn (A). ABPC, 9.37 (7,018). p: John Argyle, p: supervisor Walter Summers, d: Roy Lockwood, c: Bryan Langley, sc: Walter Summers, Beaufoy Milton from novel by Jack London, des: Duncan Sutherland, ed: F. H. Bickerton. With Paul Lukas, Lyn Harding.

My Friend, The King Film Engineering at Walton (U). Fox, 9.31 (4,243). p: Jerome Jackson, d: Michael Powell, c: Geoffrey Faithfull, sc: Michael Powell, J. Jefferson Farjeon, des: W. G. Saunders, ed: A. Seabourne. With Jerry Verno, Luli Hohenberg.

My Heart Is Calling G-B and Cine-Allianz Tonfilm at Beaconsfield (U). G-B D, 1.35 (7,459). p: Arnold Pressburger, assoc. p: Ivor Montagu, d: Carmine Gallone, c: Glen MacWilliams, sc: Richard Benson, Sidney Gilliat, Robert Edmunds from story by Ernst Marischka, des: John Harman, ed: Ralph Kemplen, sd: Harold King, MD: Louis Levy, songs Robert Stolz, lyrics T. Connor, Harry S. Pepper. With Jan Kiepura, Marta Eggerth, Sonnie Hale. (Joint production based on French and German versions made in Germany; made in Britain but registered as foreign film.)

My Heart Is Calling You See **My Heart Is Calling**

My Heart's Desire See **Heart's Desire**

My Irish Molly Argyle-British Productions at Welwyn (U). ABPC, 12.38 (6,300). p: John Argyle, d: Alex Bryce, c: Ernest Palmer, sc: Alex Bryce, Ian Walker, add. dial: W. G. Fay, from story by John Argyle, des: Duncan Sutherland, ed: F. H. Bickerton, sd: A. E. Rudolph, MD: Guy Jones. With Binkie Stuart, Tom Burke, Maureen O'Hara.

My Lord the Chauffeur British Screen Classics (U). Fox, 1.30 – made in 1927 (5,320) silent. d: B. E. Doxat-Pratt, sc: J. Hellier. With Kim Peacock.

My Lucky Star Masquerader Productions (U). W & F, 6.33 (5,750). p: Louis Blattner, d: Louis Blattner, John Harlow, lyrics Anona Winn. With Oscar Asche, Florence Desmond, Harold Huth.

My Old China Gainsborough (U). Ideal, 8.31 (3,237). p: Michael Balcon, d: W. P. Kellino, sc: Angus MacPhail. With Clifford Heatherley.

My Old Duchess See **Oh, What a Duchess!**

My Old Dutch Gainsborough at Islington (U). G-B D, 9.34 (7,552). assoc. p: Ivor Montagu, d: Sinclair Hill, c: Leslie Rowson, sc: Bryan Wallace, Marjorie Gaffney, Michael Hogan from music-hall sketch by Albert Chevalier and Arthur Shirley. With Betty Balfour, Gordon Harker.

My Song for You G-B and Cine-Allianz Tonfilm at Shepherd's Bush (U). G-B D, 7.34 (7,960). assoc. p: Jerome Jackson, d: Maurice Elvey, c: Charles Van Enger, sc: Richard Benson, Austin Melford, Robert Edmunds from Joe May's German film *Ein Lied für Dich* (1933) by Ernst Marischka, Irma von Cube, des: Alfred Junge, cost: Berleo, ed: Charles Frend, sd: Philip Dorté, MD: Louis Levy, add: music Mischa Spoliansky, lyrics Frank Eyton. With Jan Kiepura, Sonnie Hale, Emlyn Williams, Aileen Marson. (Joint production based on German film made by Joe May; made in Britain, with Riviera locations, but registered as foreign film.)

My Song Goes round the World BIP at Elstree (U). Wardour, 9.34 (6,050). p: d: Richard Oswald, c: R. Kuntze, sc: Clifford Grey, Frank Miller from story by Ernst Neubach, des: David Rawnsley, ed: Walter Stokvis, sd: B. Cook MD: Idris Lewis, music Hans May. With Joseph Schmidt, Charlotte Anders, John Loder.

Mystery of the Loch, The See **Secret of the Loch, The**

Mystery of the Mary Celeste, The Hammer Productions (A). GFD, 11.35 (7,261). p: H. Fraser Passmore, d: Denison Clift. With Bela Lugosi, Shirley Grey, Arthur Margetson.

My Wife's Family BIP at Elstree (A). Wardour, 6.31 (7,265) FT RCA. d: Monty Banks, c: Claude Friese-Greene, sc: Val Valentine, Fred Duprez from play by Hal Stevens and Harry B. Linton, as revised by Fred Duprez and Norman Lee (1931), des: John Mead, ed: A. C. Hammond, sd: C. V. Thornton. With Gene Gerrard, Muriel Angelus.

Narkover See **Boys Will Be Boys**

Natacha See **Moscow Nights**

Naughty Cinderella WB-FN at Teddington (U). WB, 1.33 (5,068). p: Irving Asher, d: John Daumery, sc: Randall Faye from story by W. Scott Darling. With John Stuart, Winna Winfried.

Naughty Husbands Geoffrey Benstead Films (A). Geoffrey Benstead, 1.30 (5,700) silent. p: d: sc: Geoffrey Benstead. James Reardon.

Navvy, The See **Real Bloke, A**

Navy Eternal See **Our Fighting Navy**

Nell Gwyn B & D at Elstree B & D (A). UA, 8.34 (6,811). p: d: Herbert Wilcox, c: Freddie Young, sc: Miles Malleson, historical adviser Tom Heslewood, des: L. P. Williams, cost: Doris Zinkeisen, ed: Merrill White, sd: L. E. Overton, MD: Philip Braham. With Anna Neagle, Sir Cedric Hardwicke.

Nelson Touch, The See **His Lordship**

Never Come Back See **Just Smith**

Never Go Home See **Irish and Proud of It**

Never Touched Me! See **Feather Your Nest**

Never Trouble Trouble Lupino Lane Productions and PDC at Cricklewood (U). PDC, 3.31 (6,775) FT Visatone. d: Lupino Lane, sc: George Dewhurst from story by Lauri Wylie. With Lupino Lane, Renee Clama, Jack Hobbs, Wallace Lupino.

New Car, The See **His First Car**

New Hotel, The PDC at Cricklewood (U). PDC, 3.32 (4,513). d: Bernerd Mainwaring, music Marc Anthony, lyrics Bruce Sievier. With Norman Long.

New Waiter, The PDC (U). PDC, 2.30 (3,582) FT, songs. p: Andre Charlot, d: Monty Banks. With Rebla, Leonard Henry.

New Year's Eve See **Indiscretions of Eve, The**

Nick's Knickers G & S Films (U). Gannon and Scarborow, registered 2.30 (3,768). d: Wilf Gannon. With Wilf Gannon.

Night Alone Welwyn Studios at Welwyn (A). Pathé, 7.38 (6,865). p: Warwick Ward, d: Thomas Bentley, c: Bryan Langley, sc: Victor Kendall, Vernon Clancey from play by Jeffrey Dell (1937). With Leonora Corbett, Emlyn Williams, Lesley Brook.

Night Birds BIP at Elstree (A). Wardour, 10.30 (8,761) FT RCA. p: d: Richard Eichberg, sc: Victor Kendall, Miles Malleson. With Jameson Thomas, Jack Raine, Muriel Angelus. (Bilingual film.)

Night Club Queen, The Twick. at Twickenham (A). Universal, 3.34 (7,970). p: Julius Hagen, d: Bernard Vorhaus, sc: Anthony Kimmins from his play (1933), des: James Carter. With Mary Clare, Lewis Casson.

Night in Montmartre, A Gainsborough at Twickenham (A). Gaumont, 7.31 (6,227) FT RCA. p: Michael Balcon, d: Leslie Hiscott, c: Sydney Blythe, sc: Angus MacPhail from play by Miles Malleson and Walter Peacock (1926). With Franklin Dyall, Hugh Williams, Heather Angel.

Night Journey Brit. Nat. at Walton (A). Butcher's, 1.39 (6,900). p: John Corfield, d: Oswald Mitchell, Bernard Willis, c: Geoffrey Faithfull, sc: Jim Phelan and Maisie Sharman from novel by Jim Phelan, *Ten-a-penny People*, des: R. Holmes Paul, ed: Dug Myers. With Geoffrey Toone, Patricia Hilliard.

Night like This, A B & D at Elstree B & D (U). W & F, 3.32 (6,600). p: Herbert Wilcox, d: Tom Walls, c: Freddie Young, sc: from play by Ben Travers (1930), music arranged Lew Stone, played by Roy Fox and his Band. With Tom Walls, Ralph Lynn, Robertson Hare, Wininfred Shotter, Mary Brough.

Night Mail Brit. Lion at Beaconsfield (A). M-G-M, 5.35 (4,935). p: d: Herbert Smith, c: Alex Bryce, sc: Billie Bristow, Charles Bennett. With Richard Bird, Henry Oscar, Hope Davy.

Night of the Garter B & D at Elstree B & D (A). UA, 4.33 (7,751). p: Herbert Wilcox, d: Jack Raymond, c: Freddie Young, sc: Austin Melford, Marjorie Gaffney from play by Austin Melford (1932) based on farce by Wilson Collison and Avery Hopwood, *Getting Gertie's Garter*, des: A. L. Mazzei. With Sydney Howard, Winifred Shotter, Elsie Randolph.

Night of the Party G-B at Shepherd's Bush (A). G-B D, 2.34 (5,658). assoc. p: Jerome Jackson, d: Michael Powell, c: Glen MacWilliams, sc: Ralph Smart from play by Roland Pertwee and John Hastings Turner, des: Alfred Junge. With Leslie Banks, Ian Hunter, Jane Baxter.

Night Porter, The G-B at Shepherd's Bush (U). Ideal, 3.30 (4.073). p: L'Estrange Fawcett, d: Sewell Collins, sc: L'Estrange Fawcett and Sewell Collins from music hall sketch. With Donald Calthrop, Trilby Clark.

Night Ride B & D-Para-Brit. at Pinewood, Great North Road (U). Paramt, 6.37 (6,489). p: Anthony Havelock-Allan, d: John Paddy Carstairs, sc: Ralph Bettinson from story by Julian Vedey. With Julian Vedey, Jimmy Hanley, Wally Patch.

Nine Days Blunder see **Cross Currents**

Nine Forty-Five WB-FN at Teddington (A). WB, 4.34 (5,308). p: Irving Asher, d: George King, sc: Brock Williams from play by Owen Davis and Sewell Collins, *9.45* (1925). With Binnie Barnes, Donald Calthrop.

Nine Till Six ATP at Ealing (A). Radio, 3.32 (6,828), p: d: Basil Dean, unit p. man: Robert Cullen, c: Robert Martin, Robert de Grasse, sc: Alma Reville, John Paddy Carstairs, add. dial:

Beverley Nichols from play by Aimée and Philip Stuart (1930), des: Clifford Pember, cost: La Rue, ed: Otto Ludwig, sd: Marcus Cooper, MD: Ernest Irving. With Elizabeth Allan, Richard Bird, Louise Hampton.

Nipper, The See **Brat, The**

No Escape WB-FN at Teddington (A). WB, 6.34 (6,295). p: Irving Asher, d: Ralph Ince, sc: W. Scott Darling. With Ian Hunter, Binnie Barnes, Ralph Ince.

No Escape Welwyn Studios at Welwyn (A). Pathé, 11.36 (7,500). d: Norman Lee, c: Bryan Langley, sc: from play by George Goodchild and Frank Witty, *No Exit* (1936), des: Cedric Dawe, ed: Lionel Tomlinson, sd: Frank Midgley. With Valerie Hobson, Billy Milton.

No Escape (1937) See **Secret Lives**

No Exit See **No Escape** (1936)

No Exit Warner Brothers at Welwyn (U). Warner Brothers, 7.30 (6,375) synchronised, Vocalion. d: Charles Saunders, c: Henry Harris, sc: Charles Saunders, music Paul Mulder. With John Stuart, Muriel Angelus.

No Funny Business John Stafford Productions at Elstree (A). UA, 3.33 (6,863). p: John Stafford, d: W. Victor Hanbury, John Stafford, c: Walter Blakeley, sc: W. Victor Hanbury, Frank Vosper from story by Dorothy Hope, des: Duncan Sutherland, ed: E. B. Jarvis, sd: C. V. Thornton, MD: Ernest Broadhurst, music Noel Gay, lyrics Clifford Grey, Desmond Carter, Noel Gay. With Laurence Olivier, Gertrude Lawrence, Jill Esmond, Frank Vosper.

No Lady G-B at Shepherd's Bush, Blackpool (U). Gaumont, 5.31 (6,474). p: L'Estrange Fawcett, d: Lupino Lane, c: Percy Strong, sc: Lupino Lane, Bert Lee, R. P. Weston from story by George Dewhurst, L'Estrange Fawcett, des: A. L. Mazzei, ed: R. E. Dearing, sd: S. A. Jolly, MD: Louis Levy, Herman Darewski and his Orchestra. With Lupino Lane, Sari Maritza, Lola Hunt.

No Limit ATP at Ealing, Isle of Man (U). ABFD, 10.35 (7,304). p: Basil Dean, d: Monty Banks, c: Robert Martin, sc:

Gordon Wellesley, Tom Geraghty from story by Walter Greenwood, des: J. Elder Wills, ed: Jack Kitchin, music Ord Hamilton and his Twentieth Century Band, songs Harry Parr-Davies, Harry Gifford, Fred E. Cliffe. With George Formby, Florence Desmond.

No Monkey Business Radius at Elstree B & D (U). GFD, 11.35 (7,051). p: Julius Haimann, d: Marcel Varnel, c: Claude Friese-Greene, sc: Roger Burford, Val Guest from story by Joe May, Karl Nott, des: A. L. Mazzei, ed: E. B. Jarvis. With Gene Gerrard, June Clyde, Renee Houston.

No More Cows See **Miracles Do Happen**

Non Stop New York G-B at Shepherd's Bush (A). GFD, 9.37 (6,472). d: Robert Stevenson, c: Glen MacWilliams, sc: Kurt Siodmak, Roland Pertwee, J. O. C. Orton, Derek Twist from novel by Ken Atiwill, *Sky Steward,* des: Walter Murton, cost: Norman Hartnell. With Anna Lee, John Loder, Francis L. Sullivan.

No Parking Herbert Wilcox at Beaconsfield (A). Brit. Lion, 6.38 (6,390). p: Herbert Wilcox, d: Jack Raymond, c: George Stretton, sc; W. G. Elliott from screen story by Carol Reed. With Gordon Harker, Irene Ware.

No Return See **Romance in Flanders, A**

Norah O'Neale See **Irish Hearts**

Northing Tramp, The See **Strangers on Honeymoon**

Norwich Victims, The See **Dead Men Tell No Tales**

No. 10. The Grove See **Shadow of Death, The**

Nothing like Publicity GS Ent. (U). Radio, 9.36 (5,848). p: George Smith, d: P. Maclean Rogers, sc: Kathleen Butler, H. F. Maltby from story by Arthur Cooper. With Billy Hartnell, Marjorie Taylor.

Not so Dusty GS Ent.-Bow Bell at Walton (U). Radio, 5.36 (6,407). p: George Smith, d: P. Maclean Rogers, c: Geoffrey Faithfull, sc: H. F. Maltby and

Kathleen Butler from story by Wally Patch. With Wally Patch, Gus McNaughton.

Not so Quiet on the Western Front BIP at Elstree (U). Wardour, premiere 5.30 (4,626) FT, songs RCA. d: Monty Banks, sc: Lola Harvey and Syd Courtenay from story by Victor Kendall. With Leslie Fuller.

Not Wanted on Voyage Dela Films British Productions at Beaconsfield (A). Brit. Lion, 2.38 (6,224). p: Alexandre Dembo de Lasta, d: Emile Reinert, sc: Harold Simpson from story by Maurice Messinger. With Bebe Daniels, Ben Lyon.

Number, Please George King at Walton (A). Fox, 7.31 (3,634). p: Harry Cohen, d: George King, sc: H. Fowler Mear, Billie Bristow, Charles Bennett. With Mabel Poulton, Warwick Ward.

Number Seventeen BIP at Elstree (U). Wardour, 7.32 (5,766). p: John Maxwell, d: Alfred Hitchcock, c: J. J. Cox, Bryan Langley, sc: Alfred Hitchcock, Alma Reville, Rodney Ackland from novel and play by J. Jefferson Farjeon (1925). des: Wilfred Arnold, ed: A. C. Hammond, sd: A. D. Valentine, music A. Hallis. With Leon M. Lion, Anne Grey, John Stuart.

Nurse Edith Cavell Imperadio in Hollywood (U). RKO-Radio, 10.39 (8,727). Registered as foreign film. p: d: Herbert Wilcox, assoc. p: Merrill White, c: Freddie Young, Joseph H. August, sc: Michael Hogan from story by Capt. Reginald Berkeley, *Dawn*, des: L. P. Williams, ed: Elmo Williams, montage Douglas Travers, sp. effects: Vernon L. Walker, sd: Richard Van Hessen, music Anthony Collins. With Anna Neagle, George Sanders, Edna May Oliver.

Nursemaid Who Disappeared, The WB-FN at Teddington (A). WB, 3.39 (7,840, later 8,103). p: Jerome Jackson, d: Arthur Woods, c: Basil Emmott, sc: Paul Gangelin and Connery Chappell fron novel by Philip MacDonald. With Arthur Margetson, Lesley Brook.

Obvious Situation, An See **Hours of Loneliness**

Odds on Love See **Two on a Doorstep**

Officers' Mess, The H. R. Rowson at Walton (U). Paramt, 5.31 (5,939) FT RCA. p: Harry Rowson, d: Manning Haynes, sc: Eliot Stannard from play by Sydney Blow and Douglas Hoare (1918). With Richard Cooper, Elsa Lanchester, Harold French.

Office Wife, The WB-FN at Teddington (A). FN, 8.34 (3,935). p: Irving Asher, d: George King, sc: Randall Faye from novel by Faith Baldwin. With Nora Swinburne, Dorothy Bouchier, Cecil Parker.

Official Secret See **Spies of the Air**

Off the Dole Mancunian Film Corp: at Albany Studio (A). APD and Mancunian Film Corp, 4.35 (8,313). p: John Blakeley, d: sc: Arthur Mertz. With George Formby, Beryl, Constance Shotter.

Oh, Boy ABPC at Elstree (U). ABPC, 2.38 (6,582). p: Walter Mycroft, d: Albert de Courville, c: Claude Friese-Greene, sc: Dudley Leslie from story by Douglas Furber. With Albert Burdon, Mary Lawson, Bernard Nedell.

Oh, Daddy Gainsborough at Islington (A). G-B D, 2.35 (6,798). p: Michael Balcon, d: Graham Cutts, Austin Melford, c: Mutz Greenbaum, sc: Austin Melford from his own play (1930) based on German play by Franz Arnold and Ernst Bach, ed: Charles Frend. With Frances Day, Leslie Henson, Robertson Hare.

Oh, Listen to the Band See **She Shall Have Music**

Oh! Mr. Porter Gainsborough at Islington (U). GFD, 10.37 (7,578). p: Edward Black, d: Marcel Varnel, c: Arthur Crabtree, sc: George Marriott Edgar, Val Guest, J. O. C. Orton from story by Frank Launder, des: Vetchinsky, ed: R. E. Dearing, Alfred Roome, sd: W. Salter, MD: Louis Levy. With Will Hay, Moore Marriott, Graham Moffatt.

O.H.M.S. G-B at Shepherd's Bush, Aldershot, (U). G-B D, 1.37 (7,813).

assoc. p: Geoffrey Barkas, d: Raoul Walsh, c: Roy Kellino, sc: Bryan Wallace, Austin Melford, Λ. R. Rawlinson from story by Lesser Samuels and Ralph Bettinson, des: Edward Carrick, ed: Charles Saunders, MD: Louis Levy. With Anna Lee, John Mills, Wallace Ford.

Oh, No, Doctor! George King (A). M-G-M, 2.34 (5,660). d: George King. With Jack Hobbs, Dorothy Boyd.

Oh, What a Duchess! BIP (U). Pathé, 1.34 (6,060). d: Lupino Lane, sc: Con West, Herbert Sargent from Fred Karno Sketch, *Mumming Birds*. With George Lacy.

Oh, What a Night! BSFP (U). Universal, 3.35 (5,319). p: Edward G. Whiting, d: Frank A. Richardson, sc: from play by Ernest Denny, *The Irresistible Marmaduke*. With Molly Lamont, James Carew.

O-Kay for Sound Gainsborough at Islington (A). GFD, 4.37 (7,797). p: Edward Black, d: Marcel Varnel, c: J. J. Cox, sc: G. Marriott Edgar and Val Guest, book and lyrics R. P. Weston and Bert Lee, from George Black's Palladium show, des: Vetchinsky, ed: R. E. Dearing, sd: G. E. Burgess, songs R. P. Weston and Bert Lee, Noel Gay, Michael Carr and Jimmy Kennedy. With The Crazy Gang.

Old Bill and Son Legeran Films, in production at Denham 12.39. p: Josef Somlo, Harold Boxall, d: Ian Dalrymple, c: Jack Whitehead, sc: Ian Dalrymple, Bruce Bairnsfather from story based on cartoon character by Bruce Bairnsfather. With Morland Graham, John Mills.

Old Bones of the River Gainsborough at Islington, exteriors at Shepperton (U). GFD, 12.38 (8.110). p: Edward Black, d: Marcel Varnel, c: Arthur Crabtree, sc: J. O. C. Orton, dial: Val Guest and G. Marriott Edgar from stories by Edgar Wallace, *Bones* and *Lieutenant Bones*, des: Vetchinsky, ed: R. E. Dearing, Alfred Roome, sd: S. Wiles, MD: Louis Levy. With Will Hay, Moore Marriott, Graham Moffatt.

Old Curiosity Shop, The BIP at Elstree (U). Wardour, 12.34 (8,576). p: Walter Mycroft, d: Thomas Bentley, c: Claude Friese-Greene, sc: Margaret Kennedy, Ralph Neale from novel by Charles Dickens, des: Cedric Dawe, ed: Leslie Norman, MD: Herman Finck. With Elaine Benson, Ben Webster, Hay Petrie.

Old Faithful GS Ent. (A). Radio, 8.35 (6,029). p: George Smith, d: P. Maclean Rogers, sc: Kathleen Butler. With Horace Hodges, Glennis Lorimer.

Old Heidelberg See **Student's Romance, The**

Old Iron T. W. Productions at Shepperton (U). Brit. Lion, 9.38 (7,262). p: d: Tom Walls, c: Mutz Greenbaum, sc: Ben Travers from his own story, des: D. W. Daniels, ed: Lynn Harrison, sd: M. Cruickshank. With Tom Walls, Eva Moore, Richard Ainley.

Old Man, The Brit. Lion at Beaconsfield (A). Brit. Lion, 12.31 (6,896) FT. p: S. W. Smith, d: Manning Haynes, c: Alex Bryce, sc: from play by Edgar Wallace, des: Norman Arnold, sd: Harold King. With Maisie Gay, Lester Matthews.

Old Mother Riley Butcher's-Hope-Bell at Cricklewood (U). Butcher's, 8.37 (6,789). p: Norman Hope-Bell, d: Oswald Mitchell, c: Jack Parker, sc: Con West from story by John Argyle, des: Frank Carter, ed: Challis Sanderson, sd: Charles E. Knott, MD: Horace Sheldon. With Arthur Lucan. Kitty McShane.

Old Mother Riley in Paris Butcher's at Walton (U). Butcher's, 8.38 (6,879). d: Oswald Mitchell, c: Geoffrey Faithfull, sc: from story by Con West, des: R. Holmes Paul, sd: Hal Fuller, MD: Percival Mackey. With Arthur Lucan, Kitty McShane.

Old Mother Riley Joins Up Brit. Nat. at Elstree former Whitehall (U). Anglo-American, 10.39 (6,563). p: John Corfield, d: P. Maclean Rogers, sc: Jack Marks, Con West. With Arthur Lucan, Kitty McShane.

Old Mother Riley, M.P. Butcher's at Walton (U). Butcher's, 8.39 (6,912). d: Oswald Mitchell, c: Geoffrey Faithfull, sc: from story by Con West and Oswald Mitchell, des: R. Holmes Paul, ed: Dan Birt. With Arthur Lucan, Kitty McShane.

Old Roses Fox Brit. at Wembley (A). Fox, 7.35 (5,457). d: Bernerd Mainwaring, c: Alex Bryce, sc: from story by Anthony Richardson. With Horace Hodges, Nancy Burne.

Old Soldiers Never Die BIP at Elstree (U). Wardour, 3.31 (5,325) FT. d: Monty Banks, sc: Val Valentine from story by Syd Courtenay and Lola Harvey. With Leslie Fuller.

Old Spanish Customers BIP (U). Wardour, 9.32 (6,215). d: Lupino Lane, sc: Lola Harvey, Syd Courtenay. With Leslie Fuller, Binnie Barnes.

Olympic Honeymoon See **Honeymoon Merrygoround**

On Approval B & D at Elstree B & D (A). W & F, 8.30 (8,839) FT WE. p: Herbert Wilcox, d: Tom Walls, sc: W. P. Lipscomb from play by Frederick Lonsdale (1927), des: L. P. Williams, sd: A. W. Watkins. With Tom Walls, Robertson Hare, Yvonne Arnaud.

Once a Thief B & D-Para-Brit. at Elstree B & D (A). Paramt, 6.35 (6,065). d: George Pearson, c: Francis Carver, sc: Basil Mason from screen story by Robert Dargavel. With John Stuart, Nancy Burne.

Once Bitten Real Art at Twickenham (A). Fox, 3.32 (4,448). p: Julius Hagen, d: Leslie Hiscott, c: Sydney Blythe, sc: H. Fowler Mear from screen story by John Barrow. With Richard Cooper, Ursula Jeans.

Once in a Million BIP at Welwyn (U). Wardour, 3.36 (6,900). p: Walter Mycroft, d: Arthur Woods, c: Ronald Neame, sc: Jack Davies, des: Cedric Dawe, ed: George Black Jr. With Charles Buddy Rogers, Mary Brian.

Once in a New Moon Fox Brit. at Shepperton (U). Fox, 12.34 (5,778). d: Anthony Kimmins, sc: from novel by Owen Rutter, *Lucky Star*. With Rene Ray, Derrick de Marney, Eliot Makeham.

Once There Was a Waltz See **Where Is This Lady?**

One Crazy Week See **Annie, Leave the Room!**

One Good Turn Leslie Fuller Pictures at Elstree Rock (U). ABFD, 6.36 (6,545). p: Joe Rock, d: Alf Goulding, c: Ernest Palmer, sc: Georgie Harris, Jack Byrd, Syd Courtenay from story by Con West, Herbert Sargent, des: A. L. Mazzei, musical numbers Cyril Ray, Jack Meskill. With Leslie Fuller, Georgie Harris.

One in a Million See **Going Gay**

One Precious Year B & D-Para-Brit. at Elstree B & D (A). Paramt, 2.33 (6,894). d: Henry Edwards, c: Stanley Rodwell, sc: Dorothy Rowan from play by Ernest Temple Thurston, *Driven* (1914), des: Wilfred Arnold. With Anne Grey, Owen Nares, Basil Rathbone.

On Guard in the Mediterranean See **Hell's Cargo**

On Secret Service BIP (U). Wardour, 12.33 (8,100). d: Arthur Woods, sc: Frank Vosper, Arthur Woods. With Greta Nissen, Carl Ludwig Diehl, Don Alvarado, Austin Trevor, Esme Percy.

On The Air Brit. Lion (U). Brit. Lion, 1.34 (7,152). d: Herbert Smith, c: Alex Bryce, sc: Michael Barringer, des: Norman Arnold, sd: Harold King. With Davy Burnaby, Betty Astell.

On the Night of the Fire G & S Films at Denham (A). GFD, 10.39 (8,109). p: Josef Somlo, assoc. p: Ian Dalrymple, d: Brian Desmon Hurst, c: Gunther Krampf, sc: Brian Desmond Hurst, Patrick Kirwan, Terence Young from novel by Frederick Lawrence Green. des: John Bryan, ed: Terence Fisher, sd: A. W. Watkins, MD: Muir Mathieson, music Miklos Rozsa. With Diana Wynyard, Ralph Richardson, Henry Oscar.

On Thin Ice Hall Mark (A). Equity British, 2.33 (5,650). d: Bernard Vorhaus. With Ursula Jeans, Dorothy

Bartlam.

On Top of the World City Film Corp: at Shepperton (U). AP & D, 1.36 (7,150). p: Basil Humphreys, d: Redd Davis, sc: Evelyn Barrie from story by Harry B. Parkinson. With Betty Fields, Frank Pettingell.

On Velvet AIP (A). Columbia, 3.38 (6,392). d: Widgey Newman, sc: John Quin. With Wally Patch, Joe Hayman.

Open All Night Real Art Twickenham (A). Radio, 10.34 (5,560). p: Julius Hagen, d: George Pearson, c: Ernest Palmer, sc: Gerard Fairlie from story by John Chancellor. With Frank Vosper, Margaret Vines.

Open House See **Pay-Box Adventure**

Opening Night Olympic Productions (A). Columbia, 2.35 (6,110) p: Charles Alexander, d: Alexander Brown. With Douglas Byng, Walter Crisham, Reginald Gardiner.

Orders Are Orders See **Orders Is Orders**

Orders Is Orders G-B Shepherd's Bush (U). Gaumont-Ideal, 7.33 (7,857). p: Michael Balcon, d: Walter Forde, c: Glen MacWilliams, sc: Sidney Gilliat and Leslie Arliss from play by Ian Hay and Anthony Armstrong, *Orders Are Orders,* dial: James Gleason, add. dial: Ian Hay, des: Alfred Junge, cost: Gordon Conway, ed: Derek Twist, sd: S. A. Jolly. With Charlotte Greenwood, James Gleason, Ian Hunter, Cyril Maude.

Other Men's Women See **Murder at the Inn**

Other Mrs. Phipps, The Real Art at Twickenham (A). FN, 12.31 (3,631) FT. p: Julius Hagen, d: Guy Newall, sc: Brock Williams. With Sidney Fairbrother, Richard Cooper, Jane Welsh.

Other People's Sins Assoc. Picture Productions at Cricklewood (A). PDC, 2.31 (5,752) FT Visatone. d: Sinclair Hill, c: Desmond Dickinson, sc: L. H. Gordon, des: Louis Delaney. With Stewart Rome, Anne Grey.

Other Woman, The Majestic Films (A). UA, 6.31 (4,207) FT Fidelity. p:

Gordon Craig, d: G. B. Samuelson, sc: from story by Olga Hall Brown, *The Slave Bracelet.* With Isobel Elsom, David Hawthorne.

Ouanga Ouanga Productions (A). Paramt, 9.34 (6,184). d: George Terwilliger. With Fredi Washington, Philip Brandon.

Our Fighting Navy Herbert Wilcox at Pinewood, Weymouth (U). GFD, 4.37 (6,739). p: Herbert Wilcox, d: Norman Walker, c: Claude Friese-Greene, sc: W. G. Elliott, Harrison Owen from screen story by 'Bartimeus', des: L. P. Williams. With H. B. Warner, Richard Cromwell, Robert Douglas, Noah Beery, Hazel Terry.

Ourselves Alone BIP at Elstree (A). Wardour, 4.36 (6,285). p: Walter Mycroft, d: Walter Summers, Brian Desmond Hurst, c: Walter Harvey, sc: Dudley Leslie, Marjorie Deans, Dennis Johnstone from play by Noel Scott and Dudley Sturrock, *The Trouble,* des: Cedric Dawe, ed: J. Corbett. With John Lodge, John Loder, Antoinette Cellier, Niall MacGinnis.

Outcast, The BIP at Welwyn (U). Wardour, 3.34 (7,000). p: Walter Mycroft, d: Norman Lee, c: Jack Parker, sc: Syd Courtenay, Norman Lee from story by Syd Courtenay and Lola Harvey, des: John Mead. sd: David Howells. With Leslie Fuller, Mary Glynne.

Out of the Blue BIP (U). Pathé, 11.31 (7,587). p: supervised J. O. C. Orton, d: Gene Gerrard, c: Ernest Palmer, Arthur Crabtree, sc: Frank Miller from musical play by Caswell Garth and Desmond Carter, *Little Tommy Tucker* (1930), des: David Rawnsley, ed: E. B. Jarvis, sd: C. V. Thornton, MD: John Reynders, music Vivian Ellis. With Gene Gerrard, Jessie Matthews, Binnie Barnes, Kenneth Kove.

Out of the Past WB-FN at Teddington (A). WB, 2.33 (4,642). p: Irving Asher, d: Leslie Hiscott. With Joan Marion, Lester Matthews.

Outsider, The Cinema House at Elstree

(U). M-G-M, 4.31 (8,480) FT RCA. p:
Eric Hakim, d: Harry Lachman, c:
Gunther Krampf, sc: Harry Lachman,
Alma Reville from play by Dorothy
Brandon (1923), des: Wilfred Arnold,
ed: G. Pollatschik and Winifred Cooper,
sd: Alec Murray, music W. L. Trytel.
With Harold Huth, Joan Barry.

Outsider, The ABPC at Elstree (A).
ABPC, 1.39 (8,220). p: Walter Mycroft,
d: Paul L. Stein, c: Gunther Krampf,
sd: Dudley Leslie from play by Dorothy
Brandon (1923), des: Cedric Dawe.
With George Sanders, Mary Maguire.

Overcoat Sam UK. Films at Shepperton
(A). M-G-M, 3.37 (3,992). p: John
Barter, John Baxter, d: Wallace Orton,
c: Jack Parker. With George Mozart.

Over She Goes ABPC at Elstree (A).
ABPC, 8.37 (6,760). p: Walter Mycroft,
d: Graham Cutts, c: Otto Kanturek, sc:
Elizabeth Meehan, Hugh Brooke from
play by Stanley Lupino (1936), des:
Cedric Dawe, ed: Flora Newton, MD:
Harry Acres, music Billy Mayerl, lyrics
Desmond Carter, Frank Eyton, 'Over
She Goes' by Michael Carr and Jimmy
Kennedy. With Stanley Lupino, Laddie
Cliff, Gina Malo, Sally Gray, Claire
Luce.

Over the Garden Wall BIP at Elstree (U).
Wardour, 4.34 (6,022). p: Walter
Mycroft, d: John Daumery, c: J. J. Cox,
sc: H. F. Maltby and Gordon Wong
Wellesley from story by H. F. Maltby,
des: David Rawnsley, ed: Leslie
Norman, sd: A. S. Ross, songs and
lyrics Vivian Ellis, Desmond Carter,
dances Ralph Reader. With Bobby
Howes, Marian Marsh.

Over the Moon LFP-Denham Films at
Denham (A). UA, 10.39 (7,112).
Technicolor (colour direction Natalie
Kalmus). p: Alexander Korda, d:
Thornton Freeland, c: Harry Stradling,
sc: Anthony Pelissier, Arthur Wimperis,
Alec Coppel from story by Robert
Sherwood, des: Lazare Meerson, cost:
Rene Hubert. With Merle Oberon, Rex
Harrison, Robert Douglas.

Over the Sticks Cinema Exlusives (U).

Fox, 1.30 (3,345) silent. p: Frank
Wheatcroft, d: G. B. Samuelson, A. E.
Coleby, sc: G. B. Samuelson.

Owd Bob Gainsborough at Islington,
Exmoor, (U) GFD, 1.38 (7,044). p:
Edward Black, d: Robert Stevenson, c:
J. J. Cox, sc: J. B. Williams, Michael
Hogan from novel by Alfred Ollivant,
des: Vetchinsky, ed: R. E. Dearing,
Alfred Roome, sd: A. Cameron, MD:
Louis Levy. With Will Fyffe, Margaret
Lockwood, John Loder.

Pagliacci Trafalgar Film Productions at
Elstree BIP (A), UA, 12.36 (8,337). Part
British Chemicolour. p: Max Schach, d:
Karl Grune, dial. sup: Leon M. Lion,
Rosse Thompson, c: Otto Kanturek, sc:
Monckton Hoffe and Roger Burford,
some lyrics John Drinkwater, from
opera by Leoncavallo, des: Oscar
Werndorff, cost: E. Stern, ed: Walter
Stokvis, sd: A. S. Ross, conductor
Albert Coates, assisted by Boyd Neel,
music arranged Hanns Eisler, dances
Wendy Toye. With Richard Tauber,
Steffi Duna.

Paid in Error George Smith Productions
at Walton (U). Columbia, 2.38 (6,119).
p: George Smith, d: P. Maclean Rogers,
c: Geoffrey Faithfull, sc: Basil Mason
from story by John Chancellor. With
George Carney, Tom Helmore, Googie
Withers.

Painted Pictures Bernard Smith (U). Fox,
4.30 (5,158) silent. d: sc: Charles
Barnett. With Haddon Mason.

Pal o' Mine Film Sales (U). Radio, 3.36
(3,864). p: d: Widgey Newman, sc:
John Quin from story by Widgey
Newman. With Herbert Langley.

Paradise Alley John Argyle (U). UK
Photoplays, 3.31 (5,097) silent. p: d: sc:
John Argyle. With John Argyle,
Margaret Delane.

Paradise for Two LFP at Denham (U).
UA, 10.37 (6,920). p: Alexander Korda,
Gunther Stapenhorst, d: Thornton
Freeland, c: Gunther Krampf, sc:
Robert Stevenson, Arthur Macrae from
story by Robert Liebmann and William

Kernell, des: Vincent Korda, cost: Rene Hubert, ed: William Hornbeck, E. B. Jarvis, sd: A. W. Watkins, MD: Muir Mathieson, Music Mischa Spoliansky, lyrics W. Kernell, ballet Vlademiroff, dances Jack Donohue, Philip Buchel. With Jack Hulbert, Patricia Ellis, Arthur Riscoe, Googie Withers.

Paris by Night See **Pyjamas Preferred**

Paris Plane Sound City at Shepperton, Croydon aerodrome (U). M-G-M, 9.33 (5,050, later 4,703). p: Ivar Campbell, d: John Paddy Carstairs, sc: Charles Bennett. With John Loder, Molly Lamont.

Parker, P.C. See **It's a Cop**

Passenger to London Fox Brit. at Wembley (A). Fox, 6.37 (5,138). d: Lawrence Huntington, c: Stanley Grant, sc: David Evans. With John Warwick, Jenny Laird.

Passing Brompton Road See **Her Reputation**

Passing of the Third Floor Back, The G-B at Shepherd's Bush (A). G-B D, 9.35 (8,152). p: Michael Balcon, assoc. p: Ivor Montagu, d: Berthold Viertel, c: Curt Courant, sc: Michael Hogan, Alma Reville from play by Jerome K. Jerome (1908), ed: Derek Twist. With Conrad Veidt, Anna Lee, Mary Clare.

Passing Shadows Brit. Lion at Beaconsfield (A). Fox, 5.34 (6,094). assoc. p: Herbert Smith, d: Leslie Hiscott, c: Alex Bryce, sc: Michael Barringer, des: Norman Arnold, sd: Harold King. With Edmund Gwenn, Aileen Marson, Barry Mackay.

Pathetone Parade of 1936, 1938 and **1939** Pathé three-reelers d: Freddie Watts, with variety acts; 1.36, 9.37, and 4.39.

Path of Glory, The Triumph Film Company at Hammersmith (U). PDC, 3.34 (6,181). d: Dallas Bower, sc: L. du Garde Peach from his own radio play. With Maurice Evans, Valerie Hobson.

Patricia Gets Her Man WB-FN at Teddington (A). FN, 3.37 (6,130). p: Irving Asher, d: Reginald Purdell, sc: Max Merritt, Maurice Kusell. With

Hans Sonker, Lesley Brook.

Pay-Box Adventure B & D-Para-Brit. at Elstree, former Whitehall (U). Paramt, 6.36 (6,148). d: W. P. Kellino, sc: from story by W. G. Elliott. With Syd Crossley, Marjorie Corbett.

P.C. Josser Gainsborough at Islington (U). W & F, 1.31 (8,044). FT RCA. p: Michael Balcon, d: Milton Rosmer, c: William Shenton, Horance Wheddon, sc: Con West and Herbert Sargent from music-hall sketch, *The Police Force* (1926), by Con West. With Ernie Lotinga.

Peace and Quiet GS Ent. at Twickenham (U). Fox, 6.31 (3,941). p: Harry Cohen, d: Frank A. Richardson, c: Basil Emmott, sc: Brock Williams, des: James Carter. With Herbert Mundin.

Peace in our Time See **Silent Battle, The**

Pearls Bring Tears GS Ent. at Walton (U). Columbia, 3.37 (5,769). p: George Smith, d: Manning Haynes, c: Geoffrey Faithfull, sc: Roy Lockwood from story by Clifford Grey. With John Stuart, Dorothy Boyd, Googie Withers.

Peg of Old Drury B & D at Elstree B & D (U). UA, 8.35 (6,870). p: d: Herbert Wilcox, c: Freddie Young, sc: Miles Malleson, des: L. P. Williams, cost: Doris Zinkeisen, dances Idjikowski. With Anna Neagle, Sir Cedric Hardwicke, Jack Hawkins, Margaretta Scott.

Peg Woffington See **Peg of Old Drury**

Penny Paradise ATP at Ealing (U). ABFD, 9.38 (6,435). p: Basil Dean, assoc. p: Jack Kitchin, d: Carol Reed, c: Ronald Neame, Gordon Dines, sc: Thomas Thompson, W. L. Meade, Thomas Browne based on an idea by Basil Dean, des: Wilfred Shingleton, ed: Ernest Aldridge, sd: Eric Williams, music and lyrics Harry Parr-Davies, Harry O'Donovan. With Betty Driver, Jimmy O'Dea, Edmund Gwenn.

Penny Pool, The Mancunian Film Corp. at Highbury (U). Mancunian Film Corp., 6.37 (8,075). p: John Blakeley, d: George Black Jr, c: Jimmy Burger, sc: Arthur Mertz, des: George Wood, ed: B. Bayley, sd: A. D. Valentine.

With Douglas Wakefield and his Gang, Tommy Fields, Luanne Shaw.

Perfect Crime, The WB-FN at Teddington (A). FN, 4.37 (6,217). p: Irving Asher, d: Ralph Ince, c: Basil Emmott, sc: Basil Dillon, des: Peter Proud, ed: Leslie Norman, sd: W. S. Nunn. With Hugh Williams, Glen Alyn, Ralph Ince.

Perfect Flaw, The Fox Brit. at Ealing (A). Fox, 6.34 (4,569). d: Manning Haynes, c: Robert Lapresle, sc: Michael Barringer. With Naomi Waters, D. A. Clarke-Smith.

Perfect Lady, The BIP at Elstree (A). Wardour, 11.31 (6,085). d: Milton Rosmer, sc: Frederick Jackson. With Moira Lynd, Betty Amann, Harry Wilcoxon.

Perfect Service See **Money Means Nothing**

Perfect Understanding Gloria Swanson Productions at Ealing, Cannes (A). UA, 1.33 (7,871). d: Cyril Gardner, assistant Thorold Dickinson, sc: Miles Malleson, Michael Powell from story by Michael Powell, des: Edward Carrick. With Gloria Swanson, Laurence Olivier, Genevieve Tobin.

Phantom Light, The Gainsborough at Islington, and in Wales (U). G-B D, 1.35 (6,852). p: Michael Balcon, assoc. p: Jerome Jackson, d: Michael Powell, c: Roy Kellino, sc: Ralph Smart, dial: J. Jefferson Farjeon, Austin Melford, from play by Evadne Price and Joan Roy Byford, *The Haunted Light,* des: Vetchinsky, ed: Derek Twist, sd: A. Birch, MD: Louis Levy. With Gordon Harker, Ian Hunter, Binnie Hale.

Piccadilly Circus See **Keep Smiling**

Piccadilly Nights Kingsway General Film Productions (U). FBO, 5.30 (8,113) FT Vocalion disc. p: d: sc: Albert H. Arch, music Harry Shalson, Maurice Winnick and his Orchestra, Ralph Goldsmith and his band. With Billy Rutherford.

Piccadilly Playtime Ace Films, 12.36 (4,510). d: Frank Green, variety from Windmill Theatre.

Pictorial Revue Pathé, 3.36 (3,663). d: Freddie Watts.

Playboy, The See **Paradise for Two**

Playing the Game See **It's a Grand Old World**

Plaything, The BIP (A). Wardour, 9.29 (6,417 silent, 5,637 sound) PT RCA. d: Castleton Knight, sc: V. Powell from play by Arthur J. Black, *Life is Pretty Much the Same*, MD: John Reynders, music Hubert Bath and Henry Stafford. With Heather Thatcher, Nigel Barrie, Estelle Brody, Marguerite Allan, Raymond Milland.

Play up the Band City Film Corporation at Ealing (U). ABFD, 11.35 (6,481). p: Basil Humphreys, d: Harry Hughes, sc; from story by Frank Atkinson. With Stanley Holloway, Betty Ann Davies, Frank Atkinson.

Please Teacher (1935) See **Things Are Looking Up**

Please Teacher BIP-ABPC at Elstree (U). Wardour, 2.37 (6,961). p: Walter Mycroft, d: Stafford Dickens, c: Otto Kanturek, sc: Stafford Dickens from musical play by K. R. G. Browne, R. P. Weston and Bert Lee (1936), des: Cedric Dawe, ed: Lionel Tomlinson, sd: C. V. Thornton, MD: Harry Acres, music Jack Waller, Joseph Tunbridge, lyrics R. P. Weston, Bert Lee. With Bobby Howes, Wylie Watson, Rene Ray.

Plunder B & D at Elstree B & D (U). W & F, 11.30 (8,839) FT WE. p: Herbert Wilcox, d: Tom Walls, c: Freddie Young, sc: W. P. Lipscomb, dial: Ben Travers from play by Ben Travers, des: L. P. Williams, tech. supervision: Byron Haskin, ed: Duncan Mansfield. With Tom Walls, Ralph Lynn, Robertson Hare, Mary Brough.

Pointing Finger, The Real Art at Twickenham (U). Radio, 12.33 (6,118). p: Julius Hagen, d: George Pearson, c: Ernest Palmer, sc: H. Fowler Mear George Pearson from novel by Rita, des: James Carter, ed: Lister Laurence, sd: Carlisle Mountenay, MD: W. L. Trytel. With John Stuart, Viola Keats.

Poisoned Diamond, The Grafton Films (A). Columbia, 12.34 (6,728). p: Fred

Browett, d: W. P. Kellino. With Anne Grey, Lester Matthews, Patric Knowles.

Poison Pen ABPC at Elstree (A). ABPC, 6.39 (7,043). p: Walter Mycroft, d: Paul L. Stein c: Philip Tannura, sc: William Freshman, Doreen Montgomery, add. dial: Esther McCracken, N. C. Hunter, from play by Richard Llewellyn (1937), des: Cedric Dawe, ed: Flora Newton. With Flora Robson, Reginald Tate, Ann Todd.

Police Force, The See **P.C. Josser**

Political Party, A BIP (U). Pathé, 1.34 (6,500). p: Walter Mycroft, d: Norman Lee, sc: Syd Courtenay and Lola Harvey. With Leslie Fuller, Enid Stamp-Taylor.

Poor Old Bill BIP at Elstree (U). Wardour, 6.31 (3,693). d: Monty Banks, sc: Val Valentine from story by Lola Harvey and Syd Courtenay. With Leslie Fuller.

Post Haste G-B (U). Gaumont-Ideal, registered 6.33 (1,911). p: Clayton Hutton, d: Frank Cadman, sc: Sidney Gilliat from Fred Karno sketch, *G.P.O.* With Jack Williams, Joey Porter.

Potiphar's Wife BIP at Elstree (A). FN-Pathé, 3.31 (7,020) FT RCA. d: Maurice Elvey, c: Jimmy Wilson, sc: Victor Kendall, adapt: Maurice Elvey and Edgar C. Middleton from the latter's play (1927), des: Clarence Elder, ed: Leslie Norman, sd: A. S. Ross. With Nora Swinburne, Laurence Olivier, Norman McKinnell.

Pot Luck Gainsborough (A). G-B D, 4.36 (6,460). p: Michael Balcon, d: Tom Walls, c: Roy Kellino, Arthur Crabtree, sc: Ben Travers from his own story, des: Walter Murton, ed: Alfred Roome, sd: F. McNally, MD: Louis Levy. With Tom Walls, Ralph Lynn, Robertson Hare, Diana Churchill.

Premiere ABPC at Elstree (A). ABPC, 10.38 (6,350). Registered as foreign film. p: Walter Mycroft, d: Walter Summers, c: Otto Kanturek, sc: F. McGrew Willis from French film. With John Lodge, Judy Kelly.

Press Button 'B' See **Twin Faces**

Price of a Song, The Fox Brit. at Wembley (A). Fox, 5.35 (6,003). d: Michael Powell, c: Jimmy Wilson, sc: from story by Anthony Gittins. With Eric Maturin, Campbell Gullan, Marjorie Corbett.

Price of Divorce, The See **Such is the Law**

Price of Folly, The Welwyn Studios at Welwyn (A). Pathé, 2.37 (4,777). d: Walter Summers, c: Bryan Langley, sc: Walter Summers, John Lee Thompson from play by John Lee Thompson, *Double Error*. With Leonora Corbett, Colin Keith-Johnston.

Price of Things, The Elinor Glyn Productions at Elstree (A). UA, 7.30 (7,756) FT RCA. d: Elinor Glyn, c: Charles Rosher, sc: Lady Rhys-Williams from novel by Elinor Glyn. With Stewart Rome, Elissa Landi, Walter Tennyson, Alfred Tennyson.

Price of Wisdom, The B & D-Para-Brit. at Elstree B & D (U). Paramt, 2.35 (6,030). d: Reginald Denham, c: Henry Harris, sc: Basil Mason, George Dewhurst from play by Lionel Brown. With Mary Jerrold, Mary Newland, Roger Livesey.

Pride of Donegal, The Harry B. Parkinson (U). Fox, 12.29 (6,412) silent. p: Harry B. Parkinson, d: J. Stevens Edwards, sc: Norman Lee.

Pride of the Force, The BIP (U). Wardour, 8.33 (6,918). d: Norman Lee, c: Claude Friese-Greene, sc: Norman Lee, Syd Courtenay, Arthur Woods from story by Syd Courtenay, Lola Harvey. With Leslie Fuller.

Primrose Path, The B & D-Para-Brit. at Elstree B & D (A). Paramt, 7.34 (6,411). d: Reginald Denham, c: Percy Strong, sc: Basil Mason from play by Joan Temple, des: Fred Pusey. With Isobel Elsom, Whitmore Humphries, Max Adrian.

Prince of Arcadia Nettlefold-Fogwell at Walton (A). W & F, 7.33 (7,106). p: supervisor Reginald Fogwell, d: Hans Schwartz, c: Geoffrey Faithfull, sc: Reginald Fogwell from musical comedy by Walter Reisch, des: A. L. Mazzei, music Robert Stolz. With Carl Brisson, Margot Grahame, Ida Lupino.

Princess Charming Gainsborough at Islington (A). G-B D, 4.34 (7,047). p: Michael Balcon, d: Maurice Elvey, c: Mutz Greenbaum, sc: and dial: L. du Garde Peach, adapt: Arthur Wimperis and Lauri Wylie from play of 1926, based on Viennese play by F. Martos, *Alexandra,* add. dial: Robert Edmunds, des: Ernö Metzner, cost: Norman Hartnell, sd: A. Douglas, MD: Louis Levy, music Ray Noble, lyrics Max Kester. With Evelyn Laye, Max Miller, Yvonne Arnaud, George Grossmith.

Priscilla the Rake See **She Was Only a Village Maiden**

Prison Breaker, The George Smith Productions (A). Columbia, 2.36 (6,286). p: George Smith, d: Adrian Brunel, sc: Frank Witty from story by Edgar Wallace. With James Mason, Marguerite Allan.

Prison Bars LFP at Denham (A). UA, 9.38 (6,993). p: Alexander Korda, assoc. p: Irving Asher, d: Brian Desmond Hurst, c: Georges Périnal, sc: Lajos Biro from French film *Prison sans Barreaux* by Arnold Pressburger des: Vincent Korda, ed: Charles Crichton, music John Greenwood. With Barry K. Barnes, Corinne Luchaire, Edna Best.

Private and Confidential See **Big Business**

Private Life of Don Juan, The LFP (A). UA, 9.34 (8,045). p: d: Alexander Korda, c: Georges Périnal, sc: story Lajos Biro, dial. and film play Frederick Lonsdale, based on play by Henri Bataille, des: Vincent Korda, cost: Oliver Messel, ed: Harold Young, Stephen Harrison, sd: A. W. Watkins, sp. effects: Ned Mann, tech. d: Marques de Portago, MD: Muir Mathieson, music Ernst Toch, 'Don Juan' theme Mischa Spoliansky, lyrics Arthur Wimperis. With Douglas Fairbanks Sr, Merle Oberon, Owen Nares, Benita Hume.

Private Life of Henry VIII, The LFP at Elstree B & D (A). UA, 8.33 (8,664). p: d: Alexander Korda, c: Georges Périnal, Osmond Borradaile, sc: Arthur Wimperis, Lajos Biro, des: Vincent Korda, cost: John Armstrong, ed: Harold Young, sd: A. W. Watkins, tech. adviser: Philip Lindsay, MD: Kurt Schroeder. With Charles Laughton, Elsa Lanchester, Merle Oberon, Binnie Barnes, Robert Donat.

Private Life of Sherlock Holmes, The See **Triumph of Sherlock Holmes, The**

Private Secretary, The Twick. at Twickenham (U). Twick FD, 9.35 (6,320). p: Julius Hagen, d: Henry Edwards, c: Sydney Blythe, sc: H. Fowler Mear, Arthur Macrae, George Broadhurst from play by Charles Hawtrey (1884) based on German play *Der Bibliotheker.* With Edward Everett Horton, Judy Gunn, Barry Mackay.

Private Wives See **That's My Wife**

Professional Guest, The George King at Walton (U). Fox, 10.31 (3,992). p: Harry Cohen, d: George King, sc: H. Fowler Mear from novel by William Garrett. With Gordon Harker, Pat Paterson, Richard Bird.

Proud Valley, The Ealing Studios (CAPAD) at Ealing (A). ABFD, 1.40 (6,840). p: Michael Balcon, assoc. p: Sergei Nolbandov and Herbert Marshall, d: Pen Tennyson, c: Glen MacWilliams, Roy Kellino, Jeff Seaholme, sc: Jack Jones, Louis Golding, Pen Tennyson from story by Herbert Marshall and Alfredda Brilliant, des: Wilfred Shingleton, ed: Ray Pitt, sd: Eric Williams, MD: Ernest Irving. With Paul Robeson, Rachel Thomas, Edward Chapman.

Public Life of Henry the Ninth Hammer Productions (U). M-G-M, 1.35 (5,472). d: Bernerd Mainwaring. With Leonard Henry.

Public Nuisance No. 1 Cecil Film Company at Beaconsfield (A). GFD, 2.36 (7,087). p: Herman Fellner, d: Marcel Varnel, c: Claude Friese-Greene, sc: Robert Edmunds, Roger Burford, Val Guest from story by Franz

Arnold, songs and music Vivian Ellis. With Frances Day, Arthur Riscoe, Claude Dampier.

Puppets of Fate Real Art at Twickenham (A). UA, 1.33 (6,541). p: Julius Hagen, d: G. A. Cooper, sc: H. Fowler Mear from story by Arthur Rigby and R. H. Douglas. With Godfrey Tearle, Russell Thorndike, Isla Bevan.

Purse Strings B & D-Para-Brit. at Elstree B & D (A). Paramt, 7.33 (6,277). d: Henry Edwards, c: Henry Harris, sc: from play by Bernard Parry. With Dorothy Bouchier, Gyles Isham.

Pygmalion Pascal Film Productions at Pinewood (A). GFD, 8.38 (8,609). p: Gabriel Pascal, d: Leslie Howard, Anthony Asquith, c: Harry Stradling, Jack Hildyard, sc: George Bernard Shaw, Cecil Lewis, W. P. Lipscomb from play by George Bernard Shaw (1914), des: Lawrence Irving, John Bryan, ed: David Lean, cost: Schiaparelli and Worth, designed Prof. Czettel, sd: Alex Fisher, MD: Geoffrey Toye, music Arther Honegger, conductor Louis Levy. With Leslie Howard, Wendy Hiller, Wilfrid Lawson, Marie Lohr.

Pyjama Nights in Paris See **Pyjamas Preferred**

Pyjamas Preferred BIF at Welwyn (U). Pathé, 12.32 (4,708). d: Val Valentine, sc: Val Valentine from play by J. O. Twiss, *The Red Dog*. With Jay Laurier, Betty Amann.

Q Planes Harefield Productions at Denham (U). Columbia, 2.39 (7,469). p: Irving Asher, exec. p: Alexander Korda, d: Tim Whelan, c: Harry Stradling, sc: Ian Dalrymple from screen story by Brock Williams, John Whittingham and Arthur Wimperis, des: Vincent Korda, Frederick Pusey, ed: William Hornbeck, Hugh Stewart, sd: A. W. Watkins, MD: Muir Mathieson. With Valerie Hobson, Ralph Richardson, Laurence Olivier.

Queen, The See **Queen's Affair, The**

Queen of Hearts ATP at Ealing (U). ABFD, 2.36 (7,165). p: Basil Dean, d:

Monty Banks, c: John Boyle, sc: Gordon Wellesley, dial: Anthony Kimmins and Douglas Furber, from story by H. F. Maltby and Clifford Grey, des: J. Elder Wills, ed: Jack Kitchin, sd: Paul Wiser, MD: Ernest Irving, songs Will Haines, Jimmy Harper, Harry Parr-Davies. With Gracie Fields, John Loder, Enid Stamp-Taylor.

Queen's Affair, The B & D at Elstree B & D and Dolomites (U). UA, 2.34 (6,935). p: d: Herbert Wilcox, c: Freddie Young, exterior locations Sepp Allgeier, sc: Samson Raphaelson, add. dial: Monckton Hoffe from musical play by Ernst Marischka, Bruno Granichstaedten and Oscar Straus, des: L. P. Williams, cost: Doris Zinkeisen, ed: Merrill White, sd: C. C. Stevens, sp. effects: Lloyd Knechtel, MD: Roy Robertson, Geraldo and his Savoy Orchestra, music Oscar Straus with numbers by Arthur Schwartz. With Anna Neagle, Fernand Graavey.

Queer Cargo ABPC at Elstree (U). ABPC, 7.38 (5,543). p: Walter Mycroft, d: Harold Schuster, c: Otto Kanturek, sc: Patrick Kirwan, Walter Summers from play by Noel Langley (1934), des: John Mead. With John Lodge, Judy Kelly, Keneth Kent.

Quiet, Please WB-FN at Teddington (A). FN, 1.38 (6,155). p: Irving Asher, d: Roy William Neill, c: Basil Emmott, sc: Reginald Purdell, Anthony Hankey. With Reginald Purdell, Lesley Brook.

Racing Romance GS Ent. (U). Radio, 9.37 (5,615). p: George Smith, d: P. Maclean Rogers, sc: from story by John Hunter. With Bruce Seton, Marjorie Taylor.

Radio Lover City Film Corp. (U). ABFD, 10.36 (5,773). p: Ernest King, d: Austin Melford, Paul Capon, c: Ronald Neame, sc: Ian Dalrymple from story by Elmer Dangerfield, music Eric Speer. With Betty Ann Davies, Wylie Watson, Jack Melford.

Radio Parade BIP (U). Wardour, 4.33 (6,314). d: Archie de Bear, Richard

Beville, c: Jimmy Wilson, sc: Claude Hulbert, Paul England. With radio stars.

Radio Parade of 1935 BIP at Elstree (U). Wardour, 12.34 (8,515) part Dufaycolour. p: Walter Mycroft, d: Arthur Woods, c: Cyril Bristow, Philip Grindrod, Claude Friese-Greene, sc: Jimmy Bunting, Paul Perez, Jack Davies from story by Reginald Purdell, John Watt, des: Clarence Elder, David Rawnsley, ed: E. B. Jarvis, sd: C. V. Thornton, MD: Benjamin Frankel, music Hans May, Arthur Young, Benjamin Frankel and others, dances Buddy Bradley. With Will Hay, Helen Chandler, Herbert Mollison.

Radio Pirates Sound City (U). AP & D, 3.35 (8,000). p: Norman Loudon, d: Ivar Campbell, sc: from story by Donovan Pedelty, music Donovan Pedelty, Roy Fox and his Band. With Mary Lawson, Leslie French, Enid Stamp-Taylor.

Radio Revue See **Radio Parade**

Radio Revue of 1937 See **Let's Make a Night of It**

Railroad Rhythm Carnival Films (U). Exclusive Film Co., 3.36 (3,788) Spectra colour. p: W. Devenport Hackney, d: A. E. C. Hopkins. With Vilma Vanna, Jack Browning.

Raise the Roof BIP at Elstree (U). FN-Pathé, 2.30 (6,990) FT, songs RCA. d: Walter Summers, music Jay Whidden, Idris Lewis, Tom Helmore. With Betty Balfour, Maurice Evans.

Rasp, The Film Engineering at Walton (A). Fox, 12.31 (4,000). p: Jerome Jackson, d: Michael Powell, c: Geoffrey Faithfull, sc: Michael Powell from story by Philip MacDonald, des: Frank Wells. With C. M. Hallard.

Rat, The Imperator at Denham (A). Radio, 11.37 (6,510). p: Herbert Wilcox, d: Jack Raymond, c: Freddie Young, sc: Marjorie Gaffney, Hans Rameau from film (1925) and play (1927) by Ivor Novello and Constance Collier, music Anthony Collins, With Ruth Chatterton, Anton Walbrook, Rene Ray.

Real Bloke, A Baxter and Barter at Cricklewood (U). M-G-M, 3.35 (6,310). p: John Barter, d: John Baxter, dc: Desmond Dickinson, sc: from story by Herbert Ayres. With George Carney, Mary Clare.

Reasonable Doubt Pascal Film Productions at Shepperton (A). M-G-M, 12.36 (6,633). p: Gabriel Pascal, d: George King, sc: Ewart Brookes from his own story. With Nancy Burne, John Stuart, Marjorie Taylor.

Recipe for a Murder See **Blind Justice**

Red Aces Brit. Lion at Beaconsfield (A). Brit. Lion, 6.30 (5,498) silent. p: Edgar Wallace, S. W. Smith, d: Edgar Wallace, sc: Edgar Wallace from his own play. With Cronin Wilson, Muriel Angelus.

Red Dog, The See **Pyjamas Preferred**

Red Ensign G-B at Shepherd's Bush (U). G-B D, 2.34 (6,221). assoc. p: Jerome Jackson, d: Michael Powell, c: Leslie Rowson, sc: Jerome Jackson and Michael Powell, dial: L. du Garde Peach, des: Alfred Junge, cost: Gordon Conway, ed: Geoffrey Barkas, sd: A. Birch. With Leslie Banks, Carol Goodner.

Red Pearls Nettlefold at Walton (A). Butcher's, 2.30 (6,536) silent. p: Archibald Nettlefold, d: Walter Forde, c: Geoffrey Faithfull, sc: H. Fowler Mear from novel by J. Randolph James, *Nearer . . . Nearer*, des: W. G. Saunders, ed: A. Culley, music Paul Mulder. With Lillian Rich, Frank Perfitt, Kyoshi Takase.

Red Wagon BIP (A). Wardour, 12.33 (9,057). p: Walter Mycroft, d: Paul L. Stein, c: J. J. Cox, sc: Roger Burford, Arthur Woods, adapt: Edward Knoblock from novel by Lady Eleanor Smith, des: John Mead, cost: Motley, ed: Leslie Norman, sd: C. V. Thornton, MD: Kurt Schroeder, London Symphony Orchestra. With Greta Nissen, Raquel Torres, Charles Bickford.

Rembrandt LFP at Denham (A). UA,

11.36 (7,913). p: d: Alexander Korda, c: Georges Périnal, Robert Krasker, sc: June Head, film play by Carl Zuckmayer, des: Vincent Korda, H. M. Waller, cost: John Armstrong, ed: William Hornbeck, Francis Lyon, tech. adviser: Johan de Meester, sd: A. W. Watkins, A. Fisher, MD: Muir Mathieson, music Geoffrey Toye. With Charles Laughton, Elsa Lanchester, Gertrude Lawrence.

Remember When See **Riding High**

Return of Carol Sawyer, The See **Return of Carol Deane, The**

Return of a Stranger, The Premier-Stafford Productions at Shepperton (A). RKO-Radio, 5.37 (6,455). p: John Stafford, d: W. Victor Hanbury, c: Jimmy Wilson, sc: Akos Tolnay and Reginald Long from play by Rudolph Lothar. With Griffith Jones, Ellis Jeffreys.

Return of Bulldog Drummond, The BIP at Welwyn (U). Wardour, 4.34 (6,400). p: Walter Mycroft, d: Walter Summers, c: Jack Parker, sc: Walter Summers from novel by 'Sapper', *The Black Gang*, des: John Mead, cost: Norman Hartnell, ed: A. S. Bates, sd: David Howells. With Ralph Richardson, Ann Todd, Francis L. Sullivan.

Return of Carol Deane, The WB-FN at Teddington (A). FN, 8.38 (6,845). p: Jerome Jackson, d: Arthur Woods, c: Basil Emmott, sc: John Meehan Jr and Tommy Phipps from story by Joseph Santley, des: Peter Proud, ed: A. S. Bates, sd: H. C. Pearson. With Bebe Daniels, Arthur Margetson, Chili Bouchier.

Return of Mr. Reeder, The See **Missing People, The**

Return of Raffles, The Mansfield Markham at Walton (A). WP, 9.32 (6,715). p: d: Mansfield Markham, c: Geoffrey Faithfull, Emil Schunemann, sc: W. J. Balef from stories by E. W. Hornung, des: W. G. Saunders, ed: A. J. Seabourne, Reginald Beck, sd: M. Rose. With George Barraud, Camilla Horn, Claud Allister.

Return of the Frog Imperator at Beaconsfield (A). Brit. Lion, 11.38 (6,813). p: Herbert Wilcox, d: Maurice Elvey, c: George Stretton, sc: Ian Hay, W. G. Elliott from play by Ian Hay based on story by Edgar Wallace, *The India Rubber Man*, des: Norman Arnold. With Gordon Harker, Una O'Connor, Rene Ray.

Return of the Rat, The Gainsborough at Islington (A). W & F, (1) 4.29 (7,612) silent, (2) 7.29 (9,127) synchronised BTP. p: Michael Balcon, d: Graham Cutts, c: Roy Overbaugh, sc: Angus MacPhail, Edgar C. Middleton, A. Neil Lyons from idea by Ivor Novello and Constance Collier, des: Alan McNab. With Ivor Novello, Isabel Jeans.

Return of the Scarlet Pimpernel, The LFP-British Cine Alliance at Denham (U). UA, 10.37 (8,228, later 7,589). p: Arnold Pressburger, Alexander Korda, assoc. p: Adrian Brunel, d: Hans Schwartz, c: Mutz Greenbaum, sc: Arthus Wimperis, Adrian Brunel, Lajos Biro based on novel by Baroness Orczy, *Triumph of the Scarlet Pimpernel*, des: Lazare Meerson, cost: Rene Hubert, ed: William Hornbeck, Philip Charlot, sd: A. W. Watkins, MD: Muir Mathieson, music Arthur Benjamin. With Barry K. Barnes, Sophie Stewart, James Mason.

Return to Yesterday Ealing Studios (CAPAD) at Ealing (U). ABFD, 1.40 (6,210). p: Michael Balcon, assoc. p: S. C. Balcon, d: Robert Stevenson, c: Ronald Neame, Gordon Dines, Jeff Seaholme, sc: Robert Stevenson, Roland Pertwee, Angus MacPhail, Margaret Kennedy from play by Robert Morley, *Goodness, How Sad*, ed: Charles Saunders, MD: Ernest Irving. With Clive Brook, Anna Lee, Dame May Whitty.

Reunion Sound City at Shepperton (U). M-G-M, 11.32 (5,476). p: Norman Loudon, d: Ivar Campbell, assist: John Baxter, sc: Herbert Ayres, suggested by an article by Reginald Hargreaves. With Stewart Rome, Antony Holles.

Reverse Be My Lot, The Joe Rock Productions at Elstree Rock (A). Columbia, 1.38 (6,020). p: Nat Ross, d: Raymond Stross, c: John Silver, sc: Syd Courtenay from novel by Margaret Morrison. With Ian Fleming, Marjorie Corbett.

Revue Parade Ace Films, registered 3.38 (3,221). d: R. A. Hopwood, variety from Windmill Theatre.

Rhapsody See **Blue Danube, The**

Rhodes of Africa G-B at Shepherd's Bush, Africa (U). G-B D, 3.36 (8,175). p: Michael Balcon, d: Berthold Viertel, African location Geoffrey Barkas, c: Bernard Knowles (studio), S. R. Bonnett (Africa), sc: Leslie Arliss and Michael Barringer, dial: Miles Malleson, from book by Sarah Gertrude Millin, des: Oscar Werndorff, cost: Joe Strassner, ed: Derek Twist, sd: A. F. Birch, Philip Dorté, MD: Louis Levy. With Walter Huston, Oscar Homolka, Peggy Ashcroft.

Rhythm in the Air Fox Brit. at Wembley (U). Fox, 9.36 (6,438). p: John Findlay, d: Arthur Woods, c: Roy Kellino, music Kenneth Leslie-Smith, James Dyrenforth, Peggy Cochrane, Bruce Sievier. With Tutta Rolf, Jack Donohue.

Rhythm Racketeer Rock Productions at Elstree Rock (A). BIED, 9.37 (7,619, later 6,621). p: Joe Rock, d: James Seymour, c: Ernest Palmer, sc: James Seymour, John Byrd from story by Betty Laidlaw and Bob Lively, ed: Sam Simmonds, songs Cyril Ray, Eddie Pola, Lerner, Goodhart and Hoffman, dances Larry Ceballos. With Harry Roy, Princess Pearl.

Rich and Strange BIP at Elstree and on location (A). Wardour, 12.31 (7,425). p: John Maxwell, d: Alfred Hitchcock, c: J. J. Cox, Charles Martin, sc: Alfred Hitchcock, Alma Reville, Val Valentine from theme by Dale Collins, des: C. W. Arnold, ed: Winifred Cooper, René Harrison, sd: Alec Murray, MD: John Reynders, Music Hal Dolphe. With Percy Marmont, Joan Barry, Henry Kendall, Betty Amann.

Rich Young Man, A See **Amazing Quest of Ernest Bliss, The**

Riders to the Sea Flanagan-Hurst Productions in Ireland (A). M-G-M, first shown in UK 12.35, registered 2.37 (3,710). p: John Flanagan, d: Brian Desmond Hurst, sc: Brian Desmond Hurst from play by John Millington Synge (1904). With Sara Allgood, Abbey Theatre players.

Riding High Embassy Pictures at Shepperton (U). Brit.Lion, 7.39 (6,195). p: George King, d: David MacDonald, c: Hone Glendinning, sc: H. Folwer Mear. With Claude Dampier, Helen Haye, John Garrick.

Rift in the Lute, The See **Birds of a Feather**

Right Age to Marry, The GS Ent. at Walton (U). Radio, 6.35 (6,230). p: George Smith, d: P. Maclean Rogers, c: Geoffrey Faithfull, sc: H. F. Maltby, Kathleen Butler from play by H. F. Maltby (1925). With Frank Pettingell, Joyce Bland.

Right to Live, The Fox Brit. at Ealing (A). Fox, 10.33 (6,551, later 6,154). p: d: Albert Parker, sc: Gordon Wong Wellesley from story by Michael Barringer. With Davy Burnaby, Pat Paterson, Richard Bird.

Ringer, The Gainsborough-Brit. Lion at Beaconsfield (A). Ideal, first show 4.31 (6,738) FT RCA. p: Michael Balcon, exec. p: Edgar Wallace, d: Walter Forde, c: Alex Bryce, Leslie Rowson, sc: Angus MacPhail, Robert Stevenson from play by Edgar Wallace (1926), add. dial: Sidney Gilliat, des: Norman Arnold, ed: Ian Dalrymple, sd: Harold King. With Franklin Dyall, Gordon Harker, Carol Goodner, John Longden.

Rise of Catherine the Great, The See **Catherine the Great**

River House Ghost WB at Teddington (A). FN, 12.32 (4,788). p: Irving Asher, d: Frank A. Richardson. With Florence Desmond.

River House Mystery, The Imeson-Foulsham Films (U). Universal, 10.35

(5,039). p: A. B. Imeson, d: Fraser Foulsham, sc: F. G. Robertson. With George Mulcaster.

Riverside Melodies Electrocord (U). Butcher's, 12.29 (4,500).

Riverside Murder, The Fox Brit. at Wembley (A). Fox, 3.35 (5,824). d: Albert Parker, sc: Selwyn Jepson, Leslie Landau from novel by Andre Steedman, *Six Dead Men.* With Basil Sydney, Judy Gunn, Alastair Sim.

River Wolves, The Real Art at Twickenham (A). Radio, 1.34 (5,089). p: Julius Hagen, d: George Pearson, sc: Terence Egan from play by Edward Dignon and Geoffrey Swaffer, *Lion and Lamb.* With Helga Moray, Michael Hogan, John Mills.

Riviera See **Dinner at the Ritz**

Road House G-B at Shepherd's Bush (A). G-B D, 11.34 (6,902). p: Michael Balcon, d: Maurice Elvey, c: Leslie Rowson, sc: Austin Melford, Leslie Arliss from play by Walter Hackett (1932), des: Alfred Junge. With Violet Loraine, Gordon Harker, Emlyn Williams.

Road to Dishonour, The See **Flame of Love, The**

Road to Fortune, The Starcraft at Twickenham, Cornwall (U). Paramt, 8.30 (5,358) FT. p: d: Arthur Varney, sc: Hugh Broadbridge from his novel *The Moorland Terror.* With Guy Newall, Doria March.

Robber Symphony, The Concordia at BIP, Nice, Austria, Switzerland (Mont Blanc) and Shepperton lot (U). Concordia (1) 4.36 (12,600), (2) 11.36 (8,150). p: Freidrich Feher and Jack Trendall, d: Freidrich Feher, c: Eugene Schüfftan, sc: Jack Trendell from story by Freidrich Feher and Anton Kuh, des: Ernö Metzner, sd: Stanley Atkins, MD: Alfred Tokayer, music Freidrich Feher, Concordia Symphony Orchestra. With Hans Feher, Magda Sonja, George Graves, Webster Booth.

Robert Burns See **Auld Lang Syne**

Rocks of Valpré, The Real Art at Twickenham, Mullion Cove Cornwall

(A). Radio, 1.35 (6,682). p: Julius Hagen, d: Henry Edwards, sc: H. Fowler Mear from novel by Ethel M. Dell, des: James Carter. With Winifred Shotter, John Garrick.

Rodney Steps In Real Art at Twickenham (U). Fox, 6.31 (3,999). p: Julius Hagen, exec. p: Harry Cohen, d: Guy Newall, sc: Brock Williams. With Richard Cooper, Elizabeth Allan.

Rolling Home Sound City at Shepperton (U). AP & D 6.35 (6,200). p: Norman Loudon, d: Ralph Ince, c: George Stretton, H. M. Glendinning, sc: Frank Launder from story by Will Fyffe and G Marriott Edgar, des: D. W. L. Daniels, ed: Rose Gardener, sd: John Byers, MD: Colin Wark. With Will Fyffe, Ralph Ince, Molly Lamont.

Rolling in Money Fox Brit. at Ealing (A). Fox, 3.34 (7,744). d: Albert Parker, sc: R. J. Davis, Sewell Stokes, Frank Atkinson from play by R. C. Carton, *Mr. Hopkinson* (1905). With Leslie Sarony, Isabel Jeans, John Loder.

Romance à la Carte GS Ent. at Walton (U). RKO-Radio, 3.38 (7,000). p: George Smith, d: P. Maclean Rogers, c: Geoffrey Faithfull, sc: Vera Allinson from story by Paul Hervey Fox. With Dorothy Boyd, Leslie Perrins, Antony Holles.

Romance in Flanders, A Franco-London Films at Hammersmith (A). Brit. Lion, 8.37 (6,897). d: Maurice Elvey, c: Sydney Blythe, sc: Harold Simpson from novel by Mario Fort and Ralph venlo, *Widow's Island.* With Paul Cavanagh, Marcelle Chantal, Garry Marsh.

Romance in Rhythm (Allied Film Production) Lawrence Huntington at Cricklewood (A). M-G-M, 9.34 (6601). p: d: Lawrence Huntington, c: Desmond Dickinson, ed: Challis Sanderson, music Carroll Gibbons and his Savoy Orpheans. With Phyllis Clare, David Hutcheson.

Romance of Seville, A BIP (U). FN-Pathé 7.30 (5,610) synchronised songs, RCA. Pathécolour. d: Norman Walker, sc: Garnett Weston and Alma Reville from story by Arline Lord, *The Majo*. With Marguerite Allan, Alexander D'Arcy, Randle Ayrton, Eugenie Amami.

Romany Love Patrick K. Heale at Isleworth (U). M-G-M, 2.31 (5,400) FT, songs Fidelytone. p: Patrick Heale, d: Fred Paul, des: Norman Arnold.

Rome Express G-B at Shepherd's Bush (A). Gaumont, 11.32 (8,484). p: Michael Balcon, assoc. p: Philip Samuel, d: Walter Forde, c: Gunther Krampf, sc: Sidney Gilliat, Frank Vosper, Ralph Stock, from story by Clifford Grey, des: A. L. Mazzei, cost: Gordon Conway, ed: Frederick Y. Smith, sd: George Gunn, sp. effects: Jack Whitehead. With Conrad Veidt, Esther Ralston, Cedric Hardwicke.

Roof, The Real Art at Twickenham (A). Radio, 11.33 (5,223). p: Julius Hagen, d: G. A. Cooper, sc: H. Fowler Mear from novel by David Whitelaw. With Russell Thorndike, Judy Gunn.

Rookery Nook B & D-HMV at Elstree B & D (U). W & F, 2.30 (9,722) FT WE. p: Herbert Wilcox, d: Tom Walls, c: Bernard Knowles, William Shenton, sc: Ben Travers, W. P. Lipscomb from play by Ben Travers (1926), sd: A. W. Watkins. With Tom Walls, Ralph Lynn, Robertson Hare, Winifred Shotter.

Room and Board See **Save a Little Sunshine**

Rosary, The Twick. at Twickenham (A). WP, 7.31 (6,320). p: Julius Hagen, d: Guy Newall, c: Basil Emmott, sc: Guy Newall from story by John McNally, des: James Carter. With Margot Grahame, Elizabeth Allan, Leslie Perrins.

Rose of Tralee Butcher's-Hope Bell at Cricklewood (U). Butcher's, 4.37 (7,207, later 5,024). p: Norman Hope-Bell, d: sc: Oswald Mitchell, c: Jack Parker, des: Frank Gilman. With Binkie Stuart, Kathleen O'Regan, Fred Conyngham.

Royal Cavalcade BIP at Elstree and Welwyn (U). ABPC, 4.35 (9,020). p: Walter Mycroft, p: personnel Frank Mills, Roy Godddard, supervising d: Thomas Bentley, d: Herbert Brenon, Norman Lee, Walter Summers, Will Kellino, Marcel Varnel, c: Jack Cox, Horace Wheddon, Bryan Langley, Leslie Rowson, Phil Grindrod, sc: Val Gielgud, Holt Marvel, Eric Maschwitz, Marjorie Deans, des: Clarence Elder, John Mead, David Rawnsley, J. A. Marchant, ed: A. C. Hammond, Sidney Cole, J. Neill Brown, commentators Roy Russell, Edward Chapman, D. A. Clarke-Smith, research Countess of Carlisle, George Black Jr, sd: S Attkins, A. E. Rudolph, MD: Idris Lewis, music arranged Walter Collins.

Royal Demand, A Mrs C. P. Williams (Moorland Film Productions) (U). Paramt, 8.33 (5,639). d: Gustave Minzenty, sc: Jane Moorland, based on painting *When Did You Last See Your Father?* With Cyril McLaglen, Marjorie Hume.

Royal Divorce, A Imperator at Denham (A). Paramt, 9.38 (7,623). p: Herbert Wilcox, d: Jack Raymond, c: George Stretton, sc: Miles Malleson from story by Jacques Thery, des: David Rawnsley, cost: Georges Benda, ed: Peggy Hennessy, sd: L. E. Overton, MD: Muir Mathieson, music Anthony Collins. With Ruth Chatterton, Pierre Blanchar, Frank Cellier.

Royal Eagle Quality Films at Elstree (BIP) (A). Columbia, 6.36 (6,212). d: G. A. Cooper, Arnold Ridley from story by Arnold Ridley. With John Garrick, Nancy Burne.

Royal Husband See **Private Life of Henry VIII, The**

Royal Jubilee See **Royal Cavalcade**

Royal Romance See **Everything is Rhythm**

Runaway Ladies International Player Pictures at Elstree (A). Exclusive Films, 6.38 (4,423). p: M. H. Booth, d: Jean de Limur, sc: remake of French film, based on story by Tristram Bernard, *Le Voyage Imprévu*. With Betty Stockfield, Hugh Wakefield, Roger Treville,

Raymond Cordy.

Runaway Romance See **She Couldn't Say No**

Rynox Film Engineering at Walton (A). Ideal, 11.31 (4,273). p: Jerome Jackson, d: Michael Powell, c: Geoffrey Faithfull, Michael Powell from novel by Philip MacDonald, ed: A. J. Seabourne. With Stewart Rome, John Longden, Dorothy Boyd.

Sabotage Sound City at Shepperton (A). Reunion Films, 2.36 (5,889). p: Norman Loudon, d: Adrian Brunel, c: George Stretton, sc: Heinrich Fraenkel, A. R. Rawlinson from story by Victor Varconi. With Joan Maude, Victor Varconi.

Sabotage G-B at Shepherd's Bush (A). G-B D, 12.36 (6,917). p: Michael Balcon, assoc. p: Ivor Montagu, d: Alfred Hitchcock, c: Bernard Knowles, c: Charles Bennett, Alma Reville, dial: E. V. H. Emmett, Ian Hay and Helen Simpson from novel by Joseph Conrad, *The Secret Agent*, des: Oscar Werndorff, Albert Jullion, ed: Charles Frend, cost: Joe Strassner, sd: A. Cameron, MD: Louis Levy. With Sylvia Sidney, John Loder, Oscar Homolka, Desmond Tester.

Safe Affair, A Langham Productions at Walton (U). M-G-M, 10.31 (4,758) FT RCA. d: Bert Wynne, sc: Eliot Stannard from story by Douglas Hoare. With Franklin Dyall, Jeanne Stuart.

Safe Bet See **It's a Bet**

Safe Proposition, A Real Art at Twickenham (U). Fox, 6.32 (4,191). p: Julius Hagen, d: Leslie Hiscott, sc: Michael Barringer. With A. W. Baskcomb, Austin Trevor.

Safety First See **Crazy People**

Said O'Reilly to McNab Gainsborough at Islington (U). GFD, 6.37 (7,634). assoc. p: Edward Black, d: William Beaudine, c: Arthur Crabtree, sc: G Marriott Edgar and Leslie Arliss from story by Howard Irving Young. With Will Mahoney, Will Fyffe.

Sailing Along G-B at Pinewood (U).

GFD, 1.38 (8,504). d: Sonnie Hale, c: Glen MacWilliams, sc: Lesser Samuels, Sonnie Hale from story by Selwyn Jepson, des: Alfred Junge, cost: Norman Hartnell, ed: Al Barnes, sd: A. C. O'Donoghue, MD: Louis Levy, music and songs Arthur Johnston, Maurice Sigler, dances Buddy Bradley. With Jessie Matthews, Barry Mackay, Roland Young, Jack Whiting.

Saint in London, The RKO-Radio at Elstree Rock (A). RKO-Radio, 6.39 (6,799). p: William Sistrom, d: John Paddy Carstairs, c: Claude Friese-Greene, sc: Lynn Root, Frank Fenton from story by Leslie Charteris, *Million Pound Day*. With George Sanders, Sally Gray.

Sally Bishop Brit. Lion at Beaconsfield (A). Brit. Lion, 10.32 (7,348). p: S. W. Smith, d: T. Hayes Hunter, c: Alex Bryce, sc: John Drinkwater from novel by E. Temple Thurston, des: Norman Arnold, ed: Arthur Tavares, sd: Harold King. With Joan Barry, Harold Huth, Isabel Jeans, Benita Hume.

Sally Comes to Town See **Shipyard Sally**

Sally in our Alley ATP at Beaconsfield (A). Radio, 7.31 (6,967) FT, songs RCA. p: Basil Dean, d: Maurice Elvey, c: Robert Martin, Alex Bryce, sc: Archie Pitt, Miles Malleson, Alma Reville from play by Charles McEvoy, *The Likes of 'er* (1923), des: Norman Arnold, ed: Otto Ludwig, sd: Marcus Cooper, songs by A. P. Herbert, 'Sally' by Bill Haines. With Gracie Fields, Florence Desmond, Ian Hunter, Gibb McLaughlin.

Sally of the Shipyards See **Shipyard Sally**

Sam Small Leaves Town British Screen Service at Highbury, Skegness (U). British Screen Service, 10.37 (6,454). p: Maurice J. Wilson, d: Alf Goulding. With Stanley Holloway, June Clyde.

Sanders of the River LFP at Shepperton, Africa (U). UA, 4.35 (8,764). p: Alexander Korda, d: Zoltan Korda, c: Georges Périnal, Osmond Borradaile, Louis Page, Bernard Browne, sc: Lajos

Biro, Jeffrey Dell from stories by Edgar Wallace, add. dial: Arthur Wimperis, des: Vincent Korda, ed: William Hornbeck, Charles Crichton, sd: A. W. Watkins, MD: Muir Mathieson, music Mischa Spoliansky, lyrics Arthur Wimperis. With Paul Robeson, Nina Mae McKinney, Leslie Banks.

Saturday Night Revue Welwyn Studio at Welwyn (A). Pathé, 10.37 (7,643, later 6,940). p: Warwick Ward, d: Norman Lee, c: Bryan Langley, sc: Vernon Clancey. With Billy Milton, Sally Gray, John Watt.

Save a Little Sunshine Welwyn Studios at Welwyn (A). Pathé, 9.38 (6,798). p: Warwick Ward, d: Norman Lee, c: Bryan Langley, sc: Vernon Clancey and Victor Kendall, add. dial: Gilbert Gunn, from play by W. Armitage Owen, *Lights Out*, des: Duncan Sutherland, ed: E. Richards, sd: A. E. Rudolph, MD: John Reynders, songs Noel Gay. With Dave Willis, Pat Kirkwood.

Say It With Diamonds Redd Davis at Walton (A). M-G-M, 3.35 (5,950). d: Redd Davis, sc: Jack Marks. With Frank Pettingell, Eve Becke.

Say It With Flowers Real Art at Twickenham (U). Radio, 1.34 (6,347). p: Julius Hagen, d: John Baxter, c: Sydney Blythe, sc: Wallace Orton, H. Fowler Mear from story by John Baxter, des: James Carter, ed: Michacl Chorlton. With Mary Clare, George Carney.

Say It With Music B & D at Elstree B & D (U). W & F, 11.32 (6,298). p: Herbert Wilcox, d: Jack Raymond, c: Osmond Borradaile, sc: William Pollock, music and lyrics Ray Noble. With Jack Payne and his Band, Percy Marmont.

Say It With Song See **Music Hall**

Scarab Murder Case, The B & D-Para-Brit. at Pinewood (A). Paramt, 11.36 (6,152). p: Anthony Havelock-Allan, d: Michael Hankinson, sc: Selwyn Jepson from novel by S. S. Van Dine. With Kathleen Kelly, Wilfred Hyde-White.

Scarlet Murder Mystery See **Scarab Murder Case, The**

Scarlet Pimpernel, The LFP at Elstree (A). UA, 12.34 (8,904). p: Alexander Korda, d: Harold Young, c: Harold Rosson, Osmond Borradaile, sc: Arthur Wimperis, Robert Sherwood, Sam Berman, Lajos Biro from novel by Baroness Orczy, des: Vincent Korda, cost: John Armstrong, ed: William Hornbeck, cost: for Merle Oberon Oliver Messel, sd: A. W. Watkins, sp. effects: Ned Mann, MD: Muir Mathieson, music Arthur Benjamin. With Leslie Howard, Merle Oberon, Raymond Massey.

Scat Burglars, The New Ideal Pictures at Hammersmith (A). M-G-M, 2.37 (4,207). p: Geoffrey Rowson, d: Leslie Rowson, c: H. Gillam, sc: Fenn Sherie, Ingram D'Abbes. With Harry Haver, Frank Lee.

Schooldays See **Things Are Looking Up**

School for Husbands J. G. & R. B. Wainwright at Shepperton (A). GFD, 8.37 (6,485). p: Richard Wainwright, d: Andrew Marton, sc: Frederick Jackson, Austin Melford, Gordon Sherry from play by Frederick Jackson (1932). With Diana Churchill, Rex Harrison, June Clyde, Henry Kendall.

School for Scandal, The Albion Film Syndicate at Elstree B & D (U). Paramt, registered 9.30, (6,910) FT, song. Raycol. d: Maurice Elvey, c: Bernard Knowles, sc: Jean Jay from play by Richard Brinsley Sheridan, des: L. P. Williams. With Basil Gill, Madeleine Carroll, Ian Fleming.

School for Stars B & D-Para-Brit. at Elstree B & D (A). Paramt, 5.35 (6,382). d: Donovan Pedelty, sc: Donovan Pedelty from story by Charles Austin. With Jean Gillie, Fred Conyngham.

Schooner Gang, The New Garrick Productions at Cricklewood, Leigh-on-Sea (U). Butcher's, 9.37 (6,487). p: d: W. Devenport Hackney, c: Jack Parker, sc: Frank Atkinson, Ralph Dawson, Iris Terry from story by W. Devenport Hackney.

Scoop, The B & D-Para-Brit. at Elstree B & D (A). Paramt, 10.34 (6,125). d: P. Maclcan Rogers, sc: Basil Mason, Gerald Geraghty from play by Jack Heming. With Anne Grey, Tom Helmore.

Scotland Yard Mystery, The BIP (A). Wardour, 1.34 (6,800). p. Walter Mycroft, d: Thomas Bentley, sc: Frank Miller from play by Wallace Geoffrey. With Sir Gerald du Maurier, George Curzon, Greta Natzler.

Scraggs Harry B. Parkinson (U). J-M-G, 3.30 (5,659) silent. p: Harry B. Parkinson, d: Challis Sanderson, sc: Challis Sanderson from story by Norman Lee. With Eric Hales.

Screen Struck UK Films at Shepperton (U). M-G-M, 3.37 (3,514). p: John Barter and John Baxter, d: Lawrence Huntington, c: Jack Parker, from story by Herbert Ayres. With Julian Vedey, Diana Beaumont.

Scrooge Twick. at Twickenham (U). Twick. FD, 7.35 (7,006). p: Julius Hagen, p: supervisor Hans Brahm, d: Henry Edwards, c: Sydney Blythe, William Luff, sc: H. Fowler Mear from novel by Charles Dickens, *A Christmas Carol*, des: James Carter, cost: L. & H. Nathan, ed: Jack Harris, Ralph Kemplen, sd: Baynham Honri, MD: and music W. L. Trytel. With Sir Seymour Hicks, Donald Calthrop.

Scruffy Vulcan Pictures at Cricklewood (U). BIED, 4.38 (5,550). d: Randall Faye, c: Desmond Dickinson, sc: from story by Margarette Houghton, des: Don Russell, ed: Dan Birt. With 'Scruffy', Billy Merson, Jack Melford.

Second Best Bed Capitol at Shepperton (A). GFD, 1.38 (6,696). p: Max Schach, d: Tom Walls, c: J. J. Cox, sc: Ben Travers from his own story, des: Walter Murton, ed: Lynn Harrison, sd: M. Cruikshank, MD: Van Phillips. With Tom Walls, Jane Baxter.

Second Bureau Premier-Stafford Productions at Shepperton (A). Radio, 12.36 (6,966). p: John Stafford, d: W. Victor Hanbury, c: Jimmy Wilson, sc: Akos Tolnay from novel by Charles Robert-Dumas, *Deuxième Bureau*, as adapted by Bernard Zimmer for French film, *Deuxième Bureau*, d: Pierre Billon. With Marta Labarr, Charles Oliver, Anthony Eustrel.

Second Mr. Bush, The Brit. Nat., in production at Welwyn 6.38, not shown until 4.40. p: John Corfield, d: John Paddy Carstairs, c: Jimmy Wilson, sc: Doreen Montgomery, Leslie Arliss from play by Stafford Dickens (1938). With Derrick de Marney, Kay Walsh.

Second Thoughts Fox Brit. at Wembley (A). 20th Century-Fox, 3.38 (5,549). d: Albert Parker, c: Ronald Neame, sc: David Evans from his own story, des: William Hemsley, ed: Peter Tanner. With Frank Fox, Evelyn Ankers, Frank Allenby.

Secret Agent G-B at Shepherd's Bush (A). G-B D, 5.36 (7,809). p: Michael Balcon, assoc. p: Ivor Montagu, d: Alfred Hitchcock, c: Bernard Knowles, sc: Charles Bennett, Alma Reville, add. dial: Ian Hay, Jesse Lasky Jr from novel by W. Somerset Maugham, *Ashenden*, and play by Campbell Dixon, des: Oscar Werndorff, Albert Jullion, ed: Charles Frend, cost: Joe Strassner, sd: Philip Dorté, MD: Louis Levy. With Madeleine Carroll, John Gielgud, Peter Lorre, Robert Young.

Secretary in Trouble See **Who's Your Lady Friend?**

Service Flat, The See **Here's George**

Secret Journey Brit. Nat. at Elstree former Whitehall (U). Anglo-American Films, 5.39 (6,045). p: John Corfield, d: John Baxter, c: Jimmy Wilson, sc: Michael Hogan from novel by Charles Dumas. With Basil Radford, Sylvia St Claire.

Secret Lives Phoenix-International Film Productions at Ealing (A). ABFD, 3.37 (7,034). p: Hugh Perceval, d: Edmond T. Gréville, c: Otto Heller, sc: Basil Mason from novel by Paul de Ste Colombe. With Brigitte Horney, Neil Hamilton.

Secret of Stamboul, The J. G. & R. B. Wainwright at Shepperton (A). GFD, 10.36 (8,311, later 7,853). p: Richard

Wainwright, d: Andrew Marton, c: Henry Harris, sc: Richard Wainwright from novel by Dennis Wheatley, *The Eunuch of Stamboul*. With Frank Vosper, Valerie Hobson, James Mason, Kay Walsh.

Secret of the Loch, The Wyndham Productions at Ealing (U). ABFD, 6.34 (7,117). p: Bray Wyndham, d: Milton Rosmer, c: Jimmy Wilson, sc: Charles Bennett, Billie Bristow, des: J. Elder Wills, music Peter Mendoza. With Sir Seymour Hicks, Nancy O'Neil.

Secret Voice, The B & D-Para-Brit. (A). Paramt, 2.36 (6,005). d: George Pearson, c: Francis Carver, sc: Margaret McDonnell from screen story by Frances Warren. With John Stuart, Diana Beaumont.

Seeing Is Believing B & D-Para-Brit. (U). Paramt, 2.34 (6,370). d: Redd Davis, sc: from screen story by Donovan Pedelty, des: Hylton R. Oxley. With Billy Hartnell, Faith Bennett.

Self-Made Lady George King at Walton (A). UA, 3.32 (6,990). p: d: George King, c: Geoffrey Faithfull, sc: Billie Bristow from novel by Douglas Newton, *Sookey*. With Heather Angel, Louis Hayward, Harry Wilcoxon.

Send 'em Back Half Dead Cecil Landeau at Elstree Blattner (U). Fox, 5.33 (4,042). d: Redd Davis. With Nelson Keys.

Sensation BIP at Elstree (A). ABPC, 12.36 (6,050). p: Walter Mycroft, d: Brian Desmond Hurst, c: Walter Harvey, sc: Dudley Leslie, William Freshman, Marjorie Deans from play by George Munro and Basil Dean, *Murder Gang* (1935), des: John Mead, ed: James Corbett, sd: C. V. Thornton. With John Lodge, Margaret Vyner.

Service for Ladies Para-Brit. at Elstree B & D (A). Parmt, 1.32 (8,400). p: d: Alexander Korda, c: Philip Tannura, sc: Eliot Crawshay Williams and Lajos Biro from story by Ernst Vajda, *The Head Waiter*, des: R. Holmes Paul. With Leslie Howard, George Grossmith, Benita Hume, Elizabeth Allan.

Servants All Fox Brit. at Wembley (U). Fox. 3.36 (3,053). d: Alex Bryce, sc: E. Lewis Waller from music-hall sketch. With Robb Wilton, Eve Lister.

Seven Sinners G-B at Shepherd's Bush (A). G-B D, 6.36 (6,286). p: Michael Balcon, d: Albert de Courville, c: Mutz Greenbaum, sc. adapt: L. du Garde Peach, sc: Sidney Gilliat and Frank Launder, add. dial: Austin Melford from play by Arnold Ridley and Bernard Merivale, *The Wrecker* (1928), des: Ernö Metzner, cost: Molyneaux, ed: M. Gordon, sd: A. Birch, MD: Louis Levy, music Bretton Byrd. With Edmund Lowe, Constance Cummings.

77, Park Lane Famous Players Guild at Walton (A). UA, 6.31 (7,991) FT RCA. d: Albert de Courville, c: Mutz Greenbaum, Geoffrey Faithfull, sc: Michael Powell from play by Walter Hackett (1928). With Dennis Neilson-Terry, Betty Stockfield. (Trilingual.)

Sexton Blake and the Bearded Doctor Fox Brit. at Wembley (U). M-G-M, 7.35 (5,892). d: G. A. Cooper, c: Alex Bryce, sc: from novel by Rex Hardinge, *The Blazing Launch Murder*. With George Curzon, Henry Oscar, Donald Wolfit.

Sexton Blake and the Hooded Terror George King at Shepperton (A). M-G-M, 2.38 (6,211). p: d: George King, c: Hone Glendinning, sc: A. R. Rawlinson from story by Pierre Quiroule. With George Curzon, Tod Slaughter, Greta Gynt.

Sexton Blake and the Mademoiselle Fox Brit. (U). M-G-M, 10.35 (5,773). d: Alex Bryce, sc: Michael Barringer from novel by G. H. Teed, *They Shall Repay*. With George Curzon, Lorraine Grey.

Sexton Blake and the Master Criminal See **Sexton Blake and the Hooded Terror**

Shadow, The Real Art at Twickenham (A). UA, 3.33 (6,752). p: Julius Hagen, d: G. A. Cooper, sc: H. Fowler Mear from play by Donald Stuart. With Henry Kendall, Elizabeth Allan.

Shadow Between, The BIP (A). Wardour, 9.31 (8,426). d: Norman Walker, c: Claude Friese-Greene, sc: Norman Walker and Dion Titheradge from screen story by Dion Titheradge. With Godfrey Tearle, Kathleen O'Regan.

Shadowed Eyes GS Ent.-Savoy Productions at Isleworth (A). RKO-Radio, 9.39 (6,194). p: George Smith, d: P. Maclean Rogers, c: Geoffrey Faithfull, sc: Roy Carter, Herbert Hill from story by Arnold Ridley, des: R. Holmes Paul, ed: V. Savosky. With Basil Sydney, Ian Fleming, Patricia Hilliard, Stewart Rome.

Shadow of Mike Emerald, The GS Ent. (A). Radio, 10.33 (5,561). p: George Smith, d: P. Maclean Rogers, sc: Anthony Richardson, Kathleen Butler from story by Anthony Richardson. With Leslie Perrins, Marjorie Mars.

Shadows BIP at Elstree (A). FN-Pathé, 3.31 (5,140) FT RCA. d: Alexander Esway, sc: Frank Miller. With Jacqueline Logan, Bernard Nedell, Derrick de Marney.

Shady Lady See **Love on the Spot**

Shakespeare Murders (1934) See **Third Clue, The**

Shakespeare Murders, The (1938) See **Claydon Treasure Mystery, The**

Sharps and Flats See **Play up the Band**

She Couldn't Say No ABPC at Elstree (U). ABPC, 11.39 (6,400). p: Walter Mycroft, d: Graham Cutts, c: Claude Friese-Greene, sc: Clifford Grey, Elizabeth Meehan, Bert Lee from musical play by Fred Thompson and Paul Gerard Smith, *Funny Face* (1927), songs James Dyrenforth and Kenneth Leslie-Smith, dances Freddie Carpenter. With Tommy Trinder, Basil Radford, Greta Gynt.

She Got What She Wanted See **Clothes and the Woman**

She Knew What She Wanted Rialto Productions (U). Wardour, 5.36 (6,910). p: d: Thomas Bentley, sc: Tom Geraghty, Frank Miller, from musical play by Fred Thompson and Paul Gerard Smith, *Funny Face* (1927), music George Gershwin. With Claude Dampier, Albert Burdon, Betty Ann Davies.

Shepherd's Warning See **House of Trent, The**

She Shall Have Music Twick. at Twickenham (U). Twick FD, 11.35 (8,310). p: Julius Hagen, d: Leslie Hiscott, c: Sydney Blythe, William Luff, sc: H. Fowler Mear, Arthur Macrae from story by Paul England, des: James Carter, music Jack Hylton and his Band, songs Sigler, Goodhart and Hoffman, dances Howard Deighton. With Claude Dampier, June Clyde, Jack Hylton.

She Wanted her Man See **Song You Gave Me, The**

She Was Only a Village Maiden Sound City at Shepperton (A). M-G-M, 2.33 (5,487). p: Ivar Campbell, d: Arthur Maude, c: George Stretton, sc: N. W. B. Pemberton and John Cousins from play by Fanny Bowker, *Priscilla the Rake*. With Anne Grey, Lester Matthews, Antony Holles, Carl Harbord.

Shilling for Candles, A See **Young and Innocent**

Shipmates O' Mine T. A. Welsh Productions at Cricklewood (U). Butcher's, 5.36 (7,850). d: sc: Oswald Mitchell, c: Robert Martin. With John Garrick, Jean Adrienne.

Ship's Concert WB-FN at Teddington (U). WB, 4.37 (4,087, later 3,914). p: Irving Asher, d: Leslie Hiscott, c: Robert Lapresle, sc: Reginald Purdell, John Dighton. With Claude Hulbert, Henry Kendall, Enid Trevor.

Shipyard Sally Twentieth Century Productions at Islington (U). 20th Century-Fox, 7.39 (7,153). p: Edward Black, d: Monty Banks, c: Otto Kanturek, sc: Karl Tunberg and Don Ettlinger from their screen story, des: Vetchinsky, ed: R. E. Dearing, Alfred Roome, sd: M. Paggi, MD: Louis Levy, lyrics Harry Parr-Davies. With Gracie Fields, Sydney Howard.

Shooting Stars Viking Films at Cricklewood (U). Viking Films, 10.37 (6,222, later 6,058 with short version 3,734). p: d: Eric Humphriss, c: Desmond Dickinson, sc: Fred Duprez.

Shot in the Dark, A Real Art at Twickenham (A). Radio, 10.33 (4,847). p: Julius Hagen, d: George Pearson, sc: H. Fowler Mear from novel by Gerard Fairlie. With Russell Thorndike, Dorothy Boyd.

Should a Doctor Tell? Brit. Lion at Beaconsfield (A). Brit. Lion, 9.30 (5,300) FT RCA. p: S. W. Smith, d: Manning Haynes, c: Alex Bryce, sc: G. B. Samuelson, Walter Summers, dial: Edgar Wallace. With Basil Gill, Norah Baring, Maurice Evans.

Show Flat B & D-Para-Brit. at Shepperton (U). Paramt, 10.36 (6,387). d: Bernerd Mainwaring. With Polly Ward, Anthony Hankey.

Show Goes On, The ATP at Ealing (U). ABFD, 3.37 (8,234). p: d: Basil Dean, c: Jan Stallich, sc: and dialogue Anthony Kimmins, Austin Melford, from story by Basil Dean and Anthony Kimmins, des: R. Holmes Paul, finale Cathleen Mann, ed: Jack Kitchin, sd: Paul F. Wiser, MD: Ernest Irving, music and lyrics Harry Parr-Davies, Eddie Pola, Bill Haines, Jimmy Harper, dances Carl Randall. With Gracie Fields, Owen Nares, John Stuart.

Shuttlecoq See **Blue Danube, The**

Side Street Angel WB-FN at Teddington (A). WB, 3.37 (5,842). p: Irving Asher, d: Ralph Ince, c: Basil Emmott. With Hugh Williams, Lesley Brook, Henry Kendall.

Side Streets Sound City at Shepperton (A). M-G-M, 3.33 (4,243). p: Norman Loudon, d: Ivar Campbell, sc: Philip Godfrey. With Diana Beaumont, Jane Wood.

Sign of Four, The ATP at Ealing (U). Radio, 5.32 (6,897). p: Basil Dean, p: supervised Rowland V. Lee, d: Graham Cutts, c: Robert Martin, Robert de Grasse, sc: W. P. Lipscombe, John Paddy Carstairs from novel by Sir Arthur Conan Doyle, des: Clifford Pember, ed: Otto Ludwig, sd: A. D. Valentine, MD: Ernest Irving. With Arthur Wontner, Isla Bevan, Ian

Hunter.

Sign, Please (1934) See **Brides to Be**

Sign Please G-B (U). Ideal, registered 2.33 (1,829). p: Clayton Hutton, d: John Rawlins, sc: Sidney Gilliat from Fred Karno sketch, *The Salesmen*. With Naughton and Gold.

Silent Battle, The Pinebrook at Denham (U). Paramt, 3.39 (6,356). p: Anthony Havelock-Allan, d: Herbert Mason, c: Francis Carver, sc: Rodney Ackland, Wolfgang Wilhelm from novel by Jean Bommert, *Le Poisson Chinois*, des: Wilfred Arnold. With Valerie Hobson, Rex Harrison, John Loder.

Silent Passenger, The Phoenix Films (A). ABFD, 6.35 (6,583). p: Hugh Perceval, d: Reginald Denham, c: Jan Stallich, sc: Basil Mason from story by Dorothy L. Sayers. With John Loder, Mary Newland.

Silver Blaze Twick. (U). ABPC, 6.37 (6,358). p: Julius Hagen, d: Thomas Bentley, c: Sydney Blythe, sc: H. Fowler Mear, Arthur Macrae from story by Sir Arthur Conan Doyle, *The Hound of the Baskervilles*, freely adapted, des: James Carter, ed: Alan Smith, Michael Chorlton, sd: Leonard Scotchbrook, Carlisle Mountenay, MD: M. de Wolfe. With Arthur Wontner, Ian Fleming, Lyn Harding.

Silver Greyhound, The WB-FN at Teddington (U). WB, 9.32 (4,244). p: Irving Asher, d: William McGann, c: Basil Emmott, sc: John Hastings Turner, Roland Pertwee from screen story by John Hastings Turner. With Percy Marmont, Anthony Bushell, Janice Adair.

Silver King, The Welsh-Pearson-Elder (U). Paramt, 6.29 (8,462) silent. d: T. Hayes Hunter, c: Bernard Knowles, Fred Ford, sc: Fenn Sherie from play by Henry Arthur Jones and Henry Herman, des: Walter Murton. With Percy Marmont, Jean Jay.

Silver Spoon, The WB-FN at Teddington (A). FN, 12.33 (5,874). p: Irving Asher, d: George King, sc: Brock Williams. With Ian Hunter, Garry Marsh, Binnie

Barnes.

Silver Top Triangle at Shepperton (U). Paramt, 1.38 (6,017). p: d: George King, c: Hone Glendinning, sc: W. G. Elliott, Dorothy Greenhill from story by Evadne Price. With Betty Ann Davies, Marie Wright, David Farrar.

Simply Terrific WB-FN at Teddington (A). WB, 2.38 (6,556). p: Irving Asher, d: Roy W. Neill, c: Robert Lapresle, sc: Basil Dillon, Anthony Hankey. With Claude Hulbert, Reginald Purdell, Patricia Medina.

Sing As We Go ATP at Ealing, Blackpool (U). ABFD, 9.34 (7,121). p: d: Basil Dean, c: Robert Martin, sc: J. B. Priestley, Gordon Wellesley from story by J. B. Priestley, des: J. Elder Wills, ed: Thorold Dickinson, lyrics Harry Parr-Davies. With Gracie Fields, John Loder, Dorothy Hyson.

Sing As You Swing Rock Studios at Elstree Rock (U). BIED, 7.37 (7,400, later 6,832). p: Joe Rock. d: Redd Davis, sc: Syd Courtenay from story by Clifford Grey, songs Cyril Ray, Clifford Grey. With Claude Dampier, Evelyn Dall, Lu Ann Meredith.

Singing Cop, The WB-FN at Teddington (U). WB, 1.38 (7,028). p: Irving Asher, d: Arthur Woods, c: Basil Emmott, sc: Brock Williams, Tom Phipps from story by James Dyrenforth and K. Leslie-Smith, songs Kenneth Leslie-Smith, dances Jack Donohue. With Keith Falkener, Chili Bouchier, Marta Labarr.

Singing Kettle See **This Is the Life**

Sir or Madam Foremost Productions (U). WB, 2.30 (6,421) silent. d: Karl Boese, sc: Eliot Stannard from novel by Berta Ruck. With Ossi Oswalda, Percy Marmont.

Sir Tristram Goes West See **Ghost Goes West, The**

Sister to Assist 'Er, A F. A. Thompson at Shepherd's Bush (A). Gaumont, 3.30 (5,719) FT Brit. Ac. p: Harry B. Parkinson, d: George Dewhurst, c: Percy Strong, sc: George Dewhurst from stories by John le Breton. With Barbara

Gott, Pollie Emery, Donald Stewart.

Sister to Assist 'Er AIP at Elstree former Whitehall (U). Columbia, 3.38 (6,506). p: Widgey Newman, d: Widgey Newman and George Dewhurst, sc: George Dewhurst from sketch based on stories by John le Breton. With Barbara George, Pollie Emery.

Sixty Glorious Years Imperator at Denham, Windsor, Balmoral, Buckingham Palace (U). RKO-Radio, 10.38 (8,575) Technicolor (colour direction Natalie Kalmus). p: d: Herbert Wilcox, c: Freddie Young, Technicolor c: W. Skall, sc: Miles Malleson, Charles de Grandcourt from story by Sir Robert Vansittart and Miles Malleson, des: L. P. Williams, cost: Doris Zinkeisen, historical adviser Tom Heslewood, ed: Jill Irving, sd: L. E. Overton, special effects Percy Day, MD: Muir Mathieson, music Anthony Collins. With Anna Neagle, Anton Walbrook, C. Aubrey Smith.

Skin Game, The BIP at Elstree (A). Wardour, 2.31 (7,933) FT RCA. p: John Maxwell, d: Alfred Hitchcock, c: J. J. Cox, Charles Martin, sc: Alfred Hitchcock, Alma Reville from play by John Galsworthy (1920), des: J. B. Maxwell, ed: René Harrison, A. Gobbett, sd: Alec Murray. With Edmund Gwenn, Edward Chapman, John Longden, Frank Lawton, Jill Esmond, Phyllis Konstam.

Skipper of the 'Osprey' ATP at Ealing (U). ABFD, 11.33 (2,764) Raycol. p: Basil Dean, d: Norman Walker, c: Gus Driss, sc: W. P. Lipscomb from story by W. W. Jacobs. With Ian Hunter, Renee Gadd.

Skylarks Reunion Films (U). Brit. Lion, 12.36 (6,750). p: John Gossage, d: Thornton Freeland. With Jimmy Nervo, Teddy Knox, Nancy Burne.

Sky Raiders, The Sovereign Films at Pinewood (A). FN, 3.38 (5,155). d: Fraser Foulsham. With Nita Harvey, Ambrose Day.

Sky's The Limit, The Jack Buchanan Productions at Pinewood (U). GFD,

11.37 (7,011). p: Jack Buchanan, d: Jack Buchanan, Lee Garmes, c: Henry Harris, sc: Jack Buchanan and Douglas Furber from story by Ralph Spence, des: Tom Morahan, cost: Rene Hubert, Paquin, ed: Francis Lyon, Michael Gordon, sd: John Dennis, MD: Van Phillips, songs Rawicz and Landauer with lyrics by Desmond Carter, and by Silver, Sherman and Lewis. With Jack Buchanan, Mara Losseff, David Hutcheson.

Sleeping Car G–B at Shepherd's Bush (A). Gaumont-Ideal, 5.35 (7,472). p: Michael Balcon, assoc. p: R. B. Wainwright, d: Anatole Litvak, sc: from story by Franz Schulz. With Madeleine Carroll, Ivor Novello, Laddie Cliff.

Sleeping Cardinal, The Twick. at Twickenham (U). WB, 2.31 (7,648). p: Julius Hagen, d: Leslie Hiscott, c: Sydney Blythe, sc: Leslie Hiscott from stories by Sir Arthur Conan Doyle, *The Empty House* and *The Final Problem*, sd: Baynham Honri. With Arthur Wontner, Ian Fleming, Norman McKinnel.

Sleeping Partners Sageen Productions at Islington (A). Paramt, 2.30 (7,826) FT and silent version p: Sir Seymour Hicks, d: Sascha Geneen, c: Karl Freund, sc: Sir Seymour Hicks from sketch by Sacha Guitry. With Sir Seymour Hicks, Edna Best.

Sleepless Nights BIP (A). Wardour, 11.32 (6,500). d: Thomas Bentley, c: J. J. Cox, sc: Victor Kendall from story by Stanley Lupino. With Stanley Lupino.

Sleuths See **Easy Money**

Small Man The Baxter and Barter at Cricklewood (U). Universal, 3.35 (6,300). p: John Barter, d: John Baxter, c: Desmond Dickinson, sc: from story by Con West. With George Carney, Minnie Rayner.

Smash and Grab Jack Buchanan Productions at Pinewood (A). GFD, 9.37 (6,930). d: Tim Whelan, c: Roy Clark, Henry Harris, sc: Ralph Spence from story by Tim Whelan.

Smiling Along Argyle Talking Pictures

(U). Equity British, 12.32 (3,520). p: d: sc: John Argyle. With Rene Ray, James Benton, Margaret Delane.

Smith's Wives Fox Brit. at Wembley (A). Fox, 2.35 (5,560). d: Manning Haynes, c: Alex Bryce, sc: Con West, Herbert Sargent from story by Ernie Lotinga based on play by James Darnley, *Facing the Music* (1899). With Ernie Lotinga.

Smithy WB-FN at Teddington (A). WB, 10.33 (4,899). p: Irving Asher, d: George King. With Edmund Gwenn, D. A. Clarke-Smith, Peggy Novak.

Smugglers' Harvest Cantaphone Productions (U). Exclusive Films, 3.38 (3,800). p: John R. Phipps, D. F. Cantley. With Hope Davy.

Soft Lights and Sweet Music Brit. Lion (U). Brit. Lion, 2.36 (7,988). p: d: Herbert Smith, c: Charles Van Enger. With Ambrose and his Embassy Orchestra.

Soldiers of the King Gainsborough at Islington, Prince's Theatre (U). W & F, 3.33 (7,271). p: Michael Balcon, d: Maurice Elvey, c: Leslie Rowson, Percy Strong, sc: J. O. C. Orton, W. P. Lipscomb, Jack Hulbert from story by Douglas Furber, des: Vetchinsky, ed: Ian Dalrymple, MD: Louis Levy, song Noel Gay. With Cicely Courtneidge, Edward Everett Horton.

Some Day WB-FN at Teddington (A). WB, 7.35 (6,217). p: Irving Asher, d: Michael Powell, c: Basil Emmott, sc: Brock Williams from novel by I. A. R. Wylie, *Young Nowhere's*, des: Ian Campbell-Gray. With Esmond Knight, Margaret Lockwood.

Someone at the Door BIP (A). Wardour, 5.36 (6,737). p: Walter Mycroft, d: Herbert Brenon, c: Bryan Langley, sc: Marjorie Deans, Jack Davies from play by Dorothy and Campbell Christie (1935), des: Cedric Dawe. With Billy Milton, Aileen Marson, Noah Beery.

Something Always Happens WB-FN at Teddington (U). WB, 6.34 (6,314). p: Irving Asher, d: Michael Powell, c: Basil Emmott, sc: Brock Williams, des: Peter Proud, cost: Louis Brooks, ed: Ralph

Dawson, sd: Leslie Murray. With Ian Hunter, Nancy O'Neil.

Sometimes Good Grafton Films at Elstree BIP (A). Paramt, 5.34 (6,102). p: F. Browett, d: W. P. Kellino, c: Jimmy Wilson, sc: Michael Barringer from story by Emily Rushforth. With Henry Kendall, Nancy O'Neil.

Song at Eventide Argyle Talking Pictures at Cricklewood (A). Butcher's, 7.34 (7,565). p: John Argyle, d: Harry Hughes, c: Desmond Dickinson, sc: from story by John Hastings Turner. With Fay Compton, Lester Matthews.

Song Birds BIP at Welwyn (U). Pathé, 10.33 (3,299). p: Freddie Watts, d: John Harlow, sc: Wallace Lupino. With Wallace and Barry Lupino.

Song for You See **My Song for You**

Song in Soho Ace Films, 12.36 (4,418). p: Frank Green, d: R. A. Hopwood. Variety from Windmill Theatre.

Song of Freedom Hammer Productions-British Lion at Beaconsfield (U). Brit. Lion, 8.36 (7,225). assoc. p: H. Fraser Passmore, d: J. Elder Wills, c: Eric Cross, Harry Rose, Thomas Glover, sc: Ingram d'Abbes, Fenn Sherie from story by Major Claude Wallace, Dorothy Holloway, des: Norman Arnold, ed: Arthur Tavares, sd: Harold King, music Eric Ansell, songs Henrik Ege. With Paul Robeson, Elizabeth Welch.

Song of Soho BIP at Elstree (A). FN-Pathé, 3.30 (6,571) FT, songs RCA. d: Harry Lachman, c: Claude Friese-Greene, sc: Arthur Wimperis, Randall Faye and Frank Launder from story by Harry Lachman and Val Valentine, musical numbers by Harry Carlton and Jay Whidden. With Carl Brisson.

Song of the Forge Butcher's at Cricklewood (U). Butcher's, 4.37 (7,400). p: Norman Hope-Ball, assoc. p: Wilfred Noy, d: Henry Edwards, c: Desmond Dickinson, sc: H. Fowler Mear from story by J. D. Lewin, ed: Challis Sanderson. With Stanley Holloway, Lawrence Grossmith.

Song of the Plough Sound City at

Shepperton (U). M-G-M, 12.33 (6,216). p: Ivar Campbell, d: John Baxter, c: George Stretton, sc: Reginald Pound. With Stewart Rome, Rosalinde Fuller.

Song of the Road UK Films at Shepperton (U). Sound City Dist., 2.37 (6,611). p: John Barter, d: John Baxter, sc: W. G. Elliott and H. F. Maltby from story by Michael Kent. With Bransby Williams.

Song Writers on Parade See **Around the Town**

Song You Gave Me, The BIP (U). Wardour, 7.33 (7,550). d: Paul L. Stein, c: Claude Friese-Greene, sc: Clifford Grey from play by Walter Reisch, *The Song is Ended*. With Bebe Daniels, Victor Varconi, Claude Hulbert, Walter Widdop.

Sons of the Sea British Consolidated Pictures at Elstree Rock (U). Grand Nat., 11.39 (7,412) Dufay colour; colour consultant Adrian Klein. p: K. C. Alexander, d: Maurice Elvey, c: Eric Cross, sc: W. G. Elliott, d. William Woolf and George Barraud, dial: Reginald Long, from story by Maurice Elvey and W. G. Elliott, des: James Carter, ed: Douglas Myers, sd: Leo Wilkins. With Leslie Banks, Kay Walsh, McKenzie Ward.

Sookey See **Self-Made Lady**

Sorrell and Son B & D at Elstree B & D (A). UA, 11.33 (8,900). p: Herbert Wilcox, d: Jack Raymond, c: Cyril Bristow, sc: Lydia Hayward from novel by Warwick Deeping, des: Wilfred Arnold, sp. effects: Lloyd Knechtel. With H. B. Warner, Margot Grahame, Winifred Shotter, Hugh Williams.

Sorry You've Been Troubled See **Life Goes On**

So This is London Twentieth Century Productions at Pinewood (A). 20th Century-Fox, 1.39 (7,474). p: Robert T. Kane, d: Thornton Freeland, c: Otto Kanturek, sc: Ben Travers from play by Arthur Goodrich (1923). With Robertson Hare, Alfred Drayton, George Sanders, Fay Compton.

Soul of Jenny Pearl See **Dance, Pretty Lady**

Source of Irritation See **Spy for a Day**
Southern Maid, A BIP at Elstree, Cheddar Gorge (U). Wardour, 10.33 (7,663). d: Harry Hughes, c: Claude Friese-Greene, Philip Grindrod, sc: Austin Melford, Frank Miller, Arthur Woods, Frank Launder from play by Dion Clayton Calthrop and Harry Graham (1920), des: David Rawnsley, cost: Norman Hartnell, ed: E. B. Jarvis, sd: A. E. Rudolph, MD: Harry Acres, Idris Lewis, lyrics Harry Graham, Adrian Ross, Holt Marvel, music Harold Fraser-Simson, and one number by George Posford. With Bebe Daniels, Clifford Mollison, Lupino Lane, Harry Welchman.

Southern Roses Capitol-Grafton at Denham (U). GFD, 9.36 (6,815). p. man: Isadore Goldsmith, d: Fred Zelnik, c: Philip Tannura, sc: Neil Gow from story by Rudolph Bernaur, des: Fred Pusey, ed: E. B. Jarvis, sd: A. W. Watkins, MD: Boyd Neel, music Johann Strauss, Hans May, lyrics Clifford Grey, dances Wendy Toye, Hedley Briggs. With Sir George Robey, Gina Malo, Neil Hamilton, Chili Bouchier.

South Riding Victor Saville Productions-LFP at Denham (A). UA, 1.38 (8,188). exec.p: Alexander Korda, assoc. p: Stanley Haynes, p: d: Victor Saville, c: Harry Stradling, sc: Ian Dalrymple, Donald Bull, from novel by Winifred Holtby, des: Lazare Meerson, ed: Jack Dennis, Hugh Stewart, sd: A. W. Watkins, sp: effects Lawrence Butler, MD: Muir Mathieson, music Richard Addinsell. With Edna Best, Ralph Richardson, Ann Todd, Glynis Johns.

So, You Won't Talk? WB-FN at Teddington (U). FN, 3.35 (7,454). p: Irving Asher, d: William Beaudine, c: Basil Emmott, sc: Frank Launder, Russell Medcraft from screen story by Tom Geraghty, des: Peter Proud, ed: A. Bates, sd: Leslie Murray, H. C. Pearson, dances Fred Leslie. With Monty Banks, Ralph Ince, Claude Dampier.

Spanish Eyes Samuelson at Twickenham (U). M-G-M, 8,30 (6,400) FT, songs, RCA. d: G. B. Samuelson. With Edna Davies, Dennis Noble. English version of foreign production.

Spanish Roses See **Spanish Eyes**

Spare Room, The PDC at Cricklewood (A). PDC, 3.32 (3,101). d: Redd Davis, sc: G. Marriott Edgar. With Jimmy Jones, Ruth Taylor.

Special Assignment See **Star Reporter, The**

Special Edition Redd Davis at Isleworth (A). Paramt, 3.38 (6,183). d: Redd Davis, c: Roy Fogwell, sc: Katherine Strueby from story by Derek Neame. With Lucille Lisle, John Garrick.

Speckled Band, The B & D (A). W & F, 3.31 (7,900) FT WE. p: Herbert Wilcox, d: Jack Raymond, c: Freddie Young, sc: W. P. Lipscombe from story by Sir Arthur Conan Doyle. With Raymond Massey.

Speed See **Man from Chicago, The**

Speed King See **Money for Speed**

Spider, The Admiral Films at Wembley (A). GFD, 12.39 (7,245). p: Victor M. Greene, d: Maurice Elvey, c: Ernest Palmer, sc: Victor M. Greene and Kenneth Horne from novel by Henry Holt, *Night Mail*, des: John Bryan. With Derrick de Marney, Diana Churchill.

Spies of the Air Brit. Nat. at Walton (A). ABPC, 4.39 (6,982). p: John Corfield, d: David MacDonald, c: Bryan Langley, air c: Sidney Bonnett, sc: A. R. Rawlinson, Bridget Boland from play by Jeffrey Dell, *Official Secret* (1938), des: Duncan Sutherland, ed: David Lean, sd: Hal Fuller. With Barry K. Barnes, Joan Marion, Roger Livesey.

Spike See **Guv'nor, The**

Splinters B & D-HMV at Elstree B & D (U).W & F, premiere 12.29 (7,565) FT, songs WE. p: Herbert Wilcox, d: Jack Raymond, c: David Kesson, sc: W. P. Lipscomb, music Carroll Gibbons and His Master's Voice orchestra. With Nelson Keys, Sydney Howard.

Splinters in the Air Herbert Wilcox at Pinewood (U). GFD, 2.37 (6,442). p:

Herbert Wilcox, d: Alfred Goulding, c: Eric Cross, sc: K. R. G. Browne and Ralph Reader, dial: R. P. Weston, Bert Lee, Jack Marks from story by K. R. G. Browne, des: Hylton R. Oxley, ed: Jill Irving, sd: L. E. Overton, music and lyrics Lerner, Goodhart and Hoffman, music and dances Ralph Reader. With Sydney Howard.

Splinters in the Navy Twick. at Twickenham (U). W & F, premier 11.31 (6,920). p: Julius Hagen, d: Walter Forde, c: Sydney Blythe, sc: R. P. Weston, Bert Lee, Jack Marks from story by H. Fowler Mear, des: James Carter, ed. Jack Harris, sd: Baynham Honri. With Sydney Howard, Lew Lake and the Splinters concert party.

Sporting Love Hammer Productions-Brit. Lion at Beaconsfield (U). Brit. Lion, 11.36 (6,166). assoc. p: H. Fraser Passmore, d: J. Elder Wills, c: Eric Cross, sc: Fenn Sherie and Ingram d'Abbes from musical comedy by Stanley Lupino (1934), songs Eric Ansell, music Billy Mayerl. With Stanley Lupino, Lu-Anne Meredith, Laddie Cliff.

Sport of Kings, The Gainsborough at Twickenham and Elstree (U). Ideal, 2.31 (8,850) FT RCA p: Michael Balcon, d: Victor Saville, c: Freddie Young, sc: Angus MacPhail from play by Ian Hay (1924), sd: A. W. Watkins. With Leslie Henson.

Spotlight Ace Films. Registered 3.38 (3,610). d: R. A. Hopwood. Variety from Windmill Theatre.

Spot of Bother, A Pinebrook at Pinewood (U). GFD, 7.38 (6,348). p: Anthony Havelock-Allan, d: David MacDonald, c: Francis Carver, sc: John Cousins, Stephen Clarkson from play by Vernon Sylvaine (1937), des: Wilfred Arnold, ed: Lister Laurence. With Robertson Hare, Alfred Drayton, Sandra Storme.

Spring Cleaning See **Women Who Play**

Spring Handicap BIP-ABPC at Elstree (U). ABPC, 5.37 (6,137). p: Walter Mycroft, d: Herbert Brenon, c: Otto Kanturek, sc: Elizabeth Meehan and William Freshman from story by Ernest A. Bryan, des: John Mead, ed: Lionel Tomlinson, sd: B. Cook. With Will Fyffe, Frank Pettingell, Maire O'Neill.

Spring in the Air John Stafford Productions at Elstree BIP (A). Pathé, 11.34 (6,700). p: John Stafford, d: W. Victor Hanbury. With Edmund Gwenn, Zelma O'Neal.

Spy for a Day Two Cities at Shepperton, in production 9.39. p: d: Mario Zampi, c: Bernard Knowles, sc: Hans Wilhelm, Emeric Pressburger, Ralph Block and Anatole de Grunwald, dial: T. Thompson from story by Stacy Aumonier, *Source of Irritation*, des: Paul Sheriff. With Duggie Wakefield.

Spy in Black, The Harefield Productions at Denham (U). Columbia, 3.39 (7,390). Presented by Alexander Korda, p. Irving Asher, d: Michael Powell, c: Bernard Browne, sc: Roland Pertwee, Emeric Pressburger from novel by J. Storer Clouston, des: Vincent Korda. Fred Pusey, ed: William Hornbeck, Hugh Stewart, sd: A. W. Watkins, MD: Muir Mathieson, music Miklos Rozsa. With Conrad Veidt, Valerie Hobson, June Duprez, Marius Goring.

Spy of Napoleon J. H. Productions at Twickenham, Elstree, Loch Lomond (U). Twick. F.D., 9.36 (9,048) p: Julius Hagen, d: Maurice Elvey, c: Curt Courant, sc: L. du Garde Peach, F. Merrick, Harold Simpson from novel by Baroness Orczy, des: A. L. Mazzei, cost: L. & H. Nathan, ed: Jack Harris, sd: Baynham Honri, MD: W. L. Trytel. With Richard Barthelmess, Dolly Haas, Frank Vosper, Francis L. Sullivan.

Squeaker, The Brit. Lion at Beaconsfield (A). Brit. Lion, 5.30 (8,300) FT. p: S. W. Smith, d: Edgar Wallace, c: Claude McDonnell, Horace Wheddon, sc: Edgar Wallace from his own play (1928), des: Dorothy Braham, sd: Harold King. With Percy Marmont, Anne Grey, Gordon Harker.

Squeaker, The LFP-Denham Films at Denham (A). UA, 8.37 (7,075). p:

Alexander Korda, d: William K. Howard, c: Georges Périnal, sc: Bryan Wallace, and Edward O. Berkman from play by Edgar Wallace (1928), des: Vincent Korda, ed: Jack Dennis, Russell Lloyd, sd: A. W. Watkins, MD: Muir Mathieson, music Miklos Rozsa, songs William Kernell and Edward O. Berkman. With Edmund Lowe, Ann Todd, Alastair Sim.

Squibs Twick. at Twickenham (U). Gaumont, 6.35 (6,947). p: Julius Hagen, d: Henry Edwards, c: Sydney Blythe, sc: Michael Hogan and H. Fowler Mear from earlier film by George Pearson, monologue by R. P. Weston and Bert Lee, des: James Carter, ed: Jack Harris, MD: W. L. Trytel, songs Sigler, Goodhart and Hoffman, dances Ralph Reader. With Betty Balfour, Gordon Harker, Stanley Holloway.

Stage Folk See **Happy Days Are Here Again**

Stamboul Para-Brit. at Elstree B & D (A). Paramt, 10.31 (6,723). d: Dimitri Buchowetski, sc: Reginald Denham from novel by Claude Farrère, *L'Homme qui Assassina* and play by Pierre Frondes: R. Holmes Paul. With Warwick Ward, Rosita Moreno. English and Spanish versions of film already made by Buchowetzki in French and German at Joinville, Paris.

Stardust See **Mad About Money**

Star Fell from Heaven, A BIP at Elstree (U). Wardour, 6.36 (6,383). p: Walter Mycroft, d: Paul Merzbach, c: Ronald Neame, sc: Dudley Leslie, Marjorie Deans, Val Guest, add. dial: W. G. Elliott, des: David Rawnsley, ed: Flora Newton, sd: A. Geary, MD: Harry Acres, music Hans May, lyrics Ruth Feiner, ballet Francis Mangan. With Joseph Schmidt.

Star of the Circus ABPC (U). ABPC, 3.38 (6,142). p: Walter Mycroft, d: Albert de Courville, c: Claude Friese-Greene, sc: Elizabeth Meehan from novel by Heinrich Seiler, *December with Truxa*, des: John Mead, ed: Lionel

Tomlinson, music Leo Leux. With Otto Kruger, Gertrude Michael, John Clements.

Star Reporter, The Film Engineering at Walton (A). Fox, 12.31 (3,997). p: Jerome Jackson, d: Michael Powell, c: Geoffrey Faithfull, sc: Philip MacDonald, Ralph Smart from story by Philip MacDonald, des: Frank Wells. With Harold French, Garry Marsh, Isla Bevan.

Stars Look Down, The Grafton at Denham, Twickenham, Ashby-de-la-Zouch, pit scenes in Cumberland (A). Grand. Nat., 12.39 (9,090). p: Isadore Goldsmith, exec.p: Fred Zelnik, d: Carol Reed, c: Mutz Greenbaum, Ernest Palmer, Henry Harris, sc: J. B. Williams from novel by A. J. Cronin, des: James Carter, ed: Reginald Beck, sd: Norman Davies, music Hans May. With Emlyn Williams, Nancy Price, Michael Redgrave, Margaret Lockwood.

Stars on Parade Butcher's at Cricklewood (U). Butcher's, 1.36 (7,360, later 4,560). p: d: Oswald Mitchell, Challis Sanderson, c: Desmond Dickinson, sc: Oswald Mitchell. With Lucan and McShane.

Steel See **Men of Steel**

Stepping Toes Baxter & Barter at Shepperton (U). BIED, 3.38 (7,348). p: John Barter, d: John Baxter, c: Jack Parker, sc: H. Fowler Mear from story by Jack Francis and Barbara K. Emary, musical numbers Kennedy Russell. With Hazel Ascot. Enid Stamp-Taylor, Jack Barty.

Stickpin, The Brit. Lion at Beaconsfield (A). Fox, 6.33 (3,980). p: supervisor Herbert Smith, d: Leslie Hiscott, c: Alex Bryce, sc: Michael Barringer, des: Norman Arnold, sd: Harold King. With Betty Astell, Henry Kendall.

St Martin's Lane Mayflower Picture Corp. at Elstree BIP (U). ABPC, 7.38 (7,691). p: Erich Pommer, d: Tim Whelan, c: Jules Kruger, Gus Drisse, sc: from story by Clemence Dane, des: Tom Morahan, cost: John Armstrong, ed: Hugh Stewart, Robert Hamer, sd: Jack Rogerson, MD: Muir Mathieson, music Arthur Johnston, lyrics Eddie Pola, Carroll Gibbons and his Orchestra, dances Philip Buchel. With Charles Laughton, Vivien Leigh, Rex Harrison, Tyrone Guthrie.

Stoker, The Leslie Fuller Pictures at Elstree Rock (A). G-B D, 7.35 (6,425). p: Joe Rock, d: Leslie Pearce, c: C. Van Enger, sc: Syd Courtenay and Georgie Harris from story by Wallace Geoffrey, des: J. Elder Wills. With Leslie Fuller, Georgie Harris.

Stolen Life Orion Productions at Pinewood, Cornwall, South of France, Dolomites (A). Paramt, 1.39 (8,253). p: d: Paul Czinner, assoc. p: Anthony Havelock-Allan, c: Phil Tannura, sc: Margaret Kennedy from novel by K. J. Benes, add. dial: George Barraud, des: John Bryan, cost: Joe Strassner, ed: Frederick Wilson, sd: W. Lindop, conductor H. Greenbaum, music William Walton. With Elisabeth Bergner, Michael Redgrave, Wilfrid Lawson.

Stolen Necklace, The WB-FN at Teddington (A). WB, 2.33 (4,444). p: Irving Asher, d: Leslie Hiscott. With Joan Marion, Lester Matthews.

Storm in a Teacup Victor Saville Productions-LFP at Denham (Λ). UA, 5.37 (7,894). exec. p: Alexander Korda, p: Victor Saville, assoc. p: Stanley Haynes, d: Victor Saville and Ian Dalrymple, c: Mutz Greenbaum, sc: Ian Dalrymple and Donald Bull from play by James Bridie based on play by Bruno Frank, *Sturm in Wasserglass*, des: Andre Andreiev, ed: William Hornbeck, Hugh Stewart, sd: A. W. Watkins, MD: Muir Mathieson, music Frederic Lewis. With Vivien Leigh, Rex Harrison, Cecil Parker.

Stormy Weather Gainsborough at Islington (A). G-B, 7.35 (6,753). p: Michael Balcon, d: Tom Walls, c: Phil Tannura, sc: Ben Travers from his own story, des: Vetchinsky, cost: Joe Strassner, ed: Alfred Roome, sd: H. Hand, MD: Louis Levy. With Tom Walls, Ralph Lynn, Robertson Hare, Yvonne Arnaud.

Strange Adventures of Mr. Smith, The George Smith Productions (U). Radio, 5.37 (6,453). p: George Smith, d: P. Maclean Rogers, sc: Kathleen Butler from story by H. F. Maltby with Gus McNaughton, Norma Varden.

Strange Boarders Gainsborough at Pinewood (A). GFD, 5.38 (7,149). p: Edward Black, d: Herbert Mason, c: J. J. Cox, sc: A. R. Rawlinson, Sidney Gilliat from novel by E. Phillips Oppenheim, *The Strange Boarders of Paradise Crescent*, des: Walter Murton, ed: Michael Gordon. With Tom Walls, Renée Saint-Cyr, Googie Withers.

Strange Cargo B & D-Para-Brit. at Elstree B & D (A). Paramt, 3.36 (6,131). d: Lawrence Huntington, c: Francis Carver, sc: from story by W. G. Elliott. With Kathleen Kelly, Moore Marriott, George Sanders.

Strange Case of the Missing Rembrandt, The See **Missing Rembrandt, The**

Strange Evidence LFP at Elstree B & D (A). Paramt, 1.33 (6,484). p: Alexander Korda, d: Robert Milton, sc: Miles Malleson from story by Lajos Biro, des: R. Holmes Paul, ed: Stephen Harrison. With Carol Goodner, Leslie Banks, Diana Napier, Frank Vosper.

Strange Experiment Fox Brit. at Wembley (A). Fox, 1.37 (6,726). d: Albert Parker, c: Ronald Neame, sc: Edward Dryhurst from play by Hubert Osborne, John Golden. With Ann Wemyss.

Strange Justice See **Case of Gabriel Perry, The**

Strangers on Honeymoon G-B at Shepherd's Bush (A). G-B D, 11.36 (6,233). assoc. p: Haworth Bromly, d: Albert de Courville, c: Mutz Greenbaum, sc: Sidney Gilliat, Ralph Spence, Bryan Wallace from novel by Edgar Wallace, *The Northing Tramp*, des: Ernö Metzner, ed: C. Randell, sd: A. F. Birch. With Constance Cummings, Noah Beery, Hugh Sinclair.

Strangehold Teddington Studios at

Teddington (A). WB, 10.31 (6,064) FT RCA p: d: Henry Edwards, c: Walter Blakeley, sc: Henry Edwards. With Garry Marsh, Isobel Elsom.

Strangler, The BIP-BIF at Welwyn (A). Pathé, 3.32 (4,125). d: sc: Norman Lee. With Jack Morrison, Moira Lynd.

Street of Lost Souls See **Woman He Scorned, The**

Street Singer, The Brit.Nat. at Pinewood (U). ABPC, 3.37 (7,700). p: Dora Nirva, d: Jean de Marguenat, c: Henry Harris, sc: Reginald Arkell from story by Paul Schiller, Jean de Marguenat, des: Erwin Scharf, ed: Douglas Myers, sd: C. C. Stevens, MD: Lew Stone. With Arthur Tracy, Margaret Lockwood, Arthur Riscoe.

Street Singer's Serenade see **Limelight**

Street Song Real Art at Twickenham (A). Radio, 3.35 (5,773). p: Julius Hagen, d: Bernard Vorhaus, c: Ernest Palmer, sc: Bernard Vorhaus and Paul Gangelin. With John Garrick, Rene Ray.

Strictly Business BIF at Welwyn (U). Wardour, 1.32 (4,155). d: Jacqueline Logan and Mary Field, c: Jack Parker, sc: Jacqueline Logan, des: Ian Campbell-Gray, sd: A. F. Birch. With Betty Amann, Carl Harbord.

Strictly Illegal Leslie Fuller Pictures at Cricklewood (U). G-B D, 2.35 (6,266). p: Joe Rock, d: Ralph Cedar, c: Desmond Dickinson, sc: Syd Courtenay and Georgie Harris from play by Con West and Herbert Sargent, *The Naughty Age*. With Leslie Fuller, Betty Astell, Georgie Harris.

Strictly in Confidence WB-FN at Teddington (A). FN, 7.33 (3,868). p: Irving Asher, d: Clyde Cook. With James Finlayson, Betty Amann.

Strike it Rich Brit. Lion at Beaconsfield (U). Brit. Lion, 10.33 (6,864). p: supervisor Herbert Smith, d: Leslie Hiscott, sc: from screen story by Michael Barringer, music Reggie Bristow. With George Gee, Gina Malo, Davy Burnaby, Betty Astell.

Student's Romance The BIP at Elstree (U). Wardour, 7.35 (7,066). p: Walter Mycroft, d: Otto Kanturek, sc: Clifford Grey from operetta by Ernst Neumann, *I Lost My Heart in Heidelberg*, des: Cedric Dawe, music Hans May. With Grete Natzler, Patric Knowles.

Such is Life Incorporated Talking Films at Shepperton (A). NPFD, 10.36 (7,465). p: Brandon Fleming, d: Randall Faye, c: Geoffrey Faithfull, sc: Brandon Fleming. With Gene Gerrard, Claude Dampier.

Such is the Law Stoll at Cricklewood (A). Butcher's, 11.30 (7,958) FT Visatone p: Oswald Mitchell, d: Sinclair Hill, c: Desmond Dickinson, sc: L. H. Gordon from story by Reginald Fogwell, des: Walter Murton, cost: Reville, Norman Hartnell, sd: Dallas Bower, MD composer: Herbert Griffiths. With Lady Tree, C. Aubrey Smith, Carl Harbord.

Sugar and Spice Gainsborough, 1930 (2 reels each), Ideal: **Al Fresco, Toyland, Black and White, Classic v. Jazz, Gypsy Land, Dusky Melodies.**

Summer Lightning B & D at Elstree B & D (U). UA, 5.33 (7,004). p: Herbert Wilcox, d: P. Maclean Rogers, sc: from story by P. G. Wodehouse, des: L. P. Williams. With Ralph Lynn, Winifred Shotter.

Sunset in Vienna Herbert Wilcox at Pinewood (U). GFD, 6.37 (6,588). p: Herbert Wilcox, d: Norman Walker, c: Freddie Young, sc: Marjorie Gaffney and Harrison Owen from story by Florence Tranter, music Lerner, Goodhart and Hoffman. With Tullio Carminati, Lilli Palmer.

Sunshine Ahead Baxter and Barter at Cricklewood (U). Universal, 12.35 (5,859). p: John Baxter, d: Wallace Orton,c: Desmond Dickinson, sc: from story by Con West, Geoffrey Orme, music Kennedy Russell and Reg Connelly. With Eddie Pola, Betty Astell, Leslie Perrins.

Sunshine Susie Gainsborough at Islington (U). Ideal,12.31 (7,918) FT RCA. p: Michael Balcon, d: Victor Saville, c: Mutz Greenbaum, sc: Angus MacPhail,

Victor Saville, Robert Stevenson from German film *Die Privatsekretarin* based on play by Franz Schulz, des: Vetchinsky, cost: Gordon Conway, ed: Ian Dalrymple, Derek Twist, sd: George Gunn, MD: Louis Levy, music Paul Abraham, lyrics Desmond Carter. With Renate Müller, Jack Hulbert, Owen Nares.

Susie in the Bath See **There Goes Susie**

Suspense BIP at Elstree (A). Wardour, 7.30 (7,100) FT RCA. d: Walter Summers, c: Theodor Sparkuhl, Hal Young, sc: Walter Summers from story and play by Patrick MacGill, des: John Mead, .ed: Walter Stokvis, Émile de Ruelle, sd: Dallas Bower. With Fred Groves, Cyril McLaglen, Mickey Brantford.

Sweeney Todd, The Demon Barber of Fleet Street George King at Shepperton (A). M-G-M, 3.36 (6,111). d: George King. With Tod Slaughter, Bruce Seton.

Sweet Devil Jack Buchanan Productions at Pinewood (U). GFD, 1.38 (6,633). p: Jack Buchanan, d: René Guissart, c: Bernard Browne, sc: Ralph Spence, des: D. W. L. Daniels. With Bobby Howes, Jean Gillie.

Sweet Inniscarra Emmett Moore Film Company in Ireland (U). Columbia, 2.34 (6,545). With Sean Rogers, Mae Ryan.

Sweet Racket See **Just Like a Woman**

Swing Ace Films, 3.38 (3,316). d: R. A. Hopwood, Variety from Windmill Theatre.

Swinging the Lead Philip Weiner, David Mackane and George Crooke Rogers (A). Universal, 1.35 (5,896). d: David Mackane. With Billy Hartnell, Moira Lynd.

Sword of Honour Butcher's at Walton, Sandhurst (U). Butcher's, 3.39 (7,570). p: d: Maurice Elvey, sc: W. G. Elliott from story by Major Dudley Sturrock. With Dorothy Dickson, Geoffrey Toone, Sally Gray.

Symphony in Two Flats Gainsborough at Islington, finished at Elstree BIP (U).

Gaumont, 7.30 (7,752) FT, songs RCA. p: Michael Balcon, d: V. Gareth Gundrey, c: Jimmy Wilson, sc: Angus MacPhail from play by Ivor Novello (1929), Jack Payne and his BBC Orchestra. With Ivor Novello, Benita Hume, Cyril Ritchard.

Take a Chance Grosvenor Sound Films at Ealing (A). ABFD, 1.37 (6,680). p: Harcourt Templeman, d: Sinclair Hill, sc: D. B. Wyndham-Lewis and G. H. Moresby-White from play by Walter Hackett (1931), des: A. C. Hammond, ed: Michael Hankinson, MD: John Reynders. With Binnie Hale, Claude Hulbert.

Take it From Me WB-FN at Teddington (U). FN, 9.37 (7,005). p: Irving Asher, d: William Beaudine, c: Basil Emmott, sc: J. O. C. Orton and John Meehan Jnr. With Max Miller, Buddy Baer, Betty Lynne.

Take my Tip G-B at Shepherd's Bush (U). GFD, 4.37 (6,422). d: Herbert Mason, c: Bernard Knowles, sc: Sidney Gilliat, Michael Hogan, Jack Hulbert from play by François de Croisset, *La Livrée de Monsieur le Comte*, des: Ernö Metzner, cost: Joe Strassner, sd: A. Birch, MD: Louis Levy, music Lerner, Goodhart and Hoffman, dances Philip Buchel. With Jack Hulbert, Cicely Courtneidge, Harold Huth, Frank Cellier.

Take Off That Hat Viking Films at Cricklewood (U). Viking Films, 6.38 (7,531, later 7,247, later 6,984). p: d: Eric Humphriss, c: Desmond Dickinson, sc: Edmund Dalby, C. Denier Warren.

Taking Ways Sound City at Shepperton (A). Universal, 12.33 (3,638). p: Ivar Campbell, d: John Baxter, sc: Leonard Morris from sketch, 'Light-fingered Freddie'. With Leonard Morris, Daisey Crossley.

Talking Feet UK Films (U). Sound City Dist., 7.37 (7,135). p: John Barter, d: John Baxter, sc: H. Fowler Mear from story by Geoffrey Orme and Jack Francis. With Hazel Ascot, Jack Barty.

Talk of the Devil B & D at Pinewood (A). UA, 12.36 (7,021). p: Jack Raymond, d: Carol Reed, c: Francis Carver, sc: Carol Reed, Anthony Kimmins, dial: George Barraud from story by Carol Reed and Anthony Kimmins. With Ricardo Cortez, Sally Eilers.

Tangled Evidence Real Art at Twickenham and Merton Park (A). Radio, 3.34 (5,136). p: Julius Hagen, d: G. A. Cooper, sc: G. A. Cooper from novel by Mrs Champion de Crespigny. With Judy Kelly, Michael Hogan.

Tattenham Corner See **All In**

Taxi for Two Gainsborough at Islington, Harrods location (U). W & F, 11.29 (6,642 silent, 6,785 synchronised) PT RCA. p: Michael Balcon, d: Alexander Esway (silent) and Denison Clift (sound), c: Jimmy Wilson, sc: Alexander Esway, dial: Ian Dalrymple, Angus MacPhail. With John Stuart, Mabel Poulton.

Taxi to Paradise George Smith at Wembley (A). Fox, 2.33 (4,042). p: George Smith, d: Adrian Brunel, sc: Adrian Brunel from play by Graham Hope, *Misconduct*. With Binnie Barnes, Garry Marsh.

Tea Leaves in the Wind See **Hate in Paradise**

Television Follies, The English Films (U). English Films, 6.33 (4,039). p: Geoffrey Benstead, d: Geoffrey Benstead, MD: Horace Shepherd. George Carney.

Television Talent Alexander Film Productions (U). Ambassador Film Productions, 11.37 (5,050). p: R. H. Alexander, d: Robert Edmunds, sc: Robert Edmunds from story by R. H. Alexander. With Richard Goolden, Polly Ward.

Tell England BIF at Welwyn, Malta (A). Wardour, 3.31 (7,850) FT Klangfilm. p: H. Bruce Woolfe, d: Anthony Asquith, Geoffrey Barkas, c: Stanley Rodwell, Jack Parker, Jimmy Rogers, sc: Anthony Asquith, add. dial: A. P. Herbert from novel by Ernest Raymond, des: Arthur Woods, ed: Mary Field, sd: Victor Peers. With Fay Compton, Carl Harbord, Tony Bruce.

Tell-Tale Heart, The Clifton-Hurst Films (A). Fox, 3.34 (4,469). d: Brian Desmond Hurst, sc: David Plunkett Greene from story by Edgar Allan Poe. With Norman Dryden, John Kelt.

Temperance Fete, The Fogwell Films at Isleworth (A). M-G-M, 1.32 (4,112). p: Reginald Fogwell, d: Graham Cutts, c: William Shenton, sc: Reginald Fogwell from stories by Herbert Jenkins, *The Adventures of Bindle*. With Sir George Robey, Sydney Fairbrother.

Ten Days in Paris Irving Asher Productions at Denham (A). Columbia, 10.39 (7,373). p: Jerome Jackson, d: Tim Whelan, sc: John Meehan Jr and James Curtis from novel by Bruce Graeme. With Rex Harrison, Karen Verne.

Ten Minute Alibi Brit. Lion and Transatlantic Film Corp at Beaconsfield (A). Brit. Lion, 1.35 (6,815). p: Paul Soskin, d: Bernard Vorhaus, c: Alex Bryce, sc: Michael Hankinson, Vera Allinson from play by Anthony Armstrong (1933), des: A. L. Mazzei. With Phillips Holmes, Aileen Marson.

Tenth Man, The BIP at Elstree (A). Wardour, 8.36 (6,098). p: Walter Mycroft, d: Brian Desmond Hurst, c: Walter Harvey, sc: Dudley Leslie, Marjorie Deans, Jack Davies, add. dial: Geoffrey Kerr, from story by W. Somerset Maugham, des: Cedric Dawe, ed: J. Corbett, sd: B. Cook, MD: Harry Acres, songs Hugh Wade and Edgar Blatt, sung by Dinah Miller. With John Lodge, Antoinette Cellier.

Terror, The ABPC at Elstree (A). ABPC, 4.38 (6,594). p: Walter Mycroft, d: Richard Bird, c: Walter Harvey, sc: William Freshman from play by Edgar Wallace (1927), des: Cedric Dawe, ed: Lionel Tomlinson. With Wilfrid Lawson.

Thank Evans WB-FN at Teddington (U). FN, 4.38 (7,015). p: Irving Asher, d: Roy William Neill, c: Basil Emmott, sc:

Austin Melford from stories by Edgar Wallace, 'Educated Evans'. With Max Miller, Polly Ward.

Thark B & D at Elstree B & D (A). W & F, 7.32 (7,014). p: Herbert Wilcox, d: Tom Walls, c: Freddie Young, sc: from play by Ben Travers. With Ralph Lynn, Tom Walls, Robertson Hare, Mary Brough.

That Night in London LFP at Elstree B & D (A). Paramt, 11.32 (7,009). p: Alexander Korda, d: Rowland V. Lee, c: Bernard Browne, sc: Dorothy Greenhill, dial: Arthur Wimperis. With Robert Donat, Miles Mander, Pearl Argyle.

That's a Good Girl B & D at Elstree B & D, South of France (U). UA, 9.33 (7,363). p: Herbert Wilcox, d: Jack Buchanan, c: Freddie Young, sc: Jack Buchanan, Douglas Furber, Donovan Pedelty from musical play by Douglas Furber (1928), des: L. P. Williams, cost: Norman Hartnell, ed: Merrill White, sd: L. E. Overton, MD: Philip Braham, music Philip Charig and Joseph Meyer, lyrics Douglas Furber. With Jack Buchanan, Elsie Randolph, Dorothy Hyson, Garry Marsh.

That's My Uncle Twick. at Twickenham (U). Universal, 3.35 (5,218). p: Julius Hagen, d: George Pearson, c: Ernest Palmer, sc: Michael Barringer from play by Frederick Jackson, *The Iron Woman*. With Margaret Yarde, Mark Daly, Richard Cooper.

That's My Wife Brit. Lion at Beaconsfield (A). Brit. Lion, 3.33 (6,031). p: supervisor Herbert Smith, d: Leslie Hiscott, c: Alex Bryce, sc: Michael Barringer from story by W. C. Stone, des: Norman Arnold, sd: Harold King. With Claude Allister, Frank Pettingell, Betty Astell.

Their Night Out BIP (U). Wardour, 3.33 (6,600). d: Harry Hughes, c: Walter Harvey, sc: Harry Hughes from play by George Arthurs and Arthur Miller (1928), des: Duncan Sutherland, ed: Walter Stokvis, sd: A. S. Ross, songs by Peter Mendoza. Claude Hulbert, Renee Houston, Binnie Barnes.

There Ain't No Justice Ealing studios (CAPAD) at Ealing (A). ABFD, 6.39 (7,262). p: Michael Balcon, assoc. p: Sergei Nolbandov, d: Pen Tennyson, c: Mutz Greenbaum, sc: Pen Tennyson, James Curtis, Sergei Nolbandov from novel by James Curtis, des: Wilfred Shingleton, ed: Ray Pitt, sd: Eric Williams, MD: Ernest Irving. With Jimmy Hanley, Jill Furse.

There Goes Susie John Stafford Productions at Elstree BIP. Pathé, 9.34 (7,200). p: d: John Stafford, W.Victor Hanbury. With Gene Gerrard, Wendy Barrie.

There Goes the Bride Gainsborough-Brit. Lion at Beaconsfield (U). Ideal, 10.32 (7,184). p: Michael Balcon, d: Albert de Courville, c: Mutz Greenbaum, Alex Bryce, sc: W. P. Lipscomb from story by Hermann Kosterlitz and Wolfgang Wilhelm, des: Norman Arnold, sd: Harold King, music Fred Raymond, Noel Gay. With Owen Nares, Jessie Matthews.

There Was a Young Man Fox Brit. at Wembley (U). 20th Century-Fox, 9.37 (5,744). d: Al Parker, c: Ronald Neame, sc: David Evans from story by Dudley Clark. With Oliver Wakefield, Nancy O'Neil.

These Charming People Para-Brit. at Elstree B & D (A). Paramt, 7.31 (7,350) FT WE d: Louis Mercanton, dial. d: Reginald Denham, sc: Hugh Perceval from play by Michael Arlen, *Dear Father* (1924), sd: A. W. Watkins. With Godfrey Tearle, Cyril Maude, Ann Todd, Nora Swinburne.

They Came by Night Twentieth Century Productions in production at Islington by 7.39. p: Edward Black, d: Harry Lachman, c: J. J. Cox, sc: Frank Launder, Sidney Gilliat, Michael Hogan and Roland Pertwee from play by Barré Lyndon (1937), sd: S. Wiles, With Will Fyffe, Phyllis Clavert.

They Didn't Know Brit. Lion at Beaconsfield (A). M-G-M, 4.36 (6,082). p: d: Herbert Smith, sc: Brock Williams. With Eve Gray, Leslie

Perrins.

They Drive by Night WB-FN at Teddington (A). FN, 1.39 (7,536). p: Jerome Jackson, d: Arthur Woods, dial. d: Anthony Hankey, c: Basil Emmott, sc: Paul Gangelin, James Curtis and Derek Twist from novel by James Curtis, des: Peter Proud, Michael Relph, ed: Leslie Norman, MD: Bretton Byrd. With Emlyn Williams.

They're Off! G-B (U). Ideal, registered 2.33 (1,721). p: Clayton Hutton, d: John Rawlins. With Flanagan and Allen.

Thief in the Night See **Jump for Glory**

Thief of Bagdad, The Alexander Korda Productions-LFP, in production at Denham in spring 1939, finished in Hollywood later. UA. Technicolor (colour direction Natalie Kalmus). p: Alexander Korda, assoc. p: Zoltan Korda, W. Cameron Menzies, d: Ludwig Berger, Michael Powell, Tim Whelan, c: Georges Périnal, Osmond Borradaile, sc: Lajos Biro, Miles Malleson, des: Vincent Korda, cost: Oliver Messel, John Armstrong, Marcel Vertes, ed: William Hornbeck, Charles Crichton, sd: A. W. Watkins, sp: effects: Lawrence Butler, scenic backings Percy Day, MD: Muir Mathieson, music Miklos Rozsa. With John Justin, Sabu, Conrad Veidt, June Duprez.

Things Are Looking Up G-B at Shepherd's Bush (U). G-B D, 1.35 (7,197). p: Michael Balcon, d: Albert de Courville, c: Charles Van Enger, sc: Stafford Dickens and Con West from story by Albert de Courville. With Cicely Courtneidge, Max Miller, William Gargan.

Things to Come LFP at Elstree old Whitehall, Isleworth, and Denham exteriors (U). UA, 2.36 (9,781, later 8,830). p: Alexander Korda, d: William Cameron Menzies, c: Georges Périnal, Robert Krasker, sc: H. G. Wells from his book *The Shape of Things to Come*, des: Vincent Korda, Frank Wells, cost: Rene Hubert, John Armstrong, Cathleen Mann, ed: William Hornbeck, Charles

Crichton, Francis Lyon, sd: A. W. Watkins, sp. effects: Ned Mann, Edward Cohen, aeronautical adviser Nigel Tangye, MD: Muir Mathieson, music Arthur Bliss. With Raymond Massey, Ralph Richardson, Leslie Banks, Edward Chapman, Sir Cedric Hardwicke.

Third Clue, The Fox Brit, at Ealing (A). Fox, 11.34 (6,579). d: Albert Parker, c: Robert Martin, Jimmy Wilson, sc: from story by Neil Gordon, *The Shakespeare Murders*. With Basil Sydney, Molly Lamont.

Third Gun, The BSFP (A). Universal, registered 8.32 (3,250). d: Geoffrey Barkas, sc: Michael Barringer. With Randle Ayrton.

Third String, The Welsh Pearson (U). Gaumont, 2.32 (5,980). p: George Pearson, T. A. Welsh, d: George Pearson, sc: George Pearson, James Reardon, A. R. Rawlinson from story by W. W. Jacobs. With Sandy Powell, Kay Hammond, Mark Daly.

Third Time Lucky Gainsborough at Islington (A). W & F, 2.31 (7,656) FT RCA. p: Michael Balcon, d: Walter Forde, c: William Shenton, sc: Angus MacPhail, add. dial: Sidney Gilliat, from play by Arnold Ridley (1929), des: Walter Murton, ed: Ian Dalrymple, sd: George Gunn. With Bobby Howes, Gordon Harker, Dorothy Boyd.

Third Time Unlucky See **Crown v. Stevens**

Thirteenth Candle, The WB-FN at Teddington (A). WB, 3.33 (6,172). p: Irving Asher, d: John Daumery, sc: Brock Williams. With Isobel Elsom, Arthur Maude.

Thirty-Nine Steps, The G-B at Shepherd's Bush (A). G-B D, 6.35 (7,821). p: Michael Balcon, assoc. p: Ivor Montagu, d: Alfred Hitchcock, c. Bernard Knowles, sc: Charles Bennett and Alma Reville, add. dial: Ian Hay, from novel by John Buchan, des: Oscar Werndorff, Albert Jullion, ed: Derek Twist, cost: Joe Strassner, ed: Derek Twist, sd: A. Birch, MD: Louis Levy.

With Robert Donat, Madeleine Carroll, Godfrey Tearle.

This Acting Business WB-FN at Teddington (U). WB, 12.33 (4,751). p: Irving Asher, d: John Daumery. With Hugh Williams, Wendy Barrie.

This Green Hell Randall Faye at Walton (A). Radio, 3.36 (6,563). p: d: sc: Randall Faye. With Edward Rigby, Sybil Grove.

This is the Life Brit. Lion (U). Brit. Lion, 9.33 (6,897). p: supervisor Herbert Smith, d: Albert de Courville, c: Alex Bryce, sc: Clifford Grey, R. P. Weston, Bert Lee. With Gordon Harker, Binnie Hale, Betty Astell, Ray Milland.

This'll Make You Whistle Herbert Wilcox at Elstree (A). GFD, 11.36 (6,750). p: d: Herbert Wilcox, c: Freddie Young, sc: Guy Bolton and Fred Thompson from musical play by Guy Bolton and Fred Thompson (1936), des: L. P. Williams, Hylton R. Oxley, ed. Frederick Wilson, Richard Wootton, sd: L. E. Overton, J. Dennis, MD: George Windeatt, music Sigler, Goodhart and Hoffman, dances Buddy Bradley. With Jack Buchanan, Elsie Randolph, David Hutcheson, Jean Gillie.

This Man in Paris Pinebrook at Denham (A). Paramt, 6.39 (7,745). p: Anthony Havelock-Allan, d: David MacDonald, c: Henry Harris, sc: Anthony Havelock-Allan from screen story by Roger MacDougall and Allan MacKinnon, des: Ralph Brinton, ed: Reginald Beck. With Barry K. Barnes, Valerie Hobson, Alastair Sim.

This Man is News Pinebrook at Pinewood (A). Paramt, 8.38 (6,947). p: Anthony Havelock-Allan, d: David MacDonald, c: Henry Harris, sc: Roger MacDougall and Allan MacKinnon from their screen story, des: Wilfred Arnold, ed: Reginald Beck. With Barry K. Barnes, Valerie Hobson, Alastair Sim.

Thistledown WB-FN at Teddington (U). WB, 3.38 (7,009). p: Irving Asher, d: Arthur Woods, c: Basil Emmott, sc:

Brock Williams from story by J. O. C. Orton and John Meehan Jr, music and lyrics Kenneth Leslie-Smith and James Dyrenforth. With Aino Bergo, Keith Falkner.

This Week of Grace Real Art at Twickenham (U). Radio, 7.33 (8,245). p: Julius Hagen, d: Maurice Elvey, c: Sydney Blythe, sc: H. Fowler Mear from story by Maurice Braddell and Nell Emerald, sd: Baynham Honri. With Gracie Fields, Henry Kendall, John Stuart.

Thoroughbred Equity British (U). Equity British, 3.32 (5,860) silent, with music sychronised. d: Charles Barnett, sc: John Argyle. With John Argyle, Margaret Delane.

Those Were the Days BIP at Elstree (U). Wardour, 3.34 (7,400). p: Walter Mycroft, d: Thomas Bentley, c: Otto Kanturek, sc: Fred Thompson, Frank Launder, Frank Miller from play by Arthur Wing Pinero, *The Magistrate* (1885), des: Duncan Sutherland, ed: E. B. Jarvis, sd: C. V. Thornton, MD: Idris Lewis. With Will Hay, John Mills, H. F. Maltby.

Those Who Love BIP at Elstree (A). FN-Pathé, 11.29 (7,929) PT, music RCA d: Manning Haynes, sc: Lydia Hayward from novel by Guy Fletcher, *Mary Was Love*. With Blanche Adele, William Freshman, Carol Goodner.

Thousand Windows See **Crime Over London**

Thread o' Scarlet Gaumont at Shepherd's Bush (A). Gaumont, 11.30 (3,186) FT Brit. Ac. p: L'Estrange Fawcett, d: Peter Godfrey, c: William Shenton, sc: R. G. Bettinson from play by J. J. Bell. With George Merritt.

Threads New Era-G. B. Samuelson (A). 3.32 (6,978). p: Gordon Craig, d: G. B. Samuelson, c: Desmond Dickinson, sc: from play by Frank Stayton. With Lawrence Anderson, Dorothy Fane.

Three Fevers see **Turn of the Tide**

Three Maxims, The Herbert Wilcox and Cie Pathé Consortium at Twickenham, Elstree BIP and formerWhitehall (U).

GFD, 6.36 (7,736). Made in UK but registered as foreign. p: d: Herbert Wilcox, c: Freddie Young, sc: Herman Mankiewicz from story by Nicholas Farkas, des: L. P. Williams. With Anna Neagle, Tullio Carminati, Leslie Banks.

Three Men in a Boat ATP at Ealing (U). ABFD, 5.33 (5,443). p: Basil Dean, d: Graham Cutts, c: Robert Martin, sc: D. B. Wyndham-Lewis, dial: Reginald Purdell, from novel by Jerome K. Jerome, music Ord Hamilton, lyrics Bruce Sievier. With Billy Milton, William Austin, Edmond Breon.

Three Men in a Cart British Screen Productions at Isleworth (U). Universal, 4.30 (5,187). silent. d: Arthur Phillips, sc: Edward Dryhurst from story by Arthur Phillips. With Frank Stanmore.

Three of a Kind See **Love on the Spot.**

Three on a Honeymoon See **Where's Sally?**

Three Witnesses Twick. at Twickenham (A). Universal, 3.35 (6,130). p: Julius Hagen, d: Leslie Hiscott, sc: H. Fowler Mear and S. Fowler Wright from novel by S. Fowler Wright. With Henry Kendall, Eve Gray.

Thunder in the City Atlantic Film Productions at Denham (U). UA, 1.37 (7,900). p: Alexander Esway, d: Marion Gering, c: Alfred Gilks, Gus Drisse, sc: Walter Hackett, Akos Tolnay from story by Robert E. Sherwood, des: David Ramon, ed: Arthur Hilton, sp. effects: Ned Mann, music Miklos Rozsa. With Edward G. Robinson, Luli Deste, Nigel Bruce, Ralph Richardson.

Ticket of Leave B & D-Para-Brit. at Elstree B & D (A). Paramt, 1.36 (6,295). d: Michael Hankinson, c: Francis Carver, sc: Margaret McDonnell from screen story by Michael Hankinson and Vera Allinson. With Dorothy Boyd, John Clements.

Ticket of Leave Man, The George King at Shepperton (A). M-G-M, 10.37 (6,354). p: d: George King, c: Hone Glendinning, sc: H. F. Maltby, A. R. Rawlinson from play by Tom Taylor, *Ticket-of-Leave Man* (1863). With Tod Slaughter.

Tiger Bay Wyndham Productions at Ealing (A). ABFD, 9.33 (6,369). p: Bray Wyndham, d: J. Elder Wills, c: Robert Martin and Alan Lawson, sc: John Quin from screen story by Eric Ansell and J. Elder Wills, des: J. Elder Wills, ed: David Lean, Ian Thomson, sd: A. D. Valentine, music Eric Ansell. With Anna May Wong, Henry Victor.

Tight Corner, A Real Art at Twickenham (A). M-G-M, 8.32 (4,409). p: Julius Hagen, d: Leslie Hiscott, c: Sydney Blythe. With Frank Pettingell, Harold French, Gina Malo.

Till the Bells Ring BSFP (U). A. L. Bayley, 4.33 (4,927). d: Graham Moffat, sc: Graham Moffat from his music-hall sketch. With the Graham Moffat family.

Tilly of Bloomsbury Sterling at Elstree B & D (U). Sterling, 4.31 (7,050) FT WE. d: Jack Raymond, c: Freddie Young, sc: W. P. Lipscomb from play by Ian Hay (1919). With Sydney Howard, Phyllis Konstam, Richard Bird.

Timbuctoo BIP at Elstree and African locations (U). Wardour, 4.33 (6,503). d: Walter Summers, c: Jimmy Wilson, Horace Wheddon, sc: Walter Summers, Arthur Woods from book *Africa Dances*, ed: Leslie Norman, sd: Alec Murray, A. E. Rudolph. With Henry Kendall, Margot Grahame.

Tin Gods BIP at Welwyn (A). Pathé, 4.32 (4,661). d: F. W. Kraemer, sc: from play by Edgar C. Middleton, des: Wilfred Arnold. With Frank Cellier, Dorothy Bartlam.

To Be a Lady B & D-Para-Brit. at Elstree B & D (A). Paramt, 7.34 (6,191). d: George King, c: Henry Harris, sc: Violet Powell from story by C. Nicholson. With Bruce Lister, Dorothy Bouchier.

To Brighton with a Bird See **To Brighton with Gladys.**

To Brighton with Gladys George King at Ealing (U). Fox, 2.33 (4,051). p: Bray Wyndham, d: George King, sc: Eliot Stannard from story by John Quin.

With Harry Milton, Constance Shotter.

To Catch a Thief GS Ent. at Walton (U). Radio, 6.36 (5,793). p: George Smith, d: Maclean Rogers, c: Geoffrey Faithfull, sc: Kathleen Butler, H. F. Maltby from story by Gordon and Margaret McDonnell. With John Garrick, Mary Lawson.

Toilers of the Sea Beaumont Film Productions at Wembley and on Sark (U). Columbia, 3.39 (7,626). p: L. C. Beaumont, d: Selwyn Jepson, Ted Fox, c: D. P. Cooper, sc: Selwyn Jepson from novel by Victor Hugo. With Mary Lawson, Clifford McLaglen, Wilson Coleman.

Tomorrow We Live Conquest Productions at Elstree former Whitehall (A). ABFD, 10.36 (6,491). p: Clayton Hutton, d. sc: Manning Haynes, c: Walter Blakeley. With Godfrey Tearle, Haidee Wright, Renee Gadd.

Tonight's the Night BIP at Elstree (U). Wardour, 12.31 (6,686). d: Monty Banks, c: Ernest Palmer, sc: Leslie Arliss, Syd Courtenay from story by Syd Courtenay and Lola Harvey. With Leslie Fuller, Amy Veness.

Tons of Money B & D at Elstree B & D (U). W & F, 12.30 (9,126) FT WE. p: Herbert Wilcox, d: Tom Walls, sc: Herbert Wilcox and Ralph Lynn from play by Will Evans and Valentine (1922). With Ralph Lynn, Yvonne Arnaud, Robertson Hare.

To Oblige a Lady Brit. Lion at Beaconsfield (A). Brit. Lion, 2.31 (6,740) FT RCA. p: Edgar Wallace, d: Manning Haynes, c: Alex Bryce, sc: from play by Edgar Wallace, sd: Harold King. With Maisie Gay, Warwick Ward.

Too Dangerous to Live WB-FN at Teddington (A). FN, 3.39 (6,693). p: Jerome Jackson, d: Anthony Hankey, Leslie Norman, c: Basil Emmott, sc: Paul Gangelin, Connery Chappell, Leslie Arliss from novel by David Hume. With Greta Gynt, Sebastian Shaw.

Too Many Crooks George King at

Twickenham (U). Fox, 8.30 (3,414) FT RCA. d: George King, sc: Billie Bristow from story by Basil Roscoe, music W. Hodgson. With Laurence Olivier, Dorothy Boyd.

Too Many Husbands Liberty Films at Isleworth (A). Liberty Films, 12.38 (5,352). p: Roy Rich, d: Ivar Campbell, c: Ernest Palmer, sc: from play by Guy Bolton, *Mirabelle* (1937). With Iris Baker, Jack Melford, Geoffrey Sumner.

Too Many Millions WB-FN at Teddington (U). WB, 9.34 (5,144). p: Irving Asher, d: Harold Young, sc: Brock Williams. With Betty Compton, John Garrick.

Too Many Wives WB-FN at Teddington (U). WB, 3.33 (5,287). p: Irving Asher, d: George King, sc: W. Scott Darling. With Nora Swinburne, Jack Hobbs.

Tooth Will Out G-B at Shepherd's Bush (U). Ideal, registered 4.33 (1,681). p. man: Clayton Hutton, d: Frank Cadman. With Jack Williams, Joey Porter.

Toreadors Don't Care See **Old Spanish Customers.**

Touch of the Moon, A GS Ent. (U). Radio, 2.36 (6,024). p: George Smith, d: P. Maclean Rogers, c: Geoffrey Faithfull, sc: Kathleen Butler, H. F. Maltby from play by Cyril Campion. With John Garrick, Dorothy Boyd.

To What Red Hell Strand and Twickenham at Twickenham (A). Tiffany Productions, (1) 10.29 synchronised (9,247), (2) 1.30 silent (8,300) FT RCA. p: Julius Hagen, d: Edwin Greenwood, c: Basil Emmott, sc: Leslie Hiscott from play by Percy Robinson (1928), music John Greenwood. With Sybil Thorndike, John Hamilton.

Traitor Spy Rialto Productions at Welwyn (A). Pathé, 12.39 (6,724). p: John Argyle, d: Walter Summers, c: Robert Lapresle, sc: Walter Summers, Jay Van Lusil, Ralph Bettinson from novel by T. C. H. Jacobs, des: Ian White, ed: E. Richards, sd: A. E. Rudolph. With Bruce Cabot, Marta

Labarr, Tamara Desni.

Transatlantic Trouble See **Take It from Me.**

Trent's Folly See **House of Trent, The.**

Triumph of Sherlock Holmes, The Real Art at Twickenham (A). G-B D, 1.35 (7,544). p: Julius Hagen, d: Leslie Hiscott, c: William Luff, sc: H. Fowler Mear and Cyril Twyford from story by Sir Arthur Conan Doyle, *The Valley of Fear*, des: James Carter, ed: Ralph Kemplen, sd: Baynham Honri, MD: W. L. Trytel. With Arthur Wontner, Ian Fleming, Lyn Harding.

Troopship See **Farewell Again.**

Tropical Trouble City Film Corporation at Walton (A). GFD, 10.36 (6,325). p: Basil Humphreys, d: Harry Hughes, c: Geoffrey Faithfull, sc: Vernon Harris from novel by Stephen King-Hall, *Bunga-Bunga*. With Douglass Montgomery, Betty Ann Davies.

Trouble B & D at Elstree B & D (U). UA, 11.33 (6,353). p: Herbert Wilcox, d: P. Maclean Rogers, sc: R. P. Weston, Bert Lee, Jack Marks from story by Dudley Sturrock, des: G. S. Stegman. With Sydney Howard, George Curzon.

Trouble Brewing ATP at Ealing (U). ABFD, 2.39 (7,814). p: Jack Kitchin, d: Anthony Kimmins, c: Ronald Neame, sc: from story by Anthony Kimmins, Angus MacPhail, Michael Hogan, des: Wilfred Shingleton, ed: Ernest Aldridge, sd: Eric Williams, MD: Ernest Irving, music and lyrics George Formby, Harry Gifford, Fred E. Cliffe. With George Formby, Googie Withers.

Troubled Waters Fox Brit. at Wembley (A). Fox, 2.36 (6,396). p: John Findlay, d: Albert Parker, c: Roy Kellino, sc: Gerard Fairlie from story by Reginald Pound and W. P. Lipscomb, ed: Cecil Williamson. With James Mason, Virginia Cherrill, Alastair Sim.

Trouble for Two Venture Films at Isleworth (U). Anglo-American Film Distributors, 5.39 (4,014). p: Alfred d'Eyncourt, d: Walter Tennyson, c: Desmond Dickinson, sc: Ian Walker.

With Anthony Hulme, Mavis Claire.

Trouble in Store WB-FN at Teddington (U). FN, 1.34 (3,586). p: Irving Asher, d: Clyde Cook. With James Finlayson, Jack Hobbs.

Trouble in the House See **Twice Branded**

Trunk Crime Charter Film Productions at Elstree former Whitehall (A). Anglo-American Film Distributors, 3.39 (4,600). p: John Boulting, d: Roy Boulting, c: D. P. Cooper, sc: Francis Miller from play by Reginald Denham and Edward Percy, des: Duncan Sutherland.

Trust Berkely See **Adventure Limited**

Trust the Navy St George's Pictures at Cricklewood (U). Columbia, 12.35 (6,490). p: Ian Sutherland, d: Henry W. George, sc: Reginald Long, Ian Sutherland from story by Arthur Rose, songs Billy Mayerl and Frank Eyton. With Lupino Lane, Nancy Burne, Wallace Lupino.

Tudor Rose Gainsborough at Islington (U). G-B D, 4.36 (7,077). p: Michael Balcon, assoc. p: Edward Black, d: Robert Stevenson, c: Mutz Greenbaum, sc: Robert Stevenson, dial: Miles Malleson, des: Vetchinsky, cost: Joe Strassner, ed: T. R. Fisher, sd: W. Salter, period adviser Tom Heslewood, MD: Louis Levy. With Nova Pilbeam, John Mills, Sir Cedric Hardwicke.

Tunnel, The G-B at Shepherd's Bush (U). G-B D, 11.35 (8,578). p: Michael Balcon, assoc. p: S. C. Balcon, d: Maurice Elvey, c: Gunther Krampf, sc: L. du Garde Peach, add. dial: Clemence Dane from screen story by Kurt Siodmak based on novel *Der Tunnel* by B. Kellerman (already used for French and German films d: Kurt Bernhardt), des: Ernö Metzner, cost: Schiaparelli, Joe Strassner, ed: Charles Frend, sd: M. Rose, MD: Louis Levy.

Turkey Time G-B Shepherd's Bush (A). G-B D, 12.33 (6,406). p: Michael Balcon, d: Tom Walls, c: Charles Van Enger, sc: Ben Travers from his own play (1931), des: Alfred Junge. With

Tom Walls, Ralph Lynn, Robertson Hare, Dorothy Hyson.

Turn of the Tide Brit. Nat. at Elstree B & D and Yorkshire (Robin Hood's Bay, Whitby) (U). G-B D, 10.35 (7,233). p: John Corfield, d: Norman Walker, c: Franz Planer, Eric Cross, sc: L. du Garde Peach from novel by Leo Walmsley, *Three Fevers*, des: A. L. Mazzei, ed: Stephen Harrison, sd: John Dennis, music Arthur Benjamin. With John Garrick, Nial MacGinnis, Geraldine Fitzgerald.

Twelve Good Men WB-FN at Teddington (A). WB, 3.36 (5,821). p: Irving Asher, d: Ralph Ince, c: Basil Emmott, sc: Sidney Gilliat and Frank Launder from novel by John Rhode *The Murders in Praed St.* With Henry Kendall, Nancy O'Neil.

Twenty-One Days Denham Films, in production at Denham 5.37 (A). Columbia, shown 4.39 (6,761). p: Alexander Korda, d: Basil Dean, c: Jan Stallich, sc: Graham Greene and Basil Dean from play by John Galsworthy, *The First and the Last*, des: Vincent Korda, ed: Charles Crichton, MD: Louis Levy. With Vivien Leigh, Laurence Olivier, Leslie Banks.

Twice Branded GS Ent. at Walton (U). Radio, 1.36 (6,142). p: George Smith, d: P. Maclean Rogers, c: Geoffrey Faithfull, sc: Kathleen Butler from story by Anthony Richardson, *Trouble in the House.* With Robert Rendel, Eve Grey, Lucille Lisle, James Mason.

Twin Faces Premier Sound Film Productions at Highbury (A). Paramt, 8.37 (6,056). p: James Edwards, d: Lawrence Huntington, sc: W. G. Elliott from story by Douglas Reekie. With Anthony Ireland, Francesca Bahrle.

Two Crowded Hours Film Engineering at Walton (A). Fox, 7.31 (4,000). p: Harry Cohen, Jerome Jackson, d: Michael Powell, c: Geoffrey Faithfull, sc: from story by J. Jefferson Farjeon, des: W. G. Saunders, ed: A. Seabourne. With John Longden, Jane Walsh.

Two Days to Live Venture Films at Isleworth (A). Anglo-American Film Distributors, 5.39 (4,200). p: Alfred d'Eyncourt, d: Walter Tennyson, c: Desmond Dickinson, sc: Ian Walker. With Richard Goolden, Phyllis Calvert.

Two for Divorce See **Her Reputation**

Two Hearts in Harmony Time Pictures at Shepperton (A). Wardour, 11.35 (6,816). p: John Clein, d: William Beaudine, sc: Robert Edmunds and A. R. Rawlinson from story by S. G. Browne, songs Eddie Pola, Franz Vienna. With Bernice Clare, George Curzon.

Two Hearts in Waltz Time Nettlefold-Fogwell at Walton (U). G-B D, 4.34 (7,200). p: Reginald Fogwell, d: Carmine Gallone, c: Geoffrey Faithfull, sc: Reginald Fogwell, John McNally from German film (by Walter Reisch, Franz Schulz, d: Joe May), des: A. L. Mazzei. With Carl Brisson, Frances Day, Oscar Asche.

Two Men in a Box Ace Films, 3.38 (4,210). d: R. A. Hopwood. Variety from Windmill Theatre.

Two on a Doorstep B & D-Para-Brit. at Elstree Rock (A). Paramt, 4.36 (6,345). d: Lawrence Huntington, c: Francis Carver, sc: W. G. Elliott, dial: George Barraud from screen story by Donovan Pedelty. With Harold French, Kay Hammond

Two's Company B & D and Soskin Productions (U). UA, 4.36 (6,616). p: Paul Soskin, d: Tim Whelan, c: Freddie Young, sc: Tom Geraghty, John Paddy Carstairs, dial: J. B. Moreton from play by Sydney Horler, *Romeo and Julia.* With Mary Brian, Patric Knowles, Ned Sparks, Gordon Harker.

Two Way Street Nettlefold at Walton (A). UA, 12.31 (3,995) FT RCA. d: George King, sc: Charles Bennett, Billie Bristow. With Sari Maritza, Harry Wilcoxon, James Raglan.

Two White Arms Cinema House at Wembley (A). M-G-M, 3.32 (7,202), p: Eric Hakim, d: Fred Niblo, c: Henry Gerrard, Henry Harris, sc: Dr Harold Dearden from his play *White Arms*, ed:

Lars Moen. With Adolphe Menjou, Margaret Bannerman, Jane Baxter.

Two Wives for Henry George Smith at Wembley (A). Fox, 1.34 (4,015). d: Adrian Brunel. With Garry Marsh, Dorothy Boyd.

Two Worlds BIP-E. A. Dupont Production at Elstree (A). Wardour, 7.30 (9,459). Registered as foreign. p: d: E. A. Dupont, c: Charles Rosher, sc: Norbert Falk, Franz Schulz and Miles Malleson from story by E. A. Dupont and Thekla von Bodo, des: Alfred Junge, sd: Alec Murray, MD: John Reynders, music Otto Stransky. With Norah Baring, John Longden, Randle Ayrton.

Tzigane See **Gypsy**

Umbrella, The Real Art at Twickenham (A). Radio, 7.33 (5,011). p: Julius Hagen, d: Redd Davis, c: Ernest Palmer, sc: H. Fowler Mear from novel by Laurence Meynell. With Kay Hammond, Harold French.

Under a Cloud Triangle at Sound City (A). Paramt, 8.37 (6,001). p: d: George King, c: Hone Glendinning, sc: M.B. Parsons from story by Gordon Francis. With Betty Ann Davies, Edward Rigby.

Underneath the Arches Twick. at Hammersmith (U). Wardour, 2.37 (6,500). p: Julius Hagen, d: Redd Davis, Sydney Blythe, sc: H. Fowler Mear from story by Alison Booth. With Flanagan and Allen, Enid Stamp-Taylor.

Under Proof Fox Brit. at Wembley (U). Fox, 2.36 (4,570). d: Roland Gillett, c: Stanley Grant, sc: E. Lewis Waller from his own play *Dudley Does it*. With Tyrell Davis, Betty Stockfield, Judy Kelly.

Under the Greenwood Tree BIP at Elstree (U). Wardour 9.29 (8,650) FT songs, RCA. d: Harry Lachman, c: Claude Friese-Greene, sc. adapt: Rex Taylor and Harry Lachman, sc: Monckton Hoffe and Frank Launder from novel by Thomas Hardy, des: Wilfred Arnold, ed: Émile de Ruelle, sd: Dallas Bower, MD: John Reynders, music Hubert Bath. With Marguerite

Allan, John Batten.

Under the Red Robe New World Pictures at Denham (U). 20th Cent.-Fox, 5.37 (7,298) p: Robert T. Kane, d: Victor Seastrom, dial. d: Romney Brent, c: James Wong Howe, Georges Périnal, sc: Lajos Biro, Philip Lindsay and J. L. Hodson from novel by Stanley J. Weyman, and play by Edward Rose (1896), scenario Arthur Wimperis, des: Frank Wells, cost: Rene Hubert, ed: James B. Clark, sd: A. W. Watkins, MD: Muir Mathieson, music Arthur Benjamin. With Conrad Veidt, Raymond Massey, Annabella, Romney Brent.

Uneasy Virtue BIP at Elstree (U). Wardour, 2.31 (7,450) FT RCA. d: Norman Walker, c: Claude Friese-Greene, sc: from play by Harrison Owen, *The Happy Husband* (1927). With Fay Compton, Edmond Breon, Margot Grahame.

Unexpected Journey See **Runaway Ladies**

Unholy Quest, The Widgey Newman, Reginald Wyer, Bert Hopkins (A). Equity British, 3.34 (5,120). d: R. W. Lotinga, sc: Widgey Newman. With Terence de Marney, Claude Bailey.

Unlucky Jim Master Productions (U). Radio, 5.36 (3,125). p: d: Harry Mark. With Tony Jones.

Unto Each Other Cinema Exclusives (A). Fox, 1.30 (7,564) silent. p: Frank Wheatcroft, d: sc: A. E. Coleby. With Harry Lorraine.

Unwritten Law, The BSFP at Wembley (A). BIFD,, 6.29 (3.020) FT BTP. d: Sinclair Hill, sc: Violet Heckstall Smith. With Ion Swinley, Rosalinde Fuller.

Up for the Cup B & D (U). W & F, 9.31 (6,870) FT WE. p: Herbert Wilcox, d: Jack Raymond, sc: Con West, R. P. Weston, Bert Lee. With Sydney Howard.

Up for the Derby B & D at Elstree B & D (U). W & F, 3.33 (6,387). p: Herbert Wilcox, d: P. Maclean Rogers, sc: R. P. Weston, Bert Lee, Jack Marks. With Sydney Howard.

Up to the Neck B & D at Elstree B & D (U). UA, 8.33 (6,638). p: Herbert

Wilcox, d: Jack Raymond, c: Cyril Bristow, sc: Ben Travers from his own story. With Ralph Lynn, Winifred Shotter.

Uptown Revue Ace Films, 4.37 (4,076). p: Frank Green, d: R. A. Hopwood. Variety from Windmill Theatre.

Vagabond Queen, The BIP (U). Wardour, (1) 5.29 silent (5,610), (2) 8.30 sound (6,672) music only, RCA disc. d: Geza von Bolvary, c: Charles Rosher, sc: Val Valentine, Rex Taylor from story by Douglas Furber, des: Hugh Gee, ed: Émile de Ruelle, MD: John Reynders. With Betty Balfour, Glen Byam Shaw, Ernest Thesiger.

Valley of Death See under **Balaclava**

Valley of Ghosts, The Brit. Lion at Beaconsfield (A). J-M-G, 3.30 (5,304). p: S. W. Smith, d: G. B. Samuelson, sc: Edgar Wallace from his own story. With Miriam Seegar, Ian Hunter.

Valley of Fear, The See **Triumph of Sherlock Holmes, The**

Vandergilt Diamond Mystery, The Randall Faye (A). Radio, 1.36 (5,284). p: d: Randall Faye, sc: Margaret Houghton from story by Michael Crombie. With Elizabeth Astell, Bruce Seton.

Vanity GS Ent. (U). Columbia, first show 12.35 (6,942). p: George Smith, d: Adrian Brunel, sc: From play by Ernest Denny. With Jane Cain. Percy Marmont.

Variety Argyle Talking Films at Cricklewood (U). Butcher's, 3.35 (7,878). p: John Argyle, d: Adrian Brunel, c: Desmond Dickinson, sc; Adrian Brunel, Oswald Mitchell, ed: Dan Birt.

Variety (1930) See **Just for a Song**

Variety Hour Fox Brit. at Wembley (A). Fox, 3.37 (5,932). d: Redd Davis. With Clapham and Dwyer.

Variety Parade Malcolm Picture Productions at Cricklewood (U). Butcher's, 11.36 (7,500). p: Ian Sutherland, Reginald Long, d: Oswald Mitchell, c: Jack Parker, sc: Oswald Mitchell from story by Con West, ed: Challis Sanderson.

Vengeance of Kali, The See **Dance of Death, The**

Verdict of the Sea Regina Films at Elstree BIP (U). Pathé, 6.32 (5,793). p: Clayton Hutton, d: sc: Frank Miller. With John Stuart, Cyril McLaglen, Moira Lynd.

Vessel of Wrath Mayflower Pictures at Elstree BIP and South of France (A). ABPC, 2.38 (8,509). p: d: Erich Pommer, c: Jules Kruger, Gus Drisse, sc: Bartlett Cormack, B. Van Thal from novel by W. Somerset Maugham, des: Tom Morahan, ed: Robert Hamer, sd: Jack Rogerson, MD: Muir Mathieson, music Richard Addinsell. With Charles Laughton, Elsa Lanchester, Tyrone Guthrie, Robert Newton.

Veteran of Waterloo, The National Talkies (U). Paramt, 7.33 (4,400). p: Harry Rowson, d: A. V. Bramble, sc: from play by Sir Arthur Conan Doyle, *A Story of Waterloo*. With Jerrold Robertshaw.

Vicar of Bray, The J. H. Productions at Twickenham and Hammersmith (U). ABPC, 3.37 (6,110). p: Julius Hagen, d: Henry Edwards, c: William Luff, sc: H. Fowler Mear from story by Ernest Anson Dyer, des: James Carter, ed: R. J. Verrall, sd: Baynham Honri, MD: M. de Wolfe. With Stanley Holloway, Margaret Vines, Esmond Knight.

Victoria the Great Imperator at Denham (U). Radio, 9.37 (10,152). Part Technicolor (colour direction Natalie Kalmus). p: d: Herbert Wilcox, c: Freddie Young, colour c: W. Skall, sc: Miles Malleson and Charles de Grandcourt from their screen story, des: L. P. Williams, cost: Doris Zinkeisen, ed: James Elmo Williams, Jill Irving, sd: L. E. Overton, period adviser Tom Heslewood, MD: Muir Mathieson, music Anthony Collins. With Anna Neagle, Anton Walbrook, H. B. Warner.

Vie de Bohème See **Mimi**

Vienna Sunset See **Sunset in Vienna**

Village Squire, The B & D-Para-Brit. at

Elstree B & D (U). Paramt, 4.35 (6,003). d: Reginald Denham, sc: Sherard Powell from story by Arthur Jarvis Black. With David Horne, Leslie Perrins, Moira Lynd.

Villiers Diamond, The Fox Brit. at Wembley (A). 20th Cent. Fox, 2.38 (4,501). d: Bernerd Mainwaring, c: Stanley Grant, sc: David Evans from story by F. Wyndham Mallock, *The Trap,* des: William Hemsley. With Frank Birch, Edward Ashley, Evelyn Ankers.

Vintage Wine Real Art at Twickenham (A). Gaumont, 6.35 (7,277). p: Julius Hagen, d: Henry Edwards, c: Sydney Blythe, sc: H. Fowler Mear from play by Ashley Dukes and Sir Seymour Hicks (1934) based on play by Alexander Engel, *Der Ewige Juengling,* des: James Carter, ed: Ralph Kemplen, sd: Baynham Honri, MD: W. L. Trytel. With Sir Seymour Hicks, Claire Luce, Eva Moore.

Viper, The WB-FN at Teddington (U). FN, 1.38 (6,781). p: Irving Asher, d: Roy W. Neill, c: Robert Lapresle, sc: Reginald Purdell, John Dighton, J. O. C. Orton. With Claude Hulbert, Leslie Brook.

Virginia's Husband George Smith at Walton (U). Fox, 9.34 (6,419). p: George Smith, d: P. Maclean Rogers, c: Geoffrey Faithfull, sc: from story by Florence Kilpatrick, *Oh Joy!* With Dorothy Boyd, Reginald Gardiner, Enid Stamp-Taylor.

Voice of Ireland, The Victor Haddick (U). International Cinematograph Company, 3.36 (4,457). d: sc: Col. Victor Haddick. With Richard Hayward, Victor Haddick.

Voice Said Goodnight, A WB-FN (U). WB, 3.32 (3,214). p: Irving Asher, d: William McGann, sc: Roland Pertwee, J. Hastings Turner from sketch by Roland Pertwee. With Nora Swinburne, Jack Trevor.

Vulture, The WB-FN at Teddington (A). FN, 2.37 (6,024). p: Irving Asher, d: Ralph Ince, c: Basil Emmott, sc: from story by Stafford Dickens. With Claude Hulbert, Lesley Brook.

Wake Up Famous Premier-Stafford at Shepperton (U). Radio, 1.37 (6,117) p: John Stafford, d: Gene Gerrard, c: Jimmy Wilson, sc: Basil Mason. With Nelson Keys, Gene Gerrard.

Waltzes from Vienna Tom Arnold at Shepherd's Bush (U). G-B D, 2.34 (7,206). p: Tom Arnold, d: Alfred Hitchcock, c: Glen MacWilliams, sc: Guy Bolton, Alma Reville from play by Heinz Reichert, Dr A. M. Willner and Ernst Marischka (1931), des: Oscar Werndorff, ed: Charles Frend, sd: A. Birch, MD: Louis Levy, music Johann Strauss the elder, Johann Strauss the younger, adapted Hubert Bath. With Jessie Matthews, Esmond Knight, Fay Compton.

Waltz Time G-B at Shepherd's Bush (A). W & F, 6.33 (7,373). p: Herman Fellner, d: William Thiele, sc: A. P. Herbert from operetta by Johann Strauss, *Die Fledermaus,* des: Alfred Junge, ed: Derek Twist, MD: Louis Levy, music Johann Strauss, Louis Levy, Lyrics A. P. Herbert. With Evelyn Laye, Fritz Schultz.

Wandering Jew, The Twick. at Twickenham (A). Gaumont, 11.33 (9,900). p: Julius Hagen, d: Maurice Elvey, c: Sydney Blythe, sc: H. Fowler Mear from play by E. Temple Thurston (1920), des: James Carter, cost: Cathleen Mann, ed: Jack Harris. With Conrad Veidt, Marie Ney, Anne Grey, John Stuart, Peggy Ashcroft.

Wanted Embassy Pictures at Shepperton (U). Sound City Dist., 2.37 (6,293). p: d: George King, c: Jack Parker, sc:

Brock Williams from his own play. With ZaSu Pitts, Claude Dampier, Finlay Currie.

Ware Case, The Associated Star Productions (CAPAD and Ealing) at Ealing, Pinewood exteriors (A). ABFD, 12.38 (6,823). p: Michael Balcon, assoc. p: S. C. Balcon, d: Robert Stevenson, c: Ronald Neame, sc: Robert Stevenson, Roland Pertwee, add. dial: E. V. H. Emmett from play by George Pleydell Bancroft (1915), des: O. F. Werndorff, ed: Charles Saunders, sd: Eric Williams, MD: Ernest Irving. With Clive Brook, Jane Baxter, Barry K. Barnes.

Warm Corner, A Gainsborough at Elstree B & D (U). Ideal, 9.30 (9,300 at trade show, 7,036 registered) FT WE. p: Michael Balcon, d: Victor Saville, c: Freddie Young, sc: Victor Saville and Angus MacPhail, from play by Arthur Wimperis and Lauri Wylie (1929) based on play by Franz Arnold and Ernst Bach, des: Walter Murton, sd: A. W. Watkins. With Leslie Henson, Heather Thatcher.

Warned Off B & D (U). M-G-M, 12.29 (6,510) silent. p: Herbert Wilcox, d: Walter West, sc: Reginald Fogwell from story by Robert Sievier. With Chili Bouchier, Queenie Thomas, Tony Wylde.

Warning, The British Projects (A). Pro Patria, 2.30 (6,692) silent. p: A. E. Bundy, d: Reginald Fogwell, sc: Reginald Fogwell from story by A. E. Bundy. With Percy Marmont, Anne Grey, Fern Andra.

Warn London British Lion at Beaconsfield (A). Brit. Lion, 5.34 (6,190). T. Hayes Hunter, c: Alex Bryce, sc: Charles Bennett, Billie Bristow from story by Denison Clift, des: Norman Arnold, sd: Harold King. With Edmund Gwenn, Leonora Corbett, John Loder.

Warren Case, The BIP at Welwyn (A). Pathé, 3.34 (6,765). p: Walter Mycroft, d: Walter Summers, c: Jack Parker, sc: Walter Summers from play by Arnold Ridley, *The Last Chance,* des: John

Mead. With Richard Bird, Nancy Burne, Diana Napier.

Watch Beverley Sound City at Shepperton (U). Butcher's, 10.32 (7,146). p: Ivar Campbell, d: Arthur Maude, c: George Stretton, sc: N. W. B. Pemberton and John Cousins from play by Cyril Campion (1928). With Henry Kendall, Dorothy Bartlam, Francis X. Bushman.

Water Gipsies, The ATP at Beaconsfield (A). Radio, 3.32 (7,177). p: Basil Dean, d: Maurice Elvey, c: Robert Martin and Robert de Grasse, sc: Basil Dean, Alma Reville, Miles Malleson from novel by A. P. Herbert, des: Norman Arnold, ed: Otto Ludwig, sd: Marcus Cooper, MD: Ernest Irving, songs by A. P. Herbert and Vivian Ellis. With Ann Todd, Ian Hunter, Richard Bird.

Way of Youth, The B & D-Para-Brit. at Elstree B & D (A). Paramt, 11.34 (5,939). d: Norman Walker, sc: Sherard Powell from play by Amy Kennedy Gould. With Henry Victor, Irene Vanbrugh. Aileen Marson.

Wedding Eve National Progress (U). Radio, 2.35 (3,531). d: sc: Charles Barnett. With Dodo Watts, Frank Titterton, Clapham and Dwyer.

Wedding Group Fox Brit. at Wembley (U). Fox, 3.36 (6,226). p: Leslie Landau, d: Alex Bryce, Campbell Gullan, c: Arthur Crabtree, sc: Selwyn Jepson, Hugh Brooke from radio play by Philip Wade, cost: Elizabeth Haffenden. With Fay Compton, Patric Knowles, Alastair Sim.

Wedding Rehearsal LFP at Wembley (U). Ideal, 7.32 (7,595). p: d: Alexander Korda, c: Leslie Rowson, sc: Arthur Wimperis, Helen Gordon from story by George Grossmith, Lajos Biro, des: Oscar Werndorff, Vincent Korda, ed: Hal Young, sd: G. Burgess, music Kurt Schroeder. With George Grossmith, Roland Young, John Loder, Lady Tree, Maurice Evans.

Weddings Are Wonderful George Smith Productions-Canterbury at Walton (A). RKO-Radio, 9.38 (7,151). p: George

Smith, d: P. Maclean Rogers, c: Geoffrey Faithfull, sc: Kathleen Butler, H. F. Maltby from play by Sydney Blow, Douglas Hoare, *Peaches* (1915), ed: Dan Birt. With Esmond Knight, June Clyde, Rene Ray.

We Dine at Seven GS Ent. at Twickenham (U). Fox, 4.31 (3,983). p: Harry Cohen, d: Frank A. Richardson, c: Basil Emmott, sc: Brock Williams, des: James Carter. With Herbert Mundin, Dorothy Bartlam.

Wednesday's Luck B & D-Para-Brit. (A). Paramt, 5.36 (6,213). d: George Pearson, sc: Ralph Neale from screen story by Edith Pryce. With Susan Bligh, Wilson Coleman.

Well Done, Henry Butcher's-Neville Clarke at Cricklewood (A). Butcher's, 1.37 (7,315). p: Neville Clarke, d: Wilfred Noy, c: Jack Parker, sc: Wilfred Noy from story by Selwyn Jepson, des: Duncan Sutherland. With Will Fyffe, Charles Hawtrey, Cathleen Nesbitt.

We're Going to be Rich 20th Cent. Productions at Denham (A). 20th Cent.-Fox, premiere 5.38 (7,208). assoc. p: Samuel G. Engel, d: Monty Banks, c: Mutz Greenbaum, sc: Sam Hellman, Rohama Siegel from story by James Edward Grant, cost: Joe Strassner. With Gracie Fields, Victor McLaglen, Coral Browne, Brian Donlevy.

West End See **Night Birds**

West End Frolics Ace Films, 3.37 (4,335). p: Frank Green, d: R. A. Hopwood. Variety from Windmill Theatre.

West of Kerry Irish Nat. Film Corp. in Ireland (U). Butcher's, 3.38 (4,300). p: Victor Taylor, d: Dick Bird, sc: Patrick K. Heale from story by Donal O'Cahil, John Duffy.

We've Got to Have Love B & N (U). B & N, 1.35 (3,300). p: Baron Nahum, d: sc: Patrick O'Brien. With Nelson Keys, Hilda Moreno, Davy Burnaby.

What a Man! Phoenix-International Film Productions at Beaconsfield (U). Brit. Lion, 1.39 (6,712). p: Hugh Perceval, d: Esmond T. Gréville, c: Ernest Palmer, sc: Basil Mason from story by Basil Mason and Jack Marks. With Sydney Howard, Vera Pearce, Jenny Laird.

What a Night! BIP at Elstree (U). FN-Pathé, 3.31 (5,330) FT RCA. d: Monty Banks, sc: story by Syd Courtenay and Lola Harvey. With Leslie Fuller.

What a Party See **Easy Money**

What Happened Then? BIP at Welwyn (A). Wardour, 9.34 (5,200). p: Walter Mycroft, d: Walter Summers, c: Jimmy Wilson, sc: Walter Summers from play by Lilian Trimble Bradley (1933), des: John Mead, ed: E. B. Jarvis, sd: David Howells. With Richard Bird, Lorna Storm.

What Happened to Harkness? WB-FN at Teddington (U). FN, 8.34 (4,729). p: Irving Asher, d: Milton Rosmer, sc: Brock Williams from story by Rowland Brown. With Robert Hale, James Finlayson.

What Shall It Profit a Woman? See **Designing Woman**

What's in a Name WB-FN at Teddington (U). FN, 10.34 (4,272). p: Irving Asher, d: Ralph Ince. With Carol Goodner, Barry Clifton.

What's On? See **Sunshine Ahead**

What the Parrot Saw Widgey Newman at Bushey (U). Butcher's, 8.35 (3,672). p: d: Widgey Newman, c: John Miller, sc: John Quin from story by Widgey Newman. With Roma Beaumont.

What the Puppy Said Widgey Newman at Bushey (U). Butcher's, 2.36 (3,568). d: Widgey Newman, c: John Miller, sc: John Quin from story by Widgey Newman. With Wally Patch, Moor Marriott.

What Would You Do, Chums? Brit. Nat. at Elstree old Whitehall (A). Anglo-American Film Distributors, 8.39 (6,733). p: John Corfield, d: John Baxter, c: Jimmy Wilson, sc: David Evans, Con West, Geoffrey Orme from radio series by Ernest Dudley, *Mr. Walker Wants to Know,* des: Duncan Sutherland. With Syd Walker, Jean Gillie.

Wheel Spins, The See **Lady Vanishes, The**

When Knights Were Bold Capitol at Elstree B & D, Warwick Castle (U). GFD, 2.36 (6,848). p: Max Schach, d: Jack Raymond, c: Freddie Young, sc: Douglas Furber and Austin Parker from play by Charles Marlowe (1907), des: Wilfred Arnold, ed: Frederick Wilson, sd: John Dennis, MD: Harry Perritt, songs Harry Perritt and George Windeatt, and Sigler, Goodhart and Hoffman. With Jack Buchanan, Fay Wray.

When London Sleeps Twick. at Twickenham (A). AP & D, 7.32 (7,025). p: Julius Hagen, d: Leslie Hiscott, sc: H. Fowler Mear, Bernard Merivale from play by Charles Darrell, ed: Jack Harris. With Harold French, Francis L. Sullivan, Rene Ray.

When the Cat's Away Central Film Productions (U). Zenifilms, registered 8.35 (3,150). p: d: Walter Tennyson. With Davy Burnaby.

When the Devil Was Well GS Ent. at Walton (U). Columbia, 3.37 (6,093). p: George Smith, d: P. Maclean Rogers, sc: W. Lane Crawford. With Jack Hobbs, Vera Lennox.

When the Poppies Bloom Again George King at Shepperton (U). M-G-M, 5.37 (4,076). p: George King, d: David MacDonald, c: James Wilson, sc: Evadne Price from story by Herbert Ayres. With Nancy Burne, Jack Livesey, John Warwick.

When We Are Married See **Don't Rush Me**

Where Is This Lady? Amalgamated Films Association at Elstree BIP (U). Brit. Lion, 11.32 (7,249). p: John Stafford, d: Ladislaus Vajda, W. Victor Hanbury, c: Walter Blakeley, sc: Sydney Blow and Ladislaus Vajda from German film (d: Billy Wilder), *Es War Einmal ein Walzer*, music composed for film by Franz Lehar. With Marta Eggerth, Owen Nares, George K. Arthur, Wendy Barrie.

Where's George? (later **Hope of his Side, The**) B & D at Elstree B & D (U). UA, 8.35 (6,343). p: Herbert Wilcox, d: Jack Raymond, Freddie Young, sc: John Paddy Carstairs from screen story by Walter Greenwood, des: Wilfred Arnold. With Sydney Howard, Mabel Constanduros, Frank Pettingell.

Where's Sally? WB-FN at Teddington (A). FN, 4.36 (6,429). p: Irving Asher, d: Arthur Woods, c: Basil Emmott, sc: Brock Williams, Frank Launder, des: Peter Proud. With Gene Gerrard, Claude Hulbert, Renee Gadd.

Where's That Fire? 20th Cent. Productions at Islington (U). 20th Century-Fox 7.39 (6,605). p: Edward Black, d: Marcel Varnel, c: Arthur Crabtree, sc: G. Marriott Edgar, Val Guest, J. O. C. Orton from story by Maurice Braddell. With Will Hay, Moore Marriott, Graham Moffatt.

Where There's a Will Gainsborough at Islington (A). G-B D, 6.36 (7,233). p: Michael Balcon, d: William Beaudine, c: Charles Van Enger, sc: Will Hay, Robert Edmunds, William Beaudine from story by Leslie Arliss and Sidney Gilliat, des: Vetchinsky, Paula Newman, ed: Terence Fisher, sd: Michael Rose, MD: Louis Levy. With Will Hay, Gina Malo, Graham Moffatt, Hartley Power.

While Parents Sleep Transatlantic Film Corporation-B & D at Elstree B & D (A). UA, 9.35 (6,708). p: Paul Soskin, d: Adrian Brunel, c: Ernest Palmer, sc: Anthony Kimmins, Edwin Greenwood, John Paddy Carstairs from play by Anthony Kimmins (1932), des: L. P. Williams, ed: Michael Hankinson, sd: Alex Fisher, music by Percival Mackey. With Jean Gillie, Mckenzie Ward.

Whirligig See **Live Again**

Whispering Tongues Real Art at Twickenham (A). Radio, 3.34 (4,951). p: Julius Hagen, d: George Pearson, sc: H. Fowler Mear from screen story by Bernerd Mainwaring. With Reginald Tate, Jane Welsh.

White Arms See **Two White Arms**

White Cargo Neo-Art Films at Twickenham and Elstree former

Whitehall (A). WP, (1) 5.29 silent (8,000), (2) 10.29 sound (7,965) FT, song RCA. p: d: J. B. Williams, Arthur Barnes, c: Karl Püth, sc: J. B. Williams from play by Leon Gordon (1924) and novel by Vera Simonton, *Hell's Playground*. With Leslie Faber, Gypsy Rhouma, Maurice Evans.

White Ensign Sound City at Shepperton (U). M-G-M, 3.34 (7,599). p: Norman Loudon, d: sc: John L. F. Hunt, c: Hone Glendinning. With Molly Lamont, Anthony Kimmins.

White Face Gainsborough-Brit. Lion at Beaconsfield (A). W & F, 5.32 (6,359). p: Michael Balcon, d: T. Hayes Hunter, c: Bernard Knowles, Alex Bryce, sc: Angus MacPhail and Bryan Wallace from play by Edgar Wallace, *Persons Unknown* (1929), des: Norman Arnold, sd: Harold King. With Hugh Williams, Nora Swinburne.

White Lilac Fox Brit. (A). Fox, 6.35 (6.055). d: Albert Parker, sc: from play by Ladislas Fodor. With Basil Sydney, Judy Gunn, Claude Dampier, Percy Marmont.

White Man's Honour See **Man Who Could Not Forget, The**

Whither Mankind? See **Things to Come**

Who Goes Next? Fox Brit. at Wembley (A). 20th Cent.-Fox, 3.38 (7,798). p: Ivor McLaren, d: Maurice Elvey, c: Ronald Neame, sc: David Evans, add. dial: Lawrence V. Green from play by James Wedgwood Drawbell and Reginald Simpson, des: William Hemsley, ed: Reginald Beck, sd: John Cox, MD: Colin Wark. With Barry K. Barnes, Sophie Stewart, Jack Hawkins.

Who Killed Doc Robin? Gainsborough at Twickenham (U). Ideal, 2.31 (3,283) FT RCA. p: Michael Balcon, d: W. P. Kellino, sc: Angus MacPhail. With Clifford Heatherly.

Who Killed Fen Markham? See **Angelus, The**

Who Killed John Savage? WB-FN at Teddington (A). FN, 11.37 (6,228). p: Irving Asher, d: Maurice Elvey, c: Robert Lapresle, sc: Basil Dillon from

novel by Philip MacDonald, *Rynox*. With Nicholas Hannen, Barry Mackay.

Whom the Gods Love ATP-Standard Film Company, Anglo-Austrian production at Ealing, Austria. ABFD, 2.36 (7,723, later 7,445). p: d: Basil Dean, c: Jan Stallich, sc: Basil Dean and Margaret Kennedy from story by Margaret Kennedy, des: Andre Andreiev and Ernst Stern, ed: Thorold Dickinson, MD: Ernest Irving, operatic excerpts played by London Philharmonic Orchestra conducted by Sir Thomas Beecham. With John Loder, Victoria Hopper, Stephen Haggard, Liane Haid.

Who's Your Father? Lupino Lane-St George's Pictures at Walton (A). Columbia, 3.35 (5,685). p: supervisor St John L. Clowes, d: Lupino Lane, sc: Lupino Lane, Arthur Rigby from play by Mark Melford, *Turned Up*. With Lupino Lane, Nita Harvey.

Who's Your Lady Friend? Dorian Film Productions at Ealing (A). ABFD, 6.37 (6,535). p: Martin Sabine, d: Carol Reed, c: Jan Stallich, Phil Tannura, sc: Anthony Kimmins from story by Julius Hoest based on Viennese play *Der Herr Ohne Wohung* and 1937 film, des: Erwin Scharf, ed: Ernest Aldridge, MD: Ernest Irving, music Robert Stolz, Vivian Ellis. With Frances Day, Vic Oliver, Betty Stockfeld.

Why Pick on Me? GS Ent. at Walton (A). Radio, 7.37 (5,859). p: George Smith, d: P. Maclean Rogers, c: Geoffrey Faithfull, sc: H. F. Maltby, Kathleen Butler from story by Con West, Jack Marks. With Wylie Watson, Jack Hobbs.

Why Sailors Leave Home BIP at Elstree (U). Wardour, 10.30 (6,385) FT, songs RCA. d: Monty Banks, c: Ernest Palmer, H. Ford, sc: Val Valentine from story by Syd Courtenay and Lola Harvey, ed: Émile de Ruelle, A. C. Hammond, sd: Dallas Bower, MD: John Reynders, music and lyrics John Reynders, Idris Lewis, Lola Harvey, Syd Courtenay, Val Valentine and others, dances Alexander Oumansky. With Leslie Fuller, Lola Harvey, Syd Courtenay.

Wickham Mystery, The G. B. Samuelson at Isleworth (A). UA, 10.31 (7,527) FT Fidelytone. p: Gordon Craig, d: G. B. Samuelson, sc: from story by John McNally, *Paperchase.* With Eve Gray, John Longden.

Widow's Island See **Romance in Flanders, A**

Widow's Might WB-FN at Teddington (U). WB, 1.35 (6,956). p: Irving Asher, d: Cyril Gardner, sc: Rowland Brown, Brock Williams from play by Frederick Jackson. With Laura La Plante, Yvonne Arnaud.

Wife in Pawn See **Strange Evidence**

Wife of General Ling, The Premier-Stafford at Shepperton (A). RKO-Radio, 4.37 (6,506). p: John Stafford, d: Ladislaus Vajda, c: Jimmy Wilson, sc: Akos Tolnay and Reginald Long from novel by Dorothy Hope and Peter Cheyney, des: Jack Hallward, Philip Bawcombe, sd: D. Blumberg. With Inkijinoff, Griffith Jones, Adrienne Renn.

Wife or Two, A Brit. Lion at Beaconsfield (A). Brit. Lion 1.36 (5,795). p: Herbert Smith, d: P. Maclean Rogers, sc: Kathleen Butler, P. Maclean Rogers from play by C. B. Poultney. With Henry Kendall, Betty Astell, Nancy Burne.

Wild Boy Gainsborough at Islington (U). G-B D, 5.34 (7,808). p: Michael Balcon, d: Albert de Courville, sc: Stafford Dickens from story by Albert de Courville and J. E. Bradford. With Sonnie Hale, Flanagan and Allen, Mick the Miller.

Wild Justice See **Case of Gabriel Perry, The**

Windbag the Sailor Gainsborough at Islington (U). G-B D, 12.36 (7,640). d: William Beaudine, c: J. J. Cox, sc: G. Marriott Edgar, Stafford Dickens, Will Hay from story by Robert Stevenson and Leslie Arliss, des: Vetchinsky, ed: R. E. Dearing, Terence Fisher, sd: G.

Burgess, MD: Louis Levy. With Will Hay, Graham Moffatt, Moore Marriott.

Windfall Embassy (U). Radio, 7.35 (5,837). p: George King, d: Frederick Hayward, sc: Randall Faye from play by R. C. Sherriff (1934). With Edward Rigby, Marie Ault, George Carney.

Windjammer BIF at Welwyn and at sea (A). Pro Patria, 9.30 (7,080) FT Klangfilm. p: H. Bruce Woolfe, Michael Villiers, d: J. O. C. Orton, c: R. J. Walker, A. J. Villiers, Jack Parker, sc: J. O. C. Orton, dial: A. P. Herbert, from book by A. J. Villiers, *By Way of Cape Horn*, ed: J. O. C. Orton, sd: Victor Peers, A. F. Birch. With Tony Bruce, Michael Hogan, Hal Gordon.

Windmill, The WB-FN at Teddington (A). FN, 3.37 (5,622). p: Irving Asher, d: Arthur Woods, c: Robert Lapresle, sc: from story by John Drabble. With Glen Alyn, Hugh Williams.

Windmill Revels Ace Films, 1.37 (4,194). p: Frank Green, d: R. A. Hopwood. Variety from Windmill Theatre.

Window Cleaner, The See **Letting in the Sunshine**

Window in London, A G & S Films at Denham, London locations (A). GFD, 11.39 (6,862). p: Josef Somlo, d: Herbert Mason, c: Glen MacWilliams, sc: Ian Dalrymple and Brigid Cooper, des: Ralph Brinton, ed: Philip Charlot. With Michael Redgrave, Paul Lukas, Sally Gray.

Wings of the Morning New World Pictures at Denham, Epsom, Ireland (U). 20th Cent.-Fox, 1.37 (7,704) Technicolor (colour direction Natalie Kalmus). p: Robert T. Kane, d: Harold Schuster, c: Ray Rennahan, Jack Cardiff, sc: Tom Geraghty from stories by Donn Byrne, des: Ralph Brinton, cost: Rene Hubert, ed: James B. Clark, commentary E. V. H. Emmett, MD: Muir Mathieson, music Arthur Benjamin. With Annabella, Leslie Banks, Henry Fonda.

Wings over Africa Premier Stafford at Shepperton (A). Radio, 9.36 (5,658). p:

John Stafford, d: Ladislaus Vajda, sc: Akos Tolnay. With Joan Gardner, Ian Colin.

Wise Guys Fox Brit. at Wembley (A). Fox, 8.37 (6,009). d: Harry Langdon, c: Stanley Grant, sc: David Evans from story by Alison Booth. With Naughton and Gold.

Wishbone, The Sound City at Shepperton (U). M-G-M, 3.33 (7,100). p: Ivar Campbell, d: Arthur Maude, sc: N. W. B. Pemberton from story by W. Townend, *One Crowded Hour.* With Nellie Wallace, Davy Burnaby.

Wishes BIP (U). Pathé, 9.34 (3,200). p: Walter Mycroft, d: W. P. Kellino, sc: Wallace Lupino. With Wallace and Barry Lupino.

Without You Brit. Lion at Beaconsfield (A). Fox, 3.34 (5,957). p: supervisor Herbert Smith, d: John Daumery, sc: Michael Barringer from story by W. Scott Darling. With Henry Kendall, Wendy Barrie, Margot Grahame.

With the Best Intentions See **Beware of Women**

Wolf's Clothing J. G. & R. B. Wainwright at Shepperton (U). Universal, 3.36 (7,267). p: Richard Wainwright, d: Andrew Marton, c: Phil Tannura, sc: Brock Williams, Evadne Price from play, *The Emancipation of Ambrose.* With Claude Hulbert, Gordon Harker.

Wolves B & D-HMV at Elstree Blattner (U). W & F, 5.30 (5,041) FT WE. p: Herbert Wilcox, d: Albert de Courville, sc: Reginald Berkeley from play by Georges Toudouze. With Dorothy Gish, Charles Laughton, Jack Osterman.

Woman Alone, A Garrett-Klement Pictures (A). UA, 7.36 (7,094). Registered as foreign film. p: Robert Garrett, Otto Klement, p: supervisor James B. Sloane, d: Eugene Frenke, c: J. J. Cox, sd: Leo Lania, Warren Chetham-Strode from story by Fedor Otzep, des: A. L. Mazzei. With Anna Sten, Henry Wilcoxon.

Woman Between, The BIP at Elstree (A). Wardour, 1.31 (6,980) FT RCA. d:

Miles Mander, c: Henry Gartner, sc: Frank Launder and Miles Mander from play by Miles Malleson, *Conflict* (1925), des: John Mead, ed: Walter Stokvis, sd: C. V. Thornton. With Owen Nares, Adrianne Allen.

Woman from China, The Edward G. Whiting (A). J-M-G, 3.30 (7,410) Silent. p: Edward G. Whiting, d: Edward Dryhurst from story by 'Cory Sala' (George Dewhurst) With Julie Suedo, Gibb McLaughlin.

Woman He Scorned, The Charles Whittaker Productions (U). WB, 5.30 (8,460) FT RCA. d: Paul Czinner, sc: Charles Whittaker from story by Paul Czinner. With Pola Negri, Hans Rehmann, Warwick Ward.

Womanhood Louis London (A). Butcher's, 11.34 (5,566). d: Harry Hughes, sc: from story by Brandon Fleming. With Eve Gray, Leslie Perrins, Esmond Knight.

Woman in White, The See **Crimes at the Dark House**

Woman to Woman Gainsborough-Burlington, with Tiffany-Stahl in Hollywood (A). W & F, 11.29 (8,039) FT and songs RCA. Registered as foreign film. p: Michael Balcon, Victor Saville, d: Victor Saville, c: Benjamin Kline, sc: Nicholas Fodor from play by Michael Morton (1921). With Betty Compson, Juliette Compton, George Barraud.

Women Who Play Para-Brit. at Elstree B & D (A). Paramt, 3.32 (7,185). d: Arthur Rosson, c: Philip Tannura, sc: Basil Mason, Gilbert Wakefield from play by Frederick Lonsdale, *Spring Cleaning* (1925), des: R. Holmes Paul. With Mary Newcomb, George Barraud.

Wonderful Story, The Fogwell Films (A). Sterling, 10.32 (7,250). p: d: Reginald Fogwell, c: Henry Harris, sc: Reginald Fogwell from novel by I. A. R. Wylie. With Wyn Clare, John Batten.

World Is Mine, The See **Dreams Come True**

World, The Flesh and the Devil, The Real Art at Beaconsfield (A). Radio,

11.32 (4,805). p: Julius Hagen, d: G. A. Cooper, sc: H. Fowler Mear from play by Lawrence Cowen, des: James Carter. With Harold Huth, Isla Bevan.

Would You Believe It! Nettlefold at Walton (U). Butcher's 5.29 (5,015) silent, music on Vocalion recording. p: Archibald Nettlefold, d: Walter Forde, c: Geoffrey Faithfull, sc: Walter Forde, H. Fowler Mear, des: W. G. Saunders, ed: Adeline Culley, music Paul Mulder. With Walter Forde, Pauline Johnson.

'W' Plan, The BIP-Burlington Film at Elstree (U). Wardour, 3.30 (9,347) FT RCA. p: d: Victor Saville, c: René Guissart, Freddie Young, sc: Victor Saville, Miles Malleson and Frank Launder from story by Graham Seton (Lt-Col. Graham Seton Hutchinson) in *Evening Standard*, des: Hugh Gee, ed: P. Maclean Rogers, sd: D. F. Scanlan, MD: John Reynders. With Brian Aherne, Madeleine Carroll, Gordon Harker.

Wrecker, The Gainsborough (U). W & F, 7.29 (6,670) silent, 6,705 synchronised) RCA. p: Michael Balcon, assoc: S. C. Balcon, d: Geza von Bolvary, c: Otto Kanturek, sc: Angus MacPhail from play by Arnold Ridley and Bernard Merivale (1927), des: Oscar Werndorff. With Carlyle Blackwell, Benita Hume.

Wrecker, The (1936) See **Seven Sinners**

Written Law, The Reginald Fogwell (A). Ideal, 9.31 (7,119) FT RCA. p: Reginald Fogwell, Mansfield Markham, d: sc: Reginald Fogwell. With Madeleine Carroll, Percy Marmont.

Wrong Mr. Perkins, The Starcraft at Twickenham (U). Fox, 1.31 (3,517). p: Harry Cohen, d: Arthur Varney, sc: Brock Williams. With Herbert Mundin.

Yank at Oxford, A M-G-M British at Denham (U). M-G-M, 3.38 (8,471). p: Michael Balcon, d: Jack Conway, assist. d: Pen Tennyson, c: Hal Rosson, sc: Sidney Gilliat, Michael Hogan, Leon Gordon, Roland Pertwee on an idea by J. Monk Saunders, add. dial: Malcolm Stuart Boylen, Walter Ferris, George Oppenheimer, des: L. P. Williams, cost: Rene Hubert, ed: Margaret Booth, Charles Frend, sd: A. W. Watkins, C. C. Stevens, MD: and music Hubert Bath. With Robert Taylor, Maureen O'Sullivan, Lionel Barrymore, Griffith Jones, Vivien Leigh.

'Yell' of a Night, A C. à Becket Williams (A). Universal, 7.32 (3,838). d: G. A. Minzenty, sc: C. à Becket Williams, G. A. Minzenty. With Mickey Brantford.

Yellow Mask, The BIP at Elstree (U). Wardour, 8.30 (8,560) FT, songs RCA. d: Harry Lachman, c: Claude Friese-Greene, sc: Val Valentine, Miles Malleson from musical play by Edgar Wallace (1927). With Lupino Lane.

Yellow Stockings ABPC at Elstree, Totnes, Sennen Cove (U). ABPC, 7.38 (6,192). p: Walter Mycroft, d: Herbert Brenon, c: Walter Harvey, sc: Rodney Ackland from play by Eden Phillpotts, des: John Mead, ed: Flora Newton, MD: Harry Acres, music Hubert Bath. With Dame Marie Tempest, Belle Chrystall, Wilfrid Lawson, Robert Newton.

Yellow Sands Welsh Pearson Elder (A). Paramt, 1.30 (6,608) d: Theodor Komisarjevsky, sc: Alicia Ramsey and Fred Paul from story by D. Wilson MacArthur. With Percy Marmont, Marjorie Mars, Georges Galli.

Yes, Madam Brit. Lion at Beaconsfield (U). Fox, 2.33 (4,110). assoc. p: Herbert Smith, d: Leslie Hiscott, sc: Michael Barringer from novel by K. R. G. Browne. With Kay Hammond, Harold French.

Yes, Madam? ABPC at Elstree (U). ABPC, 11.38 (6,974). p: Walter Mycroft, d: Norman Lee, c: Walter Harvey, sc: Clifford Grey, Bert Lee and William Freshman from musical by K. R. G. Browne, Bert Lee and R. P. Weston (1934) based on novel by K. R. G. Browne, des: Cedric Dawe, ed: Walter Stokvis, MD: Harry Acres, Music Jack Waller, Joseph Tunbridge, Harris Weston, songs R. P. Weston, Bert Lee, Clifford Grey. With Bobby Howes, Diana Churchill.

Yes, Mr. Brown B & D at Elstree B & D (A). W & F, premiere 1.33 (7,852). p: Herbert Wilcox, d: Jack Buchanan, c: Freddie Young, sc: Douglas Furber from play by Frank and Hershfield, *Geschaft mit Amerika,* music Paul Abraham, lyrics Douglas Furber. With Jack Buchanan, Elsie Randolph, Margot Grahame, Hartley Power.

You'd Be Surprised Nettlefold at Walton (U). Butcher's, 4.30 (5,992 silent, 5,960 sound) synchronised music, songs RCA. p: Archibald Nettlefold, d: Walter Forde, c: Geoffrey Faithfull, sc: H. Fowler Mear, Walter Forde, des: W. G. Saunders, ed: Walter Forde, music Paul Mulder, song Walter Forde. With Walter Forde, Joy Windsor.

You Live and Learn WB at Teddington (U). WB, 8.37 (7,230). p: Irving Asher, d: Arthur Woods, c: Basil Emmott, sc: Brock Williams, Tom Phipps from story by Norma Patterson, *Have You Come For Me?* With Glenda Farrell, Claude Hulbert.

You Made Me Love You BIP at Elstree (U). Wardour, 8.33 (6,381). d: Monty Banks, c: J. J. Cox, sc: Frank Launder from screen story by Stanley Lupino, des: David Rawnsley, ed: A. S. Bates, sd: A. E. Rudolph, MD: Harry Acres, music Noel Gay, lyrics Stanley Lupino, Clifford Grey. With Stanley Lupino, Thelma Todd, John Loder.

You Must Get Married City Film Corporation at Walton (A). GFD, 11.36 (6,110). p: Basil Humphreys, d: Leslie Pearce, c: Claude Friese-Greene, sc; F. McGrew Willis from novel by David Evans. With Frances Day, Robertson Hare, Neil Hamilton.

Young and Innocent G-B at Shepherd's Bush and Pinewood (A). GFD, 11.37 (7,569). p: Edward Black, d: Alfred Hitchcock, c: Bernard Knowles, sc: Charles Bennett, Edwin Greenwood, Anthony Armstrong, dial: Gerald Savory, from novel by Josephine Tey, *A Shilling for Candles*, des: Alfred Junge, ed: Charles Frend, MD: Louis Levy, song Lerner, Goodhart and Hoffman.

With Nova Pilbeam, Derrick de Marney, Percy Marmont.

Young Man's Fancy Ealing Studios (CAPAD) at Ealing (A). ABFD, 8.39 (6,965). p: Michael Balcon, assoc. p: S. C. Balcon, d: Robert Stevenson, sc: Ronald Neame, Gordon Dines, sc: Roland Pertwee, Rodney Ackland, E. V. H. Emmett from story by Robert Stevenson, des: Wilfred Shingleton, ed: Challis Sanderson, MD: Ernest Irving. With Anna Lee, Griffith Jones.

Young Nowhere's See **Some Day**

Young Person in Pink, The See **Girl Who Forgot, The**

Young Woodley BIP at Elstree (A). Wardour, 7.30 (7,050) FT RCA. d: Thomas Bentley, c: Claude Friese-Greene, sc: Victor Kendall, John Van Druten from play by John Van Druten (1928), ed: Émile de Ruelle, Sam Simmonds, sd: A. F. Birch. With Frank Lawton, Madeleine Carroll.

You're the Doctor! New Georgian Productions at Worton Hall (U). BIED Butcher's, (1) 10.38 (7,050), (2) 1.39 (6,077). p: George Smith, d: Roy Lockwood, c: Geoffrey Faithfull, sc: Beaufoy Milton from story by Guy Beauchamp. With Barry K. Barnes, Googie Withers, Gus McNaughton.

Youthful Folly Sound City (A). Columbia, 10.34 (6,419). p: Norman Loudon, d: Miles Mander, sc: Heinrich Fracnkel from play by Gordon Daviot. With Irene Vanbrugh, Mary Lawson, Jane Carr.

Ysani the Priestess International Productions (U). International Productions, 4.34 (3,088). d: Gordon Sherry, sc: 'invented by Raven Wood'. With Raven Wood.

Index

Included in this index, as well as the usual subjects and names in the main text of the book, are the names of film makers listed in the Film List on page 287. As this list is alphabetical, British film titles are included in the index below only where reference has been make to them in the text. Also included below are the full names of companies which appear in the Film List only in abbreviated form.

414

*Credit titles on the copy of *Waltzes From Vienna* in the National Film Archive name the art director as Werndorff, not Junge as has sometimes been said.